LANDFALLS OF PARADISE

LANDFALLS OF PARADISE

Cruising Guide to the Pacific Islands

THIRD EDITION

Earl R. Hinz

 UNIVERSITY OF HAWAII PRESS / HONOLULU

© 1993 University of Hawaii Press
All rights reserved
Printed in the United States of America

98 97 96 95 94 93   1 2 3 4 5

Library of Congress Cataloging-in-Publication Data

Hinz, Earl R.
  Landfalls of paradise : cruising guide to the Pacific Islands /
Earl R. Hinz. — 3rd ed.
    p.   cm.
  Includes index.
  ISBN 0–8248–1466–5
  1. Yachts   and   yachting—Oceania—Guidebooks.   2.
Oceania—
Guidebooks.   I. Title.
GV817.O27H56   1993
797.1'246'0995—dc20   92–42269
                                              CIP

University of Hawaii Press books are printed on acid-free
paper and meet the guidelines for permanence and durability
of the Council on Library Resources

This book, along with the accompanying charts and illustrations, is *not to be used for navigation;* it is for reference purposes only.

The contents have been carefully prepared. They are based upon personal inspection, official publications, and other data deemed reliable, with the objective of making the cruising skipper's voyage more enjoyable. Every reasonable effort has been made to achieve up-to-date accuracy, but the infinite complexities of personal observation and a constantly changing world render total accuracy impossible. Only governments, with their vast resources of money, personnel, and vessels, can achieve such reliability. Accordingly, all sailing information and directions in this book must be checked against the latest available charts, publications, and notices to mariners whenever a cruise is undertaken.

Skippers are alone responsible for the safety of their crews and their vessels, and they must plot their own courses. The author and the publisher must therefore specifically disclaim any and all personal liability for loss or risk, to persons or to property or to both, that might occur, either directly or indirectly, from any person's use or interpretation of any information contained in this book.

Cover photograph by Douglas Peebles

Designed by Paula Newcomb

CONTENTS

LIST OF CHARTS

PART III. MICRONESIA

PART IV. ISLANDS OF THE EASTERN PACIFIC

PREFACE

Aloha (ah-LO-hah) Hawaiian
Bula vinaka (boo-lah ve-NAH-kah) Fijian
Hafa adai (hah-FAH-ah-die) Guamanian
Ia orana (ee-ah or-RAH-nah) Tahitian
Ka oha (kah OH-hah) Marquesan
Kia ora (key-ah OH-ra) New Zealand Maori
Malo e lelei (MAH-low eh leh-LAY-ee) Tongan
Talofa (taw-LOW-fah) Samoan
Tiabo (sa-BOH) Kiribati
or, simply, Greetings!

However you say it, you are about to enter the domain of the friendliest people on earth—the Pacific islanders.

You are aiming to set sail on the largest of oceans, the Pacific Ocean, seen for the first time by European eyes in 1513. In that year Vasco Núñez de Balboa arrived at the western side of the Panamanian isthmus in an overland jaunt. Because the shoreline of the isthmus runs east and west at this point, Balboa called the waters Mar del Sur, or South Seas, to differentiate them from the Caribbean to the north of the isthmus, which he termed the North Sea. While the term "North Sea" has disappeared from common use, it is still common, especially in a romantic sense, to refer to the tropics and near tropics of the Pacific in both hemispheres as the South Seas.

Anyone contemplating a cruise to these South Seas could be visiting the outlying islands of the eastern Pacific; the islands of Oceania—Polynesia, Melanesia, or Micronesia; or the mysterious islands of the western Pacific—Indonesia, Malaysia, or the Philippines. Whatever you choose to call this vast and usually pacific area, there awaits a bounty of romantic adventure for the cruising sailor.

Every boat that sets out on an extended cruise will find new adventures, for no two cruising boats ever experience identical sailing conditions or island hospitality or follow the same itinerary. With more than 10,000 islands in Oceania alone from which to choose

you can be a modern-day Captain Cook and explore new places to your crew's content. Avoid the constraints of the beaten path that your friends have followed. Introduce yourself to unspoiled and uncrowded ports of call such as Pitcairn, Mangareva, Maupiti, Aitutaki, Wallis, Fanning, Kosrae, Satawal, Yap, Manus, and hundreds of others that rarely see a cruising boat.

This book, which has become the Pacific cruiser's bible, was conceived in 1976 while *Horizon* was sitting out the South Pacific tropical cyclone season in New Zealand. The first edition appeared in 1980 following *Horizon*'s return home from her own Coconut Milk Run through Polynesia.

The second edition appeared in 1986 after more years of cruising in the tropics including the Manila Galleon Run through Micronesia. Its content was expanded to include social customs of island peoples and ports of call where airline connections could be made with friends who could fly out to crew with you and share in the excitement of making new landfalls in paradise.

Now, in this latest edition, the textual and chart matter has again been updated based on continuing contact with cruisers, harbormasters, government officials, and local people throughout the islands of the Pacific Ocean. The resources of the University of Hawaii's Pacific Islands Program and its Hamilton Library, the Hawaii state library's Pacific and Hawaii section, and the Bishop Museum were all used to establish the base for this new edition.

While the format of the well-received earlier editions has, in general, been retained, much new material has been added. For instance, information about clearance procedures in and out of island countries has been expanded as well as updated, and the difficulties of carrying pets into different countries have been addressed in greater detail.

In recent years hurricanes have taken their toll of cruising boats in both the Atlantic and Pacific oceans; therefore, more detail has been added on Pacific weather in hopes that readers can avoid these disastrous storms. If they can't, then they should seek shelter in one of the possible hurricane havens also described. A recent major South Pacific tropical cyclone is analyzed to show the vigor of the high winds that accompany such storms.

A number of cruisers suggested that besides updating the myriad details involved in conducting business ashore and feeling at home in a foreign port, I include a calendar of holidays to enable them to schedule their participation in local festivities as well as to avoid overtime charges on entering harbors at the wrong time. Both reasons gave adequate incentive to include a schedule of public holidays and special events for each island group. Another common request was for some indicator of the relative cost of products and services in the various ports. Inflation and local taxation have pushed up cruising costs over the years, and planning a cruise must now include a more careful assessment of money needs en route.

The growing use of amateur (ham) radio both to "visit" with others and get and give information invited an expanded appendix on maritime mobile ham radio operations. Although restricted from business use, ham radio can be a link with family and friends left behind as well as very useful in an emergency. The many maritime mobile nets throughout the Pacific Basin provide a valuable party line for all cruisers within propagation range.

As the years have gone by, cruising philosophy has changed. In the days of Joshua Slocum, Alain Gerbault, and Harry Pidgeon, it was an escapist's game. Then came the likes of the Hiscocks, Smeetons, and Roths,

who made it into a family affair. In recent years cruisers have turned even more gregarious and now seek greater association along the way with others having salt water in their veins. The result has been a strong upsurge in cruising boats joining international yacht races in various parts of the Pacific. These are generally not "professional" races, but informal races that sharpen sailing skills and add a bit of camaraderie along the way. An appendix has been added covering international yacht races in the Pacific that have cruising classes. They start from such places as Australia, Canada, Chile, Ecuador, Hong Kong, Malaysia, New Zealand, Thailand, and the U.S. West Coast. You can find one for almost any direction your cruising itinerary takes you.

Cruise planning and procedures should not be taken lightly even though thousands of cruisers have gone before you. Stories in popular boating magazines as well as letters in the Seven Seas Cruising Association (SSCA) *Commodores' Bulletin* usually speak in glowing terms of landfalls and visitations. Generally they are right—but only if you have planned around the weather, limitations on visiting foreign islands, and the nature of services obtainable in out-of-the-way locations. *Landfalls of Paradise* gives you the needed information to make a success of your cruise.

May your winds be fair and your seas smooth!

Earl R. Hinz, WD6EYJ
Honolulu, Hawaii
1992

LANDFALLS OF PARADISE

CHART LEGEND

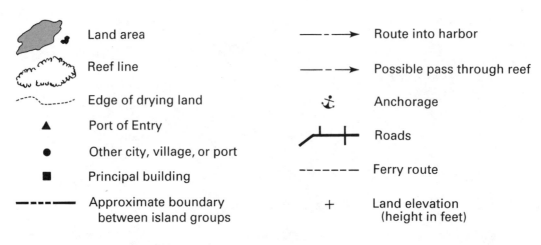

Land area		Route into harbor	
Reef line		Possible pass through reef	
Edge of drying land		Anchorage	
Port of Entry		Roads	
Other city, village, or port		Ferry route	
Principal building		Land elevation (height in feet)	
Approximate boundary between island groups			

Chart Code	Source
BA	British Admiralty, Hydrographer of the Navy, London
FR	French, Service Hydrographique et Oceanographique de la Marine, Paris
NZ	New Zealand, Hydrographic Office, Royal New Zealand Navy, Auckland
US	United States, Defense Mapping Agency, Hydrographic Center, Washington

CHAPTER 1

YOUR PACIFIC OCEAN

The Pacific Ocean offers the cruising sailor unparalleled advantages in space, exotic ports of call, weather, and hospitable peoples. It is the largest ocean of the world, covering 64 million square miles—and this does not include another six million square miles of adjoining seas. At the equator the Pacific Ocean measures 11,000 miles east to west and more than 9,000 miles north to south. Approximately 30 million square miles lie between the Tropics of Cancer and Capricorn wherein lie the majority of Pacific islands (New Zealand being a notable exception).

As a whole, the Pacific Ocean has more islands than the rest of the oceans and seas together. On a global scale the Pacific Ocean and adjoining seas cover about one-third of the earth's surface—which is more area than all the land masses of the world combined.

The Pacific Ocean is rimmed with mountains; indeed, many of its islands are mountains or mountain ranges, rising in some cases 30,000 or more feet from the ocean floor. Many of the mountains on the rim as well as in the basin itself are active volcanoes, providing a contemporary view of how land masses are formed. The island of Hawaii is probably the best known active volcano site in the Pacific, but Falcon Island in the Tonga group may be the most intriguing. Falcon Island appears and disappears at the ocean's surface as volcanic activity rises and subsides.

Earthquakes are another feature of Pacific geology occurring frequently in the mountains rimming the basin and, occasionally, in the islands of the western Pacific. Their importance to the mariner concerns the generation of tsunamis—rapidly moving seismic waves that traverse the Pacific and can raise havoc with shorelines and harbors. Fortunately, the tsunami warning system spanning the entire Pacific alerts countries to the occurrence of an earthquake and the possible generation of a tsunami.

Ferdinand Magellan was the first European to cross the Pacific Ocean in his circumnavigation of the world in the years 1519 to 1522. It was he who named it "Pacifico" because of its calm nature when he first entered it. The Pacific also has a violent face with seasonal hurricanes off Mexico and in the southwest as well as typhoons in its western waters. South of latitude 40°S are the Roaring Forties, where westerly gales almost never stop and sailing ships of yore made their record runs.

The cruising sailor can avoid the cold and gales of the higher latitudes and the seasonal tropical storms at sea by proper scheduling of passages, in return getting to enjoy the balmy weather of the tropics with all the pleasures of steady trade winds and balmy temperatures that invite rainshower bathing.

The Pacific is also "home" to the International Date Line, which regulates the dates of the world. Nominally it follows the 180th meridian and by definition separates the eastern and western hemispheres of the world. The 24-hour time change as your boat crosses the date line is certain to test the skill of your navigation. You will especially enjoy your visit to Tonga, whose local time is 13 hours fast on Greenwich, giving it the distinction of being "where time begins."

Early Migrations

The history of the Pacific islanders has been difficult to trace because the original inhabitants had no written language, and accounts of their early history were passed on only by word of mouth. Over the past several decades, however, anthropologists, archeologists, and linguistic geographers have made great strides in tracing the early migrations of these people. In particular, three developments have stood out as key steps to solving the mysteries of the dispersal of people throughout the thousands of Pacific islands: (1) the tracking of the movement of the ancient Lapita pottery makers from New Guinea to the Samoas through excavation and identification of pottery shards; (2) the proof that large double-hulled voyaging canoes could sail against the

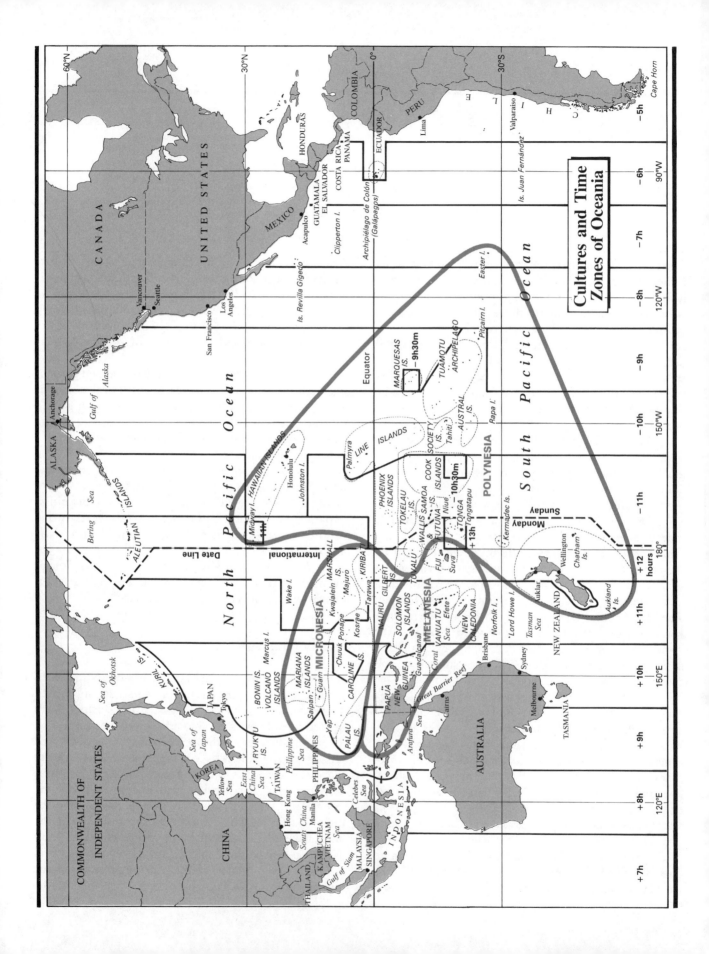

Cultures and Time Zones of Oceania

wind as demonstrated in several round-trip voyages of the Hawaiian canoe *Hokulea* between Hawaii and South Pacific destinations; and, concurrently, (3) the proof that noninstrument navigation by the stars was a credible means to guide canoes over long distances as shown by *Hokulea* on its South Pacific travels and by other vessels navigated by similar principles in the North Pacific.

Simultaneously, linguistic geographers believe they have validated the origin and development paths of the islanders' spoken language across the Pacific. The language, known as Austronesian, is consistent with the archeologists' projections of islander movement.

The eastward movement of the ancestors of the people who would later occupy the area of the Pacific Ocean known as Oceania started from Fukien province in China circa 5000 B.C. The migrants were accomplished short-distance sailors who apparently saw the possibility of adventure and new homes in the tempting islands lying east of mainland China. Their sailing skills and equipment, however, were primitive to the point that they could safely sail from island to island only by

"eyeball" navigation—at most a few hundred miles depending on the visibility of their destinations. Even with this limited capability, however, they were able to cross the Formosa Strait and begin island-hopping south through the Philippine and Celebes islands to the big island of New Guinea.

The migration did not stop there, for these were a nomadic people. They continued harbor-hopping along the north shore of New Guinea for another thousand miles east until the islands of the Bismarck Archipelago came into view. Then they crossed the small channel to what we now know as New Britain Island, where the amazing trail of Lapita pottery begins. Archeologists have uncovered Lapita pottery in the Bismarck and Santa Cruz islands, Vanuatu, New Caledonia, Fiji, Tonga, and Samoa, where it seems to have stopped, leading to the belief that there was a hiatus in the migration. The name "Lapita" comes from a site in New Caledonia where significant finds of the pottery were made.

These roving Lapita pottery makers arrived in the Fiji, Samoa, and Tonga islands about 3000–1300 B.C. They were to make these islands their home, and Samoa

The ubiquitous coconut palm provides food, drink, shelter, body covering, and ornamentation for island peoples throughout the Pacific. (Earl Hinz)

and Tonga were to become the birthplace of the Polynesian ethnic group. Before we go any further with the Polynesians in Oceania, however, something must be said about the Melanesians, who now occupy many of the island groups through which the wanderers from China passed in their eastward migration.

(Anthropologists divide the islands of Oceania into three geographic areas—Polynesia, meaning "many islands"; Melanesia, meaning "black islands"; and Micronesia, meaning "small islands." The terms are not mutually exclusive since all three areas are made up of many islands, most of which are small, and they are inhabited by indigenous people having skin tones ranging from copper to ebony.)

The Melanesians are physically quite different from the Polynesians, indicating that if the two originated from the same racial family, there has been intermarriage with other groups along the way. The two groups most likely involved can be identified by considering the five basic human groups—Australoids in southeast Asia and Australia; Bushmanoids in South Africa; Caucasoids in southern Europe and Asia; Mongoloids in China; and Negroids in equatorial Africa.

Anthropologists have deduced that the people who made the marvelous 2,000-year migration from China to Fiji, Samoa, and Tonga were Mongoloids. The original inhabitants of mainland China, they seem to have wandered far from their original homes. Besides their movement into the southwest Pacific, the Mongoloids are also credited with crossing the Bering Strait and moving southward through the Americas to Tierra del Fuego.

Anthropologists also believe that the Austroloid race occupied New Guinea, Australia, and Tasmania, having migrated to those places via an early land bridge connecting them with Malaysia. The aborigines of Australia are today's descendants of the original Australoids. The Australoids were land people, sticking to trails for transport over most of their territory. But they did come in contact with and apparently intermarried with the Mongoloids who were making their way east along the north shore of New Guinea, thus giving rise to the Melanesian ethnic group, in which the Austroloid predominates. The part of Oceania they now occupy is called Melanesia and extends as far east as Fiji.

The third ethnic group to be found within the region called Oceania is the Micronesian. Micronesians also were originally from China, and it is suggested that they migrated into their current region by two routes. One was directly from the Indonesian-Philippine islands area, bypassing the New Guinea part of the migration to Fiji. The other was a northerly migration from the islands of today's Vanuatu. This diversion may explain the linguistic and other differences between the people of the Palau and Mariana islands of western Micronesia and those in the eastern Carolines and the Marshall and Gilbert islands to the east. Racially, the Micronesians appear to be more akin to the Polynesians than to the Melanesians.

Most of what we know today as Oceania was settled between 3000 B.C. and A.D. 1000. The Polynesians sailed to and settled the islands as far east as Easter Island and as far north and south as Hawaii and New Zealand. The Micronesians moved into the atolls and the few high islands north of the equator between the Palau and the Marshall islands and the Melanesians became further ensconced in their rich islands extending from New Guinea to Fiji.

Between A.D. 1000 and the coming of the Europeans, native exploration gave way to the cultural and political development of island societies such as were eventually discovered by the Europeans. Polynesian people, in particular, developed very sophisticated civilizations in Hawaii, Tahiti, and New Zealand as well as many of the other islands. Although these societies thrived in the climate and with the resources of their areas, they were ill-prepared to deal with the overwhelming technological might of the Europeans.

European Encroachment

First to arrive were the Portuguese and Spaniards, who dominated Pacific exploration in the sixteenth century. The Spice Islands of the East Indies attracted the Portuguese to the western fringes of the Pacific via the Cape of Good Hope. It was the Spanish, however, who, having seen the wealth of Central and South America, set the stage for Pacific exploration from the east. From the time Magellan (Portuguese by birth, but a naturalized Spanish citizen) found his way through the straits at the tip of South America and crossed to the Philippines, the mighty Pacific became crisscrossed with European explorers. The Spanish and Portuguese were soon followed by the Dutch, French, and English. Most notable of the latter was James Cook, whose thorough and objective explorations from 1769 to 1779 opened the way for the developers and plunderers of the Pacific islands.

England, France, Spain, and later the United States sought riches and new colonies to support their ambitious political growth back home—at the expense of the Pacific islanders. Whaling, the sandlewood trade, and black pearling were pursued to their demise. Islanders were "contracted" for guano-mining labor on islands as far away as the coast of South America, never to return home. This infamous form of slavery was called "blackbirding." European diseases ravaged island populations, who had no natural immunity to foreign disease. Finally, the conservative Christian missionary influence spelled the end of native culture, which was centered on Pagan religions.

In the late 1800s the major world powers consolidated their Pacific colonies, annexing all unclaimed island groups. At the end of the Spanish-American War (1898), the Philippines and Guam were ceded to the United States, which also annexed Hawaii. Remaining Spanish possessions were sold to Germany, which also acquired Samoa. With the advent of World War I, however, German colonies in the Pacific were taken over by the Allies. Australia and New Zealand became governors of much of the southwestern Pacific but, more important, a quiet ally, Japan, took over the Caroline, Mariana, and Marshall islands, setting the stage for aggressive expansion that was to trigger World War II in the Pacific.

Between the two world wars the Pacific was pretty much forgotten except by the powers already in control. Japan quietly began arming the island of Truk in the Carolines in anticipation of military expansion while all the other powers simply governed the island peoples with little purpose other than to provide a good living for the colonial governors. (Note: Truk as the name of the Truk Islands existed until 1990, when, as part of the Federated States of Micronesia, their legislature elected to change the name to Chuuk. The name Chuuk will be used from here on.)

On December 7, 1941, the Pacific exploded into an inferno that was to burn for almost four years. For the first time in history communications were sufficiently well developed so that the entire world could follow the war in any part of the world, and the Pacific became instantly known to everyone. It was no longer a remote place seen only by adventurers, for now millions of military people were to become familiar with islands, atolls, island peoples, and the intoxicating grandeur of tropical geography. They may not have been able to appreciate it while in uniform, but the spell of the tropics was indelibly etched on their minds.

The war raged on, and the Japanese advanced south to New Guinea and the Solomon Islands. Finally, the industrial might and resources of the United States and its Pacific allies turned the tables in 1944 as they started an island-hopping counteroffensive that took them right to Tokyo in 1945 for the signing of the treaty that capped the Pacific War cauldron.

Things were never the same in the Pacific after that. All the Pacific islands had been touched by modern technology and politics, and the islanders felt the need to advance with the rest of the world.

Postwar political developments saw Britain shedding itself of Pacific responsibilities in order to recover from the pounding it took from Germany during the war. Australia and New Zealand again became the caretakers of many of the islands while independence moves gestated. All the former Japanese possessions were mandated to the United States to become the Trust Territory of the Pacific Islands.

The Pacific has not been without turmoil since the end of World War II, but the turmoil has been primarily political as island groups have sought to set up independent governments. While bloodshed seemed to be the way to freedom in other parts of the world, the Pacific islanders took a more patient viewpoint to gain their goals without destroying people, resources, or the goodwill of their landlords, whose help they need in the transition from colony to independent nation. Bloodless coups in Fiji, uprisings in New Caledonia, and strikes in Tahiti are the symptoms of political adjustment taking place. Cruising sailors will make themselves aware of such localized strife and not become embroiled in the politics of the host country.

Evolution of the Cruising Scene

Today there is a new look in the Pacific that has nothing to do with politics but much to do with international goodwill. The free-roaming cruising yacht is finding its way to atolls and islands, spreading person-to-person goodwill in an informal way that cannot be duplicated at the highest level of diplomacy.

Cruising yachts—crewed by people from all walks of life bonded together by a yen for seeing the beautiful Pacific and meeting new neighbors in the world—are a relatively recent phenomenon.

Such pleasure cruising started in 1898, when Joshua Slocum returned from his epic three-year single-handed circumnavigation. Slocum was no adventurer but an able seaman who proved that a small boat properly handled could sail the oceans of the world in safety. He was no diplomat in striped trousers but a common and friendly individual who was welcomed by island people for what he was and not for whom he represented. Monetary gain was not his objective, although he probably would have welcomed some additional funds to help outfit his *Spray* and keep it shipshape. Slocum was the first cruiser, and he set standards of seamanship, navigation, and goodwill that are still examples today.

Other single-handers followed in his wake: Harry Pidgeon in *Islander,* Francis Chichester in *Gypsy Moth,* and Robin Knox-Johnston in *Suhaili,* who was the first to circumnavigate nonstop. But nothing captures the hearts of the world as much as the pluck of young people who sail the world single-handed, disproving the belief that opportunities for adventure no longer exist. In 1965 Robin Lee Graham started out at age 16 and circumnavigated the world single-handed in his 24-foot sloop *Dove.* Not to be outdone by machoism, Tania Aebi took up the challenge of her father and in 1985 at age 18 began her single-handed circumnavigation in *Varuna,* a 26-foot sloop. Both Graham and Aebi thought the Pacific segment of their route the most beautiful and romantic of their itinerary.

Cruising has gone beyond the age of stunts, and it is now a family affair. Eric and Susan Hiscock have probably done more than any other persons to make cruising a way of life for people. Their circumnavigations in *Wanderer III* and *Wanderer IV* have set the stage for the cruising families of today.

There have been many other cruisers who have sailed the Pacific Ocean. You have only to visit your nearest library to get all the particulars in books of dreams fulfilled by Bill Robinson in *Varua,* Miles and Beryl Smeeton in *Tzu Hang,* Hal and Margaret Roth in *Whisper,* Irving and Electa Johnson in *Yankee,* and a host of others in more recent years.

Over the years improvements to boat design and construction, revolutionary sail materials and design, and the wonders of electronics have made blue-water cruising easier as well as more fun and have enticed thousands more to take up the sport. The numbers of boats now passaging on the blue Pacific are indeed impressive. Take those cruisers who choose to stop at Pago Pago, American Samoa, a port of call that seafaring people have loved to hate for years: in 1971 at the beginning of the cruising explosion, only 38 boats visited this port. By 1984 the number had grown to 179, and by 1987 it had reached 288. And if you don't like such a Westernized Polynesian port, continue on to Tonga, the only kingdom in the Pacific. In 1983 Tonga hosted 323 cruising boats; by 1987 the number had grown to 579. For Pago Pago and Tonga combined, that was an increase of 70 percent in just five years! The

magic of cruising the blue waters of the Pacific is enveloping more and more adventurous people every year.

This popularity is having the expected effect on the host islands. With limited facilities they are now charging for some services and tightening up entry formalities. Such change should not deter the serious cruiser, for it is happening at only a few ports of call. Honolulu, Papeete, and Rarotonga are examples, but there are hundreds of other places to go where a true island welcome still awaits the voyager.

Part of this change is the result of past excesses from the days of the beachcombers who dropped in and stayed. The excesses carried on into the days of the hippies, who were often freeloaders on an economy that was barely at the subsistence level. While the Pacific islanders are probably the most hospitable of all peoples, even they cannot continue to host the swelling numbers of yachts at the more popular ports of call.

Meanwhile, Pacific cruisers are becoming more gregarious. Ham radio was the first community tie that took hold, enabling them to stay in touch with other cruisers and even to call home to talk to those not seeking adventure on the blue Pacific. Next in the cruiser's evolution came an interest in participating in an occasional cruising race en route to the next port. Many cruisers started their sailing days in racing boats and have not lost the urge to compete, although they want to do it in more comfort than a stripped-out racing machine provides. On average 75 boats race to Hawaii every year, many with the objective of starting their Pacific cruise from Pineappleland. Appendix E lists 29 organized races in the Pacific Basin that include cruising-class entries.

The author copying traffic from radio maritime mobile amateur radio net while en route on a passage. (Betty Hinz)

For those who really want to stay with their neighbors, there are rallies whereby boats travel as an organized group from one port to another. Such was Europa 92, which circumnavigated the world in 1991–1992 with 38 boats and made many ports of call across the Pacific. While these group events often strain the resources of local ports, the peoples of Oceania have always been receptive to seafarers, and they still do their best to host cruising groups.

Some island groups, however, simply cannot accommodate the many cruising boats that come along. The Galapagos Islands is an outstanding example of a fragile ecology that was forced to curtail its hospitality to cruising boats. A combination of growing damage to the environment and a lack of a viable economy forced Ecuador to close Darwin's famous islands to random cruising-boat entry. But there are thousands more islands for cruisers to enjoy, and they are continually finding new ones. Such islands as Palmyra, Savusavu, Maupiti, Aitutake, and Niuatoputapu are taking up the slack from the loss of the Galapagos. New cruisers, new islands, and new adventure are what make the cruising life so interesting.

The growing popularity of blue-water cruising in the Pacific has also created other changes. For those who are unable to own a capable cruising boat, chartering has become an attractive option. Such worldwide charter companies as the Moorings and A.T.M. have established bases in choice Pacific cruising grounds allowing everyone to sample blue-water cruising within a two-week vacation period. The same jet airplane service that made such chartering possible by providing service between population centers of the world and the islands of paradise has also opened up opportunities for crew changes along the way so that friends and relatives can join a blue-water cruiser for a convenient leg or two.

Some of us oldtimers in the cruising game never thought it would happen, but it has—marinas replacing anchorages. When you leave your home port, you hope to enjoy the ancient ritual of anchoring off sandy beaches lined with waving coconut palms. Progress is taking its toll, however, and places like Papeete and Pago Pago now have marinas "just like home." But even they have their purpose in the cruising world, and that is to handle more boats and serve as a convenience to those who wish to use them. It's all part of the ever-changing cruising scene. The only way to beat inevitable change is to "Go now, go soon, go before it is too late" (from my *Sail Before Sunset*).

Through popular usage, two great cruising routes have evolved in the Pacific Basin. One is the well-known Coconut Milk Run that stretches from the Marquesas Islands of French Polynesia to the homey lands of New Zealand. Captain Cook and Josh Slocum pioneered this route, and it has stood the test of time. Somewhat newer (to the cruiser) is the Manila Galleon Run through the North Pacific's islands of Micronesia. Mostly unknown before World War II, the Manila Galleon Run is now a popular off-season route to the western Pacific. It follows the track of the Manila galleons, which left Acapulco every spring loaded with gold and silver to trade for the riches of spices, silks, and rare products from the islands of the mysterious Orient. For cruisers it is a wonderful opportunity to see new islands and peoples without having to wait for the South Pacific tropical cyclone season to end.

There is no turning back the tide of cruising boats setting off for adventure on the waters of the blue Pacific. Cruisers have read of the fun and satisfaction to be found in doing it themselves. Single-handers, couples, families, and pick-up crews are all partaking of the joy of cruising in the Pacific. We of the cruising community ask only that everyone "leave a clean wake."

CHAPTER 2

ROCKS AND SHOALS

Getting Along in Paradise

While a cruise in the Pacific may sound carefree and adventurous, the fact is that much of the red tape and responsibilities dreamed up by government bureaucrats will follow you throughout your cruise. Except for the uninhabited islands of the Pacific, you will have to formally enter every country you visit and be treated as a foreigner and a tourist. Your boat and everything on it will be subject to the Customs regulations of the host country and must be accounted for on entering and again on departure. You are inspected much more closely than your compatriots who arrive by air on one of those sterile tour packages, for you have the better means to smuggle and adversely influence the native population.

Everyone has read of the despoliation of the South Seas by the European and American whalers, traders, and missionaries in years past. That was all done by sea, and the countries evolved protective measures against its happening again by enacting laws and procedures to maintain control of foreigners who arrive by ship. Even though you have only a boat and not a ship, you fall under the same ancient maritime rules of entry and must pay the price in observing official procedures.

You may feel incensed over this lack of kindness to visitors who bring goodwill and money into an island economy, but there have been cruisers in recent years with just as much disregard for local property and customs as the sailors of old—stealing by living off the land, growing marijuana and peddling it to the natives, selling liquor unwisely or illegally, and taking work away from the locals in the interest of building up the cruising kitty. You may think some of these offenses petty, which they are in the sophisticated, hardened society from which you are escaping. But they are real threats to the well-being of these islanders and their communities, and therefore each island government controls visitors to its shores.

Fortunately, the people of the countries of the Pacific still live close to the sea and have a great interest in cruising sailors, who, if they abide by local laws and customs, are welcomed into the island communities. It's all a matter of respecting foreign sovereignty and protocol. Do it right and you will enjoy every landfall in paradise.

Cruise Preparations

BOAT PAPERS

Your principal boat paper is a government registration. U.S. Coast Guard documentation can be obtained from Coast Guard district offices or through a documentation broker. A state registration is also acceptable; it is usually obtained from your state's motor vehicle registration bureau or boating and waterways department. Both types of ownership require yearly renewals, which can be obtained by mail if you are overseas.

If you are only the registered owner of the boat and someone else is the legal owner, you will need additional evidence that you are the managing owner and entitled to sail the boat beyond local navigation limits. Generally, a boat whose legal owner is different from its registered owner will also have insurance, and that insurance must also carry an expanded navigation limits rider or risk voiding the policy.

Boat ownership should provide for a co-owner so that in event of the death or absence of the principal owner, a second person can rightfully execute authority over the vessel. You do not want your boat impounded in a foreign port because the owner cannot take clearance action.

Because most countries require a departure clearance from the last country you visited before they will let you enter, be sure to obtain such a departure clearance (*zarpe*) from Customs when departing any country (including the United States). In the United States it is Customs Form 1378—Clearance of Vessel to a Foreign Port.

A number of countries (those of Micronesia and

With a bone in her teeth, *Horizon* does her easting along the fortieth parallel south, on her way from New Zealand to the Austral Islands. The South Pacific hurricane season has just ended and the southeast trades are strong! (Earl Hinz)

the Galapagos Islands in particular) require a vessel to have an entry permit before arriving in their waters. These controlled-entry countries require the boat permit in addition to personal visas. Refer to specific chapters in this book for more detail. Additional information and the permits themselves can be obtained by writing directly to the countries involved (in most cases) or through an embassy or consulate. For foreign contact in the United States see Department of State (Dep/State) publication 7846—*Foreign Consular Offices in the United States*. It is best to search these out and obtain the necessary permissions before leaving the United States, where communications services and information sources are readily available.

CREW PAPERS

Individual passports are the most important crew documents to have aboard the cruising boat. They identify the nationality of the individual and make a permanent record of the person in the files of the Department of State, Foreign Office, or the like. Procedures for obtaining U.S. passports are contained in Dep/State publication 8969—*Your Trip Abroad*.

Get separate passports for each member of the family and crew traveling. Be sure to get each passport stamped and/or signed when you enter or leave a country (get a post office date stamp as a last resort), for it

not only makes interesting reading in later years, but the next country's Immigration officer will want to know from whence you came.

When a passport gets within six months of its expiration date, you had better take immediate action to get it renewed. Many countries will not process your entry if there is less than six months of valid time on your passport. Or they may only give you a 30-day visitor's permit.

Many countries require that you get a visa (usually an entry in your passport) before arrival, although you can generally obtain a limited-entry permit (good for two weeks to 30 days) after arrival on foreign shores. This may be enough time for a brief visit to a small island; but if you want to enjoy a languorous stay in places like French Polynesia, New Zealand, Hawaii (for non-Americans), and islands of the Micronesian countries, you had better apply for visas ahead of time.

It is the responsibility of the traveler to obtain visas, where required, from the appropriate embassy or nearest consular office. Visa requirements and places in the United States to apply for them are listed in Dep/State publication 9517—*Foreign Entry Requirements*. It is also possible to obtain visas en route at foreign consulates/embassies before entering the desired countries. For this reason carry a supply of two-inch by two-inch black-and-white passport-type photographs for each crew member. Note that visa requirements are often different for tourists arriving by airplane, so be certain that the visa application notes that you are arriving by boat. When applying, ask whether a visa can be renewed and for how long.

One problem with cruising is that you do not have a well-defined schedule, so it is difficult to specify a firm date of arrival. While your visa will specify a desired length of stay, the arrival date should be left as general as possible. Another solution to the timing problem is to route yourself through a country along the way that has a consul for the country requiring a visa; at that point you can better ascertain your arrival date.

A crew list is another important entry paper. There is no standard form for a crew list, but it should include date of arrival; last port of call; name of each person aboard and his or her position (all persons aboard a cruising boat, except the skipper, are listed as crew members); and the date of birth, nationality, and passport number of each person. Prepare the crew-list in quadruplicate before arrival. (This is a good reason to have a typewriter on board.)

Many boats have found it useful to have an official-looking seal or stamp made with which to emblazon documents they submit for entry or departure clearance (such as crew lists). No particular format is required, but at a minimum such a stamp should include boat name, documentation/registration number, and home port. A purveyor of seals and stamps can design one to suit your cruising needs.

HEALTH REQUIREMENTS

Although the numbers of diseases rampant in this world are growing fewer, some like yellow fever and cholera continue to show up and must not be carried to a new country. The World Health Organization offers a yellow record card (International Certificate of Vaccinations) presenting each person's recent history of vaccinations and inoculations. Each crew member should carry this card—which can be obtained from local government health organizations such as city, county, and state health clinics—with his or her passport. Let the health workers know your proposed itinerary, and they can advise you what immunizations to get. They may even offer the immunizations at reduced prices. Another source of world health information is the nearest U.S. Public Health Service office, which through its Centers for Disease Control is in contact with the World Health Organization on international medical information.

Medical services abroad are often available through the International Association for Medical Assis-

tance to Travelers (IAMAT), "a worldwide association of medical doctors to provide medical assistance to travelers who, while absent from their home country, may find themselves in need of medical or surgical care or any form of medical treatment. This is done by providing those travelers with the names of locally licensed practitioners who have command of the native language spoken by the traveler and who agree to a stated and standard list of medical fees for their services."

Before leaving home, see your family doctor and bring up to date your immunizations—tetanus, diphtheria, typhoid, and so on. If you plan to travel in malaria-ridden countries, be sure you have an adequate supply of proper antimalarial prophylactics in your medicine kit (see chapter 19). Be certain that any crew member on health maintenance drugs, has an adequate supply to last until a new supply can be obtained. Prescription drugs are sometimes difficult to obtain in foreign countries (or even out of your own state for that matter.) On the plus side, many prescription drugs are much cheaper in foreign countries, especially those with socialized medicine, and many are available without prescription.

For more detailed information of health care when traveling, write for the following two publications:

Health Information for International Travel
Government Printing Office
Washington DC 20402–9325

World Travelers Medical Information Packet
International Association for Medical Assistance
   to Travelers (IAMAT)
417 Center Street, Lewiston NY 14092
(free; donations accepted)

HANDLING FINANCES

Handling finances when cruising is principally a matter of having enough money available when arriving in a new country to satisfy entry requirements (landing bonds and financial responsibility) and to cover your expected spending needs. Six months' worth of "spending money" in cash and traveler's checks is a recommended amount.

The landing bond is to assure the authorities that you have the means to depart the country should you leave the boat for any reason. The amount of bond is equivalent to the airline fare back to your country of passport. An open airline ticket will also do the job, but cashing it in unused at a later date may be difficult.

Many countries will also demand evidence of

financial responsibility, namely, do you have enough money to support yourself for the duration of your stay? Besides normal living expenses, this also means the ability to pay for moorage and repairs to your boat. The latter could involve large sums of money should you have been dismasted or suffered other major damage while at sea.

The U.S. dollar is very popular throughout the world and the best medium of exchange there is when cruising. Select a bank at your home base that has worldwide branches. Barclays of London, Manufacturers Hanover Trust, and Citibank are good examples. The basic question is, what form should you carry your money while cruising? Traveler's checks are the safest and often the most useful, and if the checks are $20 or $50 denomination, most merchants will accept them for purchases. Larger denominations can be converted into local currency at banks. Greenbacks can be exchanged at banks—and, depending on the country, also at stores —for local currency and products. Be certain that you know the going exchange rates before exchanging money any place. Do not convert more than you need for your stay (or more than government regulations require), because every time you exchange your money, you will lose a percent or two. Be wary of black market money exchangers.

Credit cards are a worldwide institution with VISA, MasterCard, and American Express the leaders. You must have a home base setup, however, to receive the bills and match them against your receipts before paying. Delays in the overseas mail system can make this hazardous at times. American Express card members can also get travel assistance by telephone 24 hours a day. It will also advise card holders on health, visa requirements, and weather conditions in foreign countries. Their Global Assist program can help in an emergency away from home.

Obtaining money en route can be difficult. American Express will advance limited amounts of money ($500 at this time) on your credit card and offers a Moneygram service for large amounts sent from your home base. VISA and MasterCard also offer cash advances. Transfer of money by wire can be accomplished by most banks worldwide; it can take several days, but it is particularly useful for large sums. Your home bank is requested by wire to debit your account and forward the money to the requesting bank to put into your new account. Transfer of money by wire may have limits imposed by the receiving country and you must open an account to receive the money.

International postal money orders can be sent from your home base to you, but they can take weeks to clear all the banks and postal hurdles involved. They are definitely not recommended unless the country has a good postal system. Letters of credit for personal use have not worked well in the international banking system and are not recommended.

HANDLING MAIL

Since most cruising people are not intending to sever their ties with the folks back home, mail becomes a very important factor in a cruise, particularly if the younger crew members are learning their three R's at sea. Mail service is not dependable to every country of the Pacific, so choose occasional landfalls in countries with good mail connections to your home country.

The U.S. Postal Service will forward first and priority class mail to any of the U.S. territories in the Pacific and to APO/FPO addresses. Foreign mail will have to be forwarded by your home base to any foreign address. Mail to foreign countries should be sent to Poste Restante, which is the traveler's version of General Delivery. In many countries, General Delivery means local mail, and that is not what a cruiser wants. Mail marked Poste Restante, on the other hand, will be separated from the local mail. Send all mail by air since surface shipping takes, literally, months.

Don't have mail sent too far in advance of your arrival because most post offices will hold mail for only 30 days, some for only ten. Mail should be addressed

> Mr./Mrs. I. M. Person
> c/o Yacht *Wanderlust*
> Poste Restante
> Papeete, Tahiti
> FRENCH POLYNESIA

with the added note "Hold for Arrival." Other mail-holding agencies in decreasing order of dependability:

> A local resident you know
> American Express offices
> Yacht clubs
> International banks
> Port captains
> Marinas/hotels

Another option is to have your mail-forwarding service package all your mail into a box and ship it air freight by one of the worldwide airline package/courier services. This is particularly good if you are expecting catalogs, books, or other heavy products. The negative—it will have to go through Customs on arrival.

FLAG PROTOCOL

Maritime law and custom decree the use of flags for visual information exchange ranging from ship identity to requests for assistance. Cruising yachts fall under the same rules, and the correct flags must be flown (worn) at appropriate times in foreign waters.

The basic flags needed are the national flag of the boat's country of registration, a courtesy flag for the country whose waters you are entering (their merchant flag), and an international code flag Q. The national flag should measure at least one inch of fly (horizontal dimension) for each foot of boat length. The courtesy and Q flags should be at least half that size. For U.S. yachts the merchant flag is the same as the national ensign—the Stars and Stripes. Other countries may have their own merchant ship flags. The yacht ensign, Coast Guard Auxiliary ensign, and U.S. Power Squadron ensign have no international significance and should not be flown in foreign waters.

When the boat is under way, the national flag is flown from the stern staff or two-thirds the way up the leach of the aftermost sail. At anchor or in the harbor, it is flown from the stern staff only. The flag should be flown from 0800 until sunset.

When the boat is in foreign waters, nominally within the 12-mile limit, the courtesy flag is flown con-tinuously from the starboard spreader. When you actually enter a foreign port, the Q flag is raised below the courtesy flag. The Q flag says "I request pratique." It is lowered as soon as the medical officer deems your crew to be healthy, but the courtesy flag stays up.

(See back cover for proper national flags to fly as courtesy ensigns.)

Cruising Business En Route

SAFETY

Your personal safety cannot be assured in a foreign country any more than it can be at home. Some countries are more, others less, safe. Cruisers can assess the situation from newspapers, the SSCA *Commodores' Bulletin,* and a particularly valuable document from the Dep/State called *Travel Advisory.* Copies of these advisories can be obtained from

> Citizen's Emergency Center
> Bureau of Consular Affairs
> Room 4811
> U.S. Department of State
> Washington DC 20520
> Tel: (202) 647-5225

Also useful are the Dep/State booklets *Tips for Travelers* (to various countries—eight booklets in series), *A Safe Trip Abroad,* and *Tips for Americans Residing Abroad.* Listen to the Voice of America radio for news of world hot spots.

Don't traffic in drugs. Most foreign countries have more severe penalties for drug offenses than the United States, and there is very little the United States can do to help if you are caught with drugs. Read Dep/State publication 9558—*Travel Warning on Drugs Abroad.*

If you should get into trouble abroad, someone in one of the 250 consular offices around the world may be able to advise and help if you are in serious trouble. For a listing see the Dep/State booklet *Key Officers of Foreign Service Posts* (published semiannually). The State Department's Overseas Citizens' Emergency Center (Tel: [202] 647–5225) can help home base families locate a traveler abroad to deliver an emergency message. Read Dep/State publication 9402, *Tips for Americans Residing Abroad.*

If you are an American Express card holder, you can take advantage of their Global Assist program, which provides a useful number of services before you

The author's boat *Horizon* rides serenely at anchor in the lagoon at Jaluit Atoll. (Earl Hinz)

go and while you are in foreign countries. Get acquainted with the services available by calling the program hotline: (800) 554–2639.

CLEARING INTO A FOREIGN COUNTRY

There is a proper protocol to follow in entering a foreign country by yacht. Flouting a host country's laws or customs is a good way to become persona non grata and be requested to leave early, also spoiling the opportunities for cruisers following in your wake. The process of clearing into a foreign country is the most important legal process that you will go through when cruising. Do it correctly and you will have no trouble.

Many countries charge exorbitant fees for overtime clearance, so plan your arrival to coincide with normal working hours and days for the host country. Arrive at an official Port of Entry for initial clearance processing; do not stop first at intermediate ports. Seek out the quarantine anchorage or equivalent in the harbor.

The four common inspections are Health, Immigration, Customs, and Agriculture. Sometimes officers of all four will appear; oftentimes one inspector will handle more than one category. Processing may be done at anchor, at a wharf, or in an office. Until your boat has a clearance, only the skipper is permitted ashore, and no visitors are allowed on the boat.

When entering a foreign port, fly the (yellow) Q flag, requesting free pratique. The Health officer or representative will be the first on board to ascertain the health of the crew. Expect the officer to examine your passports to learn whether you have arrived from a country in which there is a known disease of concern. Should there be a serious disease in the country you are entering, the officer will advise you on proper immunizations for your stay.

Be prepared to submit to the Customs inspector a list of stores aboard including tobacco and alcohol and a separate list of high-value merchandise such as electronics, cameras, jewelry, timepieces, and the like, which, conceivably, could be sold on the local market. Tobacco and alcohol quantities are limited by most countries to those for crew use. Excess can be bonded under lock and key. Pharmaceutical drugs should be stored under lock and key and prescriptions kept with them.

Firearms are restricted in most countries, and you will have to declare them when entering a country. See Dep/State *Post Notices* for each country's restrictions on firearms or contact the country's nearest consulate before leaving home.

Some countries consider your boat as a possible article of importation. Be sure to get from Customs a written temporary importation permit for the record. If you intend to cruise to other ports of your host country, inquire of the Customs inspector about the need for a cruising permit.

Once officially cleared into the country, be certain that your boat is properly moored. The port captain, if there is one, will assign you a place in the harbor for the duration of your stay. If there is no port captain, then ask a responsible person where you can tie up or moor out of the way of shipping, which may come and go at odd hours of the day or night. Don't block local maritime operations. It would not only be undiplomatic to do so, but if you value your boat at all, you won't argue with steel-hulled copra schooners for dock space.

After clearing in with the proper officials, it is incumbent on the skipper to pay a visit to the local island chief if there is one. This initial visit should be brief and accompanied by a dignified gift. It will open many doors of cultural exchange during your visit.

CLEARING OUT OF A FOREIGN COUNTRY

So what happens when you get ready to leave? Start by informing the port captain, who will ascertain whether you owe any bills around town including wharfage or other harbor costs. Immigration will give you a clearance form and stamp your passport for the day of departure. Your final step is to visit Customs, where you will get an outbound clearance *(zarpe)* needed for entry to your next port of call. You are then ready to go. If for any reason you are delayed, stay on your boat and notify Customs; otherwise you may be required to go through the whole entering/departure process again.

Failing to properly clear out of a foreign country could put your next Port of Entry at risk. Harbormasters have an active radio and telephone network with each other permitting an exchange of information on cruising boats and the blackballing of those who do not observe the proper protocol. It is strongly advised that you pay your bills and clear through the proper authorities when departing any island country.

Pets in the Pacific

Pets are a problem for the cruising boat because the islands of the Pacific are rabies free, and all the governments work hard to keep them that way. Agriculture entry inspection varies between countries, but, generally, birds are forbidden by most countries. In the most lenient countries, four-legged pets must have a veterinary health certificate from the previous country of visit made out no more than 10 days before embarkation. The animal must also have a certificate of rabies vaccination given not less than ten days nor more than six months before embarkation.

Some countries will quarantine the animals ashore at your expense. Others will quarantine the animal on the boat and require that you post a bond of performance. The most severe restriction exercised by some countries is to ban the animal (and boat) from their waters entirely. Violations of pet importation laws are usually quite harsh and end up with the animal's being destroyed. Specific requirements are given in the State Department pamphlets *Post Report* issued individually for each country.

Before you decide to take Tabby or Rover along on your cruise, consider the following regulations for the island countries:

American Samoa: The animal is quarantined on the boat, and the owner must post a US$500 bond to assure compliance.

Australia: If you have an animal on board you will be allowed to moor in midwater only, not to tie up at a dock. You must confine the animal on board your craft and enter into an A$500 bond that it will not come ashore or come into contact with Australian animals. If you violate your bond, your animal could be destroyed, your bond forfeited, and you prosecuted.

Fiji: Any pet animal on board your boat must stay on board at all times when in Fijian waters and must not be allowed to come ashore. You will have to post a F$100 bond to assure that you will keep the animal on board. There should be no contact between your pets and animals ashore.

French Polynesia: The animal must have an antirabies vaccination and then it can be quarantined on your boat for however long you are in their waters. The entry of animals, plants, and fruits is prohibited.

Hawaii and Western Samoa: The animal must be quarantined ashore in a government facility for 120 days after receiving an antirabies vaccination. The cost in Hawaii runs US$412 for a cat and US$466 for a dog. You have no choice.

New Zealand: You must post a NZ$1,000 bond that you will keep the animal on board your boat. Animal quarantine inspectors will visit your boat three times a week to check on the animal's presence. This will cost you a minimum of NZ$150 per month depending on your location. If the animal escapes it will be destroyed. Except for clearing-in procedures, boats with pets on board must anchor out at all times. They are limited to a stay of three months regardless of immigration visa lengths.

New Caledonia: If you want to take your pet ashore it will first need to be put into quarantine for ten days for observation. You do not need to quarantine it if you do not want to take it ashore.

Tonga and Tuvalu: The animal can be landed provided that it has antirabies vaccination and an up-to-date health certificate and you have an import permit for it.

Vanuatu: The landing of animals is strictly prohibited at all times.

All other countries: An animal cannot be taken ashore no matter what the reason, but in these countries you can keep the animal on board for the duration of your stay in port. Be certain to declare all pets you have on board.

An animal, bird, or other pet picked up along the way while cruising also becomes subject to the foregoing regulations. Some countries will allow a dog to be brought ashore after a 60-day quarantine on the boat if it was born on a rabies-free island and has a valid certificate of birth. A useful guide for traveling with pets is

Traveling with Your Pet
Society for the Prevention of Cruelty to Animals
441 East 92nd Street
New York NY 10028
Cost is US$5.00 ppd.

Customs of Island People

One of the rewards of cruising is mingling with the indigenous people and learning their ways. But one must observe local protocol. Not surprisingly, the people of Oceania have different social values than Americans or Europeans have. They also tend to be more sensitive about violations of their social codes. While your hosts may say nothing (being too polite to offend you), their ardor for cruisers will cool rapidly if you disregard local customs.

Religious patterns can be a big source of trouble to the visitor. Early missionaries did such a good job of

Christianizing the islands that now the islanders have a deeper religious conviction than most visitors. The motto of Western Samoa is "Western Samoa is founded upon God." Sunday (Saturday in the case of Seventh-Day Adventists) is usually a day of rest and worship in the islands. For instance, the Tongan constitution says, "The Sabbath Day shall be sacred in Tonga forever, and it shall not be lawful to do work or play games on the Sabbath. Any agreement made or witnessed on this day shall be counted void and not recognized by the government."

Sunday also has a dress code to be observed. In the Cook Islands, for instance, it is improper to walk past a church while services are in progress without wearing a shirt. If you attend church services, men should wear trousers—long or short, but if short, knee sox should also be worn—and, of course, shoes. Women can wear long or short dresses or a blouse and slacks. Shorts and open-back dresses (and in some places, sleeveless dresses) are not acceptable.

Everyday dress standards vary considerably across Oceania; they also depend on whether you are in an urban area or in a more remote place. For instance, bathing suits (including bikinis) are permissible on most beaches but are not to be worn in town. In Tonga men must always wear shirts when off the boat. Tight or short shorts on men or women are frowned on in urban areas. Women can solve this problem by keeping a wrap-around skirt handy (called a laplap in Tuvalu, a lava-lava in Samoa, and a pareau in French Polynesia). European-style walking shorts for men are always acceptable and very comfortable in the tropics.

In the remote areas, particularly in parts of Micronesia and Melanesia, local women often go topless. That is the norm and can be discreetly followed by visitors also. But, remember, no picture taking without permission. Topless dress is rarely seen in any urban area and never complete nudity anywhere. Not until you get to certain designated beaches in Australia will you find topless swimming accepted in public. In Tuvalu exposed bras, even if part of a shorts combination, are not acceptable, so women should put on at least a T-shirt.

The people of Oceania can also be very sensitive to the street behavior of visitors. In New Guinea it is improper to show signs of affection in public or to comb your hair in public. Eating on the street is not proper etiquette in many places, including Tonga and Samoa. Do not drive a vehicle, ride a horse, or carry packages when passing in front of a Samoan *fale* (house) where chiefs are meeting. Although it may seem like a good time to explore a village, do not walk around villages while church services are in progress, and above all, do not make excessive noise.

Other, more subtle points of etiquette should be observed if you wish to keep in the good graces of the local people. When in a Samoan *fale* speak only while sitting and sit cross-legged, as it is impolite to point your feet at anyone. If for physical reasons you cannot sit cross-legged, cover your feet with a mat. Don't eat while standing in a *fale*. Never step over a baby when in New Guinea, for that is believed to hinder its further growth. In Micronesia it is frowned on to pat children on the head. If you drink kava in Fiji, tip a little of the liquid out in front of you before you drink.

The sense of humor of Pacific peoples is every bit as lively and sharp as a visitor's, but, like people anywhere, they can be offended easily by jokes or statements that place them in an inferior position. Avoid terms of ridicule like "funny money" and the plethora of lei jokes that seem so funny at cocktail parties back home. Practical jokes are a great source of amusement to the islanders, and you may well find yourself the butt of an innocent bit of local humor. Be a good sport and you will win their respect. Tread lightly with your own humor until you have been accepted by the local people, and then don't change your ways.

The peoples of Oceania are generally reserved and will wait for the visitor to set the mood of the meeting. If you show friendliness and good humor, they will respond with warmth; if you are demanding and arrogant, you will not get to enjoy South Seas hospitality.

While private property is ofttimes hard to distinguish in the quasi-communal societies of the Pacific, do not take anything without first asking permission of someone nearby. All land, buildings, trees, and fruits have some owner even though there may appear to be no boundaries or claims on the property. Compared to American and European standards of ownership, everything will appear to be free for the taking, but that isn't so. Theirs is a mostly undocumented ownership that outsiders find hard to understand until it is too late, after they have helped themselves to the fruits of paradise. Many things are indeed communal, but they require the permission of the village chief for transfer; ofttimes even food and water will fall into this class. And the one thing you do not want to do is cross the village chief!

The materialism of money also has a different connotation with the people of the Pacific islands. Once you leave the shores of Western industrialized civilization, do not tip people who help or serve you. To give service to a stranger is an honor in most islands of the Pacific.

Porpoise riding the bow waves of boats provide hours of entertainment on long passages. (Earl Hinz)

Tipping can actually be insulting. If you feel that you must reward them for their services, leave them a simple gift when you depart—something that will not make them feel indebted to you. Also, spread the joy—give small gifts to many people rather than large gifts to a few.

What makes good gifts? For the kids—chewing gum, balloons, swim trunks, and T-shirts with logos. For adults consider tobacco and matches, swim trunks for the men, cheap wristwatches, dry-cell batteries, and thong sandals. More practical gifts include hard-to-get foods, spices, and other condiments. Dried instant foods and ready-prepared foods make excellent gifts. Practically all rural people grow their own food, and gifts of melon seed packets will be very welcome. You will be surprised at how much joy modest gifts bring to people living in outlying villages.

Bartering varies throughout the Pacific, but away from major urban areas it is a way of life. (Vanuatu is one country where bartering is not common.) In some places money has no value; it is more important to have trade goods. No junk or things of little use to native people—think in terms of clothes suitable to a hot climate, small wood-carving chisels and sandpaper, knives, durable pots and pans, and fishing gear.

In bartering it is essential that both sides receive satisfaction and that no hidden defects arise after the trade. Don't give dead batteries or a radio that doesn't work or candy that has been dropped in the sand. Some cruiser coming behind you will get the backlash. Be fair but not overly generous. Don't be the cause of inflation in the local economy.

And don't give or trade items that may cause trouble in a village—no liquor unless the village chief approves, and go easy on .22 rifle shells; they are contraband in some countries, and you could get yourself into trouble.

The ancestors of today's island people lived a life close to nature, making use of natural products for their shelters and places of religious worship. Today most of those buildings have collapsed and partially returned to nature. In fact, to the untrained eye they may be indistinguishable from the surrounding bush. But show respect for those you do see by not walking across the obvious ruins or defacing them in any way though they may look like "just a pile of stones." Peoples of the Pacific are actively trying to preserve their heritage, which is so rapidly being eroded by the materialistic twentieth century.

Lastly, don't get impatient with island people. Their pace of life is far more leisurely and unpressured than in America or Europe, which is one of the reasons you are traveling in these waters. In Melanesia, Micronesia, and Polynesia, local time is usually slower than clock time. Events normally start when the people get to them, not when the hands of the clock tell them to begin.

Skipper's Responsibilities

Your boat may be only a fraction of the size of an ocean liner, but you, as skipper, will have many of the same administrative responsibilities as the captain of a

30,000-ton cruise ship. In a foreign port you are responsible for your boat and crew. Failure to observe local law or regulations or getting in trouble with the local people could result in a request to leave, a fine, or worse, the confiscation of your boat.

Many countries are insisting that cruising sailors have adequate funds to sustain the crew while the boat is visiting so that living off the local people doesn't get to be a habit. The condition of your boat will also be important because there are already enough boats cluttering the reefs of the islands because of poor navigation without having others sink in the harbor.

Your appearance and that of your crew is very important in your acceptance by the host country. Most places do not welcome hippies or nudies. An ill-kept boat or a sloppy personal appearance show a lack of consideration or even a disregard for the host country. The formalities of entry and your acceptance by the local people will be greatly enhanced by neat appearance and proper courtesy. Cruising by its nature is informal, but in a foreign land a certain amount of dignity is required to maintain the goodwill needed by the cruising fraternity.

One Last Word

The level of your cruising satisfaction depends on how much you learn before you start. You have to say to yourself "I am going to do it, I am going to do it right, and therefore I will succeed." In other words, psych yourself up for success. You will no longer be a member of a protective society with food stores on the corner, fire and police protection a telephone call away, repairmen available to fix anything that goes wrong with the material wonders of the twentieth century, lawyers to keep you out of legal troubles, and the world's finest medical help to keep your body together. You are going to leave all of that behind and go on your own to foreign lands where people don't speak your language and where they more often than not live in a subsistence economy with few, if any, benefits of modern technology. And you are going to do all of that with a wind-propelled machine that was given up as a useful form of global transportation three-quarters of a century ago!

Yes, you will do it, for that is what cruising is all about.

CHAPTER 3

PACIFIC WEATHER

Except for a few hardy adventurers who sail around the Horn and other colorful but cold places, most cruising sailors seek the milder climates of the lower latitudes. Cruising is supposed to be fun, and weather can make a big difference in how much fun you can have. But weather can be contradictory, and we find that even the pleasantness of the tropics is occasionally shattered by the violence of hurricanes. Fortunately, seasonal weather patterns on the average are repeatable, so a cruise can be planned to take advantage of good winds yet avoid the majority of the storms. Still, though you can hope to avoid tropical storms by careful planning, you will always be faced with the possibility of gale force winds at any season, so be prepared for them.

In cruising, wind is our motive power; without it we would never leave home. But with it we can cruise the length and breadth of the vast Pacific Ocean—provided that we understand the vagaries of the wind. Winds are caused by the earth's rotation and the heating and cooling of the land, sea, and air masses. On the grand scale these effects are repetitive and produce an understandable pattern of surface winds. These surface winds are shown schematically in the chart along with latitude variations of atmospheric pressure.

Doldrums

The doldrums, also known as the equatorial trough or intertropical convergence zone (ITCZ), is an area of low pressure situated between the trade winds of the two hemispheres. The width of the doldrums varies daily and seasonally but averages about 2½ degrees of latitude.

The doldrums remain north of the equator in longitudes east of 160°W. To the west of 160°W their position varies seasonally, being south of the equator between December and April and north between June and October. In the western Pacific west of 150°E longitude, however, they are virtually nonexistent during the northern hemisphere summer.

The weather of the doldrums ranges from light variable winds and often calms to squalls, heavy showers, and thunderstorms. West of 130°W the frequency of calms and variable winds is considerably less than over the waters between Central America and 130°W. The type of weather varies daily and seasonally; at times a boat may cross the doldrums and experience fine weather while another time there may be continuous squalls and thunderstorms. Generally, the weather in the doldrums is at its worst when the trades are strongest and where they meet at the greatest angle. This is essentially the eastern Pacific area.

During the southern hemisphere summer, the equatorial trough lies south of the equator between about December and April, reaching its southernmost position in February. The seasonal movement of the trough in the western South Pacific is large and so is its day-to-day movement in the vicinity of northern Australia and New Guinea. The trough averages about 150 miles in width, but it may be anywhere from 50 to 300 miles wide. The weather is similar to the doldrums of the northern hemisphere but may be more severe because of the wider angle of the converging southeast trades and northwest monsoons.

Northeast Trade Winds

The northeast trades blow on the equatorial side of the large clockwise circulation of the Pacific Ocean high-pressure area known as the Pacific high. The Pacific high lies farther north and is somewhat more intense in summer than in winter. In summer the northeast trades blow as far west as 150°E and between the doldrums and about 32°N. East of 150°, the northeast trades are remarkably persistent and steady over large areas of the ocean. Along the North American coast they are mainly

Terrestrial Pressure and Wind Systems

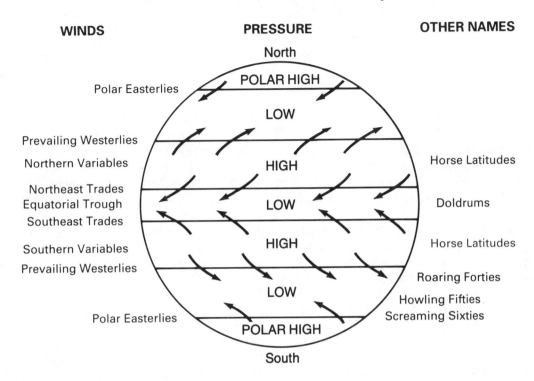

WINDS   **PRESSURE**   **OTHER NAMES**

North

POLAR HIGH

Polar Easterlies

LOW

Prevailing Westerlies

Northern Variables   HIGH   Horse Latitudes

Northeast Trades
Equatorial Trough   LOW   Doldrums
Southeast Trades

Southern Variables   HIGH   Horse Latitudes
Prevailing Westerlies

Roaring Forties

LOW   Howling Fifties
Screaming Sixties

Polar Easterlies

POLAR HIGH

South

northerly or, possibly, northwesterly. Further to the west and toward the doldrums, they are mainly easterly in the summer months.

The strength of the northeast trades averages Force 3 to 4 but occasionally freshens to Force 5 or 6. Less than 10 percent of the time will they reach Force 7.

Along the Mexican coast in the vicinity of the Gulf of Tehuantepec, north winds are particularly strong in the winter months from October to April, oftentimes reaching Force 8. The gales, which may be felt a hundred miles to sea, may last from several hours to several days and raise a short, high sea. There is less than one day per month of such winds—called Tehuantepecers—from May to September. Apart from squalls, winds of this strength are unlikely within about 600 miles of the equator.

The typical weather of the trade wind belt is fair, with scattered showers and skies half covered by small cumulus clouds known as trade wind clouds. At times the pattern is interrupted by a day or two of unsettled showery weather with occasional squalls.

In this area visibility over the open ocean is generally good, except in rain, but often a light haze restricts visibility to 8–15 miles. Showers, clouds, and haze usually increase when the wind freshens. The American coastline tends to be hazy from Mexico north because of fog and dust in the air. In the northeast part of the belt, near the American coast, there are generally fewer clouds than elsewhere, and rain is rare.

Northern Variables

The northern variables are a belt of variable winds stretching across the central Pacific at about 25°N–30°N in the winter and 35°N–40°N in the summer. In the eastern part of this belt, winds are mainly northerly in all seasons. In the west, southerly winds are prevalent in the summer giving way to southwest to northwest winds east of 150°E.

In the summer, winds are generally light and are likely to reach Force 7 only on rare occasions except in association with tropical storms. East of 140°W near the U.S. coast, north and northwest winds may reach Force 7 about four days a month. The weather is generally fair near the center of the Pacific high in summer, and rain is infrequent. Cloudier conditions prevail east and west of the high, and rain is more common to the west of it. Fog may be expected along the American coast four to five days per month in the summer.

In winter, winds occasionally reach Force 7 east of 140°W but as you progress farther west, the number of days that winds will reach Force 7 increases to six to ten days per month west of 150°E. Visibility in winter is generally good except in rain. Over the open ocean fog is not a problem.

Westerlies

North of 40°N are the westerlies, fraught with gales and fog in summer and not advised as a route in winter. The main feature of this weather is its variability resulting from the numerous depressions that move from west to east.

In winter the winds vary greatly in direction and strength, and gales are frequent. The maximum number of gales occurs between Japan and the area south of the Alaska Peninsula, and winds of Force 7 or above can be expected about half the time. Periods of overcast skies with rain or snow alternate with days of clear weather. Fog is uncommon, but the rain and snow severely limit visibility at times.

In summer the northeasterly-moving depressions are less frequent than winter and also less severe, and their tracks generally are farther north. South of 50°N, gale force winds occur only one to five days per month, and in July only one day of gale force winds is to be expected. The weather, however, can be cloudy and foggy much of the time. West of 160°W, fog can be expected five to ten days per month. East of 160°W the number of occurrences is fewer until you reach the California coast, at which place the visibility may be impaired by fog from five to ten days per month.

Southeast Trade Winds

The SE trade winds blow on the equatorial side of the oceanic high pressure area situated about 30°S. The trade winds are sustained by a semipermanent high-pressure area in the eastern part of the ocean and by the migratory high-pressure cells that move east from Australia. These trade winds are also characterized by their constancy: they have an average strength of Force 4 but occasionally rise to Force 5 or 6 over large areas. Winds of Force 7 or greater are unlikely on more than one or two days per month. Within ten degrees of the equator, strong winds are uncommon, except in short-lived squalls.

In the vicinity of South America, the trades blow from south and southeast, changing to easterly as you go further west. However, in the southern winter the southeast monsoon develops over the seas north of Australia, making the trades again southeast.

During the period of the steady southeast trades, the skies are usually half-covered with small cumulus clouds, and a slight haze limits visibility to eight to fifteen miles. Occasional showers may be expected. East of 180° and between the equator and 8°S there is a relatively dry belt that extends to the coast of South America. Although dry it is also cloudy a good share of the time, and overcast is not uncommon.

West of 140°W (but not including the foregoing dry belt), the weather tends to be unsettled and the trades unsteady from November to April. Cloudy weather with showers becomes the rule until the trades settle down again with occasional squalls from south and east.

Southern Variables

The southern variables, which extend in a belt from 25°S to 40°S in the summer to 20°S to 30°S in the winter, are generally of moderate strength. East of 85°W the winds are an extension of the southeast trades. Winds reach Force 7 or above only one to three days per month except at the southern fringe, where they may occur up to three to six days per month.

The weather is highly variable depending on where you are relative to the migrating high pressure cells that cause the variability. Near the centers the weather is usually fair, but in the adjoining troughs of low pressure, cloudy, unsettled weather is the norm, with more rainfall toward the southern edge of the belt. The rainfall at the eastern end of the belt near South America is infrequent, but cloud cover is usually heavy. Fog is common in the vicinity of the Peru current, occurring up to three to five days per month.

Westerlies or Roaring Forties

Unlike the northern hemisphere, where continental land masses interrupt and modify the flow of air, the southern hemisphere winds of the westerly wind belt can circumnavigate the earth. This unimpeded path plus a strong and constant pressure differential between the Horse Latitudes and the subpolar low creates strong winds throughout the year of Force 5 and 6. Gales are very common, especially in the winter, and winds of Force 7 or above occur five to ten days per month. The strength of these winds has earned these latitudes the title Roaring Forties; it was in these latitudes that the square-rigged ships of the 1880s made their fast runs from Australia back to the Atlantic around Cape Horn. One of the stormiest areas is west-northwest of Cape Horn, where winds of Force 7 are likely to occur on twenty days per month during the period July to September. Summer gales are less frequent and occur farther south; nevertheless, this is not common cruising ground for small boats. The weather is variable as in the other westerlies, and periods of overcast skies and rain or snow alternate with periods of fair weather. The fair weather does not hang around very long, however, and clouds are profuse. Some fog is common, up to three to five days per month.

Monsoons

Monsoonal winds are found in the waters of the Indian Ocean and the western Pacific. They can have a significant effect on sailing the western parts of Melanesia and Micronesia. The word "monsoon" is a derivative of the Arabic word *mausim* (season). Monsoons are generated by the heating and cooling of the atmosphere over the Asian land mass and, to a lesser degree, over Australia.

During the boreal summer of May to September a large, low-pressure area builds over central Asia, producing a counterclockwise air circulation and southwest winds in the western Pacific. The winds bring monsoonal rains, which are the lifeblood of the Asian continent. Squalls and thunderstorms abound, and it is a good time to sail south of the equator, especially since this is also typhoon season. As the season progresses, the winds slacken and become weak variables and the climate oppressively hot and humid.

During the boreal winter, a high-pressure area builds over the Asian continent, producing a clockwise circulation of air that strengthens the northeast trade winds. This occurs in the period October to April, making it the best time to sail the western Pacific, especially since there are few (or no) typhoons. The strongest trade wind reinforcement occurs in the earlier half of the northern hemisphere winter, tapering off in the latter half. Cruisers should carefully watch not only the typhoon patterns, but the monsoon wind patterns as well when sailing the western Pacific.

Tropical Cyclones

A unique weather phenomenon of the tropics is the tropical cyclone, which in its worst phase is the hurricane or typhoon. Because it depends on warm water as its source of energy, it is unique to the tropics. Occasionally tropical cyclones will pass from the tropics to the temperate zone, becoming extratropical cyclones. Of all storms experienced at sea, the fully developed tropical cyclone is the worst and one to be avoided by mariners in planning their itineraries. Fortunately, the regions and times of year of hurricane and typhoon generation are fairly predictable, so with a little planning these can be avoided.

A cyclone is a closed circulation about a low pressure point within a weather system as defined by isobars. Winds cross the isobars and spiral inward toward the low pressure center. The clouds also show this spiraling effect but on a grand scale visible only from satellite pictures. The tropical cyclone is of tropical oceanic origin and has no weather fronts per se; it derives its energy primarily from the warm ocean waters having temperatures in excess of 80°F. Hence, such storms rarely generate outside the tropics (although when they do, they generally travel poleward).

The formative stage is called a tropical disturbance; this is simply a situation wherein weather *seems* to be brewing. It is unsettled with clouds, rain, and squalls, and the average windspeed is not great. At this time there is no clear indication of what, if anything, is to come. The barometer will fall very slowly to the vicinity of 1010 to 1000 millibars (mbs). Its continuing fall is a sign of something significant.

When a definite closed circulation is established (in the sense of a closed isobar) and maximum sustained wind speeds are approaching 34 knots but still less than a fresh gale, the disturbance is termed a tropical depression. The center of the closed isobars is also the center of the depression. Strong winds will develop to the north and east of the developing vortex in the northern hemisphere (in the southern hemisphere they will develop to the south and east of the developing center).

As the winds further increase to sustained speeds between 34 and 63 knots, the depression becomes a tropical storm. Waves, clouds, and rain are more threatening than in the depression. Not all tropical cyclones will reach this stage. Some last only a day though strong winds may have developed briefly. Others may weaken to the tropical depression stage and then travel great dis-

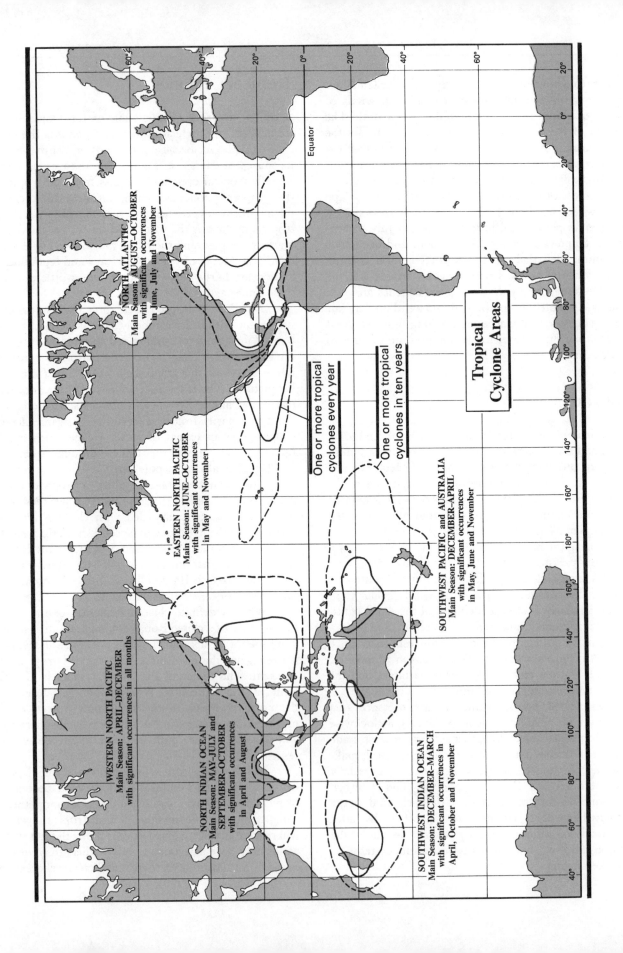

Tropical Cyclone Areas

NORTH ATLANTIC
Main Season: AUGUST–OCTOBER
with significant occurrences
in June, July and November

EASTERN NORTH PACIFIC
Main Season: JUNE–OCTOBER
with significant occurrences
in May and November

One or more tropical
cyclones every year

One or more tropical
cyclones in ten years

SOUTHWEST PACIFIC and AUSTRALIA
Main Season: DECEMBER–APRIL
with significant occurrences
in May, June and November

WESTERN NORTH PACIFIC
Main Season: APRIL–DECEMBER
with significant occurrences in all months

NORTH INDIAN OCEAN
Main Season: MAY–JULY and
SEPTEMBER–OCTOBER
with significant occurrences
in April and August

SOUTHWEST INDIAN OCEAN
Main Season: DECEMBER–MARCH
with significant occurrences in
April, October and November

Equator

tances. These may grow again or they may further weaken and dissipate. If the cyclone does intensify, the barometric pressure will rapidly fall below 1000 mbs, and high winds will form a tight, circular band around the center. The cloud and rain pattern changes from disorganized squalls to narrow, organized bands that spiral toward the center (as seen from satellite photographs). Up to this point, only a relatively small area is involved.

Hurricane status is reached when the maximum sustained winds are 64 knots or greater. As long as the barometric pressure is still dropping and the speed of the gusty and squally winds is still increasing, the tropical cyclone is still developing.

The mature stage is reached when the barometric pressure at the center stops falling and the sustained wind speeds become stabilized. However, the geographic size of the storm may continue to expand for up to a week. In the immature stage the hurricane force winds may exist only within a relatively small circle of 50 miles radius. In the mature stage this radius can increase to more than 400 miles.

Fully developed tropical cyclones with winds of hurricane force tend to move toward the west in both hemispheres. In the northern hemisphere they move about 30° north of west until in the vicinity of 25°N at which place they usually curve away from the equator and head northeast. In the southern hemisphere they usually move about 30° south of west until they reach 15°S to 20°S and then curve to the southeast. Many storms do not curve, however, but continue their westerly course until they reach a large land mass, where they quickly fill and dissipate.

Hurricanes travel at speeds of about 10 knots in their early stages increasing speed a little with latitude but seldom reaching 15 knots. A speed of 20 to 25 knots is usual after recurving with some occasionally reaching 40 knots. Not all storms follow the textbook westerly paths curving toward the poles and east. Some are very erratic, occasionally curving back on themselves, but when they do, the speed of movement is usually less than 10 knots.

The hurricane stage of a tropical cyclone is known by different names in various parts of the world as follows:

North Atlantic, Caribbean, Gulf of Mexico—
   hurricane
Mexico—hurricane or *cordonazo*
Eastern Pacific—hurricane
Haiti—*taino*
Western North Pacific—typhoon
Philippines—*baguio* or *baruio*
North Indian Ocean—cyclone
Australia area—willy-willy, cyclone, or hurricane

William Dampier, a sixteenth-century buccaneer, lived and worked with some of the most notorious pirates of history. Besides survival in combat, he had learned the ways of the weather and wrote: "Tho I have never been in any hurricane in the West Indies, yet have I seen the very image of them in the East Indies, and the effects have been the very same; and for my part I know no difference between a hurricane in the West Indies and a tuffon [*sic*] on the coast of China in the East Indies, but only the name. And I am apt to believe that both words have only one signification, which is a violent storm."

When the wind speed begins to decline steadily and the barometric pressure rises, the tropical cyclone is beginning to dissipate. This usually occurs after it has recurved poleward and eastward. Not all storms recurve into the temperate latitudes, dissipating instead over the neighboring continent; a few even die while still over tropical waters. Some tropical cyclones will dissipate within a day while others, approaching subpolar latitudes, take on a mid-latitude character and even strengthen.

Tropical cyclones generate in several different areas of the world as shown on the chart. Within the dotted lines one may expect more than one tropical cyclone every 10 years while within the solid lines one may expect one or more tropical cyclones every year. The exact number of tropical cyclones varies each year, but the average number per month and year is given for the Pacific Basin in the table. Only the western North Pacific does not have a well-defined quiescent period during the year.

ANATOMY OF A TROPICAL CYCLONE

In the austral summer of early 1990 one of the most destructive cyclones to occur in the southwest Pacific cut a swath from Tuvalu to Niue and into the open ocean beyond. It was the worst cyclone to affect Western Samoa in a hundred years. Its name was Ofa, which in the Samoan language means "love," but it showed no love for the islands in its path.

Ofa formed on February 1 near the center of the islands of Tuvalu and created gale force winds over the entire archipelago before moving southeast toward Samoa. Gale force winds extended 225 miles on either side of its path and continued until it died well into the

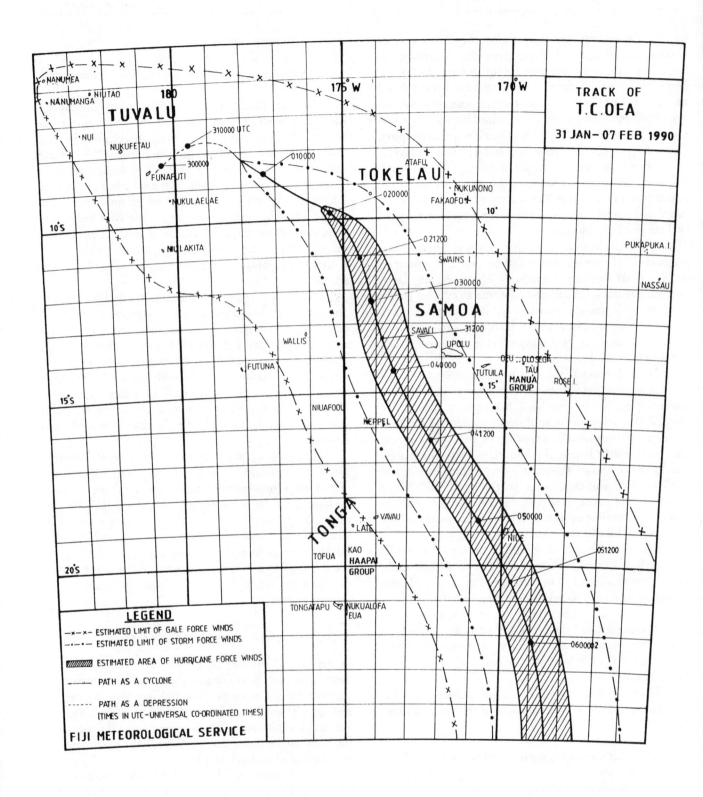

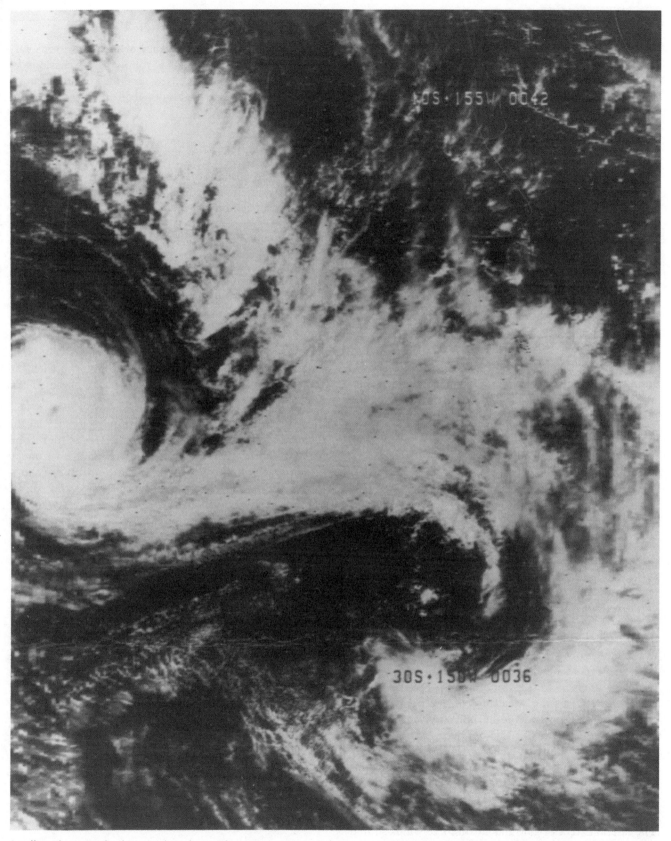

Satellite photograph of Tropical Cyclone Ofa at 0018 UTC on February 6, 1990. (NOAA Satellite Data Services Division)

Average Monthly Frequency of Tropical Cyclones

(   ) Number of tropical cyclones which became hurricanes

MONTH	EASTERN NORTH PACIFIC	WESTERN NORTH PACIFIC	AUSTRALIA- SOUTH PACIFIC
January	0 (0)	0.5 (0.2)	3.9 (1.7)
February	0 (0)	0.3 (0.1)	3.4 (1.3)
March	0 (0)	0.5 (0.2)	3.0 (1.6)
April	0 (0)	0.7 (0.5)	1.3 (0.4)
May	0.6 (0.3)	1.1 (0.7)	0.3 (0.2)
June	1.9 (1.0)	1.8 (1.0)	0.1 (0)
July	4.0 (1.9)	4.1 (2.7)	0 (0)
August	4.0 (2.4)	5.3 (3.3)	0 (0)
September	3.0 (1.9)	4.9 (3.3)	0 (0)
October	1.9 (1.0)	4.1 (3.0)	0.3 (0)
November	0.3 (0)	2.6 (1.7)	1.1 (0.4)
December	0.1 (0)	1.3 (0.7)	2.4 (1.1)
Annual total	15.8 (8.5)	27.2 (17.4)	15.8 (6.7)

Source: *Mariners Weather Log*

South Pacific ocean. Storm force winds extended outward 90 miles on either side of the path of the eye, while hurricane force and higher winds extended outward 45 miles on either side of the path. The highest winds recorded (at Apia meteorological station) reached 97 knots in gusts. Maximum winds near the center were estimated at 100 knots, and the minimum barometric reading recorded anywhere was 962.4 mbs at Alofi.

The heavy rains accompanying the winds caused moderate to very severe damage to six countries— Tuvalu, Western and American Samoa, Tokelau, Tonga, and Niue. Storm tide (combined effect of storm surge and high tide) was the major cause of destruction in several countries. The combined damage to the six countries was in excess of US$180 million. Most severely hit were the north shores of the Samoas, where much of the urban development exists and which were in the dangerous semicircle of the cyclone. The harbor at Pago Pago was protected from the north winds and waves by the island's spinal mountain range and, while anchors dragged (partly because of the poor holding ground), most boats in the harbor survived. Nothing survived in the harbors at Apia or Niue.

The accompanying chart of Ofa's track was prepared by the Fiji Meteorological Service and details Ofa's movement. As far as the cruiser is concerned, the message from Ofa is that cyclones can hit the Samoas during the normal southwest Pacific hurricane season. The lateral extent of gale and storm force winds should be carefully noted. You do not have to be close to the path of the eye to be in heavy weather.

The pattern and frequency of cyclonic storms vary with geographic area. The following discussions of tropical cyclones are based mainly on information published in or provided by the editors of the *Mariners Weather Log*.

EASTERN NORTH PACIFIC TROPICAL CYCLONES

During the months of January, February, and March there is virtually no tropical cyclone activity in the eastern North Pacific.

April—A tropical cyclone in the eastern North Pacific in April would be a rarity.

May—About once every two years, a tropical storm or hurricane develops over the ocean off Mexico during May.

June—The probability of tropical storm development rises sharply during June. One or two will develop during this month between 10°N and 20°N, the Mexican coast, and 120°W. One out of three of these storms reaches hurricane intensity.

July—Tropical cyclones tend to be quite active over the waters off the west coast of Mexico. Three to four tropical cyclones can be expected in July with at least one of them reaching hurricane force. These storms are short-lived but can be dangerous to both marine and coastal interests. They normally move west-northwestward out to sea, but sometimes they pass inland and over Baja California.

August—Over tropical waters west of Mexico four tropical cyclones usually occur in August—a monthly maximum for the year. The average duration of these storms is six days, and more than half reach hurricane strength. As in July, cyclones usually move in a west-northwesterly direction out to sea, where they almost always die after meeting with colder waters and more stable air. Occasionally, however, one recurves before it has moved too far from the coast and moves inland over Baja California or the Mexican mainland.

September—Three tropical cyclones will whirl off the Mexican coast in any given September. One, or sometimes two, will become a hurricane. These storms either originate over the waters off southern Mexico and move northwestward parallel to the coast (and sometimes inland) or develop near the Revilla Gigedeo Islands and move westward out over the open ocean.

October—In the tropical waters of the eastern Pacific, tropical cyclones are less frequent than in September, averaging fewer than two a year. Roughly half of these reach hurricane intensity at some time during their lives. October tropical cyclones follow less regular tracks than those of September. After developing off the coast of southern Mexico and Guatemala, or near the Revilla Gigedeo Islands, a large percentage of these storms will move inland over Mexico south of about 30°N.

November—Tropical cyclone activity over the eastern North Pacific drops rapidly in November, averaging only about one in every three years. None has developed to hurricane intensity.

December—Off the coast of Mexico, tropical cyclones are a rarity in December.

WESTERN NORTH PACIFIC TROPICAL CYCLONES

There is no true season for tropical cyclones in the western North Pacific. Typhoons can and do occur in every month of the year. Ninety percent of the typhoons, however, occur between early June and late December. A maximum occurs in August and a minimum (less than 1 percent) occurs in February.

January—On average one tropical cyclone can be expected each year over the western North Pacific during January. Most of the storms develop between 6°N and 10°N and west of 150°E and move toward the southern half of the Philippines. Two out of every five January tropical cyclones achieve typhoon strength.

February—Tropical cyclone activity is at the annual minimum during February. On the average, one can be expected every three years over western waters. As in the other winter months, the principal region of cyclogenesis is east of the central and southern Philippines. One out of every ten February tropical cyclones has reached typhoon intensity in the past.

March—Tropical cyclones are infrequent during March. A tropical cyclone can be looked for once every two years over the western ocean. Fewer than half of these tropical cyclones develop into typhoons. Tropical cyclones during March usually sprout east of the central and southern Philippines and west of 170°W.

April—In an average ten-year period, about nine tropical cyclones can be expected over far eastern waters. About 80 percent of these, or four out of five, have developed to typhoon strength. Tropical cyclones develop in the same region as they did in March, but the area affected by these warm-core storms has expanded northwestward to include the waters off Luzon and around Taiwan.

May—Tropical cyclones occur, on the average, slightly more than once per month. There have been some years with none in May and others with as many as four. Roughly 75 percent of these tropical cyclones become typhoons. The area of the most common development is south of 20°N, from the Carolines westward across the Philippines to the South China Sea.

June—The probability of tropical cyclone development continues to rise sharply in June. One or two develop during this month in Asiatic waters, and two out of three tropical cyclones go on to become typhoons.

July—Usually four or five tropical cyclones occur over the western North Pacific during July. More than two of these will become typhoons. These storms originate mostly over the ocean areas east of the Philippines. During their early stages, they generally move west-northwestward. After development, some may continue across the South China Sea, while others continue northwestward toward Taiwan, the coast of mainland China, Korea, or Japan. Those reaching higher latitudes generally recurve toward the northeast under the influence of the upper westerlies.

August—The frequency of tropical cyclones in the western North Pacific reaches a peak in August and September. Almost five tropical cyclones can be expected in August; three or four reach typhoon intensity. Typhoons in August are displaced farther to the north than in July and have less tendency to pass directly over the Philippines. Some move directly toward Japan and Taiwan; others may pass over Japan after recurving over the Yellow Sea. Those storms that do enter the South China Sea usually move west-northwestward into the Gulf of Tonkin and North Vietnam.

September—On the average, five tropical cyclones can be expected in the western North Pacific in September, more than any other month. More than three of these storms will achieve typhoon strength. These storms usually originate in the lower latitudes west of about 150°E and initially move west-northwestward. Some travel across the northern Philippines and the South China Sea; others recurve in the vicinity of the Philippine Sea to pass over or near the Japanese islands.

October—Three or four tropical cyclones can be expected to develop over the tropical waters of the Far East. On the average, two or three reach typhoon intensity. Most of these tropical cyclones form at low latitudes in an area extending from the Philippine Islands to 155°E. Their early movement is generally west-northwestward, and most recurve east of the Philippines or Taiwan and sweep up along the coast of Japan. A smaller number move across the Philippines into the South China Sea; a still smaller number reach the Asian mainland.

November—On the average, two or three tropical cyclones develop over the western North Pacific in November. Fewer than two of these usually reach typhoon intensity. The region of most frequent formation is in the vicinity of the central and western Caroline Islands. The tropical cyclones either travel west-north-westward over the Philippines and the South China Sea or recurve near 15°N, 132°E to pass east of the Japanese islands.

December—One tropical cyclone usually develops over the western North Pacific during December. About one out of three goes on to reach typhoon strength. The most likely area of formation is in the neighborhood of the Caroline Islands. Contrary to the events of November, very few of these storms are able to maintain their identity over the South China Sea after traversing the Philippines.

SOUTH PACIFIC TROPICAL CYCLONES

Until 1982 historical weather records affirmed that tropical cyclones in the South Pacific spawned and lived only in the northwest quadrant of the area—from 45°S to the equator and from 155°W to 110°E. The events of 1982–1983 proved differently when five tropical cyclones of hurricane intensity spawned and lived in the region 138°W to 152°W. This was an unusual event associated with disturbed weather patterns over the entire Pacific.

January—In an average year almost four tropical cyclones can be expected to occur in January. Of these, fewer than two can be expected to reach hurricane strength.

February—February brings the second highest frequency of occurrence of tropical cyclones to the South Pacific. More than three tropical cyclones can be expected with at least one attaining hurricane strength.

March—During March an average of three tropical cyclones occurs. Of these, half are expected to reach hurricane strength.

April—During April, the average number of tropical cyclones to occur is only one-half of the previous months. An average of one and one-third storms is expected to reach 34 knots or more, and of these, one-third may be expected to reach hurricane strength.

May—With May's cooler temperatures, the occurrences of tropical cyclones decrease significantly. Historical records show that only three storms can be expected to reach 34 knots or greater within an average 10-year period and that less than one storm will reach hurricane strength within an average 20-year period.

June—As water temperatures continue to cool, the frequency of tropical cyclones also decreases. Past records indicate that only two tropical storms can be expected to develop during June within an average 10-year period. Rarely will any of these storms reach hurricane strength.

July–October—Temperatures are usually too cool during these months of the austral winter to generate any tropical cyclone activity.

November—Water temperatures have now increased enough to spawn some tropical cyclone activity. In an average year, more than one storm can be expected to attain force 8 strength during November. On average over the years, fewer than half the storms will reach hurricane strength.

December—Tropical cyclone activity increases during December, producing a greater number of storms on average during any month since March. On the average, more than two tropical cyclones are observed each year. Of these, at least one will reach hurricane strength.

The Hurricane Warning System

Hurricanes are to be avoided. The best way to avoid them is to stay out of the areas in which they might appear during their usual season of occurrence. The next best way to do that is to keep track of the weather so that you will know if there is a tropical cyclone generating anywhere in your vicinity.

The countries of the Pacific Ocean monitor hurricane activity very closely since it is damaging to land areas as well as to vessels at sea. This information is transmitted over radio, and if you listen regularly to WWVH or other weather broadcasts, you will be apprised of any hurricane activity so you can take evasive action if necessary. Most of the Pacific is covered by WWVH, which gets its information from the U.S. National Weather Service.

The National Oceanographic and Atmospheric

Administration (NOAA) National Weather Service Hurricane Center in San Francisco covers the eastern Pacific; that in Hawaii, the central Pacific; the Joint Navy–Air Force Typhoon Warning System in Guam covers the western Pacific. South Pacific hurricane information is furnished by Fiji, New Zealand, Australia, and French Polynesia. In general, warnings of potentially hazardous approaching tropical cyclones will include the following information: storm type, central pressure given in millibars, wind speeds observed within the storm, storm location, speed and direction of movement, extent of the affected area, visibility, and state of the sea as well as any other pertinent information received. These warnings are broadcast on prespecified radio frequencies immediately upon receipt of the information and at specific intervals thereafter. The broadcast intervals and channels vary from one governing authority to another. Generally the broadcast interval is every six hours depending on the receipt of new information.

Detailed information on the radio broadcasts of all weather information and specific areas of geographical coverage are contained in the publication *Worldwide Marine Weather Broadcasts,* published jointly by the National Weather Service and the Naval Weather Service. It is updated annually.

Pacific Hurricane Havens

What constitutes a good hurricane haven? Consider these factors in approximate descending order of importance:

Protection from surge and waves
Shelter from the wind
Good holding ground
Good shoreline mooring points (mangroves are the best)
No hard structures like docks and seawalls to break a hull
A minimum of other water craft to crash into your boat if they break free
Local tug service to reset anchors of wayward boats
Repair facilities to put things in order afterward

While we may hope to avoid tropical cyclones in our cruising plan, our itineraries do not always work out such that we are completely away from hurricane areas during their seasons—usually because we dallied along the way, but sometimes because the season started earlier or ended later than usual. Whatever the cause for the unexpected exposure, give some thought to where you will hole up should a hurricane approach. There may be refuges from gales and storms, but there aren't many places to hide from the eye of a tropical cyclone. Hurricane Hugo in the Caribbean proved that.

Following are some of my observations on possible Pacific hurricane havens. If your favorite destination is not listed here, it is because I do not have good vibes on it as a hurricane haven.

POLYNESIA

Hawaii
The Hawaiian Islands are approached every year by hurricanes that veer off or diminish before doing much damage. During the El Niño event of 1982–1983, Hurricane Iwa hit Kauai with severe winds, and both Port Allen and Nawiliwili harbor were devastated. The Hawaiian Islands have few natural harbors and no navigable rivers offering any protection from hurricanes.

On the island of Oahu, Keehi Lagoon offers marginal protection for boats in an overcrowded anchorage with many poorly maintained boats. The holding ground is good, but there is little protection from wind. Ala Wai Boat Harbor offers marginal protection in a fully slipped area without anchoring or shore-tie space. It has good protection from waves but poor protection from wind. Kaneohe Bay has a barrier reef protecting it from waves, but little protection from northeast winds.

On the Big Island (Hawaii) only Honokohau Harbor offers any degree of protection from storms of any kind. Its biggest problem is overcrowding; all the tourist boats that normally anchor out in Kailua-Kona Roads crowd into it when bad weather threatens. There may be safety in wall-to-wall boats, but I doubt it.

French Polynesia
The islands of French Polynesia are normally not affected by tropical cyclones, but the 1982–1983 El Niño event proved that both the Tuamotus and Societies are susceptible to them. The Marquesas are too far north to receive hurricane force winds, but they do get severe gales and rains on the periphery of the hurricanes. The Austral Islands lie in the paths of hurricanes bent on becoming extratropical cyclones.

The best hurricane haven in the Society Islands may be Port Phaeton (Tahiti)—if you get there early enough to get tucked well up into the bay; otherwise, there is not much to offer. The bay is protected by a barrier reef and has good holding ground. Trees along the bank offer some shoreline ties.

Other high islands offer some deep-cut bays behind barrier reefs. It is possible to get near the heads of some of these bays for partial protection from winds, but the bays are large enough to give both wind and wave problems. Fringing reefs within the bays make shoreline mooring a problem.

Samoa

The Samoas lie at the edge of the South Pacific hurricane area; every year the islands are affected by nearby tropical cyclones. Usually storm force winds are the worst they receive, but in 1990 Tropical Cyclone Ofa pummeled them with winds to 115 knots, devastating the islands of Western Samoa and parts of Tutuila Island also.

Pago Pago Harbor escaped major damage because the winds and seas came from the opposite side of the island. Pago Pago Harbor has good protection from wind and wave from all directions except the south. It has a very poor holding ground, no shoreline ties, and numerous poorly cared-for fishing boats which could be expected to go adrift in a hurricane.

Tonga

Tonga lies well within the South Pacific hurricane belt, and some part of the lengthy chain gets hit by a hurricane every year. Cyclone Isaac hit Vavau in 1982 with the loss of several boats that were optimistically sitting out the hurricane season there. Cyclone Ofa devastated the northern Niuas atolls of Tonga in 1990. The Haapai group of low-lying atolls generally has troubles with tropical cyclones every year.

Neiafu's Vavau Harbor is the only possible haven in Tonga during cyclone season. It is surrounded by high hills giving good protection from all but easterly winds. The entry is circuitous, offering protection from waves and sudden surge action. The bottom has good holding ground, but fringing coral reefs can be a hazard in parts of the harbor.

MELANESIA

Fiji

Fiji is a mix of high and low islands with only the high islands offering any possibility of protection from tropical cyclones, of which at least two per year can be expected. The Fijian Archipelago is very large, so the chances of cyclones hitting any one spot with regularity

are small. Nevertheless, the minimal protection available makes a stay in the Fijis during hurricane season a chancy thing. Only the two big islands of Viti Levu and Vanua Levu offer any of the necessities for hurricane protection.

Near Suva off the Bay of Islands are Kumbuna Creek and the Veisania River, but you will have to get there early to reserve a place as there will be many boats seeking the same shelter. This area is not well sheltered from winds but will be from waves and sudden surge. There is good holding ground in the Bay of Islands itself and some protection from wind and seas behind the small islands and reefs closing the bay off from the main Suva harbor.

Near Lautoka are two small rivers with good protection and abundant trees along the shoreline for mooring. The space will be hotly contested by local boats. Expect much debris coming downriver from the surrounding mountains.

Solomon Islands

The Solomon Islands are generally free from tropical cyclones, but occasionally one will cross their southern islands as Namu did in 1986. It is best to sail the northern Solomons during the South Pacific tropical cyclone season. Although there are many rivers in the Solomon Islands, most are shallow and not navigable by keel boats, hence, not hurricane refuges. Only a few natural harbors like Graciosa Bay on Ndeni Island afford any degree of protection from tropical cyclones.

When visiting the Guadalcanal area, keep in mind that your closest storm refuge is Tulagi Harbor on the north side of Iron Bottom Sound. It is not perfect, but it has good holding ground and some protection from the seas and a boatyard to set things right after the blow.

New Caledonia

New Caledonia is well within the South Pacific tropical cyclone area, and boats visiting it during the cyclone season must be ready for the worst. There are no good natural harbors in New Caledonia for taking refuge from tropical cyclones.

While there is a large fleet of local sailboats at Noumea the year around, they do take a pasting occasionally from tropical cyclones as they did in early 1990. Noumea is probably the best harbor of refuge although it is large and open to wind and seas from the west. There is selective protection in the several inner harbors from certain wind directions, but in a tropical cyclone there may be a 180-degree wind shift before the blow is over. Holding ground is good. There are small tugs to help reset anchors and facilities for putting storm damage to right afterward.

MICRONESIA

The Palau, Caroline, and Marshall islands only rarely see typhoons, but they are the sites of cyclogenesis, so occasional maturing typhoons may be experienced. The southern end of the Mariana Islands is in the western Pacific typhoon belt; visits there are best made during the quiescent season. Since the western Pacific typhoon warning center is in Guam, reports on developing typhoons are timely and accurate.

Guam has limited, but useful, hurricane havens inside Apra Harbor in Piti Channel and the Harbor of Refuge at its end. Piti Channel is narrow and lined with mangroves and has good holding ground. The channel is kept open by members of the Marianas Yacht Club in their best interests. Boats moored in Piti and the Harbor of Refuge have survived typhoons while those that elected to stay on harbor moorings were lost.

To the north of Guam are the islands of Rota, Tinian, and Saipan, none of which has natural hurricane refuges. There is a small-boat refuge near Puntan Muchot on Saipan, but during a typhoon alert it is filled with local tour craft, leaving little room for cruisers unless you come early. It is like a river, with trees along the bank for mooring, good holding ground for anchors, and some wind protection.

If caught in the area of Tinian with an approaching typhoon, your best and only choice is to put into Tinian Harbor inside Sunharon Roads. Go to the shallow lagoon on the northwest side of the main wharves and anchor away from the wharf in coral sand with good holding power. There is little wind protection but good protection from the seas and some from surge.

Hurricane havens notwithstanding, your best bet is to stay out of hurricane-prone areas during hurricane seasons.

Tsunamis

Some people call tsunamis "tidal waves," but that is a misnomer. The great waves are related not to the tides but to earthquakes. The Japanese, whose homelands have been the scene of many destructive great waves, have given this phenomenon of nature the name "tsunami." The name has been accepted internationally.

The tsunami is a series of traveling ocean waves of extremely long wave length and period, generated by disturbances associated with earthquakes occurring below or near the ocean floor. As the tsunami crosses the deep ocean, its length from crest to crest may be a hundred miles or more and its height from trough to crest only a few feet. It cannot be felt or seen aboard ships in deep water nor can it be seen from the air. While in deep water the tsunami waves may reach forward speeds exceeding 600 mph.

As the tsunami enters the shoaling water of a coastline, the speed of the wave diminishes and the wave height increases. It is in shallow water that tsunamis become a threat to life and property. The arrival of a tsunami is often (but not always) heralded by a gradual recession of the coastal waters (if the trough precedes the crest) or by a rise in water level (if the crest precedes the trough). This is nature's way of warning that more severe tsunami waves are approaching. Heed this warning, for tsunami waves can crest to 100 feet and strike with devastating force.

Some particular facts are worth remembering: not all earthquakes cause tsunamis; an earthquake in your area is a natural tsunami warning; a tsunami is not a single wave but a series of waves; all tsunamis, like hurricanes, are potentially dangerous.

A Pacific-wide tsunami warning system headquartered near Honolulu monitors seismological and tidal instruments throughout the Pacific Basin. When an earthquake of sufficient magnitude to generate a tsunami occurs in the Pacific Ocean, a watch is established in all areas to determine if a tsunami has actually been generated. If it has, a warning is issued to all areas of the potential arrival of a destructive sea wave, including estimated times of arrival. Boats at sea will be unaffected, but boats in harbors could be seriously affected. The only evasive action seems to be to take the boat to sea into deeper water, where the sea wave will be less noticeable. Little information exists relative to small-boat experience in weathering tsunamis in well-protected harbors.

CHAPTER 4

PASSAGE PLANNING

To say you are going to cruise the Pacific is something of a misnomer, for there's no way you could do it all. The Pacific is vast in all dimensions—10,000 islands spread over 64 million square miles. That is a lot of opportunity for the cruising sailor, and one that calls for a little planning. Not too much, though, for cruising should not be too rigidly structured. But you do have to plan on self-sufficiency between provisioning ports, which, because of the undeveloped nature of the cruising ground, can be far apart. Then there is the matter of the time of year. Seasonal changes occur in the Pacific cruising grounds as they do elsewhere in the world. Although it may never get cold in the tropics, the seasonal changes in trade winds and monsoonal winds can affect the ease with which you make a passage. More important, the hurricanes and typhoons of the Pacific are not a sailor's best friend and should be avoided by good scheduling of passages.

Winds are the motive power for the cruising boat, and you are at their mercy on any passage, long or short. Your time en route will be determined by the winds where you are, not by Pilot Charts, the experiences of another cruising boat, or your own experiences sailing in home waters. A passage generally takes longer than you think because you plan with optimism, not anticipating adverse conditions. And though you may enjoy the sailing even on an unexpectedly slow passage, running out of food or water en route can spoil your outlook on cruising. You will find that you can't always count on rain to replenish your water tanks nor on fish to restock your larder.

Cruising should be safe, and a little thought to those factors that make up cruising safety are well worthwhile. Knowing when you are in heavily transited shipping lanes will prompt you to keep a more careful lookout for traffic. While your main objective is to keep from being run down, there is also an opportunity to speak to a ship via radiotelephone and vary the routine of a long passage. Many boats are well equipped with electronics for safety, but except for the ham radio, few of these devices can reach the breadth of the Pacific.

Consider carrying with you an Emergency Position Indicating Radio Beacon (EPIRB) for signaling that you are in distress on the sea.

Because it would probably take a long time for help to arrive, you should be able to take care of yourself under all possible emergencies that you are willing to expose yourself to. Besides having a good boat properly equipped, you will want to have adequate and sufficient crew to handle your vessel. That means planning crew needs ahead of time—not only in numbers but in capability. There is no union hall from which to get crew members. Furthermore, you want people with compatible personalities. And that takes some planning. Your friends ashore might not be friends at sea.

Last, you must give some thought to the unthinkable—pirates and hijacking. The Jolly Roger still flies in some places of the Pacific, and cruising yachts today are as fair game as the Spanish galleons were in the seventeenth century. When you leave the safety of home for adventure on the high seas, you must be able to counter those enemies of society who, like yourself, prefer to live in a marine environment.

Choosing Destinations

You may eventually be headed for a little-known South Sea island, but its geography and national sovereignty require that you stop other places first. Given a choice, you will want to enter an island group at the windward end so that you can sail to the other islands in the group without having to beat into the wind. One of the peculiarities of many island groups of the Pacific is that they are generally laid out running southeast to northwest. Hawaii, the Marquesas, Tuamotus, Cooks, Samoas, and many others lie in this position, making it of great advantage to start from the southeast and work your way up the chain enjoying scenery, sailing, and sessions with the island peoples as you go.

Unfortunately, officialdom gets in your way. All island groups and many individual islands are separate political entities requiring a visiting yacht to officially clear into its territorial boundaries at a Port of Entry. The Port of Entry is usually at the major population center of the island group—which isn't necessarily at the windward end of the island chain. Hence, you have to compromise on where to enter the chain. Some island chains have a Port of Entry at the windward end: Hilo, Hawaii; Majuro, Marshall Islands; and Noumea, New Caledonia, for example. But most, unfortunately, have their Ports of Entry sandwiched into the middle of the group, meaning that you have to bypass many interesting outlying islands on the way to your official entry. And bypass them you should, for these sovereign islands are getting pretty sticky about yachts freely transiting their waters with no regard for local custom and other regulations.

The days of casually wandering among the islands of the South Seas are over because of the number of cruising yachts on the scene. There are other reasons, too. Some cruisers are dope runners and have even been known to cultivate pot on isolated islands. Others are foragers who live off a land barely able to support the island population. Still others think in terms of the beachcombers of old who would simply settle in with the natives. No more. Island officials want to know and keep track of every yacht and crew member in their waters. While it may seem like an imposition to you, it does have its good side, and that is safety. Yachts occasionally turn up missing for a number of reasons, and the local officials would rather know where to look than have to mount a wide area search.

When you check in at a Port of Entry, inquire of the Customs officer about the need for permission to cruise the other islands of the same political group. Some countries, like New Zealand and Australia, issue cruising licenses that exempt pleasure boats of certain nations (the United States is one) from formal entry and clearance procedures at all but the first Port of Entry. Others, like the Cooks, will want to approve an itinerary of the islands to be visited. Still others, like the Tuamotu Archipelago, are still open once you have made your presence known at a proper Port of Entry. But, wherever you go, be certain that you have the proper entry and exit papers, for even the islander's bureaucracy feeds on wood-pulp products.

There is one other official nuance of island visiting —checking in at each island. You are not free to roam at will once you have cleared at a Port of Entry. You must check in with the administrator of every island that has one. It may be a civilian district officer, a military representative, or the island chief. In any case they are the

authority and must keep track of visitors. This regulation is hardly a penalty, for these people living in a somewhat isolated world usually welcome visitors; many cruisers have found their arrival to be cause for celebration. Don't forget that you are a guest and that your behavior will have a major effect on the reception afforded the next visiting yacht. It doesn't hurt to have token gifts to offer the island chief such as coffee, tobacco, some clothing, and pictures from a Polaroid camera.

Processing official papers isn't the only reason for making landfall at a Port of Entry. After a long passage you are probably interested in replenishing your supplies and even having a meal in a local restaurant. If your boat needs repairs, your entry will have to be made at a big settlement with adequate facilities and parts.

There are but a few good places to resupply or repair your boat in the Pacific, so your overall route plan should consider those few. Your major cruising needs can best be satisfied at the following ports:

> Brisbane and Sydney, Australia
> Guam, Mariana Islands
> Hong Kong
> Honolulu, Hawaii
> Noumea, New Caledonia
> Pago Pago, American Samoa
> Papeete, Tahiti
> Rabaul, New Britain
> Suva, Fiji
> Whangarei and Auckland, New Zealand

To sum up, when planning your destination you should consider the official needs of clearing into the country, replenishing your supplies, and setting your boat back in order for the next long passage. If your routine is to include frequent communication with the home port, you will appreciate having the postal, radiotelephone and telegram, and airline communications of the larger ports. Once you have taken care of all the ship's business and your personal needs, you can retire to the out islands (assuming that you have a cruising permit) to enjoy the local culture in peace and quiet.

Choosing Your Route

Over the years cruisers have developed favorite routes to follow through the Pacific Basin. The most popular is the Coconut Milk Run, which begins at the Marquesas Islands and continues through French Polynesia, the Cook Islands, the Samoas, Tonga, and Fiji to New

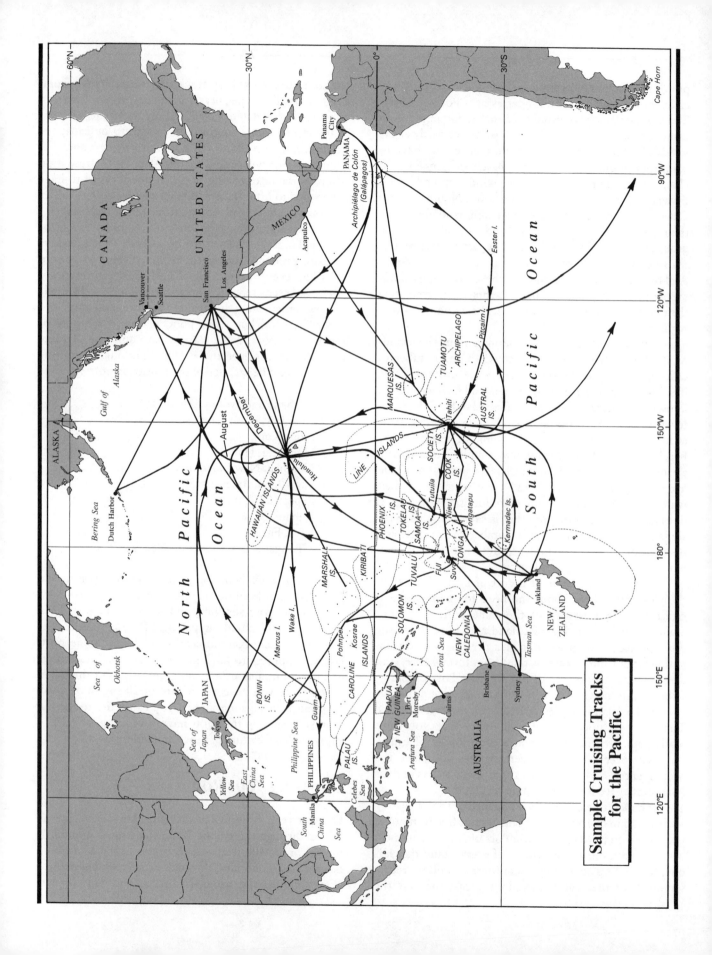

Sample Cruising Tracks
for the Pacific

Zealand. That route represents about one season of pleasant cruising. A second season continues on to New Caledonia, Vanuatu, the Solomon Islands, and Papua New Guinea. This route can be terminated at a number of places, such as Australia and Indonesia, before the South Pacific cyclone season sets in, or you can escape the season by passing into the Indian Ocean as part of a circumnavigation. For those intending to return to the U.S. mainland, the route home can either be the Coconut Milk Run in reverse or a leg north into western Micronesia and on to Japan for a return across the North Pacific Ocean.

Recent years have seen a growing interest in "cruising off the beaten path," causing many cruisers to take the Manila Galleon Run for variation. The route starts on the coast of Mexico (Acapulco was the original port of departure for the Manila galleons) and continues through the islands of Micronesia as far as Guam. This route was established in the late seventeenth century by Spanish ships taking gold and silver from Mexico to Manila, where it was exchanged for the silks and spices of Asia. A more practical route today would stop en route at Honolulu for reprovisioning and then proceed to the Marshall Islands. For boats not planning on continuing to Asia, the return trip to the U.S. mainland can be made via the North Pacific route or by going south of the equator to pick up the Coconut Milk Run in reverse.

A proliferation of international sailboat races in the Pacific now enables cruising boats to join in the fun and competition along their cruising routes without detouring far from their planned destinations. These well-organized races offer the benefits of improving sailing skills, socializing with other boats, getting valuable official approvals to enter otherwise restricted waters, and meeting different peoples. Appendix E is a compendium of such blue-water races that include cruising-class sailboats. If there happens to be a race going your way, give thought to timing your departure to take advantage of it.

Timing Your Departure

Weather patterns will dictate the timing of your departure. Most people cruise the tropics because they like the warm weather and the balmy trade winds. But as at any latitude, there is a violent side to tropical weather. Dominating your decision on when to go are the tropical cyclone patterns of the general route you want to take. Scheduling a route into an area of known cyclone activity can be a good way to ruin a voyage. Study the patterns of the tropical storms and set your routes and timing to avoid them. For possible hurricane holes in the Pacific see the section Hurricane Havens in chapter 3. Or consider sailing to New Zealand, which is partially out of the hurricane belt; a season spent there is a reward in itself.

An alternative to holing-up to avoid tangling with a hurricane is to go sailing in some other part of the Pacific. During the southern hemisphere hurricane season, cruise in the northern hemisphere and visa versa. Consider cruising among the equatorial islands, which are spared the onslaughts of hurricane force winds. But don't deliberately expose yourself to trouble. Tales of boats surviving hurricanes are heroic after the fact but downright terrifying during the experience. And then there are those you never hear about!

The seasonal nature of the trade winds also affects your planning. The trades are stronger in some seasons than in others. (Their general pattern in local waters is described later in the sections on weather accompanying each description of an island group.) Trade winds are quite dependable, disturbed only by occasional fronts that march eastward through the area. But remember that the best trade winds, those in the tropics, are easterlies carrying you west in your travels. If you want to go east you either beat your way against the trades or head for the higher latitudes. Square-riggers headed for the higher latitudes because they couldn't efficiently sail against the wind and also because they could make better time in the strong westerlies. If you opt for sailing the higher latitudes rather than beating into the trades, remember that you must be prepared for gales in any season when you sail above 35° latitude. In the local winter they will obviously be at their worst.

As a cruising sailor you will want to take advantage of seasonal wind and weather patterns. Winds are a result of high- and low-pressure cells building up over the ocean or adjacent lands. The effects of the monsoons in the western Pacific are clearly evident by noting the change in wind direction between January and July. These changes are caused by the heating and cooling of the large Asian land mass and, to a lesser extent, by the heating and cooling of Australia.

When you are planning long passages, your best source of wind data is the Pilot Chart for the area. It summarizes the average wind and weather conditions to be expected over the ocean and gives you the best overall weather pattern on which to base your cruise plan, but don't feel distressed if you eventually experience other conditions. The charts cover tens of thousands of miles, and your local conditions are but a microscopic part of the whole circulation pattern.

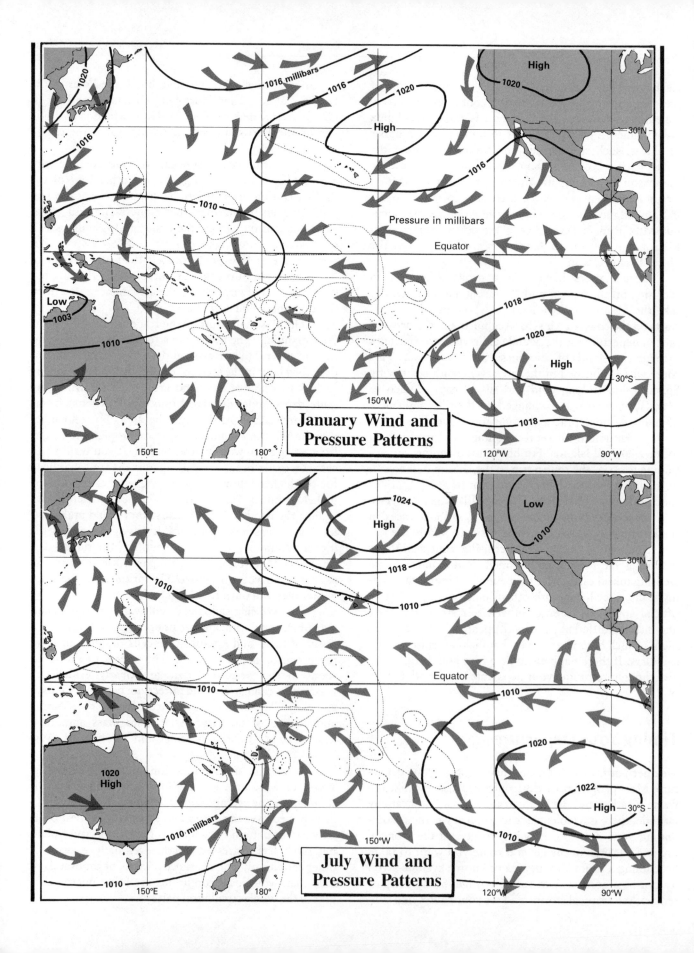

January Wind and Pressure Patterns

July Wind and Pressure Patterns

Many boats today are equipped with weatherfax machines. To a person schooled in meteorology, these can be an excellent source of weather planning information. They are, however, only another source of data from which decisions can be made and cannot make decisions themselves.

When you are near land, the weather forecasts on local commercial radio stations may give you some idea of coming winds or rain so that you can decide whether to stay put where you are or go visit the next island. On long passages your best weather reports, and probably all that is needed, are obtained from WWVH every hour. They describe the big picture from which you can determine whether your immediate weather pattern is localized or part of a major happening. (You may want to take different survival actions in each case.) On a long passage, however, there is little you can do with a weather forecast but be ready to batten down the hatches if necessary, since you usually cannot outrun a storm or get out of its way. That is the primary reason for staying out of hurricane areas. Regardless of radio weather reports, it is best for you to do your own weather forecasting by observing the sky and swells and tracking the barometer. A small low-pressure area crossing your path can create a localized gale that may never be known to the rest of the world. If you are prepared to shorten sail and have everything properly secured below decks, there is a good possibility that you can weather your own gale in safety if not comfort.

Estimating Passage Times

If you are going to race through the South Seas, then you might as well travel by jet aircraft, for cruising is not a race but a chance to enjoy an unhurried existence whether en route or at your destination. Nevertheless, you must have some idea of the length of time it will take to make a passage.

Those used to sailing the short coastal routes of a Sunday afternoon know full well that with a good wind they can hold hull speed hour after hour, so they plan accordingly. A boat's hull speed is related to its waterline length: the longer the waterline, the higher the hull speed. Typical values for monohulls are:

Waterline length (feet)	Hull speed (knots)
20	6.0
25	6.7
30	7.3
35	7.9
40	8.5

These speeds are the maximum sustainable speeds for monohulls with good winds and moderate seas and are usually attained on a broad reach or run with plenty of canvas flying. The rest of the time? Only the god of wind and sea will know. On an average a cruising boat can make between 100 and 125 miles per day over an extended passage. Sound slow? Maybe, but when you consider all the times at night when the wind goes slack and long days in the doldrums or the flat that often occurs after a squall goes through, you sometimes will feel lucky to have made that good an average. While some legs will be at hull speed, others will be fraught with slatting sails. And on still others adverse currents of one or two knots will reduce your distance made good to well below what your knot meter thinks it should be.

It is almost impossible to use speed alone to estimate the time it will take you to make a passage. Adverse currents, different points of sailing, variable winds, and navigation inconsistencies all combine to negate precise speeds made good across the bottom in the direction that you want to go. It is better to think in terms of how many days it will take you to make a passage. After you have made a number of passages and suffered through calms, squalls, and changes in wind direction, you will become quite good at estimating your boat's ability to make time on a passage. Until then, use the experience of others who have been as good sailors as you and had as fast a boat but learned that making a boat go its fastest day in and day out is less important than having a safe, pleasurable sail.

Recorded en route times for 2,000 passages on a variety of cruising boats mono and multihull were correlated; the results are shown in the table. A number of interesting observations can be made from these data. Crossings with long portions in the doldrums, such as the legs from Panama to the Galapagos, take a relatively long time. Legs to weather, such as the Honolulu–Los Angeles or San Francisco passages, also take a long time because you are essentially taking two long tacks as you circle the North Pacific high-pressure cell.

Little other correlation could be done with these data. Separating them by boat length, sailing season, or type of rig showed no consistency. Boats involved in races over these same passages showed shorter passage times but were not included in the displayed results. Appendix E contains racing speed records for a number of Pacific legs to illustrate minimum times recorded for passaging between islands.

More important than simple calendar days, however, is the safety margin that you want to allow in planning your provisions or having shoreside contacts wait

Some Recorded Passage Times

PASSAGE	GREAT CIRCLE DISTANCE (nautical miles)	DAYS EN ROUTE*	PASSAGE	GREAT CIRCLE DISTANCE (nautical miles)	DAYS EN ROUTE*
Acapulco to			Manzanillo to		
Honolulu	3,280	21–31	Hilo	2,860	21–30
Nuku Hiva	2,840	22–29	Hiva Oa	2,685	18–27
Auckland to			Noumea to		
Noumea	975	8–11	Port Moresby	1,350	11–13
Papeete	2,210	18–27	Nukualofa to		
Rarotonga	1,625	12–17	Opua	1,020	8–10
Suva	1,140	9–12	Nuku Hiva to		
Tubuai	2,010	15–22	Hilo	1,935	14–21
Bora-Bora to			Papeete	760	6–9
Hilo	2,185	16–21	Pago Pago to		
Pago Pago	1,100	9–12	Honolulu	2,265	21–30
Rarotonga	535	4–6	Panama to		
Cabo San Lucas to			Galapagos	845	9–15
Hilo	2,525	20–26	Honolulu	4,555	36–50
Nuku Hiva	2,605	19–23	Nuku Hiva	3,775	28–42
Christmas Island to			Papeete to		
Honolulu	1,160	10–13	Hilo	2,260	15–28
Fanning Island to			Rarotonga	620	7–9
Honolulu	1,050	9–12	Puntarenas		
Galapagos Islands to			(Costa Rica) to		
Hilo	4,040	38–46	Honolulu	4,240	32–27
Nuku Hiva	3,055	20–30	Rangiroa to		
Honolulu to			Hilo	2,125	18–23
Guam	3,310	20–29	Rarotonga to		
Kodiak	2,355	16–24	Niue	585	5–6
Los Angeles	2,220	19–34	Opua	1,600	14–17
Majuro	1,975	15–24	San Diego to		
Nuku Hiva	2,095	18–25	Hilo	2,170	16–24
Pago Pago	2,265	15–21	Nuku Hiva	2,820	19–32
Palmyra	955	7–9	San Francisco to		
Papeete	2,380	18–28	Hilo	2,015	15–24
San Francisco	2,080	21–26	Nuku Hiva	2,975	25–32
Seattle/Vancouver	2,355	20–28	Seattle/Vancouver to		
Kosrae to			Honolulu	2,325	18–26
Tarawa	640	6–8	Suva to		
Los Angeles to			Auckland	1,140	9–17
Hilo	2,130	16–25	Tarawa to		
Nuku Hiva	2,845	21–29	Honolulu	2,085	29–33
Majuro to					
Honolulu	1,975	22–30			

*Two-thirds of the recorded passage times were within this time span.

before getting worried. A good rule of thumb is take half again the amount of time you think it will take for the crossing.

Can you speed up your passage by using the auxiliary engine along the way? Certainly, if you carry a good supply of fuel and can put up with the noise. But unless you have a motorsailer it is not advisable to power for great distances because the average auxiliary engine installation just isn't made for that kind of service. It may be worthwhile in the doldrums or the flat of the Pacific high; otherwise save the engine for entering harbors. Passage distances are just too long for powering in the majority of cases, so you should resign yourself to becoming the best sailor possible.

This brings us to the question of how to time your arrival for a daylight entry to your destination harbor. While the principle is good, the practice is impossible. Let your arrival time take care of itself. If you arrive at night plan to stand off the harbor until daylight when you can see the navigation aids and the hazards to navigation. Time is not so precious that you should jeopardize boat and crew to save hours after you have just been days en route. Plan to drop your sails and just drift in the shadow of your destination if it is clearly visible. If it is not or if there is a strong current running or bad weather, don't stand in too close. Sail away from the harbor for a couple of hours and then sail back, timing your arrival for daylight. Remember that your boat is safer in the ocean than near an unknown or unseen shore. Sailing back and forth allows you to correct your position for current; it also occupies the crew, who might otherwise get restless.

Additional details on planning a passage from the standpoint of weather and routing can be found in *Ocean Passages of the World* published by the Hydrographer of the Navy, British Admiralty.

Two-way Radio

The most common radio in use on recreational boats today is the VHF set which in local waters is used for communications between buddy boats or to place a call through the local marine telephone operator. On a cruising boat it can also be used to talk with ships that may come into view. All ships carry VHF, and the radio operator may welcome a break from routine duties to chat with you at sea. VHF radio can also be a convenience in approaching new Ports of Entry. You can call the harbormaster and ask for specific instructions on where to go and also ask that Health, Customs, and other officials be notified of your pending arrival. Such a call, however, is not a requirement at any harbor.

Marine single-sideband radio has not proven itself of real value to the blue-water cruiser. Its high cost is not compatible with a cruising budget, it does not have the flexibility or adequate listening stations for a cruiser wandering the far reaches of the Pacific.

Undoubtedly the most useful communications means for the long-range cruising yacht is the ham rig. It is small, has a low power drain, fits the cruising budget, and has the flexibility for handling information ranging from simple position reporting to making telephone

connections with the folks back home. Like cruising itself, ham radio is a hobby, and with thousands of hams worldwide, you can have the ability to contact any part of the world.

To operate a ham radio you need a license—which you should obtain well before you plan to leave on your cruise because it will involve a little study. Without a license you will not only be illegal (a pirate), but the ham community will soon find you out and refuse to talk with you. At minimum, you need a General license to make the most of a maritime mobile ham rig. If you are a registered or documented U.S. vessel, you must have a U.S. operator's license to operate your ham rig in U.S. or international waters. (Hams on non-U.S. vessels will, of course, have to be licensed in their own countries and obtain a reciprocal operating permit from the United States to operate in U.S. waters.)

For detailed information about amateur radio, write or call:

American Radio Relay League
225 Main Street
Newington CT 06111
USA
Tel: (203) 666–1541

When you enter foreign territorial waters (usually within the 12-mile limit) you must cease operations until you can arrange reciprocal operating privileges with the country whose waters you have entered. Appendix D gives the mailing addresses of the responsible communications organizations in the various Pacific countries who can give you those privileges. You can arrange for them ahead of time by mail or wait until you arrive and get them on the spot. But do not operate in their territorial waters with your U.S. call sign or you will become persona non grata.

There has developed over the years an assemblage of maritime mobile amateur radio nets that cover the world. These nets are operated by shoreside hams with powerful rigs and directional antennas who take great pleasure in conversing with and providing services to their licensed counterparts on cruising boats. Appendix D also contains a list of the principal maritime mobile nets operating in the Pacific Basin. These nets can put you in touch with any other licensed ham in the world or provide needed services exclusive of business-related traffic, for which you must use marine single-sideband radio. Many nets will provide telephone patches to connect you with relatives and friends you may wish to contact for nonbusiness communications. This can be done in a number of foreign countries with which the United States has third-party agreements. These countries are also listed in appendix D.

If you have a serious medical emergency aboard your boat, you can get expert medical advice via a phone patch to the Memorial Hospital Medical Center in Long Beach, California. The center has doctors on duty at all times in the emergency department. They will accept collect calls from maritime mobile stations who route their phone patches through California, Nevada, Oregon, or Washington. The telephone number is (213) 595–2133.

In addition, all U.S. Public Health Service hospitals have been authorized to accept collect calls from vessels at sea having medical emergencies aboard. On the West Coast there are such hospitals at San Francisco and Seattle.

But even if you have a single-sideband marine or ham radio on board, don't depend on it for getting immediate emergency assistance. The ocean is vast, and you may be more than a thousand miles from any land or ship. Even if someone heard your call, it would take days for surface vessels to reach you. Airplanes can reach you faster if they are available, but that would only be in the vicinity of major countries that can afford such life-saving operations. It is better that you try to make yourself and your vessel self-sufficient through good equipment and seamanlike operation.

EPIRB Geographic Coverage

The Emergency Position Indicating Radio Beacon system of use to Pacific navigators operates on three frequencies—on VHF at 121.5 megahertz (mHz) (civil aviation distress frequency) and 243 mHz (military aviation distress frequency) and on UHF at 406 mHz.

One set of EPIRB listening posts is the airplane flying overhead. At 37,000-foot altitude it can provide a listening coverage of 166,000 square miles, assuming perfect propagation and good receiving equipment. But the possibility of an airplane's being overhead to hear your EPIRB's chirping is slim unless you are under one of the popular air routes illustrated in the chart. Even then, the numbers of airplanes flying some of these Pacific routes is minimal, only two or three a week. The chances that your signal will be picked up by a passing airplane are small, and that is one reason that search and rescue agencies tell you to leave your EPIRB turned on for its full battery duration.

There is also a 24-hour listening post in the sky called SARSAT/COSPAS, which is a cluster of five satellites that listen in on both VHF frequencies. Should one pass over your distress location, it will pick up your signal and relay it to the nearest ground terminal for processing. Two passes are the minimum needed for triangulation. Ground terminals, however (as the chart also shows), are not strategically situated for Pacific Ocean coverage. U.S. and Russian terminals provide coverage above 30°N in the Pacific, and terminals in South America and Australia provide spot coverage in the southern hemisphere. Since the most popular cruising grounds are south and west of Hawaii, the Pacific cruiser using VHF EPIRB frequencies can expect to be beyond coverage of the SARSAT/COSPAS system most of the time and to be covered south and west of Hawaii only by passing airplanes.

The new UHF frequency of 406 mHz for EPIRBs solves the Pacific gap problem, providing 24-hour, worldwide coverage. The satellites store the distress data when received from this frequency and automatically relay it to the ground terminals when within their line of sight. Your 406 mHz EPIRB will not only announce your emergency, but also identify your vessel, its type, and country of registration—enough data to tell the regional search and rescue organization what to look for as well as where to look for it. The VHF satellite gap in the Pacific and limited airplane flight schedules are clear arguments for equipping your cruising boat with a combined VHF/UHF EPIRB.

Even if your distress signal is heard and your location pinpointed accurately, you could still be several days from rescue because of the logistics of getting a ship to your location. There are parts of the Pacific where shipping is scarce, and you had best be prepared to survive on your boat or in your liferaft until a seaborne rescue can be made. Airplanes can drop survival equipment to you, but it will take a ship to effect the actual rescue.

Adding to Your Crew

Boat size is not a determining factor for the number of crew needed in cruising. Boats to 40 feet long are commonly single-handed, and there are many two-person crews sailing boats up to 50 feet long. Wind-vane self-steering has done much to make this possible, and one cannot help but like a mechanical crew member who works uncomplainingly for long stretches and asks little in return but some occasional tender loving care. Although there is no minimum boat-to-crew-size relation,

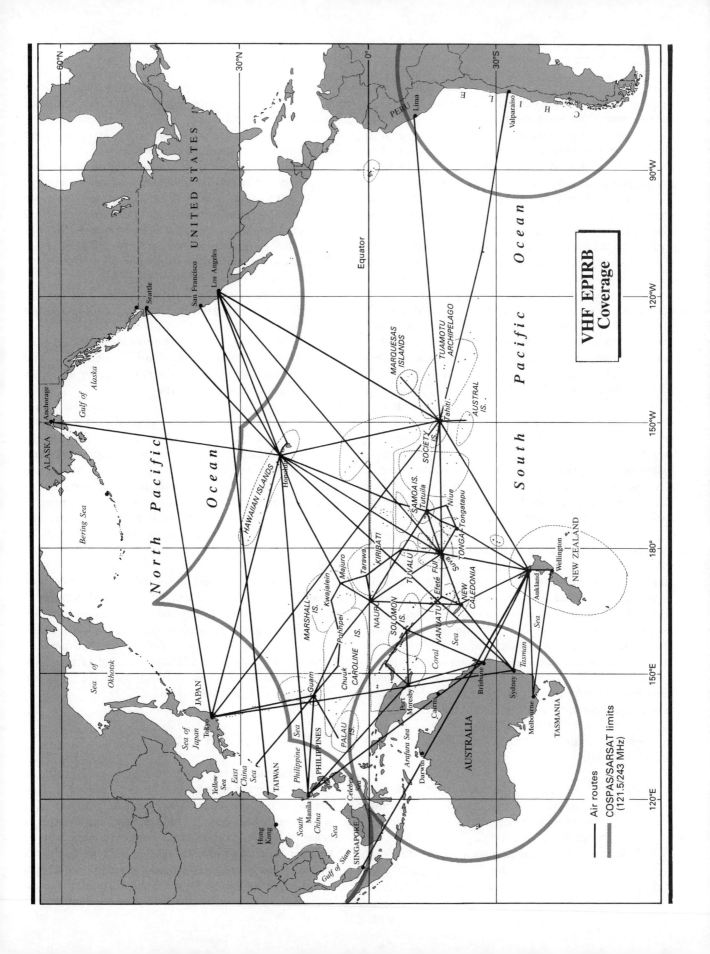

**VHF EPIRB
Coverage**

——— Air routes

——— COSPAS/SARSAT limits
(121.5/243 MHz)

there is a meaningful maximum. Boats grow pretty small at sea, and the fewer persons aboard, the fewer the problems. You will be doing no one a favor by taking unneeded crew members, particularly strangers, to share in the workload. Remember that they will also be sharing in the limited living space, and each brings a unique personality and habits to share with you.

The inherent problem with the multiple-person crew is compatibility over long passages. Even good marriages and other friendly relationships have been strained to the breaking point by long passages in small boats. To add additional persons, particularly strangers, is to court trouble.

Regardless of how you acquire your crew members, as far as Customs and Immigration are concerned, they are the responsibility of the skipper. Many countries insist that each visitor have a valid airline ticket to his or her own country. Be sure that each crew member has this ticket and leaves it with you among the ship's papers. Then if you want to part company, you can do so at your convenience, not the crew member's. Everyone, of course, should have a valid passport and health certificate. If your crew member is a national of another country, be certain of the entry eligibility of such nationals to the destination country so that you, the skipper, don't become guilty of aiding and abetting illegal immigration procedures. If visas are needed be certain that each crew member gets one ahead of time.

An early understanding between crew and skipper on how each individual is to fit into the shipboard life may preclude some rough spots later. Besides watch standing and sail changing, all crew must expect to help with the routine chores below decks such as cleaning a water closet or scrubbing down a bulkhead and should also understand that midnight raids on boat stores and water use beyond a reasonable ration won't be tolerated. The owner should also ensure what little privacy exists on a small boat by not giving the crew members carte blanche entry to parts of the boat for which access is not required in the normal pursuit of their duties.

If you have decided that your boat does need another hand aside from your family crew, the following advice is offered:

- Check your applicant out as thoroughly as possible beforehand. It is better to delay departure or do without an additional hand than have a stranger spoil your fun.
- Be frank with your applicant at the interview and demand that he or she be the same, because you will both pay for deception in the end.

- If you are confident of your own abilities, don't demand experience; go for personality and willingness to learn.
- Take only one unknown person at a time; don't load up on potential trouble.
- Agree only to take a new member to the next port and be sure he or she has a passport and sufficient finances (airline ticket at least) to travel from there alone. If the individual turns out to be good crew, you can extend the working agreement.
- If the person is on medication be certain that you know the reason for it and that he or she has an ample supply for the intended period.
- Try to determine if the person has any hangups that may be a liability. Can the person go aloft at sea to replace a broken halyard? Is he or she at home on the water? Is there a food problem? Is he or she a follower of a fad in meditation and trances? Above all, is the person clean in both a hygienic sense and in habit?
- Lastly, be certain that the individual does not take pot or any other narcotics aboard your boat. All island governments are actively fighting the introduction of the cannabis plant into their islands, and cruisers are particularly suspect in bringing it in. Governments hold the skipper responsible for the boat's crew, and some governments will confiscate the boat if nonmedical narcotics are found on board. Don't let a pothead spoil your cruise.

If you have a crew person joining you from, say, your home town, there are only a limited number of ports where it is convenient to do so from the standpoint of airline flights, convenient communications, and a safe anchorage where you can await that person's arrival. The Flotsam and Jetsam listing in each chapter makes recommendations on which ports are good and not good for making crew changes.

Preventing Collisions

Part of the fun of blue-water cruising is just roaming the oceans unfettered by schedules or the traces of society. Yet boats do turn up missing, and one wonders why. Assuming that the boat is sound and the crew capable, it is hardly likely that they would come to grief because of weather short of a hurricane. And it is hardly likely that a boat properly navigated would ground on a land mass and disappear without a trace. That leaves a collision at

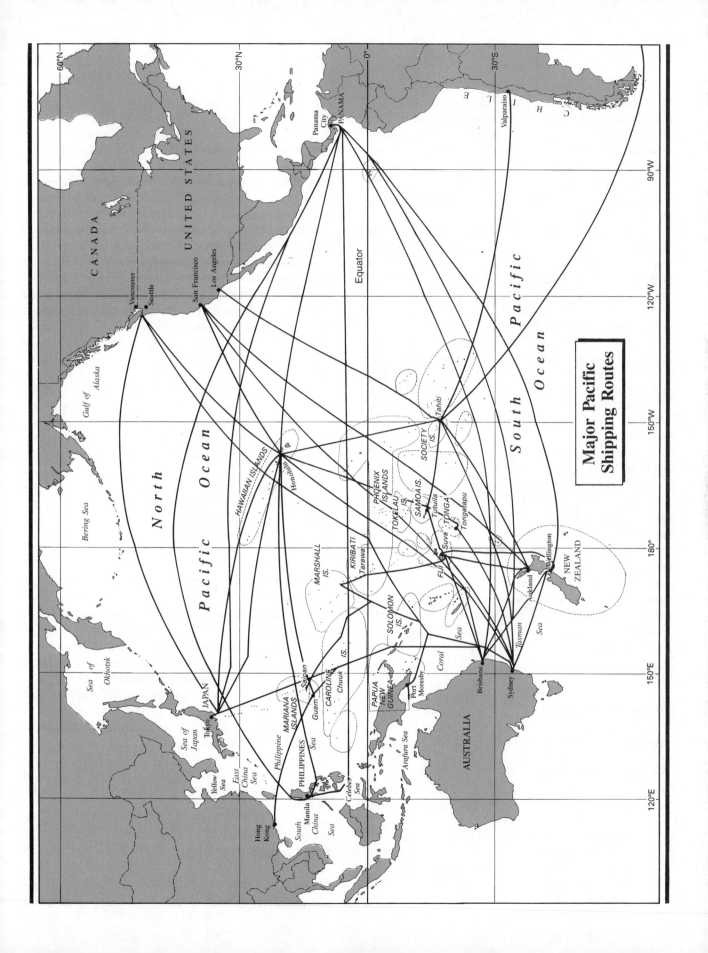

Major Pacific
Shipping Routes

sea as the likely culprit in the disappearance of a cruising boat. Anyone who has traveled the oceans knows how quickly and alarmingly a ship can appear close at hand when you think you have the whole ocean to yourself. With a dependable 24-hour watch your chances of being run down are minimal, but if there is a lapse in lookout and you are near or in steamer lanes or areas being fished by some of the large, modern fishing fleets, then trouble may be brewing.

The major steamer lanes of the Pacific Ocean are shown in the chart. But ships, like cruising boats, are not constrained to these routes and are frequently found well outside the lanes. Should you find yourself paralleling or crossing any of these routes, keep a particularly good lookout. Most ships are running on automatic pilot at sea, and their lookout may have decided to go to the galley for a cup of coffee about the time you come into view. Likewise, don't depend on their radar to sight you. In all probability it is not on or at least not being watched most of the time at sea. When you and they are near land, they are probably monitoring their radar and will note your radar reflector, assuming that they are radar-equipped.

Another potential collision possibility is with fishing fleets in active pursuit of their quarry. I myself experienced such a situation. While returning from Hawaii and about 75 miles off the California coast, I found myself enmeshed in a U.S. fishing fleet. The fishing boats showed no sign of abiding by the rules of the road, and it was necessary to take evasive action to prevent collision with the maneuvering fishing boats.

There have also been unsubstantiated reports of fishing boats taking aggressive action that had all the earmarks of casual piracy attempts. It is, undoubtedly, best to give fishing fleets a wide berth. Neither an accidental collision nor an act of piracy will improve your day at sea.

Avoiding Pirates

Piracy is robbery on the high seas, but it can also include robbery while a boat is at anchor, especially if it involves threat of bodily violence. There is no reported pirate activity in the cruising area covered by this book. It is primarily found farther west in the following locations:

> The southern islands of the Philippines and the
>   Sulu Archipelago
> The northern Philippines including Manila
>   Harbor to some extent
> Gulf of Thailand

South China Sea
The eastern coast of the Malay Peninsula
The waters surrounding the islands of Borneo—
  both Malaysian and Indonesian areas
Most of the waters of Indonesia to some extent

Who are the people that make up the pirates in these areas? They apparently come in many forms— local fishermen who see an easy chance to make material gain in their otherwise squalid world; professional pirates who do nothing else but prey on boats of all kinds, sometimes impersonating customs or police officials; rebels against local governments who need supplies; and government patrol boats operated by corrupt captains. The latter may even be tipped off by shoreside officials that a boat of some value is in transit. Whoever they are, there is little recourse for official help since the governments themselves are helpless to control them, or even worse, they condone the action.

What is it the pirates are after? Money and material goods such as gold and silver jewelry, expensive electronics, sometimes foodstuffs and yacht hardware. Human life is apparently at the bottom of their list; they seem neither to value it nor to fear threats posed by humans.

A cruising boat, armed or not, is no match for a determined band of pirates, so it is best not to leisurely cruise in any suspected area. But if you do choose to cruise in these areas, keep the following thoughts in mind:

- For some safety, travel in the company of another boat.
- Travel direct passages, staying away from the shorelines.
- Keep a low profile and good security in port.
- Keep the boat locked at all times if possible, especially when you are asleep.
- Don't let the pirates know how many persons are on board.
- Install a powerful remote-controlled searchlight away from the cabin area to help blind your pursuers.
- Above all, avoid a gunfight. It could be a losing game against pirates who have little respect for life.

On Carrying Guns

Whether or not to carry firearms has to be a personal choice. The price you pay to carry a gun is bureaucratic hassles at Ports of Entry ranging from impoundment to confiscation. Ask yourself what you really want guns for and how you would use them. Would they get you into more trouble than you can handle? Is there an alternative to firearms like more careful route planning or greater awareness of potentially dangerous ports?

Before you decide to carry a gun aboard, think out carefully the scenarios under which anything less than an Uzi, an AK-47, or some other semiautomatic weapon would be of value. Pirates carry these plus machine guns and bazookas.

In all probability your use of a gun would take place on foreign soil, and when the attack was over, you would be faced with a whole new set of problems. Did you have permission to carry a gun? Did you shoot or injure a national of your host country on their property? This can be serious because in many countries you are guilty of a crime until proven innocent by their laws, which you know little about. Is this how your cruise ends?

Isn't it better to avoid trouble on another person's turf than to try to fight your way out of it? Keep your eyes and ears alert to troublesome situations developing and be willing to move away if you see trouble brewing. Since trouble is often temporary, inquire on the radio or ask other cruisers about the safety of questionable ports of call. If you know of such places, get the word out for the safety of others. People have lost their lives in gun battles while out cruising. That certainly isn't part of the cruising game.

Guns can be both a liability and a nuisance when you're crossing national boundaries, leading to a variety of problems when entering different countries. Many countries impound firearms ashore for the duration of your stay. French Polynesia is one. What good does an impounded gun ashore do you? Other countries simply confiscate them on principle. Singapore does that unless you have obtained a firearms permit in advance. Singapore, incidentally, considers flare guns and spear guns in the same category as firearms. At best you may be permitted to put your firearms in a sealed locker aboard your vessel for the duration of your stay. American Samoa now has a law on the books banning handguns and high-powered rifles and requiring licenses for shotguns and .22 caliber rifles. Hiding a gun aboard might lead to a smuggling charge should your boat be searched for drugs or other contraband.

In the end, being friendly, maintaining a low profile, and staying out of trouble areas is your best defense against piracy.

Avoiding Hijacking

The U.S. Coast Guard warns boaters of possible danger from hijacking and acts of piracy in the Pacific Ocean.

While the incidence of known or suspected hijacking has been relatively small in the past years, the Coast Guard says that the possibility of hijacking exists in the Pacific just as it does in Atlantic, Gulf of Mexico, and Caribbean waters. The Coast Guard stresses that most of the actual hijacking incidents have been carried out by persons who came aboard with the vessel operator's permission and knowledge.

Protection for vessels and crews on the high seas and in remote or out-of-the-way places is difficult to ensure and is primarily dependent upon the alertness of vessel operators. However, the Coast Guard indicated that certain preventative measures can lessen the possibilities of hijacking.

First, vessel operators should know the crew, particularly any crew that sought out the vessel. Tag-along guests from the marina who were persuaded to make the cruise should be identified as well. Insist on positive identification of anyone who sails with you. At least one form of I.D. should have a picture or physical description of the person. Check to make sure that all passports, visas, or other documents are valid. Before departure, personally deliver or mail to a relative or trusted friend the complete crew list along with a float plan and instructions to notify the Coast Guard if you fail to arrive at your destination after a reasonable time. Let all personnel aboard your vessel know about this precaution.

When going to the assistance of anyone in apparent distress, as any good sailor is expected to do, try to notify the nearest Coast Guard radio facility or any coastal radio station or maritime mobile net and describe the situation. While preparing to render assistance, be alert to any unusual situation and be wary if the apparently distressed person insists on boarding your vessel.

When departing on a foreign cruise from a U.S. port, consider taking time to clear with the local Customs office, although this is not required of pleasure craft. In addition to providing the complete crew manifest, list on form 4455 all firearms, high-value personal property, and portable vessel equipment. Retain a certified copy to save trouble in foreign ports and in clearing Customs upon return to the United States.

PART I

Polynesia

The Polynesian triangle encompasses 10 million square miles of the most beautiful cruising waters on the surface of the earth. Within this area are more than 360 islands (Polynesia means "many islands") with a land area of 10,000 square miles excluding New Zealand. With almost 1,000 square miles of water for every square mile of land, you can now begin to understand the origin of the seafaring nature of the Polynesians. Over this vast area of the Polynesian triangle there are only 1.6 million persons (again excluding New Zealand), and two-thirds of these people live in Hawaii.

The 360 islands are not evenly distributed over this vast area. In some cases they are chains of islands rising to the surface from submerged chains of mountains. The southern Cook Islands and Austral Islands are part of the same chain, but others like the Marquesas are simply tops of closely spaced seamounts. Over the years neighboring islands have become politically associated, and today there are eleven identifiable groups of Polynesian islands. Except for New Zealand, all groups lie within the tropics, that is, between the Tropic of Cancer in the northern hemisphere and the

Island Groups of Polynesia

ISLAND GROUP	NUMBER OF ISLANDS	LAND AREA (square miles)	POPULATION† (persons)	GOVERNMENT
Hawaii	7*	6,425	1,112,000	State of the United States
Marquesas	12	492	6,800	French Polynesia—
Tuamotu	76	343	11,500	French
Society	14	646	165,000	overseas
Austral	7	63	6,600	territory
Easter Island	1	50	2,000	Colony of Chile
Pitcairn	4	2	57	British dependency
Cook	15	93	18,200	Independent
American Samoa	7	76	42,000	United States territory
Western Samoa	8	1,135	186,000	Independent
Tokelau	3	4	1,700	New Zealand territory
Tonga	170	269	101,000	Kingdom
Tuvalu	9	11	9,000	Independent
Niue	1	100	2,300	New Zealand commonwealth
New Zealand	4	102,400	3,300,000	Independent

*Inhabited islands

†Source: *The World Factbook, 1991*, Central Intelligence Agency, U.S. Government Printing Office, Washington DC 20402-9325, USA

Tropic of Capricorn in the southern hemisphere. (In a cartographic sense Easter and Pitcairn islands are also out of the tropics, but their culture and society are considered tropical.)

From the birthplace of Polynesia in Samoa and Tonga (settled in 3000 to 2500 B.C.), the Polynesians sailed their mighty double-hulled voyaging canoes to the corners of today's Polynesian triangle. Their windward journeys first made landfalls in the Marquesas between the years 100 B.C. and A.D. 200. Such landing on high islands rather than atolls is not surprising since in noninstrument navigation a sailor's awareness of an island depends to an extent on the height of the island and its richness in bird life as indicators of its presence. Following closely on the heels of their Marquesan island discoveries the Polynesian voyagers discovered and settled the Tuamotu and Society island groups between A.D. 200 and 300.

The Polynesians' great success with the double-hulled voyaging canoes guided by expert star and sea navigators enabled them to continue the exploration of other islands to the east (Easter), north (Hawaii), and south (New Zealand). This was done over the period A.D. 400 to 1100 with New Zealand being the last on the list. In the meantime scores of lesser islands such as Mangareva, the Cooks, and the Australs were added to their civilization.

But don't be surprised if you find pockets of Polynesian peoples living among the Melanesians and Micronesians. After the main Polynesian eastward migration took place, there were isolated countermigrations to the west. Coming, most likely, from Samoa for unexplained reasons, the Polynesians settled islands and atolls on the eastern flanks of Vanuatu and the Solomons. Today you will find them living on Rennell and Ballona islands and Tikopia, Anuta, and Ontong Java atolls in the Solomon Islands; on Nukumanu and Nuguria atolls in Papua New Guinea; on Rotuma Island in Fiji; on Futuna and Aniwa islands in Vanuatu; on Kapingamarangi and Nukuoro atolls in the Federated States of Micronesia; and on a few other isolated islands.

The peoples of these Polynesian outliers live a life that is little different from that their ancestors lived in pre-European times. In general the outliers are isolated and without safe anchorages. Excepting Rennell and Ballona, they are without resources of value to traders; hence, they have been left alone. Today the governments of the countries in which these islands lie are prone to want to maintain their cultures untainted by Western influences. They actively discourage visits by tourists. These distant Polynesians are said to be happy peoples because they have no malaria, no snakes, and no foreigners. May they always stay that way.

CHAPTER 5

HAWAII

The Country

Hawaii anchors the northern apex of the vast Polynesian triangle. It is a unique chain of islands that stretches for 1,600 miles across the middle of the blue Pacific in a characteristic southeast to northwest direction. The longest and most distinctly formed archipelago in Polynesia, it is made up of 132 shoals, reefs, and islands. In geologic history the visible part of the chain began its life at the western end with, in all probability, the appearance of Kure Island, now reduced by time to an atoll. While the origin of Kure and the other leeward islands of the group goes back possibly 10 million years, the chain is still growing as evidenced by the easternmost island, Hawaii, which today continues a robust volcanic growth in sight of modern man.

Between Kure and Hawaii lies an almost complete history of land formation in the Pacific Ocean. The older leeward islands have now been reduced to shoals and atolls by the irresistible weathering forces of sun and wind and erosion by rain and wave. In the middle of the chain are the last vestiges of volcanic rock such as Gardner Pinnacles, which may be merely five million years old. But it is the eight major islands at the eastern end of the chain that form the inhabited land of Hawaii. In decreasing order of size they are Hawaii, Maui, Oahu, Kauai, Molokai, Lanai, and Niihau. They, together with Kahoolawe and the lesser leeward shoals and atolls, comprise a total land area of 6,425 square miles.

There are very few wild animals and birds in Hawaii, and those that are there were mostly imported from other places. The mongoose, probably the best known of the imported animals, is responsible for there being no snakes on the islands. In addition, there are deer, pigs, and wild goats, which are hunted seasonally. The nene (pronounced "nay-nay") is the largest landbird in the islands. There are also pheasants and other game birds.

Most of the flora found on other islands throughout the Pacific are also found in the Hawaiian Islands. Crops like sugar and pineapples, however, are not indigenous to the islands.

The seas around Hawaii abound in fish. Game fish such as marlin, mahi mahi, swordfish, wahoo, skipjack, and yellowfin tuna inhabit the surrounding waters. Surf casting and shore fishing are popular pastimes with the local people. There is freshwater trout fishing on Kauai.

Although archeological evidence of settlement supports a time close to A.D. 800, it is believed that the first Polynesians arrived in Hawaii about A.D. 500. They are presumed to have first come from either the Marquesas or Society islands; later voyages are believed to have originated in both island groups.

Their voyages to Hawaii broke the pattern of easterly sailing that had been a marked success over thousands of years. Now they were striking out in a direction of greater risk, having no past experience in north-south travels. One can only surmise that their past successes in sailing to windward over long distances and finding landfalls gave them new confidence that they could find land in any direction they chose to sail. Surely they had no idea that the closest land to the north lay 2,000 miles away. To those familiar with the vast reaches of the Pacific Ocean, Polynesian seamanship and navigation were feats of staggering proportions.

Hawaii as a place name occurs throughout Polynesia in various forms as, for instance, Savaii in Samoa, Hawaiki in Aotearoa Maori mythology, Havaiki in Cook Island Maori tales, and Havaii as the ancient name for Raiatea.

Hawaii was discovered by the Western world in 1778, when British captain James Cook sighted Oahu. Cook named the archipelago the Sandwich Islands after his patron, the Earl of Sandwich, and for many years the islands were so known in the Western world. In January 1779, Cook was slain in a fight with the Hawaiians at Kealakekua on the island of Hawaii.

HAWAIIAN ISLANDS
A state within the United States

Ports of Entry

Hilo, Hawaii	19°44′N, 155°04′W
Kahului, Maui	20°54′N, 156°28′W
Honolulu, Oahu	21°19′N, 157°52′W
Port Allen, Kauai	21°54′N, 159°35′W
Nawiliwili, Kauai	21°57′N, 159°21′W

Distances between Ports in Nautical Miles
Between Honolulu and

Acapulco, Mexico	3,280
Astoria, Oregon	2,230
Bounty Bay, Pitcairn Island	3,220
Cabo San Lucas, Mexico	2,660
Christmas Island, Kiribati	1,160
Funafuti, Tuvalu	2,240
Hanga Roa, Easter Island	4,045
Kodiak, Alaska	2,355
Los Angeles, California	2,220
Majuro, Marshall Islands	1,975
Pago Pago, American Samoa	2,265
Panama City, Panama	4,555
Papeete, Tahiti	2,380
Puntarenas, Costa Rica	4,240
San Diego, California	2,265
San Francisco, California	2,080
Seattle, Washington	2,355
Taiohae, Marquesas	2,095
Tarawa, Kiribati	2,085
Vancouver, British Columbia	2,355
Wreck Bay, Galapagos	4,210

Standard Time
10 hours slow on UTC

Public Holidays and Special Events

January 1	New Year's Day—National holiday
January *	Martin Luther King Day—National holiday
February *	Narcissus Festival—Chinese New Year celebration
February *	Presidents' Day—National holiday
March 26	Prince Kuhio Day—State holiday
April 5	Buddha Day—Festival at Buddhist temples
March/April *	Easter Sunrise Service—Punchbowl Crater and other venues
May 1	Lei Day—May Day celebration
May *	Memorial Day—National holiday
June 11	Kamehameha Day—State holiday
June 11–20	Fiesta Filipina—Philippine town festivals
July 4	Independence Day—National holiday
August *	Admission Day—State holiday
September *	Labor Day—National holiday (first Monday)
October *	Discoverers' Day—National holiday
November 11	Veterans Day—National holiday
November *	Thanksgiving—National holiday
December 25	Christmas—National holiday

*Specific dates vary from year to year.

At the time of Cook's arrival, each island was ruled as an independent kingdom by hereditary chiefs. One such chief, Kamehameha, consolidated his power on the island of Hawaii in a series of battles about 1790 and then conquered Maui and Oahu. By the time of his death in 1819, Kamehameha I had united the islands under his rule and had established the Kingdom of Hawaii, which survived until 1893.

In 1820, the first American missionaries arrived from New England. Not only did they bring Christianity to a people becoming disillusioned with their ancient gods, but they represented the first of several migrations that led to the cosmopolitan character of Hawaii's people today. In the years following Cook's arrival, Hawaii had become a center of whaling activity and had opened a trade in sandalwood with China, a trade profitable for the king and the chiefs, but one that put a burden on the people who had to gather the wood. Further, the introduction of Western diseases and liquor and a breakdown of the ancient morality had created a chaotic situation. The missionaries gained great success because they aligned themselves with the chiefs against some of these evils.

The infant sugar industry required more than the available labor to work the plantations, and in 1852 Chinese were brought into the kingdom by contract. Thus began the stream of imported labor, which lasted until 1946. The first Japanese came in 1868, Filipinos somewhat later. Koreans, Portuguese, and Puerto Ricans are among the other national groups brought to the islands.

The growing importance of sugar was reflected in Hawaii's political picture during the next few decades. The sugar planters favored annexation of Hawaii by the United States to establish a firm market for the product. The Hawaiian monarchs, on the other hand, spasmodically attempted to establish and implement a policy of Hawaii for the Hawaiians. Hawaii's strategic military importance in the Pacific was recognized, particularly its potential threat to the United States if another great power were to occupy the islands. By Joint Resolution of Congress, the islands were officially annexed, and formal transfer of sovereignty was made on August 12, 1898.

The effects of the Great Depression in the 1930s were not as serious in Hawaii as they were in more industrialized areas. With growing international tensions, and particularly the aggressions of Japan in the Far East, the 1930s saw a build-up of U.S. military power in Hawaii. They also saw the binding of Hawaii closer to the mainland by Pan-American World Airways' inauguration of regular commercial air flights in 1936.

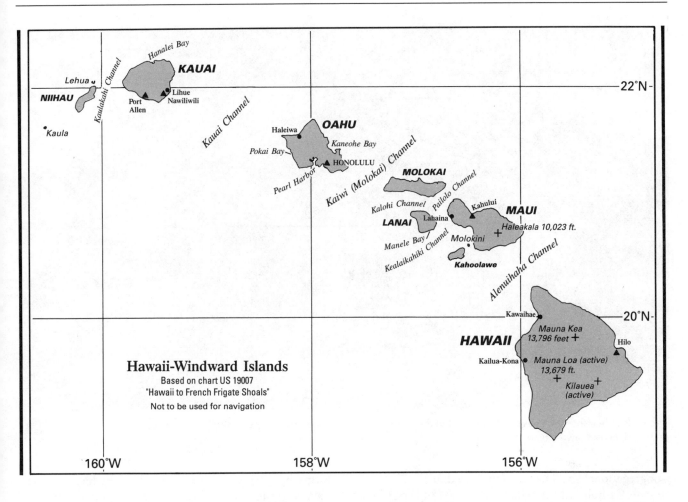

Hawaii-Windward Islands
Based on chart US 19007
"Hawaii to French Frigate Shoals"
Not to be used for navigation

International tensions burst into flame on the morning of December 7, 1941, when the first Japanese bombs fell on Pearl Harbor, causing nearly 4,000 casualties and seriously crippling the great American fleet berthed there. Hawaii quickly mushroomed into an armed camp and became the nerve center of the whole U.S. Pacific war effort. The joyous celebration of V-J Day on August 14, 1945, was heartfelt.

From the 1930s through the 1950s the dominant political theme in Hawaii was statehood. First proposed during the reign of Kamehameha III, it became a more defined goal shortly after World War I, when Hawaii's delegate to Congress, Prince Jonah Kuhio Kalanianaole, introduced a bill to that effect in Congress. More strenuous efforts were made in the 1930s and continued after World War II. All these efforts finally culminated in success in 1959, and both houses of Congress passed the necessary legislation on March 12. Hawaii officially entered the United States as the fiftieth state on August 21, 1959.

Under Hawaii's state constitution, executive powers are vested in a governor and lieutenant governor

elected every four years. The state has a bicameral legislature, which meets annually in Honolulu, the capital city.

Hawaii is unique among the states in that it enjoys only two levels of government: state and county. There are no separate municipalities and no school districts or other smaller government jurisdictions. The city and county of Honolulu (Oahu) is governed by a mayor and a nine-member city council. The other counties are each governed by a mayor and a county council.

The people of Hawaii can trace ancestry to many ethnic and national groups of the world—Asian, Polynesian, European, and others. While ancestral languages are still heard in Hawaii, English is universally used. Hawaii's citizens are U.S. citizens; nearly all of them were born under the U.S. flag and educated in U.S. schools. Since World War II, one out of three marriages in Hawaii has been interracial; such intermarriage has further contributed to Hawaii's extremely cosmopolitan population.

Hawaii's religions are as diverse as is its cultural heritage. The missionaries who arrived in 1820 were

The skills of her ancestors have not been lost to this young Hawaiian weaving baskets at the City of Refuge National Historical Park on the island of Hawaii. (Earl Hinz)

Congregationalists. They were followed in 1827 by the Roman Catholics. In the constitution of 1840, freedom of worship was guaranteed for all religions, and there are now more than two dozen religious beliefs followed in these islands.

The University of Hawaii has its main campus in Honolulu and a branch campus in Hilo. In addition to the university, there are four smaller private colleges, seven public two-year community colleges, and several business and technical schools.

Formerly under the University of Hawaii is the now independent, nonprofit East-West Center. Launched in 1960, it is providing education to students from all parts of Asia, the United States, and other areas of the world.

Hawaii's cost of living is higher than that of mainland areas, especially for housing and food. These higher costs are partially offset by the absence of heating costs and seasonal clothing requirements.

Hawaii's sources of basic income are the federal government (particularly military), tourism, agriculture, and some manufacturing. Its great cash crops are sugar and pineapple, grown on large, industrialized farms by corporate enterprises. Hawaii has the most advanced sugar technology of any area in the world—so much so that other countries have turned to Hawaii for assistance in developing sugar industries of their own. Among these are Iran and Peru. Hawaiian pineapple is world famous for its quality and the industry for its technology.

Among minor crops, macadamia nuts are rising in quantity and importance. New technology has permitted vastly increased shipments of fresh pineapple in recent years, and the same can be said of fresh papaya. Hawaii is the only state in the union that grows coffee; its Kona coffee is noted for its full body and fine aroma. The islands also export guava nectar, passionfruit (lilikoi) juice, orchids, anthuriums, and other varieties of Hawaiian flowers and foliage.

Various vegetables, as well as taro, mangoes, avocados, and citrus, are grown for consumption in the islands, and a ranching industry supplies a substantial portion of the beef consumed in Hawaii. Parker Ranch, on the island of Hawaii, is one of the largest ranches (in land area) in the United States.

Because Hawaii's people are Americans who can

trace their lineage back to virtually every country in the world, the cultural resources of the islands are steeped with Asian, Western, and Polynesian traditions, providing a colorful and fascinating environment. A cosmopolitan influence is seen everywhere in Hawaii's architecture, music, art, theater, dress, and foods. Cultures from other lands have filtered down through the generations to produce what is called today a "typical Hawaiian atmosphere."

The Bishop Museum in Honolulu is famous for its extensive collections of Pacific art and artifacts and is a center of Pacific-wide ethnological research. The Honolulu Academy of Arts is noted for its permanent collection of European, Asian, and Hawaiian art and offers a wide range of educational programs to foster art appreciation. There are noteworthy museums at Lihue on the island of Kauai and at Wailuku on Maui, at the Hulihee Palace in Kailua-Kona, and at Lyman House, Hilo.

Hawaii is a particularly attractive destination for cruising boats because of its location, weather, facilities, and the fact that it is a part of the United States. In an average year about 375 boats check into the state. About 40 percent are from the mainland, and they have made Hawaii their destination for a summer cruise. The remaining boats are either on their way to the South Pacific or are returning from there.

The Weather

The climate of Hawaii is unusually pleasant even for the tropics. Its outstanding features are (1) the persistence of the trade winds, where not disrupted by high mountains; (2) the remarkable variability in rainfall over short distances; (3) the sunniness of the leeward lowlands, in contrast to the persistent cloudiness over nearby mountain crests; (4) the equable temperature from day to day and season to season; and (5) the infrequency of severe storms.

The prevailing wind throughout the year is the northeast trade wind, which blows for more than 90 percent of the time during the summer to only 50 percent in January.

The strongest influence underlying the general circulation of air over the Hawaiian Islands area is the semipermanent high-pressure cell known as the Pacific high. The clockwise circulation around this cell, coupled with a slight deflection of the surface winds away from the high pressure, result in the northeast trades that are the dominant winds of the area.

August and September in Hawaii are normally warm and dry with persistent trade winds. Over the nearby open sea, these average 13 to 16 knots and are predominantly from the east-northeast, with directions northeast through east occurring nearly 90 percent of the time in September. However, as summer merges into fall, the trades diminish in frequency and by the end of December occur only about half the time.

The rugged and varied terrain of the islands exerts a pronounced influence on the speed and direction of the wind. Around headlands in exposed channels and to the lee of some gorges, passes, and saddles, the trades may be much stronger and gustier than over the open ocean.

In contrast, waters for as much as 10 miles leeward of the highest mountains may be entirely sheltered from the trade winds and experience instead onshore sea breezes during the day and gentle offshore land breezes at night. This sheltering and the resulting diurnal wind cycle are particularly evident off the Kona coast of the Big Island and south of Haleakala on Maui, but to some degree exist off all lee coasts. Where mountain barriers are lower, as on Kauai, Oahu, Lanai, and Molokai, the trade winds may be damped out for only a mile or two to leeward, most noticeable if they are below their usual strength.

Although the trades are often strong and gusty enough to require small craft advisories, Hawaii's strongest winds are those associated with weather systems of the October–April half-year. Beginning usually by late fall, but more commonly in winter, gale force winds may be brought into Hawaiian waters by kona storms forming within the subtropics, cold fronts moving in from the northwest, and Pacific storms migrating eastward north of the islands.

Six hurricanes have struck Hawaii since 1950, but several times that many, and a number of less intense tropical cyclones, most of them drifting west from their breeding grounds off the Mexican coast, have approached near enough for their outlying winds, clouds, and rain to affect the islands. Hurricane Iniki most recently struck the islands, passing across Kauai in September 1992. Damage to boats in harbors was extensive on Kauai, and some damage was experienced at the Keehi Lagoon anchorages on Oahu. Boats at sea rode out the storm with a good wetting but not severe damage.

It is not the winds, however, that have caused Hawaii's most significant damage but tsunamis, those massive ocean swells caused by violent undersea earthquakes, generated thousands of miles away. The size of a predicted tsunami cannot be estimated in advance.

Most of them felt in Honolulu harbor have been relatively small; the largest on record, ten feet high, struck in 1960. However, it is prudent to anticipate that even greater ones may strike. Honolulu harbor authorities require all ships to vacate the harbor before the estimated time of arrival of a sea wave, if possible.

Probably the only consistent sailing problem found in the Hawaiian waters is the roughness of the channels between the major islands. Straddling the trade winds and prevailing currents, the islands form a barrier to normal surface flows with the result that the winds and currents funnel through the channels at accelerated speeds. The channel waters develop steep waves, which make cross-channel sailing real work when the trades are strong. Night passages are generally chosen because they are more peaceful. The four principal channels, which range in width from 8 miles to 63 miles, are the Alenuihaha Channel, between Hawaii and Maui (26 miles), the Pailolo Channel, between Maui and Molokai (8 miles), the Kaiwi (Molokai) Channel, between Molokai and Oahu (23 miles), and the Kauai Channel, between Oahu and Kauai (63 miles).

Hawaii's equable temperatures are associated with the small seasonal variation in the amount of energy received from the sun and the tempering effect of the surrounding ocean. Elevation is the major control factor in determining local temperatures, although location, whether in a leeward or windward position, is also a factor. The highest temperatures reached during the day in leeward districts are usually higher than those attained in windward areas. The daily range is also greater over leeward districts where, because of less cloudiness, the maximum temperatures are higher and the minimum temperatures usually lower.

August and September are the warmest months, and January and February are the coldest. At Honolulu there is an average monthly range between a low of 74°F in January and February and a high of 80°F in August. The extreme range of temperatures at Honolulu for the five-year period of record is from a low of 57°F for January to a high of 94°F recorded in September. This spread of only 37°F between the extreme high and extreme low temperatures is small when compared with ranges at mainland U.S. ports.

All coastal areas are subject to the relatively high humidities associated with a marine climate. Humidities, however, vary considerably, with high percentages over and near the windward slopes to low percentages on the leeward sides of the higher elevations.

Because of the persistence of the northeast trade winds, even the warmest months are usually comfort-

able. But when the trades diminish or give way to southern winds, a situation known locally as "kona weather" ("kona storms" when stormy), the humidity may become oppressively high.

The word "kona" is of Polynesian origin and means "leeward." It refers to the southern winds and accompanying weather on the normally leeward slopes of the principal Hawaiian Islands which, because of the wind shift, have temporarily become the windward slopes. The konas, which occur most frequently during October through April, provide the major climatic variations of the Hawaiian Islands. During kona storms, heavy rainfall and cloudiness can be expected on the leeward coasts and slopes, which, under the usual wind pattern, receive less cloudiness and may have almost no rain. Near gales may occur, especially in areas where the air tends to funnel into sharp mountain passes near the coasts. At such times normally leeward anchorages may become unsafe for small craft.

Intense rains of the October to April "winter" season sometimes cause serious local flash flooding. Thunderstorms are infrequent and usually mild, as compared with those of the midwestern United States. Hail seldom occurs, and when it does it is small and rarely damaging to crops. Occasionally a small tornado or a waterspout moving onshore may do some damage.

Except for rare one- or two-day disruptions of interisland airplane schedules, interference to shipping or travel because of bad weather is almost unknown.

The northeast trade winds bring the rain-bearing clouds, which are caught by the mountains. Thus, there is an enormous range of rainfall with the windward sides of the islands being generally wetter than the leeward sides. Waialeale on the island of Kauai has a mean annual rainfall of 486 inches and is one of the two wettest spots on earth, although there are areas on the same island, only a few miles away, that have fewer than 20 inches of rain a year. The driest spot is Puako, on Hawaii, with a mean average of only 10 inches a year.

The complicated rainfall pattern over the islands results chiefly from the effects of the rugged terrain on the persistent trade winds. Frequent and heavy showers fall almost daily on windward and upland areas, while rains of sufficient intensity and duration to cause more than temporary inconvenience are infrequent over the lower sections of leeward areas. Considerably more rain falls from November through April over the islands as a whole than from May through October. It is not unusual for an entire summer month to go by without measurable rain falling at some points in the Maui isthmus.

Annual rainfall in the Honolulu area averages less than 30 inches along the coast (25 inches at the airport, 24 inches in the downtown area) but increases significantly inland. Parts of the Koolau Range average 300 inches or more a year. This heavy mountain rainfall sustains extensive irrigation of cane fields and the water supply for Honolulu. East (windward) of the Koolaus, coastal areas receive 30 to 50 inches annually; cane and pineapple fields in central Oahu get about 35 to 40 inches. Oahu is driest along the coast west of the Waianaes, where rainfall drops to about 20 inches a year. However, variations from month to month and year to year are considerable—more so during the cooler season, when occasional major storms provide much of the rain, than in the summer, when rain occurs primarily as showers that form within the moist trade winds as they override the mountains. Trade wind rainfall is more frequent at night, but daytime showers, usually light, often occur while the sun continues to shine, a phenomenon referred to locally as "liquid sunshine" producing beautiful rainbows.

From the dry, uninhabited atolls of the west to the lush, green islands on the east, the chain has a full variety of weather including snow at the mountain summits of Hawaii.

Cruising Notes

YACHT ENTRY

There are five Ports of Entry in the Hawaiian Islands: Hilo, Hawaii; Kahului, Maui; Honolulu, Oahu; Port Allen and Nawiliwili, Kauai. Whether coming from the continental United States or foreign ports, all yachts must clear in through one of these five ports.

Foreign yachts entering the United States at Hawaii must abide by all the Immigration, Customs, Agriculture, and Health regulations as in entering any other part of the United States. The following section describes procedures for entering yachts and nonimmigrant crew whether on foreign or U.S. yachts.

U.S. Customs has issued the following directions concerning the arrival and entry of vessels at United States ports:

  • Immediately upon arrival the following vessels must report their arrival to the nearest Customs facility:
    • A vessel arriving from a foreign port or place or arriving from the U.S. possessions of Guam, Wake, all the islands and atolls northwest of Niihau and Kauai in the Hawaiian Islands chain including Midway and Kure atolls, American Samoa, Johnston Atoll, Kingman Reef, Palmyra Atoll, and the Virgin Islands
    • A foreign flag vessel arriving from a domestic port
    • Any vessel having had contact with a hovering vessel on the high seas
  • Passengers, crew, or merchandise may not leave the vessel or be discharged until cleared by Customs.
  • Failure to report arrival, to present proper papers, or to follow the regulations regarding the entry and arrival of passengers, crew, or merchandise may result in severe penalties including fines and confiscation.

If your boat has tied up at a dock or anchored, you are considered to have entered the United States. The skipper may leave the boat for the sole purpose of notifying Customs of the boat's arrival, then must return immediately to the boat after reporting and remain on board. Customs officers will notify other departments that are involved in clearing an overseas boat into Hawaii.

CUSTOMS FOR U.S. YACHTS

U.S. yachts must report arrival from a foreign area to Customs within 24 hours and must also report any foreign merchandise aboard the vessel that is subject to duty. The report may be made by any means of communication. If an inspection is required, the Customs officer will direct the vessel to an inspection area.

All recreation vessels are being charged an annual Customs processing fee of US$25 when making first entry. There is no separate charge for Customs inspection during official business hours of 0800–1700. After-hours and Sunday/holiday inspection service will be provided at overtime rates not to exceed US$25 per boat per inspection.

Articles imported in excess of your customs exemption will be subject to duty calculated by the Customs inspector, unless the items are entitled to free entry or prohibited. Your exemptions are the same as those for any U.S. citizen traveler. (See Customs publication no. 506, *Pocket Hints for Returning U.S. Residents,* and no. 512, *Know Before You Go.*)

Although no notification is required when a U.S.

FLOTSAM AND JETSAM

Currency
Hawaii is a state of the United States and, therefore, uses the U.S. dollar ($). There are 100 cents in the dollar, and coinage is issued in denominations of 1, 5, 10, 25, 50, and 100 cents. Notes are issued in 1, 2, 5, 10, 20, 50, and 100 dollars. It is recommended that notes larger than $20 be avoided because of difficulty in cashing them at stores. The relative price of goods and services is 125. (The relative price of goods and services refers to the approximate ratio of prices between the island group and that of Washington, D.C., United States of America, at the time of writing. This is a weighted average of groceries, utilities, transportation, health costs, and miscellaneous needs. It does not include shelter or income taxes.)

Language
The indigenous language is Hawaiian, which is a Polynesian dialect. It is spoken primarily by the descended Hawaiians. The official language of Hawaii is English, and the unofficial language is pidgin. Japanese is also widely spoken as is Chinese and Filipino by persons of those national descents.

Electricity
Electricity is commonly available; it is 110v, 60 Hz AC.

Postal Addresses
Good postal service is available throughout the Hawaiian Islands. Recommended postal addresses are:

Yacht ( )
General Delivery
Hilo HI 96720, USA

Yacht ( )
General Delivery
Lihue HI 96766, USA

Yacht ( )
General Delivery
Kahului HI 96732, USA
or
Lahaina HI 96761, USA

Yacht ( )   or
General Delivery
Honolulu HI 96820, USA

Yacht ( )
c/o Hawaii Yacht Club
1739-C Ala Moana Blvd
Honolulu HI 96815, USA

Ports for Making Crew Changes
Honolulu is a recommended port for making crew changes because of its excellent airline service. It is the airline hub of the Pacific, being served by major U.S. domestic trunk carriers as well as by international air carriers from around the world. There is good domestic airline service to Kauai, Maui, and Hawaii islands. Foreign crews and foreign yachts must notify Immigration of crew changes.

External Affairs Representative
U.S. embassies and consulates

Information Center
Hawaii Visitors Bureau
Suite 801
2270 Kalakaua Avenue
Honolulu HI 96815, USA

boat departs for foreign ports, this freedom of Americans should not be taken too literally. Most countries demand a *zarpe* from your previous port as a condition of entry. Some American territories even demand one from a boat coming from another U.S. port. American Samoa will not enter your vessel coming from Hawaii, for example, unless you have a Customs clearance in hand. It is therefore wise to apply for Customs form 1378, Clearance of a Vessel to a Foreign Port, as part of your departure preparations.

Because yachts carry considerable foreign-made equipment on board, sometimes including the yacht itself, it is also wise to declare these items before departing, thereby eliminating any argument on your return about whether the duty has been paid or not. This is in lieu of trying to keep a complete file of receipts of purchase on all foreign-made equipment.

CUSTOMS FOR FOREIGN YACHTS

The master of a foreign yacht must report arrival to U.S. Customs within 24 hours and make formal entry within 48 hours. In the absence of a cruising license, vessels in this category must obtain a permit before proceeding to each subsequent U.S. port and must clear in at every port that they visit. The boats must also clear Customs prior to departing for a foreign port. Boarding charges and overtime and processing fees are the same as for U.S. yachts. A nonresident bringing a pleasure boat into the country under a duty-free customs exemption must formally enter the boat and pay applicable customs duty before selling it or offering it for sale or charter within the United States.

Cruising licenses exempt pleasure boats of certain countries from formal entry and clearance procedures at all but the first Port of Entry. The licenses can be obtained from Customs at the first port of arrival in the United States. Normally issued for no more than a one-year period, a cruising license has no bearing on the dutiability of a pleasure boat. Vessels of the following countries are eligible for cruising licenses because these countries extend the same privileges to U.S. pleasure boats: Argentina, Australia, Austria, Bahama Islands, Belgium, Bermuda, Canada, Denmark, France, Germany, Great Britain (including Turks and Caicos Islands, St. Vincent, Cayman Islands, British Virgin Islands, and the St. Christopher–Nevis–Anguilla islands), Greece, Honduras, Ireland, Jamaica, Liberia, Netherlands, New Zealand, Norway, and Sweden.

Once the cruising license has been granted, the yacht can freely cruise the domestic waters listed on the

Hanalei Bay on the north shore of Kauai is a favorite anchorage for yachts cruising the Hawaiian Islands. Many boats stop here before stepping off for the mainland. Kauai is appropriately called the Garden Isle because of its verdant growth and deep-sculpted mountains. (Hawaii Visitors Bureau)

The Ala Wai Boat Harbor on Oahu is chock-full of local boats, but except for TransPac and Kenwood Cup race weeks every summer, room can usually be found for the itinerant cruising boat passing through the Hawaiian Islands. (Earl Hinz)

license. A report of arrival must still be made at each port where there is a Customs office. But there is no requirement to go to the office or to present the vessel or its occupants for inspection. The report of arrival is generally made by telephone.

The charge for a cruising permit for any of the foregoing countries is US$9 for pleasure boats under 100 tons. Foreign pleasure boats from other than the above countries are charged US$18 for a permit to cruise within a specific Customs district (all of Hawaii is one district).

Failure to report at subsequent ports can have dramatic effects when found out. A New Zealand boat with a cruising license obtained in Seattle worked its way down the coast of the United States without checking in at ports where it stopped. By the time it got to San Francisco, Customs was on the lookout for it and impounded it on arrival. A charge equal to the value of the boat was imposed as a fine. The owner fought the fine and got it reduced to $500 by the time he got to San Pedro (Los Angeles' harbor). He was so distraught by his experience that he departed the United States at Los Angeles "never to return again." Had he followed the rules he could have enjoyed the rest of his planned cruise.

Additional information on clearing a pleasure boat into the United States can be found in Customs publication no. 544, *Pleasure Boats.*

Girls play a game of balance at Waimea Bay Park on Oahu's north shore. (Earl Hinz)

IMMIGRATION

The immigration laws of the United States deal with aliens, which includes all persons who are not citizens or nationals of the United States. In preparing for a cruise to the United States, each crew member must apply abroad to a U.S. consulate for a visa appropriate to his or her desired entry status, which in all probability will be one of the two following classes of nonimmigrants: an alien having residence in a foreign country which he or she has no intention of abandoning who is visiting the United States temporarily for pleasure or an alien crew member serving in good faith as such in any capacity required for the normal operation and service on board a vessel who intends to land temporarily and solely in pursuit of his or her calling as crew and to depart from the United States with the same vessel or some other vessel.

Since one condition for granting a visa assumes that you will arrive in the United States within the period of validity of the visa, one problem to consider is the often unpredictable schedule of a cruising yacht. It is recommended that the visa be obtained at the last possible port of call having a U.S. consulate so that the time uncertainty is minimized, but don't try to enter without a visa. A person requiring a visa who succeeds in obtaining transportation to the United States and is not in possession of a visa may be denied admission and deported.

Aliens, generally, must possess valid, unexpired visas and passports when applying for admission to the United States. A nonimmigrant must have a passport valid for a minimum of six months from the date of expiration of the period of admission authorizing him or her to enter another country during that six months.

A nonimmigrant may be admitted initially for whatever period the admitting officer deems appropriate to accomplish the intended purpose of his or her temporary stay and is permitted to stay in the United States upon these conditions:

1. That while in the United States the person will maintain the particular nonimmigrant status under which admitted;
2. That the person will depart from the United States within the period of admission;
3. That while in the United States the person will not engage in any employment unless so authorized.

If an extension of time is required, application should be made at least 15 days before expiration of the initial admission.

A nonimmigrant may be required to post a bond of not less than $500 as a condition precedent to admission to ensure that he or she will depart from the United States at the expiration of the admission time and will maintain the immigration status under which admitted.

No hard and fast rule can be laid down as to the amount of money an alien should have on arrival. Inflation is causing prices to rise in the United States as well as elsewhere. In particular, medical care is outrageously high in the United States, and medical bills could be the unfortunate yachting enthusiast's undoing.

A word of warning to skippers of U.S. yachts carrying alien crew members: Be sure that they have proper papers for entering the United States, or you will be guilty of aiding and abetting an illegal entry.

FIREARMS

Firearms and ammunition intended for legitimate hunting or lawful sporting purposes may be brought into the United States, provided that any remaining unfired ammunition is taken out upon your departure. All other firearms and ammunition are subject to restriction and import permits. A permit to carry a firearm is issued by a state or local government and is for a specified area. The laws of most states allow a person to transport firearms through the state provided that the firearms are not readily accessible. Every person arriving in the state of Hawaii with a firearm shall within 48 hours of arrival register that firearm with the chief of police of the county government. Note that hunting licenses are required in all of the United States.

AGRICULTURAL INSPECTION

It is illegal to bring many types of meats, fruits, vegetables, plants, animals, and animal products into the United States without approval from the Department of Agriculture. This approval extends to special products that may be harmful to a particular state's agriculture; hence it may differ slightly depending on your Port of Entry to the United States. U.S. yachts transiting between states are also subject to the agricultural import laws of the destination state.

The U.S. Public Health Service requires that pets brought into the country be examined at the Port of Entry to make certain they show no evidence of disease that can be passed on to humans and that they meet the requirements of other specific regulations. Pets taken out of the United States and returned are subject to the same requirements as those entering for the first time.

There is a 72-hour onboard quarantine period for cats and dogs arriving in Hawaii after which they must be shipped via air to the Animal Quarantine Center in Honolulu. The animals are quarantined at the center for a period of 120 days at a cost of US$3.80 per day for a dog and US$3.35 per day for a cat. You will also be required to pay an initial fee of US$10.00 for the booking. The full 120 days' fee must be paid in advance, but if you leave Hawaii before the 120 days are up, you can get a refund of the unused balance. Further information on bringing pets into Hawaii can be obtained from

Hawaii Department of Agriculture
P.O. Box 22159
Honolulu HI 96822
USA

FISHING LICENSES

For saltwater fishing in the state of Hawaii, there are no limits or license requirements. This is not true in the other states for either residents or nonresidents, so you must inquire when you arrive in another state.

YACHT FACILITIES

The Hawaiian Islands provide the best harbor and maintenance facilities to be found within the rim of the Pacific Ocean. Most of these facilities are in the Honolulu area, so for other than emergency services, you will do best sailing to Honolulu. The Honolulu area with its 900,000 residents also assures a good supply of food and drink plus American-style clothing. Prices are noticeably higher than on the mainland.

There are slipways and repair facilities at Ala Wai Boat Harbor, Kewalo Basin, Keehi Lagoon, and Honokohau Harbor. Fuel docks can supply all needed fuels, and good drinking water is available at all places. All boating facilities, however, are very crowded. The main Hawaiian Islands are still young islands, and erosion and coral polyps have not had time to build many natural harbors around the periphery of the islands. This lack, together with the seafaring nature of the islanders and the attraction of the fiftieth state to sailors from the mainland, keeps all facilities occupied. If you plan on a stay longer than 30 days, be prepared to shift anchorages. Boats from the mainland staying more than 90 days may be requested to register in Hawaii, but that doesn't mean that they will get any slip preference. The summer season is particularly crowded, with seasonal cruising boats arriving from the mainland as well as racing fleets descending on the islands every year from the mainland.

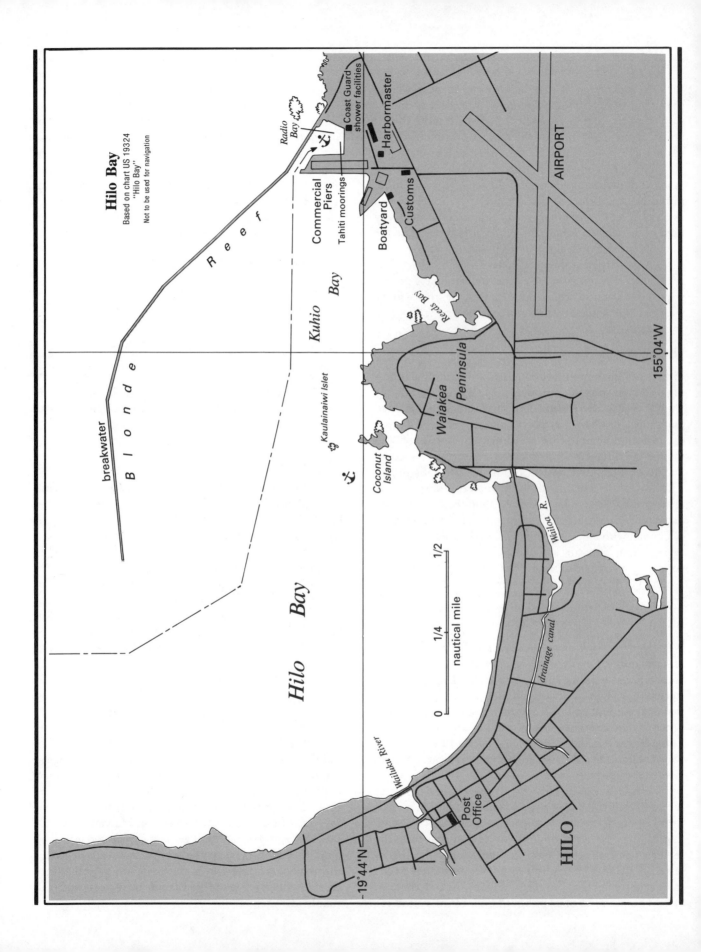

Hilo Bay

Based on chart US 19324
"Hilo Bay"
Not to be used for navigation

breakwater

B l o n d e

R e e f

Radio Bay

Coast Guard
shower facilities

Harbormaster

Commercial Piers

Tahiti moorings

Kuhio Bay

Boatyard

Customs

Reeds Bay

AIRPORT

155°04'W.

Kaulainaiwi Islet

Coconut Island

Waiakea Peninsula

Wailoa R.

Hilo Bay

Hilo Bay

1/2

1/4

nautical mile

0

drainage canal

Wailuku River

Post Office

19°44'N

HILO

The replica square-rigged *Cartha-ginian* lies to its berth alongside the harbor agent's office in the old whaling port of Lahaina, Maui. The historic Pioneer Inn is in the background. (Earl Hinz)

All the small-boat facilities in Hawaii are run by the State of Hawaii with the exception of two private marinas in Keehi Lagoon. There is a uniform scale of charges which allows free moorage for the first three days. Transient vessels can use the facilities of any one state marina only 30 days in a calendar year. Charges for transient moorings vary according to the following schedule:

Length over all (feet)	Daily charge (US$)
20–29	4.60
30–39	5.75
40–49	6.90
50–59	7.95
60–69	9.20

An additional charge of US$2 per day per person is made if you wish to live aboard during your stay.

YACHT FACILITIES AT PORTS OF ENTRY

Hilo, Hawaii

Hilo is a rather large but greatly underused harbor. It faces into the prevailing winds but is protected to a large extent by Blond Reef and the breakwater atop it. There is a designated anchorage adjacent to Kaulainaiwi Island, but the harbormaster does not want yachts anchoring out. Instead he will direct you to Radio Bay, a snug small-boat mooring area behind the main wharf.

In Radio Bay you can anchor out or moor Tahiti style to the quay. Unlike Tahiti, though, there is a significant tidal change preventing the close-in positioning needed for a stern gangway. Instead your dinghy provides your shore access. To keep this rather enclosed harbor clean, you must use the toilet and shower facilities ashore rather than any on your boat.

You can live aboard your boat for up to 30 days in Radio Bay, although you can leave your boat in Radio Bay for a longer period at the same rate while living ashore. You will also be assessed an insurance charge of US$3.

Small stores are within walking distance; major stores are in Hilo, which is a short bus ride away. There are limited repair facilities and marine parts available. If you really need major parts or work done you must go to Honolulu.

Although a nonentry port, Kailua-Kona on the leeward side of the island of Hawaii is popular among cruising boats. It is an open roadstead where you can anchor in 2 to 7 fathoms of water over a somewhat rocky bottom. Charges for anchoring space and the use of the facilities at the dock and on shore are the same as the foregoing schedule. The attraction here is the fine weather and the well-developed tourist facilities.

Another nonentry port on the island of Hawaii is Honokohau, just north of Kailua-Kona. It is the state's newest marina and provides a variety of services to yachts including fuels, food and drink, and haulout and

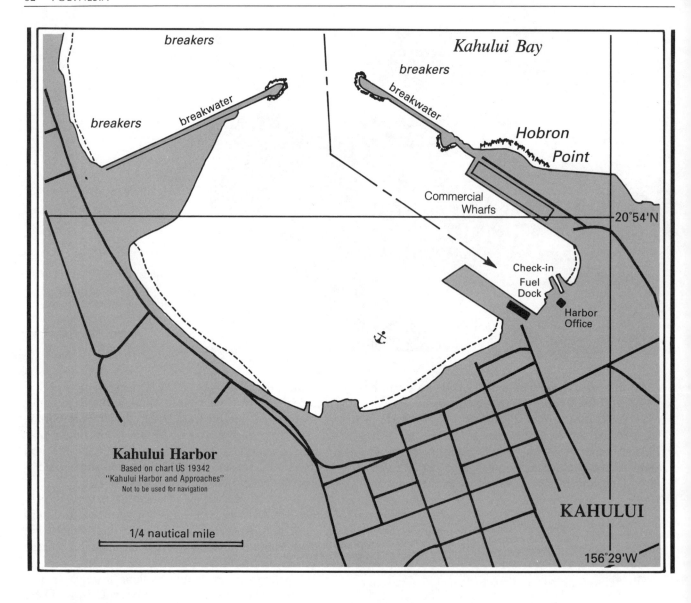

breakers

Kahului Bay

breakers

breakwater

breakers

breakwater

Hobron

Point

Commercial
Wharfs

20°54'N

Check-in
Fuel
Dock

Harbor
Office

Kahului Harbor
Based on chart US 19342
"Kahului Harbor and Approaches"
Not to be used for navigation

1/4 nautical mile

KAHULUI

156°29'W

repair services. The harbor is very crowded, but occasionally berthing space is available for the transient boat.

Kahului, Maui

Kahului Harbor, on the northeast coast of Maui, is a deepwater shipping port. Breakwaters protect the harbor from swells and waves generated by the trade winds. The harbor is approximately a third of a mile square, and small craft have plenty of anchorage room in the unimproved areas behind the breakwaters. Yachts coming from overseas ports should seek an unoccupied spot along the wharf and call the Customs officials to initiate clearance. Do not remain along the wharf any longer than necessary to conduct entry formalities as

spaces there are needed for commercial shipping. Seek an anchorage as soon as your clearance is effected.

The town of Kahului has good shopping and laundry facilities and other standard attractions, but there are no particular amenities for yachts. Engine fuels are available. For boat supplies, repairs, or other maintenance needs you will have to go to Lahaina, if minor, or to Honolulu, if major.

Most yachts favor Lahaina once formalities are completed. It is a colorful old whaling town and was once the capital of Hawaii. There is a harbor at Lahaina, but it is small and fully occupied with local craft. Anchoring is good outside the harbor in all except kona weather.

The Lahaina Yacht Club extends a guest member-

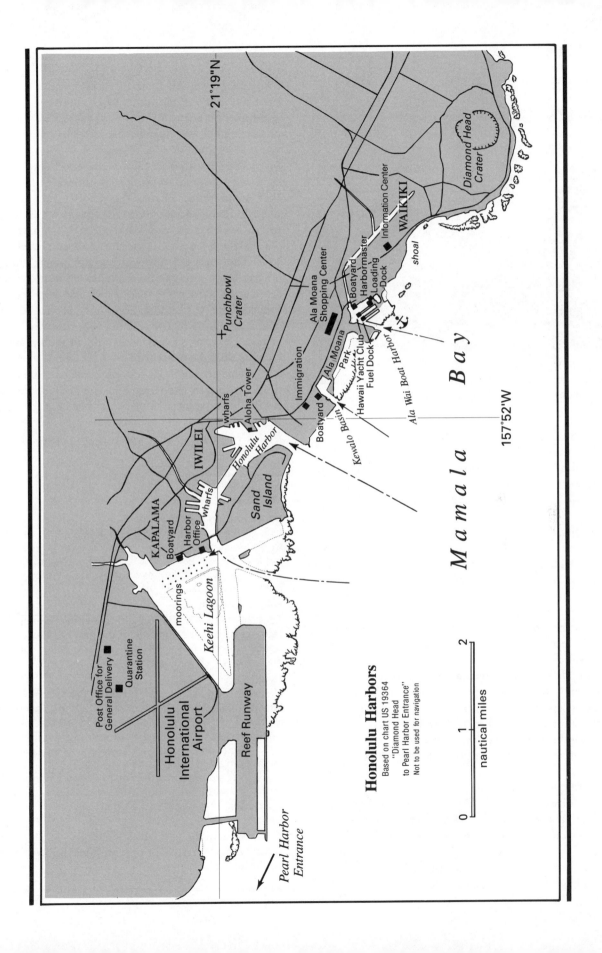

Honolulu Harbors

Based on chart US 19364
"Diamond Head
to Pearl Harbor Entrance"
Not to be used for navigation

0   1   2

nautical miles

Having every bit the spirit of the old American west, the Hawaiian cowboy, or paniolo, rides the range of beautiful Hana Ranch on Maui. (Earl Hinz)

ship to those arriving by yacht; there is no charge for the first two weeks. Hot showers are available as well as food and refreshments. If you desire to stay longer than two weeks, a special membership at a rate of US$8.50 per month for three months is available.

Honolulu, Oahu

There are several harbors of interest to yachting enthusiasts in the Honolulu area. Two are specifically boat harbors: Ala Wai and Keehi Lagoon. The other two are Kewalo Basin, which is primarily a fishing harbor —both commercial and sportfishing—and Honolulu, which is the primary deepwater port of the Hawaiian Islands. Technically, entry can be made at any of these harbors, but it is recommended that entry formalities be made at Ala Wai, which is the most popular for sailors. Immediately inside the reef is a fuel dock from which you can telephone Customs and make arrangements for clearance formalities. Then proceed to the loading dock at the southeast corner of the marina in the shadows of the high-rise buildings. Wait there for clearance officials to arrive.

After you are cleared, you can walk to the harbormaster's office or call the Hawaii Yacht Club to make berthing arrangements. Ala Wai Boat Harbor is overcrowded, but restrictions on the length of stay of nonresident yachts keeps the transient slips rotating so everyone can have a chance to use the facilities. If you go to the harbormaster you may be able to get a tempo-

rarily vacant slip for up to 30 days or space at the transient moorings in the outer row. There are toilets and showers available on the moles. Note that there is no anchoring allowed anywhere in the harbor even though you will see suitable space for it.

The Hawaii Yacht Club has guest slips available on a two-week basis with the use of the club facilities for that same time. There is a US$50 refundable key deposit. The club has room for six boats, and you can use its facilities for two weeks in any 12-month period. The berthing fee is $2.20 per foot LOA per week.

The boatyard in the harbor can handle craft up to 45 feet long. You can do the work yourself or hire the services of yard personnel, which are very expensive. Outside the yard there are many service shops for engine, rigging, electronics, and so forth, which you can engage for your special needs and probably more reasonably than the boatyard.

Provisioning and shopping of all kinds can be done on foot at the large Ala Moana shopping center nearby. Everything of a personal need can be found in the vicinity.

Every odd-numbered year the Los Angeles to

MEDICAL MEMO

Immunization Requirements
U.S. citizens coming directly from another U.S. port meet all the requirements. Crews of foreign yachts or U.S. yachts coming from foreign ports must have immunizations for cholera and yellow fever if they have transited or visited within the last six days an area currently infected.

Local Health Situation
There are no communicable diseases endemic to Hawaii but the large number of immigrants from Asia has kept a small but steady presence of some of the more common communicable diseases such as tuberculosis.

Health Services
Hawaii has excellent medical care in first-rate hospitals and qualified doctors on all the principal islands. Except for the military and the Public Health Service, all medicine is privately practiced. Medical costs are very high.

Dental and optical services are also available in most towns from private practitioners.

Drug stores carry a full line of nonprescription and prescription drugs. Prescription drugs are sold only on the order of a doctor.

Water
Tap water from the public supplies is good in all the islands. Water from private wells or streams should be considered suspect and be treated.

Honolulu race takes place with more than 70 racing boats descending on Ala Wai for the months of July and August, severely taxing the facilities. In alternate years the popular Kenwood Cup races fill the harbor to overflowing. Plan not to be there at those times.

Keehi Lagoon is located to the west of the other three harbors and is fronted by coral reefs. The cuts through the lagoon are former seaplane landing areas. The harbor has three marinas—a state marina; Arudy Keehi Marina, which also has a haulout facility for boats to 70 feet in length; and a marina run by the La Mariana Sailing Club. If space is not available at any of these marinas, there may be an empty mooring available from the state. Anchoring is no longer permitted in Keehi Lagoon.

Keehi Lagoon is being developed into several marinas, but it still has one big drawback—airplane noise from adjacent Honolulu International Airport.

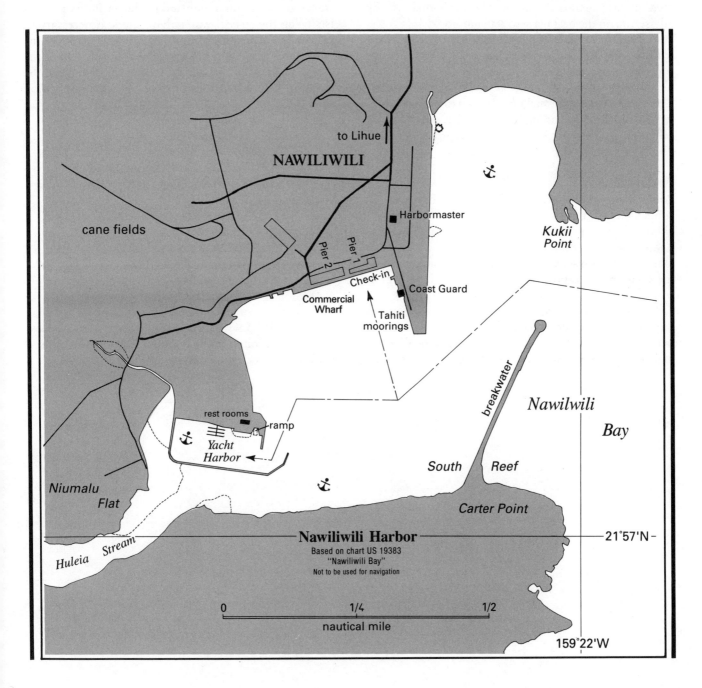

Nawiliwili, Kauai

Nawiliwili, the principal port of Kauai, is located on the southeast coast of the island. It is well protected from all winds. The outer harbor is for commercial shipping; there are some slips and some anchoring space in the inner, small-craft harbor. If you are seeking Customs clearance, it is best to tie up alongside the main wharf in an area that will not interfere with commercial activities and call Customs from there. After you are cleared, proceed to the small-craft basin. The harbormaster can advise you on the best place to set your hook.

Fuel is available at the commercial wharf via tank trucks, and potable water is piped to the wharf. Marine supplies of a general nature can be obtained in the neighboring town of Lihue as can most provisions. There are also some small shops to assist with repair work, but there are no haulout facilities. The town of Lihue is the best place on Kauai for provisioning or obtaining marine services.

Port Allen, Kauai

Port Allen facilities are inside Hanapepe Bay and are controlled by the harbormaster at Nawiliwili. There are about two dozen slips here, but all are taken up by local boats. Some Tahiti-style mooring space is available along the breakwaters of the harbor. Anchorage outside the small harbor is possible, but there is quite a surge in this bay.

The favorite yacht anchorage on Kauai is Hanalei Bay on the north side of the island. From May to October it is a safe anchorage with just enough facilities to make yacht living easy and rustic enough to be pleasant.

During the winter months, however, northers can produce surge, swell, waves, and surf, making it unpleasant if not untenable.

MARINE LIFE CONSERVATION DISTRICTS

Cruisers should be aware that many of the attractive coastal bays and bights of the Hawaiian Islands have been made into Marine Life Conservation Districts. The state's growing population and the heavy influx of tourists using the coastal waters have made it necessary to restrict many activities from these areas to preserve the marine environment for everyone's benefit. In some cases, anchoring is prohibited to prevent damage to the coral beds. The locations of these marine conservation sites are:

Oahu	Hanauma Bay
	Pupukea Bay
	Waikiki near Diamond Head
Hawaii	Kealakekua Bay
	Lapakahi
	Waialea Bay
Lanai	Manele Bay
	Hulopoe Bay
Maui	Molokini Shoal
	Honolua Bay
	Mokuleia Bay

Detailed information on allowed uses of these areas can be found in the booklet "Marine Life Conservation Districts," published by the State of Hawaii.

CHAPTER 6

FRENCH POLYNESIA

The Country

French Polynesia is an overseas territory of France consisting of 4 distinct island groups in the southeast corner of Oceania. The combined land area of all groups is a little over 1,500 square miles, and the overall population numbers about 190,000 people (more than 135,000 of them live in Tahiti). The ethnic distribution of the population is 78 percent Polynesian, 12 percent European, and 10 percent Asian—mostly Chinese. There are about 10,000 French military personnel stationed in the area in connection with the nuclear testing being conducted in the eastern Tuamotu Archipelago.

Island groups constituting French Polynesia are the Society Islands, the Tuamotu Archipelago, the Marquesas Islands, and the Austral Islands. Two small isolated islands, Rapa and Bass, lying far south of the main groups, are also part of the territory. The Society, Marquesas, and Austral groups are high volcanic islands; the Tuamotu Archipelago is composed entirely of low-lying atolls, except one, Makatea, which is a raised atoll.

The area has no native animals and only a few birds. Fish, both game and food varieties, abound near the reefs and seas throughout the area. Some islands of the western Society group are famous for the quality of the crabs found in their lagoons, and the Tuamotus are noted for the fine pearls from the oysters in their waters.

No group of islands captures the spirit and romance of the South Seas more completely than those of French Polynesia. Although known to Spanish and Dutch explorers as early as the sixteenth century, it was not until the eighteenth century that the islands came into scientific prominence with the explorations of Captain Cook. Even then, these islands half a world away from Europe were of little consequence until the ill-fated breadfruit expedition of Captain Bligh on HMS *Bounty*

in 1788. From then on the islands were to become the unwilling hosts to a multitude of explorers, whaling ships, and missionaries. French and British rivalry backed up by naval forces soon convinced the Tahitians that they would have to pledge loyalty to one or the other of the European powers for their own protection. In 1843 France took formal possession of Tahiti and Moorea and, during the remainder of the nineteenth century, annexed all the islands of the Society, Marquesas, Tuamotu, and Austral groups into what we know today as French Polynesia.

FRENCH POLYNESIA
Public Holidays and Special Events

January 1	New Year's Day—National holiday
February *	Chinese New Year—Dances and fireworks
March/April *	Good Friday, Easter, and Easter Monday— Public holidays
March 5	Gospel Arrival Day (Missionaries' Day)— Public holiday
May 1	Labor Day—Public holiday
May *	Ascension Day—Public holiday
June *	Whitsunday and Monday—Public holidays
July 11	Fête (Heiva I Tahiti)—Beginning of two-week festival
July 14	Bastille Day—Public holiday
August (2nd wk)	Polynesian Games—Pacific-wide contest at Atuona, Hiva Oa
August 15	Assumption Day—Public holiday
October *	Old Tahiti Ball—Historical costumes in Tahiti
November 1	All Saints' Day—Commemorating the dead
November 11	Armistice Day—Public holiday
December 25	Christmas—Public holiday
December 31	New Year's Eve—Illuminating of Papeete's waterfront

*Specific dates vary from year to year.

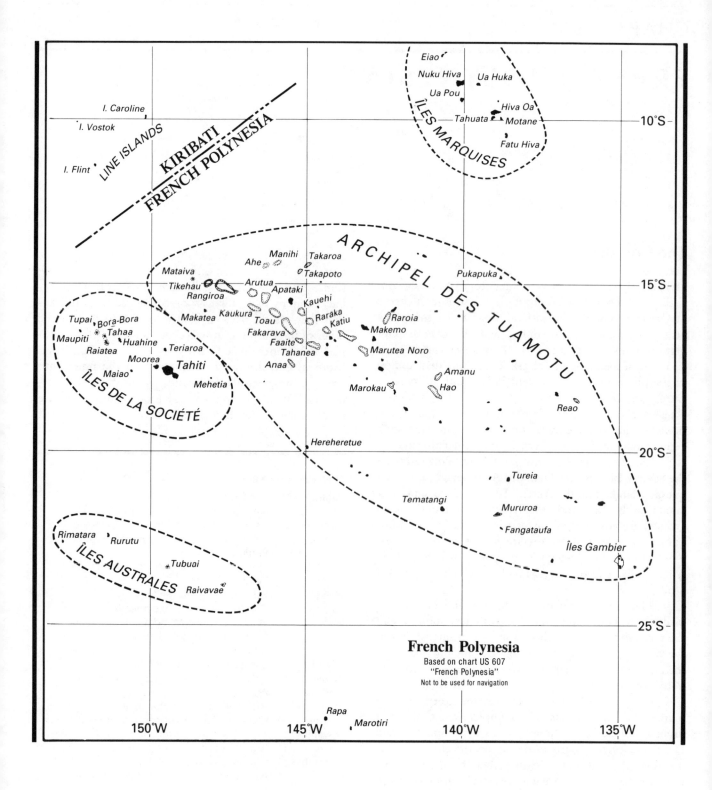

French Polynesia

Based on chart US 607
"French Polynesia"
Not to be used for navigation

FLOTSAM AND JETSAM

Currency
French Polynesia uses the Coloniale Franc Pacifique (CFP). Notes are issued for 5,000, 1,000, and 500 francs CFP and coins for 100, 50, 20, 10, 5, 2, and 1 franc CFP. The approximate rate of exchange is US$1 = CFP93. The relative cost of goods is 150.

Language
Tahitian is the indigenous language of the Society and Austral islands. It is also spoken to a large extent in the Marquesas and Tuamotu islands. There is, however, a Marquesan language and a Tuamotuan language spoken by some of the elders of those islands. French is the official language of the territory and the only one taught in the schools. English is spoken by most persons engaged in tourist businesses.

Electricity
Mostly 240v, 50 Hz AC, but some old hotels may have 110v, 60 Hz AC.

Postal Addresses
Mail to any of the outlying islands is slow and somewhat undependable, so it is recommended that your mail stop be Papeete; however, the post office at Papeete will hold mail for only 15 days. After that it is returned by surface mail to the sender. Recommended postal addresses are:

Yacht ( )
Poste Restante
Papeete, Tahiti
FRENCH POLYNESIA

For longer hold:
Yacht ( )
c/o Port Director
Papeete, Tahiti
FRENCH POLYNESIA

For AmEx card holders:
c/o American Express
B.P. 627
Papeete, Tahiti
FRENCH POLYNESIA

Ports for Making Crew Changes
Papeete is a recommended port for making crew changes as it has good international airline service from the United States, Australia, New Zealand, and France. Domestic airlines fly daily to other Society Islands such as Moorea, Huahine, Raiatea, and Bora-Bora. Service is also provided several times each week to the Marquesas, Tuamotu, and Austral islands. Immigration procedures favor making crew changes at Papeete.

External Affairs Representative
French consulates and embassies

Information Center
Tahiti Tourist Board
B.P. 65
Papeete, Tahiti
FRENCH POLYNESIA

French Polynesia lies near the center of the Polynesian triangle and is thought to have been settled about the fifth century by Polynesian mariners arriving from the islands of Samoa and Tonga. Lost in an unwritten history are the real details of settlement of the 4 island groups comprising 109 islands 1,544 square miles in area spread over an ocean area of 1,540,000 square miles. While the original center of religious and political power was on the island of Raiatea, Tahiti because of its large size and great fertility became the most populous of the Society Islands and eventually gained political power over its neighbors. Today, Tahiti is the seat of government for French Polynesia, and as a result, all the peoples of French Polynesia are known as "Tahitians" to the outside world.

The islands of French Polynesia contain a cross-section of the geologic history of Pacific land masses. The Marquesas are high islands, young in age, too new to have developed any appreciable fringing coral growth. At the other extreme, the islands of the Tuamotu Archipelago are true atolls—lagoons ringed by coral reefs that long ago swallowed up the remaining land masses. Between these two geologic extremes are the volcanic, reef-fringed islands called the Society Islands, which have become the principal islands of French Polynesia. They have fertile coastal plains of volcanic ash for growing food plus a protective barrier reef that shelters the inhabited shoreline, provides a haven for fish as well as local outrigger transportation, and now makes possible safe harbors for modern ships. Tahiti in the Society Islands is a nearly perfect combination of mountain, coastal plain, shoreline, and reef. It is not at all surprising, then, that Polynesian civilization concentrated there. This natural environment plus an intelligent people created an enviable Pacific paradise. The French rule is accepted for its benevolent nature since the local economy is supported by French financial aid. There are visible signs of political stress, however, concerned with the Tahitians' desire for independence and the cessation of nuclear testing in their islands.

The Weather

The weather over French Polynesia rivals that of Hawaii. Southeast trade winds prevail most of the year interrupted only occasionally by gales during the January to March period. The area is normally free of hurricanes with the last recorded hurricane to hit the Tuamotus in 1958 and Tahiti in 1961. That was, however, before the unusual 1982–1983 season, when two tropical storms and five hurricanes ravaged the area in the strongest El Niño event on record.

In late December 1982 Tropical Storm Lisa formed near the Marquesas, deluging the islands with rain before moving southwest to batter Bora Bora with gale force winds.

In late January 1983 Hurricane Nano ran down the eastern Tuamotus with winds of 85 knots destroying most of Hao but with no loss of life, roaring over the French nuclear test site of Mururoa, and then continuing east, where it slammed Pitcairn Island with winds of 45 to 55 knots.

In late February Hurricane Orama struck the Tuamotus, destroying villages on Anaa, Kaukura, Arutua, and Ahe and again striking Mururoa. In this hurricane the interisland vessel *Tamarii Tikehau* was lost with five lives off Kaukura.

Early March saw Tropical Storm Prema with 55 knots of wind hit the leeward Societies with heavy rains.

This was followed in mid-March by Hurricane Reva, which developed north of Rangiroa and headed southwest, devastating Mataiva on the way. Reva, with 100-knot winds, went on to batter most of the Society Islands before turning east to hit Anaa in the Tuamotus.

Hurricane Veena came to life near the Tuamotus in early April and with winds of 90 knots passed over Tahiti Iti. It continued south, passing between Raivavae and Tubuai in the Austral Islands. This storm caused much damage to boats at Papeete with upwards of 50 either sunk or cast on the reefs; most of these were later salvaged. (Many other boats survived the storm at anchor.)

Last of the unexpected storms was Hurricane William with winds of 75 knots that struck the eastern Tuamotus and Gambier Islands in late April 1983. That ended the most devastating weather recorded in French Polynesia history.

What happened that season was very different from usual weather patterns for the area. For all practical purposes, French Polynesia is outside the South Pacific hurricane belt. Hurricanes rarely appear east of 155°W in the South Pacific because the waters are usually not warm enough to support cyclogenesis. Since weather recordkeeping started in 1825, there had been only 20 recorded hurricanes in this area although a few more may have gone unrecorded for lack of reporting stations in the more isolated areas. That made the odds something like one hurricane every eight years with none since 1961. But 1983 was different with French Polynesia experiencing five hurricanes in the first four months of the year. About the only thing normal was that the occurrences all happened during the usual South Pacific hurricane months of November through April.

The suspected cause of the cyclonic activity was water temperatures that were higher than usual—about 4°C higher. This made the water warm enough to feed embryonic cyclonic storms and raise them to hurricane intensity.

The warmer waters were part of a greater environmental phenomenon that was occurring across the entire Pacific Ocean and parts of the Indian Ocean. It is believed to be related to the warm El Niño current that annually flows north along the South American coast around Christmas time. In the southern hemisphere summer of 1982–1983 it was considerably reinforced with warm surface waters flowing east from the western Pacific.

What triggers an El Niño condition is not fully understood. Two other events in 1972 and 1976 were not as severe in their effects on the overall weather patterns. Oceanographers and meteorologists are currently gathering data on water and air conditions over the equatorial Pacific. They hope to use it to develop a reliable mathematical technique for predicting the onset of an El Niño. Current results are promising.

Cruising Notes

YACHT ENTRY

The primary Port of Entry for all of French Polynesia is Papeete. Most of the entry formalities can, however, be completed at islands having a gendarme in residence. These secondary Ports of Entry are:

Marquesas Islands	Nuku Hiva
	Ua Pou
	Hiva Oa
Tuamotu Archipelago	Rangiroa
Society Islands	Moorea
	Raiatea
	Huahine
	Bora-Bora
Austral Islands	Tubuai
	Rurutu
	Raivavae

If you arrive first at any other island in any group as, for instance Mangareva, report your presence to the island chief and, with little tarrying, proceed to the nearest Port of Entry. Your presence will be made known through the administrative interisland radio, and if you don't correct your mistake, you may have difficulty later in getting your clearance papers.

CUSTOMS

Upon arrival at a Port of Entry, the owner or skipper must go immediately to Customs or the gendarmerie to make an entry declaration. The skipper will have to prove his or her identity, show boat ownership papers and a crew list with matching passports, and be ready to make up a supplies list on the official form.

Formal customs clearance is issued in the form of a "green card" for the boat, which allows the boat to stay in French Polynesia's waters free of import duty for six months. An extension of six months can be granted if your visa is extended. After one year you will have to pay a duty, which has been set at 37 percent.

When you apply for your green card, submit a planned itinerary so that the green card can reflect your movements about French Polynesia.

IMMIGRATION

Requirements for visas have changed over the years from none required to getting one before you arrive, to the present, which allows you to get one after arrival. In fact, it is better to wait until arrival because a visa obtained outside French Polynesia can be renewed only outside the Territory. You don't need a visa immediately on arrival. Americans and Canadians can get a 30-day visitor's permit to start with, then (in Papeete) you apply for a three-month visa. Your visa can be extended for another two months giving you six months in all. If you wish to stay longer, you must write a letter (do so in French) to the high commissioner asking for another three months; it may be possible to extend the visa even further under special circumstances. There is a US$30 fee for processing each visa.

Because of past bad experiences with cruising boats in French Polynesia during the South Pacific cyclone season, visas will be issued for the period April through October only. All boats are required to be out of French Polynesia waters by November 1.

Requirements state that each visitor must post a bond equal to an airline ticket price to his or her country of origin or have a ticket itself; otherwise, no visa will be issued. In the case of a cruising boat, the captain will be responsible for his crew members' visas and bonds.

MEDICAL MEMO

Immunization Requirements

Immunizations for smallpox, cholera, and yellow fever are required if you have transited or visited within the last six days an area currently infected (smallpox 14 days).

Local Health Situation

Cases of dengue fever have been reported in recent years in the Papeete area. Tropical ulcers can develop from open wounds infected by staph germs found in harbor waters. The no-no flies of the Marquesas Islands are vicious biters and can cause severe itching for days.

Health Services

In Papeete there is one government hospital and one private hospital. There are a number of private doctors in Papeete. In the outlying islands there are government dispensaries run in some cases by doctors, in others by trained medical workers, and in the smaller places by a person with some medical training. Both Nuku Hiva and Hiva Oa now have hospitals. All islands have medical radio contact with Papeete.

Limited dental and optical services are available from private practitioners in Papeete only.

There are four pharmacies in Papeete, one open on Sundays, which carry a full line of drugs from European sources. A few U.S. products are available. The dispensaries in the outlying islands stock some drugs.

IAMAT Center*

Papeete: Clinique Paofai
　　　　　Medical Director: Charles Fichter, MD

　　　　　S.O.S. Medicins Tahiti
　　　　　Iamat Coordinators: Vincent Joncker, MD
　　　　　　　　　　　　　　　F. C. Daille, MD
　　　　　　　　　　　　　　　M. P. Rosenstein, MD

*IAMAT—International Association for Medical Assistance to Travelers
417 Center Street
Lewiston NY 14092, USA

"a worldwide association of medical doctors to provide medical assistance to travelers who, while absent from their home country, may find themselves in need of medical or surgical care or any form of medical treatment. This is done by providing those travelers with the names of locally licensed practitioners who have command of the native language spoken by the traveler and who agree to a stated and standard list of medical fees for their services."

Water

Tap water is reported to be safe to drink in Papeete and the major towns of the other islands. Some of the water is treated and some is not. Water from other than the larger towns known to be treated should be considered suspect and treated before use.

Open airline tickets should be purchased directly from the airline for ease of later redemption, not through a travel agent. Cash bonds must be deposited in a local bank; be sure to choose a bank that has a branch at the island from which you will depart French Polynesia. Bond deposits do not normally draw interest, and the banks will charge a 1-percent administrative fee.

The bond deposit can be made in the United States beforehand, if the Papeete bank has a branch there, or it can be paid by cash, traveler's checks, or a wire deposit from your bank requested after arrival. The banks in Papeete to be considered are WestPac Banking Corporation, Banque Paribas, Banque de Polynaise, Banque Socredo, and Banque de Tahiti.

Again, be sure to select a bank that has a branch in whatever port of departure you plan on using. These outlying island branch banks must be notified ahead of time that you want your deposit on a certain date since they usually don't carry large sums of money such as multiple-person bond deposits. The refund will be made in cash in the same currency used for the deposit. Your Immigration clearance should also carry the notation that your bond will be picked up at a specific outer island on your departure from French Polynesia. This is one area that the cruiser must do some preliminary planning to avoid later conflict.

In addition to posting a bond you will have to show that you have adequate funds to support yourself during the length of the visa; this amounts to about US$350 per month, depending on your frugality or lack thereof.

Crew changing should preferably be done at Papeete but can be effected at any Port of Entry. The departing crew must have a confirmed reservation on a departing airline flight or be accepted on a crew list of another boat that will be departing within the unexpired visa period of the transferring crew member. The skipper of the now short-handed boat will have to sign a paper that it will leave as anticipated even though it now has one less crew member.

FIREARMS

Firearms will be impounded when you arrive; they can be recovered one hour before your scheduled departure time. (This applies to Tahiti only. On other islands your firearms will be bonded on your boat.) Ammunition carried solely for trading purposes is strictly forbidden.

PETS

The entry of any kind of pets is also prohibited, although they may be kept on board the boat during your stay if you have declared them. Pets found ashore will be destroyed.

AGRICULTURAL INSPECTION

Yachts arriving from areas infested with the rhinoceros beetle will be fumigated. This includes the islands of Fiji, Indonesia, Papua New Guinea, Palau, both Samoas, Tokelau, Tonga, and the Wallis Islands.

MARQUESAS ISLANDS

The Country

The Marquesas group of islands is the most northerly territory of French Polynesia and consists of six large and six small islands. All are elevated, ranging in height between 1,300 and 4,000 feet, and are covered with a layer of deep and very fertile soil. These islands, mountainous and cut into deep valleys, are not protected by coral barrier reefs. The jagged, tormented profile contrasts with the gentle melancholy of the valleys and the large open spaces of the plateau. There are traces of an artistic civilization seen in the Marquesan archeological remains and contemporary handicrafts.

The four southern islands of the group first became known in the West after being visited in 1595 by the Spaniard Alvaro Mendaña de Neira, who named the group Marquesas Islands in honor of the sponsor of the expedition, the Marchioness of Mendoza, wife of the

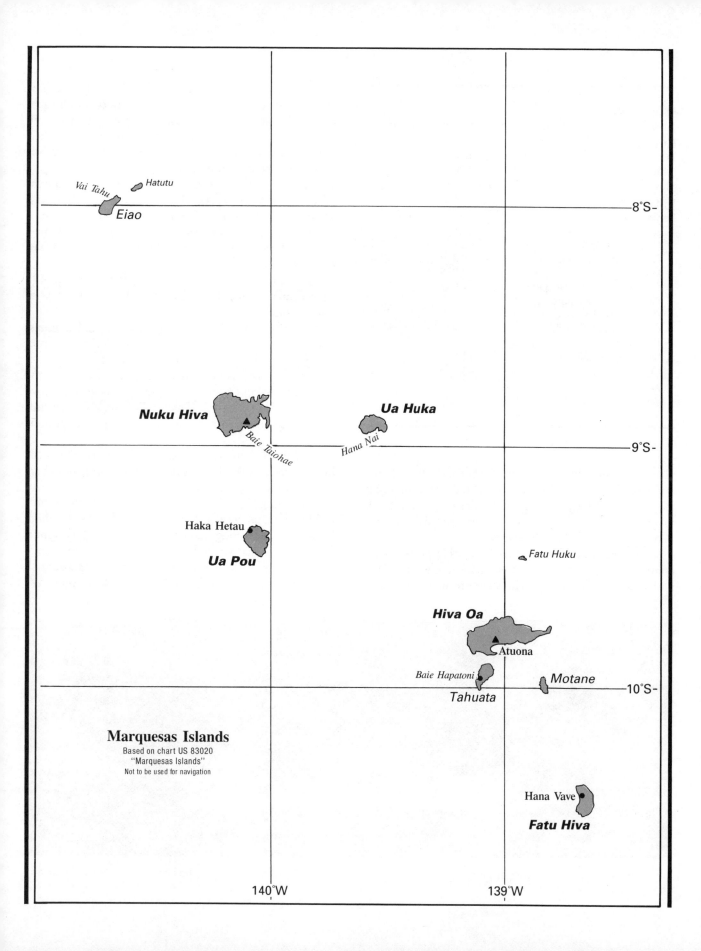

Vai Tahu Hatutu
Eiao

−8°S−

Nuku Hiva **Ua Huka**
Baie Taiohae Hana Nai

−9°S−

Haka Hetau
Ua Pou

Fatu Huku

Hiva Oa
Atuona

Baie Hapatoni Motane
Tahuata

−10°S−

Marquesas Islands
Based on chart US 83020
"Marquesas Islands"
Not to be used for navigation

Hana Vave
Fatu Hiva

140°W 139°W

MARQUESAS ISLANDS
A part of French Polynesia, an overseas territory of France

Ports of Entry

Taiohae, Nuku Hiva	8°56′ S, 140°05′ W
Haka Hau, Ua Pou	9°24′ S, 140°03′ W
Atuona, Hiva Oa	9°48′ S, 139°02′ W

Distances between Ports in Nautical Miles
Between Taiohae and

Acapulco, Mexico	2,840
Cabo San Lucas, Mexico	2,605
Christmas Island, Kiribati	1,230
Hilo, Hawaii	1,935
Pago Pago, American Samoa	1,825
Panama City, Panama	3,775
Papeete, Society Islands	755
Omoka, Cook Islands	1,065
Rangiroa, Tuamotu Archipelago	575
San Diego, California	2,820
Wreck Bay, Galapagos Islands	3,055

Standard time
9 hours 30 minutes slow on UTC

viceroy of Peru. From 1774 to 1791, Cook, Ingraham, and the Frenchman Marchand sighted the remaining islands. The Marquesas became a French protectorate in 1842 after a treaty was signed between Admiral du Petit Thouras and the native chiefs.

At one time the group had a sizable population, composed largely of blacks from Martinique and Chinese and others from Asia who were brought in to work on various types of plantations. Rainfall, which can be copious, is also erratic, and long periods of drought occurred that ultimately caused the plantations to fail. Most of the imported labor force returned to their homes, and the population in 1970 was reduced to about 5,200 native Polynesians.

The principal inhabited islands of the Marquesas group (Nuku Hiva, Ua Huka, Ua Pou, Hiva Oa, Tahuata, and Fatu Hiva) now support a population of just over 6,800. At one time in the eighteenth century, the population was estimated by European visitors to number 60,000.

The total land area of the group is about 492 square miles compared with the 407 square miles of Tahiti alone.

The group contains no indigenous land animals, but many islands contain herds of wild sheep, cattle, and pigs left behind when the plantations were abandoned. The islands do, however, have many birds, the most interesting of which is a species of ground dove found nowhere else in the Pacific. Fish are also plentiful, and waters of the area contain a variety of enormous sharks.

Half of the islands in the group are uninhabited, but all are capable of supporting rather sizable numbers of people and in the future may be settled to take care of an expanding population. The best known of the islands is Hiva Oa, a very fertile and heavily wooded high island, 23 miles long and 10 miles wide, which reputedly was the last stronghold of cannibalism in French Polynesia. In 1970 it was overrun with wild livestock brought in by former inhabitants. It is also renowned as

A powered whaleboat provides transportation between an anchored interisland trading ship in the bay at Haka Hau, Ua Pou, and the shoreline. (Earl Hinz)

the last home and burial site of Paul Gauguin, the French painter, and Jacques Brel, the Belgian singer.

Some of the Marquesan population continue to live off copra production, native handicrafts, and the sale of shells. Handicrafts include carved wood and stone, tapa (bark) cloth (both breadfruit tree—an inferior grade—and paper mulberry tree—the best), and woven hats. Many of the population are civil servants working at public works, agriculture, and so forth. Farming and fishing are carried on at the family level.

All of the Marquesas islands show an increase in liveliness during Tiurai. This coincides with preparations for Bastille Day, which is celebrated in Taiohae with pomp and good humor. The festivities are the occasion for traditional Marquesan songs and dance competitions.

Like most Pacific island groups, the Marquesas chain runs from southeast to northwest, paralleling the southeast trade winds. From any Port of Entry, one is eventually faced with sailing to windward to see all of the islands.

The Ferocious No-No Fly

Every cruiser's introduction to French Polynesia in the Marquesas is marred at the first encounter with the pesky no-no fly. These flies inhabit the beaches, valleys, streams, and other moist lowland places. The no-no looks like a tse-tse fly and quietly draws out the victim's blood after injecting an anticoagulant fluid that later causes local swelling and painful itching for up to two weeks. Vigorous scratching often results in a staph infection so easily acquired in tropical waters.

Unlike mosquitoes, the no-nos attack without any sound, and they are so small as to be almost invisible to the naked eye. They are found in almost plague proportions in parts of Nuku Hiva and in lesser numbers in the other Marquesas Islands. At one time they also existed in similar numbers in the Society Islands but were eradicated. There are two species of no-nos, the black and the white. According to local sources, the black are found predominantly on Nuku Hiva, and your skin reacts almost immediately to their bites. The white no-no is found on the other islands; its reaction is delayed as long as 24 hours after the bite.

These pests lay their eggs in the brackish water near the beaches or streams where salt and fresh water mix. Pesticides are only temporarily effective against them because the large breeding areas make it almost impossible to gain continuing control over them.

Personal protection against the no-nos is the cruiser's only salvation at the moment, for to avoid the Marquesas because of the no-no fly is to miss a big part of French Polynesia. Wear long trousers tied over shoes to protect your legs. Wear a long-sleeved cotton shirt with buttoned cuffs and collar. Cover exposed skin with a powerful bug repellant. A home-brewed bug repellant can be made by mixing equal portions of baby oil with Lysol or its Kiwi equivalent, Hexol. The smell is powerful, but it is an effective deterrent to the no-no fly. Above all, do not scratch the bites.

The Weather

These islands are in the heart of the trade wind belt, but the winds are less steady here than in the trade wind belt of the northern latitudes. Easterly winds are the most prevalent. Easterly to southerly winds taken together from April to October, which is the normal rainy season, are generally more pronounced. Easterly to northeasterly are generally more prevalent during the dry season (November to May). Among the eastern islands the average wind speed is about 11 knots while among the western islands it is about 9 knots. The highest wind speeds occur in the cooler months of July and August when the average throughout the group is 12 knots. Gales rarely occur, and the heaviest of the few squalls, insofar as scanty records indicate, occur in December.

The Marquesas Islands were on the fringe of the severe cyclonic activity that took place in French Polynesia in 1982–1983. During this time lows formed to the south, and the Marquesas Islands received torrential monsoonlike rains. There were no problems with boats as far as the winds were concerned, but it was wet! The most protected bays in situations like this are Taiohae, Tai Oa (Daniel's Bay), and Anaho Bay in the northeast corner of Nuku Hiva.

In a normal season the months of March and April are good cruising and dry in the Marquesas. If you should arrive a little early from the Galapagos or North America, just enjoy the Marquesas for a month before heading for Tahiti.

Cruising Notes

YACHT FACILITIES

There are no special facilities for yachts in any of the Marquesas islands. There are wharfs at Taiohae and

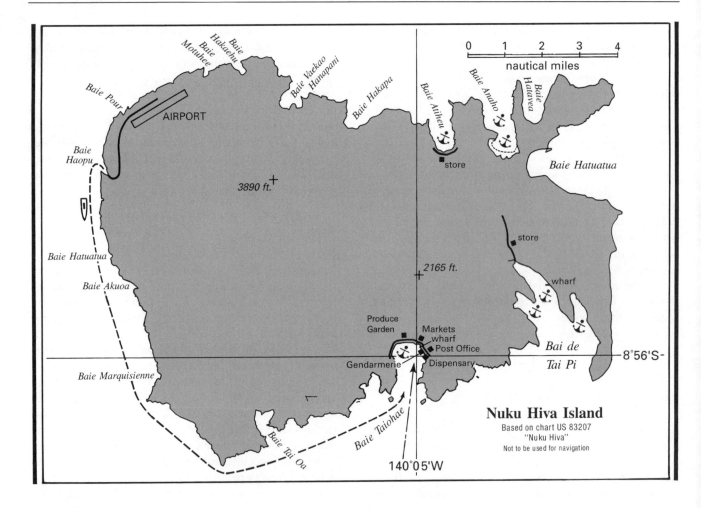

Baie
Hakaehu
Baie
Motuhee
Baie
Baie Pour
AIRPORT
Baie
Haopu
Baie Vaekao
Hanapani
Baie Hakapa
Baie Atiheu
Baie Anaho
Baie
Hatavea
0 1 2 3 4
nautical miles
3890 ft.
store
Baie Hatuatua
Baie Hatuatua
Baie Akuoa
2165 ft.
store
wharf
Produce
Garden
Markets
wharf
Post Office
Gendarmerie
Dispensary
Bai de
Tai Pi
—8°56'S—
Baie Marquisienne

Nuku Hiva Island
Based on chart US 83207
"Nuku Hiva"
Not to be used for navigation

Baie Tai Oa
Baie Taiohae
140°05'W

Atuona for the supply boats, and you can tie up to these for taking on water and fuel. There is no treatment of water in any of these islands, so be sure that you are getting your water from a clean source with no upstream pollution.

Both diesel and gasoline fuels are shipped to Taiohae for use of the local residents. It is not easy to get fuel after arrival unless you have made arrangements before the copra boat arrives. Fuel comes in drums and will (if available) be delivered to the dock, where you will have to do the pumping and carrying. It is recommended that you not depend on getting fuel in the Marquesas. Propane is available at both ports, but you will need an adapter for the metric-threaded supply bottles.

Fruits are plentiful in these islands; but since all property is privately owned, ask before you take. Marquesans are generous people, and you usually will not be denied a request; but sometimes the crops may be a little thin and the local people will need the fruit for themselves. Vegetables are not a standard table item for the local people, but some enterprising gardeners grow them for the European palate. Stores carry limited canned goods and beer, and French bread is baked every day. There is some hardware carried incidental to local living needs but no marine hardware.

PORTS AND ANCHORAGES

Taiohae Bay

Taiohae Bay is becoming the administrative center of the Marquesas Islands, and all shipping is being geared to this port. A freezer on the quai stores the catch of the local fishing co-op. A boatyard is under construction but probably will not be completed for a few more years. It will be capable of hauling local fishing boats as well as yachts.

Taiohae has grown in recent years and now offers two banks (Socredo and Indo-Suez) plus five stores and

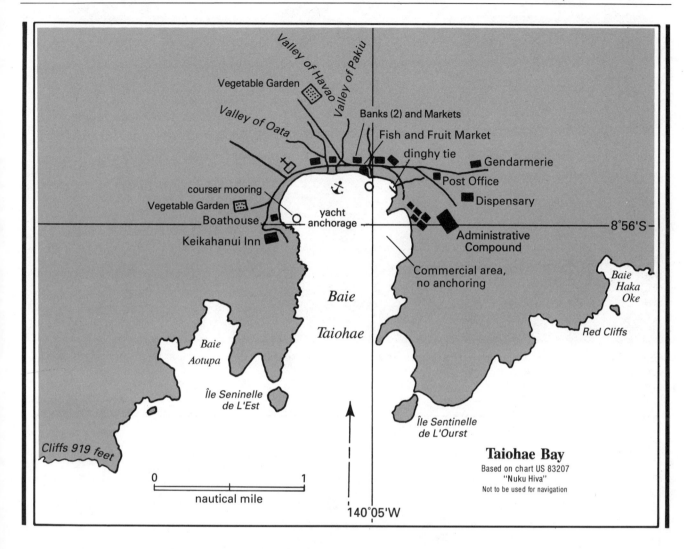

Valley of Havao

Valley of Pakiu

Valley of Oata

Vegetable Garden

Banks (2) and Markets

Fish and Fruit Market

dinghy tie

Gendarmerie

Post Office

courser mooring

Vegetable Garden

Boathouse

Keikahanui Inn

yacht anchorage

Dispensary

Administrative Compound

Commercial area, no anchoring

8°56'S

Baie Haka Oke

Red Cliffs

Baie Taiohae

Baie Aotupa

Île Seninelle de L'Est

Île Sentinelle de L'Ourst

Cliffs 919 feet

0   1

nautical mile

Taiohae Bay
Based on chart US 83207
"Nuku Hiva"
Not to be used for navigation

140°05'W

two bakeries. There is a hotel/bar "downtown" and the Keikahanui Inn/restaurant on the west side of the bay. Supplies in any and all of these establishments are dependent on the arrival of the copra schooner, so don't depend too much on reprovisioning when you get here.

When entering Taiohae Bay you may want to contact Frank and Rose Corser, who run the Keikahanui Inn. They listen to VHF channel 16 at 0900 LMT and can give you advice on where to anchor and other problems you may have.

The Keikahanui is a good place to buy tapa cloth if you do not plan on sailing to Fatu Hiva, where it is made. The inn also has the famous logbooks formerly maintained by Maurice McKittrick at his store. You probably will want to record your arrival in this timeless record. Taiohae has instituted a "water fee" for boats

amounting to 200 francs for the first day in the harbor, 100 francs for the second, and 20 francs each day thereafter. There are no other yacht charges in the Marquesas.

Do not use the post office for receiving mail at Taiohae because they will hold it for only 15 days and then send it back surface mail. Forward it in care of Maurice McKittrick or the Keikahanui Inn.

Atuona

The yacht anchorage at Atuona is in Taa Huku Bay behind a recently built breakwater. It is not a good anchorage, and a side-to-side backwash keeps yachts rolling continuously during the southeast trade wind months. The heavy rains of the 1982–1983 cyclone season also caused the bay to silt up badly, making it very

Taiohae Bay, Nuku Hiva, is a welcome sight for cruisers who have been passaging for three or four weeks from ports along the west coast of the Americas. (Rose Corser)

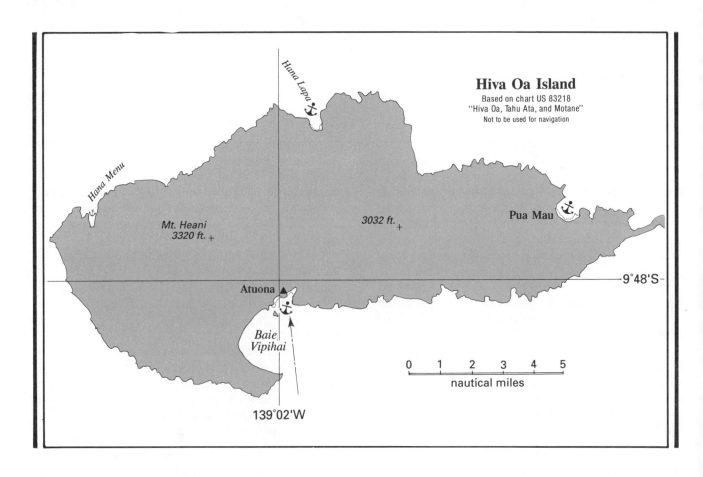

Hiva Oa Island

Based on chart US 83218
"Hiva Oa, Tahu Ata, and Motane"
Not to be used for navigation

Hana Lapa

Hana Menu

Pua Mau

Mt. Heani
3320 ft. +

3032 ft. +

Atuona

Baie
Vipihai

9°48'S

139°02'W

0   1   2   3   4   5
nautical miles

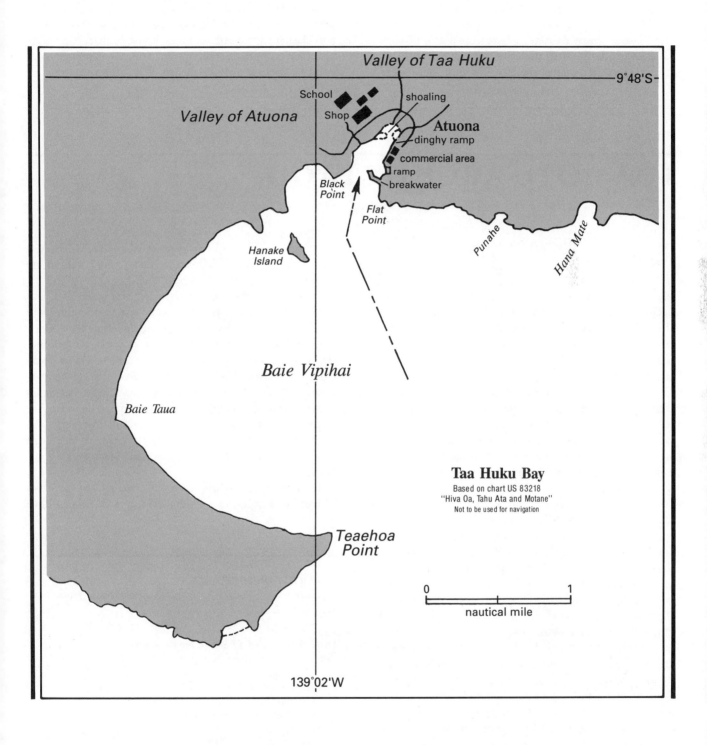

Valley of Taa Huku

School

Valley of Atuona

Shop

shoaling

Atuona

dinghy ramp

commercial area

ramp

breakwater

Black
Point

Flat
Point

Hanake
Island

Punahe

Hana Mate

Baie Vipihai

Baie Taua

Taa Huku Bay

Based on chart US 83218
"Hiva Oa, Tahu Ata and Motane"
Not to be used for navigation

*Teaehoa
Point*

9°48'S

139°02'W

0   1

nautical mile

shallow except at the entrance. There are plans to dredge the bay and make it more usable again.

The town of Atuona, where you will find stores, bakeries, and administrative offices, is a one-mile walk around the north end of the bay. Gauguin's gravesite is in the cemetery on the hill just above the village. A trade school is located on the west side of the harbor, and if you desperately need to make some boat repairs they have the equipment and space. Your own power tools will be of no use unless they are 240v, 50 Hz.

TUAMOTU ARCHIPELAGO

The Country

The Tuamotu Archipelago, also known as the Puamotu Archipelago, is an enormous arc of exclusively coral atolls lying between the Society and the Marquesas groups. There is one raised atoll (Makatea); a dozen fairly large true atolls have unbroken circular reefs; others, such as Fakarava and Rangiroa in the northern portion, are broken into numerous islets with good passages into their interior lagoons. Makatea was a profitable producer of phosphate until the deposits were exhausted in 1966. It, like the rest of the group, now has a copra economy. Some of the atolls have their income augmented by the fine pearls found in the extensive lagoon areas.

The Tuamotu Archipelago is made up particularly of dry "forested" atolls with rain the only source of fresh water. The 76 islands comprising the archipelago have a land area of 343 square miles and range from unbroken circles of coral surrounding a lagoon to glistening chains of coral islets with one or two navigable passes into the lagoon. As with most Pacific archipelagos, the Tuamotu chain stretches along a line southeast to northwest spanning a distance of 1,000 miles.

Only 30 atolls of the Tuamotus are permanently uninhabited; the rest support small populations limited by food, water, and space. In bygone days atoll populations were balanced by infanticide and migration, but today big-city attraction for youth is the prime balancing factor. An estimated 11,500 people live throughout the 46 inhabited islands. In the late 1800s, pearls and mother-of-pearl shells were the major source of income, with divers descending 50 to 100 feet to gather the valuable mollusks off the bottom. Soon, however, overgathering all but eliminated this income source, and today only experimental black pearl cultivating remains.

Atolls of the Tuamotus were first seen by European eyes in 1615. Jacob LeMaire, a Dutchman, had sailed near the northwestern end in a passage from Cape Horn (which he named) to Batavia, now part of Indonesia. So many other ships have since accidently and disastrously discovered the archipelago that it is sometimes known as the Dangerous Archipelago. In recent years many carelessly navigated yachts have added further emphasis to this gloomy name. Of all the Tuamotu atolls, Raroia is probably the best known. It was here that the raft *Kon Tiki,* captained by Thor Heyerdahl, landed in 1947 after its epic 4,300-mile, 3½-month drift from Peru. More recently, five of the atolls—Mururoa, Fagataufa, Tureia, Hao, and Anaa—have

---

TUAMOTU ARCHIPELAGO
A part of French Polynesia, an overseas territory of France

Port of Entry

Tiputa, Rangiroa	14°55′ S, 147°40′ W

Distances between Ports in Nautical Miles
Between Avatoru Pass, Rangiroa, and

Bounty Bay, Pitcairn Island	1,165
Christmas Island, Kiribati	1,170
Hilo, Hawaii	2,125
Mangareva, Gambier Islands	875
Omoka, Cook Islands	700
Papeete, Society Islands	190
Taiohae, Marquesas Islands	575

Standard Time
10 hours slow on UTC

been used by the French as the site of that nation's atomic tests. The actual detonations are carried out on Mururoa and are monitored by supporting installations on the other four.

The Tuamotuans subsist on a coconut and fish economy. The valuable nuts grow with little assistance on nearly all motus on the circumference of the atoll. Native workers visit the coconut-growing motus for the purpose of making copra out of the coconuts as they ripen. The outboard motorboat is used to convey the workers to the motus and transport the burlap-bagged copra back to the collection points.

Fish exporting is rapidly becoming the economic mainstay of the atolls. The Tahiti Islander's traditional diet of fish can no longer be satisfied by the Tahitian fishers since they are rapidly abandoning the sea in favor of "9 to 5" work in the new economy. Commercial fishing in the rest of French Polynesia has therefore taken on a new importance. One enterprising operator flies a small airplane daily into several Tuamotu atolls picking up freshly caught fish for the Tahitians' tables that night.

At the far eastern end of the Tuamotu Archipel-

Pearl farming is a growing industry in the Tuamotu Archipelago. This experimental pearl farm is in the lagoon of Ahi Atoll. (Earl Hinz)

ago, almost on the Tropic of Capricorn, are the Gambier Islands. They are often linked geographically with the Tuamotus because they appear to be the eastern terminus of the Dangerous Archipelago. In reality, though, they are a different class of islands, being mountainous instead of atolls.

The Gambiers are a cluster of five volcanic islands surrounded by a barrier reef. The highest of them is Mangareva whose Mt. Duff reaches an altitude of 1,450 feet. Today there are about 500 people, mostly Polynesians, living in the Gambiers, all of them on Mangareva. The Gambiers have gone through the same ups and downs of life due to exploration and exploitation as have other islands of the Pacific.

English sailors sighted them in 1797, but the islands saw few ships until the early 1800s, when the English mission ship *Duff* arrived. The English got a cool reception and departed, only to be followed by French missionaries, who were accepted by the local populace. That turned out to be a mistake, for the mad priest Père Laval put the islanders to work building monumental coral-stone buildings including churches, schools, houses, a monastery, wharves, and the like. Most of those monuments to overzealous persuasion now lie abandoned and deteriorating.

Mangareva enjoyed significant popularity during the whaling days of the South Pacific. Whalers stopped there to replenish their provisions with fresh fruit and meat and give the crew some welcome shore leave. With the decline of whaling, the economy languished until the French started nuclear testing in the 1970s at Mururoa Atoll in the Tuamotus 250 miles to the west. Some ancillary construction was done on Mangareva in the form of fallout shelters, and a few French Navy ships stopped by for R and R; but even that has now disappeared, and Mangareva has returned to its tranquility of old.

Of Atolls and Coconuts

The islands of the Pacific tend to be either volcanic or coral reef forms or a combination of the two. Other than that there is little similarity to the land masses upon which you will make your landfalls. For convenience, geologists classify Pacific islands in six groups that show the evolutionary change of volcanic island to an atoll. The volcanic island's life begins in the ocean depths with the bulging of the ocean bottom situated over a magma source. The bulge grows with time, forming a dome or shield until it breaks the ocean surface and erupts as a

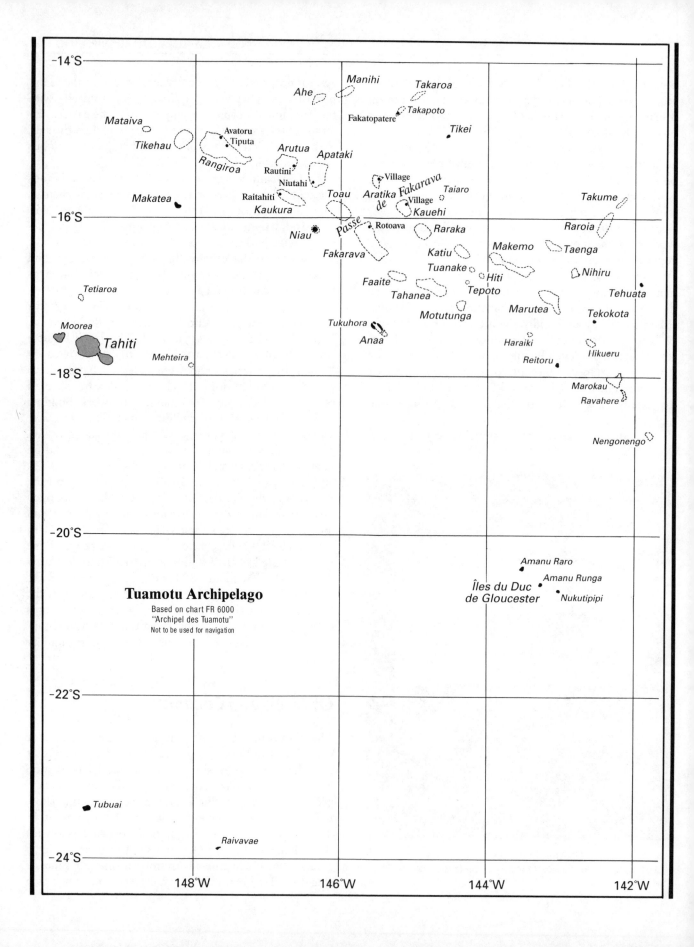

-14°S

Mataiva

Ahe Manihi Takaroa

Tikehau Avatoru Takapoto
Tiputa Fakatopatere

Arutua Apataki Tikei

Rangiroa Rautini
Niutahi

Makatea Raitahiti Toau Village
Kaukura Aratika Fakarava Taiaro
de

-16°S Village Takume
Kauehi

Niau Passe Rotoava Raraka Raroia

Fakarava Katiu Makemo Taenga

Tuanake Hiti Nihiru

Tetiaroa Faaite Tepoto

Tahanea Tehuata

Motutunga Marutea Tekokota

Moorea Tukuhora Haraiki Ilikueru

Tahiti Anaa Reitoru

Mehteira

-18°S Marokau
Ravahere

Nengonengo

-20°S

Amanu Raro

Amanu Runga

Îles du Duc Nukutipipi
de Gloucester

Tuamotu Archipelago

Based on chart FR 6000
"Archipel des Tuamotu"
Not to be used for navigation

-22°S

Tubuai

Raivavae

-24°S

148°W 146°W 144°W 142°W

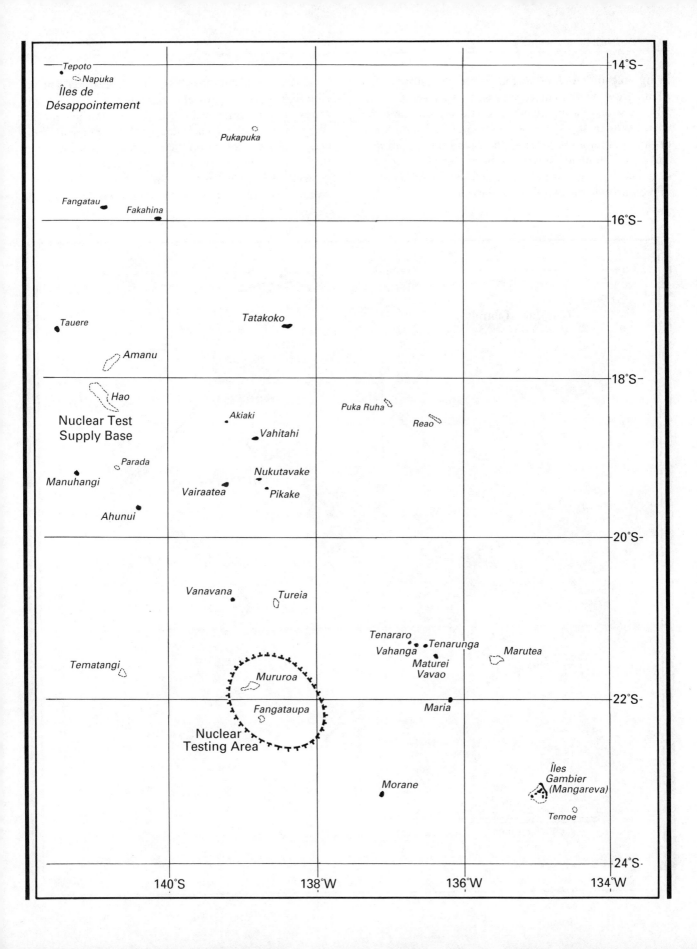

living volcano. As long as the eruptions continue, the island grows with a cinder peak and lava sides. Eventually the source of the liquid magma disappears and the island growth stops. Erosion by rain, wind, and wave begins sculpting the sides of the island and creating a soil on which plant growth can begin. At the same time in tropical seas coral polyps begin the endless building of reefs around the periphery of the island.

Reefs are composed of the skeletal remains of countless marine plants and animals that affixed themselves to the warm water shorelines of the volcanic island. Coral polyps, each smaller than a pinhead, build their limestone houses on the periphery of the land, neither rising completely above the water's surface nor growing downward more than 150 feet. In time, the volcanic islands, often hollow cones, erode away and

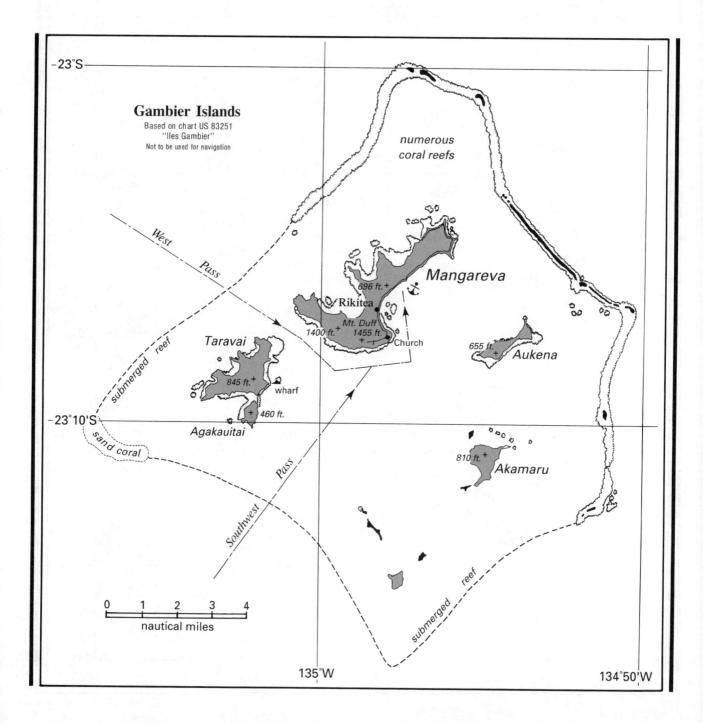

Gambier Islands
Based on chart US 83251
"Iles Gambier"
Not to be used for navigation

−23°S

numerous
coral reefs

West
Pass

submerged reef

Mangareva

696 ft. +

Rikitea

Mt. Duff
1400 ft. +   1455 ft. +
+
Church

655 ft. +

Aukena

Taravai

845 ft. +

wharf

+ 460 ft.

Agakauitai

sand coral

−23°10'S

Southwest
Pass

810 ft. +

Akamaru

submerged reef

0   1   2   3   4
nautical miles

135°W

134°50'W

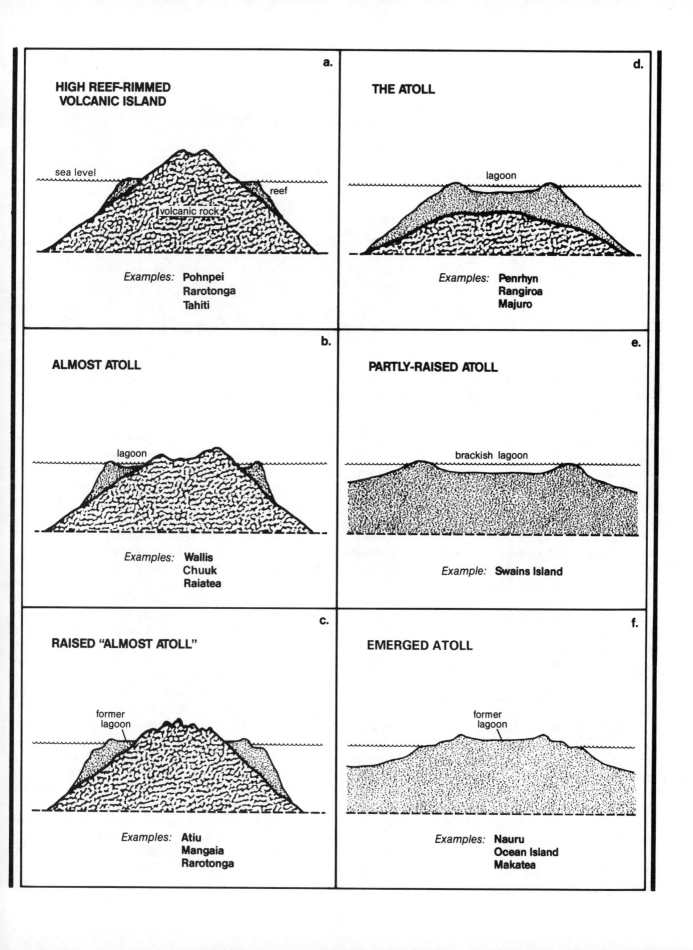

a.

HIGH REEF-RIMMED VOLCANIC ISLAND

sea level

reef

volcanic rock

Examples: **Pohnpei**
Rarotonga
Tahiti

b.

ALMOST ATOLL

lagoon

Examples: **Wallis**
Chuuk
Raiatea

c.

RAISED "ALMOST ATOLL"

former
lagoon

Examples: **Atiu**
Mangaia
Rarotonga

d.

THE ATOLL

lagoon

Examples: **Penrhyn**
Rangiroa
Majuro

e.

PARTLY-RAISED ATOLL

brackish lagoon

Example: **Swains Island**

f.

EMERGED ATOLL

former
lagoon

Examples: **Nauru**
Ocean Island
Makatea

The coral reef, which looks so dazzling from a distance, becomes a jagging and clutching death trap to any vessel that carelessly ventures too close. This is the seaward shoreline of Rangiroa Atoll. (Earl Hinz)

become submerged. This process proceeds so slowly that the prolific coral polyps manage to keep their upper domain alive near the water's surface even though their host land is slowly disappearing into the depths. The accumulating coral growth, a combination of skeletons and living polyps, forms reefs hundreds of feet above the surrounding ocean floor supported by its own living structure. The coral growth on the windward side of the island is the most prolific because the ocean currents bring abundant nutrients to the immobile polyps.

Gaps in the reef are caused by many subtle factors, but the ones of most interest to cruising boats are those caused by fresh-water streams flowing down the mountainside and preventing the build-up of saltwater-based polyps. Eventually many of the gaps become large enough to be called canoe passes and even ship's passes, but they are highly variable in depth, width, and direction, although almost always the best passes are on the leeward side of the island. It is important to remember, however, that a coral reef is a living thing and unlike other "land masses" is forever changing its shape, albeit at a glacial pace.

The final stage of volcanic island erosion combined with full coral reef development is the atoll. It is nothing but a lagoon-encircling reef, in some instances continuous and in others broken up into a series of motus or islets. From the air the motus appear as sparkling beads of a necklace. Motus vary in length from a few hundred yards to ten miles long, but they rarely exceed 300 to 400 yards in width.

To the unwary sailor the atolls represent danger. At best, they are visible for seven to ten miles in clear weather; in rain or at night, visibility can be reduced to

only a hundred yards. Reefs rising steeply from the bottom may be awash; motus rarely rise more than ten feet above sea level; and the stately coconut tree adds only another 50–75 feet of height.

Inside the lagoon is an aquarium of marine life not sustainable in the deep, turbulent open ocean. Tropical fish abound in a rainbow of colors and a fantasy of shapes, varied coral "plants" grow with delicate forms and pastel hues, and threatening coral heads rise abruptly to the surface while the coral sand bottom reflects the rays of the sun to a jade-green surface.

Vegetable life on the motus is dominated by the majestic coconut palm, whose tolerance to a salt environment and poor sandy soil is beyond belief. Coconuts are the wanderers of the Pacific. Floating for thousands of miles until cast up on a shore, they have made barren islets into lovely motus. Lying quiescent on its side in the warm tropical sun, the coconut soon sprouts into life, sending roots out through two of its eyes to seek water and food while simultaneously spikes or fronds shoot skyward through the third eye seeking the life-giving sunlight. In five to six years it has matured to the well-known graceful palm tree whose fronds rustle musically in the gentle trade winds.

The coconut palm is more than romantic prose; it is the key to life for the islanders who inhabit the atolls. The fibrous trunk is prime building material, while the giant fronds are hand woven into roof thatches of geometric beauty with lifetimes of three years. Carefully stripped, the fronds yield materials for structural lashings, baskets, mats, and essential handicraft items of all kinds. The husk of the coconut, which forms a cushion to protect the inner nut in the fall to the ground, also produces fibers for rope called sennit. It is the nut itself, however, that is the secret to life on the atoll.

A coconut takes a year to develop from a flower to a ripe nut. After reaching its mature size but long before fully ripening, the green nut is at the drinking stage, providing more than a pint of sweet, nourishing coconut milk. Not to be confused with the rancid fluid of the hard, ripe nut sold in supermarkets, the fluid of the drinking nut furnishes the island substitute for cow's milk, soda pop, and even fresh water.

More recently it has been reported that fresh coconut milk can be used in place of sterile water for some medical purposes. The addition of table salt compensates for the deficiency in sodium and chlorine and makes the milk suitable for oral rehydration of persons suffering from severe gastroenteritis.

As the nut begins to ripen, a thin, white pulp layer begins to form inside the hardening shell. This layer has the consistency of a soft-boiled egg white and, eaten with fingers or spoon, it makes a rare dessert treat. If the nut is left longer on the tree to ripen, the soft white pulp further hardens into a thick layer, while the milk turns into tasteless water. Shredded, this mature pulp ends up on cake frostings. Removed from the shell in chunks and dried in the sun, it becomes copra, from which coconut oil is extracted to be used in such widely varied items as soap, margarine, and nitroglycerine.

A coconut that is allowed to tree-ripen and that falls onto the proper surface environment (moisture, soil, light, and warmth) will start to germinate. In doing so it passes through a fourth and last food phase. Germination causes the formation of a white, spongelike substance within the nut that totally absorbs the liquid and the hard meat. This sponge has the qualities of sweet cotton candy to be eaten with the fingers. But, beware—as the life-giving sponge deteriorates, the juices become poisonous to the human system.

Another form of drink obtainable from the coconut is toddy. It starts with collecting the juice from the coconut spath (blossom) and then processing it into toddy of one form or another. One way is to boil it down into a thick brown syrup, which you can pour onto your bread as you would honey or sugar syrup. Another is to dilute the syrup with water, making a refreshing drink. A third way is to let the collected juice ferment, making it mildly alcoholic—somewhere between beer and wine. It has a very bland and slightly coconutty flavor.

A more exotic product of the coconut palm is the hearts of palm salad, sometimes called "millionaire's salad." It is made from the hearts of the new sprouts of embryo coconut trees. Extracting the heart kills the tree, but at the same time with judicious selection of which young trees are to be sacrificed to tempt the palate, a useful thinning of new growth is accomplished.

Food and drink, shelter, body covering, and ornamentation—such are the contributions of the ubiquitous coconut palm to the life in the tropics.

The Myth of the Coconut Crab

Coconut crabs live throughout the Pacific islands but not on every island. The coconut crab is a nocturnal land-dweller but deposits its eggs along shallow, inshore salt waters where many are lost when the hatching larvae sink to depths from which they can't make it ashore. The crab is large, sometimes exceeding three feet in leg span and weighing in at four to five pounds. The body is the size of a round loaf of San Francisco sourdough bread. Such a large crab is estimated to be some 30 years of age. Coconut crabs go through an annual molting process, shedding their skins (shells) once a year instead of the customary two to four times a year for aquatic crabs. The reason for this is that the coconut crab lives on terra firma and does not have the water resources to aid in more frequent molting.

The myth of the coconut crab has given it its reputation, although in truth, it is not predominantly a coconut eater. If it were, it would go hungry, since it has little innate capability for harvesting and opening coconuts. The myth, however, proceeds thusly: The coconut crab climbs the tall coconut tree and with its powerful claws wrestles a coconut free of the palm by twisting the stem until it breaks. Gravity deposits the coconut on the ground, where the crab descends to tear off the husk, break open the nut, and gorge itself on the sweet coconut meat.

Maybe coconut crabs are lazy, but the coconuts they do attack are usually already on the ground. The crab will drag one to its ground hole and start whittling away with its powerful claws. It takes a big coconut crab up to three weeks to tear its way through husk and shell and get at the coconut meat. Small coconut crabs are incapable of penetrating the husk and nut at all. Further, coconut crabs are omnivorous, living off plant and animal matter found on the ground. They will eat coconut meat, however, if it is offered to them as an opened nut. If further evidence of the naming misnomer is needed, coconut crabs are also known to live where there are no coconut palms.

It is cruel to burst the bubble of mythology with-

A popular atoll of call, Ahe has a short wharf for trading vessels that can be used by visiting yachts between times. In the foreground copra is being sun-dried. (Earl Hinz)

out offering some hope. Coconut crabs still exist on many islands and atolls, although in small numbers. Natives who harvest them in conservation areas catch only those measuring at least nine centimeters along the top of the shell, which is a 12- to 15-year-old crab. This very slow growth along with their gustatorial excellence is spelling their doom. Coconut crabs are prepared for eating by simply boiling and then eating them with the fingers and a nut cracker.

Eating the coconut crab is one thing, but catching it is another. Being nocturnal and a dull gray-green in color, it is difficult to see. If you can corner one away from its ground hole, attack it from the rear, avoiding those two awesome claws. Obviously, the crab's claws must be immobilized immediately. Another technique described to me by an islander is to chase the crab into its hole, which is too small for the crab to open its claws and fight, and then reach in and drag it out. It must work because the islander looked well fed and still had all his fingers.

The coconut crab is truly an endangered species, especially in the islands of Vanuatu, where it really hit the restaurant menus. It would be a shame if it were to disappear from the earth as so much wildlife has already done.

The Weather

The Tuamotu Archipelago, while in the nominal heart of the southeast trade wind belt, is strongly dominated by easterly winds. Over the eastern part, east to east-northeast winds are most prevalent; in the western part, the majority are from east to east-southeast. The northeasterly direction is most prevalent from November to May, and the southeasterly direction, from June to October. Some 80 percent of the annual winds are from directions between northeast and southeast.

Occasional barometric depressions cross the group, sometimes resulting in squally weather and temporary reversal of the trades into winds from westerly quadrants. These are most likely to occur from January to March but may occur earlier and later in the season. Seven severe hurricanes are on record among the islands from 1877 to 1906. Of these, three occurred in January, two in February, and one each in March and September. In December 1977, a tropical storm with winds of 34 to 63 knots moved southeast across the Tuamotu Archipelago. But the most concentrated and devastating cyclonic storms occurred in 1982–1983 (see French Polynesia, section on Weather).

Cruising Notes

YACHT FACILITIES

There are no yacht facilities in the Tuamotus. At most, villages have copra boat wharfs, which can be used for docking when copra boats are not present. Food is generally scarce except for coconuts and fish. Because of poor soil the usually common staples of the South Seas —breadfruit, bananas, and taro are not plentiful. Small stores supplied by the copra boats stock limited canned

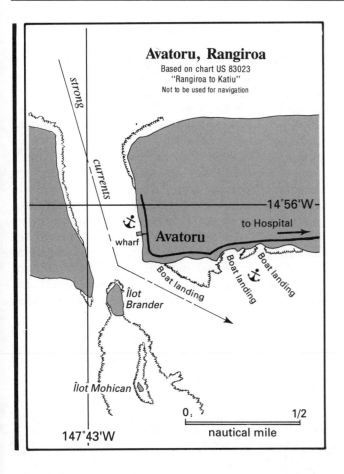

Avatoru, Rangiroa
Based on chart US 83023
"Rangiroa to Katiu"
Not to be used for navigation

strong

currents

14°56'W

to Hospital

wharf   Avatoru

Boat landing

Boat landing

Boat landing

Îlot
Brander

Îlot Mohican

0   1/2
nautical mile

147°43'W

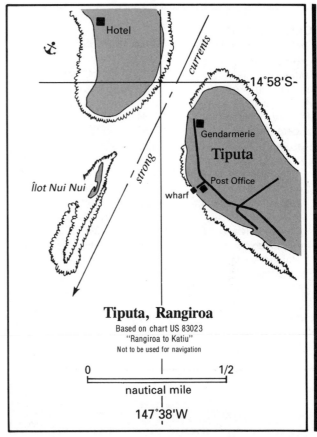

Hotel

currents

14°58'S-

Gendarmerie

Tiputa

Post Office

wharf

strong

Îlot Nui Nui

Tiputa, Rangiroa
Based on chart US 83023
"Rangiroa to Katiu"
Not to be used for navigation

0   1/2
nautical mile

147°38'W

and dry goods. Water on most atolls is collected from rainfall in cisterns and during the dry season may be in short supply, so don't depend on getting water in any atoll in the Pacific.

The hospitality of the atoll dwellers is unparalleled among the land masses of the Pacific. Because the atolls are small and sparsely populated, the people welcome a visiting boat with open arms. Some atolls of the Tuamotus have seen such a succession of cruising boats, however, that their hospitality is suffering from overwork. Among them are Ahe, Rangiroa, and Takaroa. For a truer atoll experience, cruisers should consider extending themselves over a wider area; after all, there are more than 40 atolls to visit.

SOCIETY ISLANDS

The Country

The Society group contains twelve major islands divided into a windward cluster of five and a leeward cluster of seven islands. The windward group consists of Tahiti, Moorea, Mehitia (Maitea), and Tubuai Manu, which are high volcanic types, and Tetiaroa, which is a small atoll. The leeward group includes the high islands of Raiatea, Tahaa, and Huahine; Bora-Bora and Maupiti, (which are almost atolls); and Tupai, and Mapihaa (Mopelia), which are true atolls.

Tahiti, known at one time as Nouvelle Cythere, is

SOCIETY ISLANDS

A part of French Polynesia, an overseas territory of France

Ports of Entry

Vaitape, Bora-Bora	16°30′ S, 151°45′ W
Fare, Huahine	16°42′ S, 151°02′ W
Uturoa, Raiatea	16°44′ S, 151°25′ W
Afareaitu, Moorea	17°34′ S, 149°45′ W
Papeete, Tahiti	17°32′ S, 149°34′ W

Distances between Ports in Nautical Miles

Between Papeete and

Auckland, New Zealand	2,210
Avatiu, Cook Islands	620
Avatoru Pass, Tuamotu Archipelago	190
Bounty Bay, Pitcairn Island	1,175
Christmas Island, Kiribati	1,260
Hilo, Hawaii	2,260
Mangareva, Gambier Islands	885
Pago Pago, American Samoa	1,235
Raivavae, Austral Islands	395
Rapa Iti, Austral Islands	670
Taiohae, Marquesas Islands	755

Standard time

10 hours slow on UTC

the largest and best known island of the group. It has provided the locale for so many novels and adventure stories that it has come to be associated with the typical South Seas island paradise. It was also a favorite subject of Paul Gauguin, whose paintings of island people and island life made him famous. Tahiti has an area of about 400 square miles and is formed of volcanos connected by an isthmus, making it look like a figure 8. The main peak, Mt. Orohena, has an elevation of 7,321 feet, from which the island drops precipitously to a moderately broad coastal plain. The interior is an uninhabited, trackless upland of jagged peaks and gorges covered with lush tropical vegetation. People do not live in village groups but in homes strung out around the coastal belt. This pattern is broken only by the capital city of Papeete, a modern city of more than 40,000 persons built around a coastal lagoon in the northwest corner of the island that provides the area's best and busiest harbor.

Other high islands of the group are all rugged and similar in structure to Tahiti but are smaller and lower with peaks that rise no higher than about 4,000 feet. All are populated, and their rich soils produce considerable

People who know call Bora-Bora the most beautiful island on earth. Its massive twin peaks are an ever-changing skyline as you sail the calm waters inside the surrounding barrier reef. (Earl Hinz)

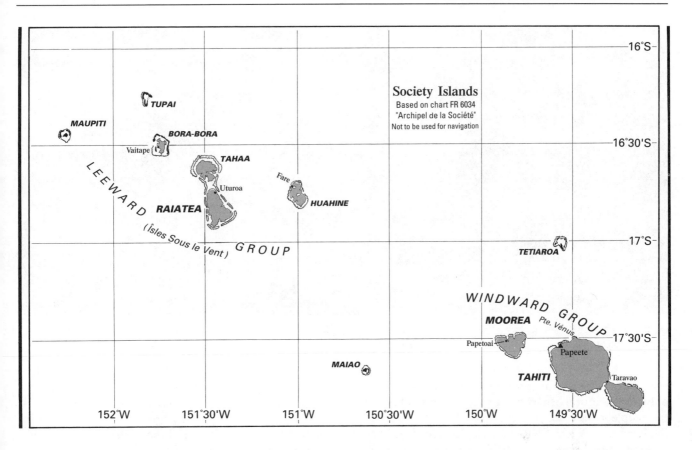

Society Islands
Based on chart FR 6034
"Archipel de la Société"
Not to be used for navigation

copra, pineapples, vanilla beans, and varieties of tropical fruits.

Papeete is the distribution center for supplies to all of the French Polynesia islands, which number more than 100 and have a total population of about 190,000. Tahiti has more than 135,000 of them. Many atolls sustain only 40 to 50 people, which seems to be the threshold size for a permanent village on an atoll.

The interisland freighters, generally small—200 to 300 tons—are diesel powered and have totally replaced the trading schooner of the romantic past. Interisland trading is conducted mainly by two companies—Donalds, which evolved from an earlier European copra-trading venture, and Wing Man Hing, which is an aggressive Chinese business in import, export, and local sales. These companies' trading ships compete in purchasing copra and selling goods throughout the French Polynesia islands. Where neither feels he can make a franc, the French navy sends its LSTs to meet the needs of the islanders. In principal, the French navy tries not to compete with the local island traders.

Papeete Harbor is also home port to the French fleet supporting the nuclear testing at Mururoa. While many South Pacific nations decry these tests, they have greatly enhanced the Tahitian economy, and one wonders what the economy will do when this source of income no longer exists.

Bora-Bora may possibly be the most beautiful island in the Pacific. Its high, sculptured, twin-peaked central mountain is surrounded by a deep lagoon inside a magnificent barrier reef on which ocean swells break into plumes of white spray. The central island has a barren appearance on its eastern flank, but agriculture has kept the western side cloaked in greenery.

During World War II Bora-Bora was a U.S. air and naval base with up to 6,000 armed forces personnel stationed on the island, whose native population has never numbered more than 2,600. Some evidence of wartime activity still exists in ruins of seaplane ramps, scattered aging quonset huts, and the island's airport runway built on the reef. In the hills are some antiaircraft guns and revetments that have become playgrounds for the local children.

Spread around the island of Bora-Bora are the remains of more than 40 *marae*s (places of worship) built by an earlier civilization. Unlike the *marae*s built of volcanic rock on the other Society Islands, the *marae*s of Bora-Bora were built with slabs of coral.

Directly inside the reef entrance to the Bora-Bora lagoon is the Bora-Bora Yacht Club, with moorings and fresh water for the cruising boat and a restaurant and bar for the tired sailor. (Earl Hinz)

Bora-Bora is a favorite stop for cruising yachts not only for its natural beauty but also for the friendliness of the people toward seagoing travelers. The anchorage off the Bora-Bora Yacht Club just inside the Teavanui Pass is good, albeit quite deep; that off the Oa Oa Hotel closer to the central area of Vaitape is somewhat shallower.

Huahine is considered the least spoiled of the major Society Islands. It is surrounded by a narrow lagoon inside a well-developed barrier reef and is separated into two parts by a strait spanned by a bridge. The two parts are known as Huahine Nui (the great Huahine) and Huahine Iti (the little Huahine). There are approximately 3,200 people on the two islands.

A major farm product of Huahine is melon. Excellent cantaloupe and watermelons are grown on the motus of the reef; these are in great demand in Papeete, where a wage income has replaced subsistence living.

Raiatae and Tahaa are surrounded by a common barrier reef and rise from the same seamount. It is possible to sail completely around both islands staying within the common barrier reef.

Raiatea, the larger of the two islands, is the second-largest island in the Society group. According to legend and some well-founded archeological research, Raiatea is the ancient Hawaiiki, which the original Polynesian migrants used as their base for later dispersal to Hawaii, the Cook Islands, and New Zealand. Before France declared a protectorate over these islands, Raia-

tea was the dominant island of the group through its religious strength. After the French took over and Christianity prevailed over the indigenous religion, the influence of Raiatea waned, and the larger island of Tahiti became the government center.

Yachting activity at Raiatea is concentrated at the main village of Uturoa at the north end of the island. For those who don't cruise in their own boats, the Moorings and ATM Charters have boats available for bareboat or skippered operations in these leeward islands. Some cruisers from the United States have built homes at Faaroa Bay, where they also keep their boats. It is a beautiful harbor and generally quite secure in prevailing winds.

The nearest neighbor isle to Tahiti is Moorea, a bare 12 miles to the west. It is rich in natural beauty with its sharp peaks, deep valleys, emerald lagoon, and two splendid bays—Cook's and Opunohu. The island covers 31 square miles and has a population of 8,000. It is often called the "getaway island" for Tahitians because it is so close to Papeete and offers a rustic retreat. As one might expect, Moorea tends to be touristy although the activities are not concentrated in any one area.

Moorea is rich in Christian history, for this is where Christianity started in these islands and spread throughout the Pacific. It is today the headquarters for the London Missionary Society (LMS) Mission in the Pacific. The first book printed in the South Seas was

The sliding roofs of these two copra sun driers are closed to keep the drying copra from being dampened by light showers. The location is the isthmus between the two islands making up Huahine. (Earl Hinz)

printed at the Port of Entry village of Afareaitu in 1817.

To the modern traveler, though, it is the famous Bali Hai Hotel that is important. Situated on the north shore, with a subsidiary location in Cook's Bay, the Bali Hai has become the epic hotel operation in French Polynesia. The Bali Hai welcomes cruising boats to anchor off their facilities and come and partake of good food and drink.

The Weather

The prevailing wind direction is easterly throughout the ocean area of the Society Islands. This holds true for every month of the year over the eastern section of the group and for most months in the western section. In the eastern section northeast winds predominate over, or are equal to, those from the southeast, except in June and July, during which months the southeast winds are about twice as frequent as those from the northeast. In the western section the southeast winds are more frequent than the northeast except in March and November.

At Papeete, however, owing to local conditions, the northeast wind prevails, except in September, when it is superseded by both north and southwest directions, and in June, when it is equaled by winds from east and southwest. Northerly winds are frequent from September to February, and southwesterly winds from April to December. Land and sea breeze effects are definitely in evidence.

The annual average wind speed at sea is 9 to 10 knots. The strongest winds average 11 to 12 knots in the southern winter months; the lightest, 6 to 8 knots in the summer season. Fresh gales have occasionally occurred in June, but these are due only to a strengthening of the prevailing winds. Up until 1982 tropical cyclones were rare, with the last one occurring in 1926 at Bora-Bora. The 1982–1983 season, however, made up for all past quiescent seasons (see French Polynesia, "Weather").

The annual rainfall is 72 inches at Papeete, of which more than a fifth occurs in December. The rainy season lasts from November through March. The driest months are July and August. On the open sea, rain is most frequent in December and January and least frequent in August. Thunderstorms are fairly common, particularly in January, February, and May.

The climate of the Society Islands is tempered by the surrounding ocean and is warm and sunny with only modest variation in temperature throughout the year. Seasons are best described by the number of days of rainfall in a month. December through February is the rainy season with from 11 to 14 days of rain per month. During the wet season temperatures will range between 81°F and 95°F with high humidity, and there will be many insects. In the dry months temperatures range between 70°F and 81°F, and there are virtually no

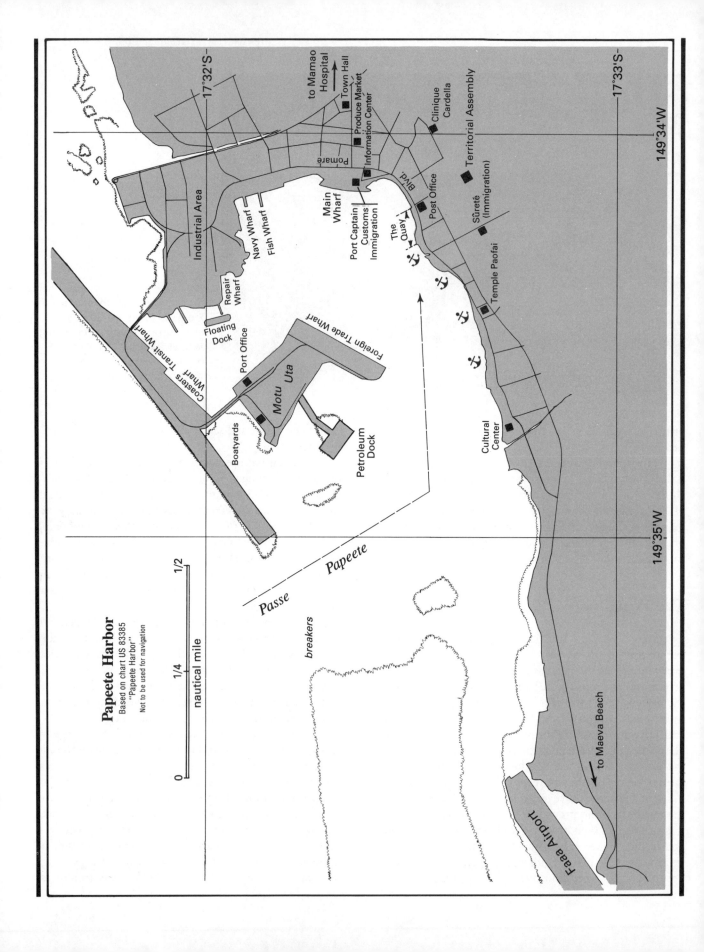

Papeete Harbor

Based on chart US 83385
"Papeete Harbor"

Not to be used for navigation

nautical mile

0   1/4   1/2

Industrial Area

Navy Wharf
Fish Wharf
Repair Wharf
Floating Dock

Coaster's Transit Wharf

Port Office

Boatyards

Motu Uta

Foreign Trade Wharf

Petroleum Dock

Main Wharf

Port Captain
Customs
Immigration

The Quay

Pomare Blvd.

to Mamao Hospital

Town Hall

Produce Market

Information Center

Clinique Cardella

Territorial Assembly

Post Office

Sûreté (Immigration)

Temple Paofai

Cultural Center

Passe   Papeete

breakers

to Maeva Beach

Faaa Airport

17°32'S

17°33'S

149°34'W

149°35'W

insects. The frequent sudden rains of this area are only of short duration, and the weather is generally good the year around.

Cruising Notes

YACHT FACILITIES

Papeete

Papeete is a very modern port and has been a port of call for ships and yachts since shortly after the days of Captain Cook. The quay is the wharf along Boulevard Pomare at which yachts tie stern-to with a bow anchor

The Captain Cook Lighthouse at Venus Point, Tahiti. This is where Cook observed the transit of the planet Venus in 1769 on behalf of the Royal Society. He named this island group in honor of the Royal Society. (Earl Hinz)

set out in the stream. You step ashore on a gangway balanced between stern and quay wall. These transom planks are generally available on the spot. Unfortunately, the limited number of these berths is outnumbered by the yachts wanting them by a factor of three or four, so the rest of the yachts anchor stern-to down the boulevard with their stern lines going to bollards installed ashore along the boulevard. Your dinghy becomes your shore boat.

A one-time fee of CFP3,600 is charged for entry and registration. Daily moorage charges in Papeete Harbor area are as follows:

LOA (meters)	Along the quay (CFP)	Along the grass (CFP)
Up to 8	225	150
8–10	375	250
10–12	525	350
12–15	900	600
15–20	1,275	850
20–25	1,875	1,250
25–30	2,550	1,700

Daily charges for electricity on the quay are CFP240 for 10a/110v or 5a/220v and CFP390 for 20a/110v or 10a/220v.

Monthly moorage charges are as follows:

LOA (meters)	Along the quay (CFP)	Anchored out (CFP)
Up to 10	6,000	3,000
10–12	8,400	4,200
12–15	10,200	5,100
Over 15	12,000	6,000

An additional charge of CFP3,000 per month is made for live-aboard privileges.

The above charges apply also to the mooring zones at Vaitupa and Maeva Beach, which are managed by Tahiti Aquatique based at the Maeva Beach Hotel. There is an additional service charge in the latter areas for showers, sanitary facilities, garbage and trash disposal, and the like. This amounts to CFP3,000 per month if anchored, CFP1,500 per month if on a mooring.

All of the following mooring and anchoring zones near Papeete are controlled by the Papeete port director, and their use must be arranged with the director or one of his agents at the mooring zone. These include

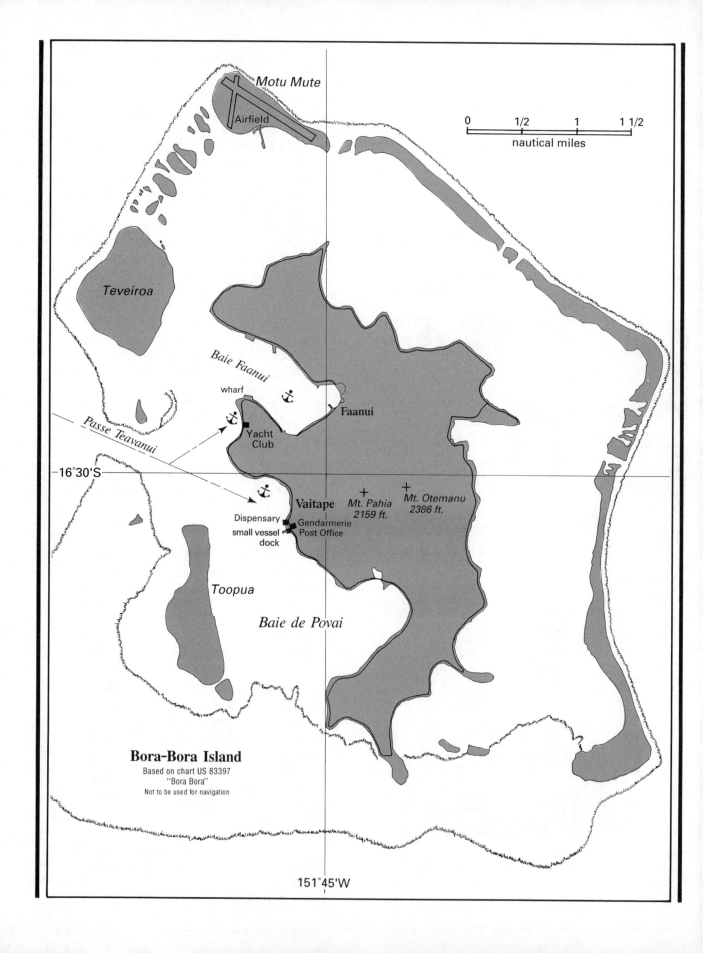

Motu Mute

Airfield

0   1/2   1   1 1/2
nautical miles

Teveiroa

Baie Faanui

wharf

⚓

Faanui

⚓

Yacht
Club

Passe Teavanui

−16°30'S

⚓

Vaitape

Mt. Pahia
2159 ft.

Mt. Otemanu
2386 ft.

Dispensary

Gendarmerie
Post Office

small vessel
dock

Toopua

Baie de Povai

Bora-Bora Island
Based on chart US 83397
"Bora Bora"
Not to be used for navigation

151°45'W

P1	Marina Taina
P2	Maeva Beach
P3	Vaitupa
P5	The quay itself
P7	Papeava

There are three private moorage zones in this area also —Marina Lotus, Aeroport, and Fare Ute—for which individual arrangements must be made directly with the owners.

The port director of Papeete rigorously controls the movement of all yachts once they have made formal entry. Trips around Tahiti or to Moorea must be cleared out and back with the port director. Trips to the outer islands must be cleared with Customs and the port director. Trips to foreign countries must be cleared with Customs, Immigration, and the port director as well as the bank that has your security bond.

Practically all services needed to repair or maintain a yacht are available in Papeete. Not all deck and engine supplies are available, however, and those that are come from French sources built to the metric measurement system. If special parts are needed, they can be ordered from the United States, New Zealand, or Australia (or almost any country) and shipped by air since Tahiti enjoys excellent air transportation services. If you do order parts from outside Tahiti, have the sender mark the package "For Yacht _____ in transit." You will not have to pay customs duty on the parts, but you will have to do a lot of paperwork to liberate them from Customs.

When you are provisioning for departure from Papeete, you should take advantage of case lot and other quantity discounts on groceries that can be obtained from some local stores. Near Maeva Beach is the Euromarche store, near the quay is Bon Marche; in addition, several distributors operate near the northeast corner of Papeete Harbor. Some will deliver to your dock.

Leeward Islands

The leeward Society Islands are gradually adding facilities for cruising boats. Raiatea, in particular, is being referred to as "the yachting center of Tahiti," primarily because of the establishment of the Moorings charter operation at Uturoa, the ATM charter operations in Faaroa Bay, and the Raiatea Carenage Services boatyard near Uturoa. The latter is a full-service yard from haulout to rigging and painting. They will also store your boat on the hard for up to a year should you have to return to your home town on business. Their address is:

Raiatea Carenage Services
P.O. Box 165
Uturoa, Raiatea
FRENCH POLYNESIA

There are no boat facilities on Bora-Bora, but there are moorings at the Bora-Bora Yacht Club and the Oa Oa Hotel. Meals are served at both places, and they have become favorites of the cruising boats. All of the leeward islands of the Society Group are replete with anchorages, bays, lagoons, sandy beaches, and friendly people. They should not be missed.

AUSTRAL ISLANDS

The Country

The Austral Islands consist of five inhabited and two uninhabited islands southwest of the Society group, arranged in a chain about 800 miles long. This range is an extension of the submerged volcanic elevations that form the Cook Islands to the north. Although classified as high islands, none of the Australs rises more than 1,500 feet above sea level. Economically, the group is unimportant, but some of them, particularly Raivavae, contain many old temples and archeological remains that are of interest to researchers.

The Austral Islands were joined to Tahiti in the early 1820s when Pomare II visited them to convert the peoples to Christianity. They have a total area of only 63 square miles, which support a current population of

AUSTRAL ISLANDS

A part of French Polynesia, an overseas territory of France

Ports of Entry

Moerai, Rurutu	22°28′ S, 151°20′ W
Mataura, Tubuai	23°21′ S, 149°29′ W
Rairua, Raivave	23°52′ S, 147°44′ W

Distances between Ports in Nautical Miles

Between Mataura and

Auckland, New Zealand	2,010
Avatiu, Cook Islands	585
Bounty Bay, Pitcairn Island	1,065
Mangareva, Gambier Islands	800
Papeete, Society Islands	350
Rapa Iti, Austral Islands	380

Standard time

10 hours slow on UTC

about 6,600. The inhabited islands are Rurutu, Rimatera, Raivavae, Tubuai, and Rapa.

Tubuai is a high volcanic island about five miles long and three miles wide. It is almost oval in shape and rises to a height of 1,385 feet. The barrier reef that surrounds it measures nine miles long and six miles wide. The annular lagoon surrounding the island is shallow throughout and not navigable by yachts. The one entrance to the lagoon is on the northwest side; it leads to the principal village of Mataura. Approximately 1,600 people live on the island.

Tubuai is a very fertile island: coffee, copra, bananas, manioc (arrowroot), and oranges are grown here. The oranges, like most of those throughout the islands of Polynesia, are ripe—and delicious—when the skin is still green.

European eyes first saw Tubuai in 1777 when Captain Cook on his third voyage of exploration visited

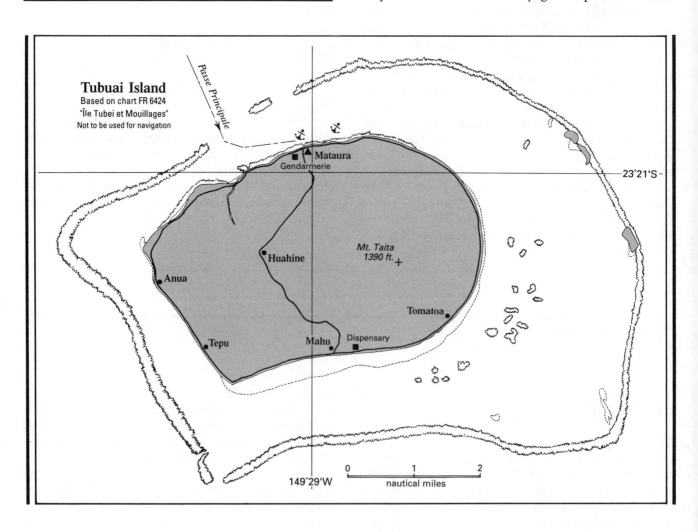

Tubuai Island
Based on chart FR 6424
"Île Tubei et Mouillages"
Not to be used for navigation

Passe Principale

Mataura
Gendarmerie

23°21′S

Huahine

Mt. Taita
1390 ft.

Anua

Tomatoa

Tepu

Mahu

Dispensary

149°29′W

0	1	2

nautical miles

All along the shoreline of Raivavae you will find canoes belonging to the local fishermen. Usually they are beached to prevent fouling or being blown away in strong winds. (Earl Hinz)

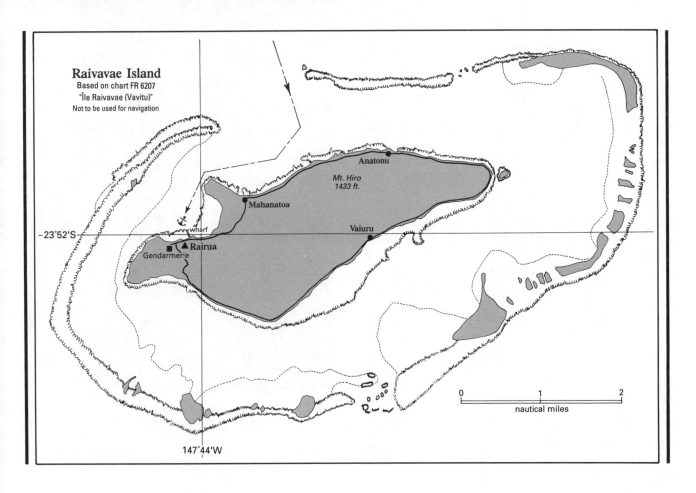

Raivavae Island
Based on chart FR 6207
"Île Raivavae (Vavitu)"
Not to be used for navigation

Anatonu

Mt. Hiro
1433 ft.

Mahanatoa

Vaiuru

wharf

−23°52'S

■ ▲ Rairua

Gendarmerie

147°44'W

0   1   2
nautical miles

there just before heading north to look for the Northwest Passage above North America. The next Europeans to visit Tubuai were the mutineers from HMS *Bounty,* who landed there in 1789 and attempted to make a settlement. The natives did not look kindly on this invasion: violence soon erupted, and 66 natives lost their lives. It was obvious to the mutineers that this would continue to be an inhospitable island for them, so they embarked once more in their quest for a haven.

In 1882 the first true missionaries arrived in the form of Christianized Tahitians. But Christianity took a severe setback the following year when an epidemic swept the islands, killing hundreds of the islanders. The Tubuaians blamed the epidemic on the anger of their old gods who were being pushed aside; modern medicine notes that the Tubuaians, like many indigenous peoples in the New World, had lived in isolation for so many generations that they had not developed even the simplest immunity to Western diseases. These deaths started the decline of the people and culture from which Tubuai never recovered.

Few people have ever heard of Raivavae Island, and even fewer have ever visited it. On the chart of the South Pacific it is but a dot at 23°52′S latitude and 147°44′W longitude, 360 miles south-southeast of Tahiti. It is a high island of considerable geologic age surrounded by a well-developed barrier reef that is just awash in most places but that also has on it some of the familiar wooded islets known as motus. While the oval barrier reef measures five miles north to south and eight miles east to west, the 1,400-foot-high volcanic mountains that form the island proper cover an area of only two by five miles. The intervening annular space is a beautiful lagoon with a coral sand and mud bottom, uncounted coral heads with many rising close to the surface, and along the shoreline a fringing reef that makes dinghy landing difficult. The blue-green lagoon, the lush green growth of the coastal plains, and the spectacularly eroded mountains give Raivavae a beauty rivaling Bora-Bora in the Society Islands.

Raivavae today is a quiet, almost subdued island with little of the gaiety and love for pleasure found on the other islands of French Polynesia, but it was not always so. In the eighteenth and nineteenth centuries Raivavae was alive with 3,000 people in a social order said to rival that of Tahiti. These early people were daring seafarers who not only voyaged to neighboring islands but north to Tahiti and Raiatea and, reputedly, even to the shores of New Zealand. Fishing was then an important part of their daily life although little is done now and, in fact, the islanders no longer seem to have

an affinity for the sea. Their early civilization developed agriculture to a fine art using terracing techniques for growing taro—the universal food of all Pacific islands.

Warfare between the districts of the island was a way of life, and the mountainous backbone of the island was in many parts made a fortress. Disaster came to Raivavae in 1826 in a very different form when a contagious, malignant fever was brought from the neighboring island of Tubuai. The disease devastated the popula-

Among the few artifacts from the past that have neither returned to nature nor been removed to distant museums is this stone tiki, which was found on the island of Raivavae. It is now on display at the Gauguin Museum on Tahiti, and tales are still told of unfortunate endings for the persons who moved it there. (Earl Hinz)

tion, reducing their numbers to an estimated 120. Unable to sustain their culture any longer, it vanished into the underbrush, and the Raivavaeans today enjoy no heritage from the past.

Captain Cook came upon Rurutu on his first voyage in 1769, but until the second decade of the nineteenth century the island had very few contacts with Europeans. It became a French protectorate in 1889 and a possession in 1900.

Rurutu is a mountainous island with a coastal strip of land protected by a continuous coral reef. The highest peak is Mt. Taatioe (1,285 feet). The main island is about 6½ miles long by 3½ miles wide. The main village is Moerai, where approximately 700 people live. It has a town hall, a school, a dispensary with one doctor plus assistants, a temple and a church, and a general store. The total population of Rurutu is about 1,600, and their economy is based solely on agriculture. They grow potatoes and carrots, arrowroot and taro, pigs and cattle. Tropical fruits are not as plentiful as on others of the Austral Islands.

If weather prevents an anchorage opposite Moerai, Avera is usually sheltered. These two villages are linked by a road 3 miles long, and you can walk from one to the other across the central uplands.

One of the main exports of the Austral Islands is handicrafts. Hats and baskets made of both pandanus and coconut fronds are available on all islands. Some wood carvings made of tou and miro woods are available in the little village of Mahu on Tubuai.

Remote Bass and Rapa islands are so far south that they differ from the rest of French Polynesia. Their climate is too moderate for most tropical growth, and they do not produce copra but concentrate on coffee, taro, and oranges. Bass Island (Morotiri) is actually a cluster of nine islands, eight of which are mere rock pinnacles rising to a maximum height of only 350 feet. They are uninhabited but are visited occasionally by fishermen.

Rapa is a small volcanic island 2,000 feet high. It is populated by approximately 300 people who are believed to have descended from a primitive, pure Polynesian stock. They are darker than most Polynesians but have the sturdy, splendid physique of that ethnic group. Special permission of the French governor is required to visit Rapa Island.

The Weather

The winds in the area of the main Austral group (excluding Rapa) are similar to those of the windward isles of the Society group. The islands lie in the trade wind belt, and the winds tend to be easterly with southeast winds dominant in June and July. The rest of the year they are equally divided between northeasterlies and southeasterlies.

Gales are infrequent, and hurricanes were practically unknown until the 1982–1983 season, which is described in detail in the "Weather" section of French Polynesia.

The climate of these islands is very healthful, and the most pleasant months for visiting are September and October. In the southern winter the temperature may drop as low as 52°F.

Cruising Notes

YACHT FACILITIES

There are no yacht facilities in the Australs. Some villages have wharfs for the copra boats, and these can be used for docking when the copra boats are not present. There are no boat supplies, but there is water piped to the docks; the water is untreated but fresh from the mountain streams. Diesel fuel is available at Tubuai.

These islands are very fertile, and there is an abundance of good fruits available but few vegetables except for taro. The small stores carry a limited variety of canned goods and dried staples.

CHAPTER 7

EASTER ISLAND

The Country

Easter Island is known by a variety of names and has been called the world's loneliest island by Thor Heyerdahl, who spent a year there studying the famous brooding statues and other archeological remains of a past civilization. The Chilean administrators call it Isla de Pascua, the islanders refer to it as Rapa Nui (distin-guishing it from Rapa Iti, which is in the Austral Islands), while the complete Polynesian name for it is Te Pito O Te Henua, meaning the Navel of the World.

Whatever you call it, from the water it is a forbidding volcanic rock whose coast is steep-to and rocky with only a few sandy beaches on its total periphery. It measures 14 miles long, seven miles wide, has a circumference of 34 miles, and is roughly triangular in shape. The land area is approximately 50 square miles. The

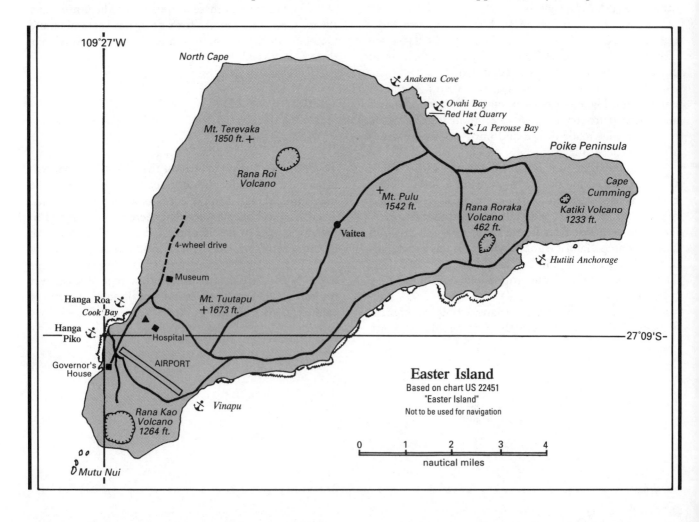

Easter Island
Based on chart US 22451
"Easter Island"
Not to be used for navigation

EASTER ISLAND
A colony of Chile

Port of Entry
Hanga Roa   27°09′ S, 109°27′ W

Distances between Ports in Nautical Miles
Between Hanga Roa and

Acapulco, Mexico	2,700
Bounty Bay, Pitcairn Island	1,120
Cumberland Bay, Juan Fernández Islands	1,625
Lima, Peru	2,030
Panama City, Panama	2,780
Papeete, Society Islands	2,290
San Diego, California	3,615
Taiohae, Marquesas Islands	2,050
Valparaíso, Chile	1,985
Wreck Bay, Galapagos Islands	1,945

Standard Time
7 hours slow on UTC

Public Holidays and Special Events

January 1	New Year's Day—Public holiday
March/April *	Good Friday, Easter, and Easter Monday—Public holidays
May 1	Labor Day—Public holiday
May 21	Naval Battle of Iquique—Public holiday
August 15	Assumption of the Virgin—Public holiday
September 9	Policarpo Toro Day—Public holiday (Easter Island annexation)
September 18/19	Chilean Independence Day—Public holiday
October 12	Columbus Day—Public holiday
November 1	All Saints' Day—Public holiday
December 8	Day of the Immaculate Conception—Public holiday
December 25	Christmas Day—Public holiday

*Specific dates vary from year to year.

land is generally high and precipitous in places, but the hills are gently rounded and covered to their summits with vegetation. Several extinct volcanoes are on the island. One, Rana Kao, at the southern end of the island rises to 1,264 feet and has a small, deep lake in its crater, which is the largest crater on the island. The highest peak of the island is Cerro Terevaka, which reaches 1,850 feet.

There are no completely sheltered anchorages on the island, but temporary anchorage can be found in many places in the lee of the island. Because of the steep-to sides of this island, boats have to anchor close in to the shoreline, where occasional rocky patches present a hazard.

Vegetation consists principally of tall grass that covers most of the island. Few trees exist, and most of these are found in the Rana Kao crater. They are known as toro miro trees and are used as the raw material for the wood carvings made by the islanders. All three volcanic craters are marshy and grow reeds. The eucalyptus growing on the island were planted by Europeans in the twentieth century. Cultivated crops include sweet potatoes, yams, bananas, sugar cane, and tobacco. Other than sheep and cattle brought in by the Europeans, there are no animals on Easter Island. Fish abound in the ocean, and lobstering along the shoreline is very popular. The local lobster—a big one without claws—can be speared in waist-deep water.

It is the unwritten history of this island that is so interesting, and its vagueness only adds mystery to the presence of almost 900 of the giant stone statues called *moai.* Anthropological and archeological evidence suggest that Easter Island was first settled about A.D. 400 by Polynesians coming, most likely, from Raiatea. A minority of researchers believe Easter Island's settlement involved voyagers from South America. Their arguments center around the *kumara* (sweet potato), which came from South America and is now found throughout Oceania. The counter to that argument is that some Polynesian voyagers did not stop their wanderings at Easter Island, but continued on east making landfall in Chile and bringing the sweet potato home to Polynesia from there. Easter Island's early civilization thrived until sometime between A.D. 600 and 1100.

A middle period of settlement and possibly the one that created the *moai* statues began about A.D. 1100 with an influx of Polynesians led by Hotu Matua. They were a slender people known as Hanau Momoka and often referred to as the "short ears." The Hanau Eepe, or "long ears," arrived somewhat later from Peru. For the next 500 years 4,000 people divided into two tribes lived on this island. Culture flourished but so did rivalries, and about the year 1600 war broke out between the two factions that all but ended life on Easter Island. The civilization that had created those mystifying stone statues destroyed itself, toppled its *moai,* and lost to the world the secret of building these 20-ton statues, but worse was yet to follow with the arrival of the first Europeans.

It was Easter Sunday in 1771 when a Dutch navigator named Jacob Roggeveen first sighted the island and named it Easter Island, a name that has been retained to this day ("Pascua" means "Easter" in Spanish). Following Roggeveen came a succession of Spanish, English, and French explorers in the late 1700s.

Near the primary school begins Avenida Policarpa Toro, named after the Chilean naval captain who was responsible for Rapanui's becoming a colony of Chile in 1888. A *moai* carved stone figure has been erected at the head of the avenue. Horses, which outnumber the human inhabitants, are still a popular form of transportation, although motorbikes are becoming increasingly prevalent. (Grant McCall)

That was the second step in the demise of the original inhabitants. They became slaves to foreigners who stopped there to replenish ships' provisions and take advantage of the depressed native population. Many islanders were taken to Peru in 1862 as slaves to work on the coastal sugar plantations. European diseases were brought back to the island, and the population was reduced to a mere 111 people by the year 1870.

Chile annexed the island in 1888, and under more settled conditions the population again started to increase. In 1966 the people of Easter Island became enfranchised Chilean citizens. Today there are 1,500 Rapa Nuieans and 500 Chileans on the island with such twentieth-century conveniences as telephones and closed-circuit television.

Easter Island is administered by an appointed civilian governor with local affairs handled by a mayor and a council of elders. A nationalized sheep farm provides communal income, which is used for building materials and equipment. Sources of personal income include selling carvings of wood and shell and providing quarters and services for tourists who come in on the twice-a-week jet airplane from Valparaiso and Tahiti.

Although there are a few Protestants, most of the island people are devout members of the Roman Catholic Church. But the past dies slowly, and many people still believe in the power of the guardian spirits or *aku aku.*

An American satellite tracking station was operated on the island from 1960 to 1970 before political issues overruled technical ones and the National Aeronautics and Space Administration was forced to close it down. A new treaty, however, between the United States and Chile in 1985 set the stage for an airport expansion to 10,000 feet surfaced and instrumented to accept emergency landings of the U.S. space shuttle. This improved airport is being used by Lan-Chile airline as well as Air France Concorde flights.

The Weather

There is only one description for the weather at Easter Island—unpredictable. Rarely does the wind stay steady from any direction for more than a few days, and then it shifts direction in a matter of minutes. A vessel left unattended in a calm leeward anchorage could quickly find itself on a lee shore. While the weather is highly unpredictable, it is never really bad. The island's position at the northwestern edge of the South Pacific high-pressure area accounts for the light, variable winds and total absence of fog.

Most of the gales of the great southern ocean pass well to the south of Easter Island, but their effects are often felt. Heavy swells generated by the storms of the Roaring Forties roll in from the south or southwest, making the southern anchorages untenable.

Summer (December, January, and February) has the best weather of the year; during that time 60 percent of the winds are between northeast and southeast at speeds of 10 to 12 knots. These are referred to as the southeast trades. The variable winds that occur are known locally as "Tangariki" and "Anoraru." Gales are virtually nonexistent at this time of the year. The current is flowing from the northeast at about 5 to 15 miles per day, and the water is at the annual maximum of 73°F.

In autumn the winds continue their variability but come dominantly from the northwest to northeast at

FLOTSAM AND JETSAM

Currency

Easter Island uses the Chilean peso as its basic unit of monetary exchange. There are 100 centisimos in a peso. The approximate rate of exchange is US$1 = 337 pesos.

Language

Spanish is the official language of Easter Island, but some of the people still speak a Polynesian tongue they call Rapa Nui. French and German are also spoken by a few people, as well as English with a Yankee accent.

Electricity

Chilean electric systems are 240v, 50 Hz AC, but you may find some 110v, 60 Hz AC supply left over from the former American military base there. The Hanga Roa Hotel is wired for 110v, 60 Hz AC.

Postal Addresses

Mail comes in at very irregular intervals, and it is recommended that you use other ports of call for mail.

Ports for Making Crew Changes

Easter Island is not a recommended port for making crew changes because of the difficult reef anchorage and generally poor communications, which would make coordination very difficult. A major airline provides service three times a week between Valparaiso and Papeete with a stopover at Easter Island. The closest port for making a change would be Papeete.

External Affairs

Chilean embassies and consulates

Information Center

Agency of National Tourism
Agustinas Street
Santiago
CHILE

---

slightly increased speeds of 10 to 15 knots. Calms are almost nonexistent during this period of the year. There are now a measureable number of gales, averaging about one a month, but major storms stay far to the south. The current has shifted to the north but dropped in speed to zero to five miles per day.

Winter (June, July, and August) is the period of the westerlies, with virtually no northeast or east winds. The winds, however, continue variable. The wind speeds have also increased to 15 to 18 knots and gales average fewer than one per month. Even with the higher winds there are more calms, averaging up to 5 percent of the time. At this time of year the southern storm tracks have moved their farthest north, and Easter Island is barely on the edge of them. The northerly

winds that occur during the winter are called "Papakino," the southwesterlies, "Vaitara."

In the spring the winds return to the easterly semicircle with virtually no westerlies blowing at all. Gales are nonexistent, but calms may occur on at least two days per month. Wind speed averages between 10 and 12 knots. The current is northerly at a speed of 10 to 15 miles per day, and the water temperature is at its lowest for the year, 65°F.

Although the climate in general may be characterized as "moderately maritime-tropical," the island enjoys two seasons—dry and rainy. Rainfall averages 52 inches annually; the monthly average is four to five inches. Winter is the rainy season, although there is some rain in every month of the year. In the summer (February and March) the weather is dry and hot. September and October are the driest months. The rain waters filter through earth of volcanic origin (porous subsoil) and create underground currents along the coastline.

Although the humidity is surprisingly constant the year around, there is daily variation ranging from 85 to 87 percent in the morning to 75 to 80 percent in the afternoon. Temperatures are fairly equable throughout the year with a daily average of 75°F and a daily average low of 63°F. January is the hottest month and August the coolest.

Cruising Notes

YACHT ENTRY

Entering formalities at Easter Island are simple and can be done at either Hanga Roa or Hanga Piko, the latter being a better harbor for sailboats of moderate draft. Call the gobernacion maritima on VHF channel 16 and announce your arrival at one of these harbors. It is best to anchor out for this exercise since surge makes lying alongside a dock a risky affair. Customs and Immigration will come out to your boat, sometimes with police and doctor accompanying them. A passport is required but no visa. The paperwork is minimal.

After the inbound clearance is effected, check with the port captain regarding the best place to anchor and future weather possibilities. As a matter of courtesy, you should also pay your respects to the mayor of Hanga Roa who, next to the island governor, is the most important person on the island.

Sailors in the past have experienced some theft of items from their boats, and you are advised not to tempt

The brooding statues of Easter Island symbolize the enigma of this remote eastern corner of Polynesia. (Barbara Marrett)

the local people. By their standards almost any cruising boat is "rich" and full of "surplus"; in addition, local culture is not founded on the rigid property code of a European-type civilization.

YACHT FACILITIES

There are no safe anchorages at Easter Island, and the prudent cruiser will always leave aboard a capable crew member who can take appropriate action should the wind suddenly shift and the anchorage develop into a lee shore. A number of small bays and coves indent the rocky coastline, and some of them have landing places for dinghies, albeit through the surf line. Four coves in particular may be usable by the cruising boat under different weather conditions. Hanga Roa on the west coast offers a good anchorage from October to April, which is the season of the southeast trades. Should a northerly gale set in, the alternative is to duck around the southwest peninsula, site of the volcano Rana Kao, and anchor in Vinapu (Ovnipoo) cove.

During the southern winter Anakena is the preferred anchorage and is probably the best all-around anchorage on the island for yachts. It is reasonably well protected from all but northerly winds; the sandy beach is quite level and suitable for dinghy landing; and there is little sea or swell that comes into the little cove. (But beware of an errant wave that may make an attempt to upset your dinghy.) Adjacent La Perouse Bay near the

"red hat" quarry is also good in the southern winter. Should severe northerly weather develop, the alternate anchorage is around the east end of Poike Peninsula at Hutuite in the sunset shadows of Rana Roraka volcano and the most famous group of stone statues. Dinghy landing here will be much more difficult, and the recommended landing is at the eastern end of the famous statues at water's edge.

At Hutuite be wary of strong down drafts that

MEDICAL MEMO

Immunization Requirements
A vaccination is required for smallpox if arriving from or having transited an infected area within the last 14 days. Typhoid immunization is also recommended.

Local Health Situation
There are no reported health problems at this time. Flies are abundant and can be a nuisance.

Health Services
A new 20-bed hospital was completed in 1976 and is fully air-conditioned. It is staffed by a doctor and two nurses. There is also a pharmacy (chemist) and a dentist at the hospital. Most medical problems can be handled at this facility. Really major medical problems would have to be transported by airplane to Chile.

Water
You should consider the water suspect and treat it.

may blow down through the valleys. At all these anchorages leave a capable crew person on board for the safety of your vessel.

The principal community on Easter Island is at Hanga Roa and, before going ashore elsewhere, you should make an attempt to anchor there for purposes of getting official clearance. Anchorage should be made outside the six-fathom line (about a quarter to a half mile offshore), thereby staying away from the numerous rocky hazards and foul grounds. With exceptional care one can come into water a fathom deep just southeast of the ruined pier.

Ships use the harbor at Hanga Piko when offloading supplies to lighters, but it appears to have no advantages for small boats and is considerably farther from town than Hanga Roa. There is a pier at Hanga Piko that can be used for dinghy landing. Be wary of staying long at Hanga Piko. One yacht having stopped there was inundated by a rogue wave that had rolled out of an apparently calm sea. You will also be under the flight path of 747 aircraft landing on the runway.

At either Hanga Roa or Hanga Piko you can arrange with local fishermen for shoreboat service at a weekly charge of US$20, but remembering that you may have to leave an anchorage rather suddenly because of a wind shift, this may not be a good bargain.

There are no boat supplies available on Easter Island and no maintenance services. Water and diesel are available, but both have to be carried to your boat via dinghy. A limited stock of canned goods can be found at the government store, and fresh fruits and some vegetables can be obtained from the local people, but these items are very expensive. Fresh meat including beef, mutton, and poultry is also available.

While at Easter Island, you should plan on an island tour. You can hire a private van (about US$75 with guide); a guided tourist van (about US$50 per person); or a horse or trail bike for a self-guided tour. The island is too big to see on foot.

Although Easter Islanders use the Chilean peso as the medium of exchange, far better bargains can be had through trading in goods not available or priced too high for the people to buy at the government store. Items of trade particularly sought by the local people are used clothing (especially jeans), shoes, fish hooks, wire, nylon rope, and even canned goods. These can also be bartered for artifacts such as carvings, shells, and shell jewelry.

CHAPTER 8

PITCAIRN ISLAND

The Country

Pitcairn is an isolated Pacific island whose base is far below the level of the sea. The lack of a coral reef surrounding it indicates its relatively recent origin. It measures about two miles long by one mile wide and at its highest point near the west end rises to a peak of 1,000 feet. Approximately half of its 1,200 acres is cultivated, although of that there are only 88 acres of flat land and another 352 acres of rolling land. The shoreline consists of formidable near-vertical cliffs of volcanic rock preventing easy access from the sea all around.

The soil is rich and fertile but very porous, being made up primarily of decomposed lava with some rich black earth. All the island is thickly covered with luxuriant growth right to the cliffs, which are skirted with thickly branching evergreen trees. Although there are no indigenous animals on the island, there are indigenous fruits and vegetables, including coconut palms, breadfruit, plantains, yams, taro, pandanus, and paper mulberry, which people throughout the Pacific use for mak-

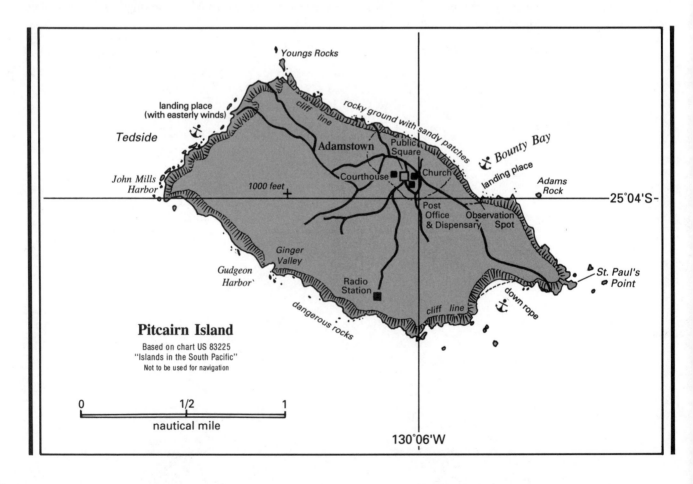

Pitcairn Island

Based on chart US 83225
"Islands in the South Pacific"
Not to be used for navigation

PITCAIRN ISLAND
A British dependency

Port of Entry
Bounty Bay   25°04′ S, 130°06′ W

Distances between Ports in Nautical Miles
Between Bounty Bay and

Hanga Roa, Easter Island	1,120
Mangareva, Gambier Islands	290
Panama City, Panama	3,590
Papeete, Society Islands	1,175
San Diego, California	3,540
Taiohae, Marquesas Islands	1,125
Tubuai, Austral Islands	1,065
Wreck Bay, Galapagos	2,755

Standard Time
9 hours slow on UTC

Public Holidays and Special Events

January 1	New Year's Day—Public holiday
January 23	Bounty Day—Public holiday
March/April *	Good Friday, Easter, and Easter Monday—Public holidays
April 25	ANZAC Day—Public holiday
June **	Queen's Official Birthday—Public holiday
October 8	Labour Day—Public holiday
December 25	Christmas Day—Public holiday
December 26	Boxing Day—Public holiday

*Specific dates vary from year to year.

**Second Saturday of the month

Note: Holidays are not celebrated on a Saturday because that is the Sabbath Day on Pitcairn Island. Holidays falling on Saturdays are celebrated on Sunday instead.

---

ing tapa cloth. Water is obtained principally from rain although in the dry season it can be obtained from intermittent springs in a valley west of the village of Adamstown.

The waters surrounding the island abound in fish —mackerel, rock cod, red snapper, and in the early southern summer, tuna. Crayfish are also plentiful, but the Pitcairners because of their religion do not eat shellfish.

All seafaring folk know the main element of Pitcairn's history, namely, its being the final settlement of the mutineers from HMS *Bounty*. The mutineers landed on Pitcairn on January 15, 1790, following the mutiny off the island of Tofua in the Tonga group on April 28, 1789. Although they found the island uninhabited, there were signs of earlier dwellers in ruins of huts and some crudely carved images, stone hatchets, fish bones, and burial sites on top of the mountain later called Lookout Ridge.

The first Europeans to sight what is now Pitcairn Island were the crew of HMS *Swallow,* Capt. Philip Carteret, commanding, in 1767. It was named after the midshipman Robert Pitcairn, who sighted it first. A description of the island was later published in the 1773 book *Hawkesworth Voyages,* which was aboard the *Bounty* and became the inspiration for the mutineers to sail east in their final pursuit of a new home after being driven off the island of Tubuai in the Austral group.

Once settled on Pitcairn the mutineers and their descendants have lived there continuously except for two brief periods when they were removed to other islands for their supposed benefit. The first occasion was in 1831, when the entire population of 87 persons was transferred to Tahiti to begin a new life under Queen Pomare. Unfortunately, disease and what they considered the amoral conduct of the Tahitians convinced them that they were better off at Pitcairn. After 24 months away from their home island they were back on Pitcairn, but in the meantime natives from Bora-Bora sailing on the French brig *Courier de Bordeaux* had vandalized their homes, and they had to rebuild many of them.

The second migration from Pitcairn took place when the entire population, now numbering 187 persons, departed on the ship *Mrayshire* for Norfolk Island, 3,200 miles to the west. Norfolk Island, a recently abandoned British penal colony with many facilities built by the prisoners, had been offered to the Pitcairners as a bigger and better place to live. Unfortunately, the British retained possession of it, and the Pitcairners became tenants only. Although it was a larger island and the living was good, many Pitcairners longed for their old home, and in 1861 two groups numbering 16 and 26 returned to their home island. From that time on Pitcairners have occupied both islands continuously.

Pitcairn Island is a British dependency with the administration directed from the Office of the Governor of Pitcairn, Henderson, Ducie, and Oeno Islands in Auckland, New Zealand. A combined education officer/government adviser is appointed to the island and acts on behalf of the Pitcairn Island Administration. The Pitcairners essentially rule themselves through an island council made up of a magistrate and eight other members. The pastor and government adviser are advisory members to this council but have no vote. There is also an island court to handle community and civil offenses, but its last case was tried in 1967.

The population of Pitcairn Island on its 200th anniversary (January 15, 1990) was 57 people: 49 islanders, the pastor and his family (5), and the education officer and his family (3). Three other Pitcairners were away in New Zealand attending schools. The population changes every year depending on how many Pitcairners are off-island and whether there are any visitors present at census time.

The economy of Pitcairn is primarily subsistence, with bartering the principal means of exchange. Most of the adults on the island are involved in some form of government work for which they are paid each month. In addition, all men must do public work for the benefit of the community.

There is no income tax on the island, and money is used mostly for off-island trade. Individual income is derived from the sale of wood carvings, woven baskets, and hats to tourists, who come by ship or small boat. The carvings are made of miro wood, which grows on Henderson Island 100 miles east-northeast of Pitcairn. Pitcairners go there once a year in their longboats to gather this wood for their carvings.

A most profitable source of revenue has been the Pitcairn Island stamps collected by philatelists the world around. The funds so obtained are used for community projects such as the maintenance of the radio station and the landing area at Bounty Bay.

Public power is supplied by a diesel generating plant and is available from 0800 to 1100 and 1700 to 2300 daily, fuel supplies permitting. Many homes also have privately owned generators to use outside of public power periods. Pitcairn homes have electric refrigerators, freezers, ovens, and many electrical appliances.

Besides church-connected activities, social life on the island consists of family picnics, fishing, and diving sports plus public dinners to celebrate birthdays. Two special birthdays are of note—Christmas Day and Bounty Day. Video viewing has taken over as a major source of evening entertainment, displacing the traditional film showings and game evenings.

Although most vegetables and fruits are grown locally, Pitcairners rely on four supply ships per year to bring bulk food stuffs, including flour, meat, cereals, canned foods, potatoes, and other modern necessities for the table. A cooperative store set up in 1967 is open two days a week; otherwise there are no other real shops. Pitcairners dress in contemporary Western fashion except for footwear, which most islanders do without except on the Sabbath.

Religion has played an important role in the lives of the Pitcairners ever since 1808, when Alexander Smith, last of the mutineers, seriously took up the Bible. (He had taken the name John Adams in his latter days.) Today the residents follow the teachings of the Seventh-

FLOTSAM AND JETSAM

Currency
The New Zealand dollar is the official currency, but U.S., Australian, and other currencies can usually be exchanged on the island. A Pitcairn Island coin has now been minted and is used along with other money. It is also a collector's item.

Language
The Pitcairners speak contemporary English to visitors, but it may occasionally be punctuated with some words and phrases having roots in the eighteenth century. Among themselves they speak an eighteenth-century English dialect mixed with Tahitian.

Postal Address
Mail comes at very irregular intervals, and it is advised that you use other ports of call for mail.

Ports for Making Crew Changes
Pitcairn is not a recommended port for making crew changes because it has no air service, shipping service is sporadic at best, and it has a difficult reef anchorage. The closest port for making a crew change would be Papeete.

External Affairs
New Zealand embassies and consulates

Information Center
Office of the Governor of Pitcairn, Henderson, Ducie, and Oeno Islands
c/o British Consulate-General
Private Bag
Auckland
NEW ZEALAND

At the center of Adamstown is the public hall and courthouse. The three doors of the building in the center are (left to right) the dispensary, library, and post office. A portion of the church entrance is to the left. (Tom Whiu)

The landing at Bounty Bay. You do not come in here on your own; anchor offshore and the Pitcairners will come out and get you in their surfboat. The landing jetty, boat shed, and canoe houses are visible, as is the "flying fox" rope running up the hill to the right. In the middle distance is St. Paul Rock. (Tom Whiu)

The Bounty Bay jetty is not all work and no play. On an otherwise quiet day, the kids of the island enjoy a refreshing swim. (Mark Balsiger/Ocean Voyages Inc.)

Day Adventists. The Pitcairners observe the Sabbath on Saturday: no work is done on that day. They do not drink alcohol in any form, nor do they smoke.

Pitcairn Island is the largest and only inhabited island of the Pitcairn District, which consists of four islands. The others are Oeno, Ducie, and Henderson atolls.

The Weather

Sitting on the edge of the tropics, Pitcairn enjoys an equable climate with moderate winds. Although there are no regular trade winds, east to northeast winds predominate with westerly winds increasing in frequency in the winter months. Mean speeds range from 11 to 15 knots, and east to southeast gales of short duration may occur perhaps a dozen times a year. Hurricanes have been experienced but are extremely rare. They are the tail ends of South Pacific cyclones occurring in the December–March time period. Most have generated in the Tuamotu Archipelago.

Mean monthly temperatures vary from around 66°F in August to 75°F in February; the absolute range recorded is 50°F to 93°F. The rainfall average for the period 1960–1974 was 71 inches annually, which was evenly spread throughout the year. July and August are the driest months, November the wettest. Relative humidity is usually upwards of 80 percent, and cloud cover averages six-tenths of the sky.

Cruising Notes

YACHT ENTRY AND FACILITIES

Although the number of yachts visiting Pitcairn Island has slowly increased over the years, the numbers are still small. In the mid-1970s an average of three yachts per year called at Pitcairn. By the mid-1980s the number had grown to about 14, where it has leveled off. Approximately half the visiting yachts arrive during April, May, and June.

If you have a ham radio aboard your boat, call Tom Christian while you are still a day or two away from the island and let him know the particulars of your boat and your ETA (see appendix D). Give him an update of your position and ETA as you approach the island, and he will arrange to have a longboat or sportboat take you ashore.

Facilities at Pitcairn for yachts or any other boats

are essentially zero. There are two landing places— Bounty Bay on the northeast side of the island and Tedside on the northwest side of the island. Both are open anchorages, and you are advised to leave a capable crew member aboard to handle the boat in case of a sudden wind shift. In Bounty Bay you can anchor in eight to ten fathoms of water having a sand bottom with some rock. If the easterly winds pick up then you must go to the Tedside anchorage where you can anchor in 12 fathoms of water.

Neither place makes a good anchorage when the wind is northwest to northeast. When that happens, there are two alternatives you may try. Down Rope Bight on the southeast shore is one. It is so named because the only way to get up or down from the plains above is by rope. The other alternative is Gudgeon Harbor off Ginger Valley on the southwest coast. There you can anchor in 12 fathoms over a sandy bottom. The Pitcairners will come and get you in one of their longboats.

If these alternatives do not work, then it is necessary to stand off the island until the weather shifts, which may be in a day or two. The islanders are known for their local weather predictions, and they will advise you of expected changes in the wind necessitating a change in anchorage.

You do not take your own dinghy ashore at Bounty Bay, the main landing place. Instead, you wait

---

MEDICAL MEMO

Immunization Requirements
Pratique is not an official entry requirement, but visiting yachts are urged not to land if they have any illness aboard or have recently visited an area having cholera, smallpox, or yellow fever.

Local Health Situation
No reported medical problems.

Health Services
The Pitcairners have learned to take care of themselves in matters of health and will extend their services to a visiting yacht in need. Medical officers of the South Pacific Health Service have made visits to the island in past years, and some help is received from doctors on ships stopping at the island. Serious illness or injury would have to be attended to elsewhere.

The only drugs available are those that the Pitcairners get from New Zealand for their own use. Use your boat supply first as you will have a better chance of replenishing your stock than they will have of replenishing theirs.

Water
You should consider the water suspect and treat it.

at anchor until one of the island boats comes out to get you. The island boat may be a motorized longboat or an outboard-powered inflatable sportboat. Because of the heavy surf, it takes experienced Pitcairners to negotiate the surfline up to the small pier and landing ramp.

Visitors are welcomed to Pitcairn Island with no official formalities. Although the islanders have developed some immunity to the diseases of civilization, do not plan on landing there if there is any illness aboard. If you want to impress your friends back home, take your passports ashore and have the chief of police stamp them for you.

Some provisions can be obtained here, especially fresh fruits, goat meat, and poultry. Water may be scarce if it has been a dry year. You should plan on buying handicraft articles not only because they are interesting but because their sale helps support the island's economy. Stamps are another "must buy" at Pitcairn.

The people here are very generous and will host you beyond your highest expectations. Reciprocate; see if there is something they need that you have on board and can part with until reaching your next port of call. This does not, however, include alcoholic beverages, ammunition, or pornographic magazines (including many not deemed pornographic in Europe and the United States).

There are no boat parts or services available and no fuels.

CHAPTER 9

COOK ISLANDS

The Country

The 15 Cook Islands are widely scattered and lie between 8 °S and 23 °S and 156 °W and 167 °W. The rectangular area of ocean within which the islands lie amounts to about 850,000 square miles. The total land area of the Cook Islands is a mere 93 square miles, half of which is on the islands of Rarotonga and Mangaia.

The Cook Islands fall into two geographic groupings: the southern group includes Rarotonga, Mangaia, Aitutaki, Mauke, Atiu, Mitiaro, Takutea, and Manuae; the northern group includes Penrhyn, Manihiki, Rakahanga, Pukapuka, Nassau, Suvarov, and Palmerston.

In the southern group of eight islands, Rarotonga, Mangaia, and Atiu are high islands while all the rest are on their way to becoming atolls with low, weathered, central volcanic cores. Rarotonga and Mangaia are the largest islands at 26 and 20 square miles area, respectively.

Rarotonga is the principal island of the whole Cook group; its rugged volcanic interior rises to a height of 2,140 feet. It is surrounded by a fringing reef with very limited boat passages and anchorages. The island has a rich soil on which many vegetables and all types of tropical and subtropical fruits thrive. Most of the islands are covered with thick evergreen bush. Mangaia and Aitutaki are the other two principal islands in the group; they, too, have limited boat passages through the fringing reefs.

The islands of the northern group are mostly dry, forested atolls differing only in size. Penrhyn is the most northerly and the largest with a 108-square-mile lagoon and three passages of which the largest, West Passage, has a 21-foot depth and a 40-yard width. The land area of this atoll is slightly more than 2,400 acres.

Suvarov is the only other island of the northern group that can be entered by small vessels. The pass depth is 15 feet, and there is only a single suitable anchorage inside. Birds abound on the island, and it has been proclaimed a bird sanctuary.

All the other islands of the northern group have small permanent populations limited by water and soil resources.

Early events in the Cook Islands' oral history indicate that the Maoris of New Zealand transited through the Cooks on some of their expeditions. However, it is less certain that they ever settled there. The first Polynesians from Tahiti may have arrived about A.D. 500. About A.D. 1300 other Tahitians sailed via the Cooks to New Zealand and back—hence the Polynesian-Maori culture in the Cooks.

Modern history begins about 1595 when the Spanish explorer Alvaro de Mendaña de Neyra saw the first of the 15 islands as he passed by Pukapuka (Danger) Island. His countryman Quiros noted Rakahanga in 1606. Captain Cook is given official credit for the Western discovery of the Cook Islands in 1774. The Cooks did not escape the *Bounty* mutiny incident. Bligh noted Aitutaki in 1789, and the mutineers of the *Bounty* called there the same year after seizing the ship in Tonga. It is said that the *Bounty* mutineers brought the first oranges and pumpkin seeds to Rarotonga.

The Reverend John Williams of the London Missionary Society first called at Rarotonga on July 25, 1823. The European and Polynesian missionaries he brought to Rarotonga soon converted the native population to Christianity, and the church gained the dominant role in Cook Island affairs. Blue laws were the result but are almost nonexistent today. The Cook Islands were put under British protection in 1888, and in 1901 administrative responsibility was taken over by New Zealand.

The people of the Cook Islands are Polynesian Maoris, akin to the people of Tahiti and the Maoris of New Zealand, whose traditions and culture they share. The estimated population of the Cooks is 18,200 people (down from 21,323 in 1971), with about 12,000 of

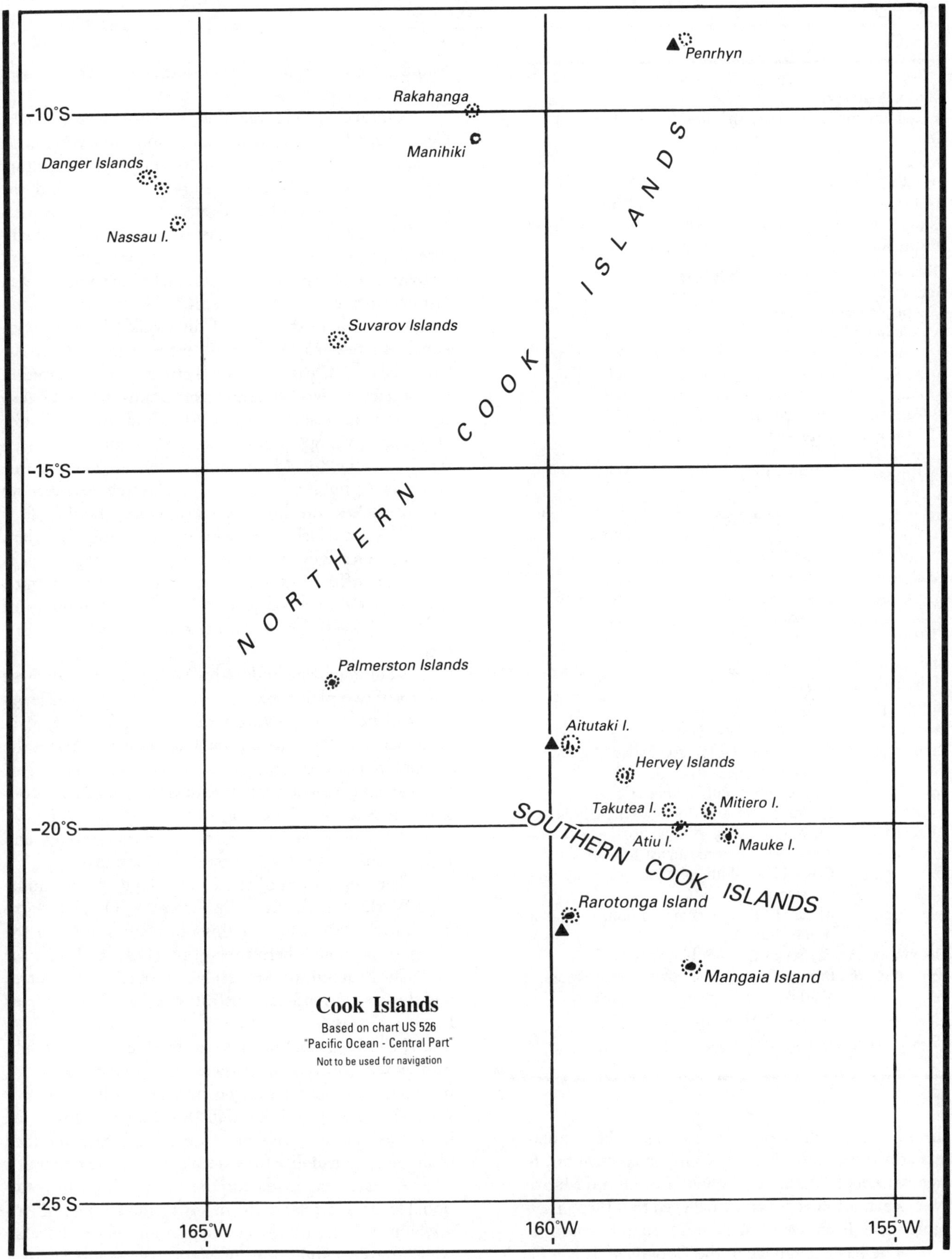

▲ Penrhyn

-10°S

Rakahanga

Manihiki

N O R T H E R N   C O O K   I S L A N D S

Danger Islands

Nassau I.

Suvarov Islands

-15°S

Palmerston Islands

Aitutaki I.

Hervey Islands

Takutea I.   Mitiero I.

Atiu I.   Mauke I.

-20°S

S O U T H E R N   C O O K   I S L A N D S

Rarotonga Island

Mangaia Island

Cook Islands

Based on chart US 526
"Pacific Ocean - Central Part"

Not to be used for navigation

-25°S

165°W   160°W   155°W

COOK ISLANDS

A self-governing country in free association with New Zealand

Ports of Entry

Omoka, Penrhyn	9°S, 158°03′W
Arutanga, Aitutaki	18°52′S, 159°40′W
Taungamiu Landing, Atiu	20°05′S, 158°10′W
Avatiu, Rarotonga	21°12′S, 159°47′W

Distances between Ports in Nautical Miles

Between Avatiu and

Apia, Western Samoa	815
Auckland, New Zealand	1,625
Alofi, Niue	585
Nukualofa, Tonga	860
Pago Pago, American Samoa	745
Papeete, Society Islands	620
Penrhyn, Cook Islands	740
Suva, Fiji	1,245
Tubuai, Austral Islands	585

Between Omoka, Penrhyn, and

Apia, Western Samoa	860
Bora Bora, Society Islands	580
Christmas Island, Kiribati	660
Kanton Island, Kiribati	895
Nukunonu, Tokelau	820
Pago Pago, American Samoa	805

Standard Time

10 hours slow on UTC

Public Holidays and Special Events

January 1	New Year's Day—Public holiday
March/April *	Good Friday, Easter, and Easter Monday—Public holidays
April 25	ANZAC Day—Public holiday
June *	Queen's Official Birthday—Public holiday
August 4	Constitution Day—Public holiday (celebrations carry on from August 1 to 10)
October 26	Gospel Day—Public holiday (open-air religious festival)
November 1	All Saints' Day—Roman Catholic candlelight procession
December 25	Christmas Day—Public holiday
December 26	Boxing Day—Public holiday (horse racing on Muri Beach)
December 31	New Year's Eve

*Specific dates vary from year to year.

them living on the island of Rarotonga. The population growth of the Cook Islands would be positive but for a steady annual migration of about a thousand Maoris to New Zealand. It is generally believed that there are now more Cook Islanders in Auckland than in Rarotonga.

The basic language of the Cook Islands is a Cook Island Maori, but almost everyone speaks English as a second language.

Cultural development is a major aspect of the Cook Islands government education policy. Among objectives are creating an active interest in culture among the Cook Islands children, teachers, and the community as a whole and ensuring the propagation and "keeping alive" of those aspects of Cook Island culture that form the basis of traditional entertainment and festivities. Each island is encouraged to develop its own distinct forms of cultural activity. Religion plays an important role in the lives of the Cook Islanders, with approximately 75 percent of them belonging to the Cook Islands Christian Church (formerly the London Missionary Society). Catholicism claims about 12 percent, and the rest are Seventh-Day Adventists, Latter Day Saints, Congregationalists, and Anglicans. Church services are held in Maori and in English. There is free compulsory public education for children between six and fifteen; several churches also operate schools.

The Cook Island economy is primarily agrarian, with commercially important crops of oranges, coconuts, and coffee, and food crops of taro, yams, manioc (cassava root), and bananas. Only a small number of cattle are raised; fish supply the protein to the islanders' diet.

Manufacturing industries with paid employment consist of two plants making pearl-shell and other jewelery and two manufacturers of clothing for New Zealand markets. The outstanding business enterprise is the canning of citrus concentrate and tomato and pineapple juices. Yachts should plan on stocking up on these products before leaving Rarotonga.

Tipping in the Cook Islands is not customary and can be insulting to these generous Polynesians.

The population of the Cook Islands grew rapidly after World War II, expanding from 14,000 in 1945 to 20,000 in 1966. Most of this population lives on the southern islands, where they grow copra and fruit for the New Zealand market. Island resources are limited, and the Cook Island administration is heavily subsidized by New Zealand.

In 1957 and 1962 steps were taken to grant substantial self-government to the islands. In April 1965 the first general election for the new legislative assembly was held, and in July the islands became self-governing in free association with New Zealand, which retained ultimate responsibility for external affairs and defense.

A place was made for the participation of traditional leaders (*arikis*) in the newly formed House of Arikis, which under the 1965 constitution was to have an advisory role on questions of Maori land tenure and tra-

The lush green interior of Rarotonga is dominated by the 2,140-foot-high Mt. Te Manga. (Earl Hinz)

dition. This marked a partial return to power of the *ari-kis*, who had been the ruling group in the typically stratified Polynesian society before the arrival of the European missionaries in the mid-nineteenth century. The missionaries had changed the society to conform to their Calvinistic ideas. In 1970, the islands still retained strong mission influence in many areas.

The Cook islanders are New Zealand citizens and enjoy entry into New Zealand.

Executive government lies with a cabinet of ministers comprising the premier of the Cook Islands and six other ministers. The premier is elected by the people; the other ministers are appointed by the premier.

The Chief Justice of the British Commonwealth is the acting head of state and the queen's representative. There is also a New Zealand representative on Rarotonga.

The culture of the Cook Islands can best be described as conservative in most ways. The people's dress is more Polynesian than other Polynesian countries, and their lifestyle holds strongly to traditional practices even though Western trends are showing up in Rarotonga. Drinking, rock music, and junk foods are in

evidence, but restrained. It is obvious that the church still retains a strong influence over the people. If you had but one hour to spend on Rarotonga to study the native people, it would be best spent attending a service of the Cook Islands Christian Church. Just hearing the magnificent voices of the islanders singing hymns is enough to justify a visit to the Cooks.

If you had a second hour to spend in Rarotonga, I would advise the more obvious—attend a performance of one of the Cook Islands dance groups. While they dance the same energetic and pulse-quickening dances as do the Tahitians, they do it with less European showmanship. Cook Islands choreographers stick closer to the story line of the legend so that you can imagine the past as your eyeballs dance to the present.

The Weather

The southeast trade winds dominate the vicinity of the Cook Islands. East to southeast winds are the most common and most dependable throughout the region. In the sea area, 15°S to 20°S and 160°W to 165°W, they comprise some 50 percent of the annual winds. Northeast winds prevail during September to April, particularly in the northern islands, but even in these months they are often equaled by easterly or southeasterly winds. In the northern islands northwesterly winds are of some importance in January and February. The average annual wind speed throughout the group is about 11 knots. The strongest winds, 12 to 14 knots, occur in July to September; the lightest, about 9 to 10 knots, occur usually in January to April. Calms are infrequent.

At Rarotonga, 25 percent of the winds are east and 25 percent southeast. South winds are next in frequency with an annual percentage of 9. These south winds are most frequent from May to September. North and northeast winds blow most often in December to February. Calms in the Rarotonga area occur about 13 percent of the time.

All the Cook Islands lie within the hurricane belt of the Southwest Pacific; thus all the islands of the group in the past have suffered from tropical cyclones. Occurrences are infrequent in this area, however, only about one every ten years. Mangaia, Palmerston, Rakahanga, and Pukapuka have all suffered severe hurricane damage in past years. While the main hurricane season extends from December through April, significant occurrences are known as early as November and as late as June. In February 1978 a hurricane hit Rarotonga, causing severe damage in the harbor. The atolls of Palmerston, Aitutaki, Mitiaro, Mauke, and Atiu were also damaged.

The author's wife (center left) enjoys an after-services chat with women of Rarotonga outside the Cook Islands Christian Church. (Earl Hinz)

Hurricanes come from the northwest in the direction of the Samoas. Gales at sea have occurred at times from May to September.

The climate is warm and humid, tempered by the trade winds. Temperatures range between 48°F and 92°F with the cooler months being from May to October. These are also the drier months.

Rarotonga has an average annual rainfall of 83 inches of which 30 inches fall in January to March and 19 inches fall in June to September. At sea, ship reports indicate most frequent rainfall in November to February and least frequent rainfall in June to October. Thunderstorms are most common from February to April and are rare from May to September.

Cruising Notes

YACHT ENTRY

The Cook Islands have been a favorite port of call for cruising boats for years. Suvarov Atoll on the route between Bora-Bora and Pago Pago, although never a Port of Entry, has been the most popular. Rarotonga, until hit by Hurricane Sally in 1987, was a good port of call for reprovisioning besides getting acquainted with a delightful people. Aitutaki, Penrhyn, and most recently Atiu are Ports of Entry with varying degrees of attractiveness to the cruising boat.

CUSTOMS

There are no charges for clearing into a Cook Islands Port of Entry during normal working hours—0800–1600, Monday through Friday. Outside normal working hours during the week and on Saturdays there is a charge of NZ$2.40 per hour; a clearance requires about two hours. On Sundays and holidays the charge starts at NZ$6.40 for the first two hours.

Prior to departing a Port of Entry for other Cook Islands, yachts need to obtain a visiting permit from the chief Immigration officer. When arriving at the other islands, check in with either the Customs officer or the resident agent. Only Takutea, Manuaue, and Nassau islands have neither. Note that although Suvarov is not an official Port of Entry, it is a National Park and has an administrator. Boats have been allowed to stop there without checking in at a formal Port of Entry.

On clearing from the Cook Islands, a departure tax of NZ$20.00 (adults) and NZ$10.00 (children 2–11) will be charged.

FLOTSAM AND JETSAM

Currency
The Cook Islands use New Zealand currency. The Cook Islands also issue their own coinage primarily for collectors. It is not exchangeable outside the Cook Islands.

Language
The indigenous language of the Cook Islands is known as Cook Islands Maori, a Polynesian dialect. English is a second language understood by everyone.

Electricity
Where electricity is available, it is 240v, 50Hz AC.

Postal Address
Yacht ( )
General Delivery
Chief Post Office
Rarotonga
COOK ISLANDS

Mail will be held for three months and then returned to sender by surface mail.

Ports for Making Crew Changes
Rarotonga is a possible port for making crew changes. It is served by international airlines operating between Auckland, Suva, Papeete, and/or Apia. Many of the outer islands such as Aitutaki and Mangaia are served by a domestic feeder airline from Rarotonga.

External Affairs Representative
New Zealand consulates and embassies

Information Center
Cook Islands Tourist Authority
P.O. Box 14
Rarotonga
COOK ISLANDS

Cook Islands women make some of the finest woven handicraft products in all the Pacific. (Earl Hinz)

IMMIGRATION

Entry to the Cook Islands requires a current passport for stays up to 31 days, and these can be arranged at any Port of Entry. If you want to stay longer than 31 days, you will have to show that you are a continuing member of the crew of the boat that will leave on time and that you have sufficient financial means to support yourself. Applications for longer stays must be made in Rarotonga 14 days before the expiration of the 31-day visitor permit. Four months is the maximum length of stay permitted. A fee of NZ$25.00 is charged for an extension.

Matters concerning immigration should be taken up with:

> Principal Immigration Officer
> Ministry of Labour and Commerce
> P.O. Box 61
> Rarotonga
> COOK ISLANDS

FIREARMS

The importation of guns and ammunition is expressly forbidden; if you arrive with firearms on board, they will be seized and held by the police for the duration of your stay.

QUARANTINE

The Cook Islands economy is based primarily on agriculture, and to avoid the introduction of diseases and pests that may be harmful to the economy, Agriculture will confiscate fresh fruits and meats and probably fumigate your boat, especially if you are arriving from ports such as Samoa, Fiji, Tonga, or Tahiti where the rhinoceros beetle exists. If you are carrying a pet on board, it must be confined to the boat during your stay. There is no requirement for posting a bond.

YACHT FACILITIES

Penrhyn
Known earlier by its native name of Tongareva, Penrhyn Atoll is 740 miles north of Rarotonga and has a lagoon easily entered by small ships. The largest pass is Taruia alongside of which is the main village of Omoka. This is the only natural deepdraft harbor in the Cook Islands. On entering fly your Q flag and tie up at the small wharf for clearance if there is no ship present. Only the skipper is allowed ashore.

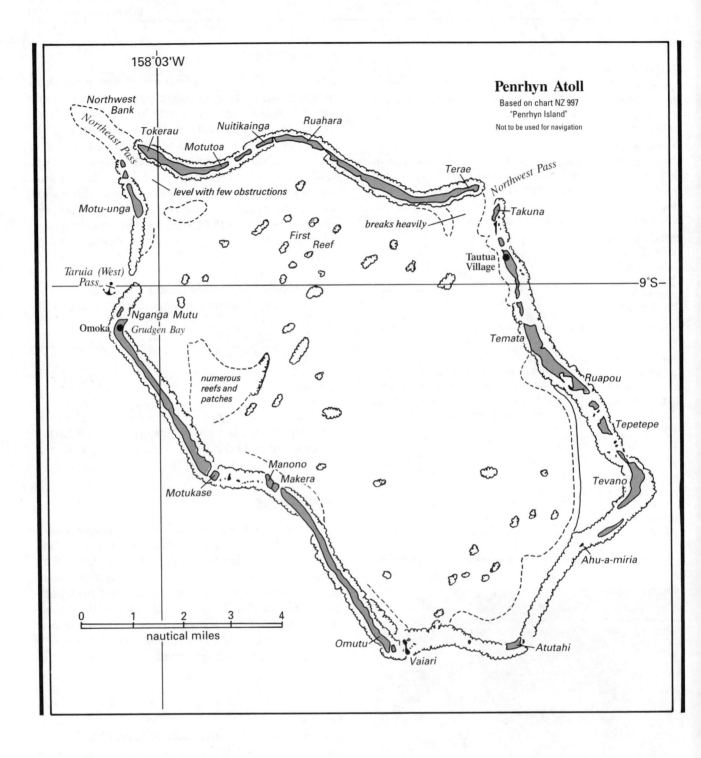

Penrhyn Atoll

Based on chart NZ 997
"Penrhyn Island"

Not to be used for navigation

158°03'W

Northwest
Bank

Northeast Pass

Tokerau

Nuitikainga

Ruahara

Motutoa

level with few obstructions

Terae

Northwest Pass

Takuna

Motu-unga

First
Reef

breaks heavily

Tautua
Village

Taruia (West)
Pass

9°S

Nganga Mutu

Omoka

Grudgen Bay

Temata

numerous
reefs and
patches

Ruapou

Tepetepe

Manono

Tevano

Makera

Motukase

Ahu-a-miria

0 1 2 3 4

nautical miles

Omutu

Vaiari

Atutahi

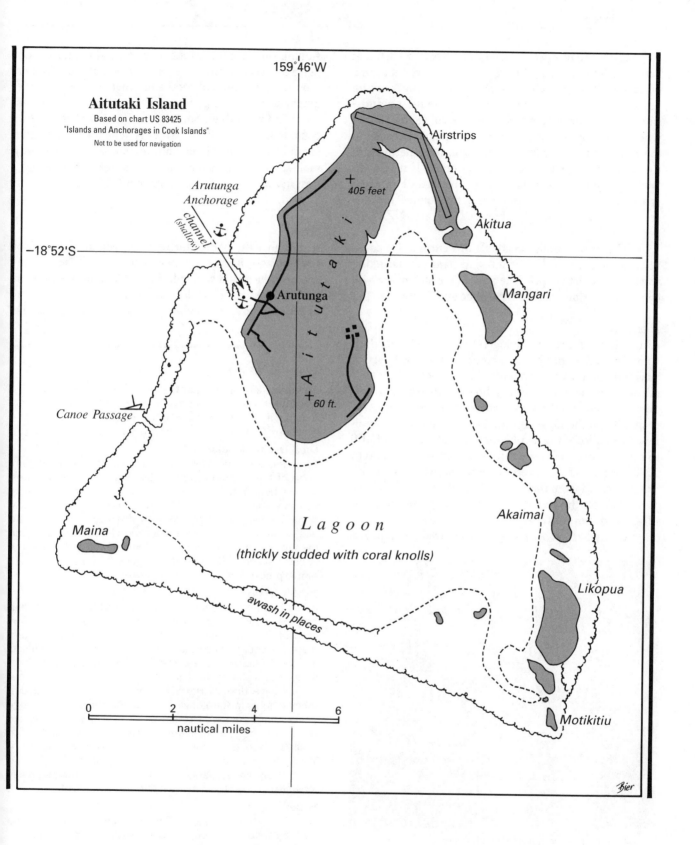

Aitutaki Island
Based on chart US 83425
"Islands and Anchorages in Cook Islands"
Not to be used for navigation

159°46'W

Airstrips

405 feet

*Arutunga
Anchorage*

Akitua

*channel
(shallow)*

−18°52'S

Mangari

● Arutunga

A i t u t a k i

+ 60 ft.

Canoe Passage

Akaimai

L a g o o n

(thickly studded with coral knolls)

Maina

Likopua

awash in places

Motikitiu

0   2   4   6
nautical miles

Bier

There are no special facilities for visiting yachts at Penrhyn. The main anchorage at Omoka can become quite unsatisfactory when the trades are strong, making it a lee shore. At such a time, it is best to request permission to move across the lagoon to the village of Tautua where you will be sheltered from the trades. Because of the pearling industry at Penrhyn, you need permission to move your boat within the lagoon. When you do anchor in the Penrhyn lagoon, try to anchor in open spaces of coral sand in order not to damage the live coral or oyster beds. Harbor charges are NZ$1.75 per day.

The only supplies available at Penrhyn are coconuts, some papaya, breadfruit, and bananas. Drinking water is in short supply. The post office at Omoka will change money and also sells gasoline and liquor.

Aitutaki

Aitutaki, an almost-atoll lying 140 miles to the north of Rarotonga, does not have a harbor for ships or boats. A pass through the reef (maximum water depth of six feet) allows shallow-draft cruising boats, lighters, and dinghies to come into a small wharf at the town of Arutanga. If you should go aground while entering this shallow pass, a local tug can be hired for about NZ$35.00 to tow you off. Shallow-draft boats can anchor in 10 to 12 feet of water at the entrance to the wharf area and can be cleared from there. Deeper-draft vessels will have to anchor on the reef flying their Q flag and wait for officials to come out.

The wharf at Arutanga can be used for reprovi-

Aitutake provides the navigator with instructions for the next leg of his voyage through the Pacific. (Earl Hinz)

sioning, but not for a long stay. Aitutaki is not a good place to reprovision, since its small population does not require large stocks of food and other supplies. You can get the usual tinned goods of the South Pacific and some fruits and vegetables. Some of the finest cabbages grown come from here. Potable water is available, but cruisers should be equipped to catch rainwater at all times. Slow mail service is available via Rarotonga, and there is a hospital with a resident doctor, but local capabilities are limited.

Atiu

Although Atiu is the third largest island in the Cook Archipelago, it is rarely visited by boats. The primary reason is lack of a secure harbor. The only shelter from the weather is on its leeward side. You will have to anchor on the reef and wait for officials to come out. Do

MEDICAL MEMO

Immunization Requirements

Immunizations for smallpox, cholera, and yellow fever are required if you have transited or visited within the last six days (smallpox 14 days) an area currently infected.

Local Health Situation

The climate of the Cook Islands is healthful, and there are none of the common tropical diseases. You will find mosquitoes but no malaria. Dengue fever is also rare, but there was an epidemic of it in 1991. Inhabitants of Rarotonga occasionally suffer from a bad form of diarrhea, and this "Raro bug" is also known to have attacked visitors. Filariasis (and the subsequent development of elephantiasis) still occurs but is being successfully treated in clinics. Visitors should take simple precautions such as wearing sandals at all times.

Health Services

A 100-bed hospital serves Rarotonga, and there is a 40-bed hospital at Aitutaki that will provide medical care at a low cost. In the other islands with populations of 700 or more, there are cottage hospitals with Fiji-trained medical officers and locally trained nurses. Radio advisory service from Rarotonga is available to these facilities. The less populated outer islands have dispensaries with trained attendants. Government schools in Rarotonga have dental clinics, and mobile dental clinics are used elsewhere. Medical and dental service (mostly for the school children) is free for Cook Islanders but available also to visitors who have emergency problems. There are a number of doctors in private practice.

Drugs are available at both hospitals or the pharmacy (chemist) in downtown Avarua. The cost is minimal.

Water

Tap water at Rarotonga is reported to be safe. Water in the outlying areas should be considered suspect and treated.

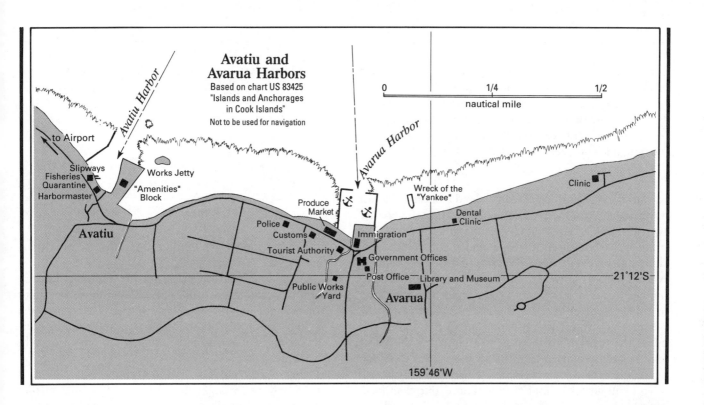

Avatiu and
Avarua Harbors
Based on chart US 83425
"Islands and Anchorages
in Cook Islands"
Not to be used for navigation

0   1/4   1/2
nautical mile

Avatiu Harbor

to Airport

Avarua Harbor

Slipways
Fisheries
Quarantine
Harbormaster

Works Jetty

"Amenities"
Block

Avatiu

Produce
Market

Police

Customs

Tourist Authority

Immigration

Wreck of the
"Yankee"

Clinic

Dental
Clinic

Government Offices

Public Works
Yard

Post Office

Library and Museum

Avarua

21°12'S

159°46'W

This is "main street" in the village of Avarua on Rarotonga. Avarua is the capital city of the Cook Islands and its largest population center. (Earl Hinz)

not leave the vessel unattended as shifting winds have caused trouble for many an anchored vessel.

Atiu is a truly rural island and not a place to provision in any sense of the word. If you go there, enjoy it for its magnificent scenery, limestone caves, native bird life, and ancient ceremonial sites.

Rarotonga

Rarotonga is the principal Cook Island and the center of government, commerce, and transportation. There are two harbors at Rarotonga—Avatiu and Avarua. The primary harbor of Avatiu is intended for commercial shipping; yachts get second choice, if any. Neighboring Avarua harbor, however, has been improved to accommodate as many as a dozen yachts at anchor. Checking in takes place at Avatiu. If there is space along the wharves at Avatiu, tie up with your Q flag flying and await the officials. If there is no room, you should at least be able to make a Tahiti-moor in a vacant spot long enough to obtain your clearance. The harbormaster will advise you what to do after you obtain your clearance. Neither harbor is safe in northerly winds, and the authorities will not permit yachts to stay there during the South Pacific cyclone season.

There is a basic berthing charge of NZ$2.00 for all boats plus daily fees for the two harbors as follows:

LOA (meters)	Daily charge (NZ$)	Minimum charge (NZ$)
up to 8	3.00	15.00
8–12	4.00	20.00
12–15	5.00	25.00
over 15	6.00	30.00

Fees are payable to the Immigration office before departure.

Haulouts can be made on the Fisheries Department slipways at a cost of NZ$2.75 per foot LOA up to a maximum of 50 feet. There is also a ten-ton crane available. Some workboat-type supplies can be purchased at the Cook Islands Trading Co., but no yacht hardware.

Fuel is available at Avatiu harbor—100 gallons or more will be brought by tank truck while smaller amounts are supplied in 44–imperial gallon drums. Potable water is available from faucets along the wharf, and toilets and showers are also on the wharf.

CHAPTER 10

SAMOA

The Country

Historians tell us that in 1722 the Dutch navigator Jacob Roggeveen sighted a new group of islands in mid-Pacific on his way west to Java, but since he calculated their position incorrectly, they continued unknown for another 46 years. In 1768 the French navigator Bougainville refound Roggeveen's islands. He saw natives paddling outrigger canoes far from shore and, thinking they were far-ranging sailors (navigators), called the island group the Navigator Islands. His assumption was wrong: these sailors, using specially designed fast outrigger canoes, were actually chasing schools of bonito, then returning every night to their villages. Since his basis for the name Navigator Islands was erroneous, the islands eventually became known to the Europeans by their native name, Samoa. Following many years of political struggles among Germany, Britain, and the United States, the islands were partitioned into Western (German) Samoa and Eastern (American) Samoa. The British withdrew their claims.

Although the Samoas are really populated by only one people (who are closely related to the Hawaiians, Tahitians, Tongans, and New Zealand Maoris), they are politically divided between Western Samoa, now an independent country, and American Samoa, a U.S. territory. Family members live in both Samoas, and they frequently travel between the islands.

The Samoan social structure is built around the *aiga,* an extended family that may take in as many as several thousand relatives. At the head of the *aiga* are *matai*s (chiefs) who guide the communal economy, which still exists to a great degree. The *matai* is responsible for control of the family lands and property, and it is also his responsibility to care for the well-being of the *aiga* and to represent it in the governing councils.

The Samoans are among the last remaining true Polynesians, and they cling steadfastly to their Samoan culture and traditions. This is called "faa Samoa" and greatly influences their acceptance of Western ways. They are friendly, generous, and totally dedicated to ceremonial and mythological practices that are centuries old.

Since the traditions and the customs of the Samoan people are so strong, visitors should defer to them in order to enjoy their visit. The influence of missionaries is obvious in the Samoan's manner of dress, which is a contradiction to the weather. Men wear long pants or lava-lavas with shirts. Women wear almost floor-length skirts and sleeved blouses. Body coverup in public is "faa Samoa," and visitors are advised to dress accordingly. Sunday is strictly a day of worship and rest.

The Weather

The sea that embraces the Samoa Islands is dominated by east to southeast winds during 57 percent of the annual observations. Easterly winds exceed southeasterly in the ratio of 2 to 1. During June to September more than half of all the winds are easterly. Northeast winds exceed southeast winds only during January to March, but the percentages of occurrence of both are comparatively low. From December to March a monsoon current from west to northwest is frequent, and in February the west wind is dominant. Calms are observed on about 20 percent of the days in the southern hemisphere summer months.

At Apia, Western Samoa, the southeast winds are infrequent, being exceeded by those from the northeast. More than half of the winds are easterly. In the southern summer season there is a noticeable current, which is deflected into the northwest. Calms are frequent, particularly in December, February, and March.

The average annual wind speed both at Apia and

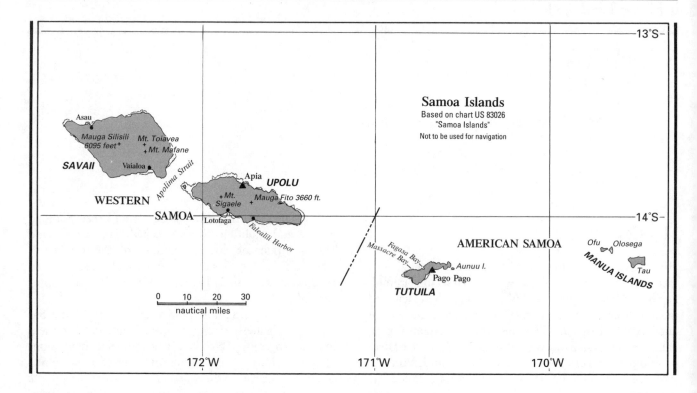

Samoa Islands
Based on chart US 83026
"Samoa Islands"
Not to be used for navigation

at sea is about 8 knots. The higher speeds at sea, some 10 to 11 knots, occur in August and September, and the lower speeds, some 2 to 7 knots, from November to April.

Gales are not uncommon at sea during most months, but those that hit the shoreline result from hurricane activity in the vicinity and occur during the southern summer. The islands of Samoa lie within the South Pacific tropical cyclone belt, and these cyclonic storms are known to occur during the months of December to April.

The analysis of Tropical Cyclone Ofa in chapter 3 is of particular importance to boats planning on staying the hurricane season in the Samoas. As attractive as the harbor of Pago Pago, American Samoa, is for an extended stay, it is not to be relied on as a hurricane haven. The surrounding mountains tend to give a false sense of security. Nowhere in the Samoas is there a harbor offering adequate protection against a severe tropical cyclone.

The Samoas experience occasional earthquakes, but these have not done significant damage in the past. Their biggest danger is in creating seismic waves causing tsunamis in other islands of the South Pacific.

Since the islands in the Samoa group are, as a whole, in close proximity to each other, the climate conditions affecting all of them will be similar. Although the islands are not far from the equator, the tropical climate is mild, equable, and healthful, with temperatures ranging between 72°F and 86°F. The cooler months are May through November. The climate varies but little during the year because of the great expanse of water surrounding the group.

With regard to rainfall, the year divides itself distinctly, but not sharply, into a dry season, May to October, and a wet season, November to April. There is a wide variation in monthly rainfall from year to year. The wettest month, January, has a range between 5 inches and 65 inches. The annual rainfall has varied in the past two decades from 130 inches to 284 inches.

Rainfall is frequent in all localities, more particularly during the southern summer season, and at sea, extending even into July. The annual rainfall at Apia is more than 100 inches, while that at Pago Pago is nearly 200 inches. The local differences are due to the considerably varying exposures among the islands. Thunderstorms are most frequent from December to March. The heaviest rainfall also occurs from December to March. During the cooler months of April to November, the trade winds make living more pleasant and comfortable.

AMERICAN SAMOA

The Country

The Territory of American Samoa is an insular possession of the United States, administered by the Department of the Interior. Comprising the eastern islands of the Samoa group, it is situated south of the equator at 14°S and about 170°W.

American Samoa is composed of seven tropical islands and is the only U.S. soil south of the equator. The islands lie some 2,300 miles southwest of Hawaii and about 1,600 miles northeast of New Zealand.

The total land area of all seven American Samoa islands is only 76 square miles. A very small amount of the land is owned fee simple by individuals, but more than 96 percent is owned communally and is regulated as to occupancy and use by traditional Samoan custom.

The total population of American Samoa is 42,000 of which 10,500 are from Western Samoa, 1,100 from Tonga, and a smattering from two dozen other Pacific countries. A large number of illegal aliens are also suspected to be present. The largest villages are Pago Pago (pronounced "pahngo pahngo") with 3,060 people, Nuuuli with 2,600, Fagotogo with 1,960, and Leone with 1,700.

A view of Pago Pago harbor looking south from the Mt. Alava (1,610 ft. high) terminus of the aerial tramway. Commercial wharves are in the center, fish canneries are in the foreground, and the yacht harbor is off to the right of the picture. (Jim Howard)

AMERICAN SAMOA
An unincorporated territory of the United States

Port of Entry
Pago Pago, Tuutila   14°17′ S, 170°41′ W

Distances between Ports in Nautical Miles
Between Pago Pago and

Alofi, Niue	290
Apia, Western Samoa	75
Auckland, New Zealand	1,560
Bora-Bora, Society Islands	1,105
Funafuti, Tuvalu	690
Neiafu, Tonga	325
Nukunonu, Tokelau	315
Mata Uta, Wallis Islands	325
Papeete, Society Islands	1,235
Penrhyn, Cook Islands	805
Rarotonga, Cook Islands	750
Suva, Fiji	670

Standard Time
11 hours slow on UTC

Public Holidays and Special Events

January 1	New Year's Day—National holiday
February *	Presidents' Day—National holiday
March/April *	Good Friday and Easter Sunday—Public holidays
April 17	Flag Day—Public holiday
May *	Memorial Day—National holiday
July 4	Independence Day—National holiday
September *	Labor Day—National holiday
October *	White Sunday—Day of honor to children
October *	Discoverers' Day—State holiday
November 11	Veterans Day—National holiday
November *	Thanksgiving—National holiday
December 25	Christmas Day—National holiday

*Specific dates vary from year to year.

The main island of Tutuila runs east and west with a spiny, jungle-covered mountain range running from one end to the other. Tutuila is almost bisected by famed Pago Pago Bay, which is recognized as one of the best harbors in the South Pacific. Governmental operations and a great portion of the commercial activities are in the bay area.

Aunuu is a small island off the southeastern shore of Tutuila. The Manua group, composed of Tau, Olosega, and Ofu, lies about 60 miles east of Tutuila. The Manua population is below 4,000. Swains Island, a small, privately owned coral atoll, is about 280 miles north of Tutuila and has a population of about 70 people. Rose Island, a small island 250 miles to the east of

Tutuila and the seventh in the American Samoa group, is a tiny, uninhabited atoll.

U.S. exploration of what is now American Samoa came 61 years before formal relations were established between the powerful nation of the northern hemisphere and the group of tiny islands in the South Pacific. U.S. interest in the islands of Samoa began with a report made by the U.S. exploring expedition that visited the islands under the leadership of Lt. Charles Wilkes in 1839. It was not until some 30 years later, however, that a formal relationship was entered into with the people of Samoa by a representative of the United States. Primarily as a result of commercial interest in obtaining harbor facilities and right for a coaling station on the shores of Pago Pago Harbor, the USS *Narragansett* visited Tutuila in 1872. Comdr. Richard Meade entered into an agreement entitled "Commercial Regulations, etc." with High Chief Mauga, the high chief of Pago Pago. While this treaty was never ratified by the U.S. Senate, it served effectively to prevent foreign influences from asserting any strong claim to the harbor.

In January 1878, a further treaty of friendship and commerce was negotiated with the leaders of the villages adjacent to Pago Pago; this treaty was ratified later in the same year. Proclaimed jointly by the United States and "the Government of American Samoan Islands," this treaty remained in force for more than 20 years.

As a result of international rivalry between Great Britain and Germany and because of warfare between various factions of the Samoan population, the United States, Germany, and Great Britain entered into a general act on June 14, 1889, for the purpose of providing for "the security of life, property, and trade of the citizens and subjects of the respective governments who were residing in or having commercial relations with the islands of Samoa." This act also had as its aim the desire "to avoid all occasions of dissensions between their respective governments and the people of Samoa" while at the same time "promoting as far as possible the peaceful and orderly civilization of the people."

Under this tripartite agreement a form of government for the islands was brought into being. However, after a trial of some ten years, it proved to be ineffective and destructive of the ends for which it was created and was superseded by the convention of 1899.

A major provision of the convention was the renunciation by Great Britain and Germany of any claims to the islands of the Samoa group east of longitude 171°W. Reciprocally, the United States renounced in favor of Germany all rights and claims with respect to

Rest and recreation have been the mission of Pago Pago businesses since the early days when it was a U.S. Navy coaling station. (Earl Hinz)

the islands of Upolu and Savaii and all other islands west of 171°W. This treaty was ratified on February 16, 1900, and on February 19 of the same year President McKinley directed the secretary of the navy to "take such steps as might be necessary to establish the authority of the United States" on the island of Tutuila and other islands of the Samoa group east of longitude 171°W.

The secretary of the navy established a naval station at Pago Pago. In 1900, deeds of cession were negotiated with the leading chiefs and orators of Tutuila and Aunuu, and on April 17 the U.S. flag was raised for the first time over these islands. On June 14, 1904, the high chief Tui Manua, king of Manua, and the other chiefs of Manua agreed also to cede their lands to the United States.

The islands remained under navy administration with Pago Pago as an active naval base from 1900 to 1951. During this time considerable progress was made in the establishment of public works and medical and educational facilities. Little was done to disturb the traditional village life of the Samoan people, who are not U.S. citizens but are classed as nationals and have unrestricted entry into the United States.

Under the terms of the deeds of cession, the United States agreed that the chiefs of the villages would be permitted to retain their individual control over their separate villages, provided that their control was in accordance with the laws of the United States pertaining to Samoa and provided that such control was not obstructive to the peace of the people and the advancement of civilization. The United States also agreed to respect and protect the individual rights of the people, especially in respect to their lands and other property. As a result of this commitment, no large tracts of Samoan communally owned land have been alienated during the years that the United States has had administrative responsibility of these islands.

In 1951, the president of the United States transferred the administration of American Samoa from the secretary of the navy to the secretary of the interior. Since that time there have been great advances in the social welfare of the people of American Samoa, as well as political advancement toward internal self-government. The latter culminated in 1978 with the election by the people of their first native governor and lieutenant governor.

Years of government support have reduced the local economy to a near welfare status. Traditional fishing and agricultural activities have almost disappeared, and the population lives on a cash economy. The only major industry that is flourishing is fish canning, and even here the fishing is done by other countries under contract to the canneries.

American Samoa is becoming an increasingly popular port of call for yachts as shown by the numbers of visiting yachts:

1971	38
1972	55
1976	85
1983	171
1984	179
1987	288

Cruising Notes

YACHT ENTRY

A boat entering American Samoa must clear at Pago Pago before going any other place in the territory. As soon as you are within VHF range of Pago Pago harbor, call harbor control on VHF channel 16 and request that they notify Customs of your pending arrival. Then

Cruising boats are rafted-up for check-in at the yacht clearance wharf alongside the Malaloa marina in Pago Pago Harbor. Other cruising boats are anchored in the background. Idle American tuna clippers are moored to the right. (Earl Hinz)

FLOTSAM AND JETSAM

Currency
American Samoa uses U.S. currency (see Hawaii for description). The relative cost of goods is approximately 100.

Language
The indigenous language of American Samoa is Samoan, but 85 percent of the population can speak English.

Electricity
Tutuila is well electrified with 110v, 60 Hz AC.

Postal Address
Yacht ( )
General Delivery
Pago Pago AS 96799
USA

Ports for Making Crew Changes
Pago Pago is a recommended port for making crew changes, having U.S. domestic airline service from Honolulu and international airline service from Auckland, Sydney, and Papeete. There also is reasonably good mail and electronic communication with the United States.

External Affairs Representative
U.S. consulates and embassies

Information Center
Director of Tourism
Government of American Samoa
P.O. Box 1147
Pago Pago AS 96799
USA

---

proceed directly to the check-in wharf at Malaloa small-boat harbor. Be prepared to berth alongside a rough concrete wharf. Do not leave your boat since you are in quarantine until cleared.

If you arrive on a weekend or holiday and want to avoid extra charges, tie up to the quarantine buoy (no. 3) if available or anchor nearby with your Q flag flying until the first working day after the holiday or weekend.

CUSTOMS

A *zarpe* from your previous port of departure is required to enter American Samoa. Even American boats arriving directly from another American port are required to have a *zarpe* from that port of entry. Customs has been adamant about this procedure.

Visitors are required by law to make a written customs declaration. There is a US$50.00 combined entering and departing fee payable to Customs.

After clearing in, walk to the harbormaster's office at the main wharf and get a mooring assignment. Failure to do this or later movement without his prior approval may draw an instantaneous $100.00 fine.

IMMIGRATION

A passport or visa is not required for U.S. citizens to enter American Samoa. A birth certificate, driver's license, or other valid identification is sufficient. All other persons must have a valid passport.

You may visit American Samoa for a period of up

to 30 days without getting special permission from the Department of Immigration. All visitors must have a return or onward airline ticket or post a cash landing bond. A boat is considered valid transportation for those whose names appear on the entry crew list and have sufficient funds for 30 days.

If you wish to stay longer than 30 days, you must apply for a permit through the Department of Immigration. Visas can be extended for a maximum of 90 days.

FIREARMS

Firearms, ammunition, and explosives of any kind are prohibited.

QUARANTINE

American Samoa is free of rabies, and pets are not allowed on shore. A bond of US$500 must be posted to assure authorities that the pet will not leave the yacht. Animals coming from rabies-free countries (as determined by a certificate of birth) can be quarantined on the boat for 60 days and then taken ashore.

YACHT FACILITIES

Tutuila is the main and largest island of American Samoa and the location of Pago Pago, which is the finest natural harbor in the South Pacific. Surrounded by steep mountains more than 1,000 feet high and with an L-shaped, reef-bordered entrance, it offers as much protection as is possible from heavy winds and high seas.

These lads were intercepted near the village of Afono on the north shore of Tutilla Island. They were bringing home baskets of breadfruit, a staple for all islanders. (Earl Hinz)

Pago Pago is not the pristine harbor dreamed of by cruisers. It reeks of fish canneries; noise from the electric generating plant is pervasive; roads are full of potholes because of the abundance of rain; and water and seabed are both heavily polluted. Such conditions should not be unexpected since this is an industrial harbor of long standing; only in recent years has tourism with its requirements for a more aesthetic environment become important. It will be a long time before this beautiful South Seas setting will attain the purity of a tourist's paradise. In the meantime, it is the finest reprovisioning port between Hawaii and New Zealand.

A small-boat harbor has been built at the west end of the main harbor, and boats can moor Tahiti-style inside it. There are no amenities although electricity can be bootlegged, and cruisers have built a shower enclosure. The "check-in wharf" is part of the marina breakwater. Improvements being made to this area will make life more pleasant for the visiting cruiser.

The mooring buoys in the inner harbor are on a first come, first served basis; otherwise there is plenty of room to anchor at the west end of this large harbor. The bottom of the harbor is muddy sand, and the abundant debris on the bottom makes secure anchoring difficult.

MEDICAL MEMO

Immunization Requirements
Immunizations for cholera and yellow fever are required if you have transited or visited within the last six days an area currently infected.

Local Health Situation
You will find mosquitoes a nuisance in American Samoa, but there is no dengue fever or malaria. Visitors are advised to have typhoid shots. In the water the crown of thorns starfish and the stonefish should be avoided, for their sting is painful and debilitating. Filariasis and elephantiasis are still evident, but cases are declining.

Health Services
There is no private medical practice in American Samoa; the LBJ Tropical Medicine Center provides a hospital and doctors. Most of the doctors are from the United States. Dental and optical services are also available at the LBJ Center. Medications are dispensed at the LBJ Center or the one pharmacy in town. A doctor's prescription will be required for certain drugs.

Water
The tap water at Pago Pago is reported to be questionable and should be treated, as should water taken at any other American Samoa stop.

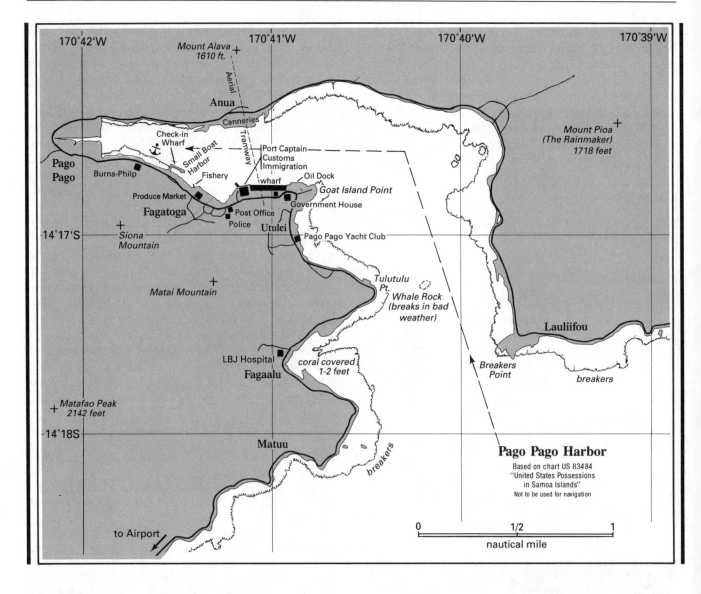

Pago Pago Harbor

Based on chart US 83484
"United States Possessions
in Samoa Islands"
Not to be used for navigation

A bigger problem is the presence of ill-kept and carelessly operated fishing boats, which are a severe danger at all times and especially so if a hurricane threatens.

The harbormaster will assign you as far as possible to your choice of mooring buoys or anchorage at the closed end of the harbor. Monthly harbor fees for the first three months are as follows:

Boat length (feet)	At anchor (US$)	On buoy (US$)
20–30	8.50	12.50
30–40	12.50	15.00
40–50	15.00	17.50
50–60	17.50	22.50
over 60	22.50	27.50

After three months' time the rates are doubled. Boats are not allowed to change locations without the permission of the harbormaster. Do not expect these low rates to continue indefinitely; the pressure of inflation is certain to drive them up in the near future.

It is also possible to rent private moorings for US$200–$250 per "hurricane season." These moorings are by and large made up of surplus or used machinery parts and should be carefully inspected before you trust your boat to them in a blow. Do not move to one of these moorings without first advising the harbormaster.

There is no slipway available for small boats. The Ronald Reagan Marine Railway caters to small ships and the fishing fleet and discourages use by small boats except on a shared basis. There are plans for a crane to lift boats onto the hard in the fisheries area, but no time schedule has been set. Other amenities are also being talked about.

Pago Pago is a good port for reprovisioning, with food products from both the United States and New Zealand. Liquor and tobacco are duty free for a departing boat. There are a number of wholesale outlets where case lots of food may be purchased. Fuel is available at the fuel dock and fresh water at all docks.

It is also worth noting that for airlines and mail,

American Samoa is considered a domestic destination, thereby enjoying low domestic airline rates to the United States as well as all first-class mail by air.

The Pago Pago Yacht Club has gained a reputation for friendliness toward cruising folk and should be visited. It is at Utulei, a long walk or short ride from Malaloa. Besides food and drink, you can mingle with locals and cruising folk and even join a Samoan canoe racing team for exercise.

WESTERN SAMOA

The Country

Western Samoa lies in the Pacific Ocean 1,600 miles northeast of Auckland, New Zealand. The main islands are formed from ranges of extinct volcanoes, which rise to 6,094 feet on Savaii and 3,608 feet on Upolu. Volcanic activity last occurred in 1911. The climate is tropical, with wet and dry seasons.

Archeological evidence suggests that Western Samoa was inhabited as early as 3000 B.C. by waves of migrants from Southeast Asia, but Polynesian oral histories and traditions do not go back beyond A.D. 1250. Samoans are the second-largest Polynesian group (after the Maoris of New Zealand) and speak a Polynesian dialect.

Samoan contact with Europe began with the visit by Dutch navigator Jacob Roggeveen; but not until 1830, following the arrival of English missionaries under John Williams, did contacts become intensive.

Between 1847 and 1861, Great Britain, the United States, and Germany established consular representation at Apia. Intrigues and jealousies among these representatives and the Samoan royal families reached a climax in 1889, when the signing of the Final Act of the Berlin Conference on Samoan Affairs brought Samoan independence and neutrality. Malietoa Laupapa was recognized as king.

After the death of the king in 1898, a dispute over succession to the throne led to adoption in 1900 of a series of conventions whereby the United States annexed

Eastern Samoa and Germany took Western Samoa. Great Britain withdrew in return for recognition of its rights in other Pacific islands.

In 1914, following the outbreak of war in Europe, New Zealand's armed forces occupied Western Samoa. In 1919 New Zealand was granted a League of Nations mandate over the territory. By the Samoa Act of 1921,

The Western Samoa police band provides stirring music every morning at 0800 preparatory to the flag-raising ceremony in front of the prime minister's office. (Earl Hinz)

WESTERN SAMOA

An independent nation.

Port of Entry

Apia, Upolu   13°50′ S, 171°55′ W

Distances between Ports in Nautical Miles

Between Apia and

Alofi, Futuna	355
Alofi, Niue	330
Auckland, New Zealand	1,555
Avatiu, Cook Islands	815
Fakaofa, Tokelau	270
Funafuti, Tuvalu	620
Neiafu, Tonga	315
Mata Utu, Wallis Islands	255
Pago Pago, American Samoa	75
Port-Vila, Vanuatu	1,165
Suva, Fiji	620

Standard Time

11 hours slow on UTC

Public Holidays and Special Events

January 1	New Year's Day—National holiday
March/April *	Good Friday, Easter, and Easter Monday—Public holidays
April 25	ANZAC Day—Public holiday
June 1–3	Independence Day—Public holiday (competitions, feasts, and speeches by talking chiefs)
October *	White Sunday—Day of honor to children
November 11	Arbor Day—Public holiday
December 25	Christmas Day—Public holiday
December 26	Boxing Day—Public holiday
December 31	New Year's Eve—Samoan bamboo fireworks, singing, and dancing

*Specific dates vary from year to year.

New Zealand made provisions for a civil administration, and progress was made in education, health, and economic development.

Some of the New Zealand government's measures were unpopular with the conservative Samoans, and a resistance movement based on civil disobedience lasted until 1936. Steps taken by New Zealand toward a more representative Samoan administration were interrupted by World War II.

In December 1946 Western Samoa was placed under a U.N. trusteeship with New Zealand as administering authority. The Samoans asked that they be granted self-government, but this petition was not accepted by the United Nations at the time.

From 1947 to 1961 a series of constitutional advances, assisted by visits from U.N. missions, brought Western Samoa from dependent status to self-government and finally to independence. In March 1953 New Zealand proposed a quickened pace of political and economic development, and a constitutional convention, representing all sections of the Samoan community, met in 1954 to study proposals for political development. Most of its recommendations were adopted by New Zealand and governed the territory's evolution toward cabinet government.

In January 1959 a Working Committee of Self-Government empowered to work out a draft constitution was established with New Zealand's approval. Cabinet government was inaugurated in October 1959, and Fiame Mattaafa, F.M. II, became the first prime minister.

At the request of the United Nations, a plebiscite was held in May 1961, and an overwhelming majority

The Apia waterfront is a typically British colonial style scene that could be right out of a Somerset Maugham South Seas novel. The famous hostelry of Aggie Grey's is just to the right of the picture. (Earl Hinz)

of the Samoan people voted for independence. In November 1961 the U.N. General Assembly voted unanimously to end the trusteeship agreement, and the New Zealand parliament passed the Independent State of Western Samoa Act, formally ending New Zealand's powers over the country on January 1, 1962.

Samoans have tended to retain their traditional ways despite exposure to European influence for more than 150 years. Most Samoans live within the traditional social system based on the *aiga,* or extended family group, headed by a *matai,* or chief. The title of *matai* is conferred upon any eligible member of the group, including women, with the common consent of the *aiga.* In addition to representing the *aiga* in village and district *fono*s (councils), the *matai* is responsible for the general welfare of the *aiga* and directs the use of family lands and other assets.

Apart from Apia, the capital and commercial center, Western Samoa has no major towns. Most people live in some 400 coastal villages, whose populations range from 100 to more than 2,000. In 1990 the population numbered 186,000. Of these, 86,500 lived on Upolu, 3,500 of them in Apia. The island of Savaii had 45,000 inhabitants. Among this population were approximately 2,500 Europeans.

Western Samoans are Christians, with 55 percent of the population belonging to the Congregational Church and 40 percent equally divided between the Roman Catholic and Methodist churches.

Education is free but not compulsory. In 1967, 95 percent of the children of primary school age went to school.

Western Samoa is divided into districts for purposes of government services in health, education, police, and agriculture. The only district officer is the administrator on Savaii.

Western Samoa's two most famous citizens are Aggie Grey and Robert Louis Stevenson. Aggie created the now-legendary Aggie Grey's Hotel in Apia out of a hamburger hut in which she served hamburgers to American military personnel passing through Western Samoa during World War II. Accommodations started with a ten-room grass and bamboo structure, short on everything but hospitality. It has since grown to 140 rooms and became the best known of South Pacific hostelries. A real treat for the cruising boat crew is a dinner at Aggie Grey's, where the atmosphere of the bygone days still exists.

Robert Louis Stevenson, well-known author of *Treasure Island* and many other books, chose to spend the last years of his life at Upolu. He built a magnificent

FLOTSAM AND JETSAM

Currency
The Western Samoa dollar is called a tala, and it is equal to 100 sene. Coins are issued in 1, 2, 3, 10, 20, and 50 sene. The approximate rate of exchange is US$1 = 2.32 tala. The relative cost of goods is 94.

Language
The official language of Western Samoa is Samoan, but English is widely used and understood by most Samoans.

Electricity
Where electricity is available it is 240v, 50 Hz AC.

Postal Address
Yacht ( )
General Delivery
Apia
WESTERN SAMOA

Ports for Making Crew Changes
Apia is not a recommended port for making crew changes. It does have some international airline service from Fiji, but the daily service connecting it with Pago Pago makes it better to change crews in Pago Pago.

External Affairs Representative
New Zealand or British consulates

Information Center
Western Samoa Visitors Bureau
P.O. Box 862
Apia
WESTERN SAMOA

Islands Style founder Sophia Rankin shows off one of the many locally designed and made projects of interest to the visitor to Western Samoa. (Earl Hinz)

house on a hill behind Apia and became known locally as Tusitala—teller of tales. He is buried atop Mt. Vaea, and a pilgrimage up the mountain is a pleasant half-day journey, but better done in the morning when it is cool. You'll travel along the "Road of Loving Hearts," so named after Stevenson's friends who first cut the trail to the top of Mt. Vaea.

Stevenson's monument carries his immortal words so appropriate to the cruising sailor:

Under the wide and starry sky,
Dig my grave and let me lie;
Glad did I live and gladly die,
And I laid me down with a will.

This be the last verse you grave for me;
Here he lies where he longed to be;
Home is the sailor, home from the sea,
And the hunter home from the hill.

Many items of memorabilia from Stevenson's life are on display at the new Robert Louis Stevenson Museum and Samoan Cultural Center at Vailima.

Cruising Notes

YACHT ENTRY

Apia is the only Port of Entry for Western Samoa. Yachts arriving in Apia should proceed to the main dock and lay alongside until greeted by the harbormaster, who will call the Health officer. After his inspection, Customs, Immigration, and Agriculture will be called. Do not leave your boat until clearance is given by Health and Immigration officers. If Customs does not come to the boat, you will have to go to them at the main entrance to the harbor property. There is an 11-tala entry fee. Passports are required of all foreigners, but no entry permit is required for visitors staying 30 days or less. Those who intend to stay longer should apply for an entry permit at the Immigration office.

If you wish to visit other harbors with your boat while in Western Samoa you will need to obtain permission from the prime minister's office. The prime minister's office will prepare a letter of permission in five copies, one for each of the departments to get their endorsement. If you plan on departing Western Samoa from one of the other ports, be certain that your letter of permission clearly states which one.

YACHT FACILITIES

The harbor at Apia is normally safe from May to November but is exposed to gales during the wet season of December through April. It is advised that yachts not plan on staying in Apia for any length of time during the hurricane season.

There are no dockside facilities at Apia. The commercial dock may be used temporarily for loading and unloading but not for overnight tieup. Yachts generally anchor inshore, where there is a good holding ground. Security of unattended yachts has been questioned in past years, so it is best to inquire of the harbormaster on the state of affairs when you arrive.

If you leave your dinghy on the beach, be sure that it is high and dry or you will find local children playing in it. Always take the oars with you or they will disappear. Your dinghy can be tied off inside the main dock, but stay clear of the harbor tugs, which may have to depart while you are gone. There are no harbor charges.

While it is recommended that you undertake all repairs and maintenance at Pago Pago, where facilities are better and supplies more adequate, you can get a haulout at Apia on slips used for small-boat maintenance. The facilities are quite rustic, however, and skilled labor hard to find.

Potable water and diesel fuel are available at the dock, and the town of Apia has a good variety of canned

MEDICAL MEMO
Immunization Requirements
Immunizations for smallpox, cholera, and yellow fever are required if you have transited or visited within the last six days (smallpox 14 days) an area currently infected.

Local Health Situation
You will find mosquitoes a nuisance in Western Samoa, and they have at times carried dengue fever. There is no malaria.

Health Services
These can be had at the Apia General Hospital and district hospitals in the outlying areas. There is no private service. Dental and optical care is also available at these hospitals. Drugs are available from the Apia General Hospital or the private pharmacies (chemists) in Apia. Prescriptions are not needed, and the prices are extremely low.

Water
Tap water at the Apia dock has been reported safe, but water in the outlying areas should be considered suspect and treated.

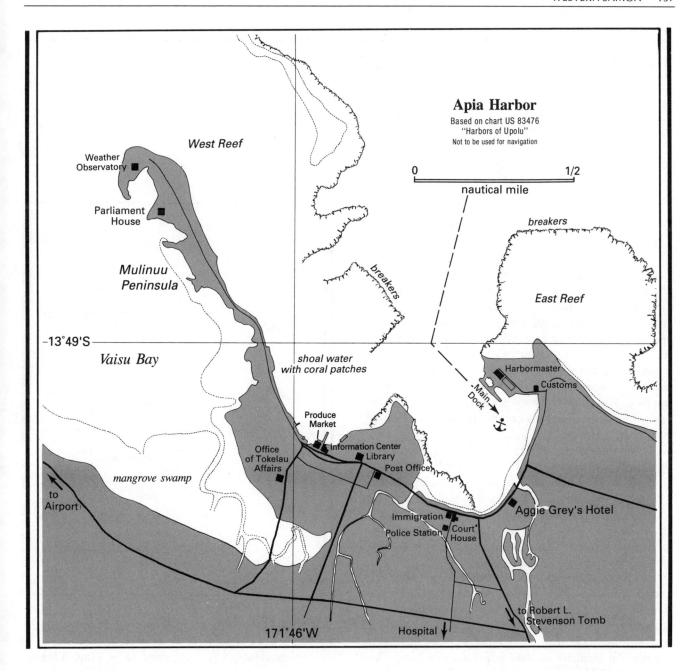

Apia Harbor
Based on chart US 83476
"Harbors of Upolu"
Not to be used for navigation

West Reef

Weather
Observatory

Parliament
House

*Mulinuu
Peninsula*

Vaisu Bay

−13°49'S

breakers

East Reef

breakers

*shoal water
with coral patches*

Harbormaster

Customs

Main
Dock

Produce
Market

Office
of Tokelau
Affairs

Information Center
Library

Post Office

mangrove swamp

to
Airport

Immigration

Police Station

Court
House

Aggie Grey's Hotel

to Robert L.
Stevenson Tomb

Hospital

171°46'W

0   1/2
nautical mile

and dried foods and much fresh fruit at reasonable prices.

On the island of Savaii there are two non–Port of Entry harbors you can visit while harbor hopping west. Saleolago Harbor is relatively indifferent, but usable in settled weather. Asau, in contrast, has been well developed with a breakwater, and anchorage can be taken in 25–30 feet of water over a sand bottom. There are numerous other anchorages in little bays around the island useful in settled weather.

CHAPTER 11

TOKELAU ISLANDS

The Country

The Tokelau group, sometimes known as the Union group, is a New Zealand dependency composed of three small atolls lying about 250 miles north of Samoa. The atolls do not lie in close proximity to each other; Faka-ofu and Nukunonu are 40 miles apart, and Nukunonu and Atafu are 50 miles apart. Each atoll is composed of a number of coral islets surrounding a central lagoon into which there are only canoe passes. The islets vary in size from 100 yards to four miles long and none is wider than 400 yards. Their maximum elevation is 10 to 15 feet above sea level.

Nukunonu was the first of the Tokelaus to be sighted by Westerners, this by Captain Edwards on the *Pandora* in 1791. The islands were put under the protection of Great Britain in 1877 and formally annexed in 1916. In 1925 the New Zealand government agreed to administer the islands, and in 1948 they were included in the boundaries of New Zealand. Tokelauans are British subjects and New Zealand citizens.

The group lies in a border area between Polynesia and Micronesia. The indigenous inhabitants are Polynesians similar to the Samoans in physical appearance and cultural life. Because of the very restricted economic and social future in the atolls, the islanders agreed in 1965 to resettle the majority of their population in New Zealand. By 1975 there were 500 Tokelauans in New Zealand. A 1990 census counted 1,700 people on the islands.

Overall administration for Tokelau lies with the administrator of Tokelau, who is responsible to the New Zealand minister of external relations and trade. In practice, most of the powers of the administrator are exercised by the Official Secretary, Office for Tokelau Affairs, which by agreement with the government of Western Samoa is based in Apia. The office coordinates the activities of the members of the Tokelau public ser-

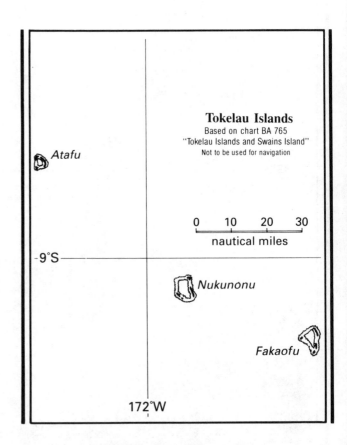

vice. (The Office of Tokelau Affairs will be moved in the near future to Fakaofu.)

New Zealand is committed to assisting Tokelau toward a greater degree of self-government and economic self-sufficiency. At present the people of Tokelau are not ready to cut the ties that bind them to New Zealand.

Fakaofu, with a population of about 660, is the most populous atoll of Tokelau. The village at Fakaofu is on a small but comparatively high motu. It is overcrowded, although emigration to New Zealand has lessened the overcrowding. A new village was established in 1960 on the larger nearby motu of Fenuafala; the school, hospital, and other facilities are there. In all, the

TOKELAU
A New Zealand dependency

Port of Entry (unofficial)
Fakaofu   9°23′ S, 171°15′ W

Distances between Ports in Nautical Miles
Between Fakaofu and

Apia, Western Samoa	270
Funafuti, Tuvalu	565
Kanton Island, Kiribati	395
Mata Uta, Wallis Islands	370
Pago Pago, American Samoa	295
Penrhyn, Cook Islands	785

Standard Time
11 hours slow on UTC

Public Holidays and Special Events

January 1	New Year's Day—Public holiday
February 6	Waitangi Day—Public holiday (commemoration of New Zealand Bay of Islands treaty signing)
March/April *	Good Friday, Easter, and Easter Monday—Public holidays
April 25	ANZAC Day—Public holiday
June *	Queen's Official Birthday—Public holiday
October *	Labour Day—Public holiday
October *	Tokehehga Day—Public holiday
December 25	Christmas Day—Public holiday
December 26	Boxing Day—Public holiday

*Specific dates vary from year to year.

An elderly Tokelauan husks drinking nuts on a sharpened wood stake driven into the ground. (Gary Brookins)

atoll of Fakaofu comprises 611 motus with a total land area of 650 acres surrounding the lagoon. Fenuafala is now the capitol of Tokelau.

In terms of land area Nukunonu is the largest of the three atolls with a land area of 1,350 acres spread over 30 islets. The 425 people who live there inhabit the adjacent islets of Nukunonu and Motusaga, which are connected by a bridge over the small pass.

Smallest of the three atolls is Atafu, which has but 500 acres spread across 19 islets. The population of about 605 all live on Atafu islet in the northwest corner of the atoll.

Two Christian denominations prevail. Almost all inhabitants of Atafu belong to the Congregational Christian Church of Samoa; on Nukunonu all are Roman Catholics; and on Fakaofu both denominations are represented, with adherents of the Congregational Christian Church forming the majority.

Each of the three atolls has a modern and well-equipped primary and secondary school for children between 5 and 18. In 1987 a national fifth form was established and opened on Nukunonu at Matiti School. Schooling is free and attendance close to 100 percent. There are also preschool classes in each village.

Village affairs are managed by a council of elders, or *fono*, comprising representatives of the families; this body also exerts influence over the *aumaga*, or village labor force. In this way the traditional form of patriarchal authority has been preserved to operate in parallel with public government officials such as the *faipule* (chief) and *pulenuku* (mayor). Local government is carried out on each atoll by an elected *faipule*, who is also magistrate. He is assisted by a village mayor, a village clerk, and other lesser officials.

Communications between the atolls and with Western Samoa is conducted by single-sideband radio. Business and medical traffic and weather reports are transmitted every four hours to Apia Radio 2AP. Shipping connections to Apia are somewhat irregular but average five times a year.

The cash economy of Tokelau is based primarily on copra with minor income from stamps and handi-

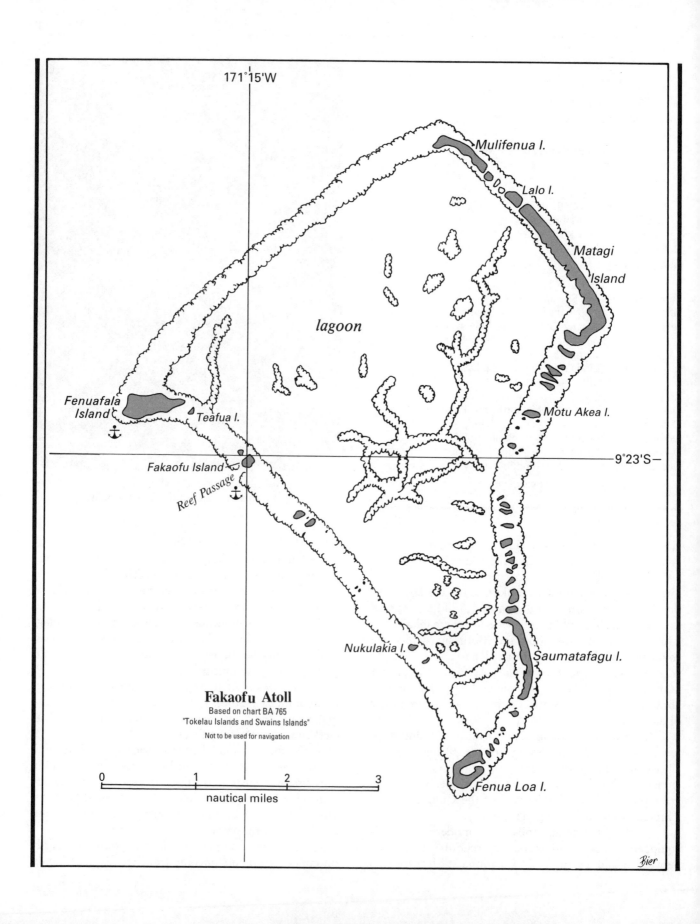

171°15'W

Mulifenua I.

Lalo I.

Matagi

Island

lagoon

Fenuafala
Island

Teafua I.

Motu Akea I.

9°23'S

Fakaofu Island

Reef Passage

Nukulakia I.

Saumatafagu I.

Fakaofu Atoll

Based on chart BA 765
"Tokelau Islands and Swains Islands"

Not to be used for navigation

0   1   2   3

nautical miles

Fenua Loa I.

Bier

crafts. Tokelau lives basically on a subsistence economy with food crops consisting of coconut, papaya, bananas, breadfruit, and taro; because of the poor soil, crops are not bountiful. Fish are the real source of food for the Tokelauans with tuna and bonita the most common species caught. Families raise pigs and poultry for additional meat. Each of the three villages operates a cooperative store handling imported products, mostly from New Zealand.

There is little farming in the accepted sense. The coarse, rubbly sand is devoid of humus and can support little vegetation other than the pandanus plant, casuarina tree, and coconut palm. One islet of each atoll is reserved for growing the tauanave, a short, stubbly tree that yields the only locally grown timber for the construction of canoes and utensils. The only food plants are a few breadfruit trees, bananas, and papaya grown in compost pits. These are supplemented by fish, fowl, pigs, and imported staples from New Zealand.

FLOTSAM AND JETSAM

Currency
Legal tender in Tokelau is the New Zealand dollar, but for convenience many transactions are made in the Western Samoan tala. Tokelau has its own dollar coinage, but it's primarily for souvenir collectors. There are no banks, so monetary transactions must be made with the local merchants.

Language
The indigenous language of Tokelau has linguistic ties with Samoan which have been strengthened with the introduction of the Bible in the Samoan language. Most Tokelauans, however, speak English.

Electricity
None except an occasional home generator.

Postal Address
You would do better to use Apia, Western Samoa, or your next port of call.

Ports for Making Crew Changes
Tokelau is not a recommended location for making a crew change. There is no air service to Tokelau, shipping is very sporadic, and all three islands have only reef anchorages. The closest port recommended for making a crew change would be Pago Pago.

External Affairs Representative
New Zealand embassies or consulates

Information Center
Office for Tokelau Affairs
P.O. Box 865
Apia
WESTERN SAMOA

Yacht *Staghound,* winner of the 1953 and 1955 TransPac Races and now a bluewater cruising boat, is anchored on the coral shelf off of Atafu Atoll, the nor ernmost of the Tokelau atolls. (Gary Brookins)

The Weather

The Tokelau group lies in the zone of the southeast trades, but northeast and north winds are common and predominate during the period November to February. The islands lie at the north edge of the South Pacific tropical cyclone region and rarely have severe tropical storms. In January 1914 a hurricane and two great sea waves washed over the island of Atafu, demolishing the church and most of the houses. Another hit the islands in January 1966. Tokelau was on the edge of gale force winds from Tropical Cyclone Ofa described in chapter 3.

The air temperature is an almost constant 82°F the year around, varying only slightly throughout the

MEDICAL MEMO

Immunization Requirements

Pratique is not a formal process in Tokelau, but visiting yachts are urged not to land if they have any illness aboard or if they have recently visited an area having cholera, smallpox, or yellow fever.

Local Health Situation

The incidence of disease in the atolls is comparatively slight. Island people suffer from some skin diseases because of the limited supply of fresh water for good hygiene, and sand and sun cause irritation of the eyes.

Health Services

Each of the three atolls has a hospital permanently staffed by Fijian-trained Tokelauan medical officers plus assistants trained in Apia, Western Samoa. Western Samoan medical officers visit the atolls regularly. Extreme illnesses or major injuries would have to be taken care of in Apia, Western Samoa, if transportation can be arranged.

The only medical drugs available are what the Tokelauan dispensaries receive from New Zealand for their own purposes.

There are no dental or optical services available.

Water

You should consider water suspect and treat it.

day and night. July tends to be the coolest month and May the warmest. The average rainfall is 115 inches per year with the highest recorded being 177 inches and the lowest 87 inches. It is not uncommon to have a daily rain of as much as three inches or more at any time of the year. In spite of the heavy rainfall, drinking water is scarce. There is no ground source of fresh water, so all the atolls depend on rainfall. Drinking water is collected from roofs of buildings and stored in concrete rain tanks for the villagers' use.

Cruising Notes

YACHT ENTRY AND FACILITIES

There are no formalities to visiting any of the atolls comprising Tokelau. Technically, however, you should check in with the Office of Tokelau Affairs in Apia and present a letter describing the yacht, reason for going, crew list, and passport information. This information will be radioed to Tokelau for approval. It may take several days for this to be done. In the meantime you can enjoy the people and sights of Apia.

If you should be coming from a different direction, it is not illegal to go directly to one of the islands and make yourself known. Common sense tells you to check in with the atoll chief and to pay a visit to the mayor of the village. Showing deference to local officials is certain to make your stay in Tokelau a more interesting experience.

Yacht facilities at the atolls are virtually zero. Channels have been blasted out of the fringing reefs at all three atolls to allow small boats to get ashore. These are not, however, harbors in any sense, and you can go into them only with a dinghy. Anchor offshore on the coral shelf leaving a crew member aboard in case your anchor doesn't hold.

Except for coconuts and fish, do not expect to get any provisions from these atolls. In a dry year even water may be scarce. You are only a two-day sail from Samoa if you are in desperate need of anything.

The Tokelau atolls are little visited by cruising yachts, but this happy situation is bound to change as cruisers become disenchanted with the crowded harbors along the beaten path and seek unspoiled islands of the South Seas. Tokelau is just such a group waiting to be discovered by the yachting enthusiast.

CHAPTER 12

TONGA

The Country

Tonga is a kingdom of some 170 islands and 101,000 people that became an independent state in mid-1970. It is the sole remaining Polynesian kingdom and has successfully retained the family-subsistence basis of its ancient culture. The people speak a Polynesian variant called Tongan and are closely related to the inhabitants of Samoa.

The islands are mixed as to type, and the combination of high volcanic and low coral forms gives the group a physical character all its own. Of Tonga's 170 islands, 134 are uninhabited because they lack fresh water, arable land, transport and or communications.

The islands are dispersed in three identifiable groups—the northern or Vavau group, the central or Haapai group, and a southern or Tongatapu group. The kingdom is bordered on the east by the deep Tonga Trench, indicating that it lies at the eastern extremity of the continental shelf. It is an area of great structural instability and vulcanism. Some of the islands are a little more active than extinct volcanic cones should be. One, Falcon Island, in the Vavau group, has a unique up-and-down character. It is a submerged active volcano that erupts periodically. When it is active, lava and ash rise above sea level, forming a clearly visible island. When the eruption is over, the unconsolidated pile is destroyed by wave action, and the island disappears until the next eruption.

Cruisers should be aware of a new and uncharted island in the group. It is called Lateiki and lies on the Metis Shoal about midway between Late and Kao. In 1979 the island measured 1,060 feet long, 400 feet wide, and 50 feet high. The island is composed of volcanic ash, pumice, and loose lava rock. This island is expected to disappear after a number of years as volcanic activity ceases and the seas erode the loose rock.

The Vavau group consists of 34 islands having a total land area of 45 square miles and a population esti-mated at 16,000, about two-thirds of whom are on Vavau, the largest island in the group. Fourteen of the other islands are uninhabited.

The Haapai group is a cluster of 36 islands of mixed form, only 20 of which are permanently inhab-ited. The largest of this group is Tofua, an active vol-cano whose crater contains a steaming lake. A few miles north of Tofua is Kao, an extinct volcano with a perfect conical peak rising to 3,400 feet. Most of the group's 20,000 people live on low coral islands in the eastern chain.

The Tongatapu group contains seven major is-lands, the largest of which is Tongatapu, a wholly coral-line island on which Nukualofa, the capital city, is situated. Roughly two-thirds of the kingdom's entire population reside on Tongatapu. Other major islands in the group include Eua, Ata, Atata, Euaki, Kalaau, and Kenatea. Ata is an ancient volcano 1,165 feet high; Euaki, Kalaau, and Kenatea are uninhabited.

Archeological evidence indicates that the islands of Tonga have been settled since at least 2500 B.C., and local tradition has carefully preserved the names of the Tongan sovereigns for about a thousand years. At the kingdom's height in the thirteenth century, the power of the Tongan monarch extended as far as Hawaii.

In about the fourteenth century the king of Tonga delegated much of his temporal power to a brother while keeping himself the spiritual authority. Sometime later this process was repeated by the second line, thus resulting in three distinct lines: the Tui Tonga with spir-itual authority (which is believed to have extended over much of Polynesia) and the Tui Haatakalaua and the Tui Kanokupolu, both with temporal authority respon-sible for carrying out much of the day-to-day adminis-tration of the kingdom.

The first Europeans to sight the Tongan archipel-ago were Dutch navigators in 1616. The main island of Tongatapu was first visited by the Dutch explorer Abel Tasman in 1643. However, continual contact with Europeans did not begin until more than 125 years

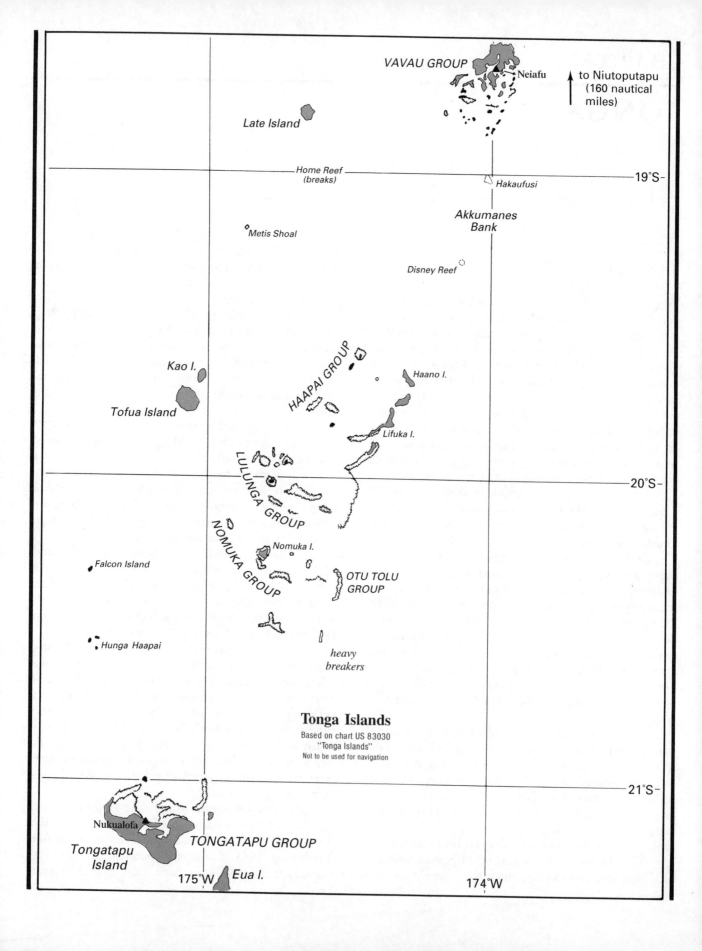

VAVAU GROUP

Neiafu

↑ to Niutoputapu
(160 nautical
miles)

Late Island

Home Reef
(breaks)

Hakaufusi

─19°S─

Akkumanes
Bank

Metis Shoal

Disney Reef

Kao I.

HAAPAI GROUP

Haano I.

Tofua Island

Lifuka I.

LULUNGA GROUP

─20°S─

NOMUKA GROUP

Nomuka I.

Falcon Island

OTU TOLU
GROUP

Hunga Haapai

heavy
breakers

Tonga Islands

Based on chart US 83030
"Tonga Islands"
Not to be used for navigation

─21°S─

Nukualofa

TONGATAPU GROUP

Tongatapu
Island

175°W   Eua I.

174°W

TONGA

An independent nation

Ports of Entry

Niuatoputapu, Niuas	15°57′ S, 173°44′ W
Neiafu, Vavau	18°39′ S, 173°59′ W
Nukualofa, Tongatapu	21°08′ S, 175°12′ W

Distances between Ports in Nautical Miles

Between Neiafu and

Alofi, Niue	280
Apia, Western Samoa	315
Pago Pago, American Samoa	325
Suva, Fiji	435

Between Nukualofa and

Alofi, Niue	365
Auckland, New Zealand	1,080
Neiafu, Vavau	165
Raoul, Kermadec Islands	510
Rarotonga, Cook Islands	860
Suva, Fiji	405

Standard Time

13 hours fast on UTC (Tonga's motto is: Where time begins)

Public Holidays and Special Events

January 1	New Year's Day—Public holiday
March/April *	Good Friday, Easter, and Easter Monday—Public holidays
April 25	ANZAC Day—Public holiday
May 4	Birthday of Crown Prince Tupoutoo—Public holiday
June 4	Emancipation Day—Public holiday
July 4	Birthday of King Taufaahau Tupou IV—Public holiday
July *	Heilala Festival (Nukualofa)
November 4	Constitution Day—Public holiday
December 4	King Tupou I Day—Public holiday
December 25	Christmas Day—Public holiday
December 26	Boxing Day—Public holiday

*Specific dates vary from year to year.

later. Captain James Cook visited the islands in 1773 and 1777 and gave the archipelago the name Friendly Islands because of the gentle nature of the Tongans he encountered. In 1789 the famous mutiny on the British ship *Bounty* took place in the water, of the Haapai group between the islands of Nomuka and Tofua.

The peaceful conditions in Tonga changed shortly after Captain Cook's last visit. The islands were torn by civil strife and warfare as each of the three lines of kings sought dominance over the others. This was the state of affairs in 1882 when the first missionaries of the London Missionary Society led by Walter Lawry of the Wesleyan Missionary Society arrived. They converted Tau-

faahau, one of the claimants to the Tui Kanokupolu line, and Christianity began to spread throughout the islands.

At the time of his conversion, Taufaahau took the name of Siaosi (George) and his consort assumed the name Salote (Charlotte), in honor of King George III and Queen Charlotte of England. In the following years he united all the Tongan islands for the first time and in 1845 founded the present royal dynasty. He was formally proclaimed King George Tupou I. He gave his country a constitution and representative parliamentary government based in some respects on the British model. In 1862 he abolished the system of semiserfdom, which had previously existed, and established an entirely alien system of land tenure whereby every Tongan male, upon reaching the age of 16, was entitled to rent for life at a nominal fee a plot of bush land *(api)* of 8¼ acres, plus a village allotment of about three-eighths of an acre for his home.

Under a Treaty of Friendship and Protection concluded with the United Kingdom on May 18, 1900, Tonga came under British protection. Tonga retained its independence and autonomy, while the United Kingdom agreed to handle its foreign affairs and protect it from external attack.

During World War II Tonga, in close collaboration with New Zealand, formed a local defense force of about 2,000 men, which saw action in the Solomon Islands. Additionally, New Zealand and U.S. troops were stationed on Tongatapu, which became a staging point for shipping.

A new Treaty of Friendship and Protection with the United Kingdom was signed in 1958 and ratified in May 1959. It provided for a British commissioner and consul in Tonga who were responsible to the U.K. secretary of state for colonial affairs. Tonga became a fully independent country on June 4, 1970, an event officially designated by the king as Tonga's "reentry into the community of nations."

You can believe whom you would—Captain Cook, who named the Tonga Islands the Friendly Islands, or Captain Bligh, who on the Tonga island of Tofua suffered his only casualty in his remarkable 3,620-mile trip in an open launch after the mutiny on the *Bounty*. The Tonga Islands are beautiful, the customs and climate in contradiction, and the economy poor, but these are a proud and independent people.

Tongans, a Polynesian group with a very small mixture of Melanesian, represent more than 98 percent of the inhabitants. The rest are Europeans, mixed Europeans, and other Pacific islanders.

The royal palace at Nukualofa is a majestic example of Victorian architecture. It is located on the waterfront surrounded by stately Norfolk pines brought from the island of Norfolk near Australia. Although the king holds court here, he no longer lives in the palace. (Earl Hinz)

For most of the twentieth century Tonga has been quiet, inward-looking, and somewhat isolated from developments elsewhere in the world. The Tongans as a whole continue to cling to many of their old traditions, including a respect for the nobility. However, the people are beginning to face the problem of preserving their cultural identity and traditions in the wake of the increasing impact of Western technology and culture. Educational opportunities for young commoners have advanced, and their increasing numbers are already too great to provide the constitutional 8¼ acre *api* for each adult male. The pressure to move to the kingdom's only urban center or to emigrate is, therefore, considerable.

The forward-looking nature of the Tongans is nowhere better seen than in their creation of five island parks and marine preserves in the Tongatapu area. The islanders realized that the heavy exploitation of the reefs was diminishing the numbers of fish, shellfish, turtles, and coral beds so they took action to preserve and, it is hoped, to reestablish the marine life. The parks not only protect their food supply but preserve a valuable natural resource for future generations.

The economy of Tonga is derived from both the land and the sea by a people who have traditionally farmed their fertile lands and fished the generous sea around them. Approximately half of Tonga's domestic income is provided by three-fourths of the people engaged in agriculture. In terms of exports, 90 percent of the income is derived from coconut oil and copra, desiccated coconut, bananas, capsicums, and tomatoes.

The men of Tonga have proved themselves skillful navigators and well trained in the art of fishing. They continue to follow the business of whaling in a small way. Using small boats and hand harpoons, they pursue the humpback whale migrating south during the winter season of July to October. When these boats return to the Nukualofa dock flying the black flag indicating a successful hunt, the local people are only too eager to buy cuts of the meat for their table use—even down to the blubber and outer skin. The number of whales caught is small compared to the number killed by the factory-ship operations of the Japanese and Russians.

While the men fish and till the fields, the women make some of the finest tapa cloth in the Pacific. There is a large cottage industry producing handicrafts, which are sold locally to Tongans and visitors and exported to other island countries, particularly American Samoa, where they are sold as tourist souvenirs.

Tonga is also noted for its postage stamps—probably the most unusual and beautiful in the world. The stamps have irregular shapes outlining the particular subject being honored (a banana is one!). They have self-adhesive backs to eliminate licking. The banana stamp is small enough to get on a postcard, but most stamps are so large that they overrun the address space. Furthermore, the Tongan postal clerks take great delight in giving you the maximum number of small denomination stamps that meet the postal requirements so your mailing will look like a Tongan public relations billboard.

The post office and treasury (bank) for Neiafu are located on the hillside above the commercial wharf in this quaint colonial structure. (Earl Hinz)

The Tongan people, while very similar in physical appearance to the heavy-set Samoans, display a more congenial disposition like the Tahitians. In the marketplace one hears lighthearted laughter as bargaining takes place between buyer and seller.

The national dress of Tonga is the skirt called a *tupenu* or *vala*. It is worn ankle length by women and knee length by men. In addition, women wear a highly decorated waistband known as a *kiekie* and men a woven mat called a *taovala* around the waist as a sign of respect for one's elders and the royal family.

Tongans are very conservative in their manner of dress. Visitors are advised to wear cover-up garments. Men who go ashore shirtless can draw a 25-paanga fine.

The Weather

Nearly 60 percent of the annual sea winds among the Tonga Islands and vicinity are from southeast to east. During May to August when the southeast winds are in their ascendency, the easterly wind components are in considerable part replaced by southwesterly to northwesterly winds. About 24 percent of the annual winds are from the northeast and south, about equally divided between the two directions. The average wind speed at sea is 12 knots while at Nukualofa it is 9 knots. The December wind speed at Nukualofa is 10 knots and in May to July, about 7 knots. At sea the range is between 13 and 11 knots during the corresponding period.

From May to November the strongest winds are generally experienced from south-southeast to east-southeast, usually accompanied by rain from these quarters lasting up to three days. On the wind shifting to the north of east, fine and settled weather may be expected for a time.

After September strong northwesterly winds with thick, dirty weather and heavy rains may occasionally be expected, but the wind does not appear to remain longer than 12 hours in that quarter and will probably shift southward and clear up.

From December to April the winds are generally easterly, but sudden and violent westerly and northwesterly squalls are common. An average year brings about three days of gales.

Tropical cyclones occur in the Tonga Islands at the rate of about one annually. They are most frequent in January and February. The hurricane season begins in November and usually ends in April. However, one such storm has been known to occur in May.

A particularly disastrous cyclone, Isaac, wreaked havoc the length of the Tongan chain in March 1982. There were 21 cruising and charter boats caught in what was thought to be the well-protected harbor of Neiafu. Six boats survived, ten were cast on shore or rocks, and five were totally lost.

The Tongan climate has less rain and is slightly cooler than other tropical areas. From May to December, the dry season, the weather is as good as any found in the tropics. Maximum temperatures average 80°F

FLOTSAM AND JETSAM

Currency

The unit of currency is the paanga; it is not tied to any fixed rate of exchange with any other currency. The paanga is divided into units of 100 called seniti (cents). Coins are issued in denominations of 1, 2, 5, 10, 20, and 50 seniti and also 1, 2, 5, and 10 paanga. The approximate rate of exchange is US$1 = 1.28 paanga. Relative cost of goods is 95.

Language

Tongan, a Polynesian dialect, is the indigenous language; however, most people also speak English.

Electricity

240v, 50 Hz AC

Postal Addresses

Name
Yacht (   )
General Delivery
Nukualofa
TONGA

Name
Yacht (   )
c/o Paradise International Hotel
P.O. Box 191
Neiafu, Vavau
TONGA

Ports for Making Crew Changes

Nukualofa is a possible port for making crew changes; it has international airline service connecting it with Auckland, Suva, and Apia. A domestic airline connects Nukualofa with Vavau, making a crew change possible there.

External Affairs Representative

British embassies or consulates

Information Center

Tonga Visitors Bureau
P.O. Box 37
Nukualofa
TONGA

with moderate humidity. During the rainy season from December to April, the maximum average temperature climbs to 90°F with high humidity. People from the temperate climes usually find this weather oppressive.

The annual rainfall at Nukualofa is 58 inches with as much as 10 inches falling in the month of April and as little as one inch falling in the months of May and July. Records from ships at sea show a considerable variation in the rainy periods, but with greatest precipitation frequencies, some 10 to 20 percent, occurring in April, July, and September to January. Each month, from 2 to 4 percent of the days have thunderstorms, with the greatest frequency in December to February. There is a measurable rainfall on about 130 days of the year. Vavau is the wettest part of the Tongan group. Nearly 20 inches of rain fell there in one month.

Cruising Notes

YACHT ENTRY

Tonga has become a very desirable port of call for cruising yachts because of its strategic location on the Coconut Milk Run to Fiji or New Zealand. A measure of its popularity is seen in the 1987 records of yacht arrivals: 342 in Vavau; 22 in Haapai; and 235 in Tongatapu. That is a twofold increase since 1983.

There are three Ports of Entry to Tonga—Niuatoputapu, Niuas; Neiafu, Vavau; and Nukualofa, Tongatapu. You can enter or clear at any of them depending on your overall itinerary.

CUSTOMS

Cruising in Tongan waters is strictly controlled. In past years renegade cruisers have trafficked in marijuana, hence the present-day restrictions. A cruising permit is required for the nearby islands; it can be obtained by writing a letter of request to the chief of police stating your desired itinerary. Remember that you are in a foreign country and abide by the laws.

Customs will impound your firearms and keep them until your departure.

The monumental Haamonga Trilithon, built about A.D. 1200, consists of two large vertical stones with a connecting stone lintel mortised into the tops of the upright pillars. The uprights are five meters high, and the visible parts are estimated to weigh between 30 and 40 tons each. (Earl Hinz)

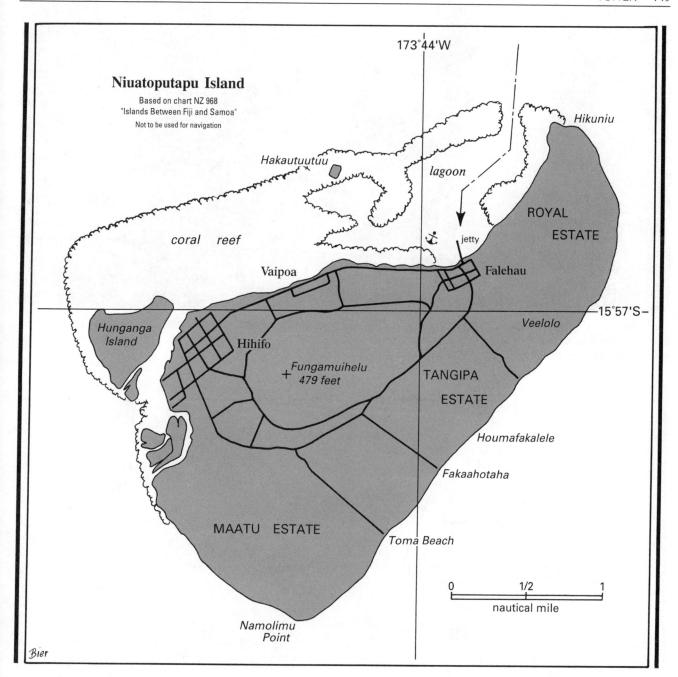

Niuatoputapu Island

Based on chart NZ 968
"Islands Between Fiji and Samoa"

Not to be used for navigation

173°44'W

Hikuniu

Hakautuutuu

lagoon

ROYAL
ESTATE

coral   reef

jetty

Vaipoa

Falehau

15°57'S

Veelolo

*Hunganga
Island*

Hihifo

+*Fungamuihelu
479 feet*

TANGIPA

ESTATE

Houmafakalele

Fakaahotaha

MAATU   ESTATE

Toma Beach

0   1/2   1
nautical mile

*Namolimu
Point*

Bier

IMMIGRATION

Passports are required of all crew. Onward tickets are not required for persons listed as crew members, who are expected to depart the islands on the boat. Proof of adequate funds will be required.

A visa is not required for a stay less than 30 days. Extensions up to six months may be granted by the principal immigration officer. Longer extensions require approval by his majesty's cabinet.

YACHT FACILITIES

Niuatoputapu, Niuas

The northernmost group of islands in the Tonga Archipelago are the Niuas, a group of three small inhabited islands—Niuafoou ("Tin Can Island"), Tafahi, and Niuatoputapu, the latter sometimes known as Keppel Island. They lie south of Western Samoa and could be a unique stop on your passage from the Samoas to Tonga. The most populated of the three is Niuatoputapu,

The wharf and shipping facilities at Neiafu, Vavau. Cruising yachts generally anchor below the hill from which this picture was taken. Cruise ships occasionally dock at this harbor for a day and the passengers inundate the town. That is a good time for cruisers to go shelling out on the reef. (Tonga Visitors Bureau)

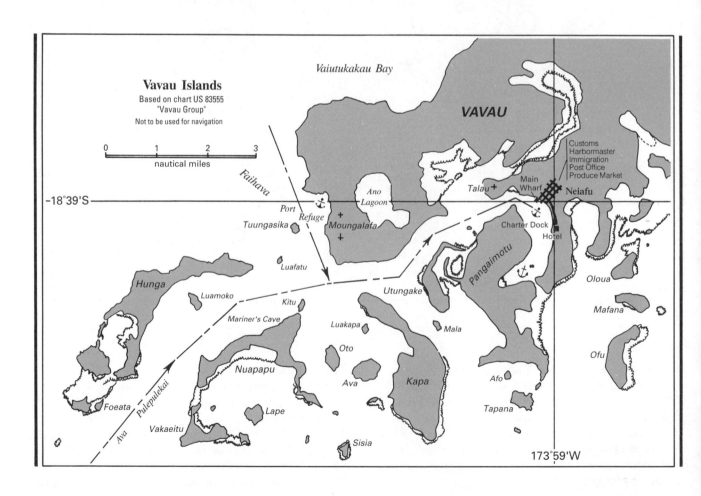

Vavau Islands

Based on chart US 83555
"Vavau Group"

Not to be used for navigation

0   1   2   3
nautical miles

Vaiutukakau Bay

VAVAU

Customs
Harbormaster
Immigration
Post Office
Produce Market

Faihava

-18°39'S

Port Refuge

Ano Lagoon

Talau

Main Wharf

Neiafu

Tuungasika

Moungalafa

Charter Dock

Hotel

Luafatu

Pangaimotu

Hunga

Luamoko

Kitu

Utungake

Oloua

Mariner's Cave

Luakapa

Mala

Mafana

Oto

Nuapapu

Ava

Kapa

Afo

Ofu

Puiepulekai

Lape

Foeata

Vakaeitu

Sisia

Tapana

173°59'W

This woman of Vavau was part of a large group weaving floor-size mats out of pandanus leaves. (Earl Hinz)

which has a small harbor protected from the trade winds by a ridge of hills about 450 feet high. This island is one of the most traditional of Tonga's 170 islands. Few cruising boats stop here.

The pass into the harbor is at the northeast corner of the island and should be attempted only in daylight. Proceed to the small trading wharf at the village of Falehau for inbound clearance. After completing entry formalities at the wharf, stand clear and anchor in 30–40 feet of water over a sand bottom.

There is well water available near the wharf, but do not expect to obtain provisions here. If you are in need of provisions, fuel, or help of any kind, it is better to continue on to Vavau. The island people, however, see so few visitors that a short stop to enjoy their culture would be worthwhile.

Neiafu, Vavau

Vavau has been the cruiser's favorite port of call in Tonga for decades because of its numerous waterways, islands, and friendly rural population. It is also the closest thing to a hurricane haven in Tonga. While most cruising boats seek haven in New Zealand during the tropical cyclone season, many boats do choose to stay at Vavau.

On first arrival and after passing down the beautiful waterway entry to Vavau, tie up at the Neiafu city dock, preferably at one end, and stay on board until your clearance is completed. All clearance formalities are handled right at the wharf. You can be cleared on Saturdays, but there is an extra charge of 15 paanga for the overtime. No clearance on Sundays. It is permissible to wait on your boat until Monday for normal clearance, but do not allow anyone to go ashore, no matter how tempting the local markets.

Neiafu offers provisions and potable water that is chemically very hard. Staples and fresh foods are available in limited but adequate quantities. Several good restaurants are available, one at the Paradise International Hotel. You can also use the hotel swimming pool, showers, toilets, and dinghy dock for ten paanga per week. The hotel has a wharf that you can use for ten paanga per day or six paanga per night. Shorepower electricity is charged extra.

The Moorings charter company operates a large number of popular charter sailboats, which are moored in this same general vicinity. Their dock is for their own use; cruisers should use the public dinghy dock inside the small breakwater near the boatyard (or the hotel's). Purchase a copy of the *Moorings Cruising Guide* used by charter boats to find all the good places to visit in the Vavau group.

Don Coleman's boatyard is adjacent to the Moorings and can handle boats to 50 tons and 60 feet. Typi-

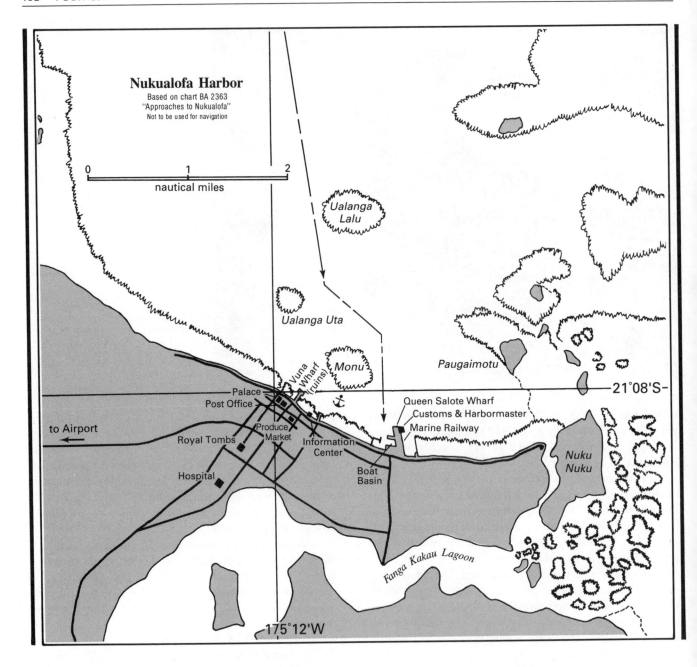

Nukualofa Harbor
Based on chart BA 2363
"Approaches to Nukualofa"
Not to be used for navigation

0   1   2
nautical miles

Ualanga Lalu

Ualanga Uta

Monu

Vuna Wharf (ruins)

Palace
Post Office

to Airport

Royal Tombs

Produce Market

Hospital

Information Center

Boat Basin

Paugaimotu

21°08'S

Queen Salote Wharf
Customs & Harbormaster
Marine Railway

Nuku Nuku

Fanga Kakau Lagoon

175°12'W

cal charges are eight paanga per foot for in and out plus one day. Outside paid labor is not permitted, but you will find labor rates very low in this yard. The yard provides general marine repair and maintenance services, but they do not have yacht hardware on hand; that must be ordered from New Zealand. Diesel fuel and gasoline are available at his dock. Personal use moorings are available from Coleman at five paanga per night. Give thought to using these moorings instead of damaging the coral seabed with your own anchor.

Cruisers should also note the sign posted in the Paradise International Hotel: "Please observe the Sunday laws. No work on Sunday—this includes running generators (noisy), banging, etc. People not respecting the law affect everybody else."

Nukualofa, Tongatapu

The Tongatapu group of islands is the main group of Tonga and the location of the kingdom's administrative offices. Tongatapu is a very flat, coralline island with

MEDICAL MEMO

Immunization Requirements

Immunizations are required for smallpox, cholera, and yellow fever if you have transited or visited within the last six days (smallpox 14 days) an area currently infected.

Local Health Situation

Insect bites can be irritating, and you should have medications on board for them. Infectious hepatitis is endemic to the islands, and gastrointestinal infections are common. Neither needs be a problem if you exercise proper hygiene and avoid contaminated food and water. Other diseases such as tuberculosis, filariases, and influenza are present but to only a minor degree.

Health Services

There are hospitals at Nukualofa, Tongatapu; Neiafu, Vavau; and Pangai, Lifuka. The three hospitals have a combined capacity of 296 beds. In addition, there are seven rural dispensaries offering a limited range of services. Private practitioners are also available at Nukualofa, and the costs are reported to be moderate.

Maintenance dental services are available at all three of the hospitals, but optical service is available only at the Vaiola Hospital in Nukualofa.

There are no private pharmacies (chemists) in Tonga. Drugs must be obtained through the hospitals.

IAMAT Center

Nukualofa: Vaiola Hospital
             Medical Director: L. Malolo, MD
             Director of Health: Supileo Foliaki, MD

Water

The water at both Neiafu and Tongatapu is barely potable and rainwater is a far better choice.

---

many interesting places to visit by car or bus. You can sit down in the very spot where Captain Cook landed to replenish his water supplies and you can see the only remaining active royal palace in the Pacific.

Entry to Nukualofa should be made only during daylight because of the plethora of reefs you must pass through. Head for Queen Salote Wharf to get Quarantine and Customs clearance. If the wharf is unoccupied, you can tie up at one end out of the way of large vessels. If it is occupied, anchor to the west of it and take your dinghy to the wharf. The latter may be preferable because the wharf can be damaging to your small boat and interisland freighters and cruise ships may want to use the wharf. After Customs and Quarantine clearance, move your boat into the Faua small-craft harbor and moor Tahiti-style along the ocean wall. Then walk downtown to the police station to obtain your Immigration clearance.

The new Faua small-craft harbor in Nukualofa is between the old "slipper" basin and the Queen Salote Wharf. It is capable of mooring 25 cruising boats Tahiti-style and has a number of side ties for loading. There are charges for the use of this small-craft harbor. They vary according to boat length. For a 40-foot boat they are approximately as follows:

Harbor dues	40 paanga per year
Light dues	25 paanga per year
Mooring	30 paanga per 3 months
Slipway	110 paanga in and out

If you choose to anchor outside the small-craft harbor, there is a charge of 13 paanga per month.

There is also a modern slipway at Nukualofa, but no marine hardware, paints, or organized workforce. "Engineering shops" in the neighborhood can repair almost any hardware on your boat. Sails can be repaired (or new ones made) at the Small Industries Center, a bus ride into the interior of the city. There is also a modern fiberglass boatbuilding plant that could help with boat repairs.

Diesel fuel is available from a truck supply; water in limited quantities is available from a storage tank. Tap water is not recommended for drinking. Ice is available from the fishery house, but it has a distinctly fishy odor.

CHAPTER 13

TUVALU

The Country

Tuvalu became an independent country on October 1, 1978, having formerly been a part of the Gilbert and Ellice Islands Colony administered by Great Britain. Tuvalu lies between 5°S and 11°S and 176°E and the 180th meridian. It extends for a distance of 360 miles in a northwesterly-southeasterly direction and is composed of nine islands with a land area of 9 square statute miles. The national waters of Tuvalu encompass approximately a quarter million square nautical miles of the Pacific Ocean.

Seven of the islands are coral atolls; two are coral reef islands with a surrounding fringing reef. The tallest objects on the islands are coconut palms, which reach a height of 60 to 80 feet above sea level at the highest point. An estimated 9,100 people inhabit the islands.

The name "Tuvalu" means "eight standing together," which are the inhabited islands. The ninth island, Niulakita, formerly had no population, but it is now occupied by about 60 people working copra.

The principal island of the group, its capital, and the only Port of Entry is Funafuti. It is an atoll consisting of 30 islets with a total land area of 625 acres on a reef surrounding a lagoon 13 miles long with a maximum width of 10 miles. The islet of Funafuti has a population of 2,700; its principal village is Fongafale. The islets of the eastern (windward) side of Funafuti atoll form an almost continuous barrier reef, but there are many gaps in the reef on the leeward side.

In 1911 Sir Edgeworth David of Sydney, Australia, bored a hole in the islet of Funafuti to prove Darwin's theory on the evolution of atolls. The bore went to a depth of 1,100 feet and revealed only sand and coral formation, a finding that was accepted as further proof of Darwin's theory.

The second most important island of Tuvalu is Vaitupu, which has a population of 1,320. Vaitupu has two lagoons, one of which can be entered at high tide by shallow-draft boats. The islets forming the atoll have a total land area of 1,400 acres with a soil that is somewhat better for agriculture than the other atolls. Vaitupu is the site of the secondary school for all of Tuvalu's students.

The ethnological history of Tuvalu suggests that it was originally peopled by Micronesians from Southeast

---

TUVALU
An independent nation
Port of Entry
Funafuti   8°31′S, 179°12′E
Distances between Ports in Nautical Miles
Between Funafuti and
  Apia, Western Samoa   620
  Fakaofu, Tokelau   570
  Honiara, Solomon Islands   1,140
  Kanton Island, Kiribati   640
  Majuro, Marshall Islands   1,050
  Mata Uta, Wallis Islands   395
  Nauru (Aiwo District)   880
  Pago Pago, American Samoa   690
  Port-Vila, Vanuatu   845
  Suva, Fiji   580
  Tarawa, Kiribati   700
Standard Time
12 hours fast on UTC
Public Holidays and Special Events
January 1   New Year's Day—Public holiday
March *   Commonwealth Day—Public holiday
March/April *   Good Friday, Easter, and Easter Monday—
                Public holidays
June *   Queen's Official Birthday—Public holiday
August 3   National Children's Day—Public holiday
October 1–2   Independence Day—Public holiday
November 10   Prince Charles's Birthday—Public holiday
December 25   Christmas Day—Public holiday
December 26   Boxing Day—Public holiday

*Specific dates vary from year to year.

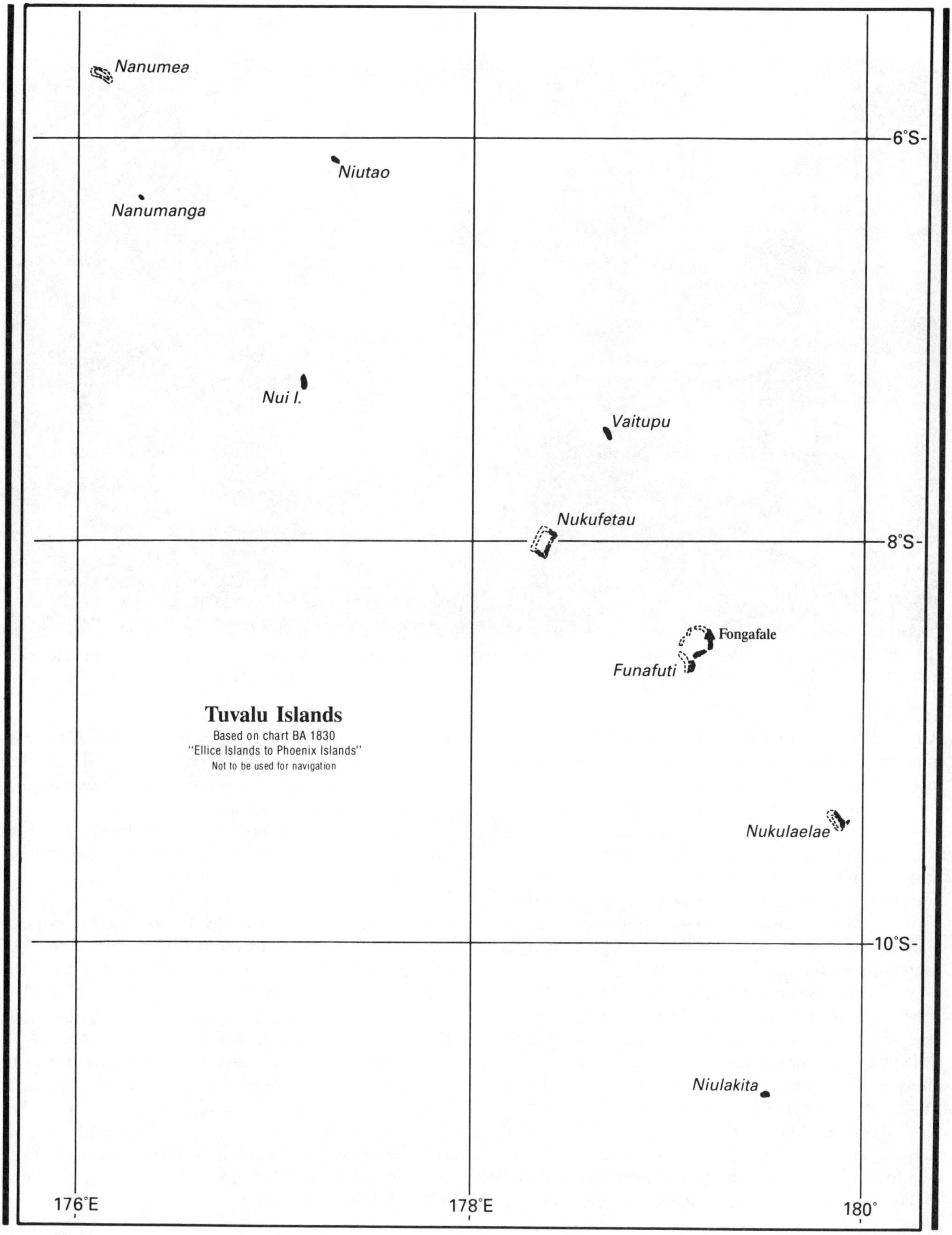

Nanumea

6°S

Niutao

Nanumanga

Nui I.

Vaitupu

Nukufetau

8°S

Fongafale

Funafuti

Tuvalu Islands
Based on chart BA 1830
"Ellice Islands to Phoenix Islands"
Not to be used for navigation

Nukulaelae

10°S

Niulakita

176°E

178°E

180°

The atoll of Nukufetau, a bare 40 miles from Funafuti, has a fairly large, shallow lagoon, which is navigable with care. Here live some of the best Tuvaluan canoe builders. Shown is a canoe made from a local tree in the rough hewn stage. (William Lobban)

Asia and Indonesia who arrived about 1000 B.C. These may have been the same people who populated Kiribati just to the north. In the sixteenth century, however, the Samoans invaded the islands and established the dominance of the Polynesian race in Tuvalu. The island of Nui in central Tuvalu is unusual because its people bear more resemblance to the I-Kiribati than to Polynesians and their language and culture are also more like the I-Kiribati. Many Tuvaluans have a trace of European ancestry because of the many whalers who visited the islands during the nineteenth century.

The first Western sighting of the islands of Tuvalu is believed to have taken place in 1568 by the Spanish explorer Mendaña on his first voyage to the Pacific. DePeyster, an English captain, "rediscovered" the islands in 1819. They were named Ellice Islands by the English hydrographer Findlay who sailed with DePeyster. (Alexander Ellice was the head of the Montreal, Canada, firm that owned De Peyster's ship *Rebecca*.) The first American into the group was Captain Barrett of the Nantucket whaler *Independence II,* who was

there in 1821. The first charting of the area was done by Lieutenant Wilkes, USN, as part of the 1840 U.S. exploring expedition. Wilkes estimated a native population of about 20,000 at that time.

Whaling was popular in the area from 1821 until 1870, and many crewmen deserted their ships to become beachcombers on the islands. Blackbirding took its toll of the islanders in the 1860s, and European diseases also took many lives. By 1890 the native population had been reduced to about 3,000. This sad state of affairs prompted the British to take jurisdiction of the islands in 1892, and in 1916 they were formally made a part of the Gilbert and Ellice Islands Colony, which they remained until their independence in 1978.

Although the adjacent Gilbert Islands were invaded by the Japanese during World War II, the Ellice Islands remained outside the fighting zone. The atoll of Funafuti, however, became a major forward base for U.S. forces until the Japanese invaders were driven from the Gilbert Islands to the north. The present airfield was a World War II airstrip that for reasons of expediency

FLOTSAM AND JETSAM

Currency

Tuvalu uses Australian notes and Tuvaluan coinage tied dollar-for-dollar to Australian currency. The approximate rate of exchange is US$1 = A$1.41.

Language

The native language of Tuvalu is closely related to modern Samoan with a sprinkling of words from the Tongan and Niuean languages. Many of the people speak English.

Electricity

If you find any electricity on these islands, it will be 240v, 50 Hz AC.

Postal Address

Yacht (   )
General Delivery
Funafuti
TUVALU

Ports for Making Crew Changes

Funafuti is not a recommended port for making crew changes because of minimum airline service and poor shipping schedules. The outer islands lack runways, and there is no seaplane service. The closest recommended ports for making a crew change would be Suva or Pago Pago.

External Affairs Representative

British or Australian embassies or consulates

---

was laid directly across the most fertile lands of the islet of Funafuti.

Most of the people of Tuvalu are Christians, with the large majority belonging to the Congregational Church founded by the London Missionary Society. Their lifestyle embodies the church, sports such as volleyball and cricket, and singing and dancing at feasts.

Tuvalu's economy is mostly agrarian, with copra being the principal crop for export. Tuvalu has a maritime school on the islet of Amatuku on Funafuti atoll where seamen are trained for overseas shipping companies. The school turns out about 60 seamen every year; about 300 are already at posts on ships of the world. Marine resources also make a contribution to the economy in the form of tuna fishing and harvesting of beche-de-mer for export to Hong Kong.

The thin, sandy soils of the atolls support only a narrow range of vegetation of which coconut and pandanus are the dominant forms. Taro is grown in pits, and there are some banana trees. Otherwise the basic foodstuffs are obtained from the sea and lagoon.

The present government of Tuvalu is an indepen-dent constitutional monarchy with the British queen as the head of state. It has a single-chamber parliament consisting of 12 members representing all the islands. Island councils (town council in the case of Funafuti) administer the needs of the separate islands. Security is provided by a chief of police and 24 officers and constables, all of whom are Tuvaluans.

The Weather

The islands of Tuvalu are seasonally affected by the intertropical convergence zone. During the period June through early October, the ITCZ lies to the north of Tuvalu, allowing full development of the southeast trades, which blow moderate to fresh and sometimes strong over the islands. The trades are predominantly east and southeast in direction. By November the ITCZ has moved south toward Tuvalu, and the northeast trades dominate with occasional winds from the north and the northwest as well.

During the November–April period westerly winds caused by low-pressure areas to the south of Tuvalu may be expected. These westerlies are the same as strike the Gilbert group and can be of gale force with violent squalls and heavy rain.

The average wind speeds from May to October are 10 to 13 knots and are quite steady. When the winds shift to any northerly direction, they become less steady. Calms occur about 5 percent of the time and are at a minimum during the July to November period.

When the trade winds are interrupted by the passage of a cold front from the temperate regions farther south, there follows a period of unsettled weather with variable winds, rain squalls, and thunder. At this time waterspouts may be seen starting from the base of low nimbus clouds. Several of these waterspouts may form at any one time; sailing craft should avoid them.

Although this area is normally outside the southwest Pacific tropical cyclone belt, a weather eye should be kept open to their possible occurrence during the period November to April. Hurricanes are known to generate east of Tuvalu and pass to the south in their journey toward Fijian waters. Though they may not pass directly over Tuvalu, gale force winds can be felt over the islands. In 1957 a hurricane passing on a west-southwest track through the central Tuvalu group caused widespread damage. In October 1972 Hurricane Bebe devastated the islands of the group.

The south equatorial current flows through the

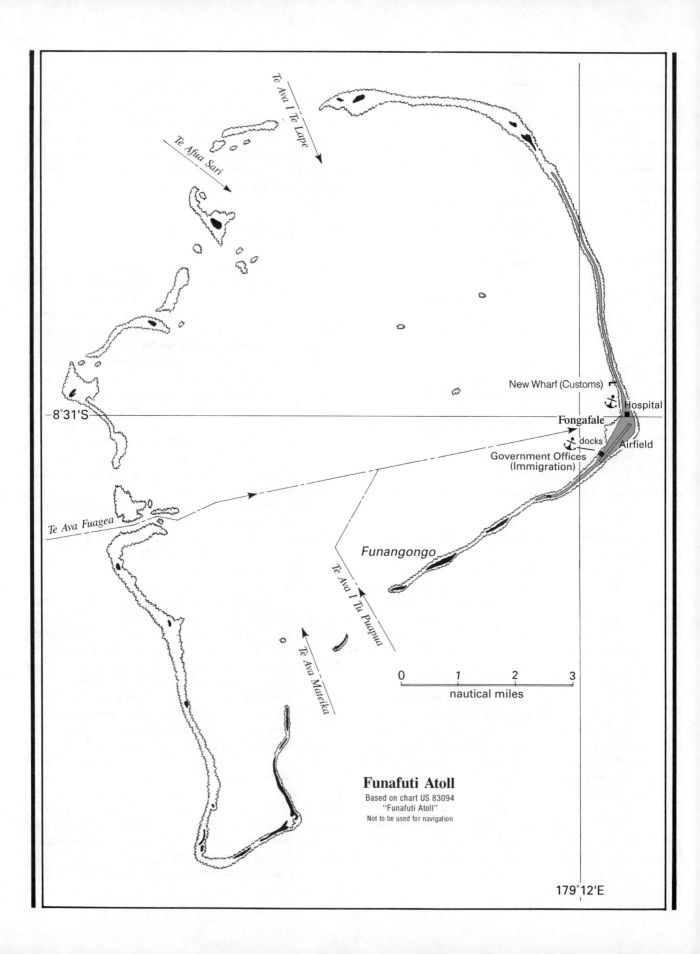

Te Ava I Te Lape

Te Afua Sari

−8°31'S

New Wharf (Customs)

Hospital

Fongafale

docks

Airfield

Government Offices
(Immigration)

Te Ava Fuagea

Funangongo

Te Ava I Tu Puapua

Te Ava Mateika

0	1	2	3

nautical miles

Funafuti Atoll

Based on chart US 83094
"Funafuti Atoll"
Not to be used for navigation

179°12'E

Tuvalu group and may reach speeds of as much as 40 miles per day, but it is variable in both speed and direction. Westerly winds may produce a measurable eastward set to the surface current that can continue for several days after the westerly wind ceases.

The climate of Tuvalu is moderate with temperatures averaging about 80 °F. Extremes are reported to be between 72 °F and 92 °F. The average rainfall for a year is about 180 inches with the wettest season between December and March. The driest months are September and October. There is measurable rainfall on over half the days of the year. A heavy rain could measure as much as four inches in one day, and there are rarely dry spells longer than ten days. Humidity ranges between 75 and 80 percent during the day, but it is tempered by the trade winds when blowing.

Cruising Notes

YACHT ENTRY AND FACILITIES

Funafuti is the only Port of Entry, and yachts should check in there before visiting other atolls. Primary entrance to the Funafuti lagoon is made through the Te Ava Fuagea Pass, although both the Te Ava i te Lape and Te Ava i te Puapua passes are clear. There are a few coral reefs to be avoided and few navigation aids.

When inside the lagoon, proceed to the new deepwater wharf at Fongafale for Customs clearance and then to the old government wharf nearer the center

MEDICAL MEMO

Immunization Requirements
A smallpox vaccination is required and also cholera and yellow fever immunizations if you are arriving 14 days after visiting or transiting an infected area.

Local Health Situation
In the late 1970s there were cases of cholera reported due to unsanitary conditions, but there have been no recent similar reports. There are no other reported health problems. Mosquitoes can be particularly bothersome.

Health Services
The Princess Margaret Hospital on Funafuti was opened in 1978. It has 36 beds, an operating room, X-ray facilities, a laboratory, and a dental clinic. Each of the other islands has a dispensary attended by medical aides and nurses.

Two opticians from New Zealand spend two weeks each year in Tuvalu taking care of eyeglass needs. An eye surgeon comes on a separate schedule from New Zealand to treat eye diseases.

Water
Water from all sources should be considered suspect and treated. Boats should capture their own rainwater.

of activities for the other clearances. There is an A$10.00 immigration entry charge during normal working hours; an additional A$6.00 charge is made for overtime. A visa is not required to visit Tuvalu, but the visitor must have a passport and an onward airline ticket or the equivalent. The maximum stay time is four months. Departure clearances are obtained at the same

Central Funafuti, showing the old wharf and the preferred yacht anchorage. (Peter McQuarrie)

places; you will need a clearance to visit other atolls of this country.

When you have finished with formalities, anchor out in front of the stone jetty where there is 15–20 feet of water over a sand bottom and use your dinghy for further visits. Beware of sunken small craft and pontoons remaining from World War II. This anchorage is well protected from the prevailing east and southeast winds, making it safe during the months of May through September. After October the summer westerlies set in, and the anchorage can become untenable.

Provisions are not plentiful, but you can fill in with some tinned goods, vegetables, and frozen meat from New Zealand. Coconuts and fish are readily available. Water can be in short supply on land, so you should take every opportunity to keep your tanks filled with rainwater. Diesel fuel can be obtained in town or at the Burns-Philp office at the main wharf.

The only other island in this group with a lagoon that can be safely entered by boats is Nukufetau. It is the only place offering shelter during strong westerly winds. The best anchorage is to the east of Coal islet, but entry must be made early because when the wind reaches Force 6, breakers form across Teafua Pass.

CHAPTER 14

NIUE ISLAND

The Country

Niue Island, visited by Captain Cook in 1774, became part of New Zealand in 1901, when the boundaries of New Zealand were extended to include the Cook Islands. The island is an elevated coral outcropping perched on top of a seamount rising from very deep water. Its area of 100 square miles makes it the largest raised coral island in the world. The central saucer-shaped plateau, rising to a height of 220 feet, is encircled by a narrow terrace about 90 feet above the water. The soil, though fertile, is not plentiful, and this feature combined with the rocky and broken nature of the country makes cultivation difficult. Niueans live mostly along the coastline in 14 villages connected by crushed coral roads.

Niue was probably settled more than a thousand years ago by migrations from Samoa and Tonga. Their descendants, even today, are found in the northern and southern villages, respectively. Cook named the island Savage Island because of the hostility of the natives. History has proven the name to be ill-advised, and it is resented by the Niueans.

The London Missionary Society attempted to land teachers on the island in 1830, but they too were repulsed. In 1849, Niuean and Samoan teachers were landed and established the first mission. The first European missionary arrived to stay in 1861.

Niue started as early as 1887 to try to become a member of the British empire, but it did not happen until 1900, when Niue was declared a British protectorate. The next year it was annexed to New Zealand.

On October 19, 1974 (Constitution Day), Niue became self-governing in free association with New Zealand. The leader of government became the premier of Niue and the executive committee became the cabinet.

Under the constitution the Niue assembly consists of 20 members elected by universal suffrage: 14 members each representing a village constituency and 6 members elected on a common roll.

It is written into the Niue Constitution Act of 1974 that New Zealand will continue to be responsible for the external affairs and defense of Niue and for providing necessary economic and administrative assistance. Niueans are British subjects and New Zealand citizens.

The pre-European population of Niue is un-

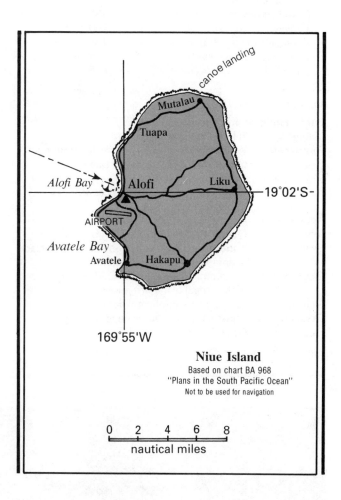

Niue Island
Based on chart BA 968
"Plans in the South Pacific Ocean"
Not to be used for navigation

NIUE
A self-governing country in free association with New Zealand

Port of Entry
Alofi   19°02′S, 169°55′W

Distances between Ports in Nautical Miles
Between Alofi and

Apia, Western Samoa	330
Auckland, New Zealand	1,340
Nukualofa, Tonga	335
Pago Pago, American Samoa	290
Papeete, Tahiti	1,160
Raoul, Kermadec Islands	755
Rarotonga, Cook Islands	585
Suva, Fiji	665

Standard Time
11 hours slow on UTC

Public Holidays and Special Events
January 1–2	Takai—Public holidays
February 6	Waitangi Day—Public holiday (commemoration of New Zealand Bay of Islands treaty signing)
March/April *	Good Friday, Easter, and Easter Monday—Public holidays
April 25	ANZAC Day—Public holiday
June *	Queen's Official Birthday—Public holiday
October 19	Annexation Day—Public holiday (anniversary of annexation to New Zealand)
October *	Peniamina's Day—Public holiday (anniversary of the arrival of the first missionary)
October *	Labour Day—Public holiday
December 25	Christmas Day—Public holiday
December 26	Boxing Day—Public holiday

*Specific dates vary from year to year.

known; the earliest figure is 5,070 people in the year 1884. From then on its population declined, reaching a low of 3,750 in 1928. It recovered to 5,200 persons in 1966 but then fell again to 3,580 in 1979. The October 1989 population stood at 2,267, a 12 percent reduction in three years. The first decline was a result of European diseases and blackbirding; the current decline is a consequence of the emigration of Niueans to New Zealand in search of economic opportunity. There are believed to be about 12,000 Niueans residing in New Zealand at any one time.

The only substantial employer of labor is the government, which employs Niueans in the education, police, public works, health, agriculture, and other departments and in the loading and discharge of vessels. Many unskilled workers are employed in public works. Most workers who do not work for wages, work on their family plantations.

The principal agricultural exports are passionfruit, honey, copra, and limes. Of the total area of the island of 64,900 acres, approximately 50,900 acres are available for agriculture, while some 13,600 acres are in forest. The remaining 400 acres are in buildings and roads.

The forests are in the interior of the island and are made up of mahogany, miro (rosewood), and sandalwood. Although there is much timber on the island, it is not exported but used for houses and other buildings. Some cattle are now being raised on the island to supplement the frozen mutton imported from New Zealand.

Niue's natural attractions are highlighted by its massive limestone caves along the coast and inland. The caves were caused by ancient submarine upheavals, which produced deep chasms in the limestone cap of the

There is no harbor at Niue, but a passage has been blasted through the fringing reef at Alofi to permit small boats to come alongside the man-made jetty. It is wise to lift your dinghy onto the jetty to prevent it from pounding on the jetty wall. The harbor was severely damaged by tropical cyclone Ofa in 1990. (Gail Jensen)

FLOTSAM AND JETSAM

Currency
Niue uses New Zealand currency. For the approximate rate of exchange see New Zealand. The relative cost of goods is 132, the result of shipping from New Zealand.

Language
The indigenous language is a Polynesian dialect peculiar to the island but closely related to that of Tonga and Samoa with some elements from eastern Polynesia. English is the official language.

Electricity
Where electricity is available it is 240v, 50 Hz AC.

Postal Address
Mail comes infrequently to Niue. It is recommended that yachts use Tonga, Samoa, Cook Islands, or New Zealand for mail drops.

Ports for Making Crew Changes
Niue is not a recommended port for making crew changes because of the difficult reef anchorage. Furthermore, generally poor communications would make coordination very difficult. Niue has twice weekly air service from Apia. The nearest recommended ports for making a crew change would be Rarotonga, Pago Pago, or Nukualofa.

External Affairs Representative
New Zealand consulates or embassies

Information Center
Niue Tourist Board
P.O. Box 67
NIUE ISLAND
South Pacific Ocean

seamount. Some caves are nearly a mile deep, and many are yet unexplored.

The Weather

The prevailing wind is from the east-southeast. Variable winds, sometimes strong, often blow from the west, northwest, and north during the summer months of November to April.

Niue is on the edge of the southwest Pacific tropical cyclone belt and occasionally has received devastating storms—1959, 1960, and, most recently, 1990, when Tropical Cyclone Ofa visited it. (See chapter 3 for details of Ofa.) Considerable damage was done to the northern and western coastal areas including roads, buildings, water supply, and shoreline landings. There was no loss of life.

The climate of Niue is mild and equable with an average mean temperature in July of 76°F and in January of 81°F. December to March is the wettest season. The average annual rainfall is 79 inches with the highest recorded being 133 inches and the lowest being 32 inches. Droughts are not uncommon. April to November is the best season to visit Niue.

Cruising Notes

YACHT ENTRY

Passports are required of all foreign visitors to Niue. A visa is not required for stays of 30 days or less, but sufficient funds and an onward airline ticket or the equivalent are required. Although visits by cruising boats are always welcome, it is preferred that they not arrive on Sunday, which is a quiet day of religion and rest on the island.

Check in with the harbormaster on arrival since Niue is free of the rhinoceros beetle, and infected yachts must be fumigated.

MEDICAL MEMO

Immunization Requirements
Smallpox vaccinations are required unless arriving from neighboring islands. Yellow fever and cholera immunizations are required if arriving within six days after leaving or transiting an infected area.

Local Health Situation
Niue, although situated in the tropics, is largely free from diseases prevalent in tropical countries. Insects in general are few, but flies and mosquitoes can be more than a niusance. The latter are carriers of dengue fever, which is an acute infection caused by a virus. The symptoms are fever, headache, and joint pains, much like the flu, which result in general debilitation that may last for a week or more. In 1980 an outbreak of dengue affected 600 of the island's population and caused four deaths. Cutaneous disease and opthalmia are more common diseases.

Health Services
All medical treatment including hospital service is provided by the government through grants from New Zealand. Visitors are not eligible for free service but must pay a nominal charge. The Lord Liverpool Hospital has 30 beds with an X-ray department, laboratory, dispensary, and out-patient service. Three dispensaries in outlying areas also provide services. Dental and optical services and drugs are available at the hospital.

Water
Drinking water is from natural springs and rainwater.

The Customs officer and doctor will clear your boat at anchor, but you must go ashore to clear with Immigration, which is handled by the police. There is a NZ$30.00 fee for the inbound clearance, but it is not always collected.

Port fees are NZ$5.00 per day.

YACHT FACILITIES

The port of Alofi is an open roadstead on the west side of the island, and yachts must anchor close in because of the very deep water. Private and fishing boat moorings previously available to cruising yachts were destroyed by Ofa. Anchoring, however, can be done in 6–8 fathoms of water in coral sand canyons. Be certain that your anchor is well set before leaving your boat. The water is exceptionally clear because there is little runoff from the island. In-the-water visibility can reach 100 feet. Surge is present in the anchorage and generally comes from the southwest, a condition resulting from southeast wind swells wrapping around the southern coast of the island.

Dinghies can be taken to shore through a natural passage in the reef that is also used by lighters when unloading ships. If you land at the jetty in Alofi Bay, it is wise to lift your dinghy onto the jetty to avoid pounding. There are landings but really no safe anchorages at Tuapa and Avatele.

The anchorage at Alofi is tenable when the normal prevailing winds are blowing from an easterly direction. However, if the wind swings into the west, it is advisable to leave immediately. If your visit wasn't completed, stand offshore until the wind returns to the prevailing direction and then return to the anchorage.

Fresh provisions on Niue may be somewhat limited depending on the amount of recent rainfall. Fresh water itself is not overly abundant, being pumped from wells in the coral base of the island. Some vegetables are available; and passionfruit, honey, and limes—Niue's main export crops—can also be purchased. Some beef, pork, and chicken can also be obtained. Fish are scarce in these deep waters.

Spirits can be purchased duty free on departure.

CHAPTER 15

NEW ZEALAND

The Country

Two main islands comprise New Zealand—the North, 44,200 square miles; and the South, 58,200 square miles. Both islands are long and narrow, 1,100 miles separating the extremity of the south from the slim tip of the north. No point is farther than 68 miles from the sea. New Zealand lies at latitudes south of the equator similar to California's position north of the equator and hence has a climate similar to that of California's coastal regions.

The country is predominantly mountainous. Alps run almost the length of the South Island with New Zealand's highest peak, Mt. Cook (12,349 feet), midway along the chain. There are 16 mountains of more than 9,840 feet. In keeping with this great alpine system is a network of glaciers, some of which reach the forests of the west coast.

As huge and permanent as the mountains seem, New Zealand has changed its shape many times, for it is a region where the earth's crust has long been changing. This is particularly true of the volcanic and thermal area that stretches in a line from just south of Lake Taupo in the center of the North Island to White Island, off the Bay of Plenty. It begins, in the central plateau, with three great volcanic peaks: Ruapehu and Ngauruhoe—which have both, from time to time, emitted steam and ash—and Tongariro. The remarkable thermal activity of this belt is most spectacular at Rotorua, where geysers spout and mud pools bubble and plop like boiling porridge.

New Zealand's deeply folded landscape has many lakes and rivers. The rivers vary from short and torrential ones along the west coast of the South Island to the long, braided, glacier-fed waters of its eastern plains and the impressively deep-flowing Wanganui and Waikato rivers that drain the volcanic plateau of the North Island.

Of the many lakes, Taupo (234 square miles) is the largest. In the south, Te Anau, Wakatipu, Wanaka, and Manapouri lie still and deep, creating classically beautiful scenery in valleys left by glaciers.

Although more than three-quarters of New Zealand is more than 650 feet above sea level, there are large expanses of easier country. The most extensive are the Canterbury Plains, which spread across 4,800 square miles of the South Island's east coast. The North Island has the rich grasslands of the Wairarapa, Manawatu, Waikato, and Taranaki rivers and the green valleys of the Auckland province.

Geologically speaking, New Zealand as it exists today is only about five million years old. Its hills and mountains are still jagged, and conversion by erosion has not progressed very far. Other than the Canterbury Plains of the South Island, there is little level land in this country, and consequently, crop farming has not developed. In contrast, the hillsides of both islands covered with lush grass interspersed between the valleys of impenetrable bush make ideal grazing grounds for sheep and cattle.

The north end of North Island is subtropical, enabling the growing of citrus fruits, while the south end of South Island has cold, snowy winters. South Island on its rugged southwestern rim has spectacular fjords and glaciers. It is this jagged and indented coastline that gives New Zealand a coastline length that approximates that of the contiguous 48 United States. Westerly winds are the rule. Rain, while seasonal, is well spread over the two islands, giving lush natural pastures, bush that is impenetrable in spots, and trees of magnificent stature.

Besides good summer weather, the yachting enthusiast is attracted to New Zealand's highly indented coastline, which provides innumerable harbors for exploration, isolation, or sanctuary from a local storm. In particular, the northeast coast of North Island is favored by the Kiwi sailor and has also become the overwhelming favorite of overseas yachts. South of East Cape to Bluff there are only a few snug harbors; even fewer exist

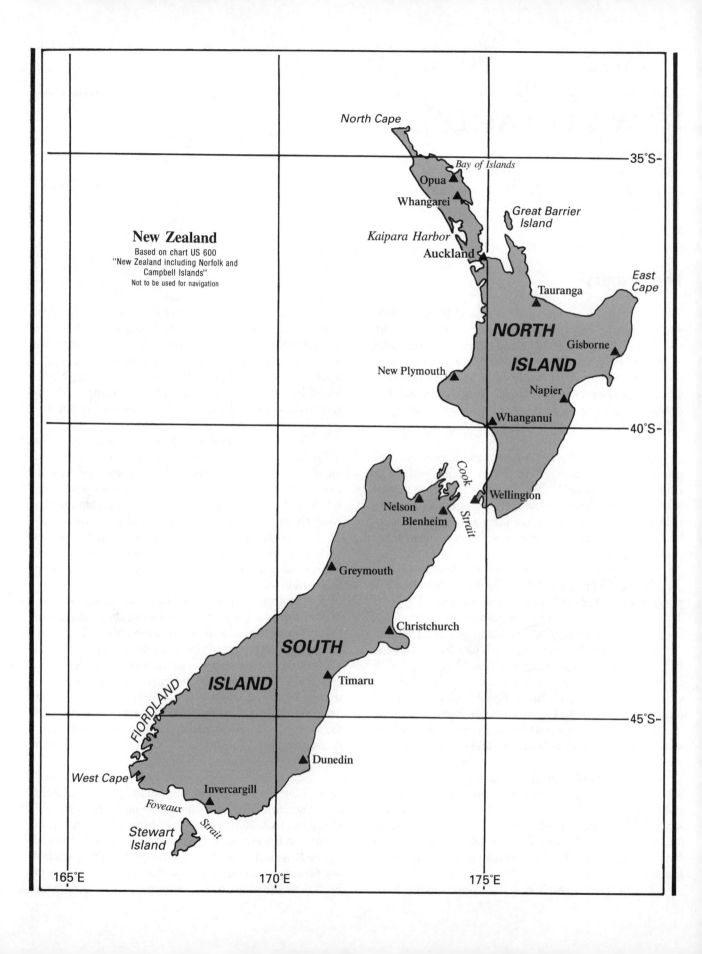

North Cape

Bay of Islands

Opua ▲

Whangarei ▲

Great Barrier
Island

Kaipara Harbor

Auckland ▲

Tauranga ▲

East
Cape

NORTH

ISLAND

Gisborne ▲

New Plymouth ▲

Napier ▲

Whanganui ▲

35°S–

40°S–

New Zealand

Based on chart US 600
"New Zealand including Norfolk and
Campbell Islands"

Not to be used for navigation

Cook

Nelson ▲

Blenheim ▲

▲ Wellington

Strait

SOUTH

Greymouth ▲

Christchurch ▲

ISLAND

Timaru ▲

FIORDLAND

45°S–

Dunedin ▲

West Cape

Invercargill ▲

Foveaux

Stewart
Island

Strait

165°E

170°E

175°E

NEW ZEALAND
An independent nation

Ports of Entry (partial)

Opua (Bay of Islands)	35°19′ S, 174°07′ E
Whangarei	35°44′ S, 174°20′ E
Auckland	36°50′ S, 174°46′ E
Tauranga	37°39′ S, 176°11′ E
Wellington	41°18′ S, 174°47′ E

Distances between Ports in Nautical Miles
Between Auckland and

Alofi, Niue	1,365
Brisbane, Australia	1,290
Noumea, New Caledonia	975
Nukualofa, Tonga	1,080
Papeete, Tahiti	2,210
Port-Vila, Vanuatu	1,195
Raoul, Kermadec Islands	585
Rarotonga, Cook Islands	1,625
Suva, Fiji	1,140
Sydney, Australia	1,275
Tubuai, Austral Islands	2,010

Standard Time
12 hours fast on UTC

Public Holidays and Special Events

January 1	New Year's Day—Public holiday
January 26	Anniversary Regatta—World's largest one-day yacht regatta (at Auckland Harbour)
February 6	Waitangi Day—Public holiday (commemoration of Bay of Islands treaty signing)
March/April *	Good Friday, Easter, and Easter Monday—Public holidays
April 25	ANZAC Day—Public holiday
June *	Queen's Official Birthday—Public holiday
October *	Labour Day—Public holiday
December 25	Christmas Day—Public holiday
December 26	Boxing Day—Public holiday

*Specific dates vary from year to year.

along the entire west coast of both islands facing the Tasman Sea. Separating the two islands is Cook Strait, which is noted for its violent winds. Here the prevailing westerlies are funneled between the mountain ranges that form the strait, and the resultant winds and currents make the Alenuihaha Channel of Hawaii look like a millpond.

The flora and fauna of New Zealand are uniquely described by their abundance—much of the flora and little of the fauna. This is the land of the great kauri tree, although the trees are also found in limited numbers on islands to the north and west as far away as Malaysia. A slow-growing tree living more than a thou-

sand years, the kauri reaches heights of more than 150 feet with the lowest limbs often 60 feet above the ground; the trunk has a girth of up to 50 feet. In once great stands, it started to disappear rapidly after the arrival of the Europeans—first for masts for English warships, then settlers' buildings and export to Australia. Now it is protected and its uses limited to those applications requiring its fine wood qualities such as boatbuilding. Kauri gum for varnish was a much sought after byproduct in the 1880s, and "gum diggers" scoured North Island for buried chunks of fossilized resin left from ancient stands of the trees. To help save the remaining kauris, faster-growing pines are now farmed to supply New Zealand's timber needs and for export.

There are some other unusual trees in this unusual country. The punga is a tree fern that reaches heights of 50 feet; and the cabbage palm is similar to the pandanus palm of tropical islands. A favorite of many is the pahutukawa tree—a massive, gnarled, many-limbed tree as big as the largest oak or Brazilian pepper tree. It grows in the most improbable spots on steep hills, rocky bluffs, and at the ocean's edge. Covered most of the year with conservative gray-green leaves, it bursts forth in summer (December and January) with brilliant crimson powder-puff flowers. The pohutukawa trees form dramatic splotches in the bush covering much of the hilly land.

New Zealand has few native land animals, but a great diversity of birds—some 250 species in all. There is the flightless kiwi, shy and nocturnal, and the fat and comical weka, also flightless. More common are the bellbird and tui; the fantail; the kaka and kea (forest and mountain parrots, respectively); the pukeko, or swamp hen; and the morepork, or native owl. The kotuku, or white heron, is a rare bird of great beauty. Rarest of all is the takhe, a large, flightless type of rail believed to be extinct and rediscovered some years ago in the remote areas of southwest Fjordland.

The only indigenous land animals are two species of bats and a rare Maori rat. Among reptiles, the lizardlike tuatara is described as a living fossil and is now found only on some offshore islands.

There is some evidence that the first New Zealand natives were lost Polynesians who arrived there by accident and not by intent. Possibly they were out fishing or in small canoes voyaging between the islands far to the north and east and were blown south to ultimately land on these islands. The time of arrival of these first inhabitants was about A.D. 500. Finding the islands to have little vegetable growth to sustain their lives, they turned to hunting the giant flightless and now extinct moa bird. Their nomadic, isolated existence lasted until A.D. 800 to 1100. At that time adventuresome Polynesians from the Marquesas and/or Society Islands started migrating throughout the vast triangular area of the Pacific formed by Easter Island, Hawaii, and New Zealand. These later Polynesian arrivals—now called Maoris—eventually eliminated the earlier race of moa hunters and established their own society based on independent tribes with a common culture.

The Maoris were the most fierce of all Polynesians, engaging constantly in warfare in which the loser could expect to be eaten. While wars were usually fought for conquest or revenge, war was also a sport with chivalrous periods. Halts in battle were frequently called to return the wounded. After the arrival of European guns, battles were sometimes extended by one side's giving additional ammunition to the other side. Guns in the hands of warring tribes together with disease reduced the Maori population from an estimated 200,000–400,000 in 1780 to a low of 42,000 in 1896. Today the Maori population numbers about 290,000.

The first European explorers to see these islands were the Dutch under Abel Tasman in 1642; subsequently, the islands were named after a Dutch province —Sea Land. The English explorer Captain Cook thoroughly explored and charted New Zealand for the first time in 1769–1777.

Following closely on the heels of the explorers were the exploiters of the period—sealers, whalers, and traders. Sealers managed to virtually exterminate the seal population found principally off the South Island by 1830 and then turned to whaling. The humpback whale became the new hunting target. These whales migrated south along the New Zealand coast in October and November to spend the summer months in the Antarctic and returned north in June and July to winter in the tropics. Their shoreline migration at slow speeds (4 knots) and their huge bulk (40 to 50 tons) were their undoing.

New Zealand whaling reached its peak in 1838. Whalers sought their R and R (resupply and ribaldry!) in a little Bay of Islands settlement called Kororareka (Maori for "tasty blue penguin"), which could boast of 30 grog shops. At one time in 1836 there were 36 whaling ships from all around the world anchored at Kororareka. While whaling greatly diminished in these waters in the following years, the town of Kororareka survived. Today it has but one pub and carries the respectable name of Russell.

Serious colonization of New Zealand began after

That good New Zealand milk is hustled to the customer by the youth brigade, assuring freshness and timeliness. Milk in paper cartons at supermarkets is replacing this delivery system. (Earl Hinz)

the Treaty of Waitangi was signed in 1840 between the Maoris and British. Traders, missionaries, and farmers from England flocked to the islands, which proved to be fertile ground for all three. While many settlements just happened, some were deliberately planned, like the bit of Scotland developed on South Island's Otago Harbor now known as Dunedin. It is New Zealand's fourth-largest city, with a population of 120,000. Christchurch on the Canterbury Plain of the South Island was a planned Church of England settlement. It is more familiar in today's world activities as the jumping-off place for Antarctic expeditions. Wellington, New Zealand's capital, was sited by the New Zealand Company on the north side of Cook Strait separating the North and South islands. The land for Wellington was bought by the New Zealand Company in 1839 from a Maori tribe that supposedly owned it. (The true ownership of land in New Zealand is very confused, however, and poses a problem for land courts even today.)

New Zealand was declared a dominion by a royal proclamation effective September 26, 1907 (Dominion Day). It achieved full internal and external autonomy by the Statute of Westminster Adoption Act of 1947, although this only formalized a situation that had existed for many years.

New Zealand has a parliamentary system of government closely patterned on that of the United Kingdom and is a fully independent member of the British

Commonwealth of Nations. It has no written constitution. Queen Elizabeth II is the sovereign and chief of state, represented in New Zealand by a governor-general.

The estimated population in 1989 totaled 3.3 million, and the annual growth rate was 0.4 percent. Of the total population, 290,000 are indigenous Maoris of Polynesian stock; the remainder are predominantly British in origin. The inhabitants of this beautiful country are fiercely holding on to old traditions, both Maori and European, while taking advantage of twentieth-century opportunities.

While other more populous countries may envy New Zealand's capacity to spread its population to an average of only 32 people to a square mile. New Zealanders, despite their heavy dependence on agriculture, are predominantly urban dwellers, with about 40 percent living in the four main centers of Auckland, Wellington, Christchurch, and Dunedin. More than 70 percent of the population lives on the North Island. The milder climate of the North Island, the expansion of the forest industries there, the specialized farming, and the building of factories near the larger local markets have helped lead to the uneven distribution of population.

New Zealand has kept political ties over the years with many of the island countries, giving their citizens free right of access to New Zealand. The result has been a steady migration of island people to New Zealand, particularly Auckland, in hopes of getting jobs in local industries. As of 1990, New Zealand's Polynesian population (excluding the indigenous Maoris) was reported to be 95,700. Western Samoans and Cook Islanders made up three-fourths of these, with Niueans, Tongans, and Tokelauans making up the rest.

Although there is no officially established church or state religion, non-Christian sects are few. About 80 percent of the people belong to four denominations—Anglican, Presbyterian, Roman Catholic, and Methodist. Church schools receive government assistance, as do other private schools, and follow curricula prescribed by the Department of Education. The literacy rate is 98 percent.

New Zealand is a strong welfare state, and interwoven into the social security network is a full range of health services for its own citizens. Public hospital treatment and medicine prescribed by doctors are free. The state pays for a portion of all doctors' bills amounting to almost half. Private hospital bills are paid in part by the state, and some private health plans exist. (Foreigners have to pay for doctors, hospital services, and medicine; costs can be quite high.)

State benefits also apply in one instance to visitors. Accident compensation exists for all visitors to the country. It's automatic, and for the visitor it is free except for a motor vehicle levy if you buy a car. Upon your arrival, coverage for personal injury due to accidents is also extended to you. Full information is available from the state insurance office.

The Weather

Because the mean atmospheric pressure tends to be greater at the northern than at the southern end of New Zealand, the general direction of the wind over New Zealand should be westerly; but it is deflected by the high mountain chains, and consequently the wind often blows up or down the coast and almost invariably through Cook Strait either from northwest or southeast. When, however, at a sufficient distance from the coast to be free of local influences, the winds generally commence at east and veer through north and west, etc., showing that they are mainly caused by depressions passing southward of New Zealand.

The high-pressure cells (anticyclones) generated over Australia march with regularity across the North Island every six to ten days, normally moving eastward

New Zealand Summer Weather Pattern

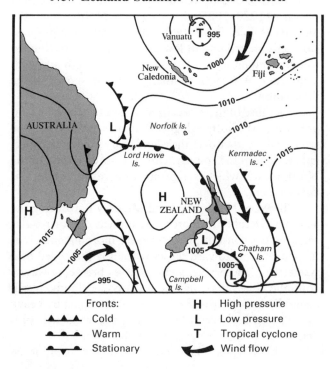

The capital of New Zealand is Wellington, at the southern tip of North Island. It is located on magnificent Lambton Harbor, but its higher latitude and blustery prevailing winds make it less attractive to the cruiser used to moderate tropical weather. (Earl Hinz)

at a speed of 300 to 400 miles per day. When the high pressure (1020–1025 mbs) is over the North Island, the weather is fine. But between the successive high-pressure cells are troughs of low pressure (1000–1010 mbs) usually containing a cold front from the south and with some rain. A typical weather pattern is shown in the illustration.

Because of these peculiarities and because the temperature in the north is higher than that in the south, the wind and weather over the islands vary greatly in different sections of the country. Only the northern end of the North Island, which is of primary interest to cruisers, is covered here.

Between North Cape and Mercury Bay during the summer (October to March), a northeasterly or regular sea breeze is constant; it starts in the morning and gradually dies away toward sunset when it is succeeded by a westerly or land breeze. Should the sea breeze, however, continue after sunset and the sky become cloudy, it will generally increase to a fresh gale accompanied by heavy rain lasting for several hours; then the wind will suddenly shift to the west and the weather clear.

These regular land and sea breezes cannot be depended on during winter, when northwest to southwest winds prevail. A north wind with cloudy weather usually terminates in a gale of short duration accompanied by rain.

A northwesterly wind is generally strong with heavy rains; it seldom lasts for more than 24 hours, the general shift being counterclockwise. With a westerly wind the weather is unsettled and squally, but when it veers to west-southwest and southwest, which it almost invariably does, fine settled weather sets in and usually continues for several days.

A strong easterly or southeasterly gale generally occurs about once in six weeks. It is accompanied by rain and thick weather, lasting from two to three days. This wind is preceded by a high barometer and generally shifts through north to southwest.

There is also an exceedingly cold southeast wind, with a clear sky and fine settled weather, which frequently continues for several days, terminating in a calm or shifting to southwest. Westerly gales generally die away at sunset within a short distance of the land, their continuance indicated by a noticeable fall in the barometer.

Between Mercury Bay and East Cape and in the Bay of Plenty, westerly breezes prevail, freshening during the day almost to a gale at times and moderating at sunset. Northwesterly gales are frequent and sometimes last three days, bringing a heavy sea into the Bay of Plenty. With strong westerly winds the weather is generally fine and clear, but in fine weather with light winds there can be a haze over the land. Northeasterly and northerly gales are indicated by a swell from the north rolling into the Bay of Plenty a day or two before.

Southeasterly winds are infrequent, but they generally blow freshly for a few hours and bring rain. Northeasterly gales in winter always work round through north to southwest.

During summer, southeasterly winds are most common in the vicinity of Cape Runaway. Strong westerly winds are frequently met 5 miles offshore while it is quite calm at Cape Runaway.

Gales accompanied by heavy rains are experienced during both winter and summer. These gales are generally preceded by a high barometer (1025 mbs) with the wind from south and east. As the barometer falls the wind increases for 12 to 18 hours followed by a sudden shift to the west and southwest. The weather rapidly clears and the barometer rises quickly. During the intervals between these gales, which occur about once a month, winds between northwest and southwest prevail, calms being uncommon.

Southeast winds are common near East Cape, sometimes lasting for several days, and are often very strong. A strong southwest gale, which is dangerous in the roadstead between Cape Runaway and East Cape, sometimes occurs; it is preceded by rollers and unsteady flows of wind.

Cyclones (low-pressure cells) traveling to the east most frequently pass south of Stewart Island and are most severe over the South Island, but sometimes their influence is felt over all New Zealand. The wind begins at northeast or north, with a falling barometer, then veers to northwest and blows hard; as the center of the storm passes eastward the barometer rises and the wind shifts (usually suddenly with heavy rain, hail, thunder, and lightning and the temperature falling several degrees) to the southwest in a strong gale; fine weather returns as the wind veers through south to southeast or east. If, however, the wind backs through west to north

Horizon moored at the Waitangi Yacht Club. Piling moorings are quite common in New Zealand, and consideration must be given to the 10 to 13 foot tidal ranges when anchoring or mooring. (Earl Hinz)

FLOTSAM AND JETSAM

Currency
The unit of currency is the New Zealand dollar. There are 100 cents in the dollar, and coins are issued in amounts of 1, 2, 5, 10, and 50 cents. Notes are issued in denominations of 1, 2, 5, 10, 20, and 100 dollars. The approximate rate of exchange is US$1 = NZ$1.68. The relative price of goods and services is approximately 119.

Language
English is the national language and understood by everybody. In addition, Maori, a Polynesian dialect, is spoken by many of the indigenous Maoris; its use is on the increase.

Electricity
New Zealand is fully electrified; the current is 240v, 50 Hz AC.

Postal Addresses
New Zealand has an extensive postal system, and you can receive your mail General Delivery at any town you choose. Since there is more than one post office in some towns, it is wise to have mail sent to the main post office. A typical address would, therefore, read:

Yacht ( )
General Delivery
Main Post Office
Whangarei
NEW ZEALAND

Yacht ( )
Opua Postal Agency
Opua, Bay of Islands
NEW ZEALAND

Yacht ( )
c/o Westhaven Marina
Ports of Auckland
P.O. Box 1560
Auckland 1
NEW ZEALAND

Ports for Making Crew Changes
Auckland is a recommended port for making crew changes because of its excellent airline service. It is served by international carriers from Sydney, London, Singapore, Honolulu, and Los Angeles. International feeder airlines connect with Papeete, Rarotonga, Nukualofa, and Suva. Domestic airlines provide connections within New Zealand to most cities and towns.

External Affairs Representative
New Zealand has embassies and consulates in the principal countries of the world. Should you be in an area where there is none, you can get assistance from any British consulate.

Information Center
New Zealand Government Tourist and Publicity Department
Private Bag
Wellington
NEW ZEALAND

or northeast, it is a sure indication that another similar storm is approaching. These changes frequently take place with considerable rapidity and succeed each other for weeks at a time. The barometer rises and falls quickly, and the weather is very unsettled.

The southwest Pacific tropical cyclone season occurs during the southern hemisphere summer months of November through March. An average year generates 11 tropical storms with winds from 35 to 64 knots and four tropical cyclones with winds in excess of 64 knots. While most of these storms originate and move well north and west of New Zealand, a few each year turn east and south, posing threats to Fiji, Tonga, Samoa, and the sailing routes to New Zealand. For this reason, the prudent cruiser intending to summer in New Zealand starts sailing south no later than November 1.

The climate is temperate without marked extremes but with sharp regional contrasts caused by the high relief of the country. It is warmest in the subtropical Northland to the north of Auckland and gets increasingly colder to the south. Rainfall is heavy in most areas, especially on the west coasts, which are exposed to the prevailing winds.

The extremes of daily temperature in New Zealand vary throughout the year by an average of only 20°F. The mean annual temperature of North Island is 57°F, that of South Island, 52°F. The temperature on the west coast of both islands is more equable than that on the east.

The abundance and frequency of rainfall are the leading features in the climate of New Zealand as a whole, and very rarely is there a month without rain in any part of the islands. On the other hand, on very few occasions is there rainfall every day of the month. The rainfall is usually more intense and frequent at night than in the daytime.

In the Auckland area winter rains bring about 4 inches per month while summer rains bring about 3 inches per month. Long-term averages show an annual rainfall of 44 inches. North of Auckland, in the section known as the Northland, around Whangarei, the average annual rainfall is greater, ranging between 60 and 100 inches per year.

The contrast between the rainfall on the east and west coasts is most striking on South Island. There the lofty Southern Alps lie broadside to the prevailing westerly winds, and on their windward slopes are condensed the vapors that have been swept by the breezes over vast stretches of ocean. Over North Island the rain bands are more irregular in form and the rainfall itself more regular over the country. Here, again, the influence of the mountains and plains on precipitation is apparent.

Thunderstorms are comparatively rare in the coastal districts except in the southwestern part of South Island. In summer the thunderstorms usually occur in the afternoon, and in the winter with the low pressure, at night.

Cruisers who take their boats up the Keri Keri River should be aware that thunderstorms can cause dramatic increases in the height of the river waters. Many boats in past years have been damaged by or lost to raging torrents in this canyon river.

Fog is rare, except at the south end of New Zealand. In September, October, and November in the Bay of Islands and in Hokianga there is sometimes a morning fog, which generally clears by mid-morning. Dense fog occurs occasionally during the winter. In the Bay of Plenty fog has continued for as long as three days, but this duration is unusual. An excellent weather information service for the North Island and the ocean beyond is provided by the Keri Keri Marine Radio Association described later in the section on Yacht Facilities under Main Ports of Entry.

Cruising Notes

YACHT ENTRY

There are 14 Ports of Entry to New Zealand. Cruising boats coming off the Coconut Milk Run usually enter at Opua, Bay of Islands, or sometimes Whangarei or Auckland. You must enter at a Port of Entry and, by law, announce your pending arrival not less than 12 hours beforehand. Should you arrive unannounced, immediately contact the nearest Customs office or the police. Normal working hours for Customs are 0800–1630 weekdays, so plan your request for clearance during that time. Request for clearance outside normal working hours could result in an overtime charge of as much as NZ$240.

CUSTOMS

Following are the procedures for cruisers to follow in entering at the most popular Ports of Entry:

Opua (subport to Whangarei)
Opua is New Zealand's most popular Port of Entry by overseas yachts; some 250 to 300 yachts clearing in every year. Sometimes as many as 10 yachts are waiting for clearance at one time. During the busy season, November through April, a Customs officer is in residence at Opua.

As you enter the Bay of Islands, call Opua harbor control on VHF channel 16; they will arrange for necessary inspections. Proceed to the wharf and tie up in the area designated "Customs." If you haven't been able to make radio contact, then telephone Whangarei Customs and someone will drive up to Opua to clear you.

Whangarei
Before arrival, it is best to radio harbor control at Marsden Point on VHF channel 16 and ask them to inform Customs of your pending arrival at Port Whangarei. A less preferable alternative is to wait until you reach the town wharf and then call Customs by telephone. All clearance procedures will take place at the town wharf. There is a NZ$50 charge made by the Northlands Harbour Board and collected at the Whangarei Marina office.

Auckland
Overseas yachts or yachts returning to New Zealand from abroad should call the Mt. Victoria signal station on 2182 kHz for instructions when entering at Auckland. The officer in charge will advise you where to meet the port doctor. Should you arrive at night, you may be advised to anchor off Compass Dolphin until daylight. Should strong winds make the anchorage unpleasant, you may request an alternate anchorage from Mt. Victoria.

Yachts can also call Auckland harbor radio on VHF channel 16 when inside Rangitoto Island. They will contact Health, Customs, Immigration, and Agriculture for you. If you do not get instructions to the contrary, proceed to the Admiralty Steps between Queen's Wharf and Captain Cook Wharf for clearance.

Yachts without radio should anchor off Compass Dolphin flying their Q flag where they will be observed from the Mt. Victoria signal station. A doctor will be sent for health clearance after which Customs will either come aboard while the boat is at anchor or, more likely, direct the vessel to proceed to Admiralty Steps.

Foreign yachts cannot move freely about New Zealand unless they are in possession of a cruising license. These cruising licenses are issued on a reciprocal basis to yachts from countries who grant the same privileges to New Zealand yachts. The United States and all members of the British Commonwealth fall into that category. Other nationalities should check with Customs on arrival.

All overseas registered yachts are entered on a temporary basis. A value for duty and/or goods and services tax (GST) will be assessed against the yacht but not subject to immediate collection. Instead it will be secured by means of a declaration by the skipper that the yacht will depart within 12 months from the date of entry. Equipment belonging to the yacht, either installed or in transit, is not subject to duty or GST, provided it will be exported with the yacht. If any equipment is landed, then Customs must be notified and taxes paid. If the boat and its goods are not exported in accordance with the entry conditions, then the owner becomes liable for payment of taxes on the boat, which include a 24 percent duty and a 12.5 percent GST. Any visa extensions that may be granted to you do not extend the 12-month term approved for the yacht. The wise cruiser will make several copies of the temporary import permit to facilitate getting exemptions on the 12.5 percent GST on exportable items.

Baggage declarations listing "personal effects" must be completed by each crew member on arrival. Personal effects means all articles that a traveler may reasonably require for personal use during the cruise such as clothing, footwear, watches, articles of adornment, toiletries, and jewelry. A limited amount of tobacco and spirits may be entered. They will be exempt from duty and the GST provided they are personal property, they are not intended for resale, and they are not imported in commercial quantities.

Certain goods cannot be imported to New Zealand at all, to wit, drugs of any kind except personal health needs, which have to be declared, and products that are banned by the Convention on International Trade in Endangered Species of Wild Fauna and Flora (CITES, pronounced "sightees"). If you suspect you have any in your souvenir collection, you must declare them. Innocent possession is not a criminal offense, but the items will be confiscated.

Where goods are purchased in New Zealand and fitted to the transient yacht, a refund of the import duty will be made upon presentation of evidence of overseas origin and your intent to export them as part of your yacht. Overseas goods purchased by you while in New Zealand for fitting to the vessel such as electronic gear, engine parts, and so forth must have an import entry form completed at time of import and a deposit made on the applicable taxes. The deposit will be refunded after the goods have been exported as part of the yacht.

Departure must be made from a Customs Port of Entry, and once you have obtained your clearance certificate, you must sail within 24 hours. Duty-free stores can be obtained from a licensed export warehouse and must be delivered just prior to a Customs officer's granting your clearance certificate.

IMMIGRATION

Citizens of countries that have a visa-free arrangement with New Zealand do not need to get a visa before arrival in New Zealand. Among those countries are Canada, France, Germany, and the United States. Altogether there are 30 such countries. In addition, Australian citizens, British citizens, and other British passport holders who have the right to live permanently in the United Kingdom need no visas.

A visitor's permit will be issued to the boat owner and crew members on arrival; it is good for an initial period of three months and is renewable by the Labour Department for a total of 12 months. Your passport must be valid for a period of three months beyond your total stay, and you cannot work in New Zealand without first obtaining a separate work permit.

It is the responsibility of the boat's captain to ensure that everybody on board has onward travel arrangements either as a continuing crew member or by other means. Crew members who are not dependents of the owner or skipper must have a letter guaranteeing their departure on the boat. If you do not intend to depart New Zealand on the boat you arrived on, then you must have an onward airline ticket or equivalent funds to travel to a country for which you have a right of entry.

If you do expect to depart from New Zealand on board the same boat, you need to have evidence of sufficient funds to support yourself while in New Zealand. In the case of a boat's crew who will live on the boat while in New Zealand, this amounts to NZ$400 per person per month. Evidence of funds can be in the form of travelers checks, bank drafts, letters of credit, or one of the following credit cards: American Express, Bankcard, Diners Club, MasterCard, or VISA. If you cannot satisfy your need for support funds by one of these methods, then you need a guarantee of accommodation and maintenance from a New Zealand "sponsor."

FIREARMS

If you are carrying any firearms, you must obtain a permit immediately on entry from the local police.

HEALTH

Yachts arriving in New Zealand are not required to undergo a health quarantine or present a certificate of deratting as are ships. The skipper is, however, responsible to report having visited any country in recent weeks that may have had plague, cholera, or yellow fever. The skipper should also report any occurrences of skin rash, fevers, chills, or diarrhea that may have occurred on the voyage or up to 3 weeks after arrival. New Zealand is a healthy country by reason of its isolation, and boats should not knowingly bring in any disease.

AGRICULTURAL INSPECTION

New Zealand's economy is highly dependent on agriculture, and it is relatively free of pests and plant diseases. Yachts arriving from overseas can introduce pests and disease not in existence. As a result, the agricultural quarantine inspection is quite thorough and may be exasperating to the crew; it is, however, necessary for the good of the host country. In brief, New Zealand agricultural inspection rules state:

- Fruits, vegetables, plant product foodstuffs, and the waste from them cannot be landed.
- Potted plants cannot be landed.
- Meat and animal products cannot be landed. All waste from these products must be disposed of in the proper garbage disposal system.
- Eggs and egg containers cannot be landed.
- Cycles, powered or unpowered, must be cleaned before landing. A written permit is required for landing such cycles.
- No garbage can be thrown overboard within the territorial sea of New Zealand (12-mile limit).
- Garbage of any kind must be disposed of on land in proper containers.

It is possible to bond certain prohibited products while you are in New Zealand, but the subsequent inspection ritual usually does not make it worthwhile. The skipper will have to complete a Master's Certificate of Compliance with the agricultural regulations.

Special attention must also be paid to bonding pets on board your boat (see chapter 3). Note, in particular, the three-month limit for keeping a pet under bond in New Zealand. If you have a pet aboard, you cannot move your boat between ports without first notifying Agriculture Inspection. Experiences of other cruisers have shown that New Zealand enforces its pet quarantine laws with considerable zeal.

YACHT FACILITIES

New Zealand is a haven for yachting probably unlike any other place in the world. Its citizens are descendants of seafarers from one hemisphere or the other, and Aucklanders claim to have more boats per capita than any other city in the world. More than one overseas yacht has made New Zealand its base for seasonal cruising in the South Pacific.

Tides around New Zealand are significant and must be considered in navigating the interesting shallow waters along the coast. Tidal ranges of 10 to 14 feet are common, producing strong tidal currents in many places. If you want to explore the shallow waters, you should procure a copy of the current New Zealand nautical almanac and tide tables.

Sea waves resulting from earthquakes in the Pacific (tsunamis) can have a serious effect on boats in harbors or anchorages along the coast. In the event of the possibility of a sea wave approaching New Zealand, the Civil Defence Organization will notify harbormasters, who will spread the word to vessels in their harbors. In major harbors the signal is five prolonged blasts on a siren. Auckland, Wellington, and Whangarei have such a warning system. At the Bay of Islands and other small harbors, the signal is passed by vehicle-mounted loudspeakers.

Being in the southern hemisphere, New Zealand has its summer in the Christmas–New Year's season. The country takes a holiday for the summer starting on Boxing Day (December 26) and continuing about six weeks. From a cruiser's viewpoint the holiday is both good and bad. The bad part is that many shops and stores close or go on limited working hours, thus preventing work from getting done on your boat. The good part is that if you are doing the work yourself, you can get bargain haulout and yard rates during the holiday season when the Kiwis are busy doing their own yachting.

YACHT FACILITIES AT MAIN PORTS OF ENTRY

Opua and the Bay of Islands

Most cruising yachts coming from the tropics make the Bay of Islands their first landfall. Besides being the most northerly Port of Entry, it is a yachting enthusiast's paradise. There are more than 50 smaller bays or inlets having good holding ground and providing good

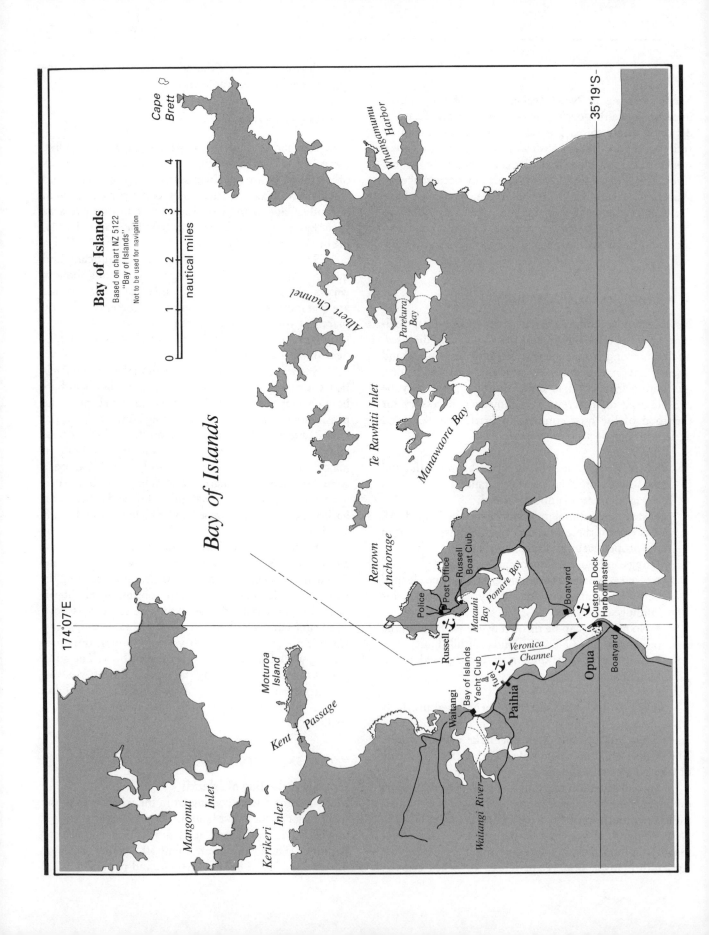

Bay of Islands

Based on chart NZ 5122
"Bay of Islands"
Not to be used for navigation

0 1 2 3 4

nautical miles

Bay of Islands

Cape Brett

Whangamumu Harbor

Parekura Bay

Albert Channel

Manawaora Bay

Te Rawhiti Inlet

Renown Anchorage

Russell Boat Club

Pomare Bay

Matauhi Bay

Police

Post Office

Russell

Boatyard

Customs Dock
Harbormaster

Opua

Boatyard

Veronica Channel

Bay of Islands Yacht Club

fuel

Waitangi

Paihia

Waitangi River

Kent Passage

Moturoa Island

Mangonui Inlet

Kerikeri Inlet

174°07'E

35°19'S

The Russell Boat Club is located on Matauhi Bay in the Bay of Islands. The waters of the bay are shallow and the bottom muddy, but it is a favorite anchorage for cruisers, who are invited to use the dinghy dock and drying grid of the Boat Club. (Earl Hinz)

Peace and tranquility reign at isolated Whangamumu Harbor. The harbor is ringed with pasture land and trees, and there is virtually no sign of contemporary civilization. Only the ruins of a whaling station on the shore remind you that this was once a busy harbor. (Earl Hinz)

weather protection. In addition, the 100 or more islands provide a variety of scenery, good beaches, and many sheltered coves for anchoring.

The town of Russell is at the head of Kororareka Bay. It was an important whaling center in the early nineteenth century. It is sheltered from the north to the southeast and has 14 feet of water abreast the end of the wharf. The bottom is black shingle and not very good holding in a blow. The wharf is used mainly by sport-fishing boats and the ferries to Paihia, but yachts can tie alongside for the purpose of taking on supplies. Though a small town, Russell burgeons with people during the holiday season; it has small but good food stores, some hardware shops, and many tourist shops. Fuel and water can be obtained at the wharf. Laundry can be done at the local camping ground.

In Matauwhi Bay there is good anchoring in water depths of 6 feet or more well sheltered from the prevail-

ing winds. The Russell Boat Club provides a dinghy dock and a pair of grids for bottom work at low tide.

Between the commercial wharf and a ferry slipway at Opua is one yacht anchorage suitable for shallow-draft vessels only. Others can anchor nearby in Veronica Channel or take one of the moorings available at a price of NZ$3.50 per day. There is also a cleaning grid near the ferry landing for vessels drawing up to 6 feet. Fresh water is available at the wharf as well as coin-operated washers, dryers, and hot showers and a dinghy landing. A contract post office operates near the wharf in conjunction with a stationery and secretarial service that offers fax and photocopying and will forward mail for the cruiser. Also nearby are a variety of small convenience stores.

There are three boatyards in the vicinity: Ashby's, Elliot's, and Deeming's. All have good reputations. Haulouts are said to be about two-thirds the cost of

The little town of Russell is a focal point for all types of boating activities and a popular holiday resort. The wharf has fuel and is the terminus for ferry services across the Bay of Islands to Paihia. (New Zealand National Publicity Studios)

MEDICAL MEMO

Immunization Requirements
No additional immunizations are required for persons from Canada, Australia, the United States, and most South Pacific islands who have not been outside those areas for the prior 14 days.

Local Health Situation
New Zealand is a very healthful country; there are no significant medical problems to be concerned about. Occasional cases of hepatitis and cholera are reported, but the diseases are not endemic. There are mosquitoes but no malaria.

Health Services
There are hospitals and registered medical practitioners in all of the cities and larger towns. The St. Johns Ambulance Service can advise on emergency medical help and also provides free ambulance service. The quality of medical service is on a par with that of any country of the world.

Optical and dental services are available in every city and most towns.

Drugs are available from chemists (pharmacies) in most towns.

IAMAT Center

Auckland	Epsom Medical Center
	310 Manukau Road
	Coordinator: Simon P. Barclay,
	MBBS, MRCGP
Wellington	IAMAT Center
	181 Willis Street
	Coordinator: Harold H. Gray, MD
	IAMAT Center
	99 The Terrace
	Coordinator: Geoffrey B. Kiddle, MD

Water
Tap water is safe to drink throughout New Zealand.

---

those in Whangarei or Auckland. Marine hardware is available locally, and there is a sailmaker in the nearby light industry center.

Besides the Russell Boating club there are four other yacht clubs in the Bay of Islands: Keri Keri Cruising Club, Bay of Islands Yacht Club, Opua Cruising Club, and Waitangi Yacht Club. Cruisers are welcome to use their facilities and join in the various sailing activities they sponsor.

The Keri Keri Marine Radio Association provides a valuable service to cruisers sailing the South Pacific as well as those making port in the Bay of Islands. The operation, headed by Jon and Maureen Cullen, maintains regular schedules on marine SSB frequency 4417 kHz at 0730 and 2030 UTC presenting weather reports for areas of your choice in the South Pacific. They also

monitor VHF channel 16 and will request Customs et al. to meet you in Opua for inbound clearances.

Unlike government services funded by taxes, Keri Keri Marine Radio is privately owned and operated and needs financial support from its users. Blue-water cruisers intending to avail themselves of the benefits of this service should join the association; annual fees are NZ$70.60. Write for further information on the wealth of services they can provide:

Keri Keri Marine Radio Association
P.O. Box 131
Keri Keri, Bay of Islands
NEW ZEALAND

Whangarei

Whangarei is an inland city of 36,500 inhabitants connected with the ocean by tidal waters which snake for 12 miles across the mud flats and sand banks to eventually meet the outflow of the Hatea River at the city center. Along the way are many pleasant anchorages such as Urquhart Bay, Parua Bay, the Nook, Onerahi, and Kissing Point. You also pass the Marsden Point oil refinery and later the general cargo wharves at Port Whangarei before coming to the town basin. When making your way upriver, stay in the center of the channel. Boats drawing more than 5 feet should travel upriver on the flood tide.

Proceed directly to the now unused city wharf for clearance and berthing assignment from the harbor agent, whose office is adjacent to the warehouse on the city wharf. You can sometimes get berthing at the city wharf where you will be rafted temporarily with other transient yachts. Usually, though, cruising boats are assigned piling moorings at NZ$3.57 daily charges. These pilings are on lease to resident yachts, but when the residents are absent, cruising boats get to use the moorings. There is no anchoring in this area.

The town basin is within dinghy and walking distance of the entire city of Whangarei, which can supply all your boat and living needs. It also provides bus connections north to the Bay of Islands and south to Auckland. Immigration and Customs offices are in Whangarei. You can obtain duty-free stores in Whangarei when you are ready to depart.

Whangarei has several boatyards capable of hauling boats up to 100 tons and has a complete line of supporting services from sailmaking to engine overhaul to electronic repair. There is also an array of chandleries selling quality boat parts and supplies. These are all within walking distance of the town basin.

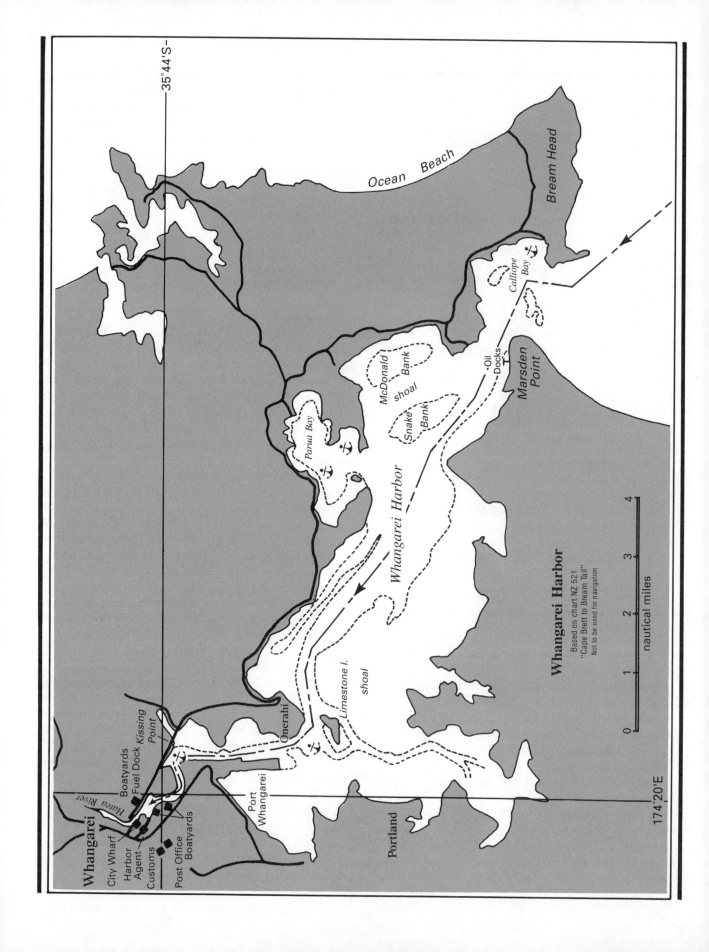

Whangarei Harbor

Based on chart NZ 521
"Cape Brett to Bream Tail"
Not to be used for navigation

0   1   2   3   4
nautical miles

35°44'S

174°20'E

Ocean Beach

Bream Head

Calliope Bay

McDonald Bank
shoal

Snake Bank

Oil Docks

Marsden Point

Parua Bay

Whangarei Harbor

Limestone I. shoal

Onerahi

Port Whangarei

Portland

Whangarei

City Wharf
Harbor Agent
Customs
Post Office Boatyards

Hatea River

Boatyards
Fuel Dock Kissing Point

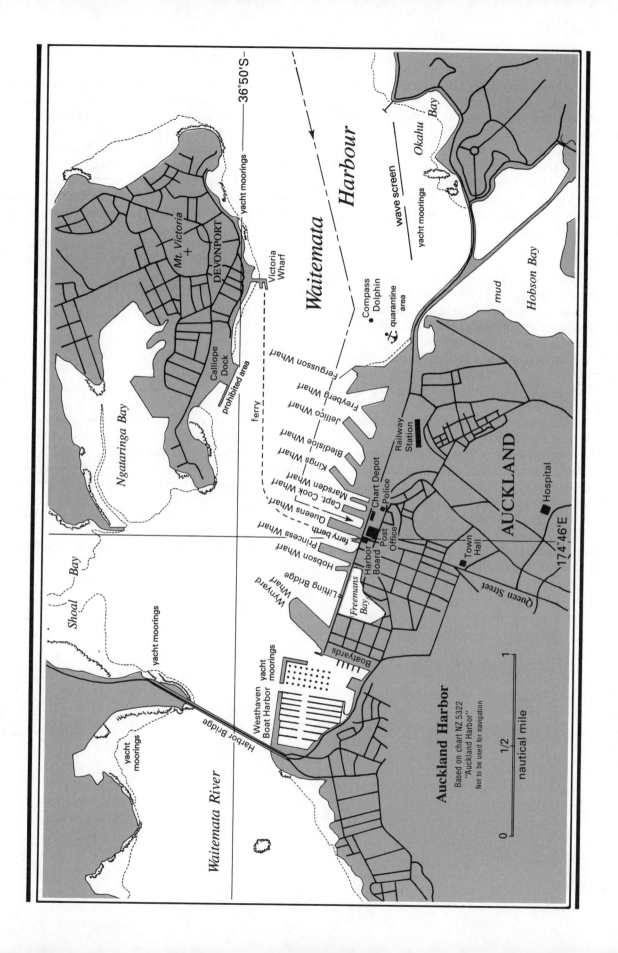

Waitemata River

Shoal Bay

yacht moorings

yacht moorings

Harbor Bridge

Westhaven Boat Harbor

yacht moorings

Boatyards

Wynyard Wharf

Freemans Bay

Lifting Bridge

Hobson Wharf

Princess Wharf

Queens Wharf

Capt. Cook Wharf

Marsden Wharf

Kings Wharf

Bledisloe Wharf

Jellico Wharf

Freyberg Wharf

Fergusson Wharf

ferry

ferry berth

Harbor Board

Post Office

Chart Depot

Police

Town Hall

Queen Street

AUCKLAND

Railway Station

Hospital

174°46'E

Auckland Harbor

Based on chart NZ 5322
"Auckland Harbor"
Not to be used for navigation

0   1/2   1

nautical mile

Ngataringa Bay

Mt. Victoria

DEVONPORT

Calliope Dock

Victoria Wharf

prohibited area

yacht moorings

36°50'S

Waitemata Harbour

Compass Dolphin

quarantine area

wave screen

yacht moorings

Okahu Bay

mud

Hobson Bay

All the boatyards have haulout facilities for doing your own work, and there are a couple of other slipways available for do-it-yourselfers. Most Kiwis and many cruising boats take advantage of the ten-foot-plus tidal range, resting their boat's keel on a water's edge grid, which allows several hours of work to be done while the tide is out. There is a grid in the town basin and another downriver at the Nook. You will find many grids around New Zealand as that is a popular way of doing routine bottomwork.

Auckland

Auckland Harbor is a large, land-locked estuary at the head of the Hauraki Gulf and one of the most secure and commodious harbors in all New Zealand. It has a total area of 73 square miles and a water frontage of 194 miles. It is completely sheltered from all gales by an outlying chain of islands and the Coromandel Peninsula at its entrance. Anchorage in the inner harbor is good in 5 to 12 fathoms of water. The tidal range is 5 to 14 feet.

Visiting yachts can tie up alongside Marsden Wharf, which at night is distinguishable by three fixed lights—red, orange, orange, arranged vertically with the red light uppermost—at the head of the wharf. There are no charges at the wharf, and both electricity and water are available. Marsden Wharf is in the center of Auckland and is convenient to all shopping. It is, however, a typical downtown wharf—noisy and dirty—and the large tidal variations make it difficult to establish a clean, secure berth alongside. The harbormaster's office is at the Queen's Wharf adjacent to the Admiralty Steps.

Most cruising boats prefer to get a berth at Westhaven Marina in St. Mary's Bay. It is Auckland's premier mooring area with 1,200 marina berths, 303 pile moorings, and 85 swing moorings. Westhaven berths are completely assigned, but the harbormaster can usually find room for transient cruising boats. Technically, liveaboards are not permitted, but by keeping a discrete low profile, cruisers have been able to enjoy this fine Auckland harbor. Holding tanks are required, and a pumpout facility is available.

If you wish to book a slip ahead of time (highly desirable), write

Westhaven Marina
Ports of Auckland
P.O. Box 1560
Auckland 1
NEW ZEALAND

or call by telephone 391-352 or VHF channel 13.

A road behind the marina leading past the haulout and service area continues into downtown Auckland, a distance of about two miles. In Auckland you can procure all the necessities and luxuries wanted for boat and self. Boatyards and boat services are too numerous to mention; suffice it to say that this city of 70,000 boats is well equipped to handle all the cruisers' needs.

There are many other marinas and anchorages in Auckland harbor; you can search them out on arrival. None is as convenient to Auckland as is Westhaven.

PART II

Melanesia

Melanesia is a Greek term meaning "black islands," referring to the dark skin tones of the indigenous inhabitants. Melanesia is far smaller than Polynesia in global area covered, but it has as large a population and land area. It is made up predominantly of high islands, some even with active or threatening volcanoes. The islands are mountainous and generally very rugged. Rainfall is quite heavy over the area, supporting heavy vegetation, and in some places dense jungles. Some of the islands have large rivers and extensive swamps, and in the past, malaria has been a serious problem. While malaria is still present, it is no longer the serious problem that it was.

The climate of Melanesia varies from distinct seasonal changes in the south, where the trade winds predominate, to hot and humid equatorial areas in New Guinea under the influence of monsoon winds. Because several of the islands are quite large, there are distinct differences in local climates ranging from snow-capped mountains to high plateaus to temperate coastal plains.

The people of Melanesia are predominantly of the Austroloid group with some softening of features due to intermarriage with the nomadic Mongoloids who were moving to the east during the period 3000 to 1000 B.C. The Austroloids, who now occupy the islands of Indonesia, Melanesia, and Australia itself, are believed to

Island Groups of Melanesia

ISLAND GROUP	NUMBER OF ISLANDS	LAND AREA (square miles)	POPULATION* (thousands)	GOVERNMENT
Fiji	332	7,055	760	Independent
Wallis and Futuna	3	93	15	French overseas territory
New Caledonia (including Loyalty Islands)	6	7,300	153	French overseas territory
Vanuatu	83	5,700	165	Independent
Solomon Islands	10	12,000	335	Independent
Papua New Guinea	626	178,000	3,823	Independent
New Guinea	(mainland)	69,700	1,950	
New Britain	1	14,600	204	
New Ireland	1	3,800	66	
Bougainville	1	41,000	103	
Admiralty group	22	800	29	
Lesser islands	600			

*Reference: *The World Factbook, 1991*, Central Intelligence Agency, U.S. Government Printing Office, Washington DC 20402-9325, USA

have come from Malaysia about 8000 B.C. over the Sunda-Sahul land bridge created during the Ice Age. There is other evidence that the aborigines were in Australia as early as 30,000 B.C., a time period not comprehendable by other than dedicated anthropologists.

It is believed that well-developed cultures existed in Melanesia by the period 2000 B.C. and that much of the early Polynesian culture was derived from them. Melanesians were not navigators like the Polynesians, and they maintained strong, independent tribal structures even on single islands. Because of this characteristic there is no semblance of a common language for Melanesia. Instead, there are hundreds of native dialects plus new languages brought in from Asia and Europe. Except for New Caledonia and Wallis and Futuna Islands, English seems to be the only common language. As each of the countries forming Melanesia has become independent, it has legislated its own national tongue.

CHAPTER 16

FIJI

The Country

Fiji is a group of 332 islands and islets centered along the 180th meridian at 18 degrees south latitude. The island of Rotuma some 240 miles north-northwest of the main group, although not geologically related, is also part of the country. The main group rises from two platforms in the submerged mountain chain of the continental shelf. Most of the larger islands are ancient volcanic peaks; many others are upthrust limestone sometimes pierced by volcanic cones; and still others are coral formations that cap elevations remaining below the surface. Excluding the outlying island of Rotuma, the Dominion of Fiji covers about 274,000 square miles of which about 97 percent is ocean.

The western platform is the broadest, and from it rise Viti Levu and Vanua Levu (the two largest, highest, and most populous islands in the group) and the smaller Yasawa and Lomaitivi groups. The eastern platform forms the base of the Lau island group, a 400-mile-long chain of some 50 islands composed mainly of raised limestone but also containing some that are predominantly volcanic and a few atolls. The combined land area of the group is 7,055 square miles.

About half the area of the high islands is covered by tropical rain forest on their windward sides. Much of the forest has been destroyed by slash-and-burn agricultural methods and is now replaced by secondary bamboo, reed, and scrub growth. On leeward sides the rain forest gives way to more open area that is dry and contains only sparse low vegetation. It is called *talasiga* (sunburned land).

Coastal areas of the high islands are usually broad and are fringed along their seaward extremities by impenetrable mangrove swamps and the usual strand vegetation. Farther inland are great stretches of sugar cane, which is the country's main money crop. The low coral islands are given over to coconut plantations,

which provide relief from the low casuarina, pandanus, and other strand vegetation.

The big islands of Viti Levu and Vanua Levu contain numerous rivers that are unusually large for the size of the island masses involved. Some of these, such as the broad Rewa in Viti Levu, are navigable by small boats and launches as far as 100 miles upstream. These rivers usually enter the sea through broad, fertile flatlands on which most of the sugar plantations are situated.

Despite evidence that Fiji has been inhabited for more than 4,000 years, little is known of the history of Fiji before the coming of the Europeans. The early reputation of the Fijian tribes as fierce maneaters, which earned the group a place on the map as the Cannibal Islands, is belied by the friendly and open manner of today's people.

The first known European to sight the Fiji islands was the Dutchman Abel Tasman in 1643. European missionaries, whalers, traders, and deserters settled during the first half of the nineteenth century. Their corrupting influence caused increasingly serious wars to flare among the native Fijian confederacies. In 1871 the Europeans in Fiji (about 2,000) established an administration under Ratu Serv Cakobau, who had become paramount chief of eastern Viti Levu some years before. A chaotic period followed until 1874, when a convention of chiefs ceded Fiji unconditionally to Great Britain.

The pattern of colonialism during the following century was similar to that in other British possessions: the pacification of the countryside, the spread of plantation agriculture, and the introduction of Indian indentured labor. Many traditional institutions, including the system of communal land ownership, were maintained.

Fijian soldiers fought for Great Britain during both world wars. The United States maintained military forces and installations in Fiji during World War II; but on the whole the war did not seriously affect the country.

In April 1970, in London, a constitutional confer-

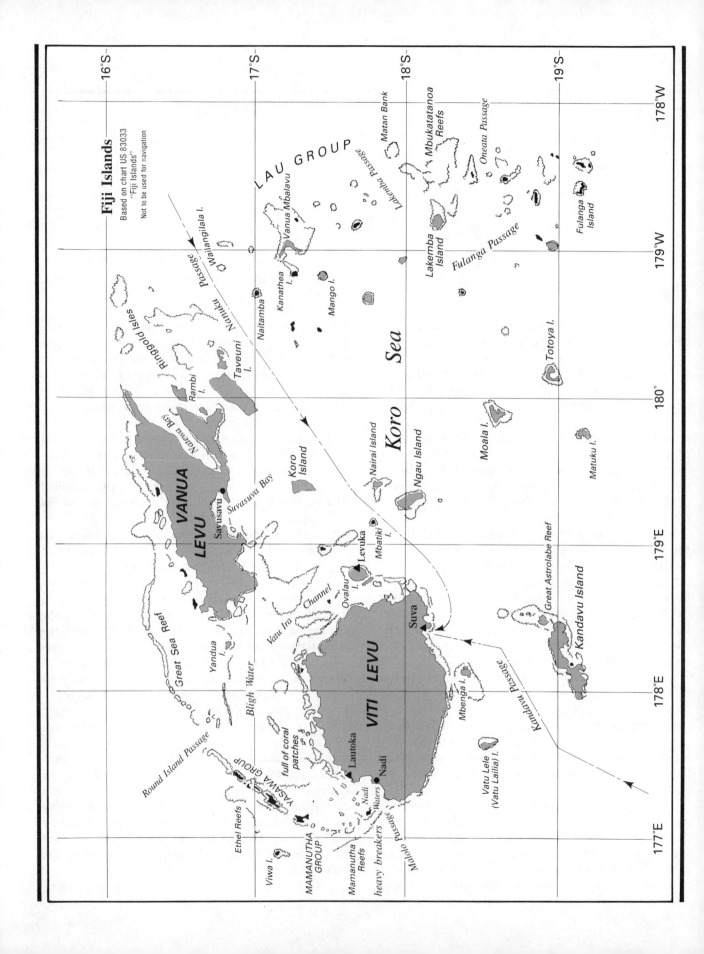

Fiji Islands

Based on chart US 83033
"Fiji Islands"
Not to be used for navigation

LAU GROUP

Matan Bank
Mbukatatanoa Reefs
Oneata Passage
Lakemba Passage
Vanua Mbalavu
Fulanga Passage
Lakemba Island
Fulanga Island

Wailangilala I.
Nanuku Passage
Naitamba
Kanathea I.
Mango I.
Totoya I.

Ringgold Isles
Rambi I.
Taveuni I.

Koro Sea

Koro Island
Nairai Island
Ngau Island
Moala I.
Matuku I.

VANUA LEVU
Natewa Bay
Savusavu
Suvasuva Bay
Yandua I.
Great Sea Reef

Levuka
Ovalau I.
Mbatiki I.
Vatu Ira Channel

Bligh Water

Round Island Passage
YASAWA GROUP
full of coral patches

VITI LEVU
Lautoka
Nadi
Nadi Waters
heavy breakers
Malolo Passage
Mamanutha Reefs
MAMANUTHA GROUP
Viwa I.
Ethel Reefs

Mbenga I.
Vatu Lele (Vatu Lailia) I.

Suva
Kandavu Passage
Great Astrolabe Reef
Kandavu Island

16°S
17°S
18°S
19°S

178°W
179°W
180°
179°E
178°E
177°E

FIJI
An independent nation

Ports of Entry

Savusavu, Vanua Levu	16°46' S, 179°20' E
Lautoka, Viti Levu	17°36' S, 177°27' E
Levuka, Ovalau	17°41' S, 178°51' E
Suva, Viti Levu	18°08' S, 178°26' E

Distances between Ports in Nautical Miles
Between Suva and

Alofi, Niue	665
Apia, Western Samoa	620
Auckland, New Zealand	1,140
Funafuti, Tuvalu	580
Honiara, Solomon Islands	1,195
Noumea, New Caledonia	720
Fakaofa, Tokelau	800
Pago Pago, American Samoa	670
Port-Vila, Vanuatu	575
Rarotonga, Cook Islands	1,245
Sydney, Australia	1,740
Tarawa, Kiribati	1,215
Vavau, Tonga	435

Standard Time
12 hours fast on UTC

Public Holidays and Special Events

January 1	New Year's Day—Public holiday
February 3	Prophet Mohammed's Birthday—Public holiday
March/April *	Good Friday, Easter, and Easter Monday—Public holidays
June *	Queen's Official Birthday—Public holiday
August *	Bank Holiday—Public holiday
October *	Diwali Festival—Public holiday
November *	Prince Charles's Birthday—Public holiday
December 25	Christmas Day—Public holiday
December 26	Boxing Day—Public holiday

*Specific dates vary from year to year.

ence agreed that Fiji should become a fully sovereign and independent nation with dominion status in the British Commonwealth effective on October 10, 1970.

Fiji's government was controlled by native Fijians until the national elections of April 1987, which were won by a coalition of parties composed predominantly of Indian voters. For the first time in history the native Fijians had been overwhelmed in an election. Two military coups occurred in quick succession; these put Fijians back in control of their country and established the Republic of Fiji in October 1988. The coups were virtually bloodless and have had no adverse effects on cruising boats visiting these islands.

The 1990 population of Fiji stood at 760,000, with 45 percent of them Fijian, 50 percent Indian, and the rest other Pacific islanders or Europeans. The Fijian government is attempting to keep the population of their islands within the capability of the islands to feed and clothe it. The urban areas still draw people away from the farm; there are about 80,000 people in Suva proper, with a total of 118,000 in the greater Suva area. Due to the military coups and the loss of political opportunities for the Indian-heritage population, Indians have been leaving Fiji in significant numbers. Records indicate a net migration loss of 9,000 person per year. The net population loss is probably greater than that because the Indian population segment has had a higher birthrate than the Fijian.

Indigenous Fijians are a mixture of Polynesian and Melanesian races resulting from the original migrations to the South Pacific centuries ago. The Indian population has grown rapidly from an original nucleus of about 60,000 indentured laborers who were brought from India between 1879 and 1916 to work in the sugar cane fields. Unlike the native Fijians, who live throughout the country, the Indians reside primarily near the urban centers and in the cane-producing areas of the two main islands.

Virtually all native Fijians are Christian—about 85 percent Methodist and 12 percent Roman Catholic. About 70 percent of the Indians are Hindu and about 25 percent are Muslim; the remainder are of other sects, including Christian.

A Sunday observance decree has made Fiji a very quiet place on the Sabbath. Businesses, except those vital to the safety and health of the people, are mostly closed. There are no organized sports or other forms of public entertainment and no assembly or processions in public places. Picnics are permitted. Restaurants are permitted to operate during limited hours. Plan your Sunday activities accordingly.

Fiji enjoys a special role in the education of Pacific islanders. It is, first of all, the home of the University of the South Pacific (USP), a multinational school supported by Fiji, Tonga, Western Samoa, Kiribati, Solomon Islands, Cook Islands, Vanuatu, Niue, Tuvalu, Nauru, and Tokelau. It receives grants from New Zealand, Australia, and the United States. Schools within the USP are Education, Natural Resources, Social and Economic Development, and Agriculture. Additionally, the Fiji School of Medicine trains doctors and doctors' assistants from the many island countries; these practitioners help maintain the health of the Pacific peoples.

The Fijian economy is mainly agrarian, with primary emphasis on sugar, copra, and root vegetables. The large sugar interests were responsible for the importation of the Indians in the late 1800s as farm workers, but most Indians have now abandoned the farms in favor of being merchants in the towns. Copra is produced from coconuts grown on Vanua Levu and the outer islands; it is processed into oil, of which about one-fourth is used in locally made foodstuffs and the rest exported.

Other farm products include pineapples, citrus, ginger, passionfruit, rice, cocoa, and tobacco. Commercial fishing, including tuna, is a growing industry, as are mining and tree farming. Tourism as a source of revenue is second only to sugar in the Fijian economy.

Notes on Kava Drinking

Throughout Fiji, as in much of Polynesia, the drinking of yaqona (pronounced "yanggona"), or kava, is a common ceremonial and social custom. Yaqona is made from the root of the pepper plant, *piper methysticum*. In days gone by yaqona was prepared by young maidens of a village, who chewed the pieces of root into a soft, pulpy mass before the water was added. Today the root is prepared with pestle and mortar or ground to powder by machine. It is usual to sun-dry the roots before powdering, but on occasions the green root is used. After the addition of the water, the gritty pieces of root are removed by passing a bundle of vegetable fiber, usually the shredded bark of the vau tree, through the liquid. More recently cheesecloth is used. Yaqona powder ready for mixing can be bought by the pound in the markets and at most small shops.

The yaqona ceremony is still important in the Fijian way of life, but today it has become a social drink as well as a ceremony. Yaqona drinking is common in Fijian villages, and the men of the village gather around the *tanoa* at the least excuse and swap yarns as the *bilo*, a half coconut shell, is passed around.

The *tanoa* is a large wooden bowl, carved from a single piece of vesi (a hardwood) usually from the island of Kabara, where the required wood is plentiful and where the skill of woodcarving has been retained. (In parts of Viti Levu, particularly inland and on the southern and western coasts, instead of a *tanoa,* a *dari* [pottery basin] without legs is used for mixing yaqona. These are handmade from red clay and fired in an oven.) Some *tanoa*s are simple, round bowls supported by up to eight or ten legs and sometimes as large as 36 inches in diameter. Others are carved in the shape of a turtle. Ceremonial *tanoa*s can be much bigger and are usually very old. Today visitors are able to buy *tanoa*s of varying sizes in the markets and curio stores.

In old Fiji birth, marriage, and death as well as such lesser events as the installation of chiefs, welcoming of important visitors, launching of canoes, and honoring of visitors all called for the correct yaqona ceremonies.

The ceremony is performed by hosts in the presence of the guest of honor and in a complicated ritual. On such an occasion, the guest of honor is seated cross-legged in front of the *tanoa* from which protrudes a thick rope of coconut fiber embellished with white cowrie shells. This is known as the Tui-ni-buli and is pointed toward the guest of honor. During the ceremony no one on pain of death may cross that line. The person to perform the ceremony is seated cross-legged behind the *tanoa;* clustered behind him is usually a group of people who chant to the rhythm of small *lali*s (hollow wooden drums) while the potion is being mixed.

At the direction of the master of ceremonies, acting on behalf of the guest of honor, water is added to the pulped root in the *tanoa.* When satisfied that the mixture is right, the master of ceremonies indicates that the preparation may continue. The yaqona is strained by passing the shredded bark of the vau tree through the liquid in the bowl. Finally, when the grit has been removed and the potion is ready for drinking, the cup-bearer comes forward bearing the *bilo.* With much ceremony and respect he presents the guest of honor with the first serving, pouring it into the personal cup of the guest, who holds it before him with both hands. When he has drained the cup in a single draft, there is a cry of "maca" (pronounced "maathaa," meaning "it is drained") accompanied by the clapping of hands.

The master of ceremonies representing the guest of honor is next to drink, and then succeeding cups are handed to senior guests in order of rank, one of the host group drinking after each guest. When all guests of rank have been honored, the ceremony is declared over. Preparations then proceed for the enjoyment of a *magiti,* or feast.

This ceremony is not performed indiscriminately by Fijians and therefore still retains great significance. The yaqona ceremony cannot be performed as a spectacle, and not all visitors to Fiji are fortunate enough to see it. Social yaqona drinking, however, is very informal, and in the large population centers there are numerous kava saloons where Fijians gather for social drinking of yaqona.

The Weather

The Fijis and vicinity are under the major influence of easterly and southeasterly winds, which, combined, blow about 65 percent of the time on the open sea and about 50 percent of the time at Suva. The southeasterly trades blow most persistently during the period June to October, varying to easterlies in February and March.

Northeast winds blow about 14 percent of the time over the area as a whole, but only in March are they more frequent than those from the southeast. The mean annual wind velocity at Suva is about 5 knots and on the open sea about 11 knots. Little month-to-month variation in strength occurs at sea: the lowest average velocity is 8 to 9 knots in February and March and 10 to 12 knots during the remainder of the year. Calms are frequent at Suva but rare at sea. Among the islands off the west and northwest coasts of Viti Levu, the southeast winds, interrupted by the lofty hills, are deflected irregularly into south to northeast winds.

Gales are occasional in all months but are most frequent from December to March during the height of

Duty-free shopping is a must while in Suva, but discount store prices in mainland USA often rival duty free prices and give you a better claim to repairs and refunds. Most of the goods are electronics, cameras, and watches from Asia. (Earl Hinz)

the tropical cyclone season. They occasionally occur in November and April also. These tropical cyclones affect the Fijis on the average about twice yearly, moving in from north or northeast. An occasional hurricane moves slowly among the islands for several days, accompanied by gales; heavy, blinding rains; and dangerous storm tides, which most severely affect the northerly slopes of the islands. These hurricanes usually originate near or west of the Samoa Islands, and mostly south of the 10th parallel, but a few are known to have originated to the north of 10°S. After leaving the vicinity of the Fijis, most hurricanes curve into the southeast and cross into extratropical waters. The course of these storms is erratic, however, and it may be years before a destructive one strikes any particular location.

Fiji's climate is typically oceanic and tropical. Temperatures are high, with maximums averaging about 84°F from January through June and dropping to about 82°F from July through December. These high levels are tempered and made quite pleasant, especially at the higher altitudes, by unfailing breezes from the sea. The southeast trade winds prevail during most of the year but are replaced by the northwest monsoon in the hot summer months. Both bring abundant rain which, nevertheless, varies in the windward/leeward pattern characteristic of Oceania.

Rainfall varies in different parts of the islands. On the southeastern coasts it is about 120 inches; inland it reaches 200 inches; on the northwest, lee side, it drops to 60 to 80 inches. Rainfall at Suva varies from 75 inches to 170 inches, with an average of 120 inches. The dry season, June to October, is not as apparent in Suva as it is on the lee coast.

Precipitation occurs on average about 20 days per month, with the greatest monthly amounts falling from December to May. Thunderstorms in the open sea are, as a rule, most frequent during those same months.

The interiors of the larger islands, which rise over 5,000 feet in places, are often drenched with as much as 300 inches of rainfall per year. The low islands, over which the winds blow without losing any of their moisture, are often so dry that drinking water is scarce. This condition is somewhat alleviated by the location of the group within the hurricane belt, where severe cyclonic, tropical storms are likely to develop, bringing water to high and low islands alike.

Overall the Fiji Islands enjoy a healthful climate presenting two seasons—December through April, when it is hot and humid; and May through November, when it is cool, dry, and exceptionally pleasant.

Cruising Notes

YACHT ENTRY

Fiji has become an increasingly popular port of call for cruising yachts, with more than 300 entering each year. Many of these come from New Zealand and Australia for a casual winter cruise. Others are involved in annual races from Sydney or Auckland to Suva. Still others are world cruisers who spend hurricane seasons in New Zealand or Australia and then visit the Fijian archipelago in the winter. Fiji is a welcome host to all cruisers, and bureaucracy is at a minimum for cruisers who follow proper entry procedures.

Entry to the Republic of Fiji must be made at one of the four designated Ports of Entry—Suva, Lautoka, Levuka, or Savusavu. The latter is a new Port of Entry. All of these ports have designated quarantine anchorages. On approaching one of these ports, radio ahead on VHF channel 16 to port control with your ETA giving a three-hour or more advance notice of your arrival. On arrival anchor in the quarantine anchorage and fly the Q flag requesting pratique. You will be cleared by the health inspector at the quarantine anchorage and then directed to another location, most likely a wharf, for the other inspections.

CUSTOMS

Yachts may visit Fiji under the following conditions of temporary entry:

• Visiting yachts may enter and be kept temporarily in Fiji without payment of Customs duty provided the conditions of the Customs Tariff Concession Code are complied with. The conditions of the code require that the vessel is the property of, or has been hired by, the tourist or temporary resident and is imported solely for his or her personal use for a period not exceeding 12 months and will not be used commercially. (If you live on your boat, the free import period is limited to six months.)
• You must report your yacht inbound at a Customs port on arrival in Fiji and must clear your yacht outbound at a Customs port before leaving Fiji. You must report your yacht inbound at, and clear outbound from, any Customs port at which you call while you are in Fijian waters.
• You will be asked to sign a copy of a notice sum-marizing other conditions relating to your yacht while it is in Fiji waters, saying that you understand and accept the conditions.
• Yachts and other vessels are subject to duty and tax on importation into Fiji. These charges are payable on your yacht if it is disposed of in Fiji, or if it is put to commercial use while in Fiji water, or if it is not exported within 12 months of the date of its arrival in Fiji.
• On first arrival you are required to make Customs entry of your yacht, and you must sign a declaration thereon that your yacht will not be used for any commercial purpose while in Fiji.
• Liquor import duties may be paid on arrival or the liquor may be bonded in a lockable locker on your boat. One liter per person is allowed while in Fiji. If you take a motorbike ashore, it will have to be licensed, and you will have to obtain insurance on it.
• No high-duty goods such as liquor, beer, tobacco, and cigarettes can be shipped duty free as stores on yachts of less than 100 net tons.
• Hours of clearance into a port are from 0800 to 1630 Monday through Friday. There is no charge during these normal working hours, but a flat overtime rate of F$35 will be charged outside normal working hours. You will also be charged a F$20 fee for a "security inspection," which was instituted at the time of the 1987 coup.

IMMIGRATION

Cruisers require permits from an Immigration officer before they disembark in Fiji. If an Immigration officer does not meet the yacht on its arrival, a message should be sent via the Customs officer to the Immigration office or a telephone call made to that office (312-622) requesting the attendance of an Immigration officer. The officer will need to be provided, by the person in charge of the yacht, with two copies of a manifest listing all persons on board. The officer will need to see every person and every such person's passport and receive from all concerned a correctly completed passenger arrival card. In addition, the officer may require onward tickets or security bonds from any person or persons aboard.

Before leaving Fiji, all such crew members should report to the Immigration office with their passports for outbound immigration clearance, specifying their date, time, and means of departure, next port of call, and ETD.

A visitor's permit will be issued for up to a six-month stay, which is the longest possible within any one year. After an absence from the country for three months, you can reapply for another six-month permit. In exceptional circumstances it may be possible to get another six-month immigration permit. A special 11-page application must be completed and submitted along with a non-refundable F$100 fee. This should preferably be done by an in-person visit to Immigration in Suva. If the application is approved, an additional fee of F$50 must then be paid.

Crew members other than bona fide owners of the boat are required to have onward tickets with documentation to enter another country or a return ticket to their

FLOTSAM AND JETSAM

Currency
Fiji issues its own currency in the form of Fiji dollars. There are 100 cents in a dollar, and coins are issued in values of 1, 2, 5, 10, and 20 cents. The approximate rate of exchange is US$1 = F$1.45. The relative price of goods and services is approximately 92.

Language
Fijian is the indigenous language of the ethnic Fijian people. Hindi is the language of the Indians in the Fiji Islands. English is the official language of the islands and is understood by just about everybody.

Electricity
Where electricity is available, it is 240v, 50 Hz AC.

Postal Addresses

Yacht ( )
General Delivery
General Post Office
Suva
FIJI

Yacht ( )
c/o Royal Suva Yacht Club
P.O. Box 355
Suva
FIJI

Ports for Making Crew Changes
Suva is a recommended port for making crew changes because of its good international airline service. Besides trunk service to Honolulu, Sydney, and Auckland, there is international feeder airline service to Port-Vila, Apia, Noumea, Nukualofa, Honiara, and Nauru. Domestic airlines provide connections throughout Fiji. The main international airport is at Nadi, not Suva.

External Affairs Representative
Australian consulates or embassies

Information Center
Fiji Visitors Bureau
G.P.O. Box 92
Suva
FIJI

country of origin. You will be required to show evidence of sufficient funds to support yourself while in the country.

FIREARMS

On arrival, all arms and ammunition must be cleared and surrendered to the Customs officer for safekeeping by the Fiji police. These may, by timely arrangement with the police (48 hours at least), be recovered before leaving Fiji.

QUARANTINE

If you wish to cruise within Fijian waters, you must obtain a clearance at each port, whether a Customs port or not, from the Coconut Pests and Diseases Board, in addition to the Customs clearance. Certain islands and places in Fiji are free of the rhinoceros beetle, and you may be proceeding from an infected to an uninfected area.

No live animals, reptiles, or birds of any kind or fresh meat, fruit, and vegetables on board the yacht may be landed or taken ashore. Restrictions on whether such goods will be permitted to remain on board after your initial arrival at a Customs port will be made by officers of the Department of Agriculture. If you have a pet on board, you will have to post a F$100 bond to assure that you will keep the animal on board.

Yachts that have been in malaria-infested countries within the previous 50 days will be required to conform to special instructions issued by the Health officer at arrival.

CRUISING PERMITS

You are not free to cruise at random within Fijian waters; you must have an itinerary approved by Customs. Although the Customs approval can be secured at any Port of Entry, Suva is the best place to do it since your next step is to visit the Fijian Affairs Board (Provincial Desk) in Suva. They will issue the documents needed to visit each of the islands on your itinerary. Fijian Affairs will also brief you on special customs and protocol to be followed at each island.

Special permission is required to visit the Lau group of islands. Do not under any circumstances stop at the Lau group without prior approval. You must go to a Port of Entry first and then get special permission at Suva for your visit. The government is very strict on this. Permission to visit the Lau group is also obtained

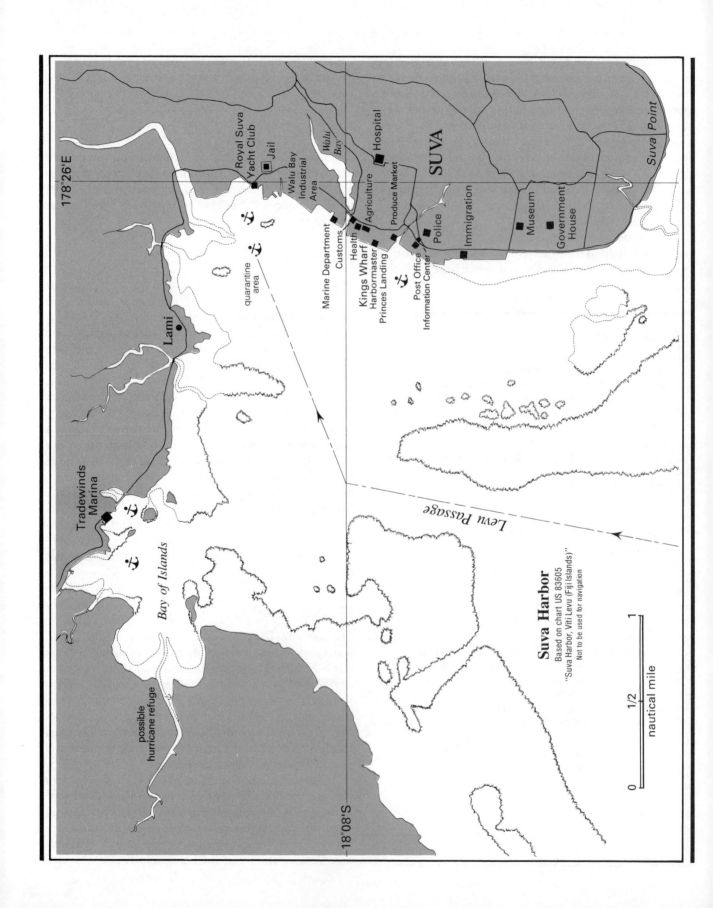

178°26'E

18°08'S

Royal Suva
Yacht Club

Jail

Walu Bay
Industrial
Area

*Walu
Bay*

Hospital

SUVA

Suva Point

Marine Department
Customs

Health

Kings Wharf
Harbormaster
Princes Landing

Agriculture

Produce Market

Police

Immigration

Museum

Government
House

Post Office
Information Center

quarantine
area

Lami

Levu Passage

Tradewinds
Marina

Bay of Islands

possible
hurricane refuge

Suva Harbor

Based on chart US 83605
"Suva Harbor, Viti Levu (Fiji Islands)"
Not to be used for navigation

0   1/2   1
nautical mile

from the Provincial Desk of the Fijian Affairs Board, but you will also need the approval of the prime minister for the visit. To expedite approval, have the following papers in hand for your first visit:

- Inbound clearance papers including visas for duration of visit
- Crew list (names, nationalities, passport numbers)
- A letter addressed to the Paramount Chief of the Lau Group, c/o Department of Fijian Affairs, identifying the Lau islands you wish to visit, the approximate dates of your visit, and your reason for wanting to visit the Lau group

The general procedure on arrival at a Lau island (or any other village on one of Fiji's islands) is to proceed to the nearest village and ask for the chief (Turaga ni Koro). Show him your papers, then make the offering of kava (see Notes on Kava Drinking) and the presenting of other items brought as gifts for the chief(s). Follow the procedures recommended by the Fijian Affairs Office. The welcoming ceremony (sevusevu) may take several hours, but it will set the tone of your visit. Don't be in a hurry, for this is part of the Fijian culture few people get to see.

YACHT FACILITIES

Suva

Upon arrival anchor near the quarantine buoy and await the arrival of the Health officer. After pratique has been granted, proceed to Kings Wharf for Customs, Immigration, and Agriculture clearance. Kings Wharf is a high concrete structure that can be damaging to a yacht's topsides, so prepare protection with adequate fenders and fender boards. While you are there, also check in with the harbormaster. You can obtain fuel and water at King's Wharf. If you lay along the wharf for other than clearing in or taking on fuel and water, you will have to pay wharf fees of F$1 per 12-hour time period.

After clearance has been granted, you can take anchorage in any of three places—the general harbor anchorage opposite the main part of town, the Royal Suva Yacht Club, or the Bay of Islands. Most skippers prefer the Royal Suva Yacht Club because it is close to town, and yacht club members and staff can be very helpful in getting you settled. Anchoring charges are F$20 per week; in addition, the club has some Tahiti-style moorings against pontoon docks at F$35 per week with electricity and water. Visitors are offered the full services of the club including showers, access to fuel dock, laundry pickup, mail handling, and a chance to join in on their social activities while you are there.

The second most popular spot is the Tradewinds Marina in the Bay of Islands. It is operated as part of the Tradewinds Resort Hotel, an establishment that is not always open. The water facilities, however, are operated separately by the Tradewinds Canoe Club, which has been in business for many years. The canoe club offers a dinghy dock, showers, mail holding service, swimming pool, trash disposal, propane BBQ, shorepower, and electricity. Rates are F$15 for yachts anchoring out and F$40–50 for Tahiti-style moorings against the dock. Bus and taxi service into Suva are available.

Slipways and workshops are available in Suva Harbor to help with yacht repairs and maintenance, but hardware and mechanical parts are scarce. The shops are set up mostly to handle ships and workboats but can help with yacht repairs.

If you are in need of parts or equipment from Australia or New Zealand, there is a unique service offered in Suva called Yacht Help. Their services range from holding mail to ordering parts to helping find a crew—just about anything a cruiser would need. If you anticipate using their services, send for their "Yacht Help Booklet." The address is Yacht Help, P.O. Box 13107, Suva, FIJI.

Fiji is often in the path of South Pacific tropical cyclones and is not the safest place to be if one passes close by. If you do plan on spending the hurricane season at Suva, check out the Kumbuna Creek and Veisania River locations on the west side of the Bay of Islands. Those two places and the Bay of Islands offer some protection from tropical storms but would probably not be adequate protection for a full-blown tropical cyclone.

Lautoka

Lautoka is Fiji's second-largest port, with plenty of anchoring room inside Vio Island just off King's Wharf or on the northeast side of Queen's Wharf. There are no fees for anchoring in this harbor. You can get your inbound clearance, as well as fuel and water, at the north end of Queen's Wharf provided there is no ship berthed there at the time of your arrival. If there is a ship there and you want immediate clearance, you will have to anchor and bring the inspection officers to your boat by dinghy. As with the other Fijian ports, it is best to call the port authorities on VHF channel 16 ahead of time to

Downtown Suva, with the large Kings Wharf in the center of the picture. The Royal Suva Yacht Club is at the far right end of the harbor waters, and the Bay of Islands is in the middle background. (Fiji Director of Information)

Lautoka is the location of one of Fiji's largest sugar mills. If you are downwind of the mill's smokestacks, you can expect your boat to get quite dirty. The boat anchorage is in the upper right corner of the picture. (Fiji Director of Information)

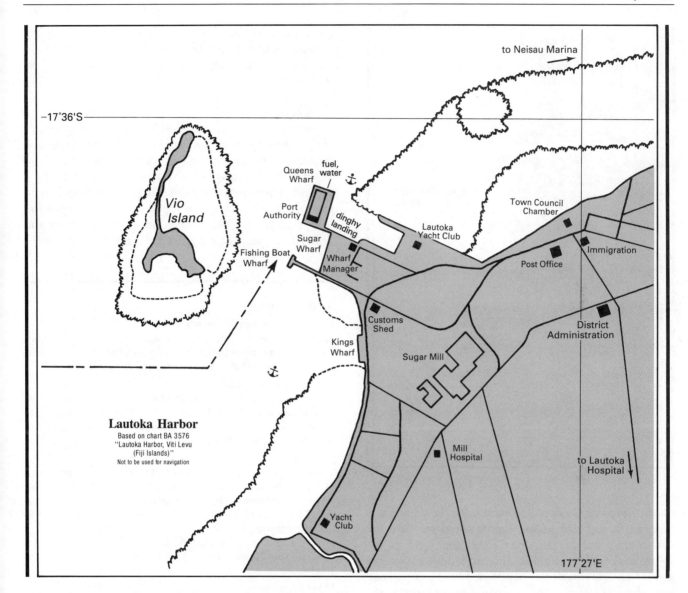

Lautoka Harbor
Based on chart BA 3576
"Lautoka Harbor, Viti Levu
(Fiji Islands)"
Not to be used for navigation

let them know your ETA. Wharf fees are F$1.36 per hour, and there is a water fee of F$5 per 250 gallons. It is also possible to get water and fuel at the fishing-boat wharf on the south side of the sugar wharf.

Lautoka is the shipping port for most of the island's sugar, and there is an interesting large sugar mill to visit a short distance from the wharf. The mill, however, puts out a black, sootlike material that makes the harbor quite dirty. Several cruising boats have found Saweni Bay about four miles south of Lautoka a much more attractive and rural anchorage.

There is a small store there, and the bus into Lautoka is inexpensive. You can also get low-cost taxi service back to Saweni Bay with your load of provisions purchased in Lautoka.

There is a possible hurricane hole just north of the Lautoka wharf in the Vitoga River. It has a mangrove shoreline and is a very dirty river, but could be tolerated in an emergency. Local cruise boats use it when threatened. Be prepared for a strong current should heavy rains occur in the mountains.

On your way to or from Suva, you may be interested in stopping at the Nadi area, a major tourist and charter boat area as well as the site of Fiji's international airport. There is an Immigration office here should you be changing crews by air.

Levuka

Before the British took over Fiji as a colony, the Fijian government was headquartered at the village of Levuka

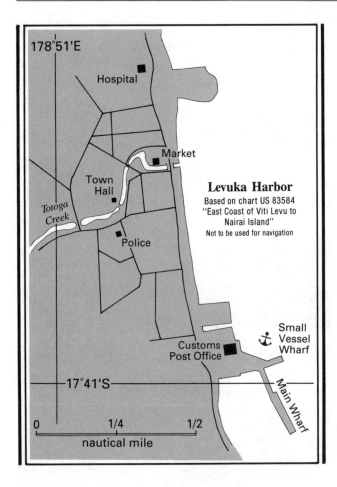

Levuka Harbor
Based on chart US 83584
"East Coast of Viti Levu to
Nairai Island"
Not to be used for navigation

good place to be during the South Pacific tropical cyclone season. Every year Levuka experiences 50–55 knot winds that create havoc among the small craft in the harbor.

Savusavu

Savusavu town on the island of Vanua Levu is an area of old plantations, a whaling station from years back, and the location of geothermal springs. The commercial center of Vanua Levu is at Labasa, which is reached by a bus ride over the mountains. Sugar cane is the main product of the area; it is shipped out of the deep-water port of Savusavu. This is Fiji's newest Port of Entry and useful for vessels coming from the north. It is a well-

on the island of Ovalau. The reason for the choice was that the large Fijian sailing canoes could sail into the harbor on a beam reach from either the north or the south, making it an ideal location to handle commerce and interisland travels by sail power. Many colonial and precolonial buildings still exist in Levuka, which the Fijian government intends to keep as a living museum of the past. It is worth a visit for its historic value.

Clearance can be effected at the north side of the small-vessel wharf where the Customs office is. If you have not radioed in your ETA, tie up at the wharf and have the skipper go to the Customs shed and announce the boat's arrival. Because of the compactness of this town, it is easier to get your clearance here than in Suva; however, if you want to get a cruising permit, you will still have to go to Suva.

After clearing in, anchor well off the wharf. The long reef will give you good protection from the seas. Water and diesel fuel are available at the wharf, and some provisions can be obtained in the local stores. Only limited repair facilities are available. This is not a

MEDICAL MEMO

Immunization Requirements

Immunizations for smallpox, cholera, and yellow fever are required if you have transited or visited within the last 6 days (smallpox 14 days) an area currently infected.

Local Health Situation

Fiji is free from most tropical diseases including malaria. Mosquitoes are a problem, however, and they sometimes carry the dengue fever virus. Infectious hepatitis and filariasis have occasionally been reported in Fiji.

Health Services

There are government hospitals and health-care centers in all of the larger towns and in most outlying districts. There are private practitioners in the larger towns for those who can afford them. Dental and optical services are also available in the larger towns.

Drugs can be purchased from the chemists (pharmacies) in the larger towns. Many U.S. drug products are stocked.

IAMAT Center

Labasa	Labasa Divisional Hospital Coordinator: Ravindra Raj, MD
Nadi	IAMAT Center 36 Clay Street Coordinator: Ram Raju, DSM
Suva	Gordon Street Medical Center Coordinator: Robin Everett Mitchell, MBBS
	Singh's Medical Clinic Cumming Street Coordinator: Parshu Ram, MBChB, MRCP, FRACP

Water

Tap water in the principal populated areas is treated and reported to be safe. Water from all other sources should be considered suspect and always treated.

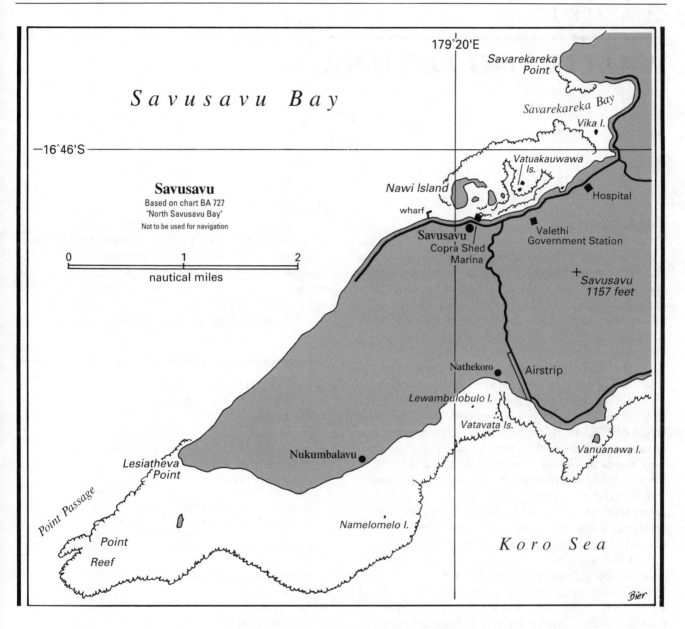

Savusavu
Based on chart BA 727
"North Savusavu Bay"
Not to be used for navigation

0   1   2
nautical miles

sheltered port, especially from the southeast, from whence most cyclonic winds blow.

The center of yachting activity is at the Copra Shed Marina in Na Kama Creek, well sheltered from winds and seas. Immigration and Customs offices are expected to be headquartered here. The copra shed, from which the marina gets its name, is Savusavu's oldest and most historic building. It has been restored and renovated to provide marina services for visiting yachts.

Berthing is available alongside the Copra Shed at F$40 per week, and two offshore "hurricane" moorings are available at F$150 per month. Shower, toilet, and mail services are available at F$15 per week. Some repair facilities are available from the famous Whippy Brothers boatbuilders. Provisions are obtainable in the village of Savusavu. The Savusavu Yacht Club is also here; membership is free for the first two weeks, but a charge of F$10 per year is charged thereafter. (Note: You can legally stay only six months in Fiji at one stretch, however.)

CHAPTER 17

WALLIS AND FUTUNA

The Country

The Wallis and Futuna Islands consist of two sections just north of the Fiji group, both of which are French Overseas Territories. They are groups of small volcanic and coral islands that have a combined land area of 93 square miles and a total population of about 15,000. Although geographically in Melanesia, the people are Polynesians who originally came from Tonga.

The Wallis group consists of the main island of Uvea and 22 outlying islets enclosed within a single barrier reef that classifies the unit as an almost-atoll. Uvea is seven by four miles in size and rises to a maximum height of 479 feet. Its population once was engaged in a flourishing copra business. Most of the palms, however, were wiped out by the rhinoceros beetle, and by 1970 the people had reverted to subsistence farming. The soil is rich, and grows virtually every type of tropical fruit in abundance, including oranges and pineapples. Uvea's encircling islets are mostly uninhabited but are used occasionally for minor agricultural and fishing pursuits.

The Futuna (sometimes called Horne) group consists of two volcanic high islands, Alofi and Futuna. These islands are higher than Uvea, rising to 2,629 and 1,310 feet, respectively. Both are well watered and densely wooded, containing valuable stands of timber that are extensively exploited as a source of cash income. The two islands have an area of about 35 square miles and a total population of about 3,000.

Wallis and Futuna were the only French territories in the Pacific to continue under a Vichy administration until after Pearl Harbor. Until 1959 they were under the jurisdiction of the administration of New Caledonia. Local government, however, had been headed by indigenous sovereigns since the time of the French-established protectorate in the late 1880s.

The Polynesian population, thought to have migrated from Tonga originally, was less than 5,000 in the 1920s. Most of the people lived on Wallis. In 1959 they chose by referendum to become a territory of overseas France, as were New Caledonia and French Polynesia. After the referendum, in which 94 percent of the voters concurred, Wallis and Futuna were removed from the jurisdiction of New Caledonia and were more closely integrated into the metropolitan political structure. The islanders were given French citizenship. The traditional law and customs of the islanders were retained under

---

WALLIS AND FUTUNA ISLANDS
An overseas territory of France

Port of Entry

Mata Uta, Wallis Islands	13°17′ S, 176°08′ W

Distances between Ports in Nautical Miles
Between Mata Uta and

Apia, Western Samoa	255
Funafuti, Tuvalu	395
Honiara, Solomon Islands	1,425
Noumea, New Caledonia	1,130
Neiafu, Tonga	345
Pago Pago, American Samoa	325
Santo, Vanuatu	990
Sigave Bay, Futuna Island	130
Suva, Fiji	430

Standard Time
12 hours fast on UTC

Public Holidays and Special Events

January 1	New Year's Day—Public holiday
March/April *	Good Friday, Easter, and Easter Monday—Public holidays
May 1	Labor Day—Public holiday
May *	Ascension Day—Public holiday
June *	Pentecost Monday—Public holiday
July 14	Bastille Day—Public holiday
August 15	Assumption Day—Public holiday
November 1	All Saints' Day—Public holiday
November 11	Armistice Day—Public holiday
December 25	Christmas Day—Public holiday

*Specific dates vary from year to year.

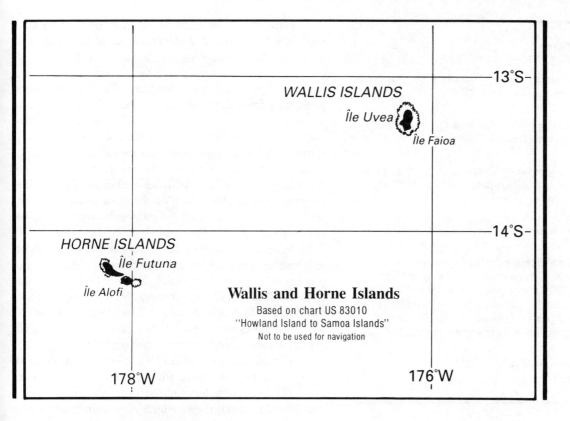

WALLIS ISLANDS

Île Uvea

Île Faioa

—13°S—

HORNE ISLANDS

Île Futuna

Île Alofi

—14°S—

Wallis and Horne Islands
Based on chart US 83010
"Howland Island to Samoa Islands"
Not to be used for navigation

178°W

176°W

the administration of the traditional rulers. Population pressure on these small and poor islands led to migration of laborers to Vanuatu, New Caledonia, and Fiji.

Wallis Island and Futuna to an even greater degree are unaffected by tourists because of their remoteness as well as the fact that they are a Polynesian group on the fringe of Melanesia. That they are French-speaking in an area of English-speaking neighbors seems to isolate them further. The result is that a visiting boat will meet islanders who are truer Polynesians than most other islanders of the Pacific.

The Wallis and Futuna Islands are administered from Noumea, New Caledonia, but ruled locally by three chiefs, one on Uvea and the other two on Futuna and Alofi.

Since copra went bust, Wallis and Futuna Islands' exports consist only of a small amount of trochus shells. The islanders would lead a pure subsistence life except for the largesse of the French government, which picks up the tab for imported food, clothing, petroleum, and transport. Fish is the main source of protein; there is, however, a rather large pig industry for local consumption. Local gardens produce taro, yams, breadfruit, pineapple, tapioca, and bananas. There is relatively little chicken but some beef.

High-quality tapa cloth decorated with traditional designs is an artifact the cruiser should be certain to purchase.

The Weather

The Wallis and Futuna Islands are only 255 miles west of Apia, Western Samoa; hence their weather patterns are similar to those described for the Samoas. The only difference is that the group is farther into the South Pacific tropical cyclone area and could be expected to experience more of the seasonal tropical storms.

One noticeable trait of the weather in the Wallis Island area is the build-up in strength of the southeast trades in September and October. While remaining consistent in direction, their strength may grow to 20 to 30 knots. This strong wind is good for sailing, but it can cause a rough entry or exit through Honikulu Pass. During the strong southeast trade winds, the lagoon passes are always on the ebb flow as a result of the ocean's water being blown across the reef on the windward side of the lagoon. Then, when the ebbing current in Honikula Pass encounters the strong waves outside the pass, there is a surface water build-up just outside the pass

FLOTSAM AND JETSAM

Currency
Wallis and Futuna Islands use the Coloniale Franc Pacifique (CFP). See French Polynesia for description.

Language
The indigenous language of the group is a Polynesian dialect similar to Tongan. French is the official language of the group.

Electricity
Limited to individual generating units except for the central district of Hanake, where public power (240 vac, 50 Hz) is available 24 hours a day.

Postal Address
You would do better to use Apia, Western Samoa; Suva, Fiji; or your next port of call.

Ports for Making Crew Changes
Neither Wallis nor Futuna is recommended as a port for making crew changes. While they have some local air service connections with Noumea, infrequent service and difficulty of communications make crew changes impractical in most cases. The closest ports for making a crew change are Suva and Pago Pago.

External Affairs Representative
French consulates and embassies

(much like a race) to bounce your boat around. Breakers will form on both sides of the pass. A good speed through the water, possibly using both sail and engine, will take you through the pass quickly.

There is some rain the year around, but most of it falls in the summer months, sometimes as a torrential downpour. These islands are in the South Pacific tropical cyclone belt and would not make a safe anchorage in the months of December through April. The mean daily temperature of about 85 °F is tempered by the consistent southeast trades, making the climate very pleasant.

Cruising Notes

YACHT ENTRY AND FACILITIES

The official Port of Entry of the Wallis and Futuna Islands is Mata Uta, Uvea, in the Wallis group. There a French administrator will process Customs and Immigration papers and ascertain the health of the crew. Visits to the Futuna group should start with a visit to the deputy administrator at Sigave Bay, Futuna Island. Passports and papers showing boat ownership are all that is required.

Care should be used in entering the lagoon surrounding Uvea. Enter at slack low water to avoid high currents in the main pass, Honikulu. Once inside, there are three bays in a row affording good anchorage with varying degrees of protection. Mua, the first bay, offers protection from the southeast trades in the lee of Faioa Island and from the northerlies by Uvea itself. Unfortunately, it is away from all the action. Just off Mua Bay, the next in line going north is the small village of Gahi. It has a pier, and some provisions are available. The third bay is Mata Uta, with an anchorage just off the fringing reefs at the village of the same name. Anchor near the small wharf and go ashore in your dinghy to check in with the gendarmerie.

Visas will be issued for a period of three months and can be extended for another three months with no posting of a bond of any kind. You need not take your boat to Mata Uta for an inbound clearance; you can go ashore at Gahi and hitchhike to Mata Uta for the minimal formalities required. If you have a two-wheeled vehicle aboard, ask for permission to take it ashore.

The anchorage at Mata Uta offers little protection from the southeast trades which, if blowing hard, can make the anchorage less than satisfactory. In that case, move to Gahi anchorage, which is well-protected from the trades.

There are few amenities for yachts at Mata Uta, which is the largest of the villages on Wallis Island. The post office, Catholic church, a bank, three grocery

MEDICAL MEMO

Immunization Requirements
No official statement, but yachts are urged not to land if they have any illness on board or have recently visited an area having cholera, smallpox, or yellow fever.

Local Health Situation
Many islanders suffer from filariasis and intestinal ailments because of poor hygiene and the freedom given the domestic farm animals. There are no reported medical problems with visitors.

Health Services
There is a hospital at Mata Uta staffed by three doctors; there are two dispensaries on Futuna with one doctor in attendance. Serious illnesses or major injuries would have to be taken elsewhere. There are no dental or optical services available in this group. Drugs are available only through the hospital and dispensaries. There is no charge.

Water
You should consider the water suspect and treat it.

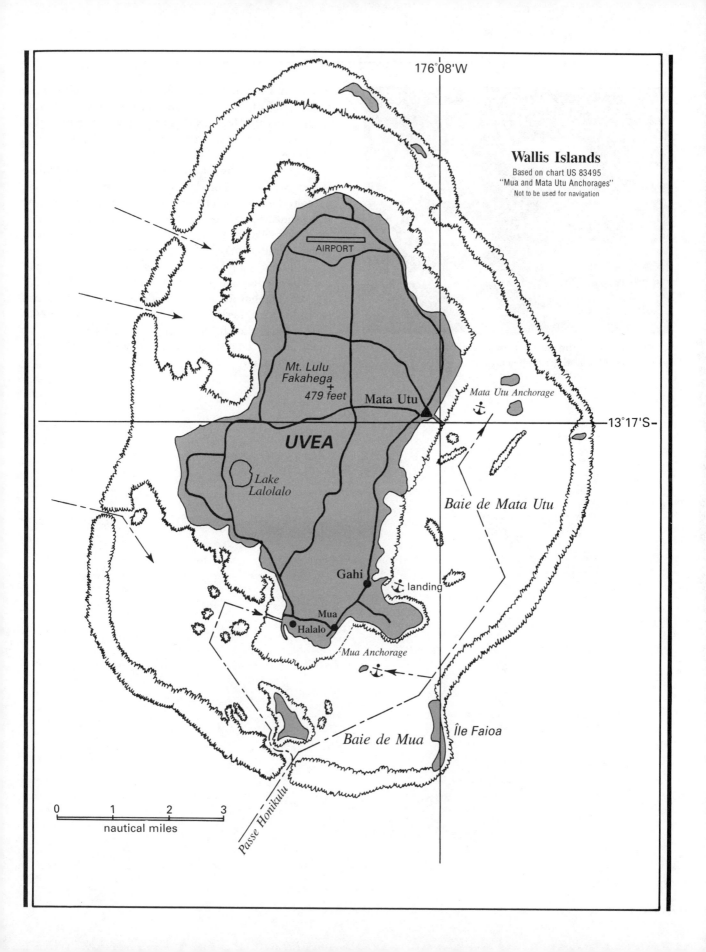

176°08'W

Wallis Islands
Based on chart US 83495
"Mua and Mata Utu Anchorages"
Not to be used for navigation

AIRPORT

Mt. Lulu
Fakahega
+
479 feet   **Mata Utu**

Mata Utu Anchorage

UVEA   13°17'S—

Lake
Lalolalo   *Baie de Mata Utu*

Gahi
                    ⚓ landing

Mua
Halalo
                Mua Anchorage

                                    ⚓

Baie de Mua   *Île Faioa*

0   1   2   3
nautical miles

Passe Honikulu

A *tutu* (woman) of the Wallis Islands standing amidst the lush greenery of the island. (F. Angleviel)

stores, and a couple of small restaurants are there. A small hotel of five rooms sits on the lagoon, offering relief from cabin fever as well as having a restaurant that specializes in seafood from the lagoon. Diesel fuel is available.

On the southwest corner of Uvea Island is Halalo Wharf, which has a dredged channel alongside it leading in from the lagoon. The pier and channel were built by U.S. armed forces during World War II. Should you be caught at Wallis during the tropical cyclone season, marginal refuge may be found at Halalo.

Futuna is a high, volcanic island and too young to have developed a barrier reef with enclosed sheltered lagoon. The harbor is a bight along the southwest rim exposed to southerly to westerly winds. It is small with little room for anchoring. Because few yachts visit this island, it may be just the place to enjoy unspoiled traditional islanders.

CHAPTER 18

PAPUA NEW GUINEA

The Country

Papua New Guinea lies in the southwest Pacific about a hundred miles northeast of Australia. It includes the eastern half of the island of New Guinea; the Bismarck Archipelago of which New Britain, New Ireland, and Manus are the largest islands; Bougainville and Buka islands in the western Solomons; and the Trobriand, Woodlark, D'Entrecasteaux, and Louisiade island groups to the east of the New Guinea mainland. The mainland (New Guinea) and the islands of Papua New Guinea with a total land area of 178,000 square miles lie entirely within the tropics.

The main island has about 40 percent of the land area. A complex system of mountains extends from the eastern end of the island to the western boundary with Indonesian Irian Jaya. Precipitous slopes, knife-sharp ridges, great outcroppings of mountains to heights of almost 15,000 feet, and broad upland valleys at altitudes of 5,000 to 10,000 feet characterize this area. Large rivers flow to the south, north, and east; few are navigable except by small boats in the lower reaches. The largest of them, the Fly, rising in the mountains of western Papua, flows more than 700 miles through the southwestern plains, and can be navigated for nearly 500 miles by shallow-draft vessels drawing less than eight feet. The same is true of the Sepik, which rises in the central cordillera and flows first northward, then east into the Bismarck Sea. Between the northern and the central range of mountains is the Central Depression, which includes the valleys of the Sepik, Ramu, and Markham rivers. On the smaller islands, mountains cover much of the area; many of them are active or dormant volcanoes, and some reach peaks of 8,500 feet.

Along most of the coasts are lowlands and rolling foothills of varying widths. Swamps cover large areas of the country, and on the southwest littoral of the mainland the great delta plain of the Dara coast forms one of the most extensive swamps in the world. The Sepik and Ramu rivers also flow for hundreds of miles through large riverine swamps of sago, bamboo, and other forest land.

The luxuriant rain forest that covers most of Papua New Guinea gives a misleading impression of widespread highly fertile soils. In fact many of the inland soils are shallow, heavily leached, and relatively infertile. Notable exceptions are the broad lowland valleys of the Markham and Ramu rivers and many highland valley systems where alluvial loams or soils of volcanic origin can be very productive. The greatest soil fertility problem is the leaching that results from heavy rainfall. This has already degraded the soils of the Sepik and Daru plains.

As a consequence of these geographic and climatic conditions, establishing adequate transport and communications facilities is difficult and expensive. These conditions inhibit the development of some of the interior areas and impact upon the entire process of social, political, and economic integration.

Little is known about the prehistory of Papua New Guinea, but it is now established that humans were in the New Guinea highlands at least by 8,000 B.C., and their probable first arrival in the area may have been as early as 30,000 B.C. There appear to have been several migrations from Asia by way of Indonesia over a great length of time, and the earliest migrants were evidently not agriculturalists but hunters who used bone and stone tools and weapons. Later migrations introduced agriculture and plants such as yams, taro, sugar cane, bananas, and green vegetables and animals such as pigs and dogs. There was no central government during the early history. Each community was virtually its own government, often with little or no contact with other areas or groups.

The first Europeans to sight New Guinea were probably the Portuguese and Spanish navigators sailing into the South Pacific in the early part of the sixteenth century. Don Jorge de Meneses in 1526–1527 accidentally came upon the principal island and is credited with

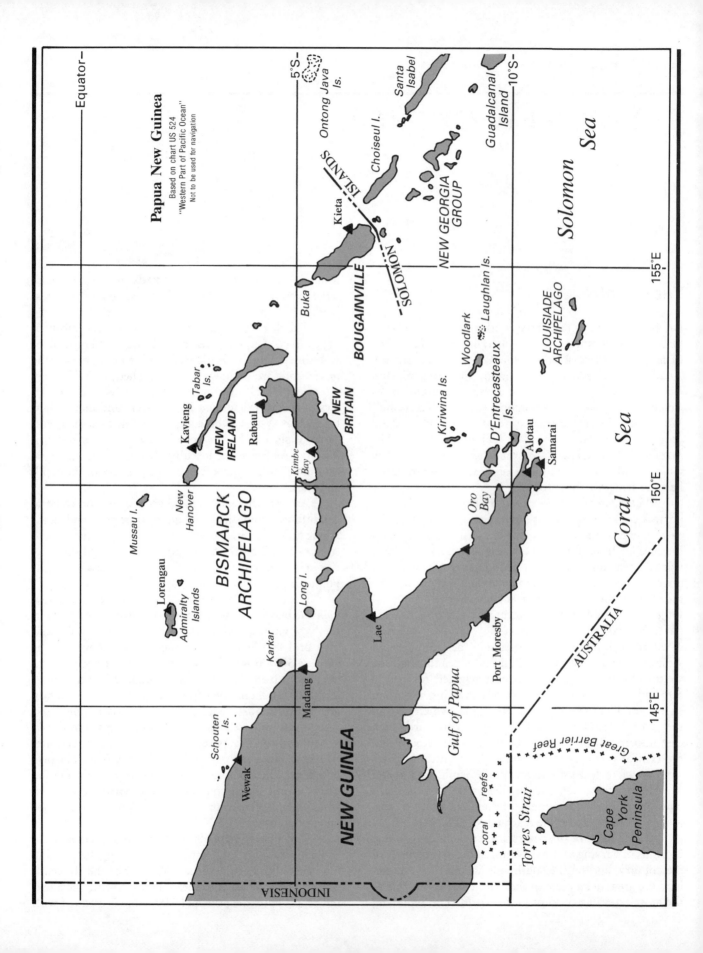

Papua New Guinea

Based on chart US 524
"Western Part of Pacific Ocean"
Not to be used for navigation

PAPUA NEW GUINEA
An independent nation

Ports of Entry (partial)

Kavieng, New Ireland	2°35′ S, 150°48′ E
Rabaul, New Britain	4°13′ S, 152°12′ E
Madang, New Guinea	5°13′ S, 145°49′ E
Kieta, Bougainville	6°13′ S, 155°38′ E
Port Moresby, New Guinea	9°29′ S, 147°08′ E
Samarai Island	10°37′ S, 150°40′ E

Distances between Ports in Nautical Miles

Between Rabaul and

Honiara, Solomon Islands	560
Nauru (Aiwo District)	910
Santo, Vanuatu	1,120

Between Madang and

Agana, Guam	1,120
Chuuk, FSM	840
Koror, Palau	1,015
Pohnpei, FSM	1,045
Yap, FSM	995

Between Port Moresby and

Brisbane, Australia	1,130
Noumea, New Caledonia	1,350
Port-Vila, Vanuatu	1,330

Standard Time
10 hours fast on UTC

Public Holidays and Special Events

January 1	New Year's Day—Public holiday
February 5	Chinese New Year—Community celebration
March/April *	Good Friday and Easter—Public holidays
April 25	Remembrance Day (ANZAC Day)—Public holiday
June 13–15	National Capital Show—Public holiday (coincides with Queen Elizabeth II's official birthday)
June/July *	Frangipani Festival—Carnival and sing-sing in Rabaul
September *	Papua New Guinea Arts Festival—Port Moresby
September *	Eastern Highlands Sing-Sing**
September 16	Independence Day—Public holiday
October 13–14	Morobe Province Agricultural Show—at Lae
December 25	Christmas Day—Public holiday
December 26	Boxing Day—Public holiday

*Specific dates vary from year to year.

**The Eastern Highlands show, largest and most famous of the sing-sings, is held in even-numbered years.

naming it Papua. The term "New Guinea" was applied to the island in 1545 by a Spaniard, Ynigo Ortis de Retez, because of some fancied resemblance between the island inhabitants and the inhabitants of the African Guinea coast. Although European navigators visited the islands and explored their coastlines for the next 170 years, little was known of the inhabitants until the late nineteenth century.

In 1884 a British protectorate was proclaimed over the southern coast of New Guinea (the area called Papua) and its adjacent islands. The protectorate, called British New Guinea, was annexed outright in 1888. The possession was placed under the authority of the Commonwealth of Australia in 1902.

As a consequence of Europe's growing need for coconut oil, Godeffroy's of Hamburg, the largest trading firm in the Pacific, began trading for copra in the islands of New Guinea. In 1884 Germany formally took possession of what later came to be called the Trust Territory of New Guinea and put its administration in the hands of a chartered company. In 1899 the German imperial government assumed direct control of German New Guinea. In 1914 Australian troops occupied German New Guinea, and it remained under Australian military control until 1921. The British government, on behalf of the Commonwealth of Australia, assumed a mandate from the League of Nations for governing the Territory of New Guinea in 1920. It was administered under this mandate until the Japanese invasion in December 1941 brought about the suspension of Australian civil administration. Following the surrender of the Japanese in 1945, civil administration of both Papua and New Guinea was restored, and under the Papua New Guinea Provisional Administration Act, 1945–1946, Papua and New Guinea were combined as an administrative union.

The Papua and New Guinea Act of 1949 formally approved the placing of New Guinea under the international trusteeship system and confirmed the administrative union of New Guinea and Papua under the title of "The Territory of Papua and New Guinea." Elections in 1972 resulted in the formation of a ministry headed by Chief Minister Michael Somare, who pledged to lead the country to self-government and then to independence before the next scheduled elections in 1976. Self-government was achieved in 1973 and full independence on September 16, 1975.

The constitution considers Her Majesty Queen Elizabeth II of the United Kingdom as head of state. She is represented in Papua New Guinea by a governor-general and makes this appointment on the advice of the Papua New Guinea National Executive Council (Cabinet) following Parliament's decision on the nominations.

The indigenous population is one of the most heterogeneous in the Pacific. Papua New Guinea has hundreds of separate communities, most with only a few hundred people. Divided by language, customs, and tradition, some of these communities have engaged in tribal warfare with their neighbors for centuries. Some groups, until recently, have been unaware of the existence of neighboring groups a few miles away. About 700 separate languages are spoken, and a significant number of them are wholly different from any other. Only a small number of them are spoken by more than a few thousand persons. While Melanesian pidgin and Hiri Motu both serve as linguae francae, neither language is universally spoken. English is spoken by the relatively small group of educated people.

In 1990 there were an estimated 3,823,000 people living in Papua New Guinea, slightly more than 31,000 of them expatriates; that number is decreasing as Papua New Guineans take over more and more of the foreign business ventures. Although the population is scattered throughout the islands, there is a concentration of them in the highlands provinces. Province populations in 1985 were estimated as follows:

Central (Port Moresby)	265,500
Western (Daru)	89,000
Gulf (Kerema)	70,000
Milne Bay (Alotau)	145,900
Northern (Popondetta)	87,600
Southern Highlands (Mendi)	254,100
Eng (Wabag)	175,300
Western Highlands (Mt. Hagen)	293,000
Chimbu (Kundiawa)	184,400
Eastern highlands (Goroka)	299,600
Morobe (Lae)	346,800
Madang (Madang)	238,400
East Sepik (Wewak)	247,900
West Sepik (Vanimo)	125,300
Manus (Lorengau)	29,000
New Ireland (Kavieng)	74,800
East New Britain (Rabaul)	149,400
West New Britain (Kimbe)	103,800
North Solomons (Arawa)	148,800

More than half the population is nominally Christian. Of these 25 percent are Catholic, 17 percent Lutheran; the balance are members of other Protestant sects. The non-Christian half of the indigenous population adheres to magico-religious beliefs and practices that are an integral part of their traditional cultures. They are numerous and diverse in character and are largely based on ancestor and spirit worship.

Papua New Guinea's economy is solidly based on both the exploitation of mineral resources and on traditional tropical crops. It has undergone rapid change over the past half dozen years. The country had a typical South Pacific plantation-oriented economy until the mid-1960s, when the first major copper mines were discovered at Panguan on Bougainville Island.

The majority of the indigenous inhabitants are subsistence farmers, but education and foreign investment are increasing the acreage given to commercial crops for export. On the coast near centers like Lae, Madang, Rabaul, and Port Moresby, there are large plantations growing coconuts, cocoa, and rubber. In the highland area of Goroka and Mt. Hagen, coffee and tea are grown. At Bulolo one of the largest plywood mills in the world is supplying all of the country's needs in this field plus a surplus for export.

Expatriate-owned plantations, which now account for less than 1 percent of the arable land, are slowly being sold back to Papua New Guinea nationals. These are usually groups of individuals laying claim to the land on the basis that it was theirs before it was alienated or individuals organized into cooperatives. The return of land is expected to continue for many years until foreign ownership is phased out entirely.

At the time of this writing travel advisories were still in existence for many parts of Papua New Guinea. Travelers were warned to stay more than 50 miles away from the border of Papua New Guinea and Irian Jaya because of hostile activities by the Indonesian secessionist group Movement for a Free Papua. Armed insurgency also exists on the islands of Bougainville and Buka, and vessels are advised to stay 12 miles offshore from these islands.

Throughout Papua New Guinea troubles have recently been reported with "rascals," local males who attack, mug, rape, and steal from others. At one time this kind of trouble was limited to the Port Moresby area and blamed on an influx of people into the capital province without enough jobs to keep them busy. It has since spread to many areas including Madang, Lae, and Rabaul. Visitors are advised to stay off the streets at night, to talk with a local administrator before hiking any trails, and to keep their boats locked and under the care of a trusted local person when they are away.

The Weather

The most noticeable feature of the climate is the seasonal change in the direction of the winds. The East Indies (of which New Guinea is part) lie along and just south of the equator, between the two trade-wind systems. In the summer of the northern hemisphere, low barometric pressure prevails on the continent of Asia, causing an indraft of air from the western Pacific. At that time the southeast trades extend northward, resulting in an air stream that crosses the East Indies from southeast to northwest and is drawn further northwestward into the low-pressure system over Asia. This movement is strengthened by the relatively high pressure prevailing over Australia at that time.

In the northern winter, pressure is high over Asia and relatively low over and to the immediate north of Australia. This distribution of pressure causes outflowing winds from Asia, which combine with the northeast trades and extend southeastward across the equator and over practically all of the East Indies.

The cause of these pressure differences is found in the large annual range of temperatures over the continents of Australia and Asia, as compared with the slight temperature changes over the adjacent ocean surfaces. As a result of the air circulation thus produced, in combination with the trades, there are pronounced seasonal changes in the winds, which are known as monsoons.

At the height of the monsoon season in the East Indies region, the winds blow with much constancy from one quarter. There is, however, considerable variation in wind direction during the transitional periods between monsoons. The general character of the weather depends upon the direction of the prevailing monsoon.

The east or "good" monsoon, which rises in the east or southeast, is relatively drier, though its moisture content increases as it progresses. It blows with greatest constancy in August. Much haziness characterizes this monsoon, especially in the southern part of the archipelago.

The west or "bad" monsoon blows from the west and northwest, reaching its maximum strength in January. Its moisture content is high, especially in the south, so that it is quite depressing compared to the east monsoon. In the vicinity of the equator there is not much difference, so far as humidity is concerned, between the two monsoons.

While these winds are known as east and west monsoons, their directions are not the same in all parts of the archipelago. In some northwestern sections, for example, the winds are northerly in the northern winter and southerly in summer. Nevertheless, they are termed east and west monsoons, and the terms are so used here.

The transitional periods occur on the average in April and in October or November. In the northern part of the archipelago the west monsoon prevails for a longer period than it does in the southern part while the east monsoon prevails longer in the south than in the north. Hence the transitional periods vary somewhat with latitude. There is also some variation from year to year in the general direction, duration, and force of the monsoons.

The average velocity of the west monsoon in January in the open sea is about 10 knots, except in the area northwest of New Guinea, where it averages about 6 knots. The velocity of the west monsoon gradually diminishes until April, when the average velocity for the region as a whole is 6 to 8 knots.

The east monsoon sets in during May and reaches its greatest speed in August, when it averages about 13 knots with the greatest wind strength (15 knots) over the Coral Sea. The east monsoon then gradually diminishes until November and December, when the average wind speed over the open sea in the region as a whole is about 8 knots.

The strongest regular winds of the region are found locally where the monsoons blow through narrow straits bordered by elevated land.

The extreme southern part of the area including the Louisade Archipelago lies within the influence of the southeast trades. The west monsoon does not reach this area with any dependability, even in January and February, and easterly and northeasterly winds continue to blow frequently in these months. In March the winds are variable, mostly easterly. From April to November the southeast trades, reinforced by the east monsoon, are felt with much constancy and force. The average speed is 12 to 15 knots, rising to gale force frequently during the prevailing east monsoon. The prevailing wind in December is from the east.

Tropical cyclones occur infrequently within 6–8 degrees of the equator; hence much of the region is free of danger from such storms. Cyclones forming or passing in neighboring higher latitudes cause heavy sea swells and sometimes strong winds and rain in the archipelago.

During the west monsoon there is much rain along the coast, and squalls are frequent. The west (wet) monsoon weakens in April, and the east (dry) monsoon becomes established in May, although the winds are variable in both months. The seasonal distribution of rainfall also depends on the topography; but as a rule the wet season extends from December to March, and the dry season reaches its height in August and September. Overall, the best months for seeing New Guinea are April through September.

Average annual rainfall is high, ranging from 80 to

FLOTSAM AND JETSAM

Currency

The Papua New Guinea dollar is called a kina ("keener") and equals 100 toea ("toyer"). Notes are issued in denominations of 2, 5, 10, and 20 kina. Coins are issued in values of 1, 2, 5, 10, 20, and 50 toea and 1 kina. The approximate rate of exchange is US$1 = 1.05 kina. The relative price of goods and services is approximately 108.

Language

More than 700 different languages are used by various tribes of Papua New Guinea. English is the official language of business and government, and pidgin and Hiri Motu are used as linguae francae.

Electricity

240v, 50 Hz AC

Postal Address

Postal service is nominally good to the Ports of Entry. An example address is:

Yacht ( )
Poste Restante
General Post Office
Port Moresby
PAPUA NEW GUINEA

Ports for Making Crew Changes

Port Moresby is a recommended port for making crew changes because it has international airline connections with Sydney, Auckland, Suva, Guam, Papeete, and Honolulu. Domestic airlines connect all the major towns of Papua New Guinea with Port Moresby.

External Affairs Representative

Papua New Guinea embassies or consulates. Use Australian if Papua New Guinea is not represented.

Information Center

Papua New Guinea Office of Tourism
P.O. Box 773
Port Moresby
PAPUA NEW GUINEA

---

100 inches for most districts. Many areas receive more than 200 inches but a few, like Port Moresby, lie in a rain shadow and record figures as low as 40 inches or less annually.

In general, there is less rainfall in the southern part of the archipelago because the rains occur chiefly with the east monsoon, which contains less moisture than the west monsoon. However, topographic effects result in very great differences in the distribution of rainfall. Although wet/dry seasons exist in many zones, this term is relative since even in the so-called dry season, precipitation ranges from two to four inches a month in most areas.

While there are no systematic records of rainfall in the open sea in this region, the rainfall records at coast stations indicate that the rains at sea are more regularly distributed through the day and the year than on the larger islands.

In the interior of the larger islands, rainfall occurs largely in the afternoon hours; this is also true along coasts when the wind blows from the interior. During the part of the year when the wind blows from the sea, the rains are distributed about equally throughout the 24 hours. Thunderstorms occur frequently, especially during the transitional periods.

The mean annual temperature is 80°F throughout this region, and the annual range of temperature is small. In the southeastern part of the area the highest temperatures occur, as a rule, in October and November, while in the northwestern part the period of highest temperatures is in April and May. The warm periods coincide with the turning of the monsoons. On the smaller islands and in the open sea, the difference in temperature between the warmest and coolest months is only about 2°F.

The daily range of temperatures is small at sea and in low areas near the sea. Day temperatures are, therefore, not excessively high, averaging for the year about 86°F as a daily maximum on the smaller islands and on the coasts of the larger islands. Night temperatures stay relatively high. For the region covered by this chapter the daily minimum at places near the sea is about 75°F as an average for the year.

Lowland humidity is uniformly high at about 80 percent, with very little seasonal variation. Fluctuations are much greater in the highlands, where temperatures are lower.

Cruising Notes

YACHT ENTRY

The Ports of Entry to Papua New Guinea are Port Moresby, Daru, Samarai, Lae, Rabaul, Madang, Wewak, Lorengau, Oro Bay, Kavieng, Kieta, Alotau, and Kimbe. Not all of these are useful to cruising boats for reasons of a poor anchorage or inadequate stores and marine services ashore. Those that have proven most useful are Port Moresby, Samarai, Rabaul, Madang, Kavieng, and Kieta. A boat arriving from Palau and other points to the north may want to make entry at Lorengau in the Admiralty Islands where many good reports have been received on the beauty of the islands and friendliness of the inhabitants.

CUSTOMS

At your first port of call in Papua New Guinea, you are required to present a departure clearance (zarpe) from your previous port of call plus the following documents:

- Passports for all crew members
- Crew list
- Stores list covering high-duty goods such as liquor and beer, tobacco products, and life-saving drugs on board
- List of arms and ammunition (which will be placed under seal on board)

Customs will issue a yachting permit for the boat for a period of two months to coincide with the visas. You must, however, still clear in at every port where there is a Customs officer stationed.

The forms required for the yachting permit can be obtained from PNG diplomatic missions or obtained after arrival. Supporting papers needed include your visa, ship's papers, financial declaration, zarpe, and planned cruising itinerary for their waters. Since permits may take up to a month to process, it would be wise to get them ahead of time and not be restricted when you arrive. There is a charge of ten kina for this permit.

If for some reason you are able and want to stay beyond six months, an import duty security deposit of 20 percent of boat value plus 3.5 percent general levy is payable. You will receive the duty deposit back on departure. The deposit does not apply to the first six months of your stay, and it is at the discretion of the Customs officer.

IMMIGRATION

Visas are required to enter Papua New Guinea. The government has become more strict on entry requirements to the disappointment of those who are attempting to make tourism a viable source of income for the country. Visas should be obtained before arrival through a PNG diplomatic mission. They will be issued for a two-month duration and must be used within six months of their approval. Passports are required for all crew members, and onward tickets must be in possession of all crew members who are not bona fide owners of the boat. The visas will require two passport-type photos. If you do not have a visa on arrival, an extra 100 kina will be charged to issue one on the spot.

For stays longer than two months, your application will be sent to Port Moresby for processing, which will involve some delay. The extension will also involve an additional fee of 100 kina per month and, possibly, a cash bond of 500 kina per person; the latter may not be required if you can prove you have sufficient funds for your stay. If you have to deposit the bond, it will not be refunded until after you leave the country. Try to avoid this situation; the refund takes six to eight weeks and is uncertain at best. Four months total appears to be the maximum stay the authorities will allow.

AGRICULTURE

As many flora and fauna diseases are not known in Papua New Guinea, you must report the presence on board your yacht of any live animals, reptiles, fish, or birds of any kind, as well as fresh meats, fruits, and vegetables. These must not be landed or taken ashore without the prior consent of a Quarantine officer.

YACHT FACILITIES

Kavieng

Kavieng Harbor is formed by three islands at the northern tip of New Ireland and is practically landlocked, offering good shelter from the west and east. When the wind blows north or south, however, the anchorage is totally exposed and can be uncomfortable. This is the principal port for the island and the headquarters of the province. Check-in can be made at the government wharf.

The north jetty and slipway are in ruins, so if you have to haul out here your only choice is the Fisheries College slipway. It may, however, take some influence to get them to haul a private yacht. Petroleum products are available by drum or tank truck. Water is piped onto the government wharf, but it should be treated before use. Small quantities of fresh meat and vegetables are available in the town.

Rabaul

Simpson Harbor at Rabaul is a deep, completely sheltered harbor, believed to be a large volcanic crater that was breached by the ocean to form an entry. It is considered to be one of the best harbors in the world. Proceed to the main wharf at the north end of Simpson Harbor to contact Customs and port officials.

You will find ample anchoring area around the periphery of this one-mile-square harbor. The reports that Simpson Harbor has a poor holding bottom are contrary to the experience of the many cruisers who stay there during the hurricane season. A good anchorage is on the east side of the bay just south of the yacht club pier.

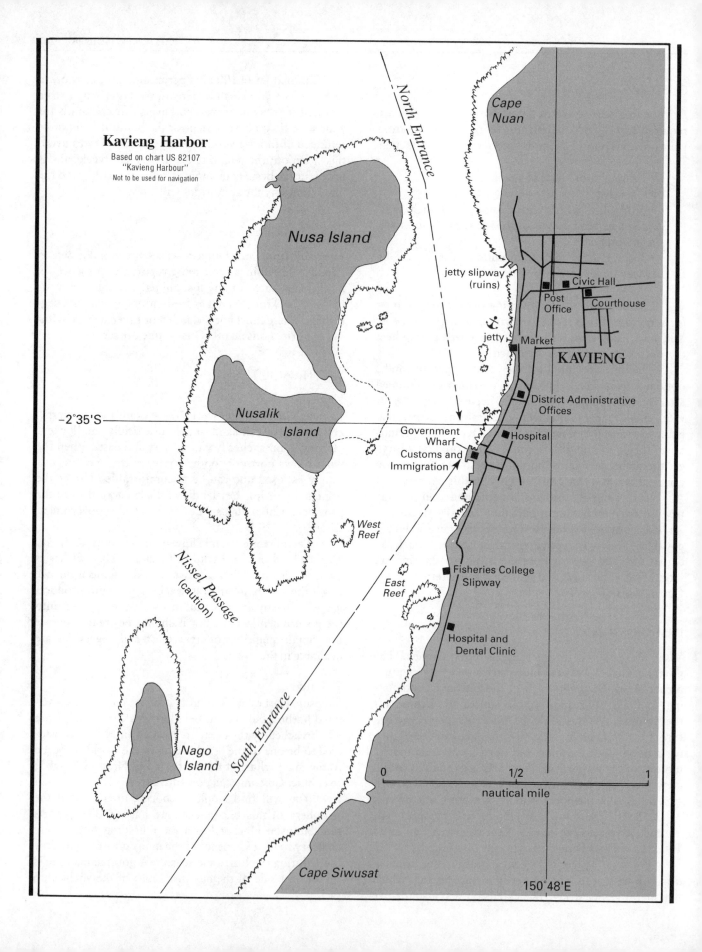

Kavieng Harbor

Based on chart US 82107
"Kavieng Harbour"
Not to be used for navigation

North Entrance

Cape
Nuan

Nusa Island

jetty slipway
(ruins)

Civic Hall

Post
Office

Courthouse

jetty

Market

KAVIENG

Nusalik
Island

-2°35'S

District Administrative
Offices

Government
Wharf
Customs and
Immigration

Hospital

West
Reef

Nissel Passage
(caution)

East
Reef

Fisheries College
Slipway

Hospital and
Dental Clinic

South Entrance

Nago
Island

0   1/2   1

nautical mile

Cape Siwusat

150°48'E

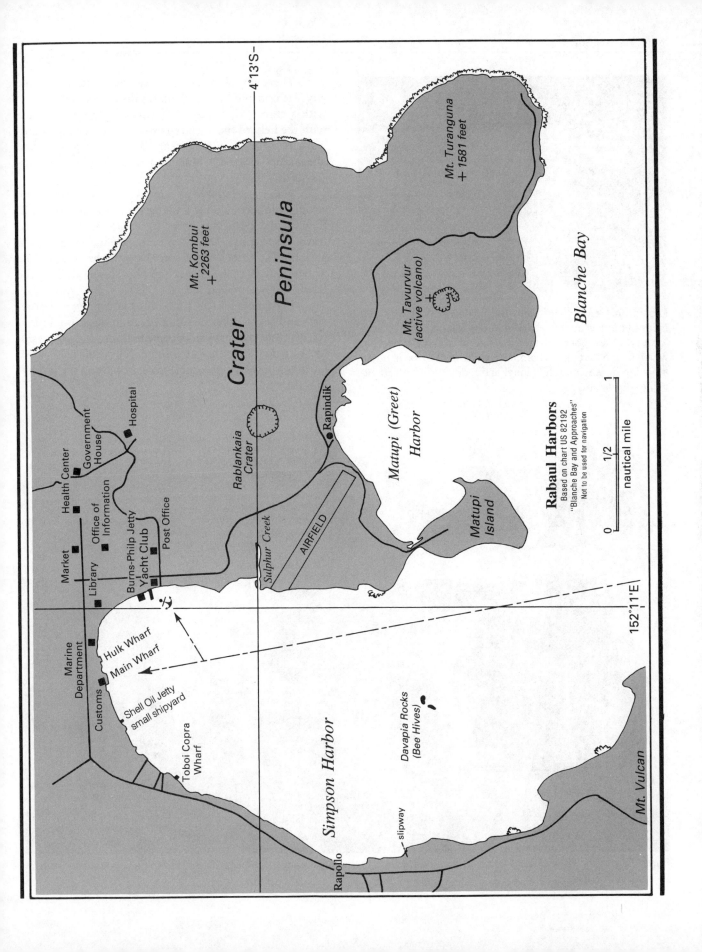

Rabaul Harbors
Based on chart US 82192
"Blanche Bay and Approaches"
Not to be used for navigation

0   1/2   1
nautical mile

Crater Peninsula

Mt. Kombui
+2263 feet

Mt. Turanguna
+1581 feet

Blanche Bay

Mt. Tavurvur
(active volcano)

Rablankaia
Crater

4°13'S–

Hospital

Government
House

Health Center

Office of
Information

Market

Library

Burns-Philp Jetty
Yacht Club

Post Office

Sulphur Creek

AIRFIELD

Rapindik

Matupi (Greet)
Harbor

Matupi
Island

152°11'E

Marine
Department

Customs

Hulk Wharf

Main Wharf

Shell Oil Jetty
small shipyard

Toboi Copra
Wharf

Simpson Harbor

Davapia Rocks
(Bee Hives)

slipway

Rapollo

Mt. Vulcan

Rabaul on New Britain Island was honeycombed with 360 miles of tunnels by the Japanese during World War II. These local tykes are posed at the entrance of a barge tunnel, in which five self-propelled harbor barges could be drawn up on a marine railway into the tunnel and hidden from Allied airplanes. (Earl Hinz)

There are slipways available adequate to handle any size cruising boat and multihulls can be hoisted out with a crane. Most needed repairs can be effected here with the help of the local repair shops. Yacht-type hardware is virtually nonexistent. Batteries, starters, and alternators can be rebuilt and diesel engine injectors serviced.

Water is available at most of the docks but has a strong sulphurous odor making it unpleasant to drink. If you take on water here, it should be filtered and treated before use. Diesel fuel and gasoline are available at John Tay's dock across from the yacht club, at the Toboi and Blanche Street wharves, and also at the Burns-Philp jetty near the yacht club.

The Rabaul Yacht Club offers hot showers, barbecues and short-order meals, a bar, and occasional movies. Visiting cruisers can become temporary members of the club for their stay at Rabaul. The club also offers cruising yachts a dependable mail drop using the following address:

Burns-Philp is the largest island trader in the South Pacific. Here sugar cane is unloaded from one of their bowloader ships in Rabaul Harbor. (Earl Hinz)

Yacht (   ) Hold for Arrival
c/o Rabaul Yacht Club
P.O. Box 106
Rabaul, New Britain
PAPUA NEW GUINEA

Rabaul is a large town of more than 40,000, so most essential provisions, supplies, and services are available here.

Rabaul Harbor is the center of an area of extreme seismic activity. Small earthquakes are almost continuous, and sulphur gases rise from the earth. As soon as you land in Rabaul, you will become aware of the situation and act accordingly. Local people are concerned, but not panicky.

Madang

The harbor at Madang is landlocked, therefore well sheltered, with good holding ground. Your initial anchoring can be done about 30 feet west of the Steamships slipway and wharf. Clearance can be accomplished here, and it is close enough to town for easy shopping and post office runs.

The main wharves are located at the northwest corner of the town, but the yacht anchorage and slipway are off Binnen Harbor near the south end of town. There are several slipways that can handle small craft, and they have workshops for engine and general repairs.

The town has a population of only about 20,000, so do not expect too much from it.

Diesel fuel and gasoline are available in drums and tank trucks, but permission must be obtained from wharf managers to use their facilities for refueling. There is no water piped to the docks, so you have to carry it in jerry jugs. There are three fairly good hardware stores in town, three "supermarkets," and an excellent "people's market" to take care of your provisioning.

The marina area offers showers, laundry facilities, and a ship's chandlery. There are garbage pickups and a coin-operated laundry facility. Visitors can get a one-month membership in the private Madang Club where you can enjoy bar and meal service as well as movies and closed-circuit TV.

The "rascal" problem has reached Madang, and unattended boats and dinghies are no longer safe. Keep them locked. A better plan is to move three miles north to the Nagada Bay area, site of the Jais Aben Resort and Research Station. It is possible to leave your boat here (with a local person on watch) and travel to the highlands to see the big sing-sing show.

Kieta

Note: Determine the status of Kieta as a Port of Call for cruising boats before you plan on visiting here. It may not be open. (See earlier discussion of travel advisories

Madang's main export is copra, which is transloaded from small copra boats to steamships in Madang Harbor. (Earl Hinz)

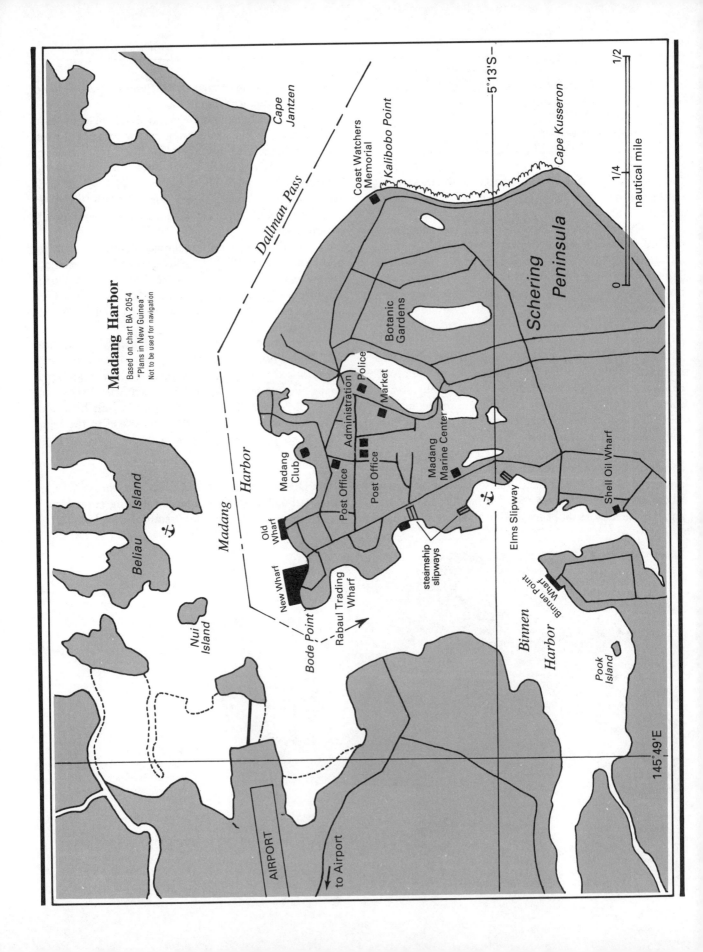

Madang Harbor

Based on chart BA 2054
"Plans in New Guinea"
Not to be used for navigation

145°49'E

5°13'S

Cape Jantzen

Dallman Pass

Coast Watchers
Memorial

Kalibobo Point

Cape Kusseron

Schering Peninsula

Botanic Gardens

Police

Market

Administration

Madang Marine Center

Madang Club

Post Office

Post Office

Madang Harbor

Old Wharf

New Wharf

Rabaul Trading Wharf

Bode Point

steamship slipways

Elms Slipway

Shell Oil Wharf

Binnen Point Wharf

Binnen Harbor

Pook Island

Beliau Island

Nui Island

AIRPORT

to Airport

0   1/4   1/2

nautical mile

in Papua New Guinea.) Although deep, Kieta is probably the best harbor on Bougainville Island. There is a small government jetty on the northwest side of the bay where you check in with Customs and other officials. After checking in, anchor south of the government jetty opposite the main town area or just south of the reef that sticks out from the land at the fisheries at the north end of the bay. There is a shoal patch of water there. If these two anchorages are unsatisfactory because of traffic or depth, then you should go north around the corner of the headland to Kobuan Bay to the yacht club.

There is no slipway here, but minor repairs can be made if you have your own parts. Limited provisions are available.

Fuel can be obtained by truck at the main wharf; occasionally it may be delivered in drums. Water is available on the wharf but through ship-size fittings only.

Kimbe

This Port of Entry is new to cruisers and a good stopover between Rabaul and Madang provided you have included it on your yachting permit itinerary. The port facility is relatively new and clean. It has free showers and dressing rooms with fresh water available. Dinghies can be tied up and locked near the pilot boat dock, which is guarded. There are no yacht facilities in Kimbe, but you can buy adequate provisions from the local trading stores to continue your cruise. There is a hotel with restaurant and bar in the town.

Port Moresby

Yachts entering Port Moresby should anchor near the Royal Papua Yacht Club and notify Customs of their presence by telephone. It is also possible to tie up to the harbor board's concrete jetty, which is used as a landing place for small craft. The four small piers between the government wharf and the L-head pier are privately owned and used for coastal shipping. After checking in, you can anchor near the yacht club or on the north side of the navy base, where the holding ground is good, but thievery may be a problem. You may also check the yacht club for the availability of Tahiti-style mooring space in their marina. These anchorages are secure during the southeast trades, although strong gusts coming off the hills may sometimes make you think differently. If the winds shift to the northwest, you can move around the peninsula and anchor off Ela Beach.

There are several slipways in Port Moresby that can handle small craft, but the prices are inordinately high. Repair services of most kinds are available, and parts can be obtained from ship's chandlers at the yacht club and in the developing business center at Waigani. The selection is rather limited, however. Diesel fuel, gasoline, and propane are available at the wharves, as is fresh water.

The Royal Papua Yacht Club at Port Moresby has showers, bar, and lunch and dinner service. It is a socially active club, and short-term membership can be obtained. Mail for yachts can be forwarded to the club. There is a drying grid at the club and sufficient tidal range for doing bottom work on most boats.

MEDICAL MEMO

Immunization Requirements

Smallpox and cholera immunizations are required of all new arrivals. Also, a yellow fever vaccination is required if you have transited within the last six days an infested area. Persons arriving from an Asian port are required to have current cholera and smallpox inoculations.

Local Health Situation

The hot, humid climate of Papua New Guinea and a still-primitive way of life away from the towns are causes for concern about personal health. Native diseases are ringworm and the New Guinea sore. There is some dengue fever. The risk of malaria exists the year around in all parts of the country including the urban areas. Malaria cases in Papua New Guinea jumped from 1 percent in 1976 to 20 percent in 1979. It is recommended that crews take malaria drugs before arrival, during their stay, and after departure from the country. It is also recommended that crews be inoculated against typhoid and tetanus.

Health Services

The major hospitals are at Port Moresby, Goroka, Lae, Madang, and Nonga. Besides these, there are 15 provincial hospitals and many government health centers and aid posts. Private doctors practice in the main cities; native medical treatments still prevail in many of the outlying rural areas.

Dental care is available at Port Moresby and the main cities. An ophthalmologist practices at Port Moresby, and an optometrist visits various parts of the country.

Drugs are available from several pharmacies (chemists) in the larger towns and also at the hospitals and health centers.

IAMAT Center

Boroko–Port Moresby Jacobi Medical Center
Tabari Place
Coordinators: James E. Jacobi, MD
Rosemary Lek, MD

Water

Tap water in Port Moresby is reportedly good, but it is recommended that all water be considered suspect and treated.

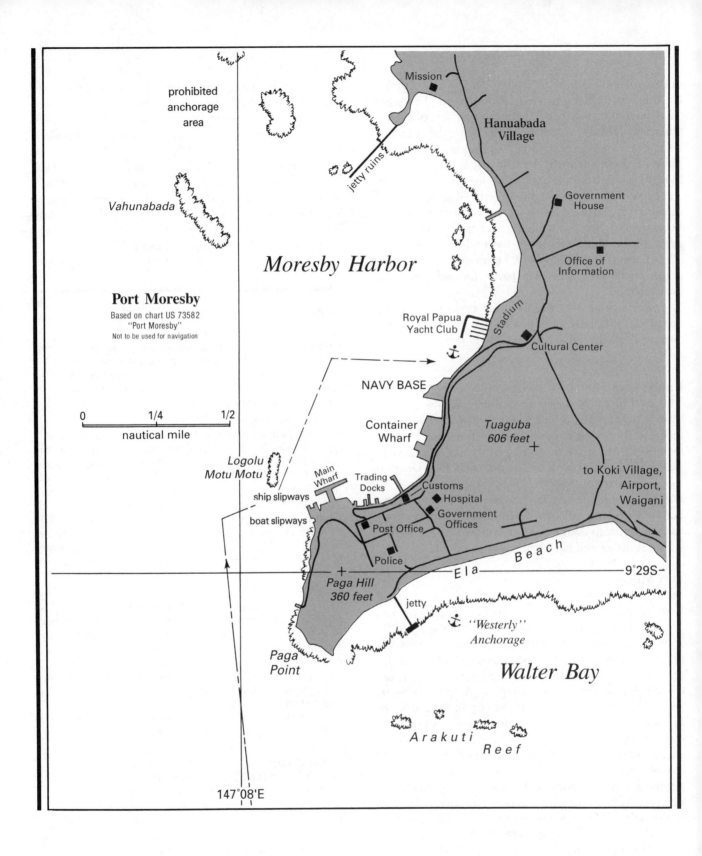

prohibited
anchorage
area

Vahunabada

Moresby Harbor

Port Moresby

Based on chart US 73582
"Port Moresby"
Not to be used for navigation

Mission

**Hanuabada
Village**

jetty ruins

Government
House

Office of
Information

Royal Papua
Yacht Club

Stadium

Cultural Center

NAVY BASE

0   1/4   1/2

nautical mile

Container
Wharf

Tuaguba
606 feet

to Koki Village,
Airport,
Waigani

Logolu
Motu Motu

Main
Wharf

Trading
Docks

Customs

Hospital

ship slipways

Post Office

Government
Offices

boat slipways

Police

E l a   B e a c h

9°29S

Paga Hill
360 feet

jetty

"Westerly"
Anchorage

Walter Bay

Paga
Point

A r a k u t i
R e e f

147°08'E

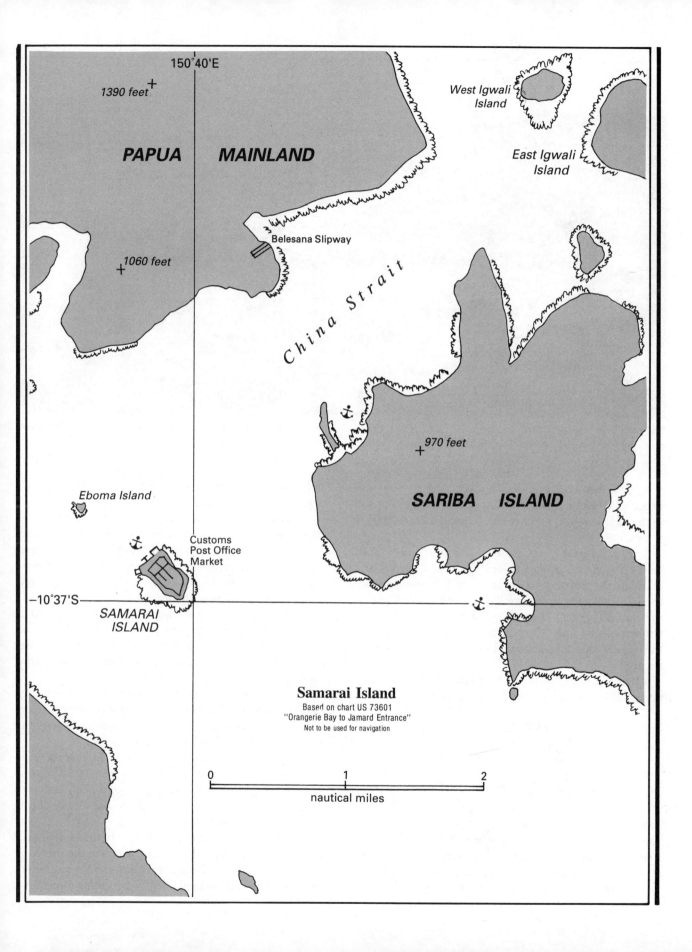

150°40'E

1390 feet +

PAPUA   MAINLAND

+ 1060 feet

Belesana Slipway

West Igwali
Island

East Igwali
Island

China Strait

+ 970 feet

SARIBA   ISLAND

Eboma Island

Customs
Post Office
Market

−10°37'S

*SAMARAI
ISLAND*

Samarai Island
Based on chart US 73601
"Orangerie Bay to Jamard Entrance"
Not to be used for navigation

0   1   2

nautical miles

The people of Hanuabada village were land dwellers at one time, but tribal warfare drove them off the land onto the stilt houses now seen in Moresby Harbor. The city of Port Moresby is seen in the background. (Earl Hinz)

The Royal Papua Yacht Club and marina are expected to move a quarter mile north of the present site in the next few years, but it will be available to cruisers as usual.

Port Moresby is a town of about 100,000 and, being the capital of Papua New Guinea, it is the best place in the country to resupply and reprovision although somewhat expensive. Duty-free stores for goods to be used after departing the country are available here. Unfortunately, Port Moresby is also the center of anti-European/American sentiment in the country, so act accordingly.

The Royal Papua Yacht Club offers cruisers a dependable mail drop at the following address:

    Yacht (   ) Hold for Arrival
    c/o Royal Papua Yacht Club
    P.O. Box 140
    Port Moresby
    PAPUA NEW GUINEA

Samarai

Samarai, on the southeastern edge of China Strait, is an island only one-tenth square mile in area. It is the southernmost Port of Entry to Papua New Guinea. It is less well known for its official status than for its colorful colonial atmosphere, left over from the days when it was a district center under Australian rule.

You can make your official entry here, buy fuel, and take on limited provisions. Up until 1968 Samarai was the capital of the Milne Bay province, but government functions have since moved up the coast to the village of Alotau. Alotau has a harbor but nothing to recommend it to the cruising sailor.

Although fuel and supplies can be purchased at Samarai, they are quite expensive. There is also a scarcity of water on this small island. Resupply is better accomplished at Port Moresby or Madang, depending on which direction you are heading.

With the removal of government functions from Samarai, its importance as a Port of Entry has decreased. Do not expect to do much business there, but visit it anyway as a picturesque port of call.

Across the China Strait from Samarai is the well-known Belesana Slipway. This is a very good slipway with a competent labor force to help with hull and engine repairs. Costs are modest and the service appreciated by the cruising sailor.

Boats using China Strait should be aware that tidal currents can run as high as 3 to 6 knots in the narrower part of the channel. Careful attention should be given to the turn of the tide as explained in the sailing directions.

CHAPTER 19

SOLOMON ISLANDS

The Country

The Solomon Islands group, situated between 5°S and 10°S and 157°E and 162°E, consists of a double row of high, continental islands formed from the exposed peaks of the submerged mountain range that extends from New Guinea to New Zealand. The group, excluding Buka and Bougainville, which are part of Papua New Guinea, are augmented by the Ontong Java atolls north of the group, the Santa Cruz Islands to the east, and the raised atolls of Rennell and Bellona to the south. These make up the new country of the Solomon Islands, formerly the British Solomon Islands.

The country has a combined land area of 12,000 square miles and a total population of about 335,000. The people are predominantly dark-skinned Melanesians. Other ethnic groups, totaling fewer than 10,000 persons, are Polynesian, Micronesian, European, and Chinese.

The double row of islands of the main group are the largest of the entire country, as follows:

Island	Size (square miles)	Population (persons)
Choisuel	980	12,600
Guadalcanal	2,500	70,000
Malaita	1,750	82,600
New Georgia	1,600	20,300
San Cristobal	1,350	18,200
Santa Isabel	1,500	14,000

All of these are volcanic, covered with steaming jungle, and have hot, humid, generally unattractive climates. Some small amounts of gold have been found in them, but major economic activity is concerned with the production of copra, coconut oil, and logging the many hardwoods found in the jungle areas.

The Ontong Java group of low atolls is small and only sparsely populated. Its few hundred people form one of the occasional pockets of Polynesians found in Melanesia. These tall, light-skinned inhabitants are engaged mainly in subsistence agriculture, but some collect trochus shells from the reefs for the export market.

The Santa Cruz group consists of three main high islands and a host of smaller outliers that are mostly coral atolls. The inhabitants of the high islands are Melanesians, of the outliers, Polynesian. Many of the smaller outliers are uninhabited.

Rennell and Bellona are both low islands of the makatea type containing deposits of phosphate. Little extraction has been done, however, and both are primarily given over to coconut palm and subsistence food agriculture. Bauxite has been mined on Rennell in an on-again, off-again operation by a Japanese company. The population of both islands is small and composed of mixed Polynesians and Melanesians.

The land mammals of the Solomons include both wild and domesticated pigs and dogs plus bush rats and bats. The reptilian dwellers include snakes, crocodiles, lizards, geckoes, and turtles. In the waters surrounding the islands are found whales, blackfish, and porpoise. A particular nuisance in these islands are the insects, among them white ants, flies, and mosquitoes. Bird life consists of cockatoos, parrots, lorries, kingfishers, ducks, eagles, hawks, hornbills, crows, and pigeons.

The first European to see the Solomon Islands was Alvaro de Mendaña de Neyra, a Spanish navigator, who sighted them in 1568, naming the island of Santa Ysabel after his wife. He also sighted and named Guadalcanal and San Cristobal. He later attempted to colonize the islands but died in the attempt; the colonizing party later went to the Philippines.

No Westerners visited for about the next two hundred years; then a succession of European explorers arrived, including Quiros, Le Maire and Schouten, Carteret, Bougainville, D'Urville, and La Perouse. By 1830 the islands were well known to the Europeans, and routine calls became commonplace.

Next followed a period of mission founding by the

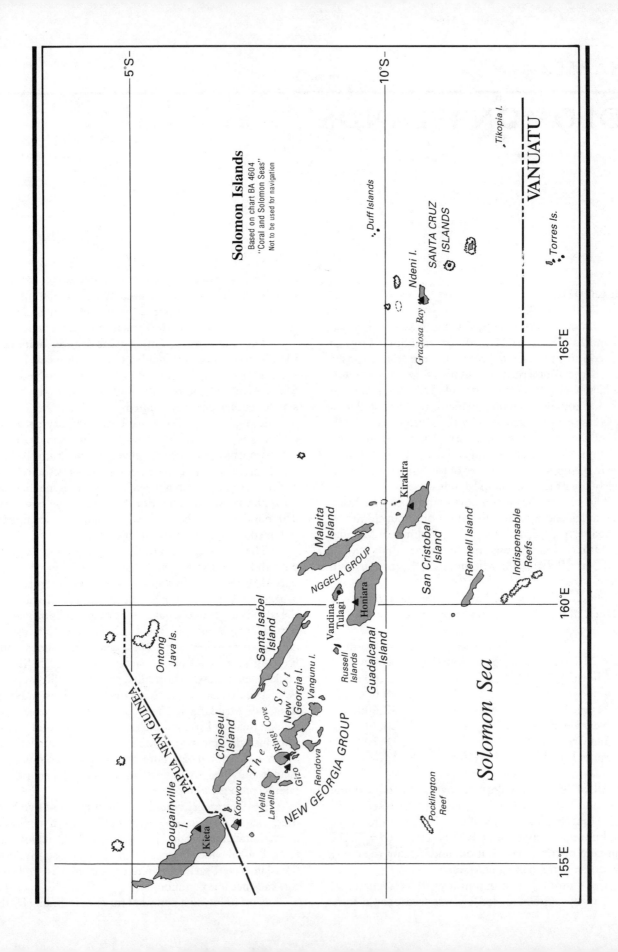

Solomon Islands

Based on chart BA 4604
"Coral and Solomon Seas"
Not to be used for navigation

SOLOMON ISLANDS
An independent nation

Ports of Entry

Korovou, Shortland Islands	7°05' S, 155°54' E
Gizo, Gizo Island	8°06' S, 156°50' E
Ringi Cove, Kolombangara	8°07' S, 157°06' E
Yandina, Banika	9°04' S, 159°14' E
Tulagi Island	9°06' S, 160°11' E
Honiara, Guadalcanal	9°25' S, 159°58' E
Graciosa Bay, Ndeni	10°46' S, 165°50' E

Distances between Ports in Nautical Miles
Between Honiara and

Auckland, New Zealand	1,830
Brisbane, Australia	1,150
Funafuti, Tuvalu	1,140
Nauru (Aiwo District)	675
Noumea, New Caledonia	855
Port-Vila, Vanuatu	695
Rabaul, Papua New Guinea	560
Suva, Fiji	1,195
Tarawa, Kiribati	1,010

Standard Time
11 hours fast on UTC

Public Holidays and Special Events

January 1	New Year's Day—Public holiday
March/April *	Good Friday, Easter, and Easter Monday—Public holidays
June *	Whit Monday—Public holiday
June *	Queen's Official Birthday—Public holiday
July 7	Independence Day—Public holiday
August 3	Bank Holiday
October 1	Solomon Islands Day—Public holiday
November 9	Prince Charles's Birthday—Public holiday
December 25	Christmas Day—Public holiday

*Specific dates vary from year to year.

French and New Zealand missionaries, but these were in general unsuccessful because of the resistance of the natives to outsiders. Murder was the most convincing resistance, and the missions had difficulty getting established.

The practice of blackbirding was conducted in the Solomons, as it was in so many of the Pacific islands. This was a system of recruiting persons for work on plantations or guano or phosphate diggings on other islands; many were taken to Australia and some as far away as South America. It was nothing better than slavery, and the native resentment was such that many Europeans in the islands were murdered. The practice was stopped in 1903, and the natives who had been sent to Australia were repatriated.

In 1893 the British established a protectorate over the southern islands to protect the Europeans who were coming in increasing numbers as traders. By 1900 all of the present Solomon Islands were placed under the protectorate. With greater security for the Europeans, large-scale plantations were developed and the South Seas trading firms of Burns-Philp and W. R. Carpenter were established.

Between 1930 and 1940 the Solomons were neglected and remained in a coconut economy, but this all changed very quickly when the Japanese started World War II in the Pacific. Japan occupied the islands in 1942, and they were turned into a furious battleground until mid-1943. During this time the Solomon Islanders distinguished themselves in aiding the Australian and British coast-watchers who reported on enemy movements and assisted in the recovery of Allied fliers.

The British protectorate capital of the Solomons had been at Tulagi in the Florida group before World War II. During the war Tulagi was totally destroyed, so when the war was over the government took up quarters in the former military buildings on Guadalcanal, near what is now Honiara. Despite Honiara's lack of a good harbor, the capital has stayed there, and new buildings have been built to replace the wartime structures.

The Solomon Islands took their independence from British rule on July 7, 1978, at which time they became an independent nation within the British Commonwealth. The national government is a parliamentary legislature with the chief minister being selected from the majority party of the Legislative Assembly. Local affairs are handled by four district governments: Western, headquartered in Gizo; Central, headquartered in Honiara; Malaita, headquartered in Auki; and Eastern, headquartered in Kira Kira.

The indigenous peoples of the Solomons are dark-skinned and heavily built. Those living near the Bougainville Straits are very dark; those in the southern areas are somewhat lighter. There are also some Gilbertese in the Gizo area, who were settled there by the British when their islands in the Gilberts group became overcrowded. These latecomers have not been assimilated too well into the social structure of the Solomon Islands.

There is no single native language for the Solomons; about 60 dialects are spoken in the various villages and islands. Because of the long occupancy of the group by the British and the presence of large numbers of Americans during World War II, English has become the main language of the islands.

Missionary stations are found on many of the inhabited islands within the country. Churches represented in the Solomons Islands are the Anglican Church, the Roman Catholic Church, the Methodist Church, the South Sea Evangelical Mission, and the Bismarck-Solomons Union Mission of the Seventh-Day Adventist Missions.

The missions have had the major responsibility for education in past years. Not until 1957 did the government take part in education, and then through the development of a secondary school program and a teachers college. Children generally live away from home when attending school. Government-sponsored and mission-sponsored students go overseas for advanced schooling. Many of the government-sponsored students attend the University of Papua New Guinea near Port Moresby. Medical training is given the Solomon Islanders at the Fiji School of Medicine. There is a modest public library at Honiara.

Agriculture is the mainstay of the islands, although there is no means for measuring accurately its importance to the economy of the land and its people. The two most valuable exports, copra and timber, are principal products of the land; cocoa also is exported. Agriculture and forestry accounted for about 23 percent of registered employment—more than any other sector except government.

Ownership and use of land also indicates the importance of agriculture, both subsistence and commercial. In 1965 it was estimated that about 96 percent of the land total, which is 12,000 square miles, was held by native people, and the land was classified according to use as bush, garden, and village land. Bushlands produce wild crops that are gathered by local residents, who also hunt animals for food in those same areas.

The major crops grown for domestic food consumption are sweet potatoes, yams, taro, and green vegetables of various kinds. The demand for these crops is increasing because of the growth of urban areas where any surplus can be marketed. Tobacco and peanuts also enjoy a local market.

Coconut, as the source of copra, is the most valuable commercial crop. Coconut plantations were initiated near the end of the nineteenth century by European traders who had been obtaining coconuts from native growers. Early enterprises were small; but after 1900 they increased in scale and in the amount of investment required. In 1904 Lever Pacific Plantations entered the Solomon Islands, and in 1908 the Burns-Philp Company initiated operations. Both firms built up large-scale plantations and enterprises for growing coconuts and processing them into copra.

Production of livestock is mostly on a small scale,

carried on more to keep weeds down on plantations than to produce beef for consumption. In 1967, however, the Guadalcanal Plains Enterprise, which was engaged in rice growing, became interested in beef production as well and established a herd of good stock on a ranch near Honiara.

Small-scale commercial fishing operations are conducted near the major population centers—Honiara, Guadalcanal; Auki, Malaita; and Gizo in the New Georgia islands; otherwise, fishing is for subsistence. Ocean products, including shells and green snails, are exported and provide welcome foreign exchange.

Since World War II, forests have been recognized as an important resource, although no survey of their potential was undertaken until 1956. Timber had been cut and exported as round logs from Gizo, Santa Isabel, and the Shortlands.

Legislation has been passed in the Solomon Islands declaring that all remaining World War II wreckage and equipment is now cultural property belonging to the government. It cannot be removed without permission, and relics with particular historical value are banned from export.

Solomon Islanders are handsome and friendly people. This young family was walking along the road to Gizo and were happy to have their picture taken. (Earl Hinz)

Solomon Islands Notes on Malaria

The chief medical officer for the Solomon Islands has prepared the following material for the information of the visitor to the Solomon Islands, which is a malarious country. Read it carefully ahead of time because the prophylaxis treatment must be started before entering a malarial region.

WHAT MALARIA IS

Malaria is a disease of the blood caused by a group of parasites that live in and destroy the red blood cells. It may be fatal. It is spread by the female anopheles mosquito. This mosquito is found in most parts of the Solomon Islands and can infect you with the disease unless you take appropriate steps to protect yourself. These steps are not difficult if you use common sense. They involve protecting yourself from bites from infective mosquitoes and regularly taking tablets called antimalarials.

PROTECTIVE MEASURES

Malaria mosquitoes bite mainly from dusk to dawn, so the greatest danger of becoming infected is during that period. The risk of this in town areas in screened quarters is almost negligible.

If you are outside during those hours, it is wise to ensure that as little of your body is exposed as possible; to that end, wear long sleeves and trousers or slacks. While sleeping in unscreened quarters, use a mosquito net.

Should you be unable to keep yourself well covered at any time for reasons of comfort and the like, carry with you and use an insect repellent.

Various types of antimalarials are available to the visitor in the Solomon Islands; these may be obtained before your visit or from the pharmacy in Honiara. Solomon Islands government hospitals in all provincial centers have only very limited supplies, but will supply in an emergency.

At the present time Maloprim or its equivalent is the drug of first choice. If you are unable to obtain this or you cannot take it for any reason, take Fansidar or its equivalent.*

---

*Since it was introduced in 1982, the antimalaria drug Fansidar has been prescribed for travelers in malaria-prone areas of Africa, Asia, and South America. Fansidar is usually well tolerated, but recent reports of severe skin reactions and even death associated with the drug have convinced doctors to rec-

Neither drug is totally recommended for prophylaxis in pregnancy or in infants under 1 month of age. However, there is no evidence that either drug is harmful to these two groups. These two drugs must not be taken if you have an allergy to sulfa drugs. In all these cases, a third antimalarial, chloroquine, is used.

This or an equivalent antimalarial, Amodiaquine, can be obtained in both adult and children's dosages. Should you decide to take either of these two antimalarials you must be aware that some resistant strains to these drugs do exist and that in the unlikely event that you develop a fever you must report for medical attention.

All of these antimalarials mentioned above are taken weekly. Another antimalarial, Proguanil (Paludrine), is also available and is effective and safe but must be taken daily.

All antimalarials must be taken in the correct dosage and regularly as prescribed. On returning to a nonmalarial country, you must continue taking your antimalarials for six weeks. If you are in any doubt, consult your doctor for advice.

THE SYMPTOMS OF MALARIA

Malaria is a common disease and mimics other diseases. Often a person with malaria may be thought to have influenza or a common cold. It is far better to err the other way and think you have malaria and seek medical attention. Someone suffering from malaria feels ill for a few days to a week before the classical form of the disease shows itself. This ill feeling is often accompanied by aches and pains and a slight to a high temperature. When the classical symptoms appear the person will react in the following way:

- There is a feeling of intense cold, which lasts from half an hour to two hours. During this time shivering occurs, which is sometimes very intense.
- The cold stage is followed by the hot stage. The patient has a high temperature, feels hot and dry, and may vomit a lot and become delirious.
- After four to five hours the sweating stage begins. The patient perspires profusely and the temperature falls.

---

ommend chloroquine, an older antimalarial agent. In some regions where malaria risks are especially high, travelers are advised to take both Fansidar and chloroquine, according to this report.

Following the first attack, similar attacks will occur at intervals of 48 to 72 hours unless the affected person is treated. A person not treated may die.

TREATMENT OF MALARIA

If you think that you have contracted malaria, you should seek immediate medical attention and treatment. Final diagnosis will be dependent upon microscopic examination of a small specimen of your blood.

WHEN YOU GET HOME

If you suffer an attack of fever or febrile illness after you leave the Solomon Islands, you should report this to a doctor and tell the doctor that you have been in a malarious country and you think you may be suffering from malaria. Malaria is not the only disease that produces fever, but your information will help the doctor to ensure the possibility of malaria is not overlooked. If it is shown you do have malaria your doctor will prescribe a further course of antimalarials to ensure that you do not suffer another attack.

A FEW POINTS

Don't spoil your stay in the Solomon Islands by getting malaria. Protect yourself and your family by taking antimalarials regularly. Don't believe people who say they don't take the tablets and never get malaria. It is not worth the risk.

The Weather

The weather of the Solomon Islands is dominated by the southeast trade winds during the period of April through October. During this period 75 percent of the winds are easterly, and 60 percent of those are east to southeast. The trades tend to be steadier and stronger over the southern part of the group, particularly in the region of the Santa Cruz Islands.

November through March the winds blow predominantly between northeast and northwest but with considerable variability including significant east and south winds. In the vicinity of the larger islands the winds are affected by daily land and sea breezes.

Between seasons the winds tend to light southeasterlies and even calms, requiring more motoring and less sailing. The winds at the beginning and end of the winter southeast trades are very docile.

The Solomon Islands are generally free from tropical cyclones, although such storms may form to the south and west of the group. After formation, these tropical cyclones tend to move to the southwest until they reach 15°S to 20°S at which time they usually curve to the southeast.

Weather, however, always has its exceptions, and May 1986 was a double exception. Not only did tropical cyclone Namu form in the month of May, which is a rarity for southwest Pacific Tropical cyclones, but it severely damaged the southern Solomons. Namu stayed put about 300 miles south of Honiara for several days, battering the islands of Malaita, Makira, and eastern Guadalcanal. Winds were estimated in excess of 70 knots, and rainfall was heavy, causing severe damage to villages. Namu later moved south and then southeast,

---

FLOTSAM AND JETSAM

Currency
The Solomon Islands has its own money issued in notes of 2, 5, 10, and 20 dollars and coins of 1, 2, 5, 10, and 20 cents as well as a 1-dollar coin. The approximate rate of exchange is US$1 = SI$1. The relative price of goods and services is 88.

Language
English is the official language of the Solomon Islands. Pidgin is commonly heard, and there are more than 60 dialects in the group.

Electricity
Where electricity is available it is 240v, 50 Hz AC.

Postal Address
Yacht ( )
Poste Restante
Honiara
SOLOMON ISLANDS

There are also post offices at Yandina, Gizo, Auki, and Kira Kira. In Honiara also check for your mail at the yacht club, where it may be forwarded for convenience.

Ports for Making Crew Changes
Honiara is a possible port for making crew changes; it has international airline connections to Suva and Brisbane. A domestic airline connects the major towns of the Solomon Islands with Honiara.

External Affairs Representative
British embassies or consulates

Information Center
Solomon Islands Tourist Authority
P.O. Box 321
Honiara
SOLOMON ISLANDS

The Solomon Islanders build their houses on stilts to minimize problems with termites and to keep the floors dry in rains. These friendly people were living in the Matanikau River valley. (Earl Hinz)

becoming a mere tropical depression just north of New Caledonia.

May to October is the drier season of the year with rainfall averaging about 5 inches per month. During the rest of the year it averages 9 to 12 inches with March being the wettest with more than 14 inches of rainfall. What the dry season lacks in rainfall, however, it makes up for in humidity. July to September the humidity stays about 73 percent. Maximum humidity occurs in March, when a high of 80 percent is reached.

The average temperature for the year is 79°F to 80°F, making it one of the most consistent climates in the Pacific.

The most pleasant time to visit the Solomon Islands is from July through September when rainfall, humidity, and temperature are at their lowest levels.

Cruising Notes

YACHT ENTRY

The principal Port of Entry into the Solomon Islands is Honiara, Guadalcanal, which is the seat of the national government as well as the central district headquarters. The other listed Ports of Entry—Korovou, Gizo, Ringi Cove, Yandina, Tulagi Island, and Graciosa Bay—are really only check-in ports allowing temporary entry, and you are obligated to formally clear in at Honiara within two weeks. You can, however, clear out from the Solomon Islands at any of the listed ports.

Although the Solomon Islands cover a vast expanse of ocean and number many islands, do not stop at any but the designated Ports of Entry when first arriving. If you have to put into any other port for reasons of safety or provisions, contact the local island administrator and proceed as soon as possible to Honiara or a designated Port of Entry for proper clearance; otherwise you may not be permitted to stay.

CUSTOMS

All vessels entering the waters of the Solomon Islands are subject to a Light Fee of SI$100 plus five cents per vessel-displacement ton. This is a user tax originally intended only for commercial ships, but it has been extended to cruising boats as well. It is best if you obtain Solomon Islands dollars before arriving so that you can pay these fees immediately and not get involved in exchange-rate bargaining before you can get to a bank. If you stay longer than four months, Customs will demand a refundable bond on the boat based on its tonnage. A 15-ton boat will have to deposit SI$4,000.

If you are carrying firearms, be aware that they will be impounded when you check into Honiara and will be returned only on departure. All liquor will be bonded on entry, and portable radios must be declared.

As in many countries, if you do not have a cruising permit from the host country, you must check in at each port where there is a Customs office even though you may have been cleared into the country elsewhere. Visiting yachts must make their presence known to the local district headquarters where they are visiting. Note that even though Auki and Kira Kira are district headquarters, they are not Ports of Entry.

Excellent charts for the Solomon Islands at a very reasonable price can be purchased from the Marine Department at Honiara.

IMMIGRATION

Passports are required of all entering visitors. British Commonwealth, U.S., and most West European citizens are not required to secure visas. A visitor's permit will be issued on arrival for a period not exceeding 3 months in any period of 12 months. In special cases, stays longer than 3 months may be granted, but you must pay a fee of SI$10 per month per person. It is also possible to apply for temporary resident permits, which cost SI$30 per month per person.

YACHT FACILITIES AT PRINCIPAL PORTS OF ENTRY

Honiara

Small craft with the help of local knowledge can anchor on either side of Point Cruz in Honiara depending on the wind. The principal anchorage, however, is on the west side near the Point Cruz Yacht Club. There you can anchor in about 8 fathoms of water close to shore with stern lines tied ashore or to the sunken barge near the club. Most boats will anchor between the Customs office on the point and the barge. The west side of Point Cruz is a safe anchorage during the winter season, April through October, but quite a surge may be experienced.

During the summer season, November through March, there is likely to be significant wind from the northwest, making this anchorage a dangerous lee

Cruising boats and other small craft anchor to the west of Guadalcanal's Point Cruz during prevailing southeasterly winds. The Point Cruz Yacht Club is in the left background, adjacent to the Mendana Hotel. (Earl Hinz)

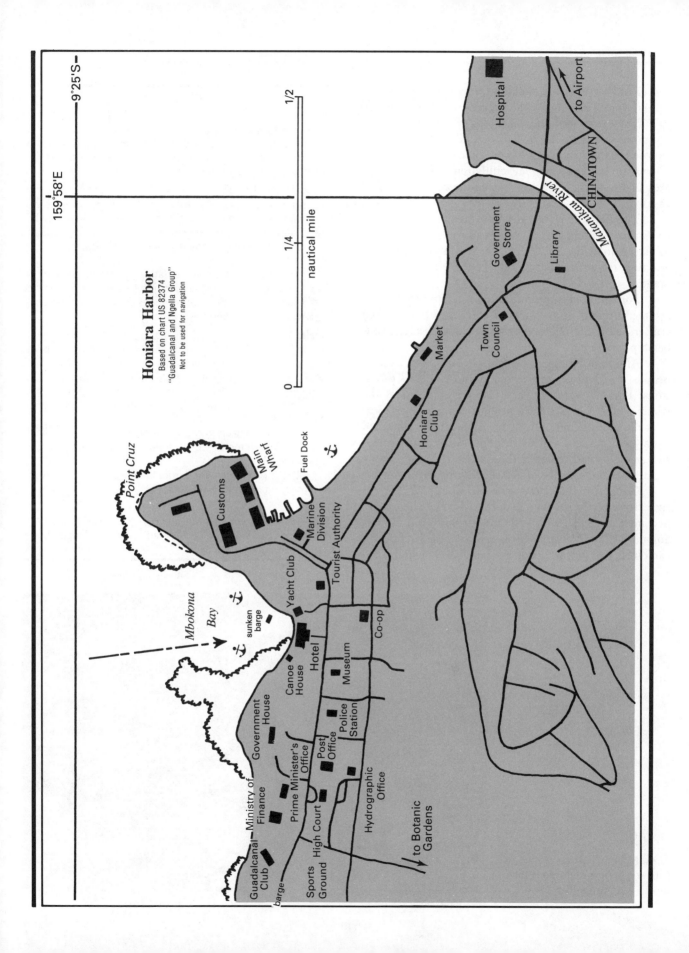

Honiara Harbor

Based on chart US 82374
"Guadalcanal and Ngella Group"
Not to be used for navigation

0   1/4   1/2
nautical mile

159°58'E

9°25'S

Point Cruz

Mbokona Bay

sunken barge

Ministry of Finance

Guadalcanal Club

barge

Sports Ground

Government House

Prime Minister's Office

High Court

Post Office

Police Station

Hydrographic Office

to Botanic Gardens

Canoe House

Hotel

Museum

Co-op

Yacht Club

Tourist Authority

Marine Division

Customs

Main Wharf

Fuel Dock

Honiara Club

Market

Town Council

Government Store

Library

Hospital

CHINATOWN

Mataniku River

to Airport

shore. At that time you should move around to the east side of Point Cruz and anchor stern-to, just east of the fuel dock. Bow and stern anchors are recommended. For more safety, sail to the harbor at Tulagi Island. The exposed nature of the Honiara anchorage was well known to the early native population who called the area Naho-ni-ara, meaning "facing the east and southeast wind."

The Point Cruz Yacht Club extends a warm welcome to all visiting yachts. You can arrange for Customs to meet you at the Point Cruz Yacht Club dinghy dock and then ferry them out to your boat for clearance formalities.

For short stays the club extends temporary honorary membership. If an extended stay is envisaged, then cruisers are requested to arrange for some form of membership.

Although Honiara is a small town, about 12,000 people, you will be able to secure most needed provisions. Potable water and fuel can be obtained at the wharf on the east side of Point Cruz. There are no local boat-repair facilities, but some help can be obtained from local garages and workshops. Fairly comprehensive ship slip and repair facilities exist at Tulagi. Some are private and some belong to the Marine Department.

Guadalcanal Island is a rapidly disappearing treasure trove of World War II relics. Most of them have become overgrown with bush and are hard to find. The Solomon Islands Visitors Bureau, nearby the yacht club, can direct you to tour operators and dive shops who can

MEDICAL MEMO

Immunization Requirements

Immunizations for smallpox, cholera, and yellow fever are required if you have transited or visited within the last six days (smallpox 14 days) an area currently affected.

Local Health Situation

This is a humid, tropical country; malaria is still present, and antimalarial treatment should be taken before arriving, while there, and for a period after leaving. (See text for Solomon Islands chief medical officer's advice on staying free of malaria.)

Tuberculosis among the native peoples is still a problem, but leprosy is almost eradicated. Hookworm is common and is best avoided by wearing shoes or sandals when walking. Avoid animal droppings.

Health Services

The main government hospital is Central Hospital with 158 beds at Honiara. There are also district hospitals at Auki, Gizo, Kira Kira, and Santa Cruz. These facilities are staffed with Fiji-trained medical officers. There are also small clinics throughout the country with mission doctors present at Munda and Atoifi.

The few dentists in the Solomon Islands are completely absorbed in helping the local population. There are no optical services.

Drugs can be obtained from the hospitals, and there is a pharmacy (chemist) in Honiara.

Water

Tap water at Honiara is supposedly good, but it is recommended that all water be considered suspect and treated.

A resident of Gizo tries his luck at catching finny protein along the town's waterfront. (Earl Hinz)

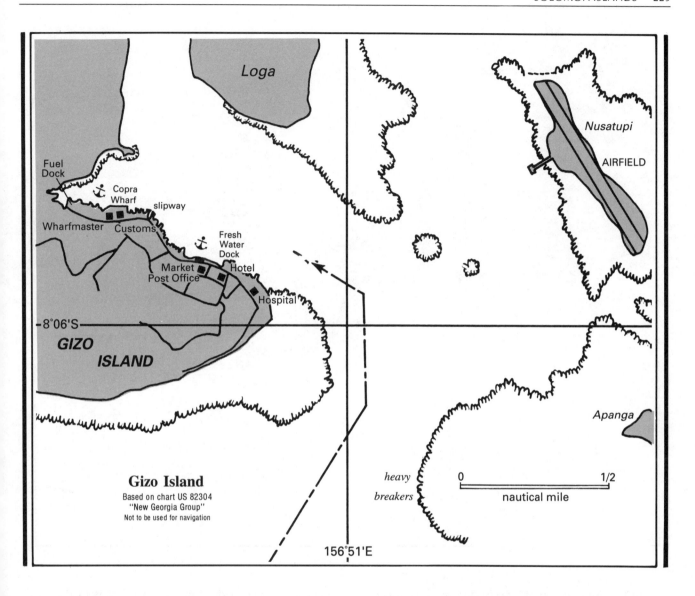

Gizo Island

Based on chart US 82304
"New Georgia Group"
Not to be used for navigation

take you to some of the more notable World War II battlegrounds and remaining relics.

Also, while in Honiara, pay a visit to the Seventh-Day Adventist Betikama Carving Center east of the airport. Carvers work there to pay for room, board, and tuition at the school, and they also bring carvings from the outlying islands to sell for the same purpose. These contemporary pieces of art are well worth taking home.

Gizo

Gizo is the headquarters for the Western district and the second most important trade center in the Solomons. Most prices are higher than in Honiara. Gizo is the copra- and cocoa-receiving port for the Western district. Limited supplies of dry provisions are available, as are potable water and some diesel fuel. Deck and engine stores are in limited supply. There are limited haulout and repair facilities at Gizo for vessels to 40 feet long.

Gizo's waterfront and main street present a rustic charm not found in the larger urban areas. The island periphery provides vivid scenes of placid lagoons surrounded by white coral beaches. From above the business center, the view of neighboring Kolombangara is spectacular.

Tulagi

About 20 miles north of Guadalcanal across what is now called Iron Bottom Sound lie the Florida Islands. One of these islands, Tulagi, was the capital of the Solomon Islands prior to World War II, but it was so badly

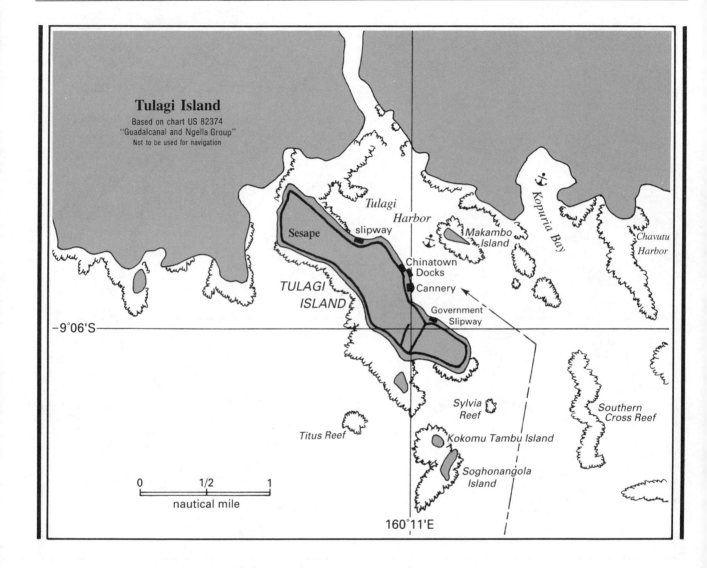

Tulagi Island
Based on chart US 82374
"Guadalcanal and Ngella Group"
Not to be used for navigation

Tulagi
Harbor

Sesape   slipway

Makambo
Island

Chinatown
Docks

Kopuria Bay

Chavutu
Harbor

Cannery

TULAGI
ISLAND

Government
Slipway

—9°06'S

Sylvia
Reef

Southern
Cross Reef

Titus Reef

Kokomu Tambu Island

Soghonangola
Island

0   1/2   1

nautical mile

160°11'E

torn up by American bombing in driving the Japanese out that a new capital was situated at Honiara. Paradoxically, Tulagi has a good harbor while Honiara has virtually no harbor at all.

Tulagi Island, however, remains the country's boatbuilding and repair center and has also added a fish cannery. If you have work to do on your boat, you can haul out here and obtain whatever craft support you need. If you only want to visit the area, you can anchor near the Sesape Boatworks at the risk of hooking your anchor onto some World War II debris; better, you may be able to tie up at the boatworks after asking permission.

The Sesape Boatworks can make fiberglass as well as other repairs and do most maintenance required on a boat. Skilled workers are available at SI$20 per hour. If

you wish to live off your boat while it is in the yard, there is a rental cottage adjacent to the yard with hot water, washing machine, and kitchen with a refrigerator and stove.

A more secure and remote harbor is Ghavutu Harbor to the east, at the northeast corner of Ghavutu Island. There you are completely isolated in a well-protected harbor.

An even more protected and isolated bay is Tokyo Bay, a few miles east of Ghavutu Island. Besides protection from the weather, there are several interesting World War II ships rusting away along the shores.

Graciosa Bay

Graciosa Bay on Ndeni Island in the Santa Cruz group is the most southeasterly check-in point in the Solomon

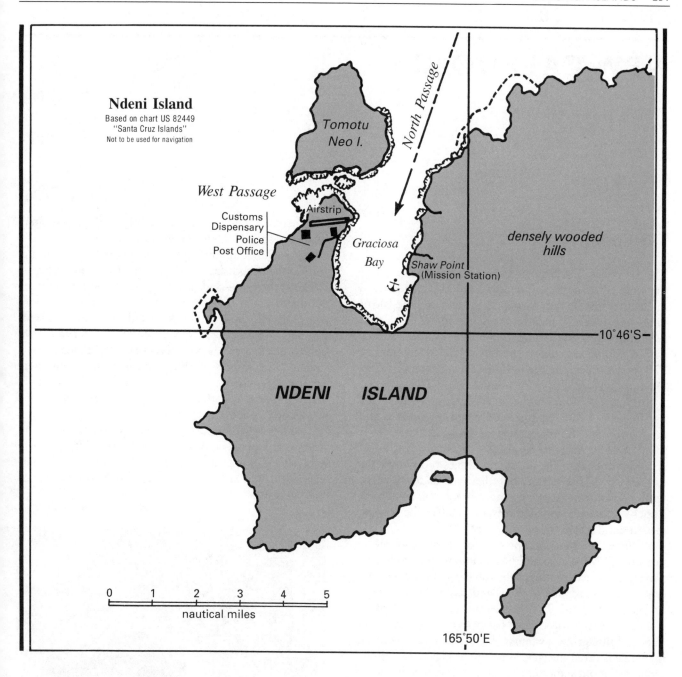

Ndeni Island

Based on chart US 82449
"Santa Cruz Islands"
Not to be used for navigation

Tomotu
Neo I.

North Passage

West Passage

Airstrip

Customs
Dispensary
Police
Post Office

Graciosa
Bay

Shaw Point
(Mission Station)

densely wooded
hills

10°46'S

NDENI   ISLAND

0   1   2   3   4   5
nautical miles

165°50'E

Islands. It is a well protected harbor, but its extreme depth makes anchoring difficult. The best anchorage is just inside Shaw Point on the east side of the bay, but this, unfortunately, is across the bay from the main settlement at Spurgeon Point where the government offices, stores, and dispensary are. There is a town wharf at Spurgeon Point you can use while getting your clearance. Customs and other offices for clearing-in purposes are about 200 yards up the hill from the wharf.

CHAPTER 20

NEW CALEDONIA

The Country

The Overseas Territory of New Caledonia consists of the main island of New Caledonia and its dependencies, made up of the Loyalty Group to the east and the Isle of Pines and Ouen Islands to the south. New Caledonia (250 miles long by 31 miles wide) is the largest island, with 6,450 square miles; the Loyalty Islands comprise 770 square miles; the Isle of Pines, 84 square miles. The Ouen Islands are dots in the ocean.

New Caledonia is the fourth-largest island in the Pacific being exceeded in size only by New Guinea and the North and South islands of New Zealand. It is mountainous, rising to an altitude of almost 5,400 feet (Humboldt Peak). The mountain ranges run almost the full length of the island, but they are discontinuous, with steep northeast slopes and more gentle southwest slopes. A barrier reef lies offshore and is the longest insular coral reef in the world.

New Caledonia occupies one of the most southerly portions of Melanesia and has a climate that, although tropical, is neither excessively hot nor damp. The eastern or windward side of the island has a heavy rainfall and is well forested. The western side in the rain shadow is drier, and the coastline is fringed erratically by tidal flats and mangrove swamps. Vegetation in the western lowlands is often meager, although at higher elevations remnants of old stands of araucaria pine can be found.

The first impression of the navigator who has been accustomed to the luxuriant vegetation of most of the Pacific islands is that New Caledonia is bare and arid. The prevailing growth is a small, drab tree, the niaouli, similar in appearance to the common eucalyptus scrubs of Australia, but that is only in some places. The coconut palm grows along the coast, and a great many valleys are filled with a luxuriant growth of the magnificent kauri pine.

There is very little animal life on New Caledonia, but there are many varieties of bright plumaged small birds and several kinds of pigeons and hawks.

In 1774 Captain Cook became the first Westerner to find the island. He named it New Caledonia because to him the pine-clad ridges bore a resemblance to Scotland. From that time to 1840, when the missionaries arrived, the island was visited by explorers, traders, and ship deserters. New Caledonia became a French colony in 1853 and was used as a penal settlement starting in 1864. Some 40,000 prisoners were sent there before it was closed as a penal colony about 1897. However, many of the prisoners and their dependents stayed on to populate the island.

The French did little to develop the island beyond using it as a penal colony. The native population was in an almost continuous state of rebellion up to 1917. During World War I, New Caledonia fought on the side of the Allies.

The ruins of the forbidding nineteenth-century prison on the Isle of Pines. France transported its undesirables to prisons in New Caledonia, and they became the ancestors of many of today's population. (Earl Hinz)

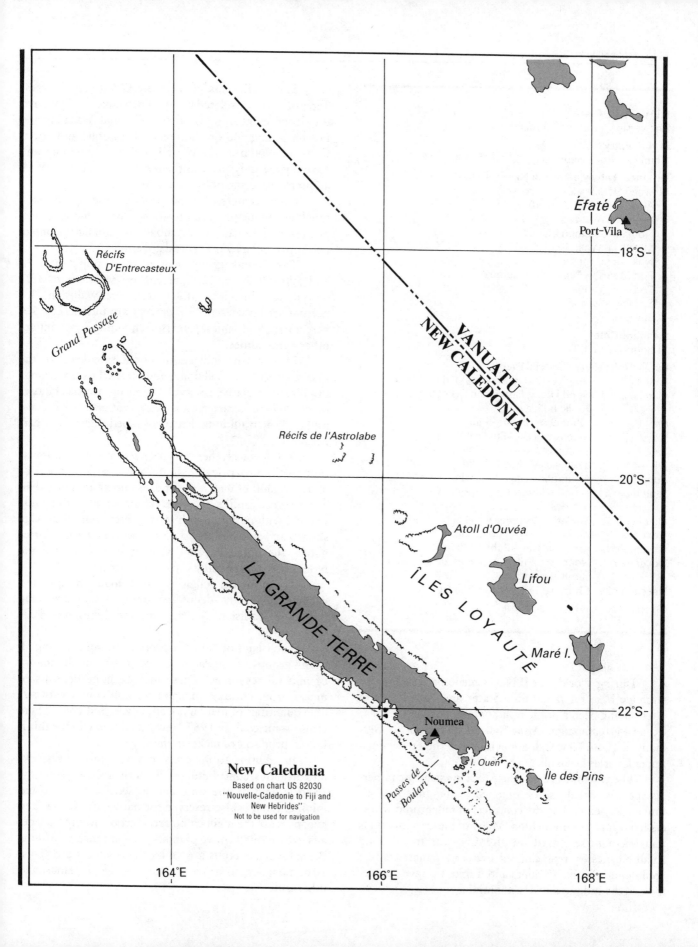

VANUATU
NEW CALEDONIA

Récifs D'Entrecasteux

Grand Passage

Récifs de l'Astrolabe

Éfaté
Port-Vila ▲

18°S

20°S

Atoll d'Ouvéa

ÎLES LOYAUTÉ

Lifou

Maré I.

LA GRANDE TERRE

Noumea ▲

I. Ouen

Île des Pins

22°S

Passes de Boulari

New Caledonia

Based on chart US 82030
"Nouvelle-Caledonie to Fiji and
New Hebrides"
Not to be used for navigation

164°E   166°E   168°E

NEW CALEDONIA
An overseas territory of France

Port of Entry
Noumea, New Caledonia   22°16′ S, 166°26′ E

Distances between Ports in Nautical Miles
Between Noumea and

Auckland, New Zealand	975
Brisbane, Australia	795
Honiara, Solomon Islands	855
Mata Uta, Wallis Islands	1,130
Nukualofa, Tonga	1,025
Port Moresby, Papua New Guinea	1,350
Port-Vila, Vanuatu	290
Sydney, Australia	1,065
Suva, Fiji	720

Standard Time
11 hours fast on UTC

Public Holidays and Special Events

January 1	New Year's Day—Public holiday
March/April *	Good Friday, Easter, and Easter Monday—Public holidays
May 1	Labor Day—Public holiday
May *	Ascension Day—Public holiday
June *	Pentecost Monday—Public holiday
July 14	Bastille Day—Public holiday
August 15	Assumption Day—Public holiday
September 24	New Caledonia Day—Sports events and parades
October 4	Braderie—Noumea street fair
November 1	All Saints' Day—Public holiday
November 11	Armistice Day—Public holiday
November *	Noumea Carnival—Parades, dances, and carnival events
December 25	Christmas Day—Public holiday

*Specific dates vary from year to year.

During World War II New Caledonia was a major strategic base for the United States and New Zealand after having been a prime military target of the Japanese expansion campaign. After the fall of France to Germany in 1940, New Caledonia followed the Free French under Charles DeGaulle.

The wartime need of the Allies for strategic minerals such as nickel and chrome led to the government's unilaterally extending the contracts of indentured workers from Java and Indochina. Many of these Indonesians and Vietnamese stayed on after the war to open up small businesses, replacing the prewar Japanese trading companies. Wallis Islanders and Tahitians have supplemented the Indonesians for nonmining work.

The inhabitants of the New Caledonia Overseas Territory are considered to be French citizens. The territory is represented in the French National Assembly and French Senate and on the French Economic and Social Council. Noumea, the capital of New Caledonia and virtually the only town in the territory, is the seat of all administrative and political activity.

Other centers of population are locally administered by municipal commissions. The commissioners' powers and functions are subject to financial control and supervision by the central government.

The island group has a total population of 153,500. Of these, 42.5 percent are Melanesian, 37.1 percent are European, 8.4 percent are Wallisian, 3.8 percent are Polynesian, 3.6 percent are Indonesian, 1.6 percent are Vietnamese, and the remaining 3 percent are other nationalities.

Most of the indigenous population lives on the east coast of New Caledonia and on the Loyalty Islands in villages on native reserves and in the towns. Houses of earthen or cement walls with thatched roofs have replaced the traditional beehive-shaped quarters of earlier days.

As elsewhere, there has been a trend of the population to the urban area. Noumea has a population of about 80,000 of which Europeans constitute more than 55 percent. Unlike Papeete, Noumea is high-profile French, with numerous white apartment buildings, chic shops, and restaurants to rival those in Paris. Fortunately, the noted Parisian hauteur is absent, and the Noumeans are generally warm and friendly.

The principal religions are Roman Catholic and various Protestant denominations. Masses are sung weekly in Wallisian, Melanesian, and Tahitian and are very colorful.

The island of New Caledonia is unique among all island groups of the Pacific in that it has an abundance of mineral resources. These include large deposits of nickel, iron, chrome, manganese, and cobalt with sizable quantities of mercury, lead, silver, and gold. There is also some coal. In 1967 New Caledonia was the third-largest producer of nickel in the world.

In addition to minerals, crops, forests, livestock, and fisheries contribute significantly to the economy. Land is held by the state and leased for farming and mining. Land is also reserved for native use. Coffee and coconuts are the main commercial crops. Many Europeans live on small coffee plantations and ranches. Among the subsistence crops grown by the islanders are yams, taro, mangoes, corn, sweet potatoes, rice, bananas, and other fruit.

A downtown Noumea street leading to the Catholic cathedral on the hill. (Earl Hinz)

Forests cover about 15 percent of the land and produce several varieties of trees of commercial value. The New Caledonian pine is found no other place in the world.

Livestock is of considerable importance; there are large herds of cattle, some pigs and sheep, and modern poultry farms near Noumea. Dairy farming is limited.

Abundant saltwater fish of good quality exist in the nearby waters, but there is proper concern for the future because of the high contamination of the shoreline by mining and smelting operations. Commercial fishing supplies only the local market, no fish are exported.

Although you can cruise inside the reef for hundreds of miles, the two most interesting cruising areas are the Isle of Pines at the southern tip of La Grande Terre and the Loyalty Islands 60 miles to the east.

From Noumea south to the Isle of Pines is a long day's cruise, because of the many reefs, only a daylight passage is recommended. Kuto Bay is the center of marine activities on the Isle of Pines. In its earlier days, the Isle of Pines was noted for two species of trees—sandalwood and pine. The sandalwood suffered the fate of all sandalwood in the Pacific—it was ruthlessly harvested and shipped to China. The New Caledonia pines (*Araucaria cookii*) ended up as building materials.

Besides the beauty of the island itself, visitors should seek out the limestone caves and the old penal colony. The caves, near the airport, are laced with stalactites and stalagmites. One cave is almost two miles long.

The ruins of the nineteenth-century penal colony are found closer to Kuto Bay but are overgrown with brush. This penal colony and one on La Grande Terre were the sole interest France had in the islands of New Caledonia, other than to keep them from falling into British hands.

For the real South Seas atmosphere, however, you must go to the Loyalty Islands. Of the three main islands—Ouvea, Lifou, and Mare—Ouvea has the best lagoon anchorage. The people of these islands are actually Polynesian, having come originally from the Wallis Islands. Their politics, however, are akin to the politics of the Kanaks (see below) along the eastern shore of La Grande Terre. The Loyalty Islands are not a Port of Entry, but you can get permission in Noumea to take your departure from them.

The winds of independence are blowing strong in New Caledonia, with the native Kanaks demanding an end to France's occupation of their islands. Curfews and restrictions on travel about New Caledonia are the rule. Peaceful at times but at other times in open rebellion, the Kanaks will settle for nothing less than the right to rule their own lands. Visitors to Noumea are advised to watch the local political situation and not get embroiled in sporadic fighting between the French and the Kanaks.

The Weather

The winds in the New Caledonia area are dominated by the southeast trades, but they vary in strength and steadiness throughout the various seasons. The trades are most dependable between November and May when about 60 percent of the winds are between east and southeast. The remaining part of the year, which is the southern hemisphere's winter, sees an increase in the southerly components of the wind although east and southeast winds still prevail and the average wind strength is greater. The western side of the island frequently experiences onshore and offshore breezes, but the east side of the island does not because of the dominant trade wind.

New Caledonia lies in the southwest Pacific tropical cyclone belt. Tropical cyclones in this area generally move south-southeast but occasionally cross from

FLOTSAM AND JETSAM

Currency
New Caledonia uses the Coloniale Franc Pacifique (CFP), the same money as used in French Polynesia. It is issued in coinage of 1, 5, 10, 20, and 50 francs and notes of 100, 500, 1,000 and 5,000 francs. The approximate rate of exchange is US$1 = CFP 93. The relative cost of goods and services is 150.

Language
Like Tahiti, New Caledonia's official language is French. Various other languages are occasionally heard including some indigenous Melanesian dialects, Vietnamese, and some Polynesian dialects. English is spoken by many business people.

Electricity
In the city of Noumea there is 240v, 50 Hz AC electricity.

Postal Addresses
Yacht ( )
Poste Restante
Noumea
NEW CALEDONIA

The government post office charges service fees for holding mail. Mail must be picked up by the person to whom addressed.

If you are staying at the yacht club
Yacht ( )
c/o Club Nautique de Calenonien
B.P. 235
Noumea
NEW CALEDONIA

Like many other harbor mail drops, the yacht mail addressed c/o the club is placed in a box for all to rifle through.

Ports for Making Crew Changes
Noumea is a possible port for making crew changes being served by international airlines that connect it with Suva, Sydney, and Auckland. A domestic airline connects Noumea with Wallis and Futuna islands and other major towns and resort areas of New Caledonia.

External Affairs Representative
French consulates and embassies

Information Center
Office Territorial du Tourisme de Nouvelle-Calédonie
B.P. 688
Noumea
NEW CALEDONIA

northeast to southwest. Strong gales from a northerly direction occur with these storms. The main season for tropical cyclones is December to March.

Noumea has an extremely pleasant climate the year around with the best part of the year from May to November. Temperatures range from 68°F in these months to 80°F in the summer months. The relative humidity hovers about 70 percent the year around.

February through April are the wettest months of the year with a monthly average rainfall of about 5 inches at Noumea, where total annual rainfall measures 40 to 45 inches. Because the mountain chains of the island lie athwart the prevailing winds, the eastern slopes get an abundance of rainfall while the western slopes get only half as much. This rain distribution results in the eastern slope being well forested with kauri, pines, and hardwood above the 1,200-foot level. The interior of the island and the dry western slopes are covered with savanna and a eucalyptus-like scrub called niaouli. Mangroves are common along the coasts.

Ships report thunderstorms to be common in this area in February and March and infrequent between June and October.

Although New Caledonia is sometimes referred to as the Island of Eternal Spring, spring as everywhere has its drawbacks, and new Caledonia has an abundance of mosquitoes.

Cruising Notes

YACHT ENTRY

Noumea is the only Port of Entry to New Caledonia and the Loyalty Islands. All yachts must make their entry there before proceeding elsewhere. Before arriving at the reef entrance, call Port Moselle on VHF channel 16 and announce your ETA. The port captain will give you instructions on where to berth in the harbor for clearance. He will also notify Customs and Immigration, who are within walking distance of the marina at Port Moselle. You can also be cleared in at the Club Nautique de Calédonien in nearby Baie de Pêcheurs.

CUSTOMS

Customs will ask for a list of serial numbers of cameras and electronic equipment you have on board, so this should be prepared in advance. Firearms and ammunition must be surrendered to Customs, who will put them in custody until your departure.

Departure clearance should be started 24 hours before you wish to leave. Clear with officials in the following order: Immigration, Customs, and port director. When departing, you can get permission to make a stop or two along the way as, for instance, to stop at the Loyalty Islands on your way east.

IMMIGRATION

A visa is not required for a stay of 30 days or less. For longer periods you will need to obtain a visa; this can be done on arrival. Four photographs and US$2.45 will be required for each person. Obviously you will need your passport and health record.

Located two miles inside the northern passage to Noumea, Amadee Island not only provides range markers for safe navigation but is a popular picnic spot for Noumeans. The lighthouse, called in French Phare Amadée, was built in 1865. (Earl Hinz)

YACHT FACILITIES

The harbor at Noumea is very good, providing extensive anchorage in 3 to 7 fathoms of water with basically a coral bottom covered with silt and sand, so there is little dragging of the anchor. While some of the harbor is virtually landlocked, there is some question how good a hurricane hole it really is. Many boats in the Baie de L'Orphelinat were lost in a 1989 tropical cyclone.

Moorage can be had at both the new Port Moselle full-service marina and the Club Nautique de Calédonien in the Baie de Pêcheurs. After checking in at Port Moselle, ask the port captain for a transient berth assignment. A visitors' dock with fresh water plumbed to it is available for short-term assignment. Longer-term berthing can be had in slip's where there is fresh water and electricity. Port Moselle is especially convenient to downtown Noumea.

The Club Nautique de Calédonien has Tahiti-style moorings costing approximately US$4.00 per day up to seven days. The cost increases for additional weeks. The club has showers, a bar and restaurant, and its regular

---

MEDICAL MEMO

Immunization Requirements
Immunizations for smallpox, cholera, and yellow fever are required if you have transited or visited within the last six days (smallpox 14 days) an area currently affected.

Local Health Situation
Insects are a nuisance. Poisonous stonefish are present in the waters, but casualties are not common. Typhoid and paratyphoid inoculations are recommended for all crew members.

There is no malaria here, but dengue fever has occasionally appeared. Intestinal parasites and enteric-type diseases are fairly common.

Health Services
Complete medical care is available at the modern 530-bed Gaston Bournet Hospital in Noumea. There are more than 17 medical centers and 23 dispensaries in the rural areas. In addition, there are 3 private clinics and 55 private-practice doctors. Medical costs, both hospital and doctor, are as high as in the United States.

Dental and optical services are available in Noumea from private practitioners.

Drugs for medical use are available in Noumea.

Water
Tap water at Noumea is reported good, but it is recommended that all other water be considered suspect and treated.

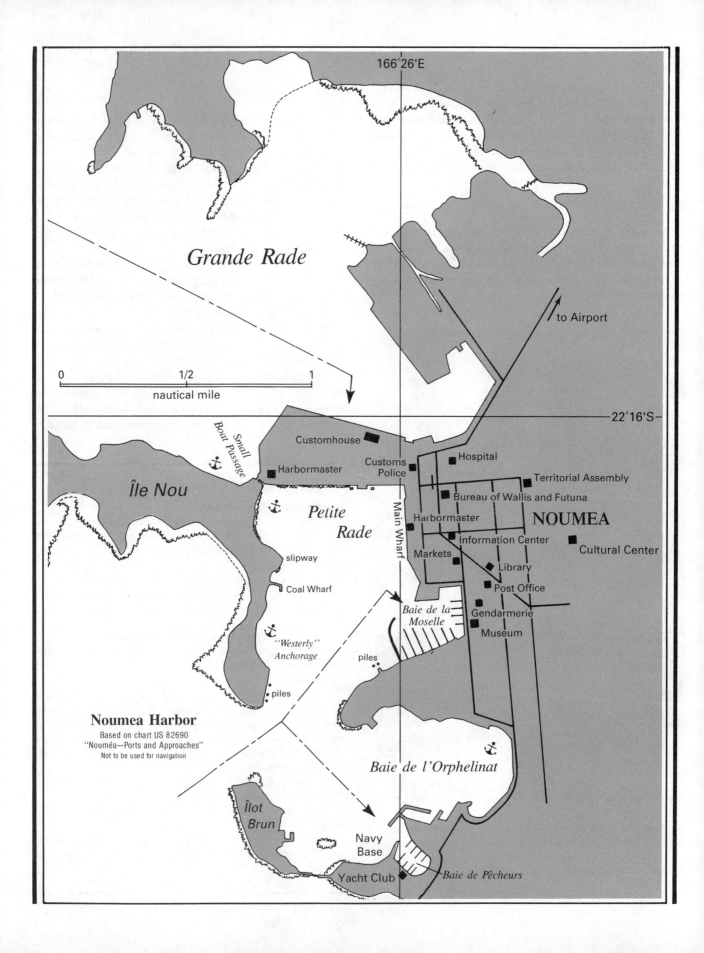

166°26'E

Grande Rade

to Airport

0   1/2   1
nautical mile

22°16'S

Small Boat Passage

Customhouse

Customs Police

Hospital

Harbormaster

Île Nou

Territorial Assembly

Petite Rade

Bureau of Wallis and Futuna

Harbormaster

NOUMEA

slipway

Information Center

Markets

Cultural Center

Coal Wharf

Library

Post Office

''Westerly'' Anchorage

piles

Baie de la Moselle

Gendarmerie

Museum

piles

Main Wharf

Noumea Harbor
Based on chart US 82690
"Nouméa—Ports and Approaches"
Not to be used for navigation

Baie de l'Orphelinat

Îlot Brun

Navy Base

Yacht Club

Baie de Pêcheurs

Noumea is the site of New Caledonia's principal hospital. (Earl Hinz)

The lifeblood of New Caledonia's economy is nickel mining. This smelter is located in Noumea's Grande Rade and is a major polluter of sea and air. (Earl Hinz)

activities are available to visitors. Its secluded location away from Noumea makes it a quieter place to stay, but it requires a short taxi ride into town.

Fuel and potable water are readily available in this harbor. Provisions of all kinds including fresh fruit and vegetables are available in the city but are high priced. A modest amount of marine hardware is available, but keep in mind that, like Tahiti, it will be designed to metric measurements. There is a modern marine boatyard with Travelift between Port Moselle and the yacht club, and adequate shops are available for repairing boat and equipment.

When strong westerly winds threaten the anchorages at the yacht club and Baie de L'Orphelinat, boats move to the westerly anchorage in the lee of Île Nou. This is only a temporary anchorage and is inconvenient to town.

CHAPTER 21

VANUATU

The Country

Vanuatu is a chain of 13 large and about 70 small islands lying between 13°S and 21°S and 166°E and 171°E. The group is composed of three sections forming a Y whose open end is in the north. Banks Island and Torres Islands form the northern legs. The central section contains the largest islands of the group, Espiritu Santo and Malekula, and a number of other islands of considerable size. The southernmost of the central section is Éfaté, the seat of national administration. The southern section consists of Eromanga, Tanna, and Aeityum, together with a few smaller islands.

The total land area of the group is approximately 5,700 square miles, of which Espiritu Santo makes up 1,400 miles. The islands are mountainous, with Mt. Talwesamana on Santo reaching 6,170 feet and neighboring Santo Peak reaching 5,500 feet. The northern islands in general are quite mountainous with several active volcanoes. Earthquakes are not uncommon. The islands are the crest of a submarine ridge. Many are raised coral plateaus with cultivable coastal strips.

The islands are well wooded and have numerous fertile valleys. They are well watered and covered by extensive rain forests containing valuable stands of kauri and sandalwood. Some of the mountain areas have small deposits of manganese, but they have not been developed.

Land fauna as in most Pacific islands has been multiplied by European importations. The indigenous fauna appears to be limited to birds, chickens, rats, and a descendant of the Asian pig. Cattle, dogs, horses, and cats are imports. Fauna of unknown origin include a crocodile that has been seen at Espiritu Santo and a species of iguana that lives on Éfaté. There are some reptiles such as skinks, geckoes, the Pacific boa, and flowerpot snakes; but they are neither numerous nor venomous.

Although there are some 61 species of birds in Vanuatu, most of them are small and shy, and you have to search all of the islands for them. The largest birds are the barn owl and peregrine falcon common to many other parts of the world. Sea- and shorebirds are quite scarce, and only rarely are frigate birds or tropic birds seen in these islands.

In contrast, marine fauna are spectacular, numerous, and sometimes dangerous. The unwary swimmer or beachcomber can come upon scorpion fish, jellyfish, cone shells that sting, and sea snakes, which are all poisonous. As if that weren't enough, there is an abundance of moray eels, barracuda, and sharks in these prolific waters.

But there is also an abundance of edible sea life such as lobster in season, tuna, bonito, sardines, sizable mackerel, and mullet for the catching. Crabs and prawns are also abundant, and no permit is required for fishing. Sea turtles are also found in these waters, but the taking of them is prohibited. It is no wonder that the early dwellers of these islands lived by and from the sea.

Pre-Western history of the islands making up Vanuatu is sketchy at best. The islands probably were an intermediate point in the early migrations of people from Asia moving into the Pacific. This Australoid migration from Asia first headed south to Australia and New Guinea about 50,000 B.C., but it wasn't until about 3000 B.C. that the migrants moved eastward into the Pacific, stopping, among other places, at the islands of Vanuatu.

Archeologists have found evidence that humans have roamed these islands since 3000 B.C. and raised pigs, dogs, and poultry and practiced an itinerant form of agriculture. Originally these people's existence was closely related to the sea, but gradually they turned to the earth, developing agriculture and making pottery for everyday use. Lapita-style pottery has been found throughout the Pacific, and in Vanuatu it dates to the 2000–1500 B.C. period. Although pottery was a staple product of early humans on Vanuatu, the making of it has died out except on Espiritu Santo's west coast,

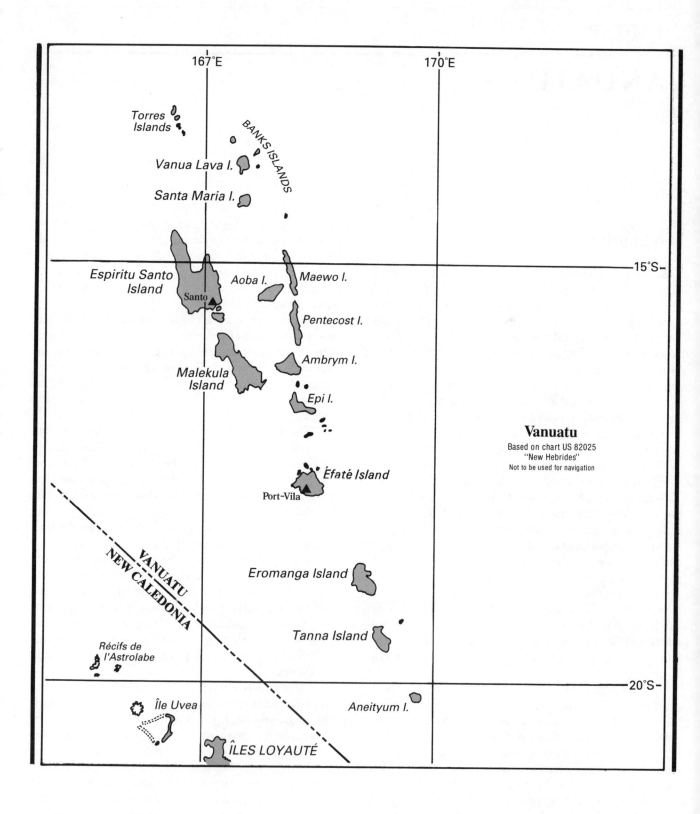

Torres
Islands

BANKS ISLANDS

Vanua Lava I.

Santa Maria I.

167°E

170°E

Espiritu Santo
Island

Santo

Aoba I.

Maewo I.

Pentecost I.

15°S—

Malekula
Island

Ambrym I.

Epi I.

Vanuatu
Based on chart US 82025
"New Hebrides"
Not to be used for navigation

Éfaté Island

Port-Vila

VANUATU
NEW CALEDONIA

Eromanga Island

Tanna Island

Récifs de
l'Astrolabe

Île Uvea

ÎLES LOYAUTÉ

Aneityum I.

20°S—

VANUATU
An independent republic

Ports of Entry
Luganville,	15°31′ S, 167°10′ E
Espiritu Santo	
Port-Vila, Éfaté	17°45′ S, 168°18′ E

Distances between Ports in Nautical Miles
Between Port-Vila and

Apia, Western Samoa	1,165
Auckland, New Zealand	1,195
Brisbane, Australia	1,025
Funafuti, Tuvalu	845
Honiara, Solomon Islands	695
Mata Uta, Wallis Islands	940
Noumea, New Caledonia	290
Nukualofa, Tonga	955
Port Moresby, Papua New Guinea	1,330
Santo, Vanuatu	145
Suva, Fiji	580
Sydney, Australia	1,335

Standard Time
11 hours fast on UTC

Public Holidays and Special Events
January 1	New Year's Day—Public holiday
February 14	John Frum Day—Cargo cult rituals on Tanna Island
March 5	Custom Chiefs' Day
March/April*	Good Friday, Easter, and Easter Monday—Public holidays
April/May*	Pentecost Jump—Land divers' rituals on Pentecost Island
May 1	Labor Day—Public holiday
May*	Ascension Day—Public holiday
July 30	Independence Day—Public holiday
August*	Assumption Day—Public holiday
August*	Toka Dance—Traditional dances and feasts on Tanna Island
October 5	Constitution Day—Public holiday
November*	National Unity Day—Public holiday
December 23–25	Christmas Holidays—Public holiday
December 28	Family Day—Public holiday

*Specific dates vary from year to year.

where pottery is still made. Little else is known about the early history of the islands except for songs and legends that have been passed down from generation to generation and are the current source of material for today's researchers into the past.

Western exploration of the islands and the start of recorded history begins in 1606 with the first landing of Pedro Ferdinand de Quiros, a Portuguese navigator in the service of Spain, on the island of Espiritu Santo.

More than a century later Bougainville visited the northern islands, naming them the Great Cyclades. Then followed visits by many other Europeans—Captain Cook in 1774, who named the group New Hebrides; La Perouse in 1778; D'Entrecasteaux in 1779, along with Dumont d'Urville the same year. Captain Bligh of *Bounty* fame sailed through here in 1789 in his amazing longboat voyage from Tonga to Timor after the *Bounty* mutiny.

Sandalwood was the first major article of foreign trade, and it was pioneered by an Irishman named Peter Dillon on the island of Tanna in 1825. The demanding Chinese market for sandalwood drove the traders to unscrupulous lengths to get the product harvested and into their ships resulting in many bloody skirmishes with the islanders.

Then followed blackbirding. Initially, the practice of recruiting natives to work on the cotton plantations in Fiji or Queensland, Australia, was almost humane, but as demand for labor and greed on the traders' part took hold, it degenerated into almost forced labor or slavery. The number returning home rarely exceeded 25 percent, and when they did come home they brought diseases with them that ravaged the home population. In 1872 Great Britain stepped in to protect the islanders, and so the New Hebrides first fell under foreign rule.

Meanwhile French interests from New Caledonia founded the Compagnie Calédonienne des Nouvelles Hebrides in an attempt to gain economic domination and subsequent political annexation of the islands. The stage was set for a confrontation between France and Great Britain over who owned the islands, with no consideration of the native population. Years of discussions, threats, and proposals between the two countries followed until in 1914 the area was declared a region of joint interest and the condominium government was born. This unwieldy administration was to last until 1980. During its existence there were two high commissioners; two sets of European laws plus native laws; and two kinds of weights, measurements, and currencies. The British and French maintained separate police forces, hospitals, and government offices, and each used its own national language. Pandemonium reigned in the condominium to the detriment of the natives of the New Hebrides islands.

The major step toward independence took place in 1978 with the formation of the government of national unity to which the French, British, and local political parties agreed. Then followed a general election in 1979 which filled the 39 seats of the new Representative Assembly. From this assembly, a prime minister was chosen. In 1980 the first president of the republic was elected and on July 30, 1980, the new country of Vanuatu was declared independent.

The population of Vanuatu according to 1990 estimates was 165,000; of these 94 percent were indigenous Melanesians, 4 percent were French, and the remainder English, Vietnamese, Chinese, and various Pacific islanders.

The populations of the different divisions of Vanuatu in 1986 were:

Éfaté region	27,200
Santo/Malo region	25,300
Tafea region	21,700
Malekula region	18,400

The urban area of Port-Vila had a population of 14,200; the urban area of Luganville, 5,600.

Unlike many other islanders in the Pacific, the ni-Vanuatu (as the people of Vanuatu are known) are still rural dwellers with only 14 percent living in so-called urban areas. Although about half the population lives near the sea, the other half lives well inland in the hills because of the prevalence of malaria near sea level.

Missionary work has played and still is playing an important role in the life of the people of Vanuatu. Most of the Protestant and the Catholic church bodies are represented here, and they are pursuing a joint effort at translating the Bible into the Bislama (pidgin) language. Mission schools are responsible for the education of about half the youth of Vanuatu.

One of the more unusual cults to be found in the Pacific is the cargo cult or John Frum Movement on the island of Tanna. The movement began in 1940–1941 and originally was an expression of rejection of the white man's religion. Today there are several thousand followers of John Frum, who believe that the Messiah will one day return to their land bringing great cargoes of worldly goods to them.

Because of a rich, volcanic soil, a tropical climate, and abundant and regular rainfall, the islands of Vanuatu are covered with luxuriant vegetation. It is not surprising, then, that the economy is primarily agrarian. Tropical food crops such as manioc, taro, yams, sweet potatoes, cabbage, and sugar cane are available the year around. During the cooler months of the southern hemisphere (June to November), temperate-zone vegetables such as tomatoes, peppers, beans, potatoes, and onions are grown. Tropical fruits are grown the year around.

Cash crops have been on the decline in recent

The small Vanuatu Cruising Yacht Club is the enthusiastic host for the annual Musket Cove Race from Fiji. It has few facilities, but the adjacent Waterfront Bar and Grill has become a gathering place for cruisers. (Earl Hinz)

years, although copra is still strong. Cocoa is also exported but to a much lesser degree. Other potential cash crops including rice, vanilla, cotton, maize, and pepper have not developed for several reasons—a shortage of manpower, tropical cyclones, remoteness of the plantations, and lack of communications. Cattle raising is another potentially good cash crop, and it is making economic headway. All in all the islands of Vanuatu are underdeveloped, with a population density of only 29 persons per square mile. Being very fertile, the islands have good possibilities for the future.

Yachts returning from Vanuatu report that the government does not like open criticism of its policies. Although Vanuatu is a democratic country, people who openly criticize the government may become personae non grata.

The Weather

The southeast trades dominate the islands of Vanuatu from May to October. More than 80 percent of the winds then blow between the east and south, with westerly winds being almost unkown. During the remainder of the year east to southeast winds still predominate, but the directions are much more variable. At Erromango Island in the south, the annual mean wind speed is 7 knots with a total of 3.4 days annually of gale force winds.

From January to March the northern part of the region experiences considerable northwest winds and many calms. In these months tropical cyclones arise in or cross the Vanuatu area, usually traveling southward. This type of storm is quite rare in the northern islands but not uncommon in the southern islands of the group.

The southern islands of Éfaté, Erromango, Tanna, Futuna, and Anatom were severely damaged by Tropical Cyclone Uma in February 1987. All of the islands at some time or other have been affected by tropical cyclones.

The climate in Vanuatu varies from tropical in the north to subtropical in the south. In the warm or wet season (November through April) the tropical air brings thundershowers and high humidity along with light winds. In the cool or dry season (May through October) the southeast trade winds bring sunny days and clear, cool nights.

There are, however, considerable variations in the climate pattern. During the dry season there are occasional days of rain while during the wet season there can be periods with little precipitation. The average annual rainfall at Port-Vila is 91 inches while at Santo it is 118 inches. The wet season also brings the threat of tropical cyclones with high and often destructive winds and always with torrential rains.

The average warm season daily temperature at Vila and Santo is 80°F while the average cool season daily temperature is 71°F at Vila and 73°F at Santo. Humidity ranges between 85 and 90 percent.

In general the average rainfall, the mean temperature, and the humidity decrease steadily from north to south through the archipelago.

Cruising Notes

YACHT ENTRY

There are two Ports of Entry to Vanuatu—Port-Vila, Éfaté; and Luganville,* Espiritu Santo. Yachts desiring to enter Vanuatu must report in at one of these ports before proceeding elsewhere in the country.

CUSTOMS

Visiting yachts may enter and remain for six months out of every two years in Vanuatu without payment of duty provided that the vessel remains the property of the owner at the time of entry. The vessel cannot be used for commercial purposes.

All visiting craft are liable for port dues of 6340 vatu for a 30-day period or part thereof. After 30 days (counting from the first date of arrival) the vessel is liable for an additional charge of 80 vatu per day. Port dues are payable at the Customs office on departure.

On completion of Customs and Immigration entry formalities, vessels desiring to visit other islands will be allowed to do so provided they have informed Customs of their plans and received formal approval.

All yachts leaving Vanuatu for a foreign port are required to obtain outward clearance from Customs and Immigration at either Port-Vila or Luganville. In approved cases, vessels will be allowed to clear outward for foreign ports via other islands within Vanuatu. Duty-free stores may be placed on board any vessel cleared from Port-Vila for a foreign port. Quantities are

*The town of Luganville is often called Santo, as is the whole island of Espiritu Santo. Luganville is the settlement that grew from the large U.S. armed forces base that was situated on the Segond Channel during World War II.

Women in the outlying areas of Éfaté Island still wash their clothes in freshwater streams. (Earl Hinz)

commensurate with the length of the anticipated voyage. If you plan on departing from Luganville, it is possible to put duty-free stores aboard under bond at Port-Vila. The skipper is honor bound not to disturb them until final departure from Vanuatu.

IMMIGRATION

Passports are required but not visas. Immigration will issue crew members an entry permit for one month to live aboard the yacht and not take up any employment. On application, Immigration can extend the permit up to four months. Crew members leaving the boat must have onward airline tickets. The skipper is responsible for repatriating crew members that leave the boat.

FIREARMS

Firearms and ammunition must be declared on arrival and surrendered to Customs. If they can be satisfactorily secured under seal on the boat, they can be left on board. If not, Customs will retain them and return them on 48-hours' notice of departure from a port of clearance.

QUARANTINE

No live animals, reptiles, birds, fresh meat, fruit, or vegetables imported with the yacht may be taken ashore. No foreign garbage can be landed in Vanuatu without permission of the Agricultural Quarantine Service.

FLOTSAM AND JETSAM

Currency
The currency of Vanautu is the vatu. The approximate rate of exchange is US$1 = 110 vatu. Because vatu are little known outside Vanuatu, you are advised to convert them to U.S. or Australian dollars before leaving the country.

Language
There are 115 indigenous languages in Vanuatu in addition to English and French, which were imposed on the people during the reign of the rather burdensome condominium government. As a result the government of Vanuatu has elected to create its own language called Bislama, which is a refinement of the pidgin English spoken by most of the ni-Vanuatu who have had contact with the Europeans. Originally it was only a spoken language, but it is now being reduced to writing and will become the lingua franca of the country. English and French continue to be official languages used mostly in business and commerce.

Electricity
Where electricity is available, it is 240v, 50 Hz AC.

Postal Address
Yacht ( )
Poste Restante
Port-Vila
VANUATU
or
Yacht ( )
Poste Restante
Luganville, Espiritu Santo
VANUATU

When addressing your mail to Vanuatu be certain to write on the envelope "Hold for Arrival". When you get to Port-Vila, check both the main post office and the Rossi Hotel for mail. The Rossi Hotel is such a well known gathering place for the cruising crowd that postal officials often send boat mail there automatically.

Ports for Making Crew Changes
Port-Vila is a possible port for making crew changes since it is connected by international airlines to Apia, Suva, Honiara, and Nauru. A domestic airline connects Port-Vila with Luganville and other major towns of Vanuatu.

External Affairs Representative
British embassies or consulates

Information Center
Vanuatu Visitors Bureau
P.O. Box 209
Port-Vila
VANUATU

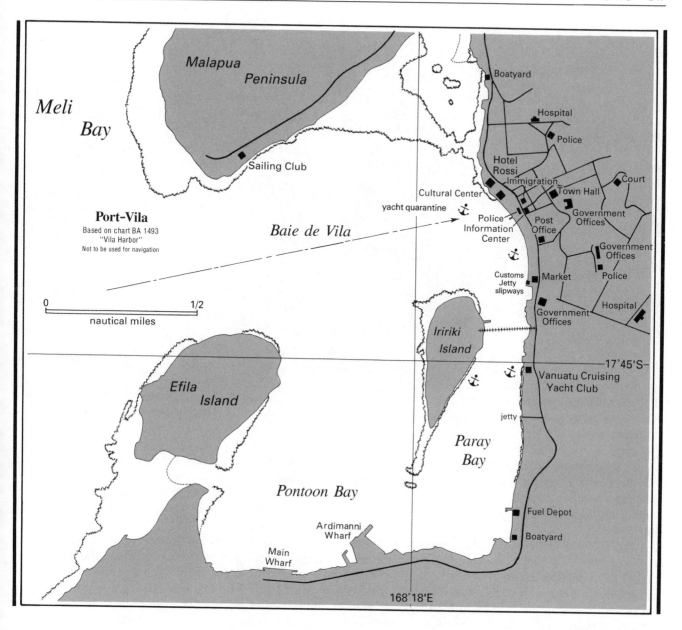

Port-Vila
Based on chart BA 1493
"Vila Harbor"
Not to be used for navigation

0 — 1/2
nautical miles

Meli Bay

Malapua Peninsula

Sailing Club

Baie de Vila

yacht quarantine

Cultural Center

Police Information Center

Boatyard

Hospital

Police

Hotel Rossi

Immigration

Town Hall

Court

Government Offices

Post Office

Government Offices

Police

Market

Customs Jetty slipways

Government Offices

Hospital

Iririki Island

Efila Island

17°45'S

Vanuatu Cruising Yacht Club

jetty

Paray Bay

Pontoon Bay

Ardimanni Wharf

Main Wharf

Fuel Depot

Boatyard

168°18'E

YACHT FACILITIES

Port-Vila

Port-Vila is the recommended Port of Entry to Vanuatu as opposed to Luganville for several reasons: it is to windward of most of Vanuatu; it is a bigger port; it is better protected; there is a better opportunity to reprovision; it is the seat of government; and duty-free stores can be purchased. Vila Harbor is a well protected inlet on the eastern side of Meli Bay affording excellent shelter from westerly winds. While the harbor is mostly free of dangers, there are fringing coral reefs that extend out from the shorelines and must be avoided.

Yachts approaching Port-Vila should radio ahead to Port-Vila radio on VHF channel 16 (or channel 60 repeater from farther out) and give an ETA. You will be directed to anchor near the large yellow quarantine buoy in front of the venerable Rossi Hotel. They will call Customs, Health, and Immigration for you. Watch for Customs and Health personnel along the fence at quayside, where they will await dinghy service to your boat. After the inspection and paperwork, Customs will direct you to the Immigration offices ashore.

After Customs has cleared your boat, you can move to one of the Tahiti style moorings along the seawall east of the Rossi Hotel. The bottom of this bay is

Iririki Island, formerly the British commissioner's residence, is now a resort, with regular shoreboat service from the Port-Vila waterfront. (Earl Hinz)

not good holding ground for mud-type anchors; fishermen or Northill are preferred. Be certain that your streamside anchor is well set because the prevailing southeast trades tend toward beam winds much of the time.

There is no private yacht club, as such, in Port-Vila, but there is a very hospitable Vanuatu Cruising Yacht Club, which serves the same purpose. You can tie up at their quay for a small fee or anchor out directly across the channel in the shadow of Iririki Island. The Vanuatu Cruising Yacht Club has a restaurant and bar as well as showers and a laundromat. It is within walking distance of town.

Provisions and deck supplies are available in Port-Vila, but prices are higher than in Suva and, being a smaller town, the selection is smaller. Although Vila is a duty-free port, if you have equipment or supplies flown in, you will have to pay duty on them. An open-air market and several stores along the sea wall make reprovisioning simple. Locally grown meat and fresh milk are available along with island fruits and vegetables. Prices for local products are sensible and lower than in New Caledonia. (Note that neither tipping nor bartering is an accepted practice in Vanuatu.)

There is no satisfactory slipway in Port-Vila for boat work. If you need a haulout, take your boat north to Luganville which, at most, is a 2-day sail away. There is a sailmaker in Vila, but few other yacht services or hardware are available. Diesel fuel, lube oil, and fresh water are available.

Port-Vila is within the area in which South Pacific tropical cyclones play havoc during the months of December through April. Local yachts seek shelter behind Iririki Island in Vila Harbor. Erakor Lagoon on the opposite side of the town of Vila has been mentioned as a possible hurricane shelter, but the channel into the lagoon is narrow and the lagoon shallow. If you do plan on going in there, take along a knowledgeable local resident as a guide.

It is permissible to leave a yacht in Vila for a season, but it should be securely anchored and left in care of a responsible person. It is probably better to leave your yacht on the hard securely tied down and in the care of a responsible person.

Luganville

Because the larger share of the agricultural population lives on the big islands in this region, Luganville is the main export shipping harbor of Vanuatu. It is a deep bay with good holding ground in a bottom of mud and

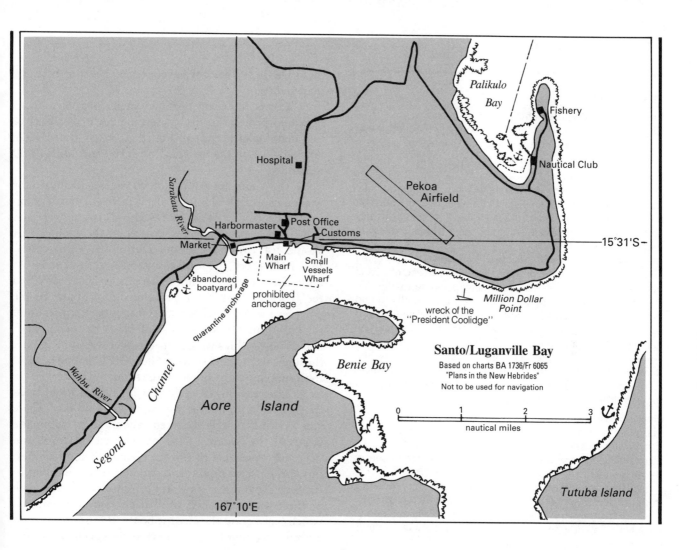

Palikulo
Bay

Fishery

Nautical Club

Pekoa
Airfield

Hospital

Sarakata River

Harbormaster

Post Office

Customs

Market

Main
Wharf

Small
Vessels
Wharf

15°31'S

abandoned
boatyard

prohibited
anchorage

quarantine anchorage

Million Dollar
Point

wreck of the
"President Coolidge"

Santo/Luganville Bay

Based on charts BA 1736/Fr 6065
"Plans in the New Hebrides"

Not to be used for navigation

Benie Bay

Wahbu River

Segond

Channel

Aore   Island

0   1   2   3

nautical miles

Tutuba Island

167°10'E

The best anchorage in the area of Luganville is in Palikulo Bay near the Nautical Club. (Earl Hinz)

MEDICAL MEMO

Immunization Requirements

Cholera and yellow fever immunizations are required if you have transited or visited within the last six days an area currently infected.

Local Health Situation

There are malaria-carrying mosquitoes in Vanuatu; antimalarial drugs should be taken before, during, and after your visit there. It has been reported that a strain of mosquitoes resistant to chloroquine has appeared; hence, Fansidar tablets are recommended.

Amoebic dysentery is also common. Water taken aboard should be treated with a strong disinfectant. Local people have been infected with hepatitis. Some marine life like the stonefish and the poisonous dart cone shells should be avoided. Coral cuts should be disinfected immediately to avoid complications resulting in fever and inflammation. The hot, humid climate requires that all cuts and abrasions be tended to quickly to prevent possible infection. During the rainy season of November to April, flies can be a nuisance. Hookworm is quite common in the local populace, and visitors should wear shoes when ashore.

Health Services

There are hospitals in Port-Vila and Luganville and dispensaries throughout the islands. Except for a private doctor at Vila, all medical personnel are government workers or members of the mission staffs. Medical costs are moderate.

There are dentists in Vila and Luganville; an optometrist from overseas makes occasional calls throughout the islands.

There are two chemists (pharmacies) in Vila and one in Luganville. In addition, supermarkets sell proprietary brands of medicine.

IAMAT Center

Bougainville House, Port-Vila
Coordinator: Jean Luc Bador, MD

Water

Tap water from public supplies in Luganville and Vila is supposedly safe. However, it would be wise to treat all water from whatever sources.

---

sand. The port is not, however, considered a good port for cruising boats because of a lack of a suitable anchorage: the Segond Channel is deep, and the port is exposed to southeasterly winds. There is a large area of prohibited anchorage because the large vessels using this port require plenty of room in both directions when berthing. (The port does not have a tug to assist in berthing maneuvers.)

Yachts requiring pratique should arrive by daylight and proceed to the quarantine anchorage west of the main wharf and anchor there with the Q flag hoisted. Customs hours are 0730–1130 and 1330–1630 weekdays.

The main wharf is not considered suitable for yachts, especially along the front face. A current of up to 1½ knots flows past it. Flood runs to the west and ebb to the east. Vessels approaching the main wharf should use extreme caution. During the cool season, May to October, the southeast wind is strong and blows onto the wharf. At times there is a heavy swell in the channel. Vessels are prohibited from lying to the wharves for extended periods without the permission of the harbormaster. Water is available at the main wharf and the small ships wharf. Fuel may be delivered in bulk through arrangements with Shell Oil Company. Most food supplies are available at the shopping center.

After clearing in at Luganville, it is recommended that you take your boat around to Palikulo Bay. There you will find a nicely sheltered anchorage far within the bay near the Nautical Club on the east side. You can make arrangements to use the Nautical Club facilities, but you must be diplomatic and courteous in doing so for they are not always warm to cruisers. To the north of the Nautical Club is the Pacific Fishing Company, which has a good slipway for boats. It tends to be busy with fishing boat business; nevertheless, you can schedule a haulout with an advance appointment. You will have to do most of the work yourself.

The Luganville Bay area has several points of historical interest. Fans of James Michener can see the fictitious isle of Bali Hai by looking east from Palikulo Peninsula. It is the island of Aoba, about 40 miles away. This entire area was a major World War II supply and staging base for the retaking of the Solomon Islands from the Japanese. Between Palikulo Bay and the town of Luganville is Million Dollar Point, where millions of dollars worth of war equipment were bulldozed into the water as the war advanced out of range. And right in Segond Channel along the shoreline are the sunken remains of the liner *President Coolidge*. It is a Scuba diver's paradise.

PART III

Micronesia

Micronesia is a Greek term meaning "small islands," and that is what the islands of Micronesia are. There are 2,000 of them, with a total land area of only 1,200 square miles covering about four million square miles of ocean. Except for Kiribati, they all lie in the northern hemisphere and span the International Date Line. Largest of the islands and the most populated is Guam, an island of coral limestone terraces on top of a submerged volcano. Most of the islands, however, are true atolls. The climate is warm but tempered by the trade winds, and rain is adequate but not abundant. In the western

part of Micronesia, typhoons are common and can occur the year around.

The Micronesian came from the Asian corridor area of Malaysia probably before 1000 B.C. and is generally more like the Polynesian than the Melanesian in features and way of life. In the far western part of Micronesia, the people are very similar to the Filipino. There are eight identifiable cultures throughout Micronesia: the Mariana Islanders (also known as Chamorros); the I-Kiribati; the Marshallese; the Eastern Carolinians; the Chuukese (Trukese); the Yapese; the

Island Groups of Micronesia

ISLAND GROUP	NUMBER OF ISLANDS	LAND AREA (square miles)	POPULATION** (persons)	GOVERNMENT
Guam	1	209	141,000	United States territory
Northern Marianas*	14	185	43,600	United States commonwealth
Marshall Islands*	34	70	43,400	Self-governing nation in free association with the United States
Federated States of Micronesia*	41	270	104,900	Self-governing nation in free association with the United States
Palau*	6	191	14,300	Self-governing nation in free association with the United States—provisional
Kiribati	33	267	70,000	Independent nation
Nauru	1	8	9,200	Independent nation

*These island groups are former members of the Trust Territory of the Pacific Islands.

**Reference: *The World Factbook, 1991,* Central Intelligence Agency, U.S. Government Printing Office, Washington DC 20402-9325, USA

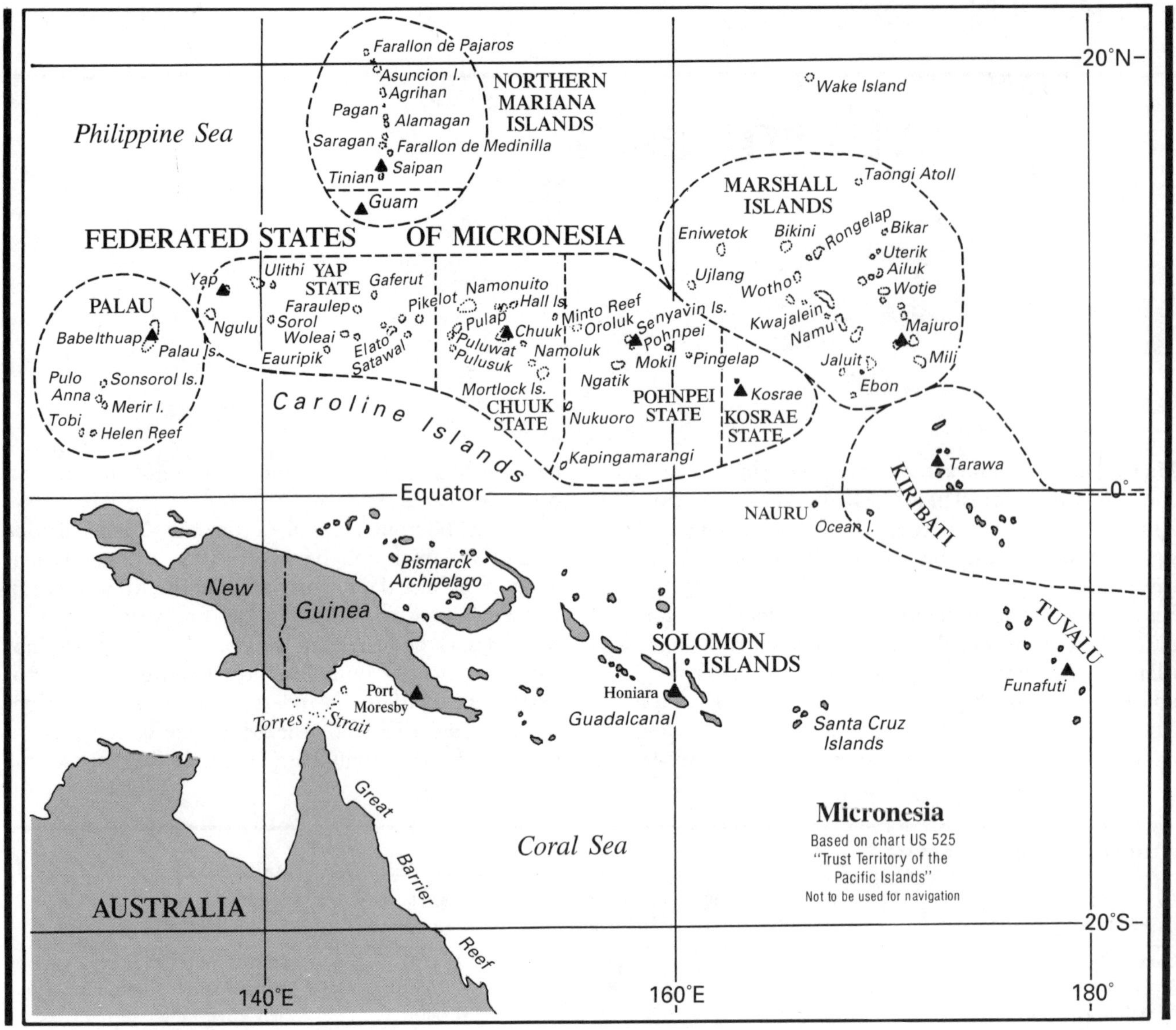

Micronesia

Based on chart US 525
"Trust Territory of the
Pacific Islands"
Not to be used for navigation

Palauans; and the Southwest Islanders. Like the Polynesians, the Micronesians were good navigators, roaming at least within their island groups so that the Micronesian culture and society has some homogeneous features. There are few natural resources on these islands and atolls, so the people support themselves predominantly through farming and fishing.

Most of Micronesia—in fact all but Kiribati, Nauru, and Guam—was a part of the Trust Territory of the Pacific Islands administered by the United States since the end of World War II. Micronesia has had a succession of rulers—Spain, Germany, Japan, and the

United States. All of the masters have left their trademarks in language and culture plus limited development of different economic "centers" in each of the groups.

The United States Trust Territory of the Pacific Islands—this lengthy title was first attached to a major segment of Micronesia in February 1947 when the United States was awarded trusteeship by the United Nations over territory surrendered by the Japanese after their defeat in World War II. The territory was first administered by the Navy Department and later by the Department of the Interior. The territory has since been dissolved, and quasi-independent nations have been created out of the former Trust Territory districts. The people of each district were given a chance to decide on the form of government they preferred. The Northern Marianas District became a Commonwealth of the United States on January 9, 1978. The Marshall Islands District became the Republic of the Marshall Islands in Free Association with the United States on May 1, 1979. The Districts of Kosrae, Pohnpei, Chuuk, and Yap united to form the Federated States of Micronesia in Free Association with the United States on October 1, 1982. The District of Palau became the Republic of Palau in Free Association with the United States on August 26, 1982. Technically, none of these new governments took effect until 1986, when the United States Trust Territory of the Pacific Islands was formally dissolved by the United Nations. Each embryo country, however, initiated its constitutionally authorized governments on the foregoing dates.

Commonwealth status and the "free association with the United States" relationship left the new countries with useful economic support and defense commitments from the United States. Besides large annual sums of economic aid being granted to them for many years, they are assured of a strong military defense by the United States. In addition, the commonwealth and all the new countries participate in the U.S. Postal System and receive the services of the Federal Aviation Administration, U.S. Weather Service, and Coast Guard. They also use U.S. dollars as currency. The benefits of free association are many, and cruisers in Micronesia will find that they, too, can use them to make their North Pacific cruise easier and more enjoyable.

CHAPTER 22

MARIANA ISLANDS

The Country

The northernmost islands of Micronesia and those closest to the Asian mainland are the Mariana Islands. They are the southern end of a long chain of submerged seamounts extending south from the Japanese archipelago. Originally called the Ladrones Islands by Magellan in March 1521, they extend from Guam in the south to Maug Island in the north, a distance of 520 miles.

The largest of the Mariana Islands is Guam at the southern end. It is composed of coral limestone terraces built on top of a submerged volcano. The islands to the north are of similar geologic formation but younger in age, so that less weathering has occurred to create fertile soil. In fact, the northernmost islands cannot support any population.

As a result of Magellan's early voyage, the Spanish took great interest in the western Pacific. The Spanish priests who accompanied the early explorers established missions in the Mariana Islands in the sixteenth century. The Catholic priests immediately set about to convert the Chamorros to Christianity but were hampered by native revolts.

The population of the Marianas at the time of the arrival of the Spanish was estimated to be in the neighborhood of 50,000 to 100,000, most of them living on Guam, Rota, and Tinian. To help the Church control the Chamorros, the Spanish soldiers took a hand in rounding up most of them and putting them on Guam; some escaped to nearby Rota in the process. The islands to the north including Tinian and Saipan were left uninhabited.

In rounding up the native Chamorros, the Spanish reduced their numbers to fewer than 5,000, living mostly on Guam. Of those, many died in a 1680 typhoon. A bad drought in 1706 resulted in years of famine, and the population fell to a low of 1,500.

Epidemics were the single biggest cause of death after the ruthless slaughter of the Chamorros by the Spanish in the name of the Church. Leprosy continued as an epidemic, depopulating the islands; and smallpox in 1849, measles in 1861, whooping cough in 1898, and influenza in 1899 wreaked additional havoc on the islanders. Interethnic marriages also caused changes, and it would be hard today to find a "true" Chamorro. Descendants of the Chamorro now number in the thousands and occupy Guam, Rota, Tinian, and Saipan with a smattering on the more northern islands.

U.S. involvement with the Mariana Islands came about as a result of the Spanish-American War, which was fought primarily in the Philippines as far as Pacific action was concerned. The United States took over Guam, which at that time seemed to be the only worthwhile island in the group, especially from the standpoint of a naval harbor. Spain, recognizing the end of its Pacific colonial empire, then sold the rest of the Mariana Islands as well as the Caroline and Marshall islands to Germany. This, then, was the political status of the Mariana Islands up to World War I.

The German oceanic empire was based mostly on commercialism and included holdings in New Guinea as well as the island groups of Samoas, Marshalls, Carolines, and Marianas. Germany's initial goal was commercial expansion, and much of its colonial administration was in the hands of copra and trading-company officials. Political expansion would naturally follow on the heels of successful commercial ventures. It probably would have except World War I interfered, and Germany lost all of its Pacific holdings.

New Zealand took over Western Samoa; Japan seized control of the Marianas (except Guam), the Marshalls, and the Carolines; and Germany's interest in New Guinea was absorbed by Australia. Between wars the Pacific was administered in four political parts—the French and British had the South Pacific, the Dutch had western New Guinea, the Japanese had Micronesia, and the Americans had Hawaii and Guam.

During World War II, Japan's aggressive land, sea, and air action took the imperial forces as far south as

New Guinea before they were stopped by the Allied forces. It took several years, but Japan was militarily defeated, and all of its holdings outside the Japanese homeland islands were put in various forms of trusteeship under the victorious Allies. Guam was returned to the United States. The island groups of Marianas, Carolines, and Marshalls were made into the Trust Territory of the Pacific Islands to be administered by the United States until self-determination by the people themselves.

Immediately after World War II Guam returned to its former status as an Unincorporated Territory of the United States. The Northern Mariana Islands elected to be a Commonwealth of the United States, a situation that came to pass in 1978. Guam continues to examine other political connections with the United States and may someday elect to become a Commonwealth, also. Uniting the Mariana Islands into one political entity would create a single powerful western Pacific island territory.

The Weather

The islands of the Marianas chain have similar weather conditions. Under ordinary circumstances, the northeast trades create easterly winds and seas in the vicinity of Guam. Northeasterly and east-northeasterly winds prevail 65 percent of the time between December and May and are strongest during these months. Westerly winds are at times experienced during the summer months as Guam is within the limits of the southwest monsoon. These winds are, as a rule, light.

Gales occasionally occur in the areas north of Palau and Guam chiefly in winter, a result of the strengthening of the northeast monsoon and trades. Sometimes, however, they occur at other seasons in connection with typhoons. Between June and November, the surface winds are quite variable. Calms are rare. In the southern islands, the winds show a slight southerly trend as early as May.

In the vicinity of Saipan and Tinian, the steadiest winds occur when the winter monsoon and the northeast trades reinforce each other. Between November and April, northeasterly to easterly winds prevail 70 percent of the time at speeds of 10 to 12 knots. During the summer monsoon (May to October) easterly winds predominate, but southerly to westerly winds also occur. Wind speeds are about 10 to 11 knots from May to July, 8 knots from August to October. Land mass effect modifies the maritime diurnal variations so that the surface winds are strongest at 0300 and weakest at 1400.

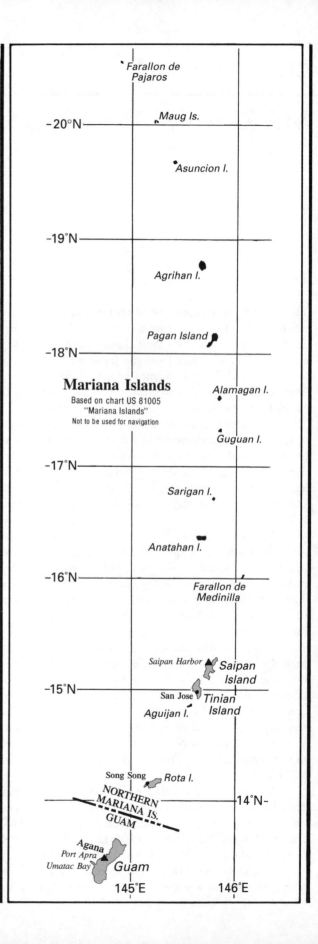

Mariana Islands
Based on chart US 81005
"Mariana Islands"
Not to be used for navigation

In the vicinity of Pagan Island, the winds are steadiest during the northeast monsoon (November through March). They usually blow from the northeast at an average speed of 15 knots. From April through June the monsoon weakens, and the prevailing winds become more easterly. During the wet season (June through November), easterly winds continue to predominate but with a greater percentage from southerly to westerly directions. The winds are mostly light, the only strong winds occurring with typhoons.

Tropical disturbances occasionally develop in the vicinity of the Mariana Islands. More often, they develop to the east and south, and in their westerly movement they generally stay south of the chain. Tropical disturbances that do develop in the vicinity of the Mariana Islands usually do so during the months of August through October.

The Mariana islands lie north of the path of western Pacific typhoons. Although most of the cyclonic activity occurs over the Philippine Sea, one or two tropical disturbances every year develop into typhoons that turn north and pass over the southern islands of the chain. Typhoon Olive swept over the Mariana Islands on April 30, 1963, causing severe damage to Saipan, Rota, and Tinian. Rarely does a typhoon, one a year at most, reach as far north as Pagan Island.

Typhoons are most common during the summer months of April through November because of the greater incidence of mid-ocean low-pressure areas during that period. The storm center, which is usually small in diameter in the early stages of formation, may be from 50 to 100 miles in diameter at the time of passage and can be quite intense near the center. January through March is relatively free of cyclonic storms in the western Pacific. Typhoons produce intense torrential rains, and winds can reach 100 knots or more.

Gales seldom occur in the vicinity of Tinian and Saipan. Winds reach gale force in the vicinity of Pagan Island from 2 to 4 percent of the time.

Thunderstorms occur frequently from July to the early part of November. December through May are relatively free of thunderstorms.

In the Mariana Islands, the rainy season occurs during the summer monsoon, at which time thunderstorms are fairly common. The wet season (July through October) has a mean monthly average of 10 inches of rain or more. The major rainfall consists of heavy showers. As a rule, the rainfall diminishes as the latitude increases.

The rainy season at Guam is from the first of July until the early part of November, with a monthly average of 8 to 15 inches. January through May is the dry period, with an average monthly fall of 2 to 3 inches. April is the driest month. The mean average rainfall is about 70 inches annually.

The rainy season at Saipan and Tinian is from July to November; the dry season lasts from December through June. During the rainy season, with the doldrum belt lying almost directly over these islands, there are increased showers and numerous thunderstorms and squalls. The dry season is characterized by fair weather, interrupted by fronts associated with northerly low-pressure centers and some showers. Saipan has an average rainfall of 86 inches per year with a monthly average of 7 inches. During the rainy season (July through October) it averages 13 inches per month. Throughout the rest of the year, the average is about 4 inches per month. April is the driest month, with an average of about 3 inches.

Pagan Island has an average annual rainfall of 60 inches. Since the mean position of the doldrum belt is always south of this island, rainfall and cloud cover are somewhat less than over the more southerly islands. The doldrum belt lies closest to this island between July and September.

The maximum development of the northeast monsoon occurs from November through March, the average rainfall then being two to three inches per month. Some rain will fall during weak cold fronts, which drift slowly across this region about twice a month. These rains usually are of short duration. Rainfall increases somewhat as the wet summer season approaches. During this season the rainfall is estimated to be about ten inches monthly, decreasing somewhat in October and November.

In Guam, the average mean temperature is 81°F, the mean maximum is 90°F, and the mean minimum is 70°F. The temperatures for the rest of the Mariana Islands are quite uniform throughout the year. January and February are the coolest months. The nights are cooler in the northern islands. Temperatures about 87°F normally occur between April and August. The daily minimums seldom fall below 74°F during the summer months.

Humidity is high throughout the year, but there is somewhat less humidity from December through May. The yearly average is about 76 percent, the January average is 68 percent, and the June average is 84 percent.

Fog and mist are rarely reported in the Guam/Saipan-Tinian areas. Visibility of less than 1¼ miles can be expected on less than one day per month.

GUAM

The Country

Guam is the most southern at 13°N latitude, most populous, and largest island of the Marianas chain. The island is 30 miles long and ranges from 4 to 8½ miles in width. It has a total land area of about 209 square miles.

The land mass was formed by the successive upheavals of a submarine volcanic mountain range and the limestone beds of the fringing coral reefs. The northern end of the island is a plateau of rolling hills set on vertical cliffs rising 300 to 500 feet above sea level. The cliffs are marked with crevices, and small caves are found at various heights in the cliffs. These were formed by the breaking of the surf against what was once the sea-level line. The island narrows in the middle around a low, dome-shaped mass of land that the islanders named the island's belly.

The tropical climate yields a lush vegetation, including vines, savanna grass, and various species of palm and other trees that would rapidly cover most of the island if not constantly cut back. The vegetation cover of the northern half of the island has a lower crown height than that of the south. The winds on the east coast of the southern half of the island have reduced vegetation on the coastal slopes, and in several places the slopes have seriously eroded.

Trees found on the island include coconut, breadfruit, banyan, ironwood, banana, and several types of flowering species. Coconuts, supplemented by rice, were used as the major food staples before the arrival of the Spanish. Wild orchids are found as well as frangipani. Flame trees and hibiscus were introduced from the other islands.

The island has a limited range of animal life. There were no quadrupeds indigenous to the island, and the only indigenous mammals that have been found are two species of bats. Rats and small, large-eared mice abound. Small deer were introduced by the Spanish in the 1770s.

The bird population suffered, as did most island animals, during the war. There are numerous shore-birds, such as the reef heron and varieties of the rail. The only true bird of prey is a short-horned owl. The only true songbird is a member of the warbler family. There are many varieties of dove, one species of tern, and no sea gulls.

Until 15 years ago, there were no snakes on Guam, although a six-inch-long scaled worm with microscopic eyes might have passed for one. Now, however, the island has rat snakes, which grow to several feet long. These are believed to have come from the Philippines in ship containers.

Sea turtles are common visitors to the island. Insect life is minimal save for the many species of mosquitoes, none of which is malarial. Scorpions and centi-

The Magellan monument at Umatac marks the landing place of Ferdinand Magellan on March 21, 1521, following a three-month, 20-day passage from the southern tip of South America. This was Western civilization's entry to the Marianas and the Philippines. (Earl Hinz)

GUAM
An unincorporated territory of the United States

Port of Entry
Apra Harbor   13°27′ N, 144°40′ E

Distances between Ports in Nautical Miles
Between Apra Harbor and

Chuuk, FSM	560
Hong Kong	1,820
Honolulu, Hawaii	3,310
Koror, Palau	700
Madang, Papua New Guinea	1,120
Majuro, Marshall Islands	1,620
Manila, Philippine Islands	1,380
Pohnpei, FSM	890
Saipan, Mariana Islands	120
Taipei, Taiwan	1,510
Tokyo, Japan	1,360
Wake Island	1,310
Yap, FSM	450

Standard Time
10 hours fast on UTC

Public Holidays and Special Events

January 1	New Year's Day—National holiday
January*	Martin Luther King Day—National holiday
February*	Presidents' Day—National holiday
March*	Discovery Day—Public holiday (commemorates Magellan's landing at Umatac Bay)
March/April*	Easter
May*	Memorial Day—National holiday
July 4	Independence Day—National holiday
July 21	Liberation Day—Commemorates liberation from Japanese occupation
September*	Labor Day—National holiday
November 11	Veterans Day—National holiday
November*	Thanksgiving—National holiday
December 8	Feast of the Immaculate Conception—Islandwide fiesta
December 25	Christmas—National holiday

*Specific dates vary from year to year.

pedes with nonlethal but painful bites are common. Large spiders sometimes reach six to ten inches in diameter.

Three different types of lizards are found on the island. The most formidable in appearance is the iguana. Although reaching larger sizes elsewhere, the Guam iguana usually grows to more than four feet in length. It preys on small birds, eggs, and chickens. It has been known to attack small dogs when cornered but generally flees when encountered.

Carbon dating from cooking pits shows the pres-

ence of humans as early as 1320 B.C. Potsherds, stone tools, and weapons found in archeological diggings indicate that the island was well populated at least 3,000 years ago and was at one time the major population and trade center for all of the Mariana Islands.

Although the origin of the Chamorros is still uncertain, on the basis of their language and way of life they are believed to be Malayo-Polynesian. They are the only oceanic people who have cultivated rice. On the basis of such evidence as this, most anthropologists agree that if the Chamorro did not themselves have origins in southeast Asia, they had prolonged contact and mixed with people who did.

The arrival of Ferdinand Magellan in 1521 brought the first contact with the West. During the second half of the seventeenth century, the Spaniards established the first permanent European settlement on Guam. The religion of the Chamorros was supplanted by Christianity. The many wars between the Spanish and Chamorros, coupled with smallpox and typhoons, resulted in reducing the population from an estimated 50,000 to 100,000 islanders in the early 1600s to about 5,000 in the late 1600s.

Spain continued in possession of Guam until the Spanish-American War of 1898. At that time the Spanish not only surrendered Guam and the Philippines to the United States, but sold the rest of their possessions in the Pacific, namely the rest of Micronesia, to Germany.

In World War I Guam became involved by the sinking of the German cruiser *Cormoran* in Apra Harbor by its own crew. Between the two world wars the island made substantial economic strides, and contacts with other parts of the world increased.

When World War II broke out in the Pacific, Guam was virtually defenseless, and the U.S. naval commander surrendered to the Japanese on December 10, 1941. The Japanese removed all Americans from the island, and for a period of 31 months the Guamanians were subject to heavy demands by the occupying Japanese forces. In 1944 U.S. forces landed on the beaches, and in one month major enemy resistance ceased.

The population in 1990 stood at 141,000, of which about 18 percent represented U.S. military personnel and their dependents. The population centers are concentrated on the coastal or narrow middle areas of the island. The capital, Agana, and its suburb, Agana Heights, are on the western side of the middle of the island.

At the time of the arrival of the Spanish, most

Religion plays a major role in the lives of Guamanians. Many of their churches are truly works of religious art. (Earl Hinz)

Chamorros on Guam lived in small villages of wood and thatch dwellings along the coast. The basic social unit was the family. Although marriages were relatively easily terminated, each man had but one wife at a time. Concubines were permitted, and unmarried males were allowed considerable sexual freedom. After puberty all males lived in the village clubhouse until they married. Each clubhouse had its secret rituals and festivals.

As a result of the initially rapid conversion to Christianity and the later reduction of the population, the values and structures of Chamorro society were rapidly eroded. By the time the Spanish lost possession of the island, there were no genetically pure indigenous people, and the islanders had lost almost all traces of their Chamorro culture. Even their language had assimilated many Filipino and Spanish elements.

Although Spanish traditions, particularly in regard to religion, have continued among the old, by 1970 this was a marginal aspect of society. The majority of Guamanians reflect the basic culture, society, and values of mainland Americans.

The Guamanians love gambling. Weekends and holidays will find cockfighting at the Sport-O-Dome in Tamuning from mid-morning to midnight. Wagering runs into the thousands of dollars on a single match. In 1976 a greyhound track offering parimutual betting on dog races was opened at Tamuning. All the time, everywhere, bingo games can be found. The Guam Recreation Center has nightly games open to the public.

U.S. administration of the Territory of Guam is provided under the 1950 Organic Act and its amendments. The territorial government of Guam is the only administrative unit on the island. All Guamanians are citizens of the United States. They do not, however, participate in national elections, nor are they represented in the U.S. Congress, although there is a representative of Guam in Washington.

The government of Guam is composed of three branches: the executive, the legislative, and the judicial. The executive branch is headed by a governor, assisted by the secretary of Guam. Both serve four-year terms. The first Guamanian governor, Manuel L. F. Guerrero, was appointed in 1963 with the confirmation of the U.S. Senate. Under the Guam Elective Governship Act of 1968, provisions were made for the popular election of the governor and the lieutenant governor.

Guam's unicameral legislature consists of 21 senators elected by legislative districts every two years.

Cruising Notes

YACHT ENTRY

The only Port of Entry for Guam is Apra Bay. Contact with the Apra harbormaster on VHF channel 16 is recommended when approaching Apra Harbor. All harbor operations are under U.S. naval control, but the port security officer at the commercial port issues all clearances for that port. Yacht clearance can be obtained at either the Cabras Island commercial port or at the Marianas Yacht Club. Upon arrival at either place, call Customs and wait on your boat for their arrival.

CUSTOMS

All yachts are required to have a clearance from their previous port of departure with the exception of a U.S.-registered vessel coming directly from another port under U.S. control and carrying only U.S. citizens. Overtime charges are levied by Customs for services outside normal working hours.

Guam is the only duty-free port under the U.S. flag in the Pacific basin. Visitors can buy goods from foreign countries at prices lower than at other U.S. ports. Products from Asia, including cameras, electronic gear, and timepieces, are of particular interest to cruisers.

IMMIGRATION

All visitors entering Guam will need to show some proof of citizenship. U.S. citizens coming directly from another political entity of the U.S. can use a driver's license, state I.D. card, or birth certificate. U.S. citizens coming from a foreign country must have a passport. There is no limit to the length of stay for U.S. citizens.

Foreign citizens are required to have a passport and a visa regardless of length of stay. The visa must be obtained before arriving.

YACHT FACILITIES

Tides and heavy swells make anchoring around the periphery of Guam hazardous. The only natural bay of commercial value is Apra Bay, formed in the San Luis de Apra Basin on the western coast of the island. Farther down the coast are Agat Bay and Umatac Bay. Guam is a good place to resupply and reprovision because it has markets and stores common to the United States with the same large variety of goods. Boat supplies are a little harder to obtain, but since Guam is served by the U.S. mail as well as many airlines, special orders from mainland United States can solve the parts problem.

Apra Harbor

Apra Harbor, an improved natural harbor, is situated off the northwest side of Orote Peninsula. Cabras Island and a breakwater that extends along Luminao Reef form the north side of the outer harbor. The commercial port for Guam is on Cabras Island. The inner harbor is

---

FLOTSAM AND JETSAM

Currency
Guam uses U.S. currency. The relative cost of goods and services is 125.

Language
English is the language of schools, government, and business, but Chamorro, the language of the ancient inhabitants of Guam (with the addition of many Spanish words during the rule of the Spanish), is still used by most local families. Tagalog and other Filipino dialects are the second language for almost 15,000 residents of Guam.

Electricity
110v, 60 Hz AC

Postal Addresses
Yacht ( )
Poste Restante
Agana GU 96910
USA

or, if you are at the yacht club,
Yacht ( )
c/o Marianas Yacht Club
P.O. Box 2297
Agana GU 96910
USA

Ports for Making Crew Changes
Guam is a recommended port for making crew changes, having good international airline service to Tokyo, Manila, and Sydney. Domestic U.S. airline service is available to Saipan, Palau, the Federated States of Micronesia, and Honolulu.

External Affairs Representative
U.S. embassies or consulates

Information Center
Guam Visitors Bureau
P.O. Box 3520
Agana GU 96910
USA

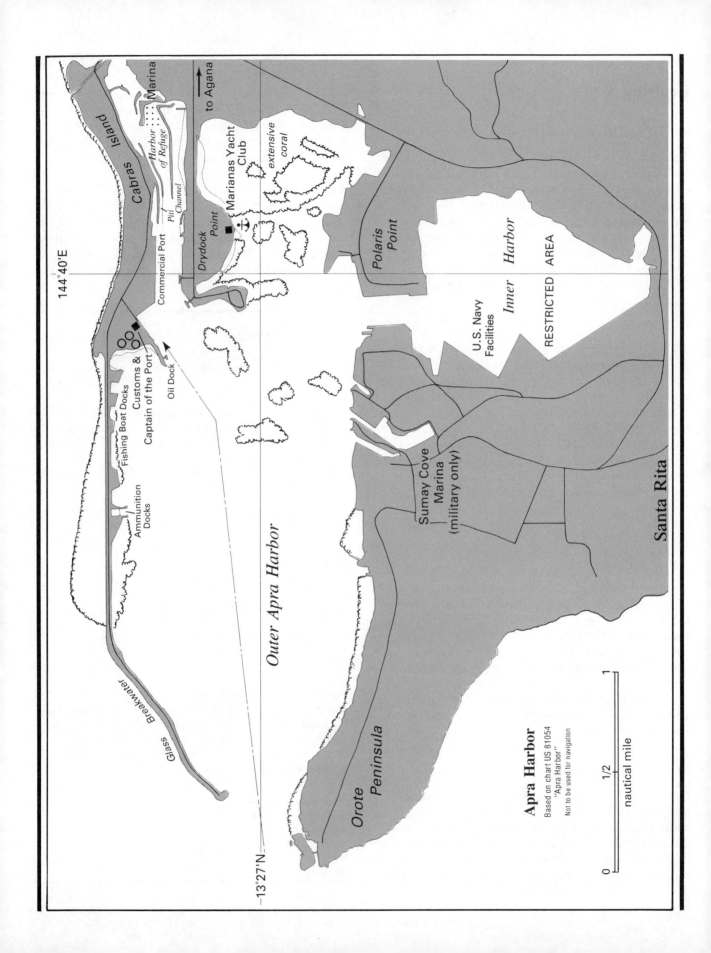

144°40'E

13°27'N

to Agana

Cabras Island

Marina

Harbor
of Refuge

Piti
Channel

Commercial Port

Drydock
Point

Marianas Yacht
Club

extensive
coral

Polaris
Point

U.S. Navy
Facilities

Inner   Harbor

RESTRICTED   AREA

Fishing Boat Docks

Customs &
Captain of the Port

Oil Dock

Ammunition
Docks

Glass Breakwater

Outer Apra Harbor

Sumay Cove
Marina
(military only)

Santa Rita

Orote
Peninsula

Apra Harbor

Based on chart US 81054
"Apra Harbor"
Not to be used for navigation

0   1/2   1

nautical mile

Guam's Agana boat basin, located in the central business district of the island, is a good place for reprovisioning but not as pleasant an anchorage as at the Marianas Yacht Club in Apra Harbor. This is the only place on Guam where a boat can be lifted onto the hard to perform bottom work. (Earl Hinz)

The underwater scenery, especially in the Cocos Island Lagoon, is spectacular. (Guam Visitors Bureau)

MEDICAL MEMO

Immunization Requirements

Smallpox vaccination is required if travel does not originate in the United States or its possessions. Immunization against cholera and yellow fever are required if you have transited or visited within the last six days an area currently infected. Typhoid, paratyphoid, and tetanus shots are recommended.

Local Health Situation

Guam is nominally free of all communicable diseases, although a measles epidemic occurred in 1984.

Health Services

There are numerous public, private, and military hospitals in Guam. The large Guam Memorial Hospital can provide all needed medical services. There is an islandwide system of health-care centers.

Dental and optical services are available at the Guam Memorial Hospital, but there is a scarcity of trained medical personnel.

Pharmacies carry a full line of nonprescription and prescription drugs. Prescription drugs are sold only on the order of a doctor.

Water

Tap water from the public supply is reported to be safe, but all other water should be considered suspect and treated.

a U.S. naval installation with extensive berthing facilities and is a restricted area.

The Marianas Yacht Club was relocated to Drydock Point and has installed 38 moorings, some of which are available on a first come, first served basis. Private aids to navigation have been installed to facilitate passage from the outer harbor into the mooring area. Cruisers who are members in good standing of other yacht clubs may receive a two-week free membership in this club. Others will have to pay $25 per week in advance. The club offers such facilities as a clubhouse, shower and toilets, barbecues, trash disposal, and a repair work area with electricity.

Complete boat-repair services including electronics repair are available at the Dillingham Shipyard at the Cabras Island Industrial Park.

Apra Harbor is extensive and safe except during the typhoon season. There is a possible hurricane hole for small boats at the eastern end of Piti Channel beyond the commercial wharves. It is called the "harbor of safe refuge," and there is a charge if you use the moorings. Piti Channel is about 8 feet deep.

Agana Harbor

Agana Bay is an open roadstead with a very steep-to bottom and great depths near the reef. There is a small-craft harbor in Agana Bay, but the reef passage and channel are narrow and very dangerous for mariners without local knowledge. Mariners unfamiliar with the channel should not attempt entry without assistance or during other than daylight hours with favorable conditions. Assistance can be requested from the harbor patrol on VHF channel 16.

The boat basin has 42 slips up to 45 feet long. Water, electrical, and telephone services are available. Boats can be hauled out on the hard with the services of a crane. There is a public market a few hundred yards from the Agana boat basin. It includes a co-op fish market selling the day's catch of local fishermen who berth their boats in the Agana boat basin.

COMMONWEALTH OF THE NORTHERN MARIANA ISLANDS

The Country

Stretching more than 400 miles north from the Territory of Guam to the lonely volcanic peaks of the northern islands, the Marianas constitute the highest slopes of a massive mountain range rising six miles up from the Mariana Trench. Here lies the boundary between the Pacific Ocean and the Philippine Sea.

The Northern Mariana Islands comprise 14 major island units having a combined land area of 185 square miles. Although the entire chain is composed of high volcanic mountains, it can be discussed in terms of a northern section of nine islands and a southern section of five islands because of differences in size, height, and soil covering the respective components.

It is believed that the Northern Marianas were set-tled as early as 1500 B.C. by an ancient seafaring race from southeastern Asia. These daring people traveled in outrigger canoes from Indonesia and the Philippines to finally reach the Northern Marianas. Their culture was an advanced one. Scientists still puzzle over the "Latte Stone" foundations, which required construction techniques apparently far beyond the scope of their ancient civilization.

The five islands of the southern section are Rota, Aguijan, Tinian, Saipan, and Farallon de Medinilla, which together have a land area twice as great as the northern section. Saipan is the largest of the group, with a land area of more than 46 square miles. Tinian and Rota are next largest in size. The other two are uninhabited and of little significance.

The southern section, larger in overall land area,

NORTHERN MARIANA ISLANDS
A Commonwealth of the United States

Port of Entry

Tanapag Harbor, Saipan   15°14′ N, 145°44′ E

Distances between Ports in Nautical Miles

Between Saipan and

Agana, Guam	120
Chuuk, FSM	585
Hong Kong	1,840
Honolulu, Hawaii	3,220
Koror, Palau	900
Madang, Papua New Guinea	1,225
Majuro, Marshall Islands	1,580
Manila, Philippine Islands	1,435
Pohnpei, FSM	885
Taipei, Taiwan	1,520
Tokyo, Japan	1,460
Wake Island	1,220
Yap, FSM	565

Standard Time

10 hours fast on UTC

Public Holidays and Special Events

January 1	New Year's Day—Public holiday
January 9	Northern Marianas Commonwealth Day—Games and arts and craft displays
January*	Martin Luther King Day—Public holiday
February 15	Annual Saipan Laguna Regatta—Sailboat races with Pacific-wide participation
February*	Presidents' Day—Public holiday
March 24	Marianas Covenant Day—Public holiday
March/April*	Easter
May 1	Law Day—Public holiday
May 2–3	St. Joseph Fiesta—Religious and social gatherings in San Jose village on Saipan
May 17	San Isidro Fiesta—Religious ceremonies, feast, and traditional dances in Chalan Kanoa village on Saipan
May*	Memorial Day—Public holiday
July 4	Independence Day—Public holiday
July 12	Micronesia Day—Public holiday
July 13–14	Our Lady of Mount Carmel Fiesta—Chalan Kanoa
September*	Labor Day—Public holiday
October*	Columbus Day
October*	United Nations Day—Parades and traditional dances
November 11	Veterans Day—Public holiday
November*	Thanksgiving—Public holiday
December 9	Constitution Day—Public holiday
December 25	Christmas—Public holiday

*Specific dates vary from year to year.

is generally lower than the northern section and tends to have rolling hillsides rather than a mountainous topography. Although the islands are of volcanic origin, there has been no recent activity. The cores are covered with limestone terraces representing former stands of coral that were thrust up from the sea in the distant past. The erosion of this limestone has produced a covering of excellent topsoil, and the well-watered islands support a good growth of vegetation.

The islands to the north of Saipan have little to offer the cruising yacht and many hazards. Starting with the island of Anatahan, about 80 miles north of Saipan, the nine northern islands show the rawness of the young volcanoes which they are. In May 1981 the volcano on Pagan Island erupted and drove the several dozen inhabitants off their island, which was turned into a blackened ash pit. On Agrihan Island the 3,000-foot volcanic crater smokes incessantly, threatening the 40 people who eke out a meager living on the island.

All of the islands have a forbidding shoreline. Steep-to cliffs of basalt with no harbors or reefs make landing difficult and sometimes impossible. The beaches are not the sparkling white sand of coral-fringed islands but black sand beaches typical of recent volcanic origin.

The northern segment of the Mariana Islands was among the first in the Pacific to be discovered by Westerners. Even before the days of Cook, Bligh, Wallis, and Bougainville, the Spanish galleons of the sixteenth century had found these islands. They gave them the artful Spanish names that have survived to this day. But more

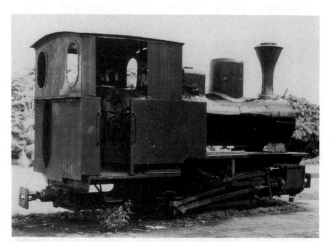

During the Japanese occupation of Saipan, sugar was the island's main crop. This aged Japanese sugar cane train locomotive survived World War II and is now on exhibit in one of Saipan's parks. (Earl Hinz)

than 400 years after their discovery by Europeans, the northern islands still remain barren and undeveloped, with a total population of only about 60 people living on Anatahan, Alamagen, and Agrihan.

Coconut palms are found on most of the islands of the Marianas chain. They grow extensively along the coasts of the dry islands but sometimes form extensive woods as existed on the great plains of Pagan Island. More or less open woods are occasionally found in the interior of the islands; and even on the coast, dense forests with little undergrowth are sometimes found. Bush-like casuarina trees grow on the dry and sandy shores.

Coconut palms, breadfruit trees, and areca palms rise above the mangroves in the ravines. More widely distributed than the forest is the savanna with its shrubs and bushes. This is the case particularly on Tinian Island, where oranges, citrons, guavas, and other fruit trees are also found.

Saipan, an oblong island dominated by the rocky, green slopes of Mt. Tagpochau, has eight villages. The largest of these, Chalan Kanoa, is a dense concentration of metal and wood houses interrupted by restored concrete shells of surviving Japanese houses or the more typhoon-proof pillbox residences recently erected by the affluent Saipanese. The main road through Chalan Kanoa, like all the major arteries around the island, has a smooth macadam surface, and slowly but surely the interior grid of narrow, dusty, potholed roads is experiencing the face-lifting effects of hot tar mix and the steam roller.

Within crowded Chalan Kanoa are found hordes of children playing in front yards shared with rusting

This Japanese prison cell at Garapan, Saipan, was reported to be the one in which Amelia Earhart, the pioneering American aviatrix, was imprisoned shortly before the start of World War II. (Earl Hinz)

auto bodies. The atmosphere is friendly and reminiscent of an Hispanic barrio. The past, however, cannot be obliterated and the occasional Shinto shrine and sounds of Oriental music remind one that these islands were under Japanese rule for 30 years. The other communities on Saipan differ but little from Chalan Kanoa with the inevitable exception of the government housing perched atop "Capitol Hill" and in a few other areas.

Saipan Island is the major producer of livestock in all of Micronesia. Swine, poultry, carabao, goats, and ducks are found on all the southern islands. Considerable vegetables are grown on Saipan, Tinian, and Rota for local use as well as shipment to Guam. Trochus shells are found in the southern Mariana Islands.

The population of the Northern Marianas is a rapidly changing figure because of both a high birth rate

FLOTSAM AND JETSAM

Currency
The Northern Mariana Islands use the U.S. dollar. The relative cost of goods and services is 125.

Language
English is the official language of the Northern Mariana Islands. The native languages are Chamorro and Carolinian. Most people between the ages of 8 and 40 can speak Japanese, and many have some knowledge of English, German, and Spanish.

Electricity
Electric power is 110v, 60 Hz AC.

Postal Address
Yacht ( )
Poste Restante
Saipan, Northern Mariana Islands CM 96950
USA

Ports for Making Crew Changes
Saipan is not a recommended port for making crew changes because of its exposed anchorage. It does have airline connections with Guam and Tokyo, but it would be better to sail to Guam to make a crew change.

External Affairs Representative
U.S. consulates and embassies
In Honolulu:
Marianas Hawaii Liaison Office
1221 Kapiolani Blvd., Suite 348
Honolulu HI 96814, USA

Marianas Visitors Bureau Information Center
P.O. Box 861
Saipan, Northern Mariana Islands CM 96950
USA

and a steady influx of foreign workers. The official 1990 population stood at 43,600, of which 48 percent (21,100) were of Northern Marianas descent and/or U.S. citizens. Resident aliens, mostly Filipinos, made up the remaining 52 percent. Saipan had a population of 39,100, Tinian Island 2,118, and Rota Island 2,311.

The government of the Northern Mariana Islands consists of a governor and lieutenant governor and a bicameral legislature made up of 9 senators and 14 representatives, all popularly elected. The formal judicial system consists of a U.S. District Court and a Commonwealth Trial Court.

After World War II the Northern Mariana Islands became part of the Trust Territory of the Pacific Islands, which was administered by the United States. In January 1978 the Northern Marianas District became a provisional Commonwealth of the United States by popular vote. When the Trust Territory was dissolved by the United Nations in 1986, the Commonwealth of the Northern Mariana Islands came into full being. Although it does not have full representation in the U.S. Congress, it does have an elected representative who advises and lobbies on affairs of the Commonwealth.

Cruising Notes

YACHT ENTRY

Tanapeg Harbor on Saipan is the only Port of Entry into all of the Commonwealth. You must enter there before visiting any other islands unless you are coming from Guam. In the latter case you can get a letter of authorization from the representative of the Northern Mariana Islands in Guam to proceed to Saipan via Rota and Tinian islands before clearing in at Saipan.

CUSTOMS

All yachts are required to have a *zarpe* from their last port of call with the exception of U.S.-registered yachts coming directly from another U.S. port (including territories) and carrying only U.S. citizens.

Entry permits for U.S. and foreign yachts cost US$10, and a fine of US$500 is imposed for being in their waters without such a permit.

IMMIGRATION

A boat entry permit is required before coming to the Commonwealth of the Northern Mariana Islands. It is obtained by writing several months in advance to the chief of immigration at the following address:

Chief of Immigration
Office of the Governor
Commonwealth of the Northern Mariana Islands
Saipan CM 96950
USA

At the same time advise the port superintendent of your pending arrival. The address is:

Port Superintendent
Commonwealth Ports Authority
P.O. Box 1055
Saipan CM 96950
USA

Make copies of both letters and take them with you because in all probability you will not receive answers; the copies will at least show that you tried to communicate with the proper authorities.

All visitors entering the Commonwealth must show proof of citizenship. U.S. citizens coming directly from another political entity of the U.S. can use a driver's license, state I.D. card, or birth certificate. U.S. citizens coming from a foreign country must have a passport the same as foreign visitors. There is no time limit on the length of stay for U.S. citizens.

Entry permits for other than U.S. citizens are issued on arrival valid for a 60-day stay. Permits authorizing presence for stays in excess of 60 days must be obtained before entry from the chief of immigration (see foregoing address). Other than U.S. citizens must also present an immunization certificate and a return or onward airline ticket and visa to their next destination.

YACHT FACILITIES

Saipan Harbor consists of two anchorages, an outer anchorage known as Garapan anchorage and an inner anchorage called Puetton Tanapag. Puetton Tanapag is protected by the barrier reef, but both anchorages are far from port facilities. Yachts are advised to head straight for pier B and tie up alongside the west face at the seaward end. The port director's office is at the base of pier C. There is a telephone there from which you can call Customs, Immigration, Health, and Agriculture officials.

Do not plan on lying alongside either pier after clearance has been obtained because there is consider-

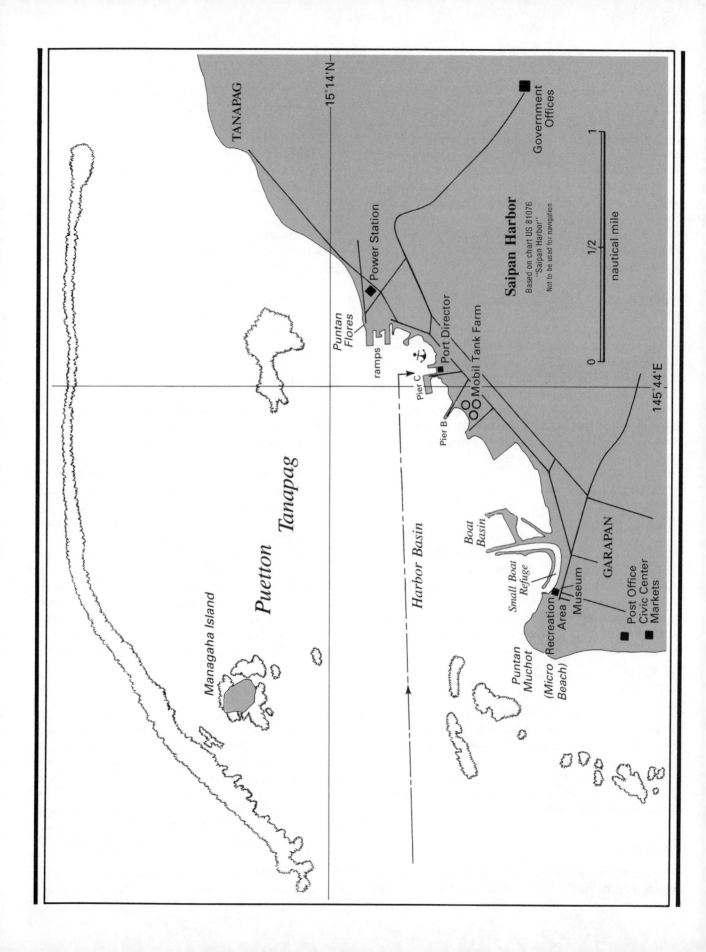

TANAPAG

15°14'N

Power Station

Puntan
Flores

ramps

Pier C

Port Director

Mobil Tank Farm

Pier B

Saipan Harbor

Based on chart US 81076
"Saipan Harbor"
Not to be used for navigation

0   1/2   1

nautical mile

145°44'E

Government
Offices

Managaha Island

Puetton Tanapag

Harbor Basin

*Boat
Basin*

*Small Boat
Refuge*

GARAPAN

*Puntan
Muchot*

Recreation
Area
(Micro
Beach)

Museum

Post Office
Civic Center
Markets

This cruising boat is moored in the casuarina-bordered small boat refuge near Puntan Muchot on Saipan. This is the only hurricane haven in the Northern Mariana Islands. (Earl Hinz)

able commercial activity; also, there is a fee of US$18 per day for the continued use of the berth. (The harbor superintendent has been known to waive that in instances when the demand for pier space is low.)

There is relatively good holding ground throughout the harbor and a minimum of coral heads, but it is a rolly anchorage. Alternately, you can move down to the small-boat basin and anchor or go inside the long channel that leads to the recreation area, but beware of the tourist boats, which are operated with heavy hands. Wherever you secure you boat while in the harbor, take precautions against theft and vandalism.

If you need a haulout, your boat can be lifted onto the dock by a crane. There are limited facilities and expertise for yacht repairs and no yacht-type hardware supplies. Diesel fuel and gasoline are available at the docks as is fresh water, which should be boiled or treated before use. Provisions are available in limited selection. Beef, pork, and fresh vegetables are obtainable as well as staple goods.

Saipan is a fairly large island, with government and commercial activities spread over much of it. The post office, civic center, and most markets are about six miles to the south of the port in the area called Chalan Kanoa. The major government and business activities are midisland in the Garapan-Tanapag area.

MEDICAL MEMO

Immunization Requirements

Smallpox immunization is required if travel does not originate in the United States or possessions. Immunization against cholera and yellow fever are required if you have transited or visited within the last six days an area currently infected. Typhoid, paratyphoid, and tetanus shots are recommended.

Local Health Situation

The Northern Mariana Islands are nominally free of all communicable diseases.

Health Services

Health-care services are provided by public facilities at no charge. There are no private physicians practicing in the Commonwealth, although there are a private dental clinic and a private oculist on Saipan.

The major health facility in the Commonwealth is Dr. Torres Hospital on Saipan. This 84-bed hospital provides inpatient and out-patient care. There are also hospitals on Rota and Tinian and dispensaries on Saipan and Agrihan. Dental services are provided at the major hospitals.

Prescription and nonprescription drugs are available at the hospital and dispensaries.

Water

The tap water in the public supply is questionable. All water should be considered suspect and treated.

Storm threats, in particular typhoons, are common in the Saipan area, and you should avoid being there in typhoon season. Unfortunately, typhoons are known to occur the year around, so even in the "off" season you should be ready with a typhoon anchoring scheme if you cannot put to sea in time. The only typhoon anchorage of any sort is in the canal that leads to the recreation area. The canal is lined with mangroves and recently has had a number of pilings installed for moorings. It is a shallow canal, expecially on the inner leg, and will be filled with many boats including the tourist boats, but it will be better than the open harbor or alongside a wharf. The harbor superintendent recommends that small craft go to the harbor at Tinian for refuge from an approaching typhoon.

There are no natural harbors in either Tinian or Rota islands, but artificial harbors have been built for small craft on both islands. These are not the greatest harbors for extended visits but can be used for a few days to see the islands.

CHAPTER 23

REPUBLIC OF THE MARSHALL ISLANDS

The Country

The Marshall Islands Archipelago consists of 34 major island units situated between 162°E and 174°E. These units contain 1,152 individual islands of low, oceanic coral formation. They are so tiny they have a combined land area of only about 70 square miles. The group is arranged in two parallel chains about 150 miles apart running generally southeast to northwest for some 800 miles between 4°N and 14°N. The eastern, or Ratak (sunrise), chain comprises 15 island units of 570 individual islands and a land area of 34 square miles.

There are no high islands in the group. Most island units (28) are atolls of the classic type, having large lagoons and a varying number of encircling islets. Kwajalein in the Ralik (sunset) chain has the largest lagoon (839 square miles); its number of component islets, 97, is second to Mili Atoll, which has 102 islets around its 295-square-mile lagoon. The smallest atoll, also in the Ralik chain, is Namorik, whose two islets enclose a lagoon of only 3¼ square miles. Five of the island units are single islands—Mejit and Jemo in the Ratak chain, and Lib, Jabwot, and Kili in the Ralik chain.

Five island units in the Ratak chain (Taongi, Bikar, Taka, Jemo, and Erikub) and three in the Ralik chain (Ailingnae, Rongerik, and Eniwetok) are uninhabited. Eniwetok and Bikini atolls were the sites of early U.S. nuclear tests, and they are still contaminated with radioactivity.

It is believed that the Marshallese came from southeast Asia many generations ago as did the ancestors of most of the Pacific islanders. Presumably they were forced out of ancestral lands by more powerful people and took to the water to find new homes. Undoubtedly many canoes and lives were lost in these voyages, but many canoes did reach land, and as a result, the Pacific islands became inhabited.

Oral traditions recount much warfare between the clans on the various atolls as chiefs sought to extend their political authority. There is no evidence that the Ratak and Ralik island chains were ever under one ruling chief nor were the chains themselves under individual rulers except for a brief recent period when Ralik was ruled as an entity.

The Marshalls were first seen by Europeans when Spanish captain Garcia de Loyasa sailed through the northern Marshalls in 1526. A few other sightings were made by Spanish captains of the galleons plying the route from Acapulco to Manila. Marshall, a British captain, "rediscovered" the islands in 1788, and the British Admiralty named them after him. The Russian ship *Rurik* under Lieutenant von Kotzebue systematically explored the islands in 1816 and 1817. Unlike the rest of the islands of Micronesia to the west, the Marshallese culture does not reflect any Spanish influence.

European and American whalers visited the area during the middle of the nineteenth century, and the Wilkes U.S. survey expedition visited there in the same period.

The Germans were first to recognize the copra trade potential; they established several copra trading stations in the late 1800s, finally annexing the islands in 1885 after a dispute with Spain over their ownership. They made their administrative headquarters on Jaluit Atoll in the southern Marshalls. The German administration continued until the outbreak of World War I, when the Japanese moved into the Marshall, Caroline, and Mariana islands. Japan's domination lasted into World War II until 1944, when the Japanese were vanquished after bloody fighting on Kwajalein and Eniwetok atolls.

After World War II, the United States assumed control of the Marshall Islands as part of the Trust Territory of the Pacific Islands. This administrative arrangement lasted until 1979, when the Marshall islanders formed their own government to be in free

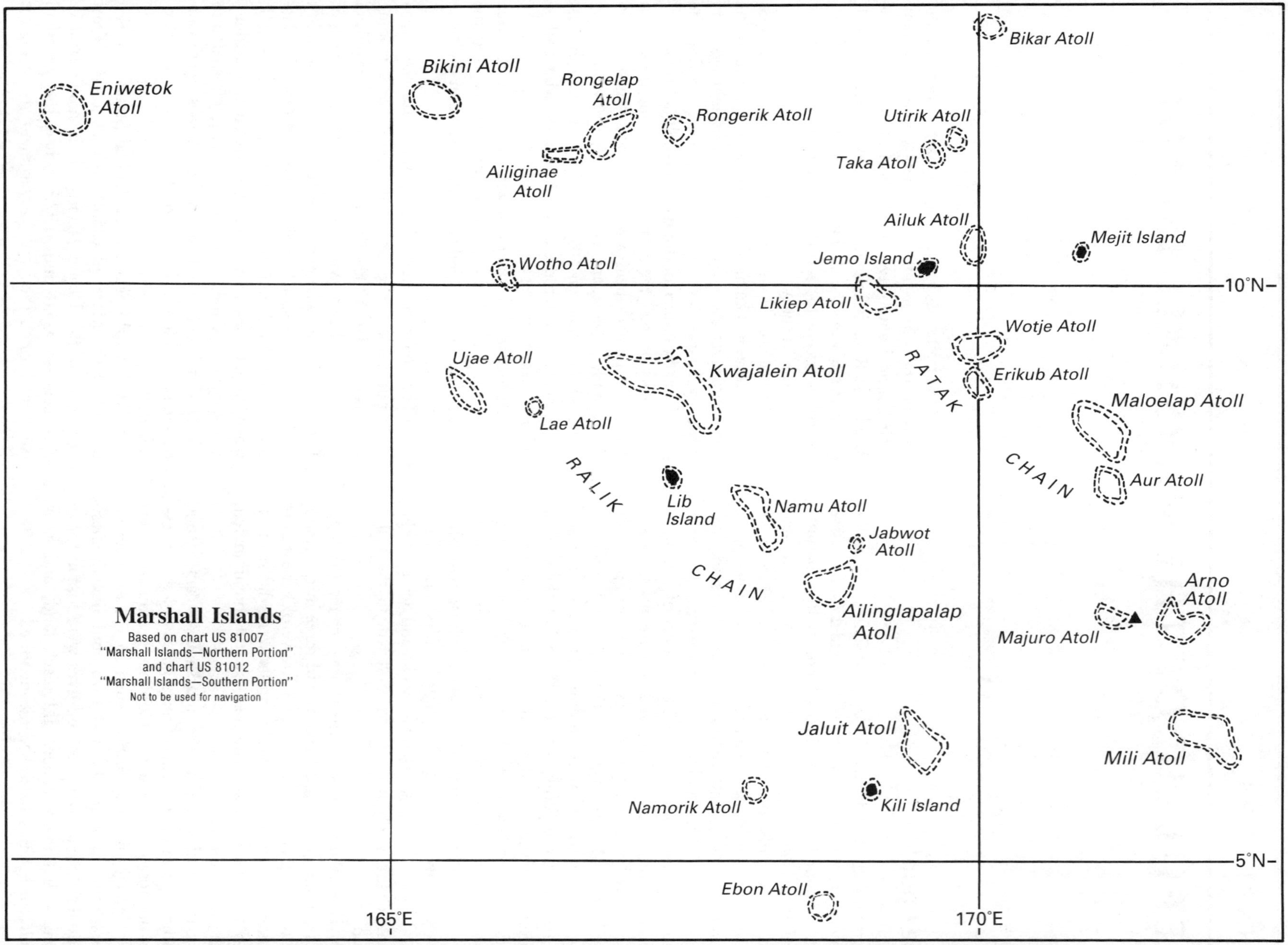

Eniwetok
Atoll

Bikini Atoll

Rongelap
Atoll

Ailiginae
Atoll

Rongerik Atoll

Taka Atoll

Utirik Atoll

Bikar Atoll

10°N—

Mejit Island

Ailuk Atoll

Jemo Island

Wotho Atoll

Likiep Atoll

Kwajalein Atoll

Wotje Atoll

Erikub Atoll

Maloelap Atoll

Aur Atoll

RATAK

CHAIN

Arno
Atoll

Majuro Atoll

Ujae Atoll

Lae Atoll

RALIK

Lib
Island

Namu Atoll

Jabwot
Atoll

Ailinglapalap
Atoll

CHAIN

Mili Atoll

Jaluit Atoll

Kili Island

Namorik Atoll

Ebon Atoll

170°E

5°N—

165°E

Marshall Islands

Based on chart US 81007
"Marshall Islands—Northern Portion"
and chart US 81012
"Marshall Islands—Southern Portion"
Not to be used for navigation

MARSHALL ISLANDS

A self-governing country in free association with the United States

Ports of Entry

Uliga, Majuro	7°06′ N, 171°22′ E
Ebeye, Kwajalein	8°43′ N, 167°44′ E

Distances between Ports in Nautical Miles

Between Majuro and

Agana, Guam	1,620
Chuuk, FSM	1,165
Ebeye, Kwajalein	235
Honolulu, Hawaii	1,975
Koror, Palau	2,190
Kosrae, FSM	505
Nauru (Aiwo District)	530
Pohnpei, FSM	785
Saipan, Mariana Islands	1,580
Tarawa, Kiribati	360
Tokyo, Japan	2,440
Wake Island	780
Yap, FSM	1,980

Standard Time

12 hours fast on UTC

Public Holidays and Special Events

December 31/

January 1	New Year's Days—Public holidays
January *	Martin Luther King Day—Public holiday
February *	Presidents' Day—Public holiday
March/April *	Good Friday and Easter—Public holidays
May 1	Constitution Day—Public holiday
May *	Memorial Day—Public holiday
July 4	Independence Day—Public holiday
July 12	Micronesia Day—Public holiday
September *	Labor Day—Public holiday
October *	United Nations Day—Parades and traditional dances
November 11	Veterans Day—Public holiday
November *	Thanksgiving—Public holiday
December 25	Christmas—Public holiday

*Specific dates vary from year to year.

association with the United States. The provisional republic became official in 1986 when the U.N. trusteeship was formally dissolved.

Physically, the Marshallese are closely related to the Polynesians to the east. They are of medium stature with light brown skin and hair varying from wavy to straight. Because of a century of contact and intermarriage with Asian and European peoples, their physical characteristics are becoming modified.

The 1988 population of the Marshall Islands was 43,380, with almost 20,000 living on Majuro Atoll. The second most populous atoll is Kwajalein with more than 9,000 people, most of whom reside on the islet of Ebeye, the native housing community in support of the U.S. Army base at Kwajalein.

Since the end of World War II, the Marshallese population has been expanding rapidly as a result of one of the highest birthrates in the world. Today 50 percent of the population is under 15 years of age; and all the signs of overpopulation are beginning to show, particularly on Ebeye and Majuro atolls.

The Marshallese language is closely related to the other languages of Micronesia spoken in the Gilbert and Caroline islands. It belongs to the large family of languages known as Malayo-Polynesian found throughout the Pacific and even in parts of Southeast Asia and Madagascar. There is some dialectal difference between the Radak and Ralik chains, but this is disappearing as transportation and other forms of communications bring people closer together. Because of the long and vigorous occupation of the islands by the Japanese, many of the older Marshallese still speak Japanese.

Land is of paramount importance to the Marshallese people, whose agricultural economy is founded on copra production and who depend on food coming directly from the land as well as the adjoining sea. Though climatic conditions are favorable in the Marshall Islands, the soils are poor compared to those of high islands such as Pohnpei, Kosrae, and Chuuk to the west; thus the variety of plants that can be grown is limited. Coconut and pandanus palms are the most plentiful, furnishing food and building and handicraft materials.

Marshallese handicrafts are considered among the best in the Pacific; the women excel in weaving mats, fans, hats, handbags, and the like. The main cash crop is copra, the dried meat of the coconut. Marshallese copra is of excellent quality, bringing a premium price on the world market. Almost 50 percent of the copra produced in the countries of the former Trust Territory comes from the Marshall Islands. A copra processing mill opened in 1980 at the new seaport in Majuro can produce US$5 million worth of oil annually. Additional cash income for many Marshallese comes from employment at the U.S. military installation at Kwajalein Atoll and in the government offices at Majuro. Breadfruit, banana, and papaya trees are important food sources although difficult to grow. Arrowroot (tapioca root) and some taro are grown.

Indigenous animals on these small, low islands are few. The surrounding ocean and the lagoons, however,

A World War II Japanese aircraft relic is a playground for kids on Maloelap Atoll. (Vicky LeHuray)

are rich in marine life. Fish and shellfish of all kinds abound, and turtles come in to lay eggs as do seabirds, providing other sources of food for the islanders. Pigs and chickens brought in by ships in earlier years are primary sources of protein in the Marshallese diet.

The Marshallese society is matrilineal with descent traced through the female line. Land rights and clan memberships are transmitted through the mother to her children. Everyone inherits land rights, and land is considered the most valuable asset the Marshallese have. Family ties have been strong with the system providing security for all members of the family. Westernization, however, is destroying the social fabric of the family as younger members flock to wage-producing jobs at Kwajalein and Majuro, leaving only the older people on the other islands.

The Weather

The Marshall Islands are climatically divided by the effects of the north equatorial current and the equatorial countercurrent into the northern and southern Marshalls with the approximate boundary at 8°30′N.

The northeast trade flows persistently into the Marshall Islands blowing strongest from December to March during which time it runs steadily over the whole area. The trades are strengthened to Force 7 with considerable frequency during the winter months; but winds of Force 9 or higher are rarely experienced. It becomes weaker and is much less steady over the south and west portions of the group from July to November. It is weakest in September and October. At this time considerable southerly and southeasterly winds are experienced. Calms are also rare throughout the area. Lowest wind speeds occur in August.

In the southern Marshalls, the northeast trades predominate from December to April, with moderate speeds from points between east and northeast. In some years, however, the trades fail or appear only sporadically and are replaced by moderate east to southeast winds. From May on, east to southeast winds increase in frequency, becoming predominant in the autumn months. In this season the winds are light and changeable, frequently interrupted by calms. Occasionally, however, violent west to southwest winds reach gale force.

The winds tend easterly at Jaluit and attain speeds

of 11 knots in December and 4 knots in August. Calms occur on the average of 4 to 6 percent of the time over the south portion.

In the northern Marshalls, the winds blow chiefly from the east and northeast throughout the year. These trade winds are more constant in direction during the winter months, from December through March. Their speed then is about 18 knots. During the remainder of the year when the trade wind belt has shifted to the north, the winds are generally lighter and more variable in both direction and velocity.

The winds are generally easterly in the vicinity of Eniwetok Atoll. A maximum speed of 39 knots has been reported in December while a maximum speed of 19 knots was reported at Ujelang Atoll. Lowest wind speeds occur in August. At this time Ujelang Atoll reported a speed of 8 knots. Eighty-five percent of the winds in the vicinity of Utirik Atoll blow between north-northeast and east throughout the year. Calms are rare over the northern Marshalls.

FLOTSAM AND JETSAM

Currency
The Marshall Islands use the U.S. dollar. The relative price of goods and services is 108.

Language
Marshallese is the indigenous language of the country, but nearly everyone speaks English.

Electricity
Electric power is 110v, 60 Hz AC.

Postal Address
Yacht ( )
Poste Restante
Majuro MH 96960
USA

Ports for Making Crew Changes
Majuro is a possible port for making crew changes; it has reasonably frequent airline service to Honolulu. Most of the Marshall Islands are connected by a domestic feeder airline.

External Affairs Representative
U.S. consulates and embassies
In Honolulu contact: Republic of the Marshall Islands
1441 Kapiolani Blvd., Suite 1910
Honolulu, HI 96814
USA

Information Center
Marshall Islands Tourist Commission
Majuro MH 96960
USA

Observations of the field of motion over the Marshall Islands show that tropical disturbances tend to originate in the region. Stations in the eastern Marshalls show wind changes before those in the west, that is, the disturbances move from east to west. Records show that typhoons seldom orginate in or move over the Marshall Islands.

In the northern Marshalls, gales are infrequent; if they occur, they usually occur during the summer and autumn, and they come from the southeast. In January 1978, a tropical storm of short duration with winds of 40 to 45 knots was 150 miles south of Eniwetok moving northward.

Thundersqualls are fairly common except in January and February, when they are relatively infrequent. In the southern Marshalls, thundersqualls are most common during the interval between July and November. Most are of light to moderate intensity, often accompanied by heavy rainfall. Jaluit reports a mean maximum of three days per month with thundersqualls in July.

Precipitation is at a minimum from December through May. Winter and spring are considered to be the dry seasons, the exception being Jaluit Atoll. Rainfall is heavier in the southern part of this area. Precipitation increases during the summer months. The period of maximum rainfall extends from July through November except at Jaluit Atoll.

Rainfall is heavy in the southern Marshalls. It reaches an annual average of 159 inches, with every month averaging more than 9 inches. April and May have more than 16 inches, and September has 13 inches. Cloudbursts from which more than an inch of rain falls are frequent. Rainfall usually occurs as moderate to heavy showers or squalls.

Rainfall is heavy and well distributed through all months at Jaluit Atoll, where rain occurs on an average of 20 days per month, except in February, which is usually the least rainy month of the year. Jabor, on Jaluit Atoll, records the highest annual rainfall, more than 150 inches. At Jabor, high monthly readings occur during the period April through July.

In the northern Marshalls, the rainfall is lowest during the time of trade winds, when it averages about 3 inches per month. The heaviest rain occurs from September through November. At Ujelang Atoll the average annual rainfall is 83 inches; farther north at Bikini Atoll it is less. The mean amount at Eniwetok Atoll ranges from 1 inch in January to 8 inches in September; Eniwetok also records the lowest annual rainfall in the Marshalls, about 45 inches.

Temperatures are relatively constant throughout the year, with the high mean being 83°F and low being 81°F. During the dry season (December through May), temperature extremes range from a minimum of 71°F to a maximum of 98°F. During the wet season (June through November) temperature extremes range from a minimum of 67°F to a maximum of 98°F.

Relative humidity is high during all months. During the day, the relative humidity ranges from about 89 percent at 1100 to 73 percent at 1400.

Cloudiness reaches a minimum during the winter months, averaging 40 percent sky coverage at Ujelang Atoll. The maximum is reached during the summer months at Eniwetok Atoll, where the average cloud cover is 70 percent through the year.

Visibility is usually good to excellent, except during heavy rain squalls. Fog rarely occurs.

Cruising Notes

YACHT ENTRY

There are two Ports of Entry to the Marshall Islands— Majuro Atoll and Ebeye Island in Kwajalein Atoll. Unless you have business with the U.S. Army Kwajalein Atoll Command, it is strongly recommended that you make your entry at the republic's capital on Majuro.

Baskets woven of pandanus leaves are a favorite handicraft product of the women of the Marshall Islands. This basket maker lives at Rita at the leeward end of Majuro Atoll. (Earl Hinz)

CUSTOMS

When approaching Majuro Atoll, call ahead on VHF channel 16 to the port director and/or to Customs and inform them of your ETA, also giving a brief description of your vessel along with the number of crew. If you get no specific berthing instructions from your call, proceed to the new pier in Uliga and take a berth distant from commercial boats. The skipper can go ashore to the

---

MEDICAL MEMO

Immunization Requirements

A valid international certificate of smallpox vaccination is required from travelers who, within the preceding 14 days, have been in any country of the world infected by smallpox. Other vaccinations or health measures may be imposed at time of entry. It is strongly recommended that all travelers have up-to-date tetanus and typhoid inoculations.

Local Health Situation

The Marshall Islands are nominally free of all communicable diseases. Principal diseases endemic in the Marshall Islands are dysentery, hookworm, infectious hepatitis, and intestinal parasites. The people of Majuro were plagued in 1982 with widespread intestinal disturbances.

The island of Ebeye in Kwajalein Atoll is reported to have recurrent epidemics of influenza and diarrhea as a result of extreme sanitation problems in an overcrowded area. The bacteria level in the lagoon is reported to be 25,000 times the safe level established by the World Health Organization.

Medical problems such as these are not surprising in view of the disregard of many islanders for sanitary toilet practices. Habits that were not particularly harmful when the population was smaller and there were no European diseases to take their toll in the twentieth century.

Health Services

There are no private doctors, dentists, or health services in the Marshall Islands. There are general hospitals at Majuro, Ebeye, and the military base at Kwajalein. The major hospitals also have dental clinics. In addition, there are 44 dispensaries throughout the atolls. Fees are generally less than those charged in the United States. Limited optical services are available at the general hospitals.

Prescription and nonprescription drugs are available at hospitals and dispensaries.

You should be aware that hospitals and dispensaries are staffed by moderately trained personnel and that modern techniques, equipment, and drugs are at a minimum except for the Kwajalein military base hospital.

Water

Tap water from the public supply at Majuro is of questionable purity, and all water except that which you collect from rain on your own boat should be considered suspect and treated.

government offices at Dalap in the southeast corner of the atoll to check in with Customs and Immigration. The rest of the crew should remain on board. Dress protocol is rigid; when you visit the capitol building, wear long trousers and a shirt with sleeves—no shorts, tank tops, or swim suits. Take with you the ship's papers, passports, crew list, and your visit permit, if you obtained one ahead of time. Check in also with the port director when you arrive. There is a paperwork fee of US$20 for port clearance.

If you intend to visit other of the Marshall Islands (and you should to get a better impression of the Marshall Islands than you will get at Majuro), you will need an outer island visit permit. This permit is ob-

tained from the Outer Island Affairs Office at the capital; there is no charge for it.

IMMIGRATION

A vessel permit must be obtained beforehand from the chief of immigration. Write to the following address to get a form and any other current instructions:

Chief of Immigration
Marshall Islands
    Government
Majuro MH 96960
USA

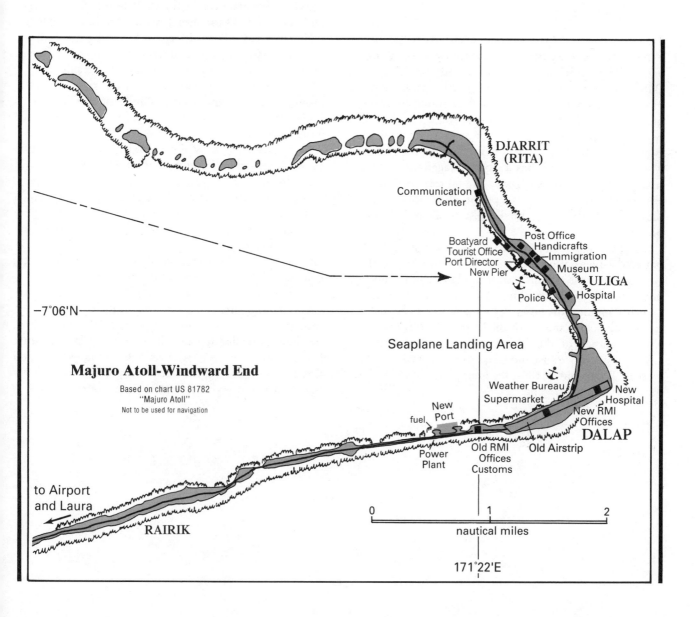

Majuro Atoll-Windward End

Based on chart US 81782
"Majuro Atoll"
Not to be used for navigation

If you are on a short time schedule or you do not hear from the chief of immigration before your planned departure (it takes several months to get a reply), you can check with the Marshall Islands Liaison Office in Honolulu. Generally, as long as you have filed the permit request and have retained a copy of it, the chances are you will have no trouble on entry. Recent experience indicates that cruising boats are also getting visit approval after arrival at Majuro.

Visit permits of up to six months can be obtained and can be extended. A passport is required for each crew member as the Marshalls are no longer a U.S. Territory.

YACHT FACILITIES

Majuro lagoon is a large, natural harbor; it has been wire-dragged in the eastern half to remove isolated coral heads. The principal anchorage is off the island of Dalap in the southeastern corner, where protection is offered from the northeast trades. The bottom is a layer of sand over a coral base. Boats with some local knowledge can also anchor at the far western end of the lagoon off the island of Laura. Laura, known as Majuro's outer island, has a small village with a smattering of stores. It is more rustic and far cleaner than the eastern end of Majuro, except for disposable diapers blown by the trades to finally rest on Laura's lagoon beach.

The original harbor facility is at Uliga. The old battered T-pier has been replaced by a new L-pier with a warehouse at the lagoon end. It can be used by cruising boats for temporary berthing while checking in, fueling, or provisioning; for any other purposes, it is far better to anchor just to the north of the pier or in the southeastern corner of the lagoon. There is a charge of US$5.50 per day to use the Uliga pier. The new seaport west of Dalap has a 180-foot long pier, but it is used mostly by heavy shipping.

There are a few boatbuilding shops along the waterfront north of the L-pier. They can take care of most yacht repair needs. There is also a reasonable hardware store in town. Heavy machine work can be accomplished at Pacific International in the new seaport region. There is no adequate slipway for hauling a boat, but Pacific International at the new seaport can lift a boat up to 65 tons out of the water onto the hard using a land crane. Electronic repairs can also be accomplished by a shop in the north Uliga area, but you had better have a detailed circuit diagram of your piece of equipment for the technician to work from.

Most of the burgeoning population of the Marshall islands lives on Majuro and most of the business activity takes place on the three islands of Djarrit, Uliga, and Dalap (DUD for short), which are linked together with causeways. Post office, banks, and a museum are in Uliga. Most government offices are now on Dalap. Djarrit, also known as Rita, is principally residential.

A sealed road starting in Rita runs 30 miles around the east and south islands of the lagoon to Laura. It is the longest road in the former islands of the Trust Territory.

Provisioning in Majuro is fairly good. It has two supermarkets plus a number of small stores. You will find United States, New Zealand, and Japanese products on the shelves. Bread is baked daily. Locally grown fresh fruits and vegetables are limited in variety; there are some imported ones, but they generally suffer from too many days at sea. Papaya and breadfruit are available in season. Fuel can be obtained from the Mobil dealer on the wharf south of the L-pier.

Beer and soft drinks are plentiful, and liquors are generally the finest brands and quite expensive. Although liquor, wine, and beer are sold on Majuro, drinking is prohibited on all the outer islands. Don't bring liquor ashore if you visit the outer islands and don't give liquor to the local people from the outer islands when they visit your yacht at anchor.

CHAPTER 24

FEDERATED STATES OF MICRONESIA

The Country

The Federated States of Micronesia became the third provisional self-governing political entity to be formed within the Trust Territory. It consists of the states of Kosrae, Pohnpei, Chuuk (Truk), and Yap; all were formerly districts within the Trust Territory.

The 41 islands comprising the Federated States span about 28 degrees of longitude from Kosrae in the east to Yap in the west. These are the Caroline Islands. From north to south they span about 12 degrees of latitude, all north of the equator. The sea area covered is nearly 800,000 square miles. The land area of all of the islands is a mere 270 square miles.

The islands vary widely in appearance and topography. Kosrae and Pohnpei are both mountainous islands, with Pohnpei rising to an inspiring height of more than 2,000 feet. Circled by one of the largest barrier reefs in the world, Chuuk lagoon holds a captive fleet of half-submerged mountain peaks looking like brooding hulks in the dusk. While many of Chuuk's larger central islands compete with Pohnpei's and Kosrae's lush peaks, Chuuk state's outer island groups—the Halls, Namonuitos, Westerns, and Mortlocks—resemble dream atolls of the South Pacific. Yap seems like a combination of two different islands—or two worlds. Along the sea are mangrove swamps, sandy beaches, and quiet villages shaded by the highest and handsomest palms in all Micronesia. But Yap's uplands—parched meadows of pandanus and scrub growth—could pass as a scene from a Western movie.

While different in appearance, the islands also differ vastly in size. Pohnpei and the old whaling port of Kosrae always surprise the visitor by their size, their rolling hills, seldom visited peaks, curving mangrove swamps, and unkempt forests. But there are also plenty of minuscule two-palmed islets like the ones seen in shipwreck cartoons.

If you expect to find white coral sand beaches throughout all islands of the Pacific, you will be disap-

FEDERATED STATES OF MICRONESIA

Public Holidays and Special Events

January 1	New Year's Day—Public holiday
January *	Martin Luther King Day— Public holiday
February *	Presidents' Day—Public holiday
March/April *	Easter
May 1	Constitution Day—Public holiday
May *	Memorial Day—Public holiday
July 4	Independence Day—Public holiday
July 12	Micronesia Day—Public holiday
September *	Labor Day—Public holiday
October *	United Nations Day—Parades and traditional dances
November 11	Veterans Day—Public holiday
November *	Thanksgiving—Public holiday
December 25	Christmas—Public holiday

*Specific dates vary from year to year.

pointed to know that some islands are different. On Chuuk, Pohnpei, and Kosrae, mangrove swamp and tidal mud flats are far more common, although there are enough beaches to satisfy the eager swimmer.

The flora and fauna of the Federated States are just as varied as the states themselves. Dominated by graceful coconut palms, the outlying coral atolls have the kind of vegetation one would expect to find on any similar sandy island—palms, and occasional breadfruit, banana, and pandanus. The high islands of Pohnpei and Chuuk are heavily overgrown, from tidal flats festooned with mangrove to sloping hillsides of coconut palms and hilltops canopied by stands of trees 100 feet tall. Yap's coconut trees are considered the best in Micronesia, and seed nuts are an item of export. But Yap can also claim some surprising uplands—red clay, expanses of grassland and pandanus, gullies and washouts.

The bat is considered the only indigenous mammal. The dog, pig, and rat were introduced by voyaging islanders. Water buffalo, horses, cattle, goats, and cats came in the post-European period from Europe and America. Also introduced into Pohnpei were deer,

FLOTSAM AND JETSAM

External Affairs Representative
U.S. consulates and embassies
In Honolulu: Federated States of Micronesia
                 3049 Ualena Street, Suite 408
                 Honolulu HI 96819
                 USA

which flourished in the dense, verdant rain forests of the interior.

Although landbirds are relatively scarce, the small, bright-green Pohnpei parrot can be seen around the Village Hotel in Pohnpei. Marine and shorebirds abound—the gull, tern, albatross, gannet, frigate bird, golden plover, duck, and heron. There are no poisonous land snakes in the Federated States, although some sea snakes are poisonous. Lizards are plentiful, and geckoes are everywhere, happily going about dining on insects and mosquitoes. There aren't enough geckoes, however, to control all the mosquitoes, so repellent sprays, screens on hatches, and burning mosquito coils are all necessary for comfort at times.

Most of the fauna are under water, where the color and drama of the seas can rival the native life above the surface. There are sharks, eels, bonito, barracuda, sea bass, sea slugs, crabs, lobsters, shrimps, langusta, oysters, clams, turtles—the list is endless. For the seafarer, dinner is often only a hull-thickness away.

The islands vary likewise in rainfall. Pohnpei claims countless streams and waterfalls flowing the year around. In some of the outlying atolls, however, rain running off metal roofs must be trapped and hoarded through the dry months. Pohnpei averages 182 inches annually. Kosrae's average ranges from 185 inches at Lelu to 300 inches in the interior. Chuuk and Yap have 110 inches a year. The wettest period for all of the states is usually between May and November.

The western end of the Federated States falls within the typhoon belt, although typhoons have been known to visit all of the states at some time or other. Hardly a year passes without the onslaught of one or more of these storms ranging from the "coconut" typhoons, which blow nuts off the trees, to winds in excess of 100 knots, which do severe damage. The U.S. Weather Service with meteorology stations on all of the state capital islands provides early warning to alert all boats at sea and those in harbors of the coming wind.

The population of the Federated States of Micronesia stood at 105,000 in 1990, an increase of 43 per-

cent over the 1980 census. In 1990 Kosrae had 7,000 people; Pohnpei 31,000; Chuuk 54,000; and Yap 13,000.

The Federated States of Micronesia graduated from Trust Territory rule in three steps. In 1980, the Compact of Free Association with the United States was approved; in 1982 it was formally accepted; in 1986 the United Nations Trust Territory authority was terminated for all but Palau. In that same year there began an economic changeover in which the United States began granting direct economic aid to the Federated States amounting to approximately US$755 million over 15 years, plus continuing program assistance in the form of weather service, postal service, aviation support, and marine navigation aids. The United States will retain international obligations such as consular assistance and defense.

A new capitol for the Federated States has been built in mountainous Palikir, Pohnpei, on the site of a

MEDICAL MEMO

Immunization Requirements
A valid international certificate of smallpox vaccination is required from travelers who, within the preceding 14 days, have been in a country any part of which is infected. Other immunizations or health measures may be imposed at the time of entry. It is strongly recommended that all travelers have an up-to-date tetanus vaccination.

Local Health Situation
All the islands of the Federated States are nominally free of communicable diseases. Some diseases endemic to the islands but not widespread are dysentery, hookworm, infectious hepatitis, and intestinal parasites. Chuuk suffered a severe cholera epidemic in 1982.

Health Services
There are no private doctors, dentists, or medical service facilities in the Federated States. There is one general hospital in each state capital offering hospital and out-patient care; there is also a dental clinic. These facilities are staffed by professional personnel. The Kosrae hospital has 35 beds, Pohnpei has 116 beds, Chuuk has 125 beds, and Yap has 55 beds. In addition, there are dispensaries in the outlying areas: 12 in Pohnpei, 53 in Chuuk, and 14 in the Yap group. Fees charged are considerably less than in the United States.

Prescription and nonprescription drugs are available at the hospitals and to a limited extent at the dispensaries.

Water
Tap water from the public supplies at the state capitals is reportedly safe, but all water should be considered suspect and treated. The high-island capitals of the four states all have ample rainfall to allow collection of pure water on your own boat.

World War II Japanese airfield. The capitol's nine buildings were designed to reflect the culture of the four states. The building roofs are of Kosrean design with Chuukese canoe-edge shapes. Yapese stone money has been designed into the eaves, and Pohnpeian basalt rock has been simulated over columns and posts. The former capitol buildings in Kolonia have been turned over to the state government of Pohnpei.

Cruising Notes

YACHT ENTRY

The official Ports of Entry for the Federated States of Micronesia are:

Kosrae	Lelu and Okat harbors
Pohnpei	Kolonia Harbor
Chuuk	Weno anchorage
Yap	Tomil Harbor and Ulithi anchorage

CUSTOMS

All yachts, including those of U.S. registry and sailed by U.S. citizens, must have a vessel permit to enter the waters of the Federated States. This is now an independent country and no longer a part of the U.S. Trust Territory. The vessel permit should be obtained in advance from:

Chief of Immigration and Labor
Federated States of Micronesia Government
P.O. Box 490
Kolonia, Pohnpei FM 96941
USA

You can check with the Federated States Liaison Office in Honolulu for more information regarding this permit.

Vessels with valid entry permits must make formal entry at one of the listed Ports of Entry. The fact that a vessel has already made entry in one state does not exempt it from clearing in at another state. Vessels that intend to stop at outlying islands en route between states should make certain they get a coastal cruising clearance from their port of departure.

A vessel in distress may anchor or land at any port for the purpose of effecting repairs or acquiring provisions. The person in command, however, must immediately notify the nearest state or federal government representative of their appearance and proceed to an official Port of Entry thereafter.

IMMIGRATION

U.S. citizen tourists entering the Federated States of Micronesia need proof of citizenship only; however, boat crews should always carry passports for entry to other countries. Non-U.S. citizen tourists must have a valid passport and a multiple reentry visa obtained ahead of time. Check the latest requirements for your country of origin. All persons entering the Federated States for more than 30 days or for purposes other than tourism must have a visitor entry permit approved in advance by the chief of immigration. Each of the four states of the Federated States handles its own immigration. You can obtain 30-day visitor permits at each Port of Entry, thus giving you as much as 120 days total in the Federated States. Visa extensions beyond the initial 30 days can be obtained in increments of 30 days up to a maximum of 90 days. A fee of US$10 per 30-day extension is charged.

KOSRAE

The Country

Kosrae is the easternmost island of the Caroline group and is a state in the Federated States of Micronesia. It is

a high, triangular island measuring 42 square miles in area. The interior of the island is mountainous with the highest peak in the north, Mt. Mutunte (Buache), rising 1,946 feet and the highest peak of all, Mt. Fwinkol

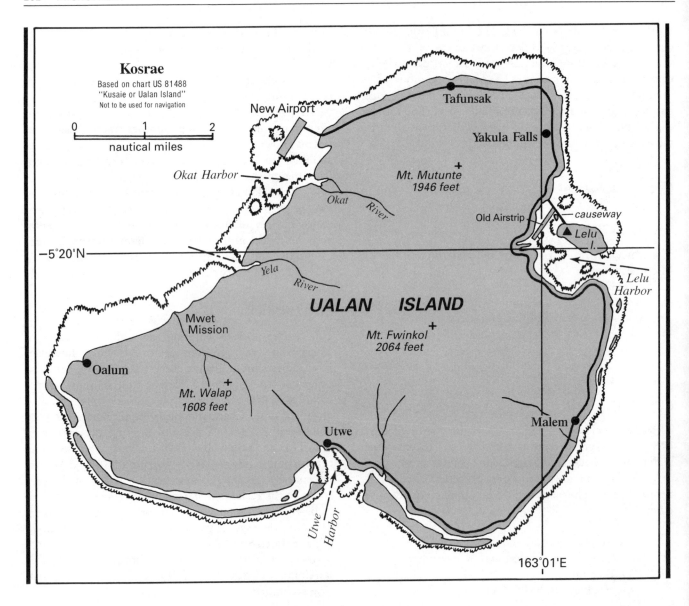

Kosrae

Based on chart US 81488
"Kusaie or Ualan Island"
Not to be used for navigation

0   1   2
nautical miles

New Airport

Okat Harbor →

Okat River

Tafunsak

Yakula Falls

+
Mt. Mutunte
1946 feet

Old Airstrip

causeway

▲ Lelu
Lelu I.

−5°20'N

Yela River

Lelu Harbor

UALAN   ISLAND

Mwet Mission

+
Mt. Fwinkol
2064 feet

● Oalum

+
Mt. Walap
1608 feet

Malem ●

Utwe ●

Utwe Harbor

163°01'E

(Crozer), rising 2,064 feet in the center of the island. Between the two is a lush valley spanning the island with Lelu Harbor to the east and Okat Harbor to the west.

Legend claims that at the beginning of time a woman was permanently placed in a reclining position by angry gods and became Kosrae. Seen from a distance, the island's distinctive skyline does appear to outline the profile of a woman lying on her back, hair spreading out behind her head. To the geologist, though, Kosrae is the remains of a classic shield-shaped volcano, dissected by erosion and increased in size by coral reef growth. Five main rivers fed by mountain streams cut through the lush interior jungle and in turn feed bath houses and canals.

Overall the island is hilly and covered with dense forests whose timber was highly prized in the past for shipbuilding. The island is composed primarily of basalt and is so fertile that almost any tropical plant can be grown there. Kosrae is said to be one of the most beautiful islands in the Pacific and is often called the Garden Island of Micronesia.

Kosrae Island is fringed by a coral reef extending offshore up to a mile on its northwestern side. After heavy rains, muddy waters extend far offshore, making it difficult to identify the reefs. Inside the reef are many islets composed mainly of mangroves. The coastal lowlands are narrow in most areas, and there is no lagoon as such. There are, however, three harbors of which

KOSRAE
A member of the Federated States of Micronesia

Ports of Entry
Lelu, Kosrae	5°20' N, 163°01' E
Okat, Kosrae	5°21' N, 162°57' E

Distances between Ports in Nautical Miles
Between Lelu and

Agana, Guam	1,195
Chuuk, FSM	680
Honiara, Solomon Islands	905
Honolulu, Hawaii	2,465
Kavieng, Papua New Guinea	875
Koror, Palau	1,705
Majuro, Marshall Islands	505
Nauru (Aiwo District)	420
Pohnpei, FSM	320
Tarawa, Kiribati	640
Tokyo, Japan	2,225
Yap, FSM	1,500

Standard Time
11 hours fast on UTC

Lelu is the principal one; Okat is being developed and Utwe is used only by fishermen.

Kosrae once was the rendezvous point for U.S. whaling ships operating in the Pacific. It was also the temporary home of the pirate Bully Hayes, who lost his ship on the reef at Utwe Harbor in 1874 and settled on the island until driven away by British warships.

Kosrae was first seen by European eyes when the Spaniard Sarveda sighted the island in 1529. It wasn't reported again until 1804 when the American whaler *Nancy,* Captain Crozer commanding, stopped there. He named it Strong's Island. The whaler *Coquille* stopped there in 1824, spending ten days, and *Coquille*'s captain estimated that the local population numbered about 5,000.

Whaling ships were the main visitors to Kosrae with the trade starting in 1830 and reaching its peak in 1850. Overkilling of the mammals caused whaling to decline in the 1860s, and the whalers went elsewhere to pursue their trade. Part of the reason for the whaling activity in the vicinity of Kosrae was the friendliness of Awane Lepalik I, known to visitors as King George. He

Copra making is a family affair near the town of Malem on Ualan Island. (Earl Hinz)

welcomed the whalers and their crews during his reign in the years 1837 to 1854, and the whalers enjoyed fraternizing with Kosraean women while in port. During the period 1852 to 1856, 75 whaling ships called at Kosrae. In October 1856 there were 20 whaling ships anchored in the harbor at Lelu.

The population of Kosrae was on a severe decline in these years; a trader named Kirkland estimated it to be between 1,400 and 1,700 in the year 1851. An influenza epidemic in 1855 killed 113 islanders, and by 1865 the population was down to 950; by 1868 it was down to 600.

In 1870 the German trading firm of Godeffroy and Sons opened a copra trading station on Kosrae, and in 1885 they raised the German flag, establishing rights to trade, fish, and use the island as a coaling station for their ships. During this period the population reached its historical low of 200 people (in 1880).

Japanese rule began on the island in 1914, when, as a result of the start of World War I in Europe, the Japanese took over most German possessions in the Pacific. They established their own colony of 25 Japanese on Kosrae in 1935. It was destined to grow to several thousand during World War II.

Kosraean involvement in World War II was minimal because Kosrae was not a strategic island. A minor U.S. bombing raid was made on it in 1942, and it was occupied with little resistance by U.S. forces in 1945.

With the formation of the Trust Territory in 1947, Kosrae was made a part of the Pohnpei district. In 1977 it became a district of its own and in 1980 became part of the Federated States of Micronesia. In 1990 the population stood at 7,000.

The Kosraean people are of medium stature and slender with a light brown skin, occasional epicanthic eyefolds, heavy hair (sometimes straight and sometimes curly), and relatively sparse beard and body hair.

The language of the Kosraean people is somewhat similar to Marshallese, and like most of the languages of Micronesia, it has vocabulary and grammatical elements common to the basic Malayo-Polynesian linguistic stock. The Kosraean language has a highly developed "polite form" that is used when addressing members of high social position.

The Kosrean economy is primarily agrarian and at a subsistence level except for welfare and government operations money allotted by the United States. Although nonarable mountains comprise 75 percent of the land, there are good soils washed down from the mountains onto coastal plains and an abundance of rain and sunshine to warm the heart of any farmer. The lower hillsides along the coasts are suitable for tree crops such as citrus, breadfruit, and banana and some low-crop cultivation. Below the lower hillsides are the fresh-water swamps where taro is grown. Coconuts are found on plots of sandy loam, which is also where most of the population lives. Beyond the taro patches and coconut groves lie the mangrove swamps that provide construction materials and firewood.

The primary crops of Kosrae are coconuts, bananas, breadfruit, taro, and yams. Crops of lesser importance but of more interest to the European palate are tapioca root, limes, oranges, and tangerines with occasional small plantings of foreign vegetables such as Chinese cabbage, green beans, watermelons, squash, and sweet potatoes. With the exception of sweet potatoes, these crops require little attention after being planted. Farming thus consists largely of keeping the land free of jungle growth until a crop is harvested.

Pigs are the principal source of meat, and most households raise pigs for use on important family, village, or church occasions. A few natives hunt the wild pigs in the interior to sell or trade.

A great variety of fish provides additional protein for the needs of the people. The fish are caught with hook, spear, and net in the sheltered tidal waters between reef and shore. The abundant tuna and other large game fish in the offshore waters are caught from small day boats.

Fresh-water canals fed from the rushing mountain streams are still used by many Kosraeans to move about the island; but the canals are very narrow in places and obstructed by trees and sand. The fresh-water canals flow into the lagoon inside the reef providing additional miles of waterways for transportation by canoe.

Lelu, the main village on Kosrae, is on the island of the same name. It is connected to the main island of Ualan by a 2,400-foot-long constructed causeway wide enough for two lanes of traffic. Lelu was the former residence of the aristocracy of Kosrae and is today the center of social, economic, religious, and political activity. Much of this is bound to change in the future with the completion of the new state governmental center being built across the harbor on the main island.

Lelu's population is about 2,000 and, as Lelu Island is less than one-sixth square mile in area, there is no room for growing crops. Consequently, most Leluans have farms on the main island surrounding the harbor. In addition to tending their main island crops, Leluans also visit the main island in times of drought to get fresh water and to bathe in the mountain streams. Otherwise their fresh-water needs are met through rain catchment systems and cistern storage.

In the village of Lelu is an area called Insaru, Ruins of the King's Residence. These ruins, built of crisscrossed hexagonal basalt logs that bear a striking resemblance to the famous ruins of Nan Madol in Pohnpei, represent several centuries of civilization. Nan Madol history mentions the valiant Isokelekel and his Kosraean warriors who vanquished the Pohnpeians. These warriors' reputation of invincibility is such that, to this date, the word "Isokelekel" uttered by a Kosraean youth to a Pohnpeian amounts to an undisguised challenge.

The Weather

The eastern Caroline Islands are swept by the northeast trades. East-northeast or east winds blow almost constantly from December through April at an average speed of 9 knots. From May through November, east to southeast winds increase in frequency and predominate during the months of September through November with average speeds of 5 knots. These averages are for land stations; winds over the open waters would be slightly stronger. Over the open sea, winds are usually strongest about 0300 and lightest about 1400 local time.

Kosrae Island is in the eastern Carolines on the south margin of the northeast trades, which dominate from December through April, and is swept by northeasterly winds of 10 to 15 knots during that period. The northeast trades move northward in June and July, and light variable winds and calms prevail until the southeast trades become dominant. The southeast trades are weaker and less constant than the northeast trades. In November and December, the wind system shifts southward again, and the island has another period of doldrums.

Tropical cyclones sometimes originate over the island; but they are rare, especially during the winter months, and the island generally escapes the brunt of such storms. Gales rarely occur. Typhoon Abby formed north of Kosrae in December 1979 and reached tropical storm strength between Kosrae and Pohnpei. Maximum winds reached 60 knots northeast of Chuuk. Abby eventually gained typhoon strength before reaching Iwo Jima, where the storm fell apart.

Kosrae Island's temperature averages 80°F throughout the year with little change during the 24-hour day. This constant warm temperature combined with an average annual rainfall measuring 185 inches at Lelu and up to 300 inches in the interior yields an average humidity of about 80 percent. Out of the wind, this can be uncomfortable, but when a breeze is blowing, the climate is quite comfortable.

Fresh water is plentiful, although periods of low rainfall may occur in January and February, forcing the inhabitants of Lelu Island to obtain water from the numerous ever-flowing mountain streams on the main island.

While Kosrae normally has a benign climate, a tsunami hit the island in 1890, causing many deaths.

FLOTSAM AND JETSAM

Currency
The U.S. dollar is the official medium of exchange.

Language
The native tongue, Kosraean, is commonly spoken by the Kosraeans among themselves. English is the second language and is spoken by everybody involved in business or government.

Electricity
Electric power, where available, is 110v, 60 Hz AC.

Postal Address (U.S. Postal Service)
Yacht ( )
Poste Restante
Lelu, Kosrae FM 96944
USA

Ports for Making Crew Changes
Kosrae is not a recommended port for making crew changes because it lacks direct service from a major airline hub. Either Majuro or Kolonia would make better crew-change ports.

Information Center
Tourism Division
Department of Economic Development
Kosrae State
Kosrae FM 96944
USA

Cruising Notes

YACHT FACILITIES

There are three harbors on Kosrae—Lelu to the east, Utwe to the south, and Okat on the west. Utwe has no

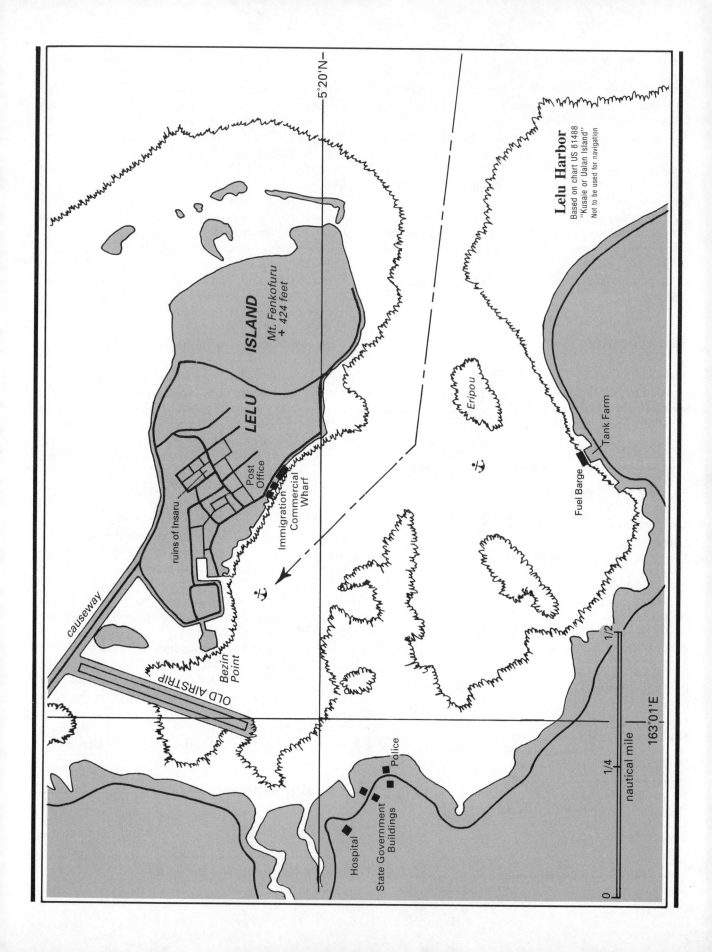

Lelu Harbor

Based on chart US 81488
"Kusaie or Ualan Island"
Not to be used for navigation

5°20'N–

LELU ISLAND

Mt. Fenkofuru
+ 424 feet

ruins of Insaru

Post Office

Immigration
Commercial Wharf

causeway

Bezin Point

OLD AIRSTRIP

Eripou

Fuel Barge

Tank Farm

Hospital

State Government Buildings

Police

163°01'E

0   1/4   1/2

nautical mile

Horizon anchored in Lelu Harbor just outside one of the entrances to the ruins of Insaru. (Earl Hinz)

The lush, jungle-like growth of the high islands of Micronesia is typified by the island of Kosrae. The picture taken from atop Mt. Fenkofuro on Lelu Island shows Lelu harbor to the left and the causeway to Ualan Island on the right. (Earl Hinz)

facilities and is used mainly by local fising boats. Scuba divers find diving on the wreck of Bully Hayes' ship *Leonora* of interest in this harbor.

Okat is the new commercial harbor on the west side of the island. It is adjacent to the airport and connected to the populated side of the island by a nominally good road. It has no facilities for cruising boats and is away from the island activities.

Lelu is the preferred harbor for cruising boats. It is sheltered from southwesterly winds by the mountains of the interior and from northeasterlies by Lelu Island on which Mt. Fenkofuro rises to 424 feet. Mangroves and fringing reefs border the harbor. Depths in the harbor range from 4 to 17 fathoms and the fringing reefs are steep-to.

Radio communications with Lelu beforehand are not possible because they have no marine radio facilities. In fact, the only radio station on Kosrae outside of the government communications facility is the broadcast station.

There is a commercial dock, about 300 feet long, along the waterfront of Lelu, but it is not recommended for yacht use because of its height and rough construction. It is preferable to anchor farther into the harbor. The best anchorage during prevailing northeasterly winds is off the large church in Lelu in about 7 fathoms of water over a black sand bottom. Do not anchor too near the commercial dock as large freighters come in without the help of pilots or tugs and turn around abreast of the commercial dock.

There are several dinghy landing spots in the vicinity of the business district, all within a short row from the anchorage. Ashore there is no public transportation, but with luck, you may be able to rent a car or thumb a ride along the potholed roads of the islands.

Some provisions are available but no yacht hardware. Repairs would be difficult to get done here because there are few shops and fewer technically qualified workers. Diesel fuel and gasoline are obtainable at the Mobil Oil floating dock across Lelu Harbor from the commercial dock. Water is usually available from private supplies along the shoreline but must be carried in cans out to your boat.

POHNPEI

The Country

Pohnpei state in the eastern part of the Caroline Archipelago consists of nine island units that contain 163 individual islands and a total land area of 133 square miles. Pohnpei is a high oceanic formation that completely dominates the district, accounting for all but four square miles of its land area and more than 80 percent of its population. The other eight units making up the 163 islands are all low coral atolls of insignificant size. (Pohnpei Island and nearby Pakin and Ant Atolls were once known as the Senyavin Islands.) About 31,000 people live in Pohnpei state.

Pohnpei Island is a rugged mountain peak rising to an altitude of 2,579 feet. It has fertile soil and abundant rainfall that results in a dense covering of luxuriant tropical growth. Under Japanese administration the island underwent intense agricultural development and in 1970 still produced large quantities of coconuts, breadfruit, bananas, taro, and yams.

The eight atolls combined have a population of less than 1,000; Oroluk and Ant atolls are uninhabited. The two atolls of Kapingamarangi and Nukuoro, isolated in the southern portion of the state, are unique in that their inhabitants are physically and culturally Polynesian rather than Micronesian.

Pohnpei is known for its spectacular waterfalls—a scintillating byproduct of high mountains and abundant rainfall. To the east of Kolonia is the dramatic Nanpil River, which in its lower reaches has slow-moving pools of refreshing water for bathing and washing clothes. As you follow the overgrown jungle trail upward into the mountain forests, you reach the spectacular two-step Nanpil waterfall, which drops 80 feet over the lower

POHNPEI
A member of the Federated States of Micronesia

Port of Entry
Kolonia, Pohnpei   7°N, 158°13′ E

Distances between Ports in Nautical Miles
Between Kolonia and

Agana, Guam	890
Chuuk, FSM	380
Honiara, Solomon Islands	990
Honolulu, Hawaii	2,685
Kavieng, Papua New Guinea	725
Koror, Palau	1,415
Kosrae, FSM	320
Majuro, Marshall Islands	785
Saipan, Mariana Islands	885
Tarawa, Kiribati	945
Tokyo, Japan	1,990
Yap, FSM	1,200

Standard Time
11 hours fast on UTC

step and another 30 feet over the upper step. An abandoned Japanese hydroelectric plant can be seen to the side of the muddy path.

In the Madolenihmw district near the ancient ruins of Nan Madol is the great Kapirohi waterfall, reached after a mile's walk through vibrantly green and lush forests. Here the visitor can dive from waterfall ledges into a crystal-clear pool of cold mountain water. To the sailor who has been denied the simple pleasure of fresh-water baths for weeks at sea, Kapirohi offers priceless relaxation and fun.

The history of this area is predominantly that of Pohnpei, the largest and most populous island in the state. In pre-Western history, the entire island was ruled by the Saudeleurs, a dynasty of island chieftains who resided at Nan Madol off the southwestern shore of Madolenihmw Harbor. This rule continued until the end of the eleventh century, when the fortress city of Nan Madol was mysteriously abandoned.

Ruins of Nan Madol provide almost unbelievable evidence of the ability of ancient peoples to build struc-

Aging rock structures along mangrove-choked waterways are all that remain of the eleventh-century city of Nan Madol. Temwen Island, on which Nan Madol stands, is the property of the Nahmwarki (chief) of the municipality of Madolenihmw, and permission must be obtained from him to visit the ruins. He will extract a few dollars in payment from each visitor for this permission. (Earl Hinz)

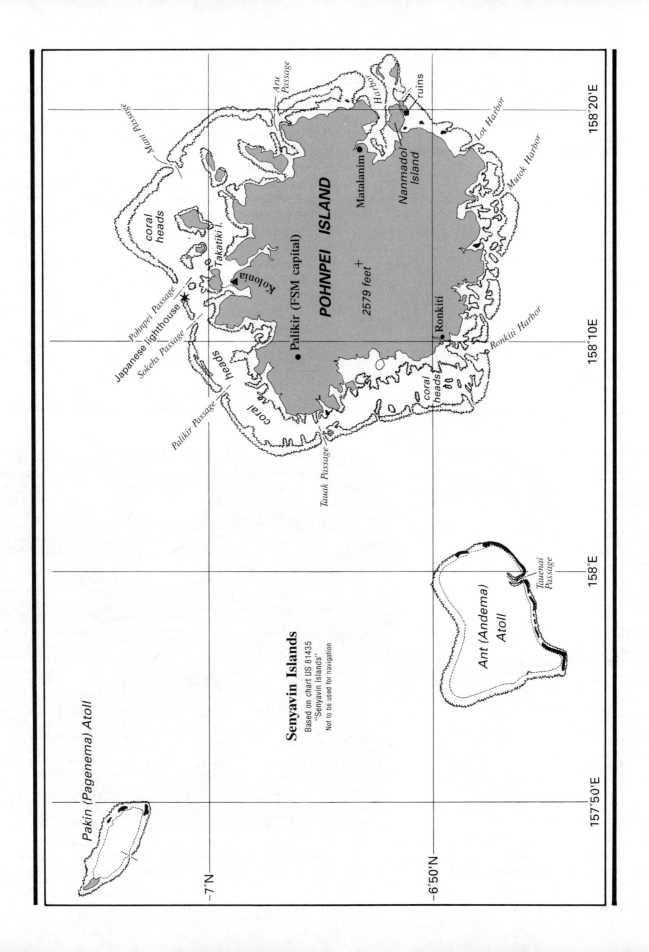

Pakin (Pagenema) Atoll

Senyavin Islands

Based on chart US 81435
"Senyavin Islands"

Not to be used for navigation

Mant Passage

coral heads

Aru Passage

Harbor

ruins

POHNPEI ISLAND

Matalanim

Nanmadol Island

Lot Harbor

Mutok Harbor

Takatiki I.

Kolonia

Palikir (FSM capital)

2579 feet

Japanese lighthouse

Pohnpei Passage

Sokehs Passage

Ronkiti

Ronkiti Harbor

coral heads

Palikir Passage

coral heads

Tauak Passage

158°20'E

158°10'E

158°E

157°50'E

7°N

6°50'N

Ant (Andema) Atoll

Tauenai Passage

tures without the aid of modern mechanical equipment. Nan Madol consisted of nearly a hundred artificial islets created of quarried basalt rock resting on the coral reef. It was a veritable Venice of the Pacific, covering hundreds of acres of tidal flats. The sources of the huge basalt logs, some weighing an estimated 16 tons, are a mystery, considering the logistics of moving and hoisting them in place. One obvious source of these logs, because of the nature of the rock itself, is Sokehs Rock on the north side of the island—25 miles away by water and impossible to reach by land!

Following the rule of the Saudeleurs, the ancient government was reorganized into independent political units consisting of the areas of Madolenihmw, Kiti, and Uh plus a fourth area of then lesser significance that now comprises the important districts of Net and Sokehs. There were two lines of chiefs (nobility) in control, the Nahnmwarki and the Nahniken. The rule of the Nahnmwarkins was absolute, and all the lands in their respective municipalities belonged to them.

The chieftains in the two lines of nobility preserved a pattern of matrilineal marriages, thus retaining chiefly prerogatives and associated material wealth within the respective matrilineal clans. Portions of this system persist today, bestowing upon current chiefs some of the social and material benefits claimed by their ancestors. The system provides many of the social and economic controls by which the current-day society is organized and maintained. Throughout the outer islands making up the state of Pohnpei, however, are different forms of local government using the traditional chieftainship, without the complexity of the Pohnpeian system of nobility and commoner.

Protestant missionaries established schools on Pohnpei in the middle of the nineteenth century, and their influence soon spread to the outer islands. They reduced the indigenous languages to writing, translated portions of the Bible, and trained a portion of the local populace to read and write. Pohnpeian lay missionaries carried their new teachings to the people of the Mortlock Islands and eventually were able to bring some people from the Mortlocks to Pohnpei following destructive typhoons in the Mortlocks early in that century.

During this period whalers and traders appeared, disrupting the island life. Even the American Civil War was felt when the Confederate cruiser *Shenandoah* caught 4 New England whaling ships in Lohd Harbor, Madolenihmw, and burned them to the waterline.

German traders were aggressively busy during this time but were driven out when the Spanish took formal control of the island by papal decree. Among other things, the Spanish built a walled town in the Bay of Ascension, now the site of Kolonia. Some of the ruins are still in evidence today.

After the Spanish-American War of 1898, the Germans purchased the Spanish holdings in the Pacific, including Pohnpei. The former Spanish town was renamed Kolonia by the German governor. The German administration had a profound influence on the social and political structure of the island, and German commercial interests developed a strong copra economy for the island. The people of Pohnpei were, however, little more than slaves to the Germans. The community of Sokehs rebelled in 1910, but the rebellion was quickly put down by German naval forces.

At the start of World War I, the Japanese occupied Pohnpei along with most of the German-held islands north of the equator. Following the war, Japan was given mandate over the former German possessions in the Caroline, Marshall, and Northern Mariana islands. The Japanese actively colonized and exploited the islands and strongly fortified some of them, like Chuuk, Kwajalein, and Peleliu. Pohnpei was made a principal administrative center and was not militarily fortified.

The Japanese instituted intensive cultivation and commercial agricultural production, for which the island is particularly well suited. They built a mill to process manioc flour and a refinery for sugar, which was converted to an alcohol plant in World War II. In doing all of this, they colonized the island with Japanese until they outnumbered the Pohnpeians. These Japanese were repatriated in 1945 and 1946.

A native Pohnpeian is born into one or more of 20 island clans. A person's clan is that of his or her mother, and he or she may not marry inside it. The island itself is divided into the five formerly independent areas now known as municipalities. In each of these are the traditional two lines of chiefs, the Nahnmwarki and the Nahniken, who effectively rule, although their absoluteness and land ownership have been severely diminished. After the beginning of the U.S. administration, democratic native governments began to develop, further diminishing the chiefs' authority; nevertheless, the deference and respect shown them has been retained.

Within the state of Pohnpei are two distinct races of people—the Polynesians of the atolls of Kapingamarangi and Nukuoro, who are generally taller, heavier, and covered with noticeable body hair; and the Micronesians, of medium stature and slender build with a light brown skin, occasional epicanthic eyefolds, heavy hair (sometimes straight and sometimes curly), and relatively sparse beard and body hair.

The people of Pohnpei state speak two distinct native languages—Polynesian and Pohnpeian. The people of the southern atolls of Kapingamarangi and Nukuoro speak a western Polynesian dialect with few, if any, Micronesian intrusions. The Pohnpeian language is spoken on the rest of the islands, with some regional variations. All of these languages have some common vocabulary and grammatical elements placing them in the Maylayo-Polynesian linguistic stock. The Pohnpeian language also has a highly developed "polite form" of speaking, which is used to address members of high social classes.

Like most Micronesians, the people of Pohnpei are gardeners and fishers, but unlike the other Micronesians, Pohnpeians live in scattered farmsteads and hamlets rather than in villages. Even this situation, is changing however, as the cash economy of Kolonia and the Westernized educational system draw young people away from the ways of their elders.

The rich soil, abundant rainfall, and dazzling sun team up to make agriculture a sure thing to any who take time to plant crops. While traditional crops such as coconuts, bananas, taro, papaya, and tapioca root are the most common, there are some gardeners who grow European foods for the expatriates and visitors to the islands. Lucky is the cruiser who can find the produce before it is snapped up by the hotels and restaurants.

While fish and pigs are abundantly available locally, much frozen meat is imported from the United States. Beef, chicken, and processed meats are handled by most stores and highly favored by the Pohnpeian palate.

Pohnpei's one agricultural export is pepper. It is grown on the plateaus of the western side of the island by independent farmers who cultivate pepper plots that were formerly part of large plantations. The pepper is processed by a government mill at the site of the old Japanese agricultural station on the outskirts of Kolonia. Every visiting yacht should take some of this pepper along when it departs the area.

Kolonia is the main town and state capital of Pohnpei and the former location of the government of the Federated States of Micronesia. It bears a striking resemblance to a town out of the Old West, with its wide main street and generally ramshackle buildings of weathering wood and rusting galvanized iron. While it is called the main street because of the location of the post office and tourist commission office, still it does not have the principal stores on it. Small general stores, movie houses, and modest restaurants line the street, along with abandoned buildings ready for demolition.

A second major street runs along the old dock area on the east side of Kolonia. There you will find fresh produce markets, several large general stores of interesting antiquated layout, the government dock, and hardware stores.

The streets of Kolonia were recently paved, improving the town's image and saving the many cars that use the streets large repair bills. Simultaneously, though, along with smoother riding came a drastic increase in the number of traffic accidents, an increase that is of great concern to the community.

A road around the island has also recently been completed, making it possible for the first time to drive all around the island without backtracking. The unstable nature of the coastal lands and the heavy rains demand continuous maintenance of the road to prevent potholes developing.

Most of the European history of Pohnpei Island is contained in and around Kolonia. The Spanish built

Excellent wood carvings are made by the Polynesians from Kapingamarangi Atoll who now live in Porakiet village on Pohnpei. The wood used is mangrove, which has a reddish hue, a beautiful grain pattern, and is very hard. Only hand tools are used by the woodcarvers, who make custom carvings at moderate prices. (Earl Hinz)

Fort Alphonso XIII in 1899, and some of the walls still stand in the center of town. They were followed by the Germans who in 1907 built a magnificent church, but the Japanese destroyed it, leaving only the bell tower standing. Although the Japanese built many structures, few survive. The agricultural station is one, the hydroelectric plant on the Nanpil River, another.

The cruiser who collects artifacts in his travels will be overwhelmed by the woodcarvings available in Porakiet village up the hill from the yacht harbor. Often referred to as "Kapingi" village, it is the home for several hundred Polynesians from the atoll of Kapingamarangi several hundred miles to the south. Overpopulation of the atoll caused many of them to move to Pohnpei, and they took their woodcarving skills and industriousness along with them. Today they hand carve replicas of sharks, fish, turtles, and other sea life out of tough red mangrove wood. Unlike the woodcarvers of the Marquesas, the Kapingis do not use a chain saw even for cutting down the mangrove trees; everything is done with hand tools—from forest to finished product.

Here in Porakiet you will also note the Polynesian way of life. Houses have thatched roofs, the people wear lava-lavas, and the men still go fishing in swift sailing canoes. Breadfruit, coconut palms, and bananas are cultivated for family use, and the village is notably clean compared to its surroundings.

Finally, you must become familiar with sakau, the social drink of Pohnpei. Sakau is closely related to the kava of Fiji and is used for ceremonial drinking as well as social drinking. By listening intently for the bell-like sound of the root being pounded by stones, you may find your way to a sakau group encounter.

The Weather

The eastern Caroline Islands are swept by the northeast trades. East-northeast or east winds blow almost constantly from December through April at an average speed of 8 knots. From May until December, east to southeast winds increase in frequency and predominate in September through November, with an average speed of 5 knots. The average speeds are for land locations; winds over the open sea are usually stronger. Gales rarely occur. Over the open sea the winds are strongest about 0300 and lightest about 1400.

In the vicinity of Pohnpei Island the northeast trades predominate at all seasons of the year and blow with great steadiness over the northern part of the area between November and April. Winds are more variable

FLOTSAM AND JETSAM

Currency
The U.S. dollar is the official medium of exchange.

Language
The native tongue, Pohnpeian, is commonly spoken by Pohnpeians among themselves. English is the second language and is spoken by everybody in government and business.

Electricity
Electric power, where available, is 110v, 60 Hz AC.

Postal Address (U.S. Postal Service)
Yacht ( )
Poste Restante
Kolonia, Pohnpei FM 96941
USA

Ports for Making Crew Changes
Kolonia is a possible port for making crew changes, having reasonably frequent service from Honolulu and Guam. There is no internal airline service.

Information Center
Pohnpei Tourist Commission
P.O. Box 66
Kolonia, Pohnpei FM 96941
USA

and are marked by occasional shifts to southeasterly and southerly between July and November, although easterly winds still predominate.

The northeast trades blow from December to March over Pohnpei Island. During April, east to southeasterly winds increase in frequency, becoming predominant by September and October. During this season, the winds are light and variable with frequent calms. Sudden, violent westerly to southwesterly winds sometimes occur with the better developed storms, and they occasionally attain gale force. Gales have been reported during the trades but are estimated to occur less than 5 percent of the time.

The doldrums belt moves northward over Pohnpei Island in June and July, when the northeast trades give way to the southeast trades. Considerable squalliness and rainfall occurs at this time over the open sea. The doldrums move southward in November and December and cause a secondary increase in squalliness and precipitation.

Showers and squalls are frequent and occur at any time of the year. Squalls are sometimes violent and have an average duration of 20 minutes. Thick cumulonimbus clouds immediately precede these squalls, bringing gusty winds and heavy rain. Thunderstorms are rare,

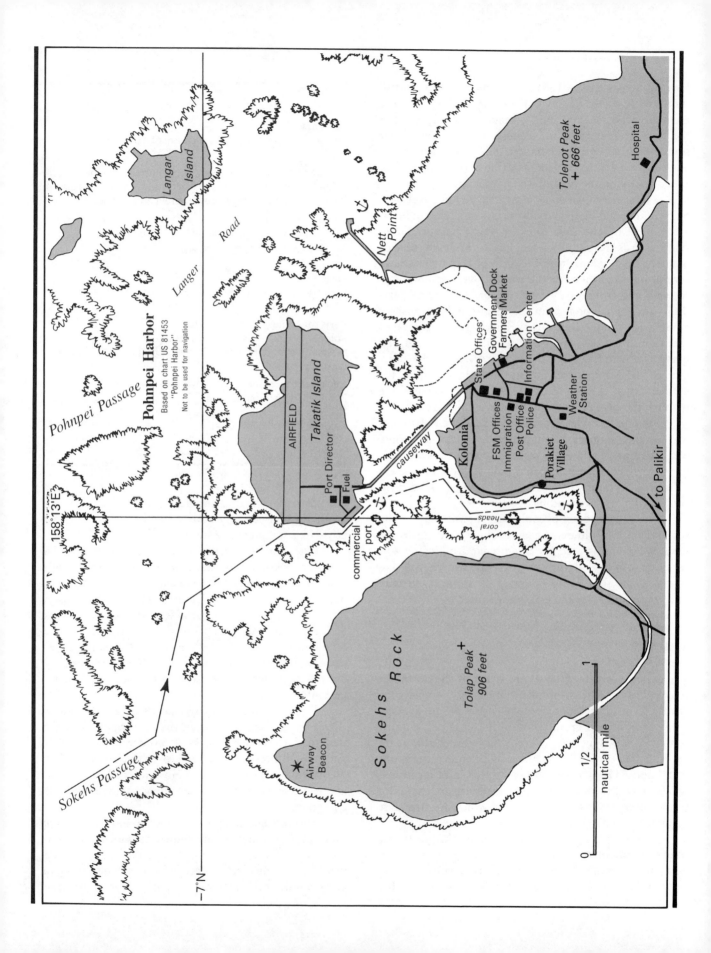

Pohnpei Harbor

Based on chart US 81453
"Pohnpei Harbor"
Not to be used for navigation

Pohnpei Passage

Sokehs Passage

Langar Island

Langer Road

158°13'E

−7°N

AIRFIELD

Takatik Island

Port Director

Fuel

commercial port

causeway

coral heads

Nett Point

State Offices

Government Dock

Farmers Market

Information Center

Kolonia

FSM Offices

Immigration

Post Office

Police

Porakiet Village

Weather Station

Tolenot Peak
+ 666 feet

Hospital

to Palikir

Sokehs Rock

Tolap Peak
+ 906 feet

Airway Beacon

0   1/2   1

nautical mile

with an annual average of about 17 distributed throughout the year.

Typhoons have sometimes occurred over Pohnpei, but they are rare during the winter months. A typhoon did hit Pohnpei on April 20, 1904. It was called a "fire of spray," meaning a twisting wind. Trees and plants were destroyed, and houses were leveled. The low islands outside Pohnpei were destroyed by the typhoon, and many people died.

Pohnpei Island is very wet, with rain falling practically every day from March to December. One inch of rain falls on about five days of each month. January and February, the so-called dry months, have in excess of 9 inches. On the average, the rainfall amounts to 10 to 20 inches per month the year around.

Cruising Notes

YACHT FACILITIES

The commercial port for the island of Pohnpei is at the southwest corner of Takatik Island with access to Kolonia by way of a causeway. The deep-water channel through the reef in the shadow of Sokehs Rock is known as Sokehs Passage; only a very few boats, mostly local fishing boats, use Pohnpei Passage, the old passage farther to the east. Sokehs Passage can be navigated right up to the commercial dock by sailboats broad-reaching on the trade winds.

Check-in takes place at the commercial dock, where you will have to find a vacant spot between freighters and copra boats. The state Department of Transportation is just outside the main gate to the dock area, and they will handle calls to Customs and Immigration for you. Meanwhile, have your crew stay aboard the boat until final clearance is given.

The yacht basin is at the inner end of Sokehs Harbor, and you have to traverse a maze of coral reefs to get there. It is best if you have some local knowledge aboard to do it. Otherwise, the best combination is a high tide at noon on a clear day with a crew member aloft in the rigging to guide your boat safely through the reefs.

The small-boat anchorage at the south end of the harbor has water 10 to 20 feet deep, clear of reefs, but with a slippery holding bottom. Pay out up to 175 feet of anchor rode without snubbing up on it and let it settle in the mud for a few days and you will have reasonable holding. Even then in a strong blow you will want to tend your anchor carefully.

There is no public transportation available, although some cars call themselves taxis. You must either

The yacht harbor at Pohnpei looks larger than it really is, for it is filled with broad expanses of coral. The "deep water" route from the commercial docks follows the mangrove-lined shore along the right edge of the picture. (Earl Hinz)

The distinct profile of Sokehs Rock has made it a Pacific landmark. (Earl Hinz)

rent a car or walk the mile and a half to town. In Kolonia you will find the post office, numerous small supermarkets, a handicraft co-op, and a large number of small general stores. The farmers' market is across town, near the old Kolonia pier, along with some hardware stores with rather meager stocks.

Boat-repair facilities are along the causeway leading from Takatik Island to Kolonia. While not very sophisticated, they can handle most urgently needed repair work. Few boat supplies are available other than the crude hardware used on local fishing and utility boats.

Fuel can be purchased from the Mobil Oil tank farm just outside the main gate to the docks, but arrangements must be made a day ahead for delivery of fuel in 55-gallon drums. Fresh water is available at the dock at a price of US$1.00 per 100 gallons upon arrangement with the harbormaster. With so much rainfall, you should be able to capture all the fresh water you need for your boat with on-board rain catchers.

CHUUK

The Country

Chuuk state consists of 15 major island units made up of 290 individual islands with a combined land area of 49 square miles. About 40 of the islands are inhabited, and many of the rest are used as food islands; that is, they are used by inhabitants of nearby islands to grow crops and to raise livestock. Excluding Chuuk itself, all the island units are low coral formations of undistinguished configuration; 12 are typical atolls; 2 (Nama and Pulosuk) are single islands.

Chuuk, which accounts for about 75 percent of the district's total land area, is an interesting complex of 11 high volcanic islands enclosed by a coral ring that is broken into 87 tiny, low, coral islets. The formation is comparable to that of an atoll, but the presence of the

Children play on an abandoned Japanese World War II tank on Satawan atoll, which is part of Chuuk State. (Gary Brookins)

CHUUK STATE
A member of the Federated States of Micronesia

Port of Entry

Weno, Chuuk	7°27′ N, 151°50′ E

Distances between Ports in Nautical Miles

Between Weno and

Agana, Guam	560
Honolulu, Hawaii	3,025
Kavieng, Papua New Guinea	605
Koror, Palau	1,030
Kosrae, FSM	680
Majuro, Marshall Islands	1,165
Manila, Philippine Islands	1,865
Pohnpei, FSM	380
Saipan, Mariana Islands	585
Tarawa, Kiribati	1,315
Tokyo, Japan	1,820
Wake Island	1,120
Yap, FSM	825

Standard Time
11 hours fast on UTC

high islands within the lagoon rules out the use of that term. The encircling reef, which in places has a diameter of 40 miles, contains several passages into the lagoon affording excellent anchorage for large ships.

The islands of Weno, Dublon, Fefan, Uman, Udot, and Tol are the major interior high islands of Chuuk. All are mountainous and heavily wooded, except in a few places where cultivation, fire, and erosion have reduced them to grasslands. Tol Island, which has a peak rising to more than 1,400 feet, is the highest. About two-thirds of the state's total population lives on these six high islands.

At one time, millions of years ago, Chuuk Atoll was one big island, a rolling mountainous hulk with today's Udot Island at its approximate center. Slowly, the island sank (and is still sinking, though at an infinitesimal rate). Now only the highest peaks of the prehistoric mountains remain. The result is the mighty Chuuk lagoon, 40 miles across, with 11 main islands and numerous smaller ones caught in a coral circle. There is saddle-shaped Weno, the state capital; three-peaked Udot; rolling agricultural Fefan (named for its resemblance to a reclining woman); the abandoned Japanese naval base of Dublon, its peak resembling a transplanted Mt. Fuji; and, not least of all, the ominous peak of Tol, a tropical Matterhorn with a height of 1,400 feet —tall enough to attract and hold rain clouds on otherwise sunny days.

Outside the lagoon are smaller island groups, low atolls even further advanced in geological age: the Halls and the Mortlocks, Namonuitos, and Westerns.

With just 49 square miles of land area, Chuuk state has the largest population of the Federated States —54,000 according to 1990 figures. It also has the two most populous municipalities in the Federated States— Weno with 15,000 and Tol with 10,000.

Linguistic and anthropologic evidence indicates that the Chuukese may have preceded the Polynesians in the eastward movement. Oral history also contains legends that speak of migrations from the island of Kosrae farther east.

The pre-Western history of Chuuk, told in story, relates to periods of interisland fighting by the people within the lagoon—the coastal people against the arrogant mountain people from inside the lagoon. The

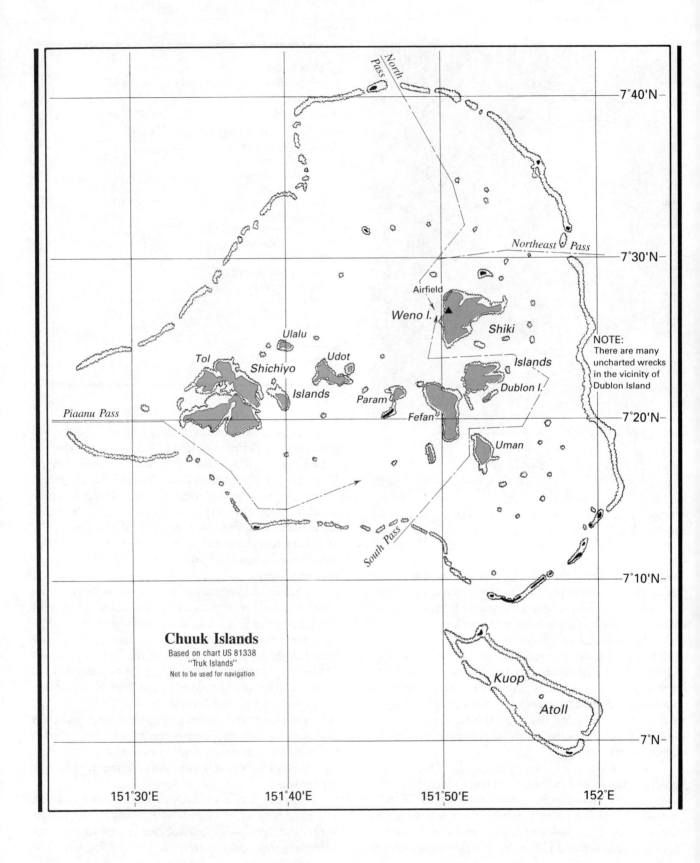

North Pass

Northeast Pass

Airfield

Weno I.

Shiki

Ulalu

Tol

Shichiyo

Udot

Islands

NOTE:
There are many
uncharted wrecks
in the vicinity of
Dublon Island

Islands

Param

Dublon I.

Piaanu Pass

Fefan

Uman

7°20'N

South Pass

7°10'N

Chuuk Islands
Based on chart US 81338
"Truk Islands"
Not to be used for navigation

Kuop

Atoll

7°N

7°40'N

7°30'N

151°30'E   151°40'E   151°50'E   152°E

mountain people were eventually driven off and fled to the atolls of Namoluk and others nearby, some returning later.

Western history starts with the first European sighting of the islands probably by Alvaro Saavedra in 1528 and by Alonso de Arellaño and Lopé Martin in 1565. The lagoon, however, did not become well known until after Dublon visited it in 1814. Following that the Russians and French sent expeditions under Krusenstern, Freycinet, Kotzebue, Duperrey, Lutke, and d'Urville to explore the islands. Duperrey was the first to make an extensive map of the lagoon during the year 1824, the islands were for a time known as the Hogalu Islands.

At the time of these early European explorations, the Chuukese were already making regular round trip voyages to Guam, trading goods for iron and steel implements.

The peak whaling years of 1830 to 1860 brought increased contact with Western people, although less than some of the other islands of the Carolines. It was really not until the 1860s and the development of the copra trade that outside influence became dominant on Chuuk. During this period the islands were under nominal control of the Spanish, which lasted until the Spanish-American War.

Missions were an early influence on Chuukese culture beginning in about 1879. The result is that Chuukese today are mostly Christian, either Catholic or Protestant faiths.

From 1899 until World War I, the Germans controlled Chuuk, abolishing the interisland warfare and encouraging the Chuukese to plant more coconut trees. They expanded the copra business to the point where the native economy became a cash economy. During this period (1906 and 1907) the first comprehensive treatise on Chuukese culture was produced by Kramer, a German anthropologist.

Following the start of World War I the Japanese took over the Chuuk Islands, developing an extensive commercial fishing industry and further expanding the copra business. Large numbers of Japanese were transported there, and in 1935 there were 2,000 Japanese nationals working on the islands. As the Japanese, in defiance of the League of Nations, developed Chuuk as the Gibraltar of the Pacific in anticipation of military moves against the other islands of the Pacific, their numbers increased until they had 35,000 persons on Chuuk by the end of World War II.

The Chuukese culture from a functional standpoint follows matrilineal lines with descendants being

There are more than World War II shipwrecks in the vast Chuuk lagoon; there is also an abundance of fish for the Chuukese tables. These two women were netting anchovy-size fish when we motored by them. Note the "butterfly" net in the hands of the woman to the right. (Earl Hinz)

able to trace common descent in the female line from a remembered ancestor. Until recently lineages were localized in villages where they owned land, and the members of the descent line formed a cooperative work group. The lineage chiefs formed the highest political authority in most cases.

Chuukese culture, however, must be viewed in terms of the Chuuk area comprising about 15 island groups within a radius of 150 miles from the main almost-atoll of Chuuk proper. These outer islands include Pulap, Puluwat, and Pulusuk to the west; Namonuito, Murilo, and Nomwin to the north; Nama, Losap, and Namoluk (the upper Mortlocks) to the southeast; and the lower Mortlocks farther away—Satawan, Lukunor, and Etal. The islands to the north and south were roughly at right angles to the trade winds, making sailing easy, so there was a greater cultural exchange with those islands. To get home from islands to the west, the sailing canoes had to beat against the trade winds, and therefore did not develop such a great cultural exchange. In the world of sailing, nothing has changed!

Prior to the Japanese takeover of Chuuk, the

island of Dublon in the Chuuk lagoon had become a trading center with the outer islands to the south and east. The people of the Chuuk lagoon islands to the west —Tol, Udot, and Ululu—would come to Dublon and trade for the products brought there by the outer islanders to the south and east. This trade pattern caused the Japanese to make Dublon their administrative and trading headquarters.

The outer islands have always depended on Chuuk proper as a supplier of food, particularly preserved breadfruit, which can be transported long distances. In times of disaster, such as when a typhoon destroyed the entire breadfruit crop on an atoll, the outer islanders could get help from Chuuk.

All the people of Chuuk state speak the Chuukese language, which is an offshoot of the Malayo-Polynesian language. Each island, however, has its own dialect, and it is possible to tell which island a person is from by the person's dialect. Generally the dialects are mutually understandable, although those of the Puluwat and Pulusuk atolls to the west are sometimes difficult for other Chuukese to understand.

The high islands of the Chuuk lagoon are all surrounded by fringing coral reefs, and there may be a narrow belt of sandy beach or rock before the swampy coastal belts lying between shore and hill. These lower lands are heavily wooded except where cultivation or fire has denuded them; then they are usually coarse grasslands with occasional outcroppings of bedrock. The soils tend to be red silt clay loams and often silt mixed with basalt boulders. The interiors of the islands are rocky basalt, sometimes in plateaus and in other places rising steeply to narrow ridges and sharp peaks. Overall, the soils of the high islands are fertile and support a dense vegetation with varied flora.

In contrast, the soil of the low islands is typically that of atolls—coral sand with some black loam created by the decomposition of plant life. Because there is so little soil that is cultivable on an atoll, the little there is, is used extensively.

The landscape of Chuuk is composed of strand forest at the shorelines, managed secondary forests on the lower and mid uplands alternating with grasslands, and remnants of the primary forests on the steep slopes at the higher elevations. Strand growth consists of mangrove, especially in the muddy swamp areas with slight wave action, or of wild hibiscus and other low tree species. Vines and coarse herbs fill in particularly where humans have abandoned an area. Tall elephant grass covers many acres of coastal swampland, especially along the inner shores of the larger islands.

The secondary forest growth is mostly planted breadfruit and coconut trees. The remnants of the high primary forests on the mountain tops and the steep slopes consist of trees endemic to Micronesia and in some cases to Chuuk itself. Some are quite tall, reaching up to a hundred feet with little herbaceous growth underneath.

Villages tend to be spread along the shoreline and lower slopes where it is not too swampy or steep. Most of the dry land near the shore is inhabited, and one village seems to blend in with the next. Some villages are, however, quite compact, with the residences surrounded by clearly defined agricultural plots. Houses are built along both traditional and modern lines. The traditional houses are thatch dwellings with pole frames lashed together with coconut husk fibers called sennit. Frame buildings, using mostly imported materials, have board or metal walls and metal roofs put together with nails. The latest in housing is a one-story structure of poured concrete or a cement-block dwelling with metal roof. A variant of this is the one-story concrete dwelling with a second story made as a framed building.

Gardens are usually small plots adjacent to a dwelling or set among the important breadfruit and coconut trees. Row crops consist mostly of sweet pota-

---

FLOTSAM AND JETSAM

Currency
The U.S. dollar is the medium of exchange.

Language
The native tongue, Chuukese, is commonly spoken by the Chuukese among themselves. English is the second language and is spoken by everybody in government and business.

Electricity
Electric power, where available, is 110v, 60 Hz AC.

Postal Address: (U.S. Postal Service)
Yacht ( )
Poste Restante
Weno, Chuuk FM 96942
USA

Ports for Making Crew Changes
Chuuk is a possible port for making crew changes, having reasonably frequent airline service to Honolulu and Guam. There is no internal airline service.

Information Center
Office of Tourism and Commerce
Chuuk State Government
Weno, Chuuk FM 96942
USA

toes and some tapioca. Other crops grown include bananas, sugar cane, squash, papaya, green beans, green peppers, Chinese cabbage, cucumbers, watermelons, and pineapples. Limes, oranges, and mangoes are also found on the high islands. The gardens are usually intermixed with many different plants in one plot.

The most important subsistence crops are breadfruit (eaten fresh or preserved in pits for the off season) and taro. Green leafy vegetables are not an important part of the Chuukese diet, although several are grown. Pigs and chickens are also raised, but their use is restricted to special occasions.

The principal island of Chuuk state is Weno. The heart of the town making up this island is in the saddle between two steep, knobby hills. Here in the saddle stand the hospital, state offices, high school, and courthouse—all new and modern. Along the shore there is a mixture of architecture with the new metal post office and warehouse and concrete bank and office buildings blending with older rusting metal and driftwood-finish structures.

The beauty of Chuuk does not lie so much with its "modern" buildings as it does with its setting. A visitor can look beyond the drabness of the Westerners' attempt to urbanize nature and see a breathtaking gallery of mountaintop islands—Tol, Udot, Dublon, and others rising out of a sparkling blue lagoon.

Not all the beauty lies above the waterline, for in this immense lagoon is some of the most spectacular underwater scenery in the world. Starting with the natural coral growth of the reefs, one finds it to be a fairyland of color and shape inhabited by fish of wondrous color, too curious of people to be afraid. Humans themselves have added to the attractions of this underwater Disneyland of the Pacific. In the latter days of World War II, the Americans caught much of the remaining Japanese fleet at anchor in Chuuk lagoon and sent more than 60 vessels to the bottom in a fiery melee that partially revenged the attack on Pearl Harbor. The ships found not so much a watery grave as a chance to become actors in the underwater drama that is Chuuk lagoon today. Diving is a natural adjunct to cruising, and nowhere is it better than in Chuuk lagoon.

The Weather

The Caroline Islands are under the influence of the doldrums belt from June through November. During this period, heavy rains, thunderstorms, and violent squalls will sometimes offer hazards. Cumulus and cumulonim-bus clouds with ceilings sometimes as low as 500 to 1,000 feet for short periods, poor visibility, lightning, and confused seas accompany the more intense of these storms. Most are of short duration and seldom cover an area larger than 20 or 25 miles in diameter. The storms usually move from east to west and occur most frequently at about 0600.

Northeasterly trades blow almost constantly from December to May over the Mortlock and Chuuk islands. The average speed is about 15 knots with an occasional gust of 30 knots. Light, variable winds can be expected from July to December. The influence of the doldrums is felt for a longer period (June to November) over the Mortlocks. During May and June, the trades decrease in force and intensity, with more east and south winds. As a rule, the winds increase during the morning hours and decrease during the night.

In the Chuuk group the northeast trades are very steady. Between November and June 85 percent of the winds flow from north-northeast to east directions. By July, however, the indraft of the summer monsoon carries easterly to southerly winds from this area into Asian waters. Then through October, the trade winds are overshadowed by various southerly to westerly breezes with an average 13 percent of calms.

Northward of the Chuuk Islands is a region of typhoon development. As a rule, however, such storms do not reach full development until they pass west of Guam. They occur more frequently in late summer or autumn.

Much rain occurs in all months in the eastern Caroline Islands. The Chuuk Islands receive an average 121 inches annually with a maximum of 12 inches per month occurring in July and August and a minimum of 6 inches in January. January, February, and March show average rainfall somewhat under 10 inches per month. Thunderstorms are common between May and October.

The Mortlock Islands usually have their heaviest rainfall between June and October. Winter and early spring, the so-called dry season, has an average of seven or eight inches of rainfall per month. The rain falls mostly at night with a maximum during the early morning hours, usually decreasing rapidly after sunrise. Minimum rainfall and cloudiness can be expected between 0900 and 1400.

A tropical ocean climate prevails in the Chuuk Islands, producing a mean temperature of about 80°F with a daily variation of only 10°F. Humidity is also very constant at about 83 percent.

Cruising Notes

YACHT FACILITIES

The capital of Chuuk state is on Weno Island near the northeast pass to the lagoon. There is no detailed chart of this area because the United States is still using primarily Japanese chart information. Japanese headquarters before and during World War II were on adjacent Dublon Island, and the main ship anchorage then was Eten anchorage, which is well charted.

Today's Chuuk harbor is on the west side of Weno Island in an area called Uola Road. Caution must be exercised when approaching Weno Island for, as the U.S. *Sailing Directions* say, "Weno Island is fringed with reefs and fronted by dangers." Besides the reefs there are innumerable wrecks of Japanese warships in these waters.

The main harbor facility, Baker Dock, has a 300-foot-long pier at its north entrance where a visiting yacht can tie up to check in and reprovision. Some dockage facilities also exist inside the south entrance to the small harbor.

The state offices, hospital, and some stores are a short distance to the northeast of the harbor in the saddle between the hills. The famous Chuuk Trading Company, a general store with an amazing line of merchandise, is across the road from Baker Dock as are the post office and some additional stores.

Some fresh foods can be obtained on Weno, and many canned products are available. At the latest report, prohibition was in force on the island of Weno to reduce the number of alcohol-related crimes. Other islands of the lagoon permit the sale of beer, wine, and other alcoholic beverages.

While most provisions can be found at the Chuuk Trading Company and other stores, few boat supplies are available any place in Chuuk. Gasoline and diesel fuel are available at the docks. There are no repair facilities for boats. Although potable water is said to flow through the water lines at the dock, the cholera epidemic of 1982 should be enough to warn yachts not to

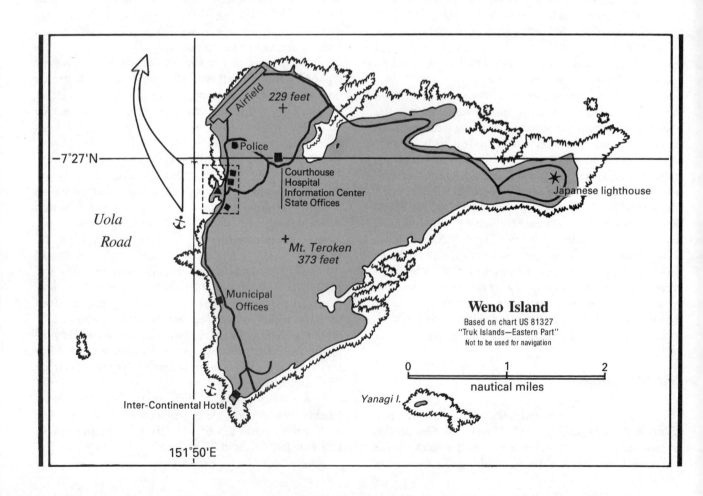

Weno Island
Based on chart US 81327
"Truk Islands—Eastern Part"
Not to be used for navigation

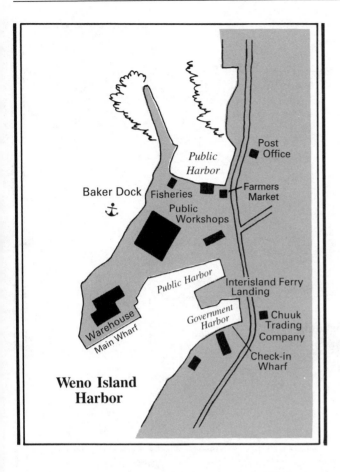

Weno Island Harbor

A seaplane ramp on the island of Dublon has become the laundry for a local woman. (Earl Hinz)

use any public water. It is better to collect rainwater on board your own boat.

Yachts visiting the capital island of Weno should pay particular attention to their safety while there. Alcohol-related crimes have in the past occurred regularly. Several thefts and one vicious beating of an American husband-wife crew took place in 1982. A number of visiting yachts have found the anchorage area south of the harbor in front of the Inter-Continental Hotel a more pleasant place to stay.

YAP

The Country

Yap state consists of 16 island units that contain 145 individual islands with a total land area of 46 square miles. The units include the Yap islands proper, five single-island formations, and ten atolls. Four of the island units—Gaferut, West Fayu, Pikelot, and Olimarao—are usually uninhabited, as are many of the small island components of the other units. In 1990 about 65 percent of the state's total population of 13,000 resided on the Yap islands proper.

Yap "proper" is made up of four major islands—Rumung, Map, Gagil-Tomil, and Yap—separated by narrow passages and surrounded on various shores by fringing or barrier reefs or both. The total land area of these four islands is about 39 square miles. The main island, Yap, is divided in the north portion by a range of hills, 585 feet high at its highest elevation, which separates the inhabited east- and west-coast villages. The southern end flattens out to coastal plains more nearly resembling the low-island formations. Roads extend several miles north of Colonia, along the east coast of the main island, and to the southern tip. Vehicle travel to some parts of the island is difficult and to others

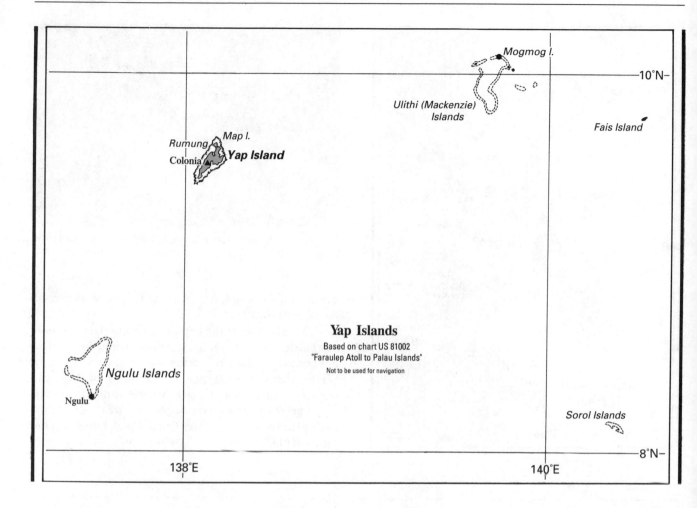

Yap Islands
Based on chart US 81002
"Faraulep Atoll to Palau Islands"
Not to be used for navigation

impossible. Canoes and small boats are still the major form of intraisland transportation.

The outer islands to the east are low atolls with the exception of Fais, which is a raised coral atoll. During the Japanese occupation of Fais, phosphate was mined for fertilizer. Most of the atolls have lagoons although a few are without, making landings difficult during heavy surf. The largest of the atolls is Ulithi which was an important staging area for the U.S. fleet during the closing days of World War II.

Only Yap, Ulithi, and Woleai, the largest of the major islands, are inhabited. In the other atolls, particularly the Ulithi and Woleai group, are numerous unpopulated islands so small that they are little more than coral dots on the ocean. The origins of the outer islanders are unknown, and their folklore sheds little light on the question.

The first Westerner to see the islands constituting Yap state was probably the Portugese captain Diego DaRocha in 1526, but little happened as far as further European contact was concerned until the emergence of the copra trade in the Pacific. The Spanish government proclaimed its sovereignty over the islands in 1874. The British and the Germans protested, and the dispute was submitted to the pope for adjudication. He ruled in favor of the Spanish but gave the Germans free trade in the area.

In 1885 the Spanish set up their headquarters on Yap to administer the whole of the Western Carolines. It was staffed by a governor, secretary, physician, and 50 Filipino soldiers. They were accompanied by six Capuchin priests and lay brothers.

Aside from the missionary activities, the Spanish had little involvement in the islands, whereas the Germans were heavily involved in the copra business. In 1899 Yap, along with the remaining island possessions of Spain, was sold outright to Germany, which set up headquarters on Yap with branches in the Marianas and Palau.

The German occupation was efficient from both a

YAP STATE

A member of the Federated States of Micronesia

Ports of Entry

Colonia, Yap	9°30′ N, 138°08′ E
Falalop, Ulithi	10°01′ N, 139°08′ E

Distances between Ports in Nautical Miles

Between Colonia and

Agana, Guam	450
Chuuk, FSM	1,200
Falalop, Ulithi	105
Honolulu, Hawaii	3,750
Koror, Palau	255
Kosrae, FSM	1,500
Madang, Papua New Guinea	995
Majuro, Marshall Islands	1,980
Manila, Philippine Islands	1,050
Pohnpei, FSM	1,200
Saipan, Mariana Islands	565
Tokyo, Japan	1,575

Standard Time

10 hours fast on UTC

---

political standpoint and a business standpoint. The Germans were skillful rulers and were able to maintain law and order much more effectively with native police than the Spanish were with their military garrison.

During the period of German occupation much of the Pacific telephone cable was completed. A German firm completed the Yap-Guam, Yap-Celebes, and Yap-Shanghai sections in 1905. The cable provided a brief economic stimulus to Yap trade but foreshadowed later international complications over cable operation. Between 1919 and 1921 the United States and Japan became embroiled in a major international dispute over the cable system.

German control of the Yap Islands passed to the Japanese in 1914 when Japan occupied most of the islands of the western Pacific at the beginning of World War I. They exploited the islands for food and later established military bases that were to become key elements in their attempt to expand their empire in World War II. The only island of the Yap group to be captured by U.S. forces prior to the Japanese surrender in 1945 was the island of Ulithi. Its spacious lagoon was desired as a staging area for the Pacific fleet's final drive on the Japanese homeland.

Yap is probably best known for its stone money. "Coins" vary in size from 6 inches in diameter to wheels 12 feet in diameter. The money is always circular with a hole through the center so it can be carried on a pole. The material is aragonite, which has a crystalline pattern and the hardness of marble. The raw material for these stone wheels was, surprisingly, found not on Yap but on the island of Palau almost 300 miles away. The effort required to quarry the stone, carve it into wheels, and transport it to Yap is what gave the money its value. You might think that stone money was a difficult medium of exchange to handle, but it really wasn't. Stone money was rarely handled or moved from its place of "deposit." It was really more a measure of the wealth of the individual and was highly visible to all.

No history of Yap can be complete without introducing "His Majesty" Captain O'Keefe, an enterprising American trader and ship owner, or a scalawag, depending on your point of view. After being shipwrecked on Yap in 1871, O'Keefe established a trading headquarters there during the late Spanish and early German rule. His trading took him throughout the western Caroline Archipelago, along the coasts of New Guinea and the Philippines, and as far north as Hong Kong.

O'Keefe's success was largely a result of his keen appreciation of the Yap culture and an understanding of the significance of stone money. He was able to motivate the Yapese to sail with him to Palau and there quarry the stone money, which he transported back to Yap. The workers, in turn, supplied him with much copra and trepang, which he marketed in Hong Kong at a fabulous profit. Not a man to stop short of total success, O'Keefe continued to captain one of his trading vessels and was eventually lost at sea in a tropical storm.

The most important form of property in Yap is land, almost all of which is owned by the Yapese. Land not only provides subsistence and building materials, but also determines one's status and role in the community. A man becomes a chief or magician because of the land he holds, and Yapese often say "the man is not chief, the land is chief."

The majority of Yapese subsist on an economy of gardening, harvesting, and fishing. Crops include taro, yams, sweet potatoes, bananas, Polynesian chestnuts, breadfruit, papayas, oranges, cassava, coconuts, pineapple, and tobacco. Chickens and pigs are raised, but they are eaten only on special occasions.

Another crop, and an unusual one, is the betelnut. The areca palm, which bears the betelnuts, was probably not an indigenous plant but was introduced from other places well in advance of the arrival of the Spanish. Betelnuts are about the size of a small chicken egg, orange in color and covered by a fibrous husk. The meat of the nut is wrapped in a leaf of the pepper vine with a

Roads of any kind are scarce in Yap, and we reached this rural residence after a one-mile walk along a well-used foot trail bordered with flaming red hibiscus shrubs. (Earl Hinz)

small amount of burnt coral lime and then chewed but never swallowed. The reaction of the lime and betelnut produces a blood-red color. Betelnut chewing results in a discoloration and eventual destruction of tooth enamel. It has a mild narcotic effect on the chewer and also kills certain intestinal parasites.

Fish are an important source of protein to these islands whose waters contain bountiful marine resources. Fish traps, spears, large nets, and the hook and line are all used. Stone fish weirs are clearly discernible from the air as huge arrows in the shallow waters of the lagoons. The Yapese go fishing in the boats and canoes they have built completely without the use of nails.

Orange-colored shell necklaces—some adorned with the teeth of dugongs or whales—and pearl oyster shells are other forms of valuables used in ceremonial exchanges, settlements of disputes, and for funerals, marriages, and other important rites.

Western-style clothes are worn by Yapese living and working in Colonia (not to be confused with Kolonia on Pohnpei Island) and by others when visiting the state capital; but in all of the villages, traditional attire is worn. Yapese clothing is simple and scanty in this warm climate but not without meaning. A man wears a loin cloth called a *thu* and upon reaching early manhood adds a bunch of hibiscus bark which passes between the thighs and is attached front and back to the thu. In the past, the color of a man's thu denoted his social standing.

A woman's dress is a full and heavy-waisted grass skirt. Upon reaching womanhood she adds a black cord looped around the neck. Yapese women are skilled in the weaving of cloth for use in clothing or household articles.

The traditional Yapese house is large with a hexagonal floor and a steep thatched roof that juts out all around. This type of dwelling is, however, being replaced by smaller, flimsier, and less aesthetic houses with corrugated metal or thinly thatched roofs. Most villages also have a large men's house where the men of the village get together to talk and sleep.

The early Spanish missionary influence is strongly felt in Yap, where 90 percent of the people are Christians, most of them Roman Catholic. There is one Protestant mission on Yap proper. The native religion with its priest-magicians and sacred places still functions and commands respect even among many of the Christians. There are noted to be, however, fewer and fewer young men being trained in the native religious practices.

The language of the Yap islands belongs to the Malayo-Polynesian language family that extends from Malaysia to Easter Island. Yapese, however, is so distinctly different from other languages as to be unintelligible even to other Micronesians. The Ulithians residing only 100 miles from Yap speak a language more related to Chuukese.

As small as the Yap Islands are, enough dialectal differences exist in the different regions that a Yapese is able to distinguish the regional origin of another Yapese by subtle speech differences.

Yapese is a complex language with 13 vowel sounds and 32 consonants. Its grammar has numerous tenses and some "extra" (to English speakers) features such as the distinction in number between singular, dual, and plural. Yapese vocabulary is rich and adequate to cover any local situation. Where new materials and concepts have been introduced by foreigners, foreign words have been adopted into the Yapese vocabulary.

Changes in foreign administration have left the Yapese largely bilingual. Many speak both Yapese or Ulithian and Japanese. Many also speak English, and a few speak Palauan and German.

The Yapese experienced a severe decline in their population after contact with the Europeans. From a high of about 10,000 people in 1869, the population steadily declined through the period of Japanese administration, when it hit a low of 2,500. After World War II there was an appreciable growth as indicated by the 1990 population of 13,000 living in the state.

The Yapese have long fascinated anthropologists studying what is changing and what is unchanged in the most reserved, most socially complicated of Micronesia's islands. You don't have to be a scholar to wonder at Yap or to speculate about what is past or yet to come. The state capital of Colonia is a study in contrasts with the properties of the modern world—motorcycles, beer, and juke boxes—absorbed into a culture of grass skirts, loin cloths, and betelnut. Away from Colonia, and not too far away at that, life continues little changed in a world of tranquil beaches, thatched roofs, stone money, and ceremonial dances. On such outer islands as Ulithi, Faraulep, Woleai, Eauripik, and Satawal, life goes on much as it did a half century ago.

A Yapese canoe typical of those found throughout the Caroline Islands. (Continental Airlines)

Women of Lamotrek atoll in the Western Carolines (a part of Yap State) participate in an evening fireside sing, which pits the voices from the northern islets of the atoll against those from the southern islets. (Gary Brookins)

FLOTSAM AND JETSAM

Currency
The U.S. dollar is the official medium of exchange.

Language
The native tongue, Yapese, is commonly spoken by the Yapese among themselves. English is the second language and is spoken by everybody in government and business.

Electricity
Electric power, where available, is 110v, 60 Hz AC.

Postal Address (U.S. Postal Service)
Yacht ( )
Poste Restante
Colonia, Yap FM 96943
USA

Ports for Making Crew Changes
Colonia is a marginal port for making crew changes because of inadequate airline service. Airline service from Guam and Honolulu is infrequent, and seats are sometimes not available at Colonia. Guam would be a better port for changing crew.

Information Center
Office of Tourism and Commerce
Yap State Government
Colonia, Yap FM 96943
USA

The Weather

The northeast trades are firmly established in January when northeast or east winds blow 89 percent of the time with an average speed of 6 knots but occasionally exceeding 25 knots. The trades prevail from February through May with a gradual decrease in frequency to 68 percent in May and a slight decrease in speed. During June the trades weaken noticeably and the winds veer to the southeast.

The doldrum belt oscillates back and forth over the Yap Islands area from July through September and is the principal climatic control during this period. It is accompanied by light, variable winds, mostly with a southerly component, and frequent calms. Strong and gusty winds occur with periods of squally weather. In October light southwest winds prevail, although northeast trades become reestablished during November and December.

Gales average one a month in March and may occur occasionally at other times. Wind speeds during the entire year are somewhat higher over the open ocean.

Typhoons sometimes occur in the Yap Islands area, usually in May and June but sometimes later in the

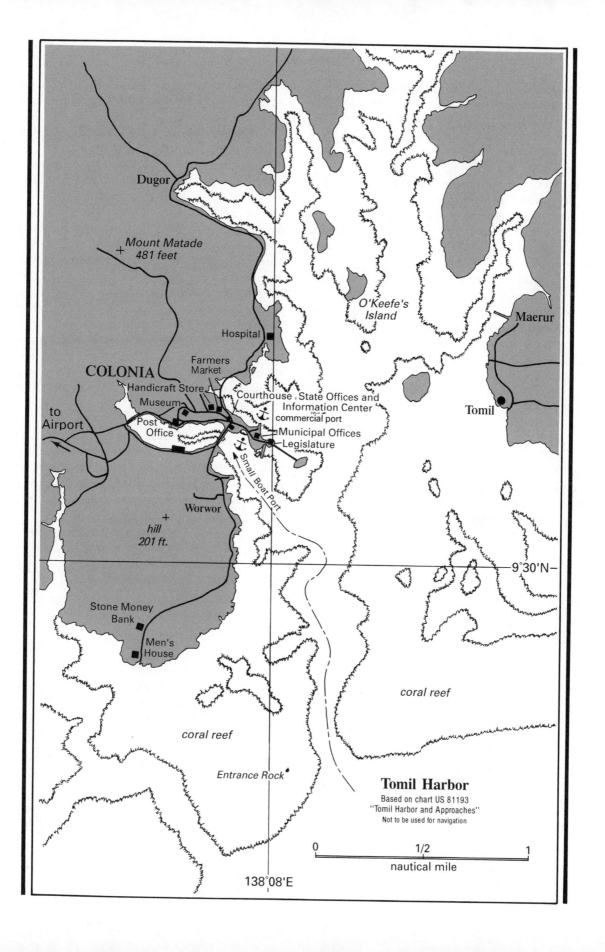

Dugor

Mount Matade
481 feet

Hospital

Farmers
Market

COLONIA

Handicraft Store

Museum

Post
Office

to
Airport

O'Keefe's
Island

Maerur

Courthouse , State Offices and
Information Center
commercial port

Municipal Offices
Legislature

Tomil

Small Boat Port

Worwor

hill
201 ft.

9°30'N—

Stone Money
Bank

Men's
House

coral reef

coral reef

Entrance Rock

Tomil Harbor

Based on chart US 81193
"Tomil Harbor and Approaches"
Not to be used for navigation

0   1/2   1

nautical mile

138°08'E

year. Although the nominal path of typhoons is north of Yap, three or four per year pass close enough to affect the weather at Yap. Typhoons centered north of Yap cause heavy showers and increasing winds from the west. The swell is heavy from the northwest and causes a heavy, confused cross sea.

In the vicnity of Yap Islands during the period July through September, the light, variable winds leave the surface calm, except for the choppy seas that develop during squalls. For the remainder of the year the prevailing winds maintain a swell of about 4 feet in height and 150 feet in wave length in the open sea.

Fog is virtually unknown, and visibility is usually very good, except during heavy rains. It has been estimated that visibility below 1¼ miles occurs only once or twice a month from July through September and not more than once a month during the remainder of the year.

Cruising Notes

YACHT FACILITIES

Colonia
The main port for Yap state is at Colonia on Yap Island. It is reached through a 1½-mile-long passage bordered by fringing reefs, making it imperative that you hold to the designated channel. There are numerous fish weirs and traps along the sides of the channels to add to your cares when entering.

The small-craft wharf at Colonia is 230 feet long; depth alongside at mean low water is 13 feet. Space permitting, yachts can tie alongside to get entry clearance. There are also several smaller piers that can be used if empty. Diesel fuel, gasoline, and fresh water are available at the small-craft wharf. There are no slipways or other facilities to work on boats, nor is there any boat hardware available. Government workshops may be able to assist with minor boat or equipment repairs.

The village of Colonia is very small, and everything is within walking distance of the wharf. State offices, post office, and bank are all situated along the southern edge of the peninsula near the port facilities. Across the narrow peninsula to the north are the farmers' market and handicraft store. Fresh fruits and vegetables of limited variety and staple goods are available at the market and local stores, but not in great abundance.

Ulithi
Ulithi is a Port of Entry to Yap, and clearance can be effected at the new government dock at Falalop. Neither fuel nor water is available here, and only locally grown produce in limited quantities can be purchased. There is a medical dispensary on Falalop as well as on Mog Mog.

CHAPTER 25

REPUBLIC OF PALAU

The Country

Palau (Belau) is the westernmost country of the Caroline Archipelago. It consists of six island units that include 349 individual islands with a total land area of 191 square miles. The group is formed directly by the exposed peaks or indirectly by coral capping on still-submerged elevations along the outer edge of the Asian continental shelf. Thus all its islands are classified as continental rather than oceanic in form.

The major island unit is the one known as the Palau cluster. Its main elements are Babelthuap, Koror, Peleliu, and Angaur islands, which are high volcanic islands, and Kayangel Island, which is Palau's only true atoll. The cluster also includes 338 tiny rock islands of little significance. Only the five main islands and three of the lesser ones are permanently inhabited. All but 192 of Palau's total population of 14,000 is concentrated on these islands. All the islands except Angaur and Kayangel are enclosed within a single barrier reef.

Babelthuap is a sizable island that dominates the cluster. It is about 27 miles long, and its area of 153 square miles makes it the second largest single land mass in Micronesia. Although classified as a high island, Babelthuap is not mountainous. It is, rather, an area of gently rolling hills, which reach a maximum height of about 700 feet. The island has one of the few real lakes in the Carolines, Lake Ngardok, which is 3,000 feet long and 1,000 feet wide with a depth of 11 to 12 feet. Most of Babelthuap is composed of volcanic material, but its southeastern corner is raised coral limestone.

Koror Island, which is the capital of Palau, and the war-littered islands of Peleliu and Angaur to the south of Babelthuap are high, rugged formations of raised limestone with considerable portions of exposed volcanic materials. Like Babelthuap, they are covered with a dense growth of trees and bushes in great variety. Kayangel Island, 28 miles north of Babelthuap, but still in the main island complex, is a picture-perfect low

coral atoll having a number of islets encircling its lagoon.

The five other island units of Palau are the tiny islands of Sonsorol, Pulo Anna, Merir, Tobi, and Helen Reef to the south. Tobi and Helen Reef are within 200 miles of New Guinea. These islands are all raised limestone formations. Sonsoral, Tobi, and Pulo Anna have populations of 55, 75, and 15 respectively. The land spit of Helen Reef is inhabited only by birds and turtles while the islet of Mirir is mosquito-ridden; shore parties are advised to wear long-sleeved shirts and full-length trousers when going ashore.

Most of Palau's 191 square miles of land is concentrated in a central cluster of islands stretching 125 miles from the northern tip of Babelthuap to the south beach of Angaur. Babelthuap has ten villages hugging its coastal plains; almost no one, including Palauans, has ventured far into the interior of the jungled island. Just off the southern flanks of Babelthuap is a quite different array of islands—a gay flotilla of emerald hillocks, formerly called the Rock Islands, but now more aptly termed the Floating Garden Islands—dozens and dozens of them laced across the sea.

Wildlife on the Palau islands is relatively scarce. The bat is the only truly indigenous mammal, with dogs, pigs, rats, water buffalo, horses, cattle, goats, and cats arriving by ship during the European period. Palau boasts some of the more unusual animal life, having both the saltwater and New Guinea crocodile. At one time the dugong was quite in evidence, but it has become a rare creature of recent years. The dugong or sea cow is thought to be the basis of the mermaid myth, but those sailors who have observed the creature at close range insist that the resemblance is only slight. Whatever its charms, the dugong is now protected by law from human harm of any kind. There is also a variety of snakes such as the tree snake, mangrove snake, and boa on land and the venomous sea snake in the water.

There is no recorded history of Palau's early years, but folklore and legends have kept many traditions

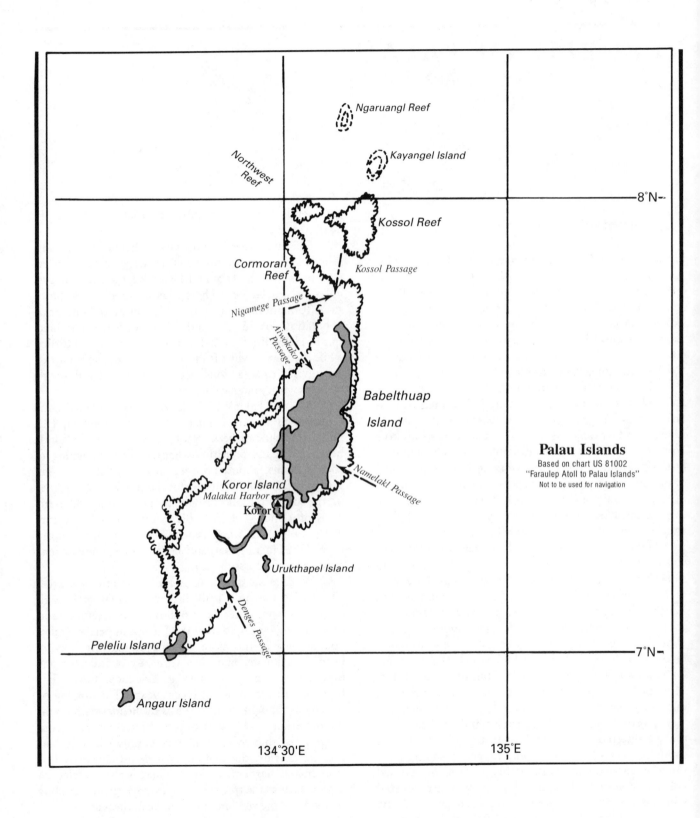

Ngaruangl Reef

Kayangel Island

Northwest Reef

8°N

Kossol Reef

Cormoran Reef

Kossol Passage

Nigamege Passage

Aiwokako Passage

Babelthuap Island

Palau Islands
Based on chart US 81002
"Faraulep Atoll to Palau Islands"
Not to be used for navigation

Namelakl Passage

Koror Island
Malakal Harbor
Koror

Urukthapel Island

Denges Passage

Peleliu Island

7°N

Angaur Island

134°30'E

135°E

PALAU

A provisional self-governing country in free association with the United States

Port of Entry

Koror, Koror Island   7°20′ N, 134°29′ E

Distances between Ports in Nautical Miles

Between Koror and

Agana, Guam	700
Honolulu, Hawaii	3,995
Kosrae, FSM	1,705
Madang, Papua New Guinea	1,015
Majuro, Marshall Islands	2,190
Manila, Philippine Islands	905
Pohnpei, FSM	1,415
Saipan, Mariana Islands	815
Tokyo, Japan	1,725
Yap, FSM	250

Standard Time

9 hours fast on UTC

Public Holidays and Special Events

January 1	New Year's Day—Public holiday
January*	Martin Luther King Day—Public holiday
February*	Presidents' Day—Public holiday
March/April*	Easter
March 15	Youth Day
May*	Palau Annual Fair—Handicraft sales, sports events, parades, and traditional music
May 1	Constitution Day—Public holiday
May 15	Senior Citizens Day
May*	Memorial Day—Public holiday
July 4	Independence Day—Public holiday
July 9	Constitution Day—Public holiday
September*	Labor Day—Public holiday
October*	United Nations Day—Parades and traditional dances
November 11	Veterans Day—Public holiday
November*	Thanksgiving—Public holiday
December 25	Christmas—Public holiday

*Specific dates vary from year to year.

alive. Until its first contact with Europeans, Palau was a world unto itself, with a culture all its own. Occasionally people drifted in canoes from the Philippines, from Indonesia, and from other islands to the west, but these were assimilated into the Palauan culture. About the time of the first Western contact in 1783, the Palauan world was divided into the competing embryonic semistates of Babelthuap and Youlthuap. Capitals for the governing village clusters were at Koror and Melekeok, respectively, and diplomatic exchanges occurred between the aristocratic chiefs of the chronically warring semistates.

Some evidence of these earlier cultures are preserved in stone such as the eerie "Stonehenge" near the northern tip of Babelthuap, which is locally called the House of Giants. It is a row of five-ton stones surmised to have supported an *abai,* or meeting house, capable of sheltering thousands of persons. Along the east coast are scattered other reminders of Babelthuap's undeciphered past: the stone paths of Ngaraard and the dock and the stone heads at Melekeok.

Since being sighted by the sixteenth-century voyagers, Palau has known a succession of foreign rulers. Spain's rule, beginning in the eighteenth century, was ended by the Spanish-American War. Germany's occupation ended with the appearance of Japanese gunboats in 1914 at the beginning of World War I. Japan's mandate was finished and America's started with the Japanese defeat in World War II. Each of these foreign rulers left distinctive marks on Palau in language, religion, and architecture.

First called Los Palaos by the Spaniards after the native *praus,* or canoes, the group of 6 major islands and 343 islets comprising the area came to be called Palau in the eighteenth century.

Direct administration by Spain was not established until 1885, when the Palau group was ruled by a resident governor at Yap. From 1885 through 1889 Spanish rule was exercised through the Jesuit priests in residence. Their chief influences were the introduction of Christianity and the alphabet and their success in putting a stop to intervillage warfare.

Palau was sold to Germany in 1899 along with the rest of the Caroline and Mariana Islands (except Guam which became a U.S. Territory after the Spanish-American War.) German concerns were directed at increasing the economic potential of the islands without disturbing the aboriginal chieftainship structure any more than necessary. The Germans introduced a program of coerced coconut planting and sanitary measures to stem the epidemic of Western contagious diseases. They established phosphate mining on Angaur Island where Palauans, for the first time, met fellow Micronesians from such distant islands as Chuuk and Pohnpei.

Germany, however, was not able to realize the benefits of these developments before Palau was taken over by the Japanese forces at the beginning of World War I. Together with the other German islands of the Pacific, Palau became part of a League of Nations mandate granted to Japan in 1920.

The Japanese occupation of Palau can be viewed in three distinct administrative time periods: (1) 1914 to 1922, when the Japanese navy ruled the islands and a conscientious effort was made to follow the German precedent of development through working with the native institutions; (2) 1922 to 1942, when the islands were under the civilian rule of the Japanese South Seas Bureau and the goals were intensive economic expansion, rapid colonization, and increasingly direct rule; and (3) the wartime period of 1942 to 1945, when the Japanese rule deteriorated as a result of the pressure of military needs and the attrition of food supplies.

In the early 1930s the Japanese Home Office applied pressure to make the islands pay, and increased emphasis was placed on mining, agriculture, and commercial fishing. Since the supply of local manpower was inadequate, Japanese, Okinawan, and Korean colonists were introduced until the colonists outnumbered the natives by one and a half to one.

Under the Japanese, the Palauans came to realize and appreciate the values of education and modernization even though universal education was limited to three years of elementary schooling that stressed speaking ability. No attempt was made to school them in understanding the administrative and technological means by which a modern economic state is formed. Palau as a whole prospered under Japanese entrepreneurship. Almost every available economic resource in the area, from fishing to charcoal manufacture, was exploited; but the Palauans received only minimal side benefits from the resulting prosperity.

The Japanese had been covertly fortifying Palau and other islands of the Pacific during the 1930s in defiance of the League of Nations mandate. War, however, did not come to Palau until September 15, 1944, when an Allied invasion force attacked Angaur and Peleliu. A planned four-day takeover that turned into a ten-week battle showed how well the Japanese had fortified the islands and manned them for defense. Losses amounted to 1,800 Americans dead and 8,000 wounded. The Japanese suffered 14,000 dead.

When the United States assumed administration of the Palaus under the Trust Territory of the Pacific mandate, the Palauans were encouraged by the new Western democratic concept and the doctrine of free economic enterprise. They were eager to accelerate the process of economic change started under the previous administration. The continued progress is evident in building construction, transportation, sawmills, furniture industries, and the like owned and operated by Palauans. Palau today is headed on an irreversible and occasionally rocky road toward cosmopolitan modernization, partly from outside suggestion but largely from internal momentum over the years.

The Palauan people are a composite of several races indicating a long history of racial intermingling. Its geographical position has placed it on the threshold of the Pacific, and numerous waves of migration passed through the area into Oceania. Today one can observe racial blends including Polynesian, itself a complex racial blend; Malayan with its strong Mongoloid strain; and Melanesian. The Mongoloid admixture has been deepened in recent years through Japanese involvement, and most recently, the Caucasian strain has been added.

Aboriginal Palauan culture was a relatively complex one for Oceania since it combined high island and atoll environments. It combined the taro and yam agriculture of the women with the fishing and hunting skills of the men. Palauan villages have always been situated along the coastline or on a waterway leading to the reef-protected tidal waters. The many islands and rivers were ideal for supporting subsistence economy of a large population. One can find on many of the islands numerous terraced hillsides, now abandoned, on which an expanded population sought its existence.

The aboriginal political unit was the village, led by the chief's council and united in confederations that in turn had their councils of chiefs. The village organizations consisted of ten totemic clans hierarchially oriented through the mother's lineage in a system that exists today. The official 1990 census put Palau's population at 14,300.

Palauan history and culture can be studied in the Palau Museum on Koror, which houses handicrafts, artifacts, and documents dating more than a hundred years back in history. A traditional *abai* has been built on the museum grounds, and next door is the Entomology Station, where well-groomed examples of Palauan flora and fauna are displayed.

The most famous product of Palauan craftsman is the storyboard—a long, wooden plank artfully carved to illustrate local legends. Other traditional handicrafts include ornate wooden money jars and turtleshell ornaments formerly worn as jewelry.

Koror, with its population of about 7,000, may be the settlement with the most distinctive individual character. To be sure, the houses by and large rely on the corrugated metal so incongruously commonplace throughout Micronesia. The roads are just now beginning to see paving over the lengths of pitted obstacle courses. About Koror there linger the traces of a distinguished pre–World War II community, and it may be this sense of the past that renders the present tolerable and the future promising. Palauans can remember when Koror, with a population almost six times the current figure, was the bustling administrative center of the Jap-

Palau is noted for its storyboards —legends of the past told in wood carvings and paintings. The community house of Airai on Babelthuap Island is one large storyboard. Note the solar panels on the roof ridge for generating electricity. (Earl Hinz)

anese Trust Territory. Today only traces remain—a sadly abbreviated stretch of paved road called "geisha lane," a Shinto shrine, seaplane ramps, Japanese-type houses, or, more likely, tin and wood shanties perched on much wider concrete foundations and entered by a flight of imperial steps. In Japanese times the population of Koror was overwhelmingly non-Palauan, but after World War II Palauans moved into the ruined colonial city and claimed it as their own. Today Koror is a growing commercial center with hotels, movie theaters, numerous bars, countless stores, and a growing sense of its own potential. Fishing and tourism both have firm footholds in Palau today, and chances are that Palau will become one of the most rapidly developed of the former Trust Territory districts.

On January 1, 1981, Palau provisionally became the Republic of Palau in Free Association with the United States. It will be governed by a full democratic government modeled after the United States with executive, legislative, and judicial branches. The legislative branch consists of an elected House of Delegates and a Senate. Each of the 16 states that make up the republic wil be represented. To preserve traditional laws and customs, the president will be advised by a Council of Hereditary Chiefs representing the 16 states of Palau. Koror was the district center in the Trust Territory and has been retained as the government seat for the new republic.

The future course of action for full independence

FLOTSAM AND JETSAM

Currency
The U.S. dollar is the official medium of exchange.

Language
The native tongue, Palauan, is commonly spoken by the Palauans among themselves. English is the second language and is spoken by everybody involved in government and business.

Electricity
Electric power, where available, is 110v, 60 Hz AC.

Postal Address (U.S. Postal Service)
Yacht ( )
General Delivery
Koror, Palau PW 96940
USA

Ports for Making Crew Changes
Koror is a possible port for making crew changes, with reasonably frequent airline connections to Guam. However, Guam itself would be a better crew-change port.

External Affairs Representative
U.S. consulates and embassies
In Honolulu: Palau-Hawaii Liaison Office
                1441 Kapiolani Blvd., Suite 1120
                Honolulu, HI 96814, USA

Information Center
Palau Tourist Commission
Koror, Palau, PW 96940
USA

The rock islands of Palau form one of the most beautiful areas of Micronesia. Wave action undercuts the soft limestone of the islands, giving the smaller ones the appearance of giant mushrooms. (Continental Airlines)

of the Republic of Palau is uncertain. The United States wants to retain access, including the transit of nuclear submarines, to parts of the islands for defense. Palau's present constitution forbids the presence of any nuclear devices. This disagreement has prevented the termination of the trusteeship for this country even though all the other islands of the former Trust Territory have been released from trusteeship. The picture is further complicated by the Philippine government's refusal to extend the leases on Subic Bay Naval Station and Anderson Air Force Base on Luzon. Palau is the nearest neighbor to the Philippines that could provide the needed facilities. It appears there will be more years of debate and negotiation before Palau becomes an independent country in free association with the United States. In the meantime, the headquarters of the Trust Territory of the Pacific Islands will remain on Palau serving this one remaining political entity under its jurisdiction.

The Weather

Palau is under the influence of the trades and monsoons, with northeasterly winds in the winter months and winds tending westerly in the summer. In the traditional Palauan calendar, the winter months are known as *ongos,* meaning "northeast," which is the direction of the prevailing winds at that time. The summer period is known as *negebard,* meaning "southwest" or the direction of the prevailing monsoonal wind in the summer.

The Palau Islands lie on the eastern edge of the monsoon belt; here the northeast trades and the north-east monsoons merge, creating winds of 12 to 14 knots on the open ocean in the winter and spring months of December through April. In May the winds over this area diminish and blow mostly from the east, at which time the southwest monsoon is beginning to set in. In summer and in early autumn, July to October, the southwest monsoon prevails over the area. In October and November the northeast trades again become established, setting up winds of 12 to 14 knots during the winter months. Between the periods of the northeast trades and the southwest monsoon, the winds may be variable.

Rain occurs at all seasons in the Palau Islands area, but it is least during the period of the northeast monsoon. Squally conditions, however, appear to occur more frequently from November to January, as the northeast monsoon is gradually established against the variable south to easterly winds of preceding months. Thunderstorms are rare from January to April but fairly common from May through August.

At Babelthuap, 148 inches of rain occurs annually, with 20 inches in July and slightly more than 7 inches in March. Rainfall is somewhat lighter over the open sea. Precipitation occurs on about 50 percent of the days from February through April and on approximately 75 percent during July through September. The heaviest rains occur during the early morning with a secondary maximum soon after sunset.

While gales seldom occur in the Palau area, typhoons do, on the average of two a year. September is the most common month, but July, August, and October have almost as many. Typhoons are least frequent during February. The normal typhoon movement is north of the Palau Islands heading west at 12 to 13 knots. The typhoon diameters are usually small, if that is any consolation.

Typhoon Mike roared through the Koror area in November 1990 with 200 mph winds doing much damage. The local fishing and other boats were severely hit.

Cruising Notes

YACHT ENTRY

The official Port of Entry for the Republic of Palau is the commercial port at Malakal Harbor. Most cruising boats stay at Malakal Harbor when visiting Koror and its environs.

CUSTOMS

There is a one-time entry tax of US$50 on each boat payable after arrival; this applies to recreational as well as commercial vessels. There are no charges for Customs inspection per se, but overtime charges of approximately US$5 per hour are charged for clearing in on weekends and outside of normal working hours during the week.

MEDICAL MEMO

Immunization Requirements

A valid international certificate of smallpox vaccination is required from travelers who, within the preceding 14 days, have been in a country any part of which is infected. Other immunizations or health measures may be imposed at the time of entry. It is strongly recommended that all travelers have a tetanus inoculation.

Local Health Situation

All of the islands of Palau are nominally free of communicable diseases. Some diseases endemic to the area but not widespread are dysentery, hookworm, infectious hepatitis, and intestinal parasites.

Health Services

There are no private doctors, dentists, or health service facilities in Palau. There is a general hospital in Koror providing hospital and out-patient care; there is also a dental clinic; both are staffed by professional personnel. Each of the other states has a smaller dispensary-type hospital. Fees charged are considerably less than those in the United States.

Prescription and nonprescription drugs are available at the main hospital and, to a lesser degree, at the smaller hospitals.

Water

Tap water from the public supply at Koror is reportedly safe, but all other water should be considered suspect and treated. At one time hookworm larvae were reported to be found in the water, but this is no longer true.

Across the Ngemelachel peninsula from the commercial harbor at Malakal is a small boatyard that can handle boats to approximately 20 tons displacement. Although once modern, it has been rendered somewhat obsolete by lack of maintenance. (Earl Hinz)

After you have officially entered Palau and wish to cruise the other islands of the group, get permission from Immigration as well as from the principal chief of the island group. You will find diplomacy a great ally in enjoying these islands.

IMMIGRATION

All yachts including those of U.S. registry sailed by U.S. crews must have a vessel permit to enter the waters of Palau. The permit request should be sent well ahead of the planned visit to:

Chief of Immigration
Ministry of Justice
Republic of Palau
P.O. Box 100
Koror, Palau PW 96940
USA

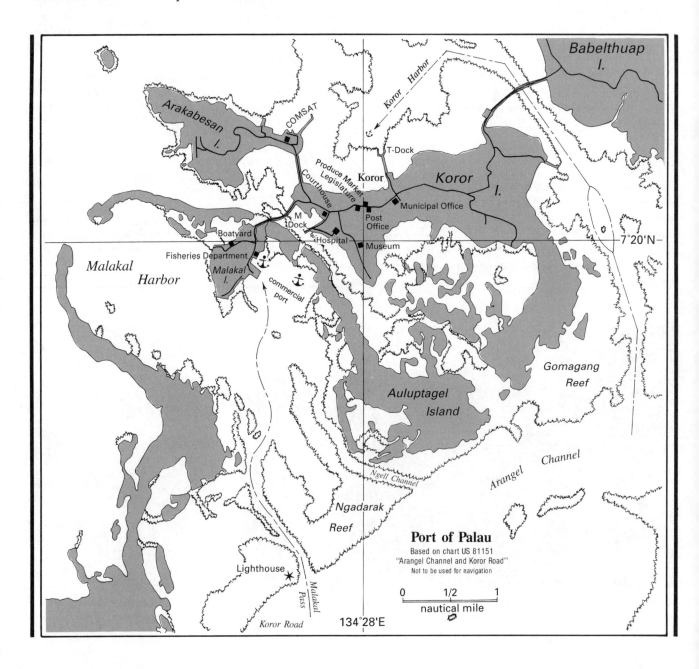

Port of Palau

Based on chart US 81151
"Arangel Channel and Koror Road"
Not to be used for navigation

0   1/2   1
nautical mile

The fee for processing this form is US$75 and covers the first 30 days of your stay. If the fee is not paid before arrival, it is doubled to US$150 payment after arrival. It is possible to get a 30-day permit extended for another 30 days provided that the boat and crew have been on their good behavior for the initial 30 days. Permit extensions beyond the initial 30 days are charged an additional US$100 per 30-day extension.

U.S. citizens entering Palau need proof of citizenship; all others must have a valid passport and a multiple reentry visa. Check the latest requirements for your country of origin. All persons entering Palau for more than 30 days or for purposes other than tourism must have a visitor entry permit approved in advance by the chief of Immigration.

YACHT FACILITIES

Palau's main harbor facilities are on the east side of Malakal Island and consist of one main wharf 510 feet long and several smaller ones, plus a number of deteriorated ones now unusable. It is not advisable to lie alongside the main wharf overnight because sudden high winds and rain squalls may buffet your boat against the concrete wharf. There is good anchorage 200 yards off the wharf.

On the opposite side of Malakal Island is a boatyard that can handle fishing boats up to 100 tons. They carry some miscellaneous boat hardware, mostly for fishing boats. The Fisheries Department alongside the main wharf has some additional supplies.

A second harbor lies to the north of Koror Island. It is called Koror Harbor and is used mostly for interisland trading boats. A small-craft basin exists between the two arms of the pier making up T-dock at the end of Ebadulis pier. You can tie up there for business ashore.

A third harbor and dock, known as M-dock, lies on the south side of Koror Island and is used mostly by local boats who can thread their way safely through the reefs. This area is the most convenient to town but depends on local knowledge of the reefs for safe entry.

The commercial center of the main town of Koror is within walking distance of all three docks; it includes stores, post office, laundromat, bank, hospital, and other small businesses. Causeways and bridges connect the islands of Arakabesan, Malakal, Koror, and Babelthuap. All your immediate needs can be taken care of on foot. The bridge connecting the islands of Koror and Babelthuap, built in 1977, is one of the world's longest single-span bridges.

One finds in Palau an endless array of islands, natural harbors, and sheltered passages, most of which can be visited by the cruising yacht exercising due caution for the fringing reefs throughout the area.

CHAPTER 26

KIRIBATI

The Country

The Republic of Kiribati—made up of the Gilbert Islands, Phoenix Islands, and some parts of the Line Islands—officially came into existence on July 12, 1979, some 87 years after Captain Davis of the British ship *Royalist* first hoisted the Union Jack at Abemama in 1892, making the island a British protectorate. In the interim the Gilbert Islands were a part of the Gilbert-Ellice Islands Colony.

The name of the new republic, Kiribati, is pronounced "kiribas." The Gilbertese alphabet contains only 13 letters and *s* is missing; however, *t* followed by *i* is pronounced as *s*. Kiribati is the Gilbertese spelling for "Gilberts." As another example, the island of Betio in Tarawa Atoll is pronounced "bay-sho." Kiritimati is the Gilbertese of Christmas. The people of Kiribati do not refer to themselves as Kiribatians but as I-Kiribati.

Kiribati consists of 33 islands situated approximately 4 degrees on either side of the equator and stretching from 157°W to 173°E, a distance of about 2,400 miles. The ocean area covered approaches 1½ million square nautical miles. The eastern components—consisting of 8 islands each in the Line and Phoenix groups—are in Polynesia. The western component—consisting of 17 islands all in the Gilbert group—is in Micronesia.

Despite the extent of the ocean area occupied, the total population was only 70,000 in 1990 with 40 percent of those living on Tarawa Atoll. Like most other Westernized islands of the Pacific, the people are leaving the outer islands to seek work in the government center, and they have concentrated themselves in the southern islands of Tarawa Atoll.

All the islands of the republic are low atolls except for Banaba (Ocean Island), which is a raised atoll. The soil of these atolls is a porous mixture of decomposed coral and sand that is incapable of retaining what moisture it does receive. Only pandanus, casuarina, sedges,

and the ubiquitous coconut palm can survive, and even these are sparse. The islanders dig pits in which they are able to accumulate sufficient compost to make a soil that they plant with babai, a swamp taro. But generally the population in the drier parts of Kiribati subsists on coconuts, fruits of the pandanus, and the fish that abound in the lagoons and surrounding ocean. Pressure

---

KIRIBATI

An independent republic within the British Commonwealth

Ports of Entry

Banaba (Ocean) Island	0°52′ S, 169°35′ E
Tarawa	1°21′ N, 172°55′ E
Kiritimati (Christmas) Island	1°59′ N, 157°27′ W
Tabuaeran (Fanning) Island	3°51′ N, 159°22′ W

Distances between Ports in Nautical Miles

Between Tarawa and

Banaba, Kiribati	240
Kanton Island, Kiribati	955
Kiritimati (Christmas), Kiribati	1,780
Funafuti, Tuvalu	700
Honiara, Solomon Islands	1,010
Honolulu, Hawaii	2,085
Majuro, Marshall Islands	360
Nauru (Aiwo District)	380
Fakaofu, Tokelau	1,120

Standard Time (Gilbert Islands)

12 hours fast on UTC

Public Holidays and Special Events

January 1	New Year's Day—Public holiday
March/April*	Island Arts Festival—Held every three years (1993, 1996, etc.)
March/April*	Good Friday, Easter Sunday, and Monday—Public holidays
July 12	Independence Day—Public holiday
August 3	Youth Day—Public holiday
December 25	Christmas Day—Public holiday
December 26	Boxing Day—Public holiday

*Specific dates vary from year to year.

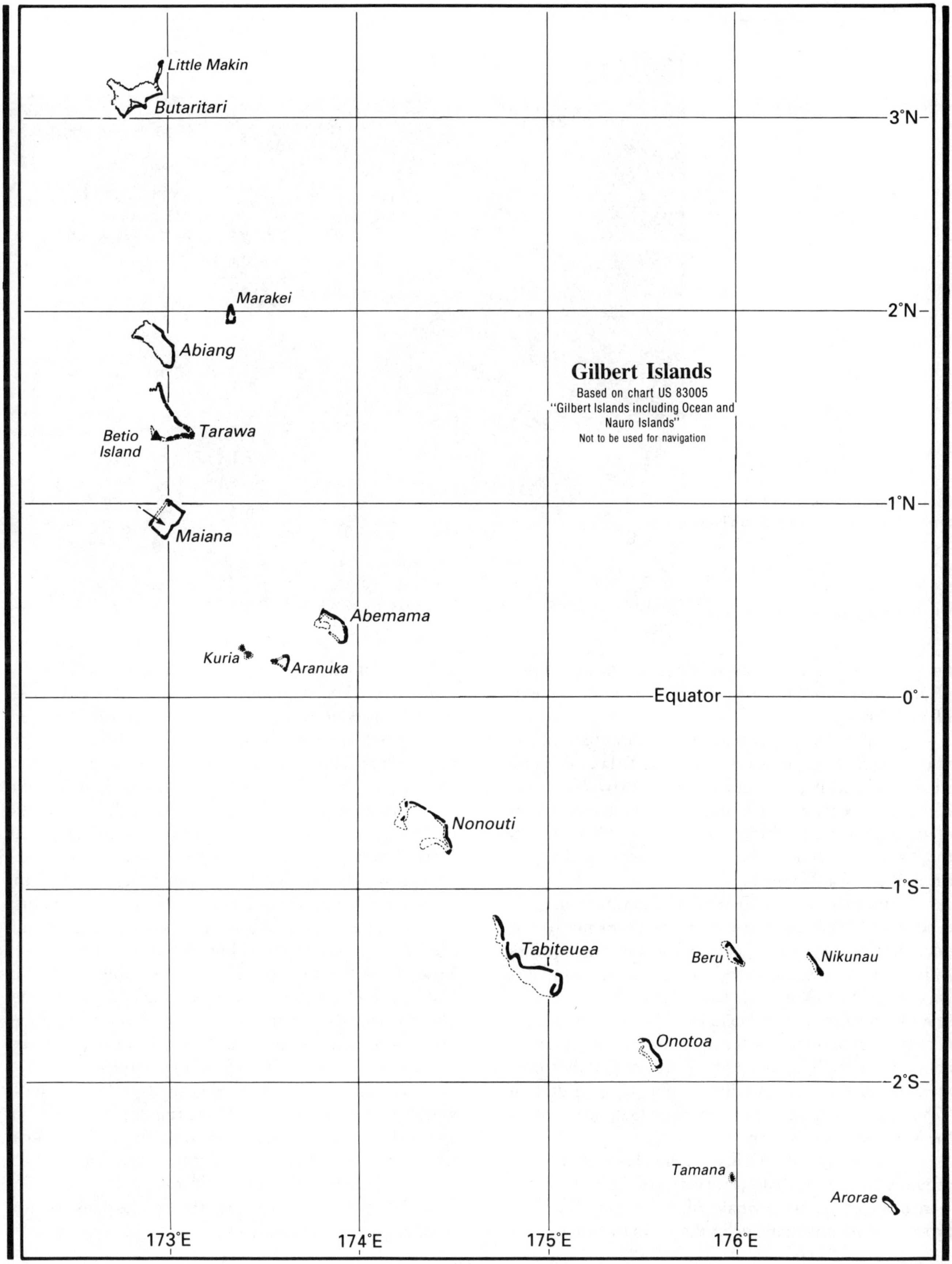

Little Makin

Butaritari

3°N

Marakei

2°N

Abiang

Gilbert Islands
Based on chart US 83005
"Gilbert Islands including Ocean and
Nauro Islands"
Not to be used for navigation

Betio
Island

Tarawa

1°N

Maiana

Abemama

Kuria

Aranuka

Equator — 0°

Nonouti

1°S

Tabiteuea

Beru

Nikunau

Onotoa

2°S

Tamana

Arorae

173°E   174°E   175°E   176°E

Copra is the sole export from Kiribati's Fanning Island. Jacob is displaying copra dried in the large trays. The trays are pushed under the low roof in the background when rain threatens. (Earl Hinz)

on the land is sometimes overtaxing, and groups of people must be removed to areas where food is more plentiful and varied.

Banaba was one of three major phosphate islands in the Pacific being mined for fertilizer (Makatea in the Tuamotus and Nauru were the other two). Now only Nauru is actively mined. Profits from the Banaba phosphate were shared between the country of Kiribati and the Banabans, who for the most part are now living on the island of Rabi in the Fijis.

Although the I-Kiribati believe that they are descendants of Samoans, there is little real evidence to support that or any other genealogical theory. The first Europeans to see the islands were the Spanish; it is believed that de Quiros sighted Butaritari in 1606. Captain Byron stopped at Nikinau in 1765, but it was a random process of discovery for the other islands, spanning about 50 years. The island group was originally named after the British captain Gilbert, who stopped there in 1788 in the company of Captain Marshall, after whom the Marshall Islands are named.

The waters of Kiribati were favorite hunting grounds for sperm whales, and many of the early traders were deserters from the whale ships. Blackbirding (slave procurement) ran rampant in the period from 1850 to

1875, and it led to the creation by Britain in 1877 of the Office of the High Commissioner for the Western Pacific to settle differences between native peoples and the traders. Kiribati was later joined to the Ellice Islands to form the Gilbert-Ellice Islands Colony, which lasted until 1976, when the Ellice Islands separated to form Tuvalu.

Since the Guano Act, passed by the U.S. Congress in 1856, there had been a friendly controversy with Great Britain regarding ownership of eight islands in the Phoenix group and six in the Line group. In 1979 the United States relinquished claim to all of them, and they are now an unquestioned part of Kiribati. These islands are Caroline, Christmas, Flint, Malden, Starbuck, and Vostock in the Line group and the atolls of Birnie, Gardner, Hull, McKean, Phoenix, and Sydney, together with the islands of Kanton and Enderbury in the Phoenix group. The United States will, however, continue some joint ventures on the island of Kanton.

The Gilbert Islands were virtually unknown to the world before World War II. During the early days of 1942 the Japanese occupied several of the Gilbert Islands as part of their expansionist move. They heavily fortified Betio Island in Tarawa Atoll.

After the Japanese southward expansion was stopped at Guadalcanal, the U.S. forces next wanted

Betio Island is an outdoor museum of World War II relics, ranging from Japanese concrete bunkers, which were no match for 16-inch naval guns, to American landing craft that got hung up on the reef due to an error in tidal predictions. This Japanese coastal rifle supposedly came from Singapore after the fall of that city. (Earl Hinz)

Betio as an air base from which to attack the Marshall Islands to the north. In 1943 a great seaborne force comprising hundreds of U.S. ships and airplanes and thousands of marines descended on the strongly fortified Japanese at Betio, and history was made. Seventy-six hours later Betio was a denuded island, and the Japanese force of 4,500 persons ceased to exist. Today only the rusting hulks of tanks, amphtracks, and landing craft dot the water, while on land rusting coastal batteries point to peaceful skies and concrete bunkers sit beneath swaying palm trees and the bright laundry of the island women.

The first European missionary to land in Kiribati was the Reverend Hiram Bingham, a Protestant of the American Board of Commissioners for Foreign Missions from Boston. He established a mission on Abaiang in 1857. Hawaiian and Samoan missionaries spread the new faith through the other Ellice and Gilbert Islands. In 1888 Catholic priests of the Sacred Heart Order began work on the island of Nonouti, and other religious faiths have more recently arrived. Christianity is largely represented in today's Gilbert Islands by the Gilbert Islands Protestant Church and the Roman Catholic Church.

The parliamentary form of government chosen by the I-Kiribati for their new country was based on their knowledge of English government. The Kiribati government is made up of a president, a cabinet, and a House of Assembly. The president and the ministers forming the cabinet are selected from among the 35 members of the elected Assembly.

At island level, local councils are elected, and the elected member of Parliament is an ex-officio member of the council. Each island also has a district administrative officer.

Village government in Kiribati centers on the traditional village *maneaba* (meeting place). It is here, since time immemorial, that the leaders of the village decided the issues by consensus.

There are no local governments in the Phoenix or Line Islands nor on Banaba. A cabinet minister, however, represents the Phoenix and Line islands groups.

The capital of Kiribati is at Tarawa Atoll with government headquarters on the island of Bairiki. Most business and commerce, however, and some government offices are on the adjacent island of Betio.

With the exhaustion of the phosphate resources on Banaba in the 1970s, the economy of Kiribati reverted to copra production and fishing. At present copra is a subsidized crop because of low market prices, but it is

FLOTSAM AND JETSAM

Currency
Kiribati uses Australian currency. The approximate rate of exchange is US$1 = A$1.41.

Language
Gilbertese is the indigenous language of the islanders, but English is the official language understood by just about everybody.

Electricity
Where electricity is available, it is 240v, 50 Hz AC.

Postal Address
Yacht ( )
Poste Restante
Betio, Tarawa
KIRIBATI

Note: Even if your mail is addressed to Betio, it may end up at the Hotel Otintai or the post offices at Bairiki or Bikenibu.

Ports for Making Crew Changes
Tarawa is not a recommended port for making crew changes because of poor airline connections. Although Air Tungaru flies between Honolulu and Tarawa, it does so only about once a week. Twice-weekly flights go to Nauru, but that is still not a good port. (See next chapter.) The closest recommended crew-change port is Majuro.

External Affairs Representative
British consulates or embassies
In Honolulu: Consulate of Kiribati
                  850 Richards Street
                  Honolulu HI 96813, USA

Information Center
Government Tourist Officer
P.O. Box 261
Bikenibeu, Tarawa
KIRIBATI

---

still the country's best cash crop. Fishing is being aggressively developed because of the abundance of fish in the waters of the islands. Third in importance of the country's exports is handicraft manufacture, particularly products such as baskets, mats, and hats made from pandanus palms. Although the people of the urbanized islands of south Tarawa depend on a cash economy, all the rest of the population remains on a subsistence economy.

The Phoenix Islands are sparsely populated, most of the people having moved to the Solomon Islands, where living conditions are better. Kanton (Canton) Island retains a few people as caretakers of rather extensive facilities left over from days when the United

States had activities there. Kiritimati, Tabuaeran, and Teraina (Christmas, Fanning, and Washington islands) are copra producers; Kiritimati, additionally, is being developed as a sportfishing center.

The Weather

The southeast trade wind season extends from March to November through the Gilbert Islands. It is characterized by more or less steady trade winds blowing from the east-southeast and very little rainfall. There is actually no specific doldrum period, although calms and catspaws occur quite often in June and July.

The westerly season, November to March, finds strong winds blowing from southwest and northwest, occasionally reaching gale strength. They do not blow regularly nor do they reach gale force every season. Westerly winds with strong squalls may be felt during other parts of the year also.

Westerlies are of particular concern to yachts since most atolls of the Gilbert group lack good protection on the western sides of the lagoons. The westerlies usually announce their coming with a precursor of a heavy westerly swell a day or two in advance of the gale and high banks of cirrus and cirrostratus clouds moving in from the west. Winds of gale force may last from three days to a week and alternately shift from southwest to northwest. When the wind veers to north or northeast, the westerly has usually run its course. Modern weather reporting from Banaba generally gives adequate early warning of the coming of a westerly so that boats and ships can deploy proper ground tackle and set an anchor watch.

During the September to March period, strong squalls may bring northeast winds and make many anchorages lee shores. The squall is usually signified by a heavy bank of black clouds like a line squall moving in from the east and northeast. These squalls usually hit with sudden and violent force producing a short, steep sea. They may last up to six hours. Yachts should normally be anchored with long scope to assure readiness should one of these squalls hit when the boat is on its own.

The region is outside of the usual belt of tropical storms. Only one hurricane has been known to cross Kiribati, and that occurred in December 1927 at 3°N, 173°E.

The westerly season is the rainy season although it doesn't rain every day. With the exception of Butaritari and Little Makin, Kiribati can be said to be in the dry zone. Rainfall at Tarawa is about 55 inches annually, but there are occasional drought years when the rainfall may be as low as 5 inches. Heavy, prolonged rains are uncommon particularly in the atolls south of the equator, which can experience years of drought.

Island contours are too low to provoke much precipitation from the clouds borne by the constant southeast trade winds that blow over the islands; consequently, fresh water is usually at a premium. The territory is too far east to be affected very much by the northwest monsoon. It does, however, lie within the narrow belt of the intertropical front where cyclonic storms originate and from which occasionally heavy rain will fall.

The climate of the Gilbert group is uniformly hot but not unduly oppressive during the season of the southeast trades. Temperatures then range in the low 80s, which is quite comfortable unless it is a calm day. During the October to March period, the atmosphere can feel quite humid and even oppressive during the day, but evenings are cool and comfortable.

In the vicinity of the Phoenix Islands, winds are easterly with 90 percent of them between east-northeast and east-southeast. Wind speeds range between 12 and 15 knots with moderate seas. The period from January to May brings the worst weather with rain squalls and northwesterly winds reaching Force 7 to 9. The seas become rough, sometimes breaking at harbor entrances, preventing the passage of vessels in or out.

There are few seasonal differences in the climate in this area. Temperatures range from nightly lows of 75 °F to daytime highs of 95 °F. Annual rainfall varies from 8 to 40 inches.

It should be noted that the equatorial countercurrent flowing eastward runs just to the north of the Gilbert Islands. This current can be used to great advantage when sailing to the east as it gives a boost of 1–2 knots in your passage compared to the normal half knot of westerly current to the north or south of the countercurrent.

Cruising Notes

YACHT ENTRY

There are four Ports of Entry to the Republic of Kiribati —Betio on Tarawa is the main port for all Kiribati; Banaba and Kiritimati are alternate Ports of Entry; Fanning can provide clearance only for a visit to itself.

CUSTOMS

Entering at Tarawa you are properly expected to call the Marine Guard on SSB marine radio 24 hours in advance and give them an ETA. If you do not have SSB marine radio, call them on VHF channel 16 when within radio range. When within the reef, anchor in the outer harbor

The tiny harbor at Betio is a beehive of activity day and night. *Horizon* takes her place alongside a cargo-handling barge long enough for the skipper to check in with officials. Copra-fattened cockroaches big enough to handle your dock lines make it chancy to stay very long. (Earl Hinz)

across from the large pier at Betio and wait for officials to come out by boat to give you clearance.

If you do not have radio on board, enter the lagoon and simply anchor in the outer harbor with your Q flag flying and stay aboard. Most improper, but also most effective and acceptable, is to motor right into the inner harbor and tie up alongside the wharf or a lighter with your Q flag flying and stay aboard. This is just improper enough to get quick action from Customs, which has an office on the wharf. They will notify the Health officer, who is also nearby on Betio island, and call Immigration to come from the neighboring island of Bairiki.

You will need the usual documents for an entry clearance—a *zarpe* from your last port, passports, crew list, and an open boat for inspection. There is an entry paperwork fee of approximately A\$10, which Customs will collect after you have had time to go to the bank and convert your dollars into Australian currency.

As a rule, Customs will not clear you from the outer islands to another country; you must return to Tarawa for your final outbound clearance. Immigra-tion makes the argument for this procedure based on past experience wherein cruising boats have stayed for months in the outer islands living off the land and the generosity of the people. They want to discourage that practice. Under "unusual" circumstances, however, they will give you an outbound clearance via an outer island notifying the outer island that they have done so.

IMMIGRATION

Visas are required of all persons except citizens of the United Kingdom and the British Commonwealth. Visas are good for three months and can be obtained from British consulates for a fee of A\$9.00. Yachts arriving without visas can obtain limited-stay visas on the spot; 30- or even 60-day visits are possible.

All inquiries regarding immigration procedures should be addressed to:

Principal Immigration Officer
P.O. Box 75
Bairiki, Tarawa
KIRIBATI

YACH FACILITIES

Tarawa

The main anchorage at Tarawa is in the southwestern part of the lagoon off Betio Island. There is a coral sand bottom at about 4 fathoms and plenty of room for visiting yachts among the anchored Kiribati fishing boats and freighters. Avoid anchoring in the fairway that extends straight out from the moles because it is a busy place in the daytime and sometimes at night. You can take your dinghy into the inner harbor and leave it in an out-of-the-way corner with no worries about its security.

Although you can bring your boat into the inner harbor for clearance, it is inadvisable to stay there for any length of time. The harbor is small (about 450 feet square), and it is busy with fishing boats, ferryboats, lighters, tugs, small interisland boats, and shoreboats for the Marine Training School. Also, this is a copra exporting country with copra from the outer islands handled on the lighters to which you will tie in most cases. You have never seen such monstrous cockroaches as those that dwell on the copra lighters, to say nothing of the rhinoceros beetles that get aboard your boat.

The anchorage at Betio is secure in prevailing winds and strong easterlies. It is, however, exposed to

---

MEDICAL MEMO

Immunization Requirements
Immunization for smallpox, cholera, and yellow fever are required if you have transited or visited within the last six days (smallpox 14 days) an area currently infected.

Local Health Situation
Sanitation standards at Tarawa are poor even to this day, and diarrheal diseases are endemic. The crowding of people into the south islands of the atoll has far exceeded the capacity of the sanitary system with adverse effects on health. Cruisers are advised to have cholera inoculations and observe good health practices while in Kiribati.

Health Services
There is a 160-bed general hospital at Bikenibeu and a 10-bed general hospital at Betio. There are also dental clinics at Bikenibeu and Betio. All of the inhabited outer islands have dispensaries. No optical service is available.

On Kiritimati there is a small hospital with a medical officer in residence; dental work is confined to extractions. Serious emergencies can be evacuated by U.S. Coast Guard airplane to Honolulu.

Water
All water should be considered suspect and treated before use. Rainwater collected on the yacht is the best and safest water available.

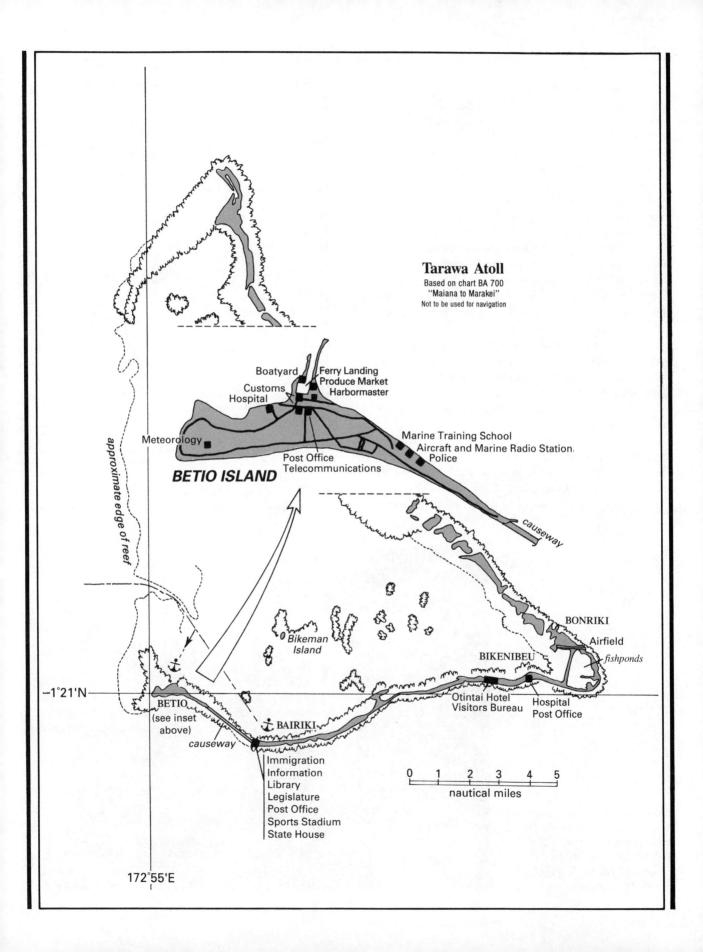

Tarawa Atoll

Based on chart BA 700
"Maiana to Marakei"
Not to be used for navigation

Boatyard   Ferry Landing
Customs   Produce Market
Hospital   Harbormaster

Meteorology

Marine Training School
Aircraft and Marine Radio Station
Police

Post Office
Telecommunications

BETIO ISLAND

approximate edge of reef

BONRIKI

Airfield

fishponds

*Bikeman
Island*

BIKENIBEU

−1°21′N

BETIO
(see inset
above)

causeway

⚓ BAIRIKI

Otintai Hotel
Visitors Bureau

Hospital
Post Office

Immigration
Information
Library
Legislature
Post Office
Sports Stadium
State House

causeway

0   1   2   3   4   5

nautical miles

172°55′E

the westerly squalls that occur in the winter months, so have good ground tackle set. From Betio it is possible to transit most of the lagoon in good sunlight and with local knowledge aboard.

Visibility in the waters of the lagoon is generally poor because of coral particles carried in suspension. This murkiness greatly reduces the effectiveness of eyeball navigation from the spreaders, so great care must be taken when moving about outside the buoyed channels.

There is a slipway available in the harbor for boats up to 90 feet long and 45 tons. Mechanical, electrical, and refrigeration workshops can do most repairs necessary to make your vessel seaworthy, although no yacht hardware is available. Some electronic repairs can be made by the technicians of the government telecommunications department.

You can get diesel, gasoline, and kerosene fuels as well as lubricating oil at the oil dock. Fuel should be filtered because it comes from drums; you will need your own containers for lube oil.

Fresh water is usually in short supply, especially in the summer months. You can buy it from the Utilities Board for A$5.00 per 500 gallons, which is really just the delivery charge to the dock. Ask for rainwater as it is the purest. Well water is brackish and heavily chlorinated ever since the cholera epidemic of 1977.

Tarawa is not a good reprovisioning port for

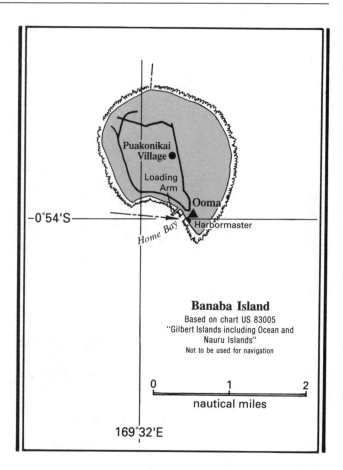

Banaba Island
Based on chart US 83005
"Gilbert Islands including Ocean and Nauru Islands"
Not to be used for navigation

Banana is one of three villages on Kiribati's Christmas Island. The other two are London and Poland, so named during the days of atmospheric nuclear testing in the 1960s. (Earl Hinz)

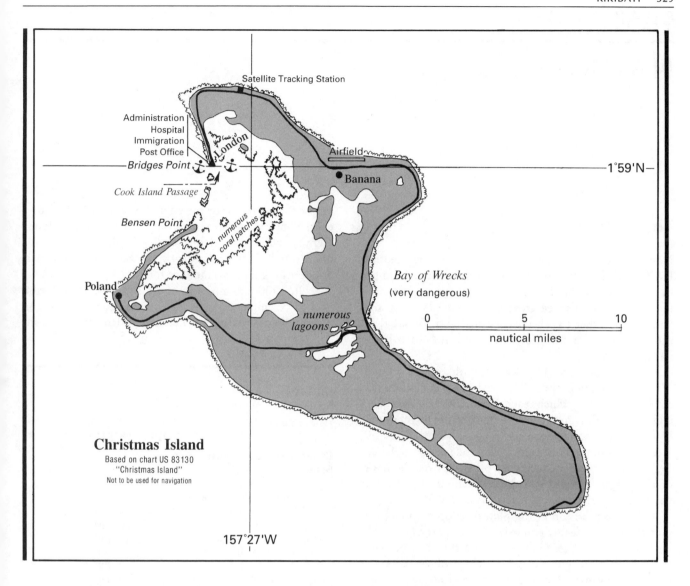

Satellite Tracking Station

Administration
Hospital
Immigration
Post Office
Bridges Point

London

Airfield

Banana

— 1°59'N —

Cook Island Passage

Bensen Point

numerous coral patches

Poland

Bay of Wrecks
(very dangerous)

numerous lagoons

0   5   10

nautical miles

Christmas Island
Based on chart US 83130
"Christmas Island"
Not to be used for navigation

157°27'W

yachts. Only local foods such as bananas, breadfruit, papayas, coconuts, fish, and chickens are available. Frozen foods and other European-type goods come from Australia on a monthly (more or less) container ship and are quite expensive. Liquor, beer, and wine are available but also quite expensive.

Banaba

Banaba Island is rarely visited because of its topography —raised coral atoll with no harbor. Anchorage must be taken on the narrow coral shelf near the cliffs, avoiding the fringing reefs.

Christmas Island (Kiritimati) and Fanning Atoll (Tabuaeran)

The Kiribati Line Islands of Christmas and Fanning and the U.S. atoll of Palmyra have become favorite stops of cruising boats traveling to the south of Hawaii. All three are described in detail in my book *Pacific Wanderer*.

CHAPTER 27

NAURU

The Country

Nauru is an oval-shaped island in the west-central Pacific 32 miles south of the equator. It is about 12 miles in circumference and contains eight square miles of land. It is one of three great phosphate islands in the Pacific (the other two being Ocean Island [Banaba] in the Gilbert group and Makatea Island in French Polynesia).

The island is slightly domed, with a narrow band of coastal lowlands about 300 yards wide encircling the cliffs of the dome, which reach about 200 feet high. The level plateau thus formed is the floor of the former atoll lagoon and contains deposits of phosphate that are 50 feet deep in some places. Encircling the island is a fringing reef whose outer edge drops off sharply to the floor of the sea and provides no inlet or safe anchorage for vessels that arrive for cargoes of phosphate.

Because the top of the plateau is open mined for phosphate, it is deeply gouged, leaving no room for villages or farms. These are on the narrow coastal rim, where a belt of light but fertile soil produces coconut palms, casuarina, a few root crops, and the usual strand vegetation. In the interior of the island there is a small, brackish lagoon slightly above sea level.

The 1990 population of 9,200 was 58 percent Nauruan, 26 percent other Pacific Islanders, 8 percent Chinese, 8 percent European. They live in small settlements scattered throughout the island. The Nauruans are a mixture of the three Pacific groups: Melanesian, Micronesian, and Polynesian. Their origin and how they came to the island are unknown. Their language, Nauruan, gives no clue as to their origin. The structure of their language and many of its words have no relationship to either Polynesian or Melanesian languages. Most of the people speak English, and all understand it. Nauruans all profess to be Christians.

The first European to visit Nauru was Captain John Fearn on the British whaling ship *Hunter* in 1798. He named it Pleasant Island. Europeans had little con-

tact with the island for the next 90 years. In 1888, however, Nauru was annexed by the German empire. Under German rule, Christianity and schooling were introduced, and the translation of the Bible into Nauruan gave the language its standard form.

In 1900 an employee of the British-owned Pacific Islands Company, working guano deposits in the Pacific, discovered that a piece of petrified wood from

NAURU
An independent nation

Port of Entry

Aiwo District	0°32′ S, 166°55′ E

Distances between Ports in Nautical Miles

Between Nauru and

Funafuti, Tuvalu	880
Honiara, Solomon Islands	675
Honolulu, Hawaii	2,445
Kosrae, FSM	420
Majuro, Marshall Islands	530
Banaba, Kiribati	160
Port-Vila, Vanuatu	1,030
Rabaul, Papua New Guinea	910
Suva, Fiji	1,255
Tarawa, Kiribati	380

Standard Time
11 hours 30 minutes fast on UTC

Public Holidays and Special Events

January 1	New Year's Day—Public holiday
January 31	Independence Day—Public holiday
March/April*	Easter
May 17	Constitution Day—Public holiday
October 26	Angam Day—Public holiday. Angam Day commemorates occasions in history when the size of the Nauruan population surpassed 1,500, which is considered the minimum necessary for survival. Angam literally means "homecoming."
December 25	Christmas Day—Public holiday

*Specific dates vary from year to year.

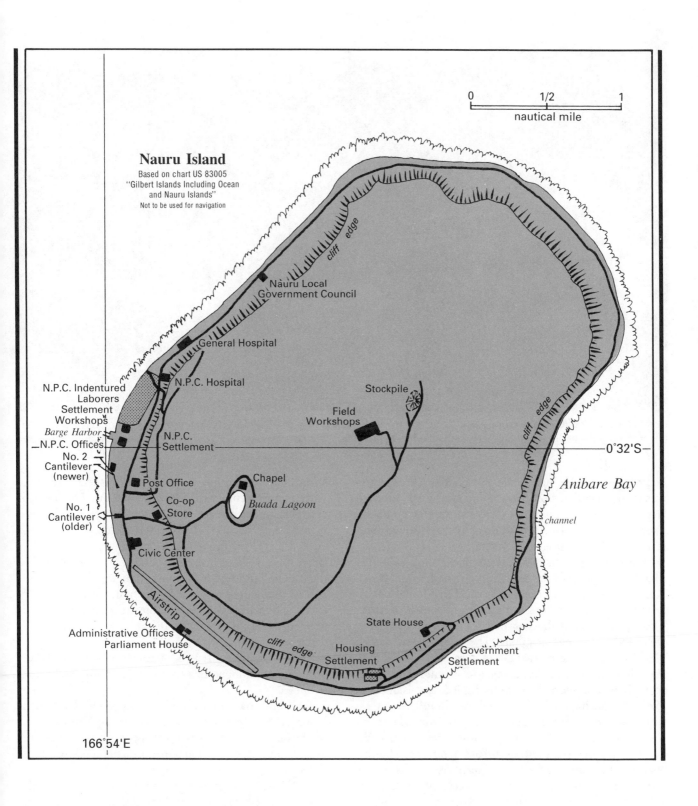

Nauru Island

Based on chart US 83005
"Gilbert Islands Including Ocean
and Nauru Islands"
Not to be used for navigation

0   1/2   1
nautical mile

cliff edge

Nauru Local
Government Council

General Hospital

N.P.C. Hospital

N.P.C. Indentured
Laborers
Settlement
Workshops
Barge Harbor
N.P.C. Offices

No. 2
Cantilever
(newer)

No. 1
Cantilever
(older)

N.P.C.
Settlement

Post Office

Co-op
Store

Civic Center

Administrative Offices
Parliament House

Airstrip

cliff edge

Chapel

Buada Lagoon

Stockpile

Field
Workshops

cliff edge

0°32'S

Anibare Bay

channel

State House

Housing
Settlement

Government
Settlement

166°54'E

Coral pinnacles looking like a moonscape are all that is left after the phosphate (aged guano) is removed to eventually become fertilizer. Almost the entire island has been devastated by the mining, which has brought a rich economy to the Nauruans. (Earl Hinz)

Nauru was actually high-grade phosphate rock. When it was confirmed that both Nauru and Ocean islands had large amounts of phosphate deposits, the Pacific Phosphate Company (also British-owned) was formed and started mining Nauruan phosphate.

In 1914 an Australian detachment took over the island in the name of the British empire and, after World War I, the island was made a Trust Territory of Great Britain, with Australia assuming administrative control. The years between the world wars were peaceful and dedicated to mining phosphate. The beginning of World War II was signaled by two German raiders sinking five phosphate ships and damaging the cantilever loading gear. Japanese marines then occupied the island in 1942, deporting 1,200 Nauruans to Chuuk island as laborers. Australian forces reoccupied the island in 1945, and about 700 of the deportees were returned, the rest having perished in forced labor at Chuuk. Nauru was again made a trust territory of the same powers and remained so until an agreement was signed in late 1967 making the island an independent republic and an associate member of the British Commonwealth.

Nauru's constitution, adopted by an elected constitutional convention in 1968, established a republic with a parliamentary form of government. The unicameral parliament consists of 18 members elected by universal adult suffrage. The president (chief of state) is elected by the parliament from among its own members for a three-year term corresponding to that of parliament. The president in turn appoints four or five members of parliament to serve concurrently as cabinet ministers. The cabinet is responsible to parliament and is obliged to resign as a body in the event of a no-confidence vote.

A supreme court was established by the constitution, and parliament may create lower courts and courts of appeal.

Nauru has no capital city as such. Parliament House and government offices are in the Yaren district on the ocean and opposite the airport. Locally, Nauru is divided into 14 districts grouped into eight electoral districts.

Nauru's economy is based almost totally on the mining of high-grade phosphate ore. It exports about two million tons a year, and its gross national product varies with the world market price of phosphate. Its per

A Gilbertese brakeman works the train carrying phosphate from the fields to the mill for crushing and eventual loading on ships for export. (Earl Hinz)

FLOTSAM AND JETSAM

Currency
Nauru does not have its own currency but uses Australian dollars. The approximate rate of exchange is US$1 = A$1.41.

Language
Nauruan is the indigenous language, but English is spoken by nearly everybody. Only the English language is written.

Electricity
Where electricity is available, it is 240v, 50 Hz AC.

Postal Address
Yacht ( )
General Post Office
NAURU

Ports for Making Crew Changes
Nauru is not a recommended port for making crew changes because of the difficult reef anchorage. Nauru has twice-weekly feeder airline service provided by Air Nauru to Pago Pago, Auckland, Suva, Honiara, Port-Vila, Guam, Majuro, and Tarawa. The closest recommended crew-change ports are Majuro or Honiara.

External Affairs Representative
Australian consulates or embassies

capita income is exceeded only by that of the Persian Gulf oil states. At the present rate of extraction, phosphate resources are expected to be exhausted by 1995. Revenue from the phosphate is invested in long-term trust funds that have been established to take care of the Nauruans when the phosphate has been depleted.

An independent commission of inquiry headed by a Sri Lankan judge was established in 1988 to persuade the governments of Australia, New Zealand, and Britain to accept responsibility for rehabilitation of the island's surface, which now looks like a moonscape at best. The rehabilitation could be one of the greatest conservation issues of the century. The defendants say that the mining agreement made in 1968 by all four parties was just and comprehensive and cleared the defendants of any further responsibility. The issue is still not settled.

There are no taxes; the costs of government and the large statutory trust fund are paid from phosphate revenues. The government subsidizes all imports, so food and other necessities are available at a nominal cost.

Practically everything required on Nauru has to be imported. Apart from some pigs, chickens, dogs, and cats, there are no animals on the island, and the erratic rainfall severely limits the local cultivation of food. The one exception is fish, which abound in the surrounding sea, but the absence of a suitable fishing harbor restricts the catch. Thus, almost all of Nauru's food and, occasionally, water (36 million gallons annually) are imported from Australia. There are weekly shipments of fresh fruit and vegetables from Australia and New Zealand but no fresh milk.

The Weather

The prevailing winds during the months of March through October are from the northeast to east and rarely stronger than Force 4 or 5. Winds are, surprisingly, affected by the island, with winds stronger near shore, especially at night. Nauru is not in the normal hurricane belt, but southwesterly storms occasionally occur.

Nauru's wet season occurs between November and February; the average annual rainfall is 80 inches. Extremes reached a low of 12 inches in 1950 and as much as 180 inches in 1930 and again in 1940.

Being on the equator, Nauru is naturally hot, but the heat is tempered by the trade winds. In the shade, the temperatures range between 76°F and 93°F with a humidity between 70 and 80 percent.

The best time to visit Nauru is during the dry season, when the trade winds are the steadiest and safe moorage can be had in the lee of the island.

Cruising Notes

YACHT ENTRY

When Nauru is in sight, contact the marine department on channel 16 for instructions on mooring. If no ship is present, you will be given permission to tie up to a mooring buoy.

Visas are required for extended stays; they can be obtained through Australian consulates. If there is no Australian consulate in your area, write directly to

Immigration Department
Government of Nauru
NAURU

requesting a visa. Give all the pertinent particulars of your boat and crew in your first letter plus anticipated dates of visit. Do it well in advance because mail is sometimes slow.

MEDICAL MEMO

Immunization Requirements
Cholera and yellow fever certificates are required for persons coming from or transiting an infected area.

Local Health Situation
There are no reported medical problems of consequence.

Health Services
There are two hospitals on the island—the government hospital and the Nauru Phosphate Corporation hospital. They are staffed by doctors, dentists, and various assistants. The NPC hospital was originally intended to serve only the corporation staff and employees but is now supplementing the government hospital in cases requiring more extensive medical equipment than the government hospital has.

Medical and dental care are free for the Nauruans and the employees of the corporation. Visitors can receive treatment at either hospital at a nominal cost. There are no private medical practitioners on the island. Visitors who wear glasses are advised to carry a spare pair with them as it takes weeks to get replacements from Australia.

Water
Nauru has inadequate water supplies for its own population, so you should not assume that you can replenish your water supply on the island. Drinking water on the island should be considered suspect.

Bulk carriers are loaded offshore with the crushed phosphate. Cantilevered conveyor belts move the phosphate from mill to ship's hold. (Nauru Phosphate Commission)

YACHT FACILITIES

Yacht facilities are almost nonexistent, with anchoring impossible around the fringing reef because of the great depths. A barge basin has been blasted out of the coral reef for use by cargo boats, launches, and the local fishermen. Dinghies can use it, but yachts are forbidden because it is shallow, and a strong westerly would prevent departure. Yachts are not allowed to remain overnight. If you desire a second day's visit, stand offshore during the night and return to the buoy in the morning.

Limited supplies are available since nothing is grown on the island; it is all shipped in from Australia. You can purchase small amounts of canned goods and alcoholic beverages. Tobacco products are available at duty-free prices. Do not ask for water (unless dying of thirst) since that is a scarce commodity on the island. Diesel fuel is available.

Many mosquitoes breed in the stagnant pools of water created by the surface mining of phosphate. Fortunately, there is no dengue fever or malaria reported here. If you are going to Nauru, put screens on your boat and take along plenty of mosquito coils.

Part IV

Islands of the Eastern Pacific

One need not venture far into the Pacific Ocean to find tropical islands. Several exist just 600 miles off the west coasts of the Americas. Unfortunately, they are not the types of islands of which paradise is made. Instead they tend to be rocky, barren, and without comfortable harbors.

Off the coast of Mexico are the Revilla Gigedo Islands, a possession of Mexico. They are uninhabited except for a small village on Isla Socorro, the largest of the four-island group. There is a Mexican navy base on Socorro, and yachts must have a clearance from the naval officials to land on any of the islands. Neither water nor provisions are available here; but trading material is very welcome, and you may get some items of local interest to take back home.

The Revilla Gigedo Islands are of volcanic origin; the only vegetation is low cactus, sage, and some grass. There are no true harbors; but adequate shelter can be found in a number of coves, and dinghy landings can be made in moderate weather on sandy beaches.

Farther south is Clipperton Island, a dependency of France but not part of French Polynesia. It is an atoll with an enclosed lagoon of brackish water. At one time there was believed to have been a usable passage into the lagoon. The island is about five miles in diameter and has wild pigs and birds in abundance. At various times it has been inhabited but with no degree of permanence. As many as a hundred people lived on it in the early 1900s, when a British firm was mining phosphate there. Anchorage can be taken off the southwest side in a coral sand bottom, but a capable crew member should be left on board for security.

Most famous of the eastern Pacific island groups are the Galapagos Islands, which straddle the equator on the route from Panama to French Polynesia. They are worthy of a cruising stop if you can get official permission. Details of the Galapagos Islands are given in this section.

South of the Galapagos and out of the tropics but still in a region of good weather are the Juan Fernandez Islands, a possession of Chile. These islands have long been used as a watering stop for sailing ships coming up the coast from Cape Horn. The story of Alexander Selkirk, put ashore on the main island of Isla Más a Tierra, was fictionalized by Daniel Defoe in *Robinson Crusoe,* and the island is often referred to as Robinson Crusoe Island. The other two islands are called Alexander Selkirk and Santa Clara.

The Juan Fernandez Islands, population about 700, are a district of the Chilean province of Valparaiso. The capital is the village of St. John the Baptist on Isla Más a Tierra. A primary school and a Chilean air base are located at St. John. Water and some provisions are available, and fish are plentiful. The local waters teem with tuna, salmon, and lobster, which are commercially fished. Scuba diving is very popular with visitors to these remote islands.

Except for the Galapagos, the islands of the eastern Pacific are rarely visited by cruising yachts and may just be of interest to the adventurous cruiser who is exploring the west coast of the Americas.

The reader is referred to another of my books, *Pacific Wanderer,* for greater details on these outlying islands of the eastern Pacific.

CHAPTER 28

GALAPAGOS ISLANDS

The Country

The Galapagos Islands, also known as the Archipélago de Colón, is a group of 13 major islands and several minor ones. They are volcanic in origin and are geologically very young. Darwin estimated the number of extinct volcanoes at 2,000. The oldest rocks found in the Galapagos are about five million years old and the youngest about one million years old. The physical characteristics of the islands—striking lava flows, interesting basalt formations, and beautiful sand beaches—are very dramatic. The principal islands are:

Island	Size (miles)	Area (square miles)	Height (feet)
Isabela	74 × 45	2,249	4,900
Santa Cruz	17 × 23	389	2,835
San Salvador	20 × 13	203	2,974
Fernandina	18 × 18	245	4,900
San Cristóbal	26 × 10	195	2,350

The Galapagos Islands are a province of Ecuador administered by the Ecuador Forestry Service. The seat of government is at Puerto Baquerizo Moreno, San Cristóbal Island. All native mammals, reptiles, and birds are protected. In 1959 the government of Ecuador and the internationally recognized Charles Darwin Foundation, with the help of UNESCO and other scientific organizations, established a biological research station at Academy Bay, Santa Cruz Island.

The Galapagos lie astride the converging El Niño current from the Gulf of Panama and the Humboldt current from the south. The currents flow side by side to the west-northwest around the islands but not always maintaining the same position. The waters of the northern islands could have temperatures as high as 80°F while the waters around the southern islands could have temperatures as low as 60°F.

Coastal areas and all the smaller islands are covered with bushes and small trees. The most striking plants are the cacti. After rains, which are scarce, desert annuals will spring up, flower, and quickly die. There is a striking contrast between vegetation of the dry, coastal areas and the dense growth on the heights. Fog, rain, and mist create a forest of ferns, lichens, orchids, and

---

GALAPAGOS ISLANDS
A province of Ecuador

Ports of Entry

Academy Bay	0°45′ S, 90°18′ W
Wreck Bay	0°54′ S, 89°37′ W

Distances between Ports in Nautical Miles
Between Wreck Bay and

Easter Island	1,945
Guayaquil, Ecuador	590
Honolulu, Hawaii	4,210
Mangareva, Gambier Islands	2,955
Más a Tierra, Juan Fernandez Islands	2,055
Nuku Hiva, Marquesas Islands	3,050
Panama City, Panama	845
Pitcairn Island	755
San Diego, California	2,550

Standard Time
6 hours slow on UTC

Public Holidays and Special Events

January 1	New Year's Day—Public holiday
March/April*	Prelenten Carnival—Local festivals
March/April*	Good Friday, Holy Saturday, and Easter Sunday
May 1	Labor Day—Public holiday
May 24	Battle of Pichincha—Public holiday
July 24	Bolivar's Birthday—Public holiday
August 10	National Independence—Public holiday
October 12	Columbus Day—Public holiday
November 2	All Souls' Day—Public holiday
December 24/25	Christmas—Public holidays

*Specific dates vary from year to year.

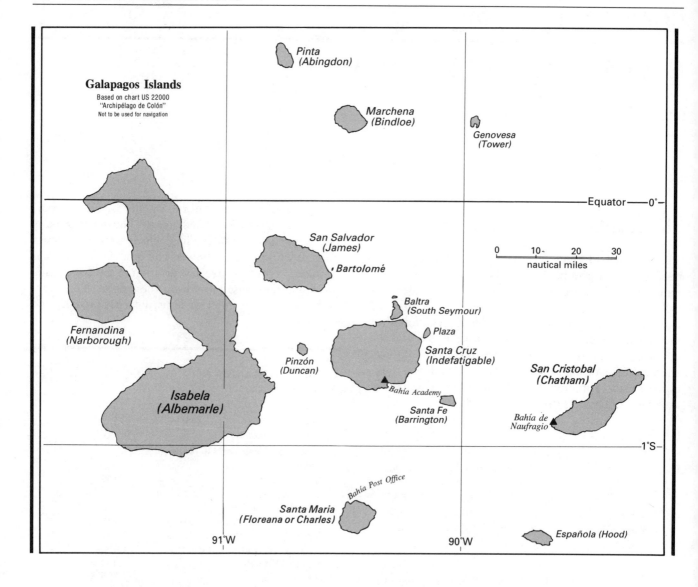

Galapagos Islands
Based on chart US 22000
"Archipélago de Colón"
Not to be used for navigation

Pinta
(Abingdon)

Marchena
(Bindloe)

Genovesa
(Tower)

Equator — 0° —

San Salvador
(James)

• Bartolomé

0   10-   20   30
nautical miles

Baltra
(South Seymour)

Plaza

Santa Cruz
(Indefatigable)

Fernandina
(Narborough)

Pinzón
(Duncan)

Bahía Academy

San Cristobal
(Chatham)

Isabela
(Albemarle)

Santa Fe
(Barrington)

Bahía de
Naufragio

— 1°S —

Bahía Post Office

Santa Maria
(Floreana or Charles)

Española (Hood)

91°W

90°W

creeping plants—a true rain forest only miles from desert land.

One usually thinks of the fauna when the Galapagos Islands are mentioned. Native land mammals are limited to two species of the rice rat, all others having been introduced by visitors to the islands. Marine mammals, however, are plentiful, including sperm and killer whales, which are occasionally sighted off the northern coast of Isabela Island. In addition, there are the bottlenose dolphin and common dolphin. The cold water of the Humboldt current supports colonies of two species of sea lions. Fur seals, at one point on the verge of extinction, can now be seen around some of the islands.

Reptiles are probably the most dramatic of the native animals. Even the name "Galapagos" suggests a

reptilian world: in Spanish it means "giant tortoises." All the reptiles in the islands, except the sea turtles, are indigenous only to the Galapagos. Among the reptiles found on the islands are the giant tortoise, lava lizard, and land iguana. Along the coasts one finds many kinds of sea turtles and the marine iguana.

There are a variety of land- and seabirds. Although some are found in other tropical lands, some very unusual birds are found only here. Among these are the Galapagos penguin and the flightless cormorant. Nearly all the landbirds are unique to the islands. Darwin noted 23 different species on San Salvador and commented that they were incredibly tame. There are still many with no fear of humans.

Because of the location of the Galapagos in relation to the plankton-rich Humboldt current, fish thrive around the waters of the archipelago. Large sharks, tuna, lobster, and crayfish abound.

The Galapagos Islands were discovered by Tomás de Berlango, Bishop of Panama, in 1535, when his ship was caught in a current that pulled him off course in his voyage from Panama to Peru. In his accounts to Emperor Carlos V of Spain, he includes descriptions of the incredibly tame wildlife, the huge tortoises, and unusual iguanas. In the decades that followed, the archipelago received the name Islas Encantadas (Bewitched Islands) because of the currents that tricked navigators and made the islands "appear" and "disappear" unpredictably.

During the seventeenth century, English pirates found the islands to be a useful refuge and often made visits to restock their vessels with food and water. They in turn stocked the islands with goats, pigs, and cattle so they could resupply themselves with fresh meat when returning. Unfortunately, they also found the giant tortoises an excellent source of fresh meat; ships took thousands of these defenseless creatures to sea, storing them in their holds until the men required fresh meat at sea. The effect on the tortoise population was devastating, and some species are now extinct. The others are carefully protected and are being raised under controlled conditions at the Darwin Research Station at Academy Bay on Santa Cruz Island.

From 1780 to 1860 the islands were visited by many British and American whalers, who killed thousands of the Galapagos fur seals. These visitors also captured and stored the tortoises in their ships' holds for fresh meat supplies, and again the population of these giant reptiles suffered.

Ecuador annexed the group in 1832 and at-

Cruising boats in the channel between Santiago Island (San Salvador) and the small neighboring island of Bartolomé. The barren nature of these islands is clearly evident. (Douglas Bernon)

One of the most famous post offices in the world—the mail barrels on Santa Maria Island. These have been in use in one form or another ever since the days of the whalers. (Bernadette Bernon)

FLOTSAM AND JETSAM

Currency
The Galapagos Islands use Ecuadorian currency. The Ecuadorian dollar is called a sucre; it is equal to 100 centavos. The approximate rate of exchange is US$1 = 870 sucres.

Language
The official language of the Galapagos Islands is Spanish. English is spoken by many people in business and government.

Electricity
Where electricity is available, it is 110v, 60 Hz AC.

Postal Address
Yacht ( )
Poste Restante
Academy Bay, Isla Santa Cruz
Galapagos Islands
ECUADOR

Note: A historic communications means exists at Post Office Bay on the north coast of Santa Maria Island. This was a crossroads in the whaling days and the location of an old barrel in which whalers put letters to be picked up later by some homeward-bound vessel. It is still used by cruising boats for the novelty of it.

Ports for Making Crew Changes
Baltra is not a recommended port for making crew changes even though there are daily flights from Quito, Ecuador. Problems with just getting permission to cruise these islands are sufficient without complicating them by changing crew members. The closest ports for making a crew change are Panama or Papeete.

External Affairs Representative
Ecuadorian consulates or embassies

Information Center
Ecuadorian Tourist Commission
P.O. Box 2454
Quito
ECUADOR

tempted to use it as a colony and a penal settlement but without much success. Charles Darwin, serving as naturalist on the British ship HMS *Beagle* when it visited the Galapagos in 1835, formulated his theory of evolution based largely on the observations he made on the islands. In the early 1930s a group of Germans attempted to set up a colony; the colony failed, but some of the group's descendants are still on the islands. Today the Galapagos Archipelago is a national park of Ecuador.

There are no indigenous people in the archipelago. It has an approximate population of 6,000 Ecuadorians and 300 permanent foreign residents. Most of the Ecuadorians live a subsistence life; but with more government employment available and the flourishing biological research station at Academy Bay, there promises to be some improvement in the standard of living. Ecuador has, since 1959, denied permanent residency permits to non-Ecuadorians.

Academy Bay is the most popular stop in the Galapagos Islands because of the Darwin Research Station. Charter boats operate from here, and it is a principal stop for cruise ships and local boats bringing tourists from the airport on Baltra Island. There is a small hotel, and the presence of the station research staff, together with the tourists, has made the settlement at Puerto Ayoro, Academy Bay, less rustic than Puerto Baquerizo Moreno at Wreck Bay.

Besides the airport at Baltra Island, there is also an Ecuadorian naval base there.

The Weather

Although the island group lies on and near the equator, the climate is tempered by the cold Humboldt current.

The southeast trade wind is the prevailing wind and blows between southeast and southwest. From April to December the trade winds blow with great regularity, and gales are unknown. Calms are frequent from January to April with occasional light squalls from the northwest. Heavy rollers occasionally break upon the northern shores during the rainy season, but no wind of any consequence accompanies them.

Thundershowers occur between November and March, but the rainfall is unequally distributed, with most falling at higher elevations of the larger islands. The greater part of the islands are, in general, embraced in a dry zone, which rises to about 800 feet. Maximum rainfall is 48 inches per year at the wettest point. Fog and occasional drizzles may be found at the lower levels. Because the rains are brought by the southeast trades, the fertile land is all on the southeast sides of the islands and at the higher levels. Fresh water is generally very limited.

Thick fog has been reported at sea near the archipelago in April and September.

The preferred season for visiting the Galapagos is between December and May. Then there is more sun with only occasional downpours but, unfortunately, light winds. The poorest month is September, when it is overcast with drizzles and is relatively cool. This is known as the Garua season. Commercial travel is at a low ebb at this time.

Cruising Notes

YACHT ENTRY

For centuries the Galapagos Islands have been an attraction to seafarers. Initially this was a place of refuge and reprovisioning for explorers, pirates, and ships of commerce; more recently it has become a popular port of call for cruising yachts. At one time cruising yachts could stop at all islands of the archipelago without prior arrangements. The very popularity of the islands, however, caused the Ecuadorian government to take a more active role in administering them. First they placed them under the Ecuadorian navy, designating all the waters a frontier zone. Then they placed all the land areas under the Forest Service as a national park, and that is the way matters stand today.

Along with the formal administration went severe restrictions on casual yacht visits. For a time, yachts were prohibited altogether, but then the restrictions were relaxed to allow yachts en route to other destinations, to visit for a three-day period, which is the way it is today. Cruising yachts can stay for three days in either Puerto Baquerizo Moreno, San Cristóbal Island, or Puerto Ayora, Santa Cruz Island. If you stay three days in one port, you are deemed to have used up your three-day quota and will, in all probability, not be permitted additional time at the other port. Cruisers in general have said that Puerto Ayora is the more attractive port of the two.

During your three-day stay you are allowed to go ashore on both these islands, visiting the local inhabitants and forest reserves and purchasing such supplies as are available. You cannot go to other islands during the three days with your boat. It is possible, however, to charter a local tour boat with a naturalist guide and visit nearby islands within the three-day limit, leaving your boat at anchor.

Should your yacht have real (not imagined) operating problems requiring a stay longer than three days, permission may be granted by the port captain to extend the period. He will, most likely, send a mechanic to your boat to verify the degree of distress you are experiencing. At best, pleading *force majeure* only eight or ten days out of Panama is a transparent argument that only makes stops at these islands more difficult for future cruisers.

CUSTOMS

In Puerto Ayora your entry clearance is processed at the port captain's office in the northwest corner of the harbor. There is a dinghy dock available below his office for check-in use. No special Customs inspection is made, but firearms must be declared and bonded on board, and pets of any kind must stay on board your boat. Entry charges are as follows:

Arrival and departure fees
Monday through Friday	US$8 each
Saturdays	US$16 each
Sundays and holidays	US$32 each
Light and buoyage fee	US$3 per gross ton
Anchorage fee	US$0.10 per foot LOA per day
Municipal landing fee	US$2.25

IMMIGRATION

Immigration formalities are handled ashore by the police department. Passports are required, and there is a US$4 charge per person.

EXTENDED VISITS

If you want to use your own boat to visit the other islands or desire to stay well beyond the technical limit of three days, you must first apply for the Yacht Tourist Permit in accordance with Ecuadorian Decree No. 812: "Regulation for the concession of permits to foreign vessels to visit the territorial sea, the coast and islands of the Galapagos Archipelago for scientific, cultural, or tourist purposes." For a copy of the decree, write:

> Embassy of Ecuador
> 2535 15th Street NW
> Washington, DC 20009, USA

The number of permits issued ranges between zero and five or six per month, and your chance of getting one even with perseverance and patience is quite small. Scientific or cultural reasons stand the best chance.

In effect you must deal with two different Ecuadorian agencies in this matter. While your formal permit should be sent to the Ecuadorian embassy or the nearest Ecuadorian consulate, copies of it with letters of application (all in good Spanish) should also be sent to:

> Armada del Ecuador
> Direccion General de Intereses Maritimos
> Quito
> ECUADOR

and

> Director
> Programa Nacional Forestal
> Ministerio de Agricultura y Ganaderia
> Quito
> ECUADOR

The letters of application should contain the particulars of your boat and crew, your itinerary, and the experience and background of the captain. Filing the decree papers and the two letters of application should be done at least a year in advance and followed up quarterly. If you have a nearby Ecuadorian consulate, they may also be of help.

PARK VISITS

Whether on a three-day or extended-permit stay (usually limited to ten days), there are certain requirements to be met. You will be charged a US$40 fee for a one-calendar-year admission to the Galapagos National Park if you visit any of the islands other than your entry port. You must also hire a naturalist guide at US$25–50 per day plus meals, to accompany you either on your own boat or a charter boat. There are about 40 recognized landing places throughout the islands. The Ecuadorian navy has park surveillance boats that check on cruising and charter boats operating in the archipelago.

YACHT FACILITIES

There are no special facilities for yachts in the Galapagos Islands, only those that are shared with the ships that come from Ecuador and the needs of the local charter boats. Cruisers should not plan on making any repairs or taking on water or any provisions in the Galapagos Islands; all of that should be taken care of on the mainland and be adequate for boat and crew to reach the Marquesas or other next port of call.

Wreck Bay

Yachts anchor out, usually on a single hook, and crews take dinghies into the beach or the small pier. The navy will sell fuel and water to you in your jerry jugs. There are some staples and limited water available in the town

---

MEDICAL MEMO

Immunization Requirements
Immunizations for yellow fever and smallpox are required if you have transited or visited an infected area within the last 14 days (yellow fever six days).

Local Health Situation
The climate of the Galapagos is healthful, and there are none of the diseases common to the tropics. Although the parent country of Ecuador is a malaria risk, the risk does not extend to the Galapagos Islands.

Health Services
There are hospitals at both Wreck Bay and Academy Bay, but major medical problems would have to be taken care of at Quito, Ecuador. Air service is available for an emergency. Limited drugs are available in the dispensaries. There is now a dentist at Wreck Bay.

Water
Water is in limited supply and is sometimes brackish. All water should be considered suspect and treated before use. Water may be unavailable during the dry season.

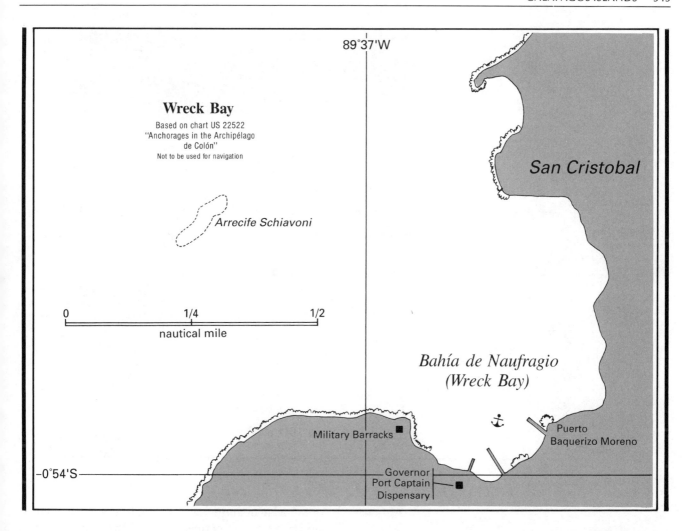

Wreck Bay

Based on chart US 22522
"Anchorages in the Archipélago
de Colón"
Not to be used for navigation

Arrecife Schiavoni

89°37'W

San Cristobal

0   1/4   1/2

nautical mile

*Bahía de Naufragio
(Wreck Bay)*

⚓

Puerto
Baquerizo Moreno

Military Barracks

Governor
Port Captain
Dispensary

-0°54'S

of Puerto Baquerizo Moreno, and an open market has a modest selection of fresh fruits and vegetables. This town is the headquarters for the navy and the national police and is the administrative center for the islands. Sights of interest to visitors are not in abundance on this island, and fewer people speak English here than at Academy Bay. For a three-day visit it would not be as attractive as Academy Bay.

Academy Bay

The best anchorage at Academy Bay is close under the cliffs near the European settlement. Anchor parallel to the cliffs with bow and stern anchors. The port captain's office is only a short row away, and there is a dinghy dock for persons seeking a clearance.

Academy Bay offers a better but still limited choice of provisions than does Wreck Bay. Fresh vegetables are

sometimes available because of the European community living nearby. Bananas, citrus fruits, bakery goods, and fresh beef are also generally available. Water on this island is brackish and should not be used, but distilled water can now be purchased in limited quantities at a price of US¢12 per gallon.

Although there is a boatyard here, do not depend on making any major repairs because of the limited time you will have. Several mechanics have businesses servicing the local charter boats, so if you have a mechanical problem, they can help fix it. Spare parts are not available, but the mechanics can arrange to get them via air delivery from the mainland.

There is a drying grid here which with spring tides can accept boats up to 6½-foot draft; however, you really don't want to waste your time on bottom work unless it is a real emergency.

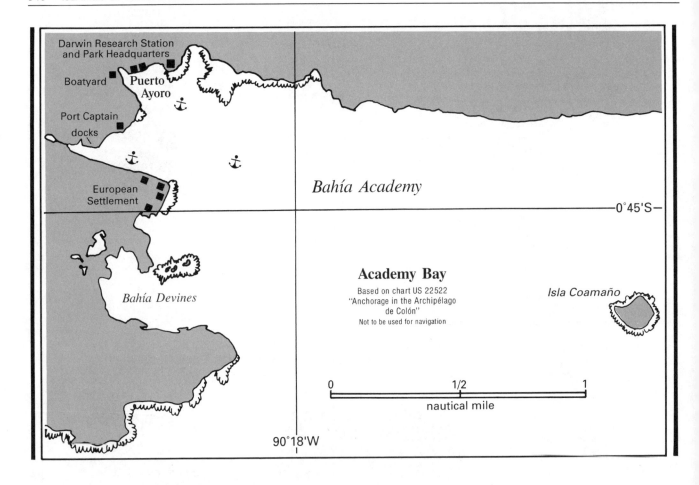

Darwin Research Station
and Park Headquarters

Boatyard

Puerto
Ayoro

Port Captain

docks

European
Settlement

Bahía Devines

Bahía Academy

0°45'S

Academy Bay

Based on chart US 22522
"Anchorage in the Archipélago
de Colón"

Not to be used for navigation

Isla Coamaño

0   1/2   1

nautical mile

90°18'W

Marine iguanas basking in the sun. Like all the rest of Darwin's creatures, these animals are unafraid of man. (Bernadette Bernon)

Fuel in quantity is not available in Academy Bay. If you are short, get permission from the port captain to stop at Aeolian Cove, Baltra Island, on your departure from the Galapagos Islands. This navy base will sell you fuel; it is reportedly clean, but as with all fuel obtained at such island fuel stops, it should be filtered. Limited water is also available on Baltra.

APPENDIXES

APPENDIX A

TRILINGUAL DICTIONARY FOR PORT ENTRY

Coastal Navigation

ENGLISH	FRENCH	SPANISH	ENGLISH	FRENCH	SPANISH
anchorage	mouillage	fondeadero	low	bas	bajo
bar	barre	barra	marina	marina	puerto deportivo
bay	baie	bahia	mean (average)	moyen	media
beacon	balise	baliza	mountain	mont	monte
black	noir	negro	mud	boue	lodo
breakers	brisants	rompiente	north	nord	norte
broad (wide)	large	vasto	pass	passe	paso
cape	cap	cabo	peak	pic	pico
channel	chenal	canal	península	péninsule	península
chart	carte	carta náutica	point	pointe	punta
cliff	falaise	acantilado	port (side)	babord	babor
coast	côte	costa	quay	quai	embarcadero
coral	corail	coral	red	rouge	rojo
cove	anse	caleta	reef	récif	arrecife
current	courant	corriente	river	rivière	río
danger	danger	peligro	roadstead	rade	rada
depth	profondeur	profunidad	rock	rocher	roca
east	est	este	sand	sable	arena
flat	basse	plano	sea	mer	mar
gulf	golfe	golfo	seaward	vers le large	hacia la mar
harbor	port	puerto	shoal	haute-fond	bajío
head	tête	cabeza	shoal bank	banc	bajío
headland	nez	promontorio	small	petit	chico
high	haut	alto	starboard (side)	tribord	estribor
hill	colline	cerro	steep	raide	empinado
hill, bluff	morne	escarpa	south	sud	sur
house	maison	casa	surf	surf	resaca
island	île	isla	tide	tide	marea
islet	îlot	islote	tower	tour	torre
jetty	jetée	malecón	town	ville	pueblo
lagoon	lagon	laguna	valley	vallée	valle
landing place	débarcadère	desembarcadero	village	village	pueblo
large	grand	grande	white	blanc	blanco
light	feu	luz	west	ouest	oeste
lighthouse	phare	faro	wreck	naufrage	naufragio

Entering a Foreign Port

ENGLISH	FRENCH	SPANISH
accident and illness	accident et maladie	accidentes y enfermedad
act of God	fortune de mer	accidents
anchorage	mouillage	fondeadero
appeal	appel	apelación
bill of health	pattente de santé	patente de sanidad
bonded stores	provisions entreposées, en franchise, sous douane	víveres precintados
certificate of clearance	certificate de déblaiement	zarpe
certificate of registry	permis de séjour	patente de navegación
cook	cuisinier	cocinero
courtesy flag	ensign pavillon de courtoisie	bandera de cortesía
crew	équipage	tripulación
customs clearance	libre-sortie, congé de douane	despacho de aduana
customs office	bureau de douane	aduana
doctor	docteur	médico
flags	pavillons	banderas
harbormaster's office	bureau de capitaine de port	oficio de capitán del puerto
immigration officer	agent du service de l'immigration	oficial de immigración
insurance certificate	certificat d'assurance	póliza de seguro
man overboard	homme à la mer	hombre al agua
mate	second, chef de quart	segundo, piloto
mooring place	point d'accostage	amarradero
mooring prohibited	accostage interdit	amarradero prohibido
navigator	navigateur	navegante
passport	passeport	pasaporte
pilot book	instructions nautique	derrotero
pratique	libre-pratique	platica
ship's articles	rôle d'équipage	rol
ship's company	équipage	compañía naviera
ship's log	livre de bord	cuademo de bitacora
ship's papers	papiers de borde	documentación
shipwreck	naufrage	naufragio
skipper	chef de bord	patrón
temporary	temporaire	provisional
weather forecast	prévisions météo	pronóstico
yacht club	yacht-club	club náutico; club de yates

Services in a Foreign Port

ENGLISH	FRENCH	SPANISH
accident	accident	accidente
auxiliary	auxiliaire	auxiliar
bakery	boulangerie	panadería
bank	banque	banco
bus	autobus	autobús
butcher shop	boucherie	carnicería
chandlery and ship's chandler	quincaillerie, accastillage et fournisseur de marine	pertechos y almacen de effectos navales
careening grid	gril de carénage	dique de peine, carenero
compass adjuster	compensateur de compas	compensador de compáses
dairy	laiterie	lechería
dentist	dentiste	dentista
diesel engine	moteur diesel	motor diesel
diesel oil	gas-oil, mazout	gas-oil
doctor	docteur	medico
drinking water	eau potable	agua potable
electrical system	système électrique	instalación eléctrica
engine oil	huile de moteur	petrolero de motor
fish market	marchand de poisson	pescaderia
garage	garage	garaje
gasoline	gazoléne	gasolina
gasoline engine	moteur à gaz	motor de gasolina
greengrocer	marchand de légumes	verdulero
grocer	épicier	tendero de ultramarinos
hospital	hôpital	hospital
illness	maladie	enfermedad
ironmongery or hardware store	quincaillerie	ferretería
kerosene	pétrole	petróleo
maintenance	entretien	mantenimiento
market	marché	mercado
outboard engine	moteur hors-bord	motor fuera de bordo
painting	peinture	pintura
pharmacist, chemist	pharmacien	farmacéutica
pilot	pilote	piloto
post office	la poste	correo
railway station	gare	estación de ferroviario
sailmaker	voilier	velero
shipyard	chantier naval	astillero
slip, slipway	cale de magasin	veraddero
stamps	timbres	sellos
tide tables	table des marées	tabla de mareas
tow	remorque	remolque

APPENDIX B

GLOSSARY OF CRUISING WORDS

Anchorages: Examination anchorage—an anchorage at which boats wait until entry examination is complete. Quarantine anchorage—an anchorage set aside for ships in quarantine. Q flag is flown here.

Archipelago: A large, geographically related group of islands.

Atoll: An annular-shaped coral reef enclosing a lagoon. There may or may not be islets on the reef.

Atollon: A small atoll on the periphery of a larger one.

Barrier reef: A coral reef roughly paralleling the shoreline and separated from it by a channel of water.

Coastal plain: That strip of flat land running along the coastline separating water and mountain.

Copra: The dried white meat of the coconut.

Coral: The hard, calcareous substance secreted by the coral polyp for the purpose of providing it a home. Coral may be dead or alive.

Coral island: An island composed principally of coral. It may be a full atoll, a solid island, or simply an accumulation of debris on a coral reef.

Coral reef: A reef composed principally of coral growth.

Fjord (fiord): A long, narrow arm of the sea between high cliffs.

Force majeure: Implied permission by international maritime convention to temporarily stop in any port for repairs or provisions necessary for safety of vessel and/or crew.

Free port: A port where the host country has waived import and export duties, usually to expand trade.

Fringing reef: A coral reef adjacent to land with no navigable water between it and the shoreline.

Grid: Parallel timbers laid in shallow water on which small boats can be grounded as the tide recedes. Bottomwork can be done on the boat between tides.

Haven: A place of refuge for vessels away from the fury of wind and waves. Usually accessible under all conditions of weather.

Hurricane: A cyclonic storm with winds in excess of 64 knots.

Indigenous: Native to the country.

Insular: Surrounded by sea (an island).

Island: A land area smaller than a continent and entirely surrounded by water.

Lagoon: The area of water within an atoll. It may be saltwater as a result of a connection with the ocean, or it may be brackish as a result of fresh water mixing with saltwater seeping through the annular reef structure.

Marina: A constructed area with berths and facilities for maintaining and storing yachts.

Motu: An islet with some vegetation situated on a reef.

Passage: A channel for navigating a boat through a reef. Also a sea journey between specific points.

Pidgin: A simplified language form used by islanders in conversing with English-speaking people.

Port of Entry: A port where officials of a country examine a vessel and grant entry of goods and people to that country.

Pratique: Permission granted to a vessel to enter a country after determining that the vessel has a clean bill of health.

Q flag: My vessel is healthy and I request free pratique (health clearance). Also called the "yellow jack."

Quarantine: The isolation of a vessel until it is determined that it is a healthy vessel and can be granted pratique.

Quay: A stone or masonry structure along a shoreline against which vessels moor to transfer cargo.

Reef: A localized area of rock or coral that is a hazard to navigation. It may or may not be above the water.

Seamount: An undersea mountain.

Shoal: A localized shallow area that is a hazard to navigation. Usually sand or mud.

Slips: Floating or fixed structures to accommodate boats adjacent to land.

Slipway: A marine railway built to haul small vessels out of the water for repairs.

Tropics: That portion of the earth situated between the Tropics of Cancer and Capricorn and spanning the equator.

Tropical storm: A cyclonic storm with winds between 35 and 64 knots.

Tsunamis: Fast-moving waves caused by a submarine earthquake; capable of traveling thousands of miles; erroneously called tidal waves.

Vigia: An uncertain or hidden danger previously reported in a general area. Both existence and position are doubtful.

Voyage: The full length of a sea journey, made up of one or more passages.

Waterspout: A tornado over the ocean in which a funnel-shaped pendant descends from a black cloud and with violent rotating motion draws up water or anything else from the surface of the ocean.

Zarpe (Spanish): A departure clearance usually given by the Customs official; gives the vessel permission to leave and, in effect, is a letter of introduction to next port of call.

APPENDIX C

MASTERING THE THREE R'S AT SEA

There is no better schoolroom than the world of nature, and the child traveling in the Pacific aboard a cruising yacht is probably the luckiest of all students, for that child gains an intimate knowledge of living a self-sufficient life. The clean life of sailing and the adventure of visiting new lands will give a depth of learning and appreciation for life not attainable in a classroom. What better way is there for a child to understand the meaning of One World than to mingle with peers in other lands and learn about their way of life?

Nevertheless, the absence of formal education needed to prepare one to compete in today's sophisticated society is one drawback for the school-age child at sea. While it may be fun to sail the oceans of the world, it is not fun to return home and find yourself unprepared for the job market or without the educational prerequisites for college. Cruising parents must give serious thought to filling the academic educational gap their children could suffer.

Fortunately, a number of qualified academic institutions in the United States (and probably elsewhere) have prepared correspondence courses equivalent to classroom studies, and these have been accredited by national and state education boards. They are made specifically for the student who must study away from the classroom for any of a variety of reasons and have proven useful to the cruising student. The following pages summarize the programs of four recognized correspondence schools serving student needs through high school. With these courses taken at sea and the actual experience of visiting the countries of the Pacific Basin, the cruising child will have a more satisfying education than could be provided in any classroom.

1. Calvert School
    Tuscany Road, Baltimore MD 21210, USA
    Grades: Kindergarten through 8

"The Calvert Home Instruction Courses are built from the regular Day School curriculum of the Calvert School —a distinguished independent school in Baltimore, Maryland. Consequently, the teachers who prepare these courses are in daily touch with the student's problems and are in a position to advise the parent in practically every matter pertaining to the student's education.

"No teaching experience or training on the part of the parent or home teacher is necessary. A specially prepared manual is supplied with every course, showing the parent exactly what to do every step of the way and giving helpful guidance and encouragement for both parent and child.

"Calvert School was founded in 1897. In 1905, through the establishment of its Home Instruction Department, the benefits of Calvert education were extended to parents and children everywhere."

How It Operates

Each grade is planned for a school year of about nine months. As a result of the individual instruction you will give your child, however, you will be able to make the schedule flexible and may adapt the courses to the needs and abilities of the child. The daily amount of time you will need will vary; but it is well to plan upon three and a half to five hours, depending upon the pupil and the grade. If your child needs as much as two years for the completion of a single course, the school permits that length of time; most pupils, however, complete each course in a school year by following a regular schedule that occupies the morning hours.

Texts and Materials

This is a totally packaged course including lesson manual, textbooks, workbooks, and supplies for the school year. The average weight of a Calvert Course is 18–23 pounds. Tuition fee includes shipment of course materials by book post or parcel post. If foreign delivery by air express is desired, additional funds must be sent.

Tuition Fees

Kindergarten	$225.00
Grades 1–4	385.00
Grades 5–8	415.00
Advisory Teaching Service	
Grades 1–4	190.00
Grades 5 and 6	200.00
Grades 7 and 8	215.00

Special Services

Individual subject courses are also offered for the eighth-grade student; these may be taken for separate credit or collectively as the complete eighth-grade course noted above. Individual courses offered are English, history, mathematics, reading/literature, and science. The Advisory Teaching Service is also available for the individual course.

2.   **University of Nebraska-Lincoln**
     Independent Study High School
     Nebraska Center for Continuing Education
     33rd and Holdrege Streets
     Lincoln NB 68583, USA
     Grades: 9 through 12

"The Independent Study High School has been in existence since 1929. The program is fully accredited by the North Central Association of Colleges and Schools and by the Nebraska State Department of Education. This accreditation allows us to grant a high school diploma upon completion of specific requirements. Courses may also be taken for personal interest or to supplement the local school curriculum.

"Each student that enrolls in one of our courses must have a local supervisor. The supervisor is an important person in the student's relationship with the Independent Study High School. Supervisors are not teachers and need not have the background to help the student with the subject matter of the course."

How It Operates

Each course is planned for 18 weeks—a semester's work. A schedule of estimated time for each unit is listed in the Material for the Student at the beginning of each unit. A student who expects to complete the course in 18 weeks should follow this schedule closely. The minimum time requirement for the completion of a one-semester course is five weeks from the time the first lesson is received by the Division of Continuing Studies.

The registration for an independent study course is one full year. At the end of the year the student must pay a renewal fee to continue work in good standing.

The supervisor receives materials, sets specific study times, monitors examinations, reviews with the pupil the corrected examinations, and maintains a working paper file for the student's use. In addition, the supervisor provides encouragement to the student. Parents and relatives are usually not approved to supervise examinations. Special permission must be obtained from the principal for parents to supervise examinations.

Texts and Materials

The necessary materials (texts, kits, and other supplies) are available from the school or can be procured separately in the case of textbooks. Course material is normally shipped by surface mail, but air mail is also available at an extra cost. Air freight shipment is recommended for overseas delivery. Material lost in shipping will normally be replaced at no cost, after the appropriate waiting period, but transportation costs will be assessed to the customer.

Tuition Fees

Tuition for each one-semester ¼ Carnegie unit (5 credit hours) course is $71.00 for nonresidents. The cost of materials varies with each course.

Special Services

Tuition can be refunded on a prorated basis for legitimate reasons submitted by the supervisor within a 60-day period. Enrollment can be made by telephone, fax machine, or mail. VISA, MasterCard, and American Express are accepted.

3.   **Independent Study by Correspondence**
     University of Florida, Division of Continuing
       Education, Gainesville, FL 32611, USA
     Grades: 9 through 12

"Independent Study by Correspondence is designed for a large number of individuals for whom no other means of guided learning is practicable. For any of a number of legitimate reasons, many persons find it impossible to enroll in scheduled classes. The educational needs of these persons are very real and to deny them is unwarranted. For these educationally disadvantaged persons, Independent Study by Correspondence seeks to provide those learning opportunities which are essential in assisting each individual to make the greatest contribution to society. For those unable to avail themselves of classroom instruction, Independent Study by Correspondence fills a void.

"In addition to the many specific opportunities provided by this widely accepted method of instruction, this method is believed to aid the development of self-discipline, desirable learning habits and the ability to organize thinking and utilize knowledge resulting from study."

How It Operates

High school courses are designed to include the subject content of one semester's work in a comparable high school class; each course carries ¼ unit of high school credit. If a full unit is desired, then two sequential courses in the one subject representing two semesters of work must be completed.

A period of one year from the date of enrollment is allowed for the completion of a course. An expired enrollment may be reinstated for a period of six months by paying a fee of $20.00. No enrollment may be continued in force for more than 15 months. The minimum time for completion of a course is one month. A maximum of four lessons per week will be accepted for grading.

Although there is no limit on the number of correspondence courses that may be carried simultaneously, the recommended maximum is three.

Each course is based on a study guide and consists of 8 to 17 written assignments. Each assignment contains a written portion that is prepared on special paper and sent to the instructor for grading. Unsatisfactory assignments must be reworked before credit can be given for the course.

Texts and Materials

The required texts and materials can be purchased from independent distributors or ordered from the school as part of the registration. The school will send courses overseas as requested (via air mail or surface mail) at cost and without additional handling charges.

Tuition Fees

The enrollment fee for each ½ unit course is $75.00. Textbooks and other materials are additional.

Special Services

Partial refund of tuition will be made if the student withdraws within two months of starting the course, nothing thereafter. Used books still being used in the correspondence course and in usable condition will be purchased back. This does not include phonograph records.

Independent Study by Correspondence courses are also available at the college level. Brochures containing complete description of courses and textbook costs are available on request. Prices subject to change.

4.   **Home Study International**
       P.O. Box 4437
       Silver Spring MD 20914-4437, USA

"Home Study International offers instruction to children who are unable to attend class or prefer to choose this alternative. Children who are in foreign countries; who are in isolated areas; who need to keep up with school while they travel with their parents; and children who need Christian education when no school is available may enroll. Home Study International is accredited by the Accrediting Commission of the National Home Study Council, Washington, D.C. USA. The course writers are exceptional professionals in their specialties and most hold degrees at the master's or doctorate levels."

How It Operates

Each course has been written by an expert in the field and is graded by a qualified teacher. Most students who have successfully completed correspondence work do as well as or better than students in the classroom.

For grades K–6 the mother (or some other chosen person) acts as a teacher's assistant, using plans prepared and presented in the syllabus for the specific grade. Frequent messages from the HSI supervisor encourage a high level of work. The supervisor grades the test papers sent in for each six-week period. It is not necessary to maintain the schedule suggested by the syllabus, but it is the best plan. Most HSI courses yielding semester credit have a midterm and a final examination for each semester for students in grades 7–12.

From the date of enrollment Home Study International allows one year for the completion of a correspondence course. A student who is unable to complete a course within one year may request an extension of time for a period of one year with payment of a $50.00 fee.

Texts and Materials

In order to offer quality programs to its students, HSI uses textbooks and other materials produced by academic publishing companies. Students are not required to purchase educational material from HSI; however, such purchase is usually convenient and assures the exact version/edition required for the course. The purchase of textbooks and supplies is cash only. Overseas shipments are sent surface mail unless otherwise indicated. Allow up to six months for surface mail. Airmail transmittal of lessons and books can be arranged according to information in the bulletin.

Tuition Fees

Kindergarten (full year, all subjects)	$130.00
Grades 1–6 (full year, all subjects)	186.00
Junior high school (full year, one subject)	170.00
High school (one unit of credit)	260.00
College (per semester hour credit)	95.00

There is a one-time nonrefundable enrollment fee of $50.00. Tuition may be made by monthly payments.

Special Services

Several college-level courses are offered in religion, business administration, education and psychology, English and speech, history, geography and sociology, languages, mathematics, and science. A student may withdraw from a course with a partial refund of tuition based on the number of lessons submitted. Enrollment fee and shipping and handling charges are nonrefundable.

Prospective students should request a free bulletin for the most current information.

APPENDIX D

INTERNATIONAL MARTITIME MOBILE AMATEUR RADIO

Although your voyage may take you through international waters, as long as you operate from a U.S.-registered vessel or hold a U.S. amateur license, you must comply with all provisions of the Federal Communications Commission (FCC) rules. Further, you may operate within the territorial waters of another country only if you have the permission of that government in advance.

An amateur mobile station operated on board a vessel must comply with all the following special conditions:

1. The installation and operation of the amateur mobile station shall be approved by the master of the vessel.

2. The amateur mobile station shall be separate from and independent of all other radio equipment, if any, installed on board the vessel.

3. The electrical installation of the amateur mobile station shall be in accord with the rules applicable to vessels as promulgated by the appropriate government agency.

4. The operation of the amateur mobile station

ITU Regions

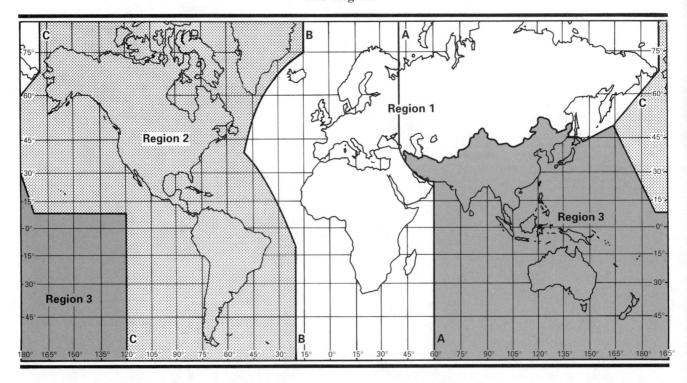

shall not interfere with the efficient operation of any radio equipment installed on board the same vessel.

5. The amateur mobile station and its associated equipment, either in itself or in its method of operation, shall not constitute a hazard to the safety of life or property.

The International Telecommunication Union, the world body regulating telecommunications, including amateur radio, has divided the world into three regions. The accompanying chart shows the boundaries. While you are sailing or anchored in international waters, it is good amateur practice to follow your call sign with the words "maritime mobile" and the number of the ITU region in which you are located. It is important to note that you are permitted to operate only on those amateur frequencies specifically allocated to the region you are in at the time of operation.

While you are in international waters, you may pass third-party traffic, including phone patches, to the United States. You may not handle or pass such traffic to other countries, except those with whom the United States holds third-party agreements. There are never any exceptions to these rules, and thoughtless violations of the rules can cost the Amateur Radio Service the good reputation it has earned over the years, especially among those countries that are not strong advocates of the Amateur Radio Service. Foreign governments are quick to monitor, observe, and record such violations, and to use them against amateurs in crucial conferences of the International Telecommunication Union.

Courtesy American Radio Relay League

Mailing Addresses to Request Reciprocal Operating Permits

You cannot operate your ham rig within the territorial limits of another country unless you are in possession of a guest or reciprocal operating permit issued by that country. These permits also specify the operating frequencies you can use while in that country's waters. Following are the addresses of the official contacts for obtaining such permits:

COOK ISLANDS (ZK1)
Chief, Telecommunications
Government of the Cook Islands
Chief Post Office
Rarotonga
COOK ISLANDS

EASTER ISLAND (CE0A)
Radio Club de Chile
Casilla 13630
Santiago de Chile
CHILE

FEDERATED STATES OF MICRONESIA (V6A)
Director of Communications and Transportation
Federated States of Micronesia
Kolonia, Pohnpei, FM 96941
USA

FIJI (3D2)
Ministry of Information, Broadcasting, Television,
  and Telecommunications
P.O. Box 2225
Government Buildings
Suva
FIJI

FRENCH POLYNESIA (FO0)
Le Directeur
de l'Office des Postes et Telecommunications
Papeete, Tahiti
FRENCH POLYNESIA

GALAPAGOS ISLANDS (HC8)
Guayaquil Radio Club
P.O. Box 5757
Guayaquil
ECUADOR

KIRIBATI (T3)
Controller of Telecommunications
Ministry of Communications
P.O. Box 72
Bairiki, Tarawa
KIRIBATI

MARSHALL ISLANDS (V7)
National Telecommunications Authority
Government of the Marshall Islands
Majuro, Marshall Islands, MH 96960
USA

NAURU (C2)
Director of Telecommunications
Republic of NAURU

NEW CALEDONIA (FK)
Office des Postes et Telecommunications
14 Rue Edouard Glasser
Noumea
NEW CALEDONIA

NEW ZEALAND (ZL)
NZART Reciprocal Licensing Bureau
23 Lydia Street
Greymouth
NEW ZEALAND

NIUE (ZK2)
Director of Telecommunications
P.O. Box 37
NIUE ISLAND

PALAU (KC6)
Director of Commerce
Ministry of Natural Resources
P.O. Box 100
Koror, Palau, PW 96940
USA

PAPUA NEW GUINEA (P2)
The Manager
Spectrum Management Department
Radio Regulatory and Licensing Branch
Post & Telecommunications Corporation
P.O. Box 1783
Port Moresby
PAPUA NEW GUINEA

PITCAIRN ISLAND (VR6)
Tom Christian, VR6 TC
P.O. Box 1
Adamstown
PITCAIRN ISLAND

SOLOMON ISLANDS (H4)
Posts and Telecommunications
General Post Office
Honiara
SOLOMON ISLANDS

TOKELAU ISLANDS (ZK3)
Office of Tokelau Affairs
c/o New Zealand High Commission
Apia
WESTERN SAMOA

TONGA (A35)
General Manager
Tonga Telecommunications Commission
P.O. Box 46
Nukualofa
TONGA

TUVALU (T2)
The Secretary to the Chief Minister
Government Offices
Funafuti
TUVALU

UNITED STATES (A, K, N, W)
(See note at end of listing)

VANUATU (YJ)
The Postmaster
Post and Telegraphic Office
Port-Vila
VANUATU

WALLIS AND FUTUNA ISLANDS (FW)
Service des Postes et Communications
Mata Uta
TERRITORIE DES ÎLES WALLIS ET FUTUNA

WESTERN SAMOA (5W)
Director
Post and Telecommunications Department
Apia
WESTERN SAMOA

Note: The Federal Communications Commission issues all amateur radio licenses for the United States, its territories and possessions. The following is a list of the territories and major possessions plus one state in the Pacific Ocean:

American Samoa (KH8)	Midway Atoll (KH4)
Guam (KH2)	Northern Marianas (KH0)
Hawaii (KH6)	Palmyra Atoll (KH5)
Johnston Atoll (KH3)	Wake Atoll (KH9)

Foreign amateur radio operators wishing to operate in Hawaii or the above U.S. possessions or territories of the Pacific should write to:

District Field Office
Federal Communications Commission
P.O. Box 1030, Waipahu HI 96797 USA
Courtesy of American Radio Relay League

Maritime Mobile Nets of the Pacific

TIME UTC[a]	FREQUENCY kHz[a]	NET NAME AND AREA COVERED	NET[b] MANAGER
0100 (D)	21407	Maritime Mobile Net—Pacific and Indian Oceans	W6BYS
0130 (D)	28313	Novice/Tech Traffic Net—Pacific Ocean	—
0200 (M–F)	7290	Hawaii Interisland Net	KH6B
0200 (D)	14313	Seafarer's Net—Central and Eastern Pacific Oceans	K6QTR
0220 (D)	14315	John's Wx Net—Norfolk Island and South Pacific	VK9JA
0300 (D)	28480	Ten Meter Maritime Mobile Net	—
0400 (D)	14115	DDD Net—Pacific Ocean	VE7DB
0400 (D)	14313	Pacific Maritime Net	KH6UY
0400 (D)	14318	Arnold Net—South Pacific (Wx)[c]	ZK1DB
0400 (D)	14075	Pacific CW Traffic Net	KH6HIJ
0500 (D)	21200	Australia–New Zealand–Africa Net—Pacific and Indian Oceans	VK3PA
0530 (D)	14303	Swedish Maritime Net	—
0630 (M)	14180	Pitcairn Net—South Pacific Ocean	VR6TC
0700 (D)	14265	Pacific Islands Net	—
0700 (D)	14310	Marianas (Guam) Net	—
0715 (D)	3815	Bay of Islands Net	ZL1BKD
0800 (D)	14303	United Kingdom Net—Pacific Ocean	—
0800 (D)	14315	Pacific Interisland Net	P29JM & KX6QU
1200 (D)	14320	SEA Net—Southeast Asia, Indonesia, and Australia	WB8JDR
1600 (D)	7238	California—Baja Net	N6ADJ
1630 (M–F)	14340	California–Hawaii Net	—
1630 (F)	21350	Pitcairn Net—South Pacific Ocean	VR6TC
1700 (M–F)	7240	Bejuka Central American and Panama Net	HP3XWB
1700 (D)	14329	Skippers Net—Pacific Ocean	KH6OE
1700 (D)	14340	California–Hawaii Net	K6VDV
1730 (M–F)	14115	DDD Net—Pacific Ocean	VE7CEM
1730 (M–F)	14292	Sourdough Net—Alaska and Pacific	KL7IJT
1800 (MWSa)	14285	Kaffee Klatch Net—Hawaii and Tahiti	KH6S
1800 (D)	7076	South Pacific Cruising Net	WA2CPX
1900 (D)	2738	Children's Hour—Society Islands	—
1900	7255	Western Pacific Net	—
1900 (D)	7285	Shamaru Net—Hawaii	KH6BF
1900 (M–F)	14305	Confusion Net—Pacific Ocean	W7GYR
1900 (D)	14329	Bay of Islands Net—New Zealand	ZL1BKD
1900 (M–Sa)	14342	Mañana Net—Mexican waters	KB5HA
1900 (M–S)	14340	Mariana Islands Net	—
2000 (D)	7095	Harry's Net—Pacific (Wx)[c]	KL7MZ
2100 (D)	14315	Tony's Net—South Pacific Ocean (Wx)[c]	ZL1ATE
2200 (Tu)	21350	Pitcairn Net—South Pacific Ocean	VR6TC
2200 (M–F)	21412	15-Meter Pacific Maritime Net, California–Hawaii	KH6CO
2230 (S–Th)	21404	Pacific Maritime Mobile Net	—
2310 (M)	14285	California to South Pacific Net	—
2400 (D)	14320	SEA Maritime Mobile Net—Asia, Japan, and Australia (Rowdy's Net)	VS6BE
As needed	14325	Hurricane Net	—

The following is not a ham radio set, but it is very useful near New Zealand:

0600 (D)	4419.4	John's Wx[c] from Keri Keri, NZ	Marine SSB

Notes: [a]Subject to change due to propagation
[b]Subject to change due to availability of manager
[c]Weather

PACIFIC SAILBOAT RACES WITH CRUISING CLASSES

Many cruising boats take the opportunity to join an international sailboat race when it is headed in the same direction as they are. The reasons are many—some like to race, others seek the companionship of buddy-boats, while still others see it as a way to get difficult paperwork done expeditiously. This last advantage is a major reason for the popularity of the annual Darwin (Australia) to Ambon (Indonesia) race, which lures 30 to 40 racing and cruising boats with its highly coveted Indonesian cruising permit.

Many sailboat races throughout the Pacific have cruising classes, and if you can schedule your presence properly, a lot of fun and adventure await you. These pages list the popular international races in the Pacific in which there are cruising classes. Included are the names and addresses of the sponsoring clubs to which you can write for more complete information about entering.

Sponsors of International Yacht Races in the Pacific

Ancient Mariners Sailing Society
P.O. Box 6484
San Diego CA 92166
USA

Bay of Islands Yacht Club
P.O. Box 205
Paihia
NEW ZEALAND

Club Nàutico Oceànica de Chile
Avenida Valparaiso 507
(3rd floor)
Valparaiso
CHILE

Cruising Yacht Association
of Northern Territories
GPO Box 3439
Darwin, NT
AUSTRALIA

Cruising Yacht Club of Australia
New Beach Road
Darling Point, NSW 2077
AUSTRALIA

Fremantle Sailing Association
Fremantle
Western Australia
AUSTRALIA

Island Yachting Association
P.O. Box 24-054, Royal Oak
Auckland
NEW ZEALAND

Japan Yachting Association
1-1-1 Jinnan, Shibuya-ku
Tokyo
JAPAN

Musket Cove Yacht Club
Private Mail Bag
Nadi Airport
FIJI

New Zealand Yachting Federation
P.O. Box 4173
Auckland
NEW ZEALAND

Nippon Ocean Racing Club
Sempakushinko Bldg.
15-16 Toranomon 1-chome
Minatoku 105
JAPAN

Ocean Racing Catamaran Association
c/o Victor Stern
279 Ravenna Drive
Long Beach CA 90803
USA

Osaka Port Promotion Association
2-1-2 Chikko, Minato-ku
Osaka 552
JAPAN

Pacific Cup Yacht Club
2269 Chestnut Street, #111
San Francisco CA 94123
USA

Pan-Pacific Yacht Race Committee
13-33 Morinomiyachuo 2-chome
Chuo-ku, Osaka 540
JAPAN

Phuket King's Cup Secretariat
37 Soi Petchburi 15
Petchburi Road, Pyathai
Bangkok 10400
THAILAND

Ponsonby Cruising Club
P.O. Box 47-010
Ponsonby, Auckland
NEW ZEALAND

PORLASI
J1. Prapatan 18,
Jakarta Pusat 10410
INDONESIA

Royal Hong Kong Yacht Club
Kellet Island
HONG KONG

Royal New Zealand Yacht Squadron
P.O. Box 904
Auckland
NEW ZEALAND

Royal Papua Yacht Club
P.O. Box 140
Port Moresby
PAPUA NEW GUINEA

Royal Selangor Yacht Club
Jalan Limbongan
42000 Port Klang
Selangor Darul Ehsan
MALAYSIA

Royal Vancouver Yacht Club
3811 Point Grey Road
Vancouver, British Columbia
CANADA V5R 1B3

Salinas Yacht Club
Guayaquil
ECUADOR

San Diego Yacht Club
1101 Anchorage Lane
San Diego CA 92106
USA

Singlehanded Sailing Society
P.O. Box 1716
Mill Valley CA 94942
USA

Tahiti Yacht Club
Arue, Tahiti
FRENCH POLYNESIA

TransPacific Yacht Club
1508 Santiago Drive
Newport Beach CA 92660
USA

Pacific Ocean International Blue-Water Races

NAME OF RACE	COURSE (Great Circle distance and record time)	WHEN RUN	SPONSORING CLUB(S)
Australia start			
Challenge Bank Bali Classic	Darwin, Dampier, Fremantle, and Singapore to Bali (940 nm [Darwin])	May 1983; biennial thereafter	Fremantle Sailing Club
Ambon	Darwin to Ambon (600 nm)	Annual (July/Aug.)	Cruising Yacht Association of Northern Territories
Nissan Coral Sea Classic	Cairns to Port Moresby to Townsville (1,435 nm)	Biennial (Apr./May)	Royal Papua Yacht Club
WestPac New Caledonia	Sydney and Brisbane to Noumea (1,058 nm [Sydney])	Biennial (odd years; Sep.)	Cruising Yacht Club of Australia
Hobart	Sydney to Hobart (630 nm; 2d/14h/36m/56s)	Annual (Dec. 26 start)	Cruising Yacht Club of Australia
Suva	Sydney to Suva (1,740 nm)	Biennial (even years; alternating with Auckland start)	Cruising Yacht Club of Australia
Yamaha Osaka Cup (doublehanded)	Melbourne to Osaka (5,300 nm; 28d/06h/39m/10s)	Quadrennial (1991, 1995, etc.; Mar.)	Nippon Ocean Racing Club and Osaka Port Promotion
Canada start			
Maui	Victoria to Maui, Hawaii (2,310 mi; 09/23h/15m/59s)	Biennial (even years; July)	Royal Vancouver Yacht Club
Chile start			
Mil Millas	Valparaiso to Robinson Crusoe Island and return (912 mi)	Biennial (even years; Feb.)	Club Náutico Oceánico de Chile
Ecuador start			
Regata Oceánica (Galapagos Cup)	Salinas to Galapagos and return (1,102 nm)	Triennial in Sep. 1993–1996	Salinas Yacht Club
Hong Kong start			
Corum China Sea Race Series	Hong Kong to Manila plus local races at each end (650 nm)	Biennial (even years; Apr.; alternates with San Fernando Race)	Royal Hong Kong Yacht Club
Dunhill San Fernando Race	Hong Kong to San Fernando, Philippine Islands (530 nm)	Biennial (odd years; Mar.; alternates with China Sea Race)	Royal Hong Kong Yacht Club
Indonesia start			
Celebes Race	Ambon to Bitung (425 nm)	Sept. Follow-on to Darwin-Ambon Race	PORLASI
Japan start			
Tokyo Cup	Tokyo to Guam (1,335 nm, 5d/12h/41m)	Annual in Dec.	Japan Yachting Association
Malaysia start			
Raja Muda Series	Port Klang to Langkawi (235 nm)	Annual (Nov.; feeds to Phuket King's Cup Regatta)	Royal Selangor Yacht Club

NAME OF RACE	COURSE (Great Circle distance and record time)	WHEN RUN	SPONSORING CLUB(S)
New Zealand start			
Great South Pacific Regatta	Auckland to Nadi to Port-Vila to Noumea (1,950 nm)	Annual (Aug./Oct.)	Ponsonby Cruising Club and Musket Cove Yacht Club
Noumea Race	Auckland to Noumea (970 nm)	Biennial (even years; Sep.; alternates with Australia start)	Royal New Zealand Yacht Squadron
Port-Vila Race	Auckland to Port-Vila (1,195 nm)	Biennial (Apr.; alternates with Papeete finish)	New Zealand Yachting Federation
Papeete	Auckland to Papeete (2,210 nm)	Biennial (Apr.; alternates with Port-Vila finish)	New Zealand Yachting Federation
Yamaha Fukuoka Cup	Auckland to Fukuoka, Japan, via Suva and Guam (5,500 nm; 28d/12h/57m/08s)	Quadrennial (1989, 1993, etc.; Apr. start)	Nippon Ocean Racing Club
Pacific Ocean Triangle	Bay of Islands to Papeete to Noumea to Auckland (5,675 nm)	Random years (last held 1989)	Bay of Islands Yacht Club and Tahiti Yacht Club
Tonga Rally	Russell to Nukualofa, Tonga (1,100 nm)	Annual (May)	Island Cruising Association
Thailand start			
Phuket King's Cup Regatta	Phuket, Thailand, and Andaman Sea	Annual (Dec.; follows Raja Muda series)	Phuket King's Cup Secretariat
United States start			
Classic TransPac	Los Angeles to Honolulu (2,225 nm; 8d/11h/01m/45s)	Biennial (odd years; July)	TransPac Yacht Club
West Marine Pacific Cup	San Francisco to Kaneohe, Hawaii (2,070 nm)	Biennial (even years; July)	Pacific Cup Yacht Club
Race for Life (Doublehanded)	San Diego to Honolulu (2,265 nm; 12d/10h/11m/31s)	Biennial (odd years; July)	San Diego Yacht Club
Hiroshima Cup	Honolulu to Hiroshima, Japan (3,710 nm)	June (random years; last run in 1989)	Nippon Ocean Racing Club
Pan-Pacific	Los Angeles to Osaka, Japan (5,970 nm; 34d/06h/28m)	Single event (starts Apr. 24, 1994; later starts also from Brisbane, Shanghai, Pusan, Vladivostok)	Pan-Pacific Yacht Race Committee
Singlehanded TransPac	San Francisco to Hanalei Bay, Kauai, Hawaii (2,126 nm; 10d/10h/03m/43s)	Biennial (even years)	Singlehanded Sailing Society
Ancient Mariners	San Diego to Lahaina, Maui (2,215 nm; 13d/05h/52m)	Approx. triennial (last in 1991)	Ancient Mariners Sailing Society
Multihull TransPac	Los Angeles to Honolulu (2,225 nm; 6d/22h/41m/12s)	Inactive	Ocean Racing Catamaran Association
Tahiti TransPac	Los Angeles to Tahiti (3,560 nm; 17d/7h/57m/57s)	Inactive (last run in 1978)	TransPac Yacht Club

INDEX

ABOUT THE AUTHOR

Earl R. Hinz, a veteran cruiser, has sailed 40,000 Pacific miles, most of them on his 41-foot ketch *Horizon.* He has visited the far reaches of the Pacific—including the popular Coconut Milk Run and the Manila Galleon Run—and has sailed in the TransPacific Yacht Races to Tahiti and Honolulu. Hinz is also an experienced writer and has authored numerous works, among them *Pacific Wanderer, The Offshore Log, Sail before Sunset,* and *The Complete Book of Anchoring and Mooring.* He is currently a contributing editor to *Cruising World* and writes regular features for *Pacific* and *Ocean Navigator* magazines. He lives aboard his trawler *Kumulani* in the Ala Wai Boat Harbor, Honolulu.

Production Notes

Composition and paging were done on the
Quadex Composing System and typesetting
on the Compugraphic 8400 by the design
and production staff of University of
Hawaii Press.

The text typeface is Sabon and the
display typeface is Compugraphic Optima.

Offset presswork and binding were done by
The Maple-Vail Book Manufacturing Group.
Text paper is Glatfelter Offset Vellum,
basis 50.